W9-BZD-541

JAMAICA

OLIVER HILL

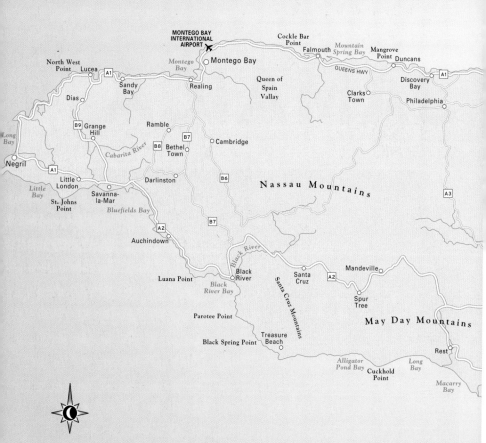

C a r i b b e a n   S e a

MONTEGO BAY
INTERNATIONAL
AIRPORT

Cockle Bar
Point

*Mountain
Spring Bay*   Mangrove
Point   Duncans

North West
Point   Lucea   Falmouth
                                                QUEENS HWY
*Montego
Bay*   Montego Bay   Discovery   A1
                                                              Bay
A1   Clarks
          Sandy   Town   Philadelphia
          Bay   Realing
                              Queen of
Dias   Spain
                              Vallay
B9   Grange
       Hill   Ramble
*Long
Bay*   B7
                    B8   Cambridge
Cabarita River   Bethel
                          Town
A1   B6   N a s s a u   M o u n t a i n s
Negril   Little
                London   Darlinston
*Little
Bay*   A3
          St. Johns   Savanna-
          Point   la-Mar   B7
          Bluefields Bay
                    A2
          Auchindown

                              Black River
                                          Black   Santa   A2   Mandeville
Luana Point   River   Cruz
                    *Black   Spur
                    River Bay*   *Santa Cruz Mountains*   Tree
                                                                    M a y   D a y   M o u n t a i n s
Parotee Point
                              Treasure
Black Spring Point   Beach   Rest

                                        *Alligator
                                        Pond Bay*   Cuckhold   *Long
                                                     Point   Bay*
                                                                          *Macarry
                                                                          Bay*

0   10 mi

0   10 km

JAMAICA

St. Anns Bay

St. Anns Bay

Bamboo

A1

Ocho Rios

A1

Port Maria Bay

Port Maria

Golden Grove

A3

Annotto Bay

Palmetto Point

A4

Buff Bay

Savanna Point

Hope Bay

Ewarton

Wag Water River

Castleton

Port Antonio

Boston

A4

Linstead

A3

B1

Rio Grande

John Crow Mountains

Reach Falls

A1

Bog Walk

Blue Mountain Peak 7,402ft

Manchioneal

Blue Mountains

May Pen

A2

Spanish Town

Kingston

Bull Bay

Amity Hall

Bushy Park

Kingston Harbour

Bull Bay

Freetown

Great Salt Pond

NORMAN MANLEY INTERNATIONAL AIRPORT

Morant Bay

Port Morant

Rio Minho

Old Harbour Bay

Salt Island Lagoon

Salt Pond Bay

A4

Morant Bay

Folly Bay

Sandy Bay

Green Goat Island

Old House Point

Rocky Point

Rocky Point

Portland Point

Caribbean Sea

DISCOVER JAMAICA

It's hard to argue with the assertion Jamaicans make that theirs is a blessed island. Little beats simple luxuries like picking a fresh mango from a tree for breakfast, bathing in a crystal clear waterfall, or sitting in the shade to watch the sun climb the sky while hummingbirds flit about on a gentle breeze heavy with the scent of tropical flowers. The very name Jamaica pays homage to the island's natural endowment, retaining a close phonetic approximation to the name given by the island's first inhabitants, the Tainos, which translates as "land of wood and water." It's an apt description, given Jamaica's lush tropical forests and mountainous terrain crisscrossed by countless rivers.

Jamaica has been a pioneer of Caribbean tourism since the late 1800s when a booming banana trade between the north coast and the northeastern United States created the opportunity for visitors to discover the island's natural beauty and perpetual warmth. Since Jamaica's independence in 1962, the government has based its eco-

Pelican Bar off Parottee Point takes the prize for the most unique bar in Jamaica.

nomic development strategy largely on creating an attractive tourism market to woo visitors from cold northern winters to the island's tropical climate and calm Caribbean waters. Today the results of a tourism-centered approach have been fully realized, with virtually every kind of accommodation imaginable available, from rustic country-style cottages to luxurious staffed villas and all-inclusive resorts.

Jamaica's resorts successfully incorporate the warmth of the country's people while pampering and indulging their guests to no end. Hot stone massages and candlelit gourmet dinners accompanied by soft reggae and lapping waves are just the beginning. Many of Jamaica's resorts have perfected the art of ensuring complete satisfaction to such a degree that it's entirely possible for guests to miss the depth and color of the island's culture beyond the resort walls. But it is outside the hotel gates where visitors are most likely to appreciate the ongoing evolution of a nation barely 50 years old, where there is no monopoly on truth or reality, and where preachers – religious, musical, and political – lend vibrancy to everyday life.

Ironically, it wasn't the tropical climate or endless natural beauty

Dancers at Passa Passa Street Dance in Kingston compete for the flashiest getup and wickedest *whine*.

that brought worldwide attention to Jamaica in the 20th century. It was a young man growing up with the odds stacked against him in the ghetto of Trench Town who managed to make his truthful message heard above the din of political violence and clashing Cold War ideologies of the 1970s. Robert Nesta Marley, along with band members Peter McIntosh and Bunny Livingston, became a beacon of hope, not just for disenfranchised Jamaicans, but for sufferers the world over. Bob Marley grew into a global force on par with Che Guevara in terms of his ability to evoke the revolutionary spirit. Today countless singers keep Marley's legacy alive and fuel Jamaica's music industry, the most prolific on the planet.

Though he is lauded as a beloved son by the Jamaican government as much as by the Jamaican people, Marley's message was not always embraced on an institutional level. Even today a conspicuous double standard persists where Rasta musicians tour the world as symbols of Jamaica's enchanting, mystical allure, while their calls for change in their beloved homeland are ignored decade after decade. Similarly, in a country with an overwhelmingly black majority, Jamaica's African heritage is still caught in a tug-of-war, embraced

Cliff jumping is a favorite pastime for tourists and locals alike at Rick's Café on Negril's West End.

by some and shunned by others. Progressive Jamaican thinkers like Paul Bogle, George William Gordon, and Marcus Garvey were finally acknowledged as national heroes decades after their deaths, but their enduring impact has perhaps been more tangible abroad where their ideas formed the foundation for civil rights struggles that would come decades later in the United States and the United Kingdom. Still, in Jamaica these leaders helped inspire the Rastafarian movement, which encompasses only a small percentage of the Jamaican population but has made a deep impact on the nation's cultural identity and continues to draw a mass following. Its emphasis on harmony with nature and physical and spiritual fitness offers an alternate worldview for countless Jamaican youth who find themselves caught in a materialistic society increasingly influenced by imported pop culture.

In reality Jamaica is a place where the struggle to get by encourages any degree of corruption, from petty thievery to governmental mismanagement. Crime and violence are present in very real terms but perhaps even more so in the national psyche, where ghetto thugs are romanticized like the gangsters of old Western movies. But there

Redemption Song, a sculpture by Laura Facey, stands in Emancipation Park in New Kingston.

is little legitimacy to the often-cited stereotype that Jamaica is a dangerous place. Jamaicans are overwhelmingly a peace-loving, church-going people who have incomparable warmth of character. Outside the ghettoes the dangers are no greater than anywhere else in the world. Visitors to the island have little reason to worry about safety, and those who travel around the island independently will find they are welcomed at every roadside stop for jelly coconut, jerk pork, and pepper shrimp. Even at dance sessions in the heart of downtown Kingston, enjoyment and brotherly love are upheld as the guiding principles, and violence is not tolerated.

Jamaica is a destination not to be missed. It has lush forests full of tropical flowers and colorful birds, and a varied topography dotted with spectacular natural features – caves, white-sand beaches, swimming holes, waterfalls, and majestic mountain peaks. It offers jerk-seasoned meats, fresh-caught seafood, and an endless list of exotic fruits. Most importantly, however, the Jamaican people are magnetic. Warm, charismatic, and down to earth, they are naturally fit hosts eager to share the best their island has to offer.

Participants gather for the annual Watt Town Revival celebrations in rural St. Ann.

Contents

MAP CONTENTS

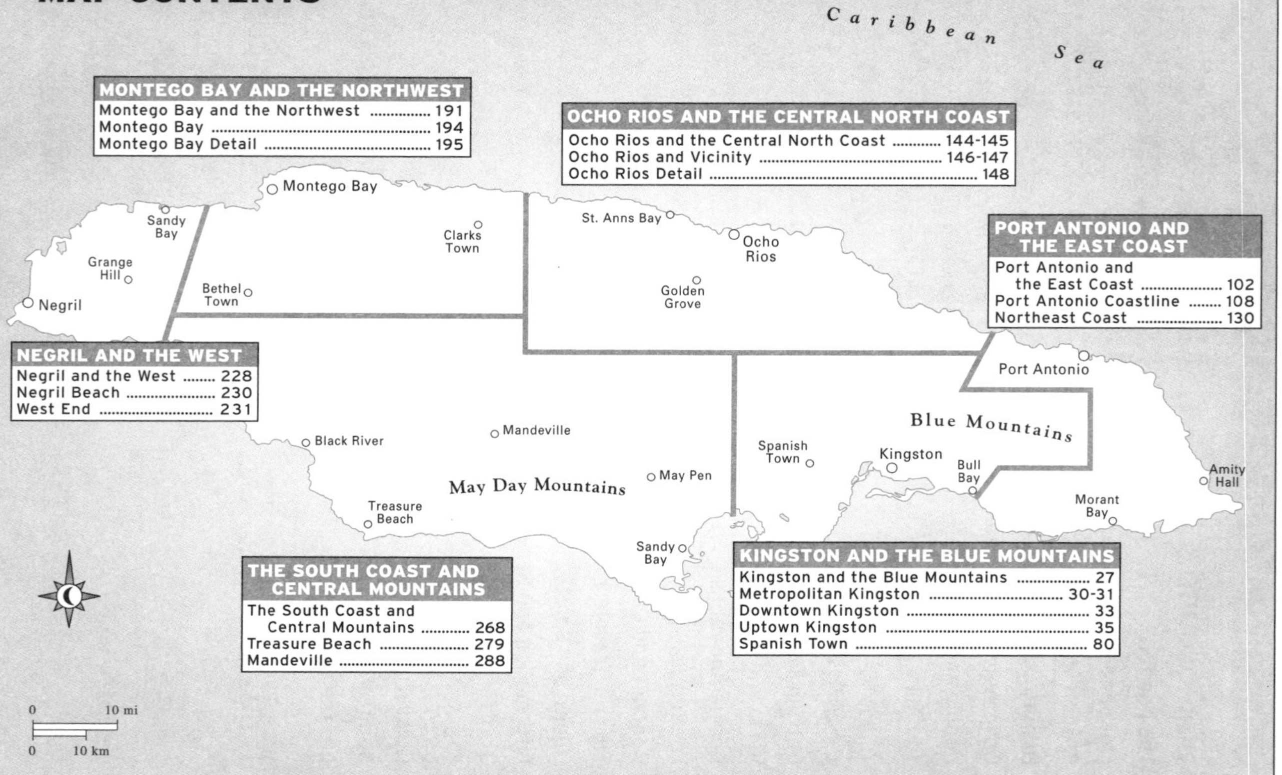

Caribbean Sea

Amity Hall

Morant Bay

Blue Mountains

Bull Bay

Port Antonio

Kingston

Spanish Town

St. Anns Bay

Ocho Rios

Golden Grove

May Pen

Sandy Bay

May Day Mountains

Clarks Town

Mandeville

Montego Bay

Treasure Beach

Black River

Bethel Town

Sandy Bay

Grange Hill

Negril

West End

0   10 mi

0   10 km

The Lay of the Land

KINGSTON AND THE BLUE MOUNTAINS

Metropolitan Kingston, or Town as it's called across the island, is an energetic city that never fails to impress. There's no sugarcoating the juxtaposition of poverty and excess that defines everyday reality in the island's capital, but once the initial shock wears off, visitors find an enticing city with some of Jamaica's most important historical and cultural sites, great restaurants, and a pulsating nightlife. Recording studios and art galleries abound, heritage sights like Fort Charles and the Bob Marley Museum are within easy reach, and enticing nightlife offers the best food, music, and clubs on the island.

St. Andrew, the parish that envelops Kingston, includes a large swath of the Blue Mountain range, which rises from the city's northern edge to where cool air, fresh coffee, and spectacular views surround the majestic peaks.

In neighboring St. Catherine, the old Spanish capital Spanish Town stands as a reminder of Jamaica's colonial past. Along the coastline, fishing villages in Hellshire and Old Harbour Bay make great day-trip destinations and offer some of Jamaica's best seafood.

PORT ANTONIO AND THE EAST COAST

Jamaica's easternmost parishes contain much of the Blue Mountains and the whole of the John Crow Mountain range. Port Antonio has an infectious charm and old-world culture that lingers in luxurious villas and hilltop resorts. It's a place naturalists confuse with heaven, where Jamaica's most picturesque beaches and rivers have been preserved in their natural states. Maroons still inhabit the region's interior, where they lead hiking trips to lush forests, waterfalls, and challenging peaks. If you love water, try lazily floating down the Rio Grande on a bamboo raft, climbing Reach Falls, or getting a massage at the hot springs in Bath. Despite Portland's claim as the first Caribbean tourist destination, it has, to its benefit perhaps, been excluded from the massive development projects of the past 50 years. As a result, the area's natural beauty remains its principal draw.

OCHO RIOS AND THE CENTRAL NORTH COAST

Boomtown Ocho Rios, or "Ochi" as Jamaicans call it, is the most visited place in Jamaica—in terms of the sheer number of tourists that pass through. The throngs of people that step off cruise ships stay predominantly on the western side of town, trapped in a maze of duty-free stores and other hustles, making the eastern side of Ochi much quieter. The strip of coast from Mahogany Beach to the mouth of the White River is the nicest around, where world-class destination hotels and villas dot the water's edge.

Contrasting with the hustle and bustle of Ocho Rios, St. Mary parish is about as laid-back as it gets, with several plantation tours available among its hills and mountains and quiet fishing villages instead of waterfront resorts.

MONTEGO BAY AND THE NORTHWEST

Montego Bay is Jamaica's "Vibes City," known for a rebellious past and vibrant present. As the capital of St. James parish, MoBay, as it's often called, has been a center of economic activity since the arrival of the Spanish conquistadores.

Beaches in and around MoBay are a strong draw, and the town erupts with activity at several points throughout the year for festivals and events. Rivers along the eastern and western borders are suitable for rafting, and MoBay has an excellent yacht club with a lively social calendar.

Neighboring Trelawny has some of the most rugged terrain on earth, where limestone rock is riddled with caves and underground rivers. Along the Trelawny coast, Falmouth is a jewel of Georgian architecture, where renovation efforts are focused on restoring the town's fleeting glory.

NEGRIL AND THE WEST

Jamaica's western end has been the site of much tourism development over the past 30 years. Once a quiet fishing village, Negril has become Jamaica's most popular beach resort destination. Negril offers recreational activities from water sports to horseback riding, mountain biking to cliff jumping, but the most popular activity is simply relaxing in the sun. Inland a wetlands area and gentle hills are excellent for hiking and birding.

Little Bay, a small fishing village just east of Negril, is a reminder of the slow pace of tourism in the 1970s, with other attractive, low-key coastal areas farther east along the South Coast in Bluefields, Belmont, and Whitehouse.

The parish of Hanover retains an old-world charm, where two upscale resorts and a smattering of villas attract the rich and famous.

THE SOUTH COAST AND CENTRAL MOUNTAINS

St. Elizabeth parish along the South Coast defines "off-the-beaten-track." Waterfalls, alligators, and seafood are some of the main attractions. Treasure Beach, a string of bays and fishing villages, is Jamaica's community tourism heartland. Little Ochie, straddling the St. Elizabeth–Manchester border, has some of the best seafood on the island.

Manchester has been an important and popular hill station for centuries, where the English gentry would spend their summers in the luxury of cool highland air. The hemisphere's oldest golf course is located in the heart of the small and bustling capital of Mandeville. Clarendon, farther east, is a small parish with swaths of unexplored coastline and a unique ethnic heritage. The Leeward Maroons have their base in the interior along the border of St. James, St. Elizabeth, and Trelawny parishes.

Planning Your Trip

For its relatively small size, Jamaica is a diverse country in every sense, with a mature and diversified tourism economy. The offerings for visitors are as varied as the topography and depend largely on what people are prepared to spend in terms of time and money, and which activities pique their interest. Two weeks allows first-time visitors to get a good grasp for Jamaica by visiting several destinations across the island. It's easy to spend US$2,000 per week for a couple, but it's also feasible to get by on US$50 a day or less, including lodging, food, and budget transportation.

Most visitors to Jamaica book a hotel through an agent or all-inclusive resort for the entire length of stay on the island. While this may be the simplest option, you will be sacrificing freedom of movement and likely forgoing visits to other parts of the island. Even though the country is relatively small, a trip from Montego Bay to Kingston is exhausting, even in a private vehicle—let alone by public transportation. A trip from Montego Bay to Kingston and back will take the better part of a day and leave little time for sightseeing, and visiting the far eastern part of the island is not practical for a day trip. The best way to visit different regions is to book a two- or three-night stay in each hub of interest and allow for stops at sights along the way. Switching hotels every day is exhausting and unnecessary.

The island is small enough to pick three or four hubs as a base over a two-week period. Many hotels and most villas have a minimum per-night stay, which varies from three to seven nights depending on the season. Smaller and more humble accommodations, however, impose no such restrictions.

Deciding where to base yourself depends largely on the experience you're going for. For culture and music, Kingston is the only choice, and can easily consume a week, with a short trip to the Blue Mountains thrown in if you're not looking to rush through.

For natural splendor, there's no place like Portland, even though it remains the most remote parish in terms of road quality. If you plan to visit Portland for the better part of your trip, consider flying into Kingston, which is only a few hours away, compared to five hours or more from the airport in Montego Bay.

St. Ann and St. Mary along the north coast both have destination resorts where visitors typically stay for a week; independent travelers have plenty of options for spending a few days in Robin's Bay, Oracabessa, or Ocho Rios, the region's hub.

Montego Bay is a hip resort town with a semblance of reality beyond tourism. The small city makes a good stopover point for a one- or two-night stay either on arrival or departure. Most of the area's must-see sights can be visited in a few days, and beyond that there is little to keep ambitious travelers in Montego Bay, barring a specific event to attend. Neighboring Trelawny parish is an adventurer's paradise, with great caving, hiking, and birding in the interior and sleepy communities along the coast.

For a beach party scene every day of the week, it's Negril. In spite of rampant harassment on its once-peaceful Seven-Mile Beach, Negril has an infectious charm, especially in its quieter corners like Bloody Bay and along the West End. A week in Negril can pass very quickly into a month, and it's easy to see why so many vacationers from up north forgot to leave. There are several good day trips from Negril that can alleviate the feeling of being stuck on the beach. Other areas of Westmoreland parish deserve as much, if not more, time than Negril if you're not looking to be entertained by all the bells and whistles.

For quaint, windswept fishing villages, Treasure Beach is the place. It's a favorite destination for writers and artists who spend weeks or months in quiet study there. If you're looking to unwind and check out some nearby sights in the middle of a 10-day tour of the island, two or three nights make the trip worth it.

WHEN TO GO

While Jamaica has typically been marketed as a choice destination for escaping the winter blues, it can be just as good, if not better, in the heart of the northern summer, when temperatures are comparable or even cooler than in places as far north as New York, especially in the breezy heights of the Blue Mountains.

While it is important to note that Jamaica's **rainy season** runs from June through October, in the absence of a large front, rainfall often lasts only a few minutes and shouldn't be cause for concern in planning a trip. Even **hurricane season,** from August to November, can be fairly sunny in a good year.

An important consideration in determining when to go is the **high and low season** that many establishments use to set their rates. High season generally runs **December 15–April 15,** when accommodations can be twice as costly as during the low season. Some establishments set their own specific dates, and others vary pricing at other specific dates throughout the year like Easter, Thanksgiving, and the week between Christmas and New Year's. If escaping the winter blues is not your first priority, traveling to Jamaica during the low season can be much more cost-effective. Check with each establishment when planning a trip to see how prices vary from high season to low season.

The Jamaican calendar is filled with annual events, many of which are worth considering in planning a trip. Check the *Annual Events Calendar* in the *Background* chapter if your schedule is flexible. Attending a music festival like Rebel Salute, Follow Di Arrow, Sumfest, or Sunsplash is one of the best ways to jump out of the tourist box and appreciate Jamaica's most respected art form alongside regular Jamaicans from all walks of life. If music isn't your thing, there are several other annual events, like the Calabash Literary Festival held every April in Treasure Beach, or the fishing tournament held in Port Antonio every October.

WHAT TO TAKE

What to take depends entirely on the nature of your trip. Most all-inclusive hotels have semi-formal dress codes (i.e., a collared shirt, no sandals) for their high-end restaurants; if church or a business meeting is in order, formal attire is highly recommended, as Jamaicans take proper dress very seriously.

If nobody needs to be impressed, however, Jamaica can be the most casual place on earth, where esteemed members of society sometimes refuse to wear shoes for greater proximity to Mother Earth, and nude beaches abound at private hotels like Couples, Grand Lido, and Hedonism. Having said that, it might be perceived as a sign of disrespect to enter places of business without a shirt.

Cool, light-colored cotton clothes are best for the heat and humidity. Obviously so is your favorite bathing suit. For cool evenings, pack a long-sleeve shirt.

Many travelers to Jamaica are surprised to find that Jamaican men rarely wear shorts, while jeans and full suits are common everyday attire. It is not necessary to buy an entire wardrobe of Hawaiian shirts before your trip, and in a pinch plenty are sold in gift shops across the island with the requisite "Jamaica, no problem" scrolled across the breast.

You'll definitely want to bring your most flashy getup if you're planning a night on the town. In nightclubs like Asylum and Quad in Kingston, women are remarkably dressed up; men will come dressed in their shiniest shoes and most "criss" jacket to "flex" in the corner till the dance floor heats up.

For hiking in the higher heights of the Blue Mountains, a sweatshirt, parka, boots, and warm socks can be extremely helpful, especially if you encounter rain.

Explore Jamaica

THE BEST OF JAMAICA IN TWO WEEKS

Two weeks is a good length for a trip to Jamaica and provides enough time to get some time in on the beach while also venturing beyond the sun and sand for a mix of adventure, culture, and heritage tourism. Highlights include Negril's West End, a few days in quiet Belmont, Kingston's culture and nightlife, and Portland's aristocratic history and lush natural beauty.

Day 1

Arrive at the airport in **Montego Bay,** check-in for two nights, and dine at the Boathouse Grill or the more casual and every-bit-as-good Scotchie's. Hit up a bar for an evening drink to gauge the scene along the Hip Strip.

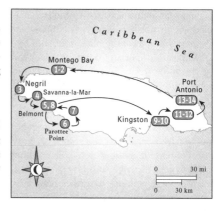

Day 2

Take tours of **Rose Hall** and **Greenwood Great House** in the morning. Then visit **Doctors Cave Beach** in the afternoon. Have dinner at Day-O Plantation followed by a play at Fairfield Theatre.

Day 3

Drive west to Negril for cliff jumping by late morning. Visit **Royal Palm Reserve** in the afternoon to fish and check out the waterfowl, then visit **Bongo's Farm** for sunset. Dine at the one-of-a-kind Hungry Lion on the West End.

Day 4

In the morning, drive southeast to Savanna-la-Mar and then turn inland to **Mayfield Falls.** Spend the morning exploring the falls and gardens. On the return back to Negril, take the northern route stopping to visit Alexander Bustamante's birthplace at Blenheim before enjoying grilled lobster at the Office of Nature on the beach of **Bloody Bay.** Back in Negril, watch the sunset from the cliffs at Why Not? Thai Kitchen.

Day 5

Check out of your hotel and drive east toward **Belmont,** stopping at **Blue Hole Garden** and **Roaring River** along the way. Settle into a beachside cottage at Horizon Cottages and dine on fresh seafood or fried chicken across the road.

Day 6

Drive south to Parottee Point and head to **Pelican Bar,** a one-of-a-kind watering hole and ramshackle fried fish joint located a mile offshore on a sandbar. Go snorkeling and enjoy fried fish and a cold beer. On your way back to Belmont, stop in **Black River** for a boat trip into the morass. Have dinner at Cloggy's or Riverside Dock.

Day 7

Drive inland and take a tour of **Appleton Estate** in the morning, followed by a stop on **Bamboo Avenue** for jelly coconut and a visit to **Y.S. Falls** in the afternoon. Pull over in **Middle Quarters** for fresh shrimp on the way back to Belmont, where you will spend another night.

Day 8

In Belmont, visit **Peter Tosh Memorial Garden** in the morning followed by a nature hike with Rasta Bryan. Depart in the afternoon for **Kingston,** arriving in time for dinner at Habibi's.

Day 9

Downtown sights in the morning could include the National Gallery, a stroll along Ocean Boulevard, and a visit to Liberty Hall. Visit Legend Cafe at the Bob Marley Museum for lunch and take a tour in the early afternoon. Stop by **Hope Botanical Gardens** for a juice at Ashanti Garden before heading back down to **Devon House** for ice cream and shopping. Go out on the town at night in New Kingston.

Day 10

Visit the Mutual Gallery and then head out to **Fort Charles** in **Port Royal** by mid-morning, followed by lunch at Gloria's. Take a boat to **Lime Cay** for a swim in the afternoon. Dinner at Fisherman's Cabin before returning to Kingston to go out on the town and hit the hay.

Days 11 and 12

Drive northeast from Kingston into the **Blue Mountains** for hiking in Holywell and two nights at Woodside. Stop at **Strawberry Hill** and splurge on a beer to check out the view—it's well worth it.

Start the next day with early-morning birding at the **Twyman's Estate** fueled by a fresh roasted pea-bean blend, the connoisseur's choice. Have lunch at The Gap Cafe, followed by an afternoon swim in the spring-fed pool at Woodside and then a home-cooked dinner.

Day 13

Leave for **Port Antonio** via Buff Bay immediately after breakfast. Check in to Jamaica Heights Resort and take a swim and then a nap. Wake up for lunch at Cynthia's and a swim on **Winnifred Beach.** Hit Roof Club or La Best in the evening to scope out the local scene.

Day 14

If you have a rental car, head back to MoBay in early morning. Otherwise, get up early and drive to **Reach Falls,** arriving by mid-morning. Climb the falls and return to **Port Antonio,** stopping in Boston to sample the jerk. If you have a driver, get dropped off at the Port Antonio airport and splurge on a charter plane to MoBay to catch your return flight.

THRILL-SEEKER'S CIRCUIT

For adventure travelers looking for adrenaline rushes and non-stop adventure punctuated with a bit of relaxation, this strategy focuses on the most exciting highlights on the island like stunning views, big waves, and mountain biking. As in any itinerary, a rental car offers the most freedom to enjoy activities and sights at your own pace without feeling pressured by waiting times, but this itinerary can work with a charter car or even by route taxi for those on a tight budget.

Days 1 and 2

Arrive in **Montego Bay,** which offers **whitewater rafting** within an hour's drive and **windsurfing** right by the airport. Get the heart pumping for the first day with one of these activities, and wind down at the MoBay Yacht Club in the evening before a night on the town.

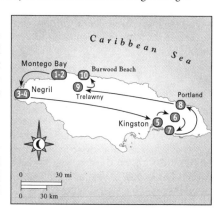

Days 3 and 4

Two days in **Negril** follow, where **cliff jumping** and **mountain biking** are the principal daytime activities, with a trip to **Mayfield Falls** or **Blue Hole Garden** thrown in. Spend the night back in Negril.

Day 5

Transfer to **Kingston,** stopping at **Y.S. Falls** on the way to test the **zipline** and **rope swing.** One night in Kingston allows for experiencing the island's best nightlife at a nightclub or street dance.

Day 6

Head up to the **Blue Mountains** for an overnight at Whitfield Hall in order to hit the peak in the morning of the seventh day. Typically hikers depart in the early morning hours to catch sunrise on top of the mountain when the sky tends to be clear.

Day 7

Descend to **Bull Bay** in the morning for a day at Jamnesia. Spend the night if the surf warrants, otherwise continue on to **Port Antonio,** stopping at **Bath Fountain** for an invigorating massage on the way.

Day 8

Go **deep sea fishing** off the Portland coast with Captain Paul or spend a day at **Blue Hole** and **Winnifred Beach.** If the surf's good at Boston or Long Bay, grab a board and hit the waves.

Day 9

Depart for **Trelawny,** stopping at **Somerset Falls** and the Human Service Station en route to Time N Place in Trelawny.

Day 10

Kite surfing or **windsurfing** on **Burwood Beach** near Starfish Trelawny for the day, with dinner at Fisherman's Inn or Glistening Waters and a boat trip on the **Luminous Lagoon** at night. Transfer to **Montego Bay** to depart the island the next morning.

SPA LOVER'S DREAM VACATION

Get pampered at the most professional spas and enjoy the more "rootsy" side of Jamaica's health tourism offerings. This 10-day itinerary is ideal for couples seeking a pampered escape. It also offers a glimpse of Jamaica's varied landscape across the different parishes and the island's most romantic spots. This itinerary includes visits to some of the more upscale hotels and spas and is not for those on a tight budget. Since relaxing is an important part of this itinerary, those unaccustomed to driving in Jamaica will want to leave the driving to somebody else. All the accommodations listed in this itinerary can arrange transportation.

This tour is based on two- or three-night stays at the island's premiere spa resorts. Other noteworthy spas that could be added to this itinerary should you approach another region include **Jackie's On The Reef** in Negril, **Milk River Bath and Spa** on the South Coast, **Nirvana** and **Jencare** day spas in Kingston, and **Round Hill Spa** in Hanover. Most all-inclusive resorts have good spa facilities, including **Grand Lido, Couples,** and **Sandals,** which carries the Red Lane brand at all its resorts.

Days 1 and 2

Arrive in Kingston. Transfer to Royal Plantation Resort or Jamaica Inn in **Ocho Rios,** where the Red Lane and Kiyara Spas wait for your first treatment followed by dinner at the hotel.

Visit Coyaba Gardens in the morning, and head to the White River Valley to see the Spanish Bridge. Tube down the river in the afternoon, or go rafting on the White River for more excitement. Stop by Reggae Beach for a dip and sunset before dinner at Toscanini.

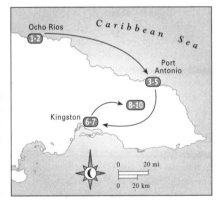

Days 3-5

Transfer to Tiamo Spa Villas in **Port Antonio** with a charter flight from Boscobel or by chopper from Ocho Rios. Upon arrival in Port Antonio, relax at San San Beach and stop by the Portland Gallery before dinner at Dickie's Banana (by reservation).

Take a morning dip at the Blue Lagoon or snorkel with Dennis Butler around Navy Island. Have lunch in Boston Bay followed by a climb up Reach Falls in the afternoon.

Spend the morning of your fifth day at Frenchman's Cove or Winnifred Beach. Enjoy lunch on the beach—jerk at Frenchman's or Cynthia's on Winnifred.

Days 6 and 7

Transfer to **Kingston,** stopping to swim and lunch in Long Bay at Chill Out. Pass through Bath for an invigorating treatment from a Rastafarian masseur. Arrive in Kingston for a night at Terra Nova. Visit the Mutual Gallery, dine at Market Place, and go out on the town for a dance performance or play.

Spend the morning sightseeing around Kingston after a visit to Shakti Mind Body Fitness. Lunch at Velissa's before heading up to stay at Strawberry Hill or Woodside in the Blue Mountains, stopping by Belcour Lodge on the way.

Days 8-10

Have a spa treatment and spend the morning by

the pool at **Strawberry Hill.** Then go hiking and birding in Holywell National Park and take a tour of Old Tavern Estate in the afternoon.

Start with an early morning hike up to Catherine's Peak with a remedial spa treatment in the afternoon at Strawberry Hill. Relax and dine on the terrace.

Brunch at Strawberry Hill on the last morning and transfer to Norman Manley airport (one hour) in Kingston for departure.

ECOTOURISM IN PARADISE

Hikes, birding, secluded beaches, and mangrove tours are indispensable to a greater appreciation of Jamaica's natural wonders. Jamaica is a relatively small island, and can be traversed in about six hours without stopping, but the diversity and ruggedness of the island's landscape makes it exhausting to try to fit in too much. Transportation is an important consideration when planning an eco-vacation, as many of the less-visited sights are remote and require a rental car. Excursions into remote parts of Cockpit Country and into the Blue Mountains require a four-wheel-drive vehicle, but for most places SUVs are not necessary and the expense is not justified. Barrett Adventures operates island-wide, and is the best charter outfit for helping to coordinate transportation for part of or an entire trip.

Day 1
Arrive in **Montego Bay** and head directly to **Good Hope Plantation** in Trelawny. Relax and dine in the **Great House.**

Day 2
Go horseback riding in **Cockpit Country** in the morning, with lunch back at the Great House. Head to **Burwood Beach** in the afternoon for windsurfing or kite-surfing lessons. Have dinner at Time N Place.

Day 3
Head deep into Cockpit Country for a visit to **Windsor Caves** and a dip near the source of the Martha Brae. Dinner back at Good Hope.

Day 4
Depart in the morning for **Tensing Pen** in **Negril.** Spend the afternoon jumping off the cliffs and relaxing by the pool.

Day 5
Visit **Royal Palm Reserve** in the morning and **Mayfield Falls** in the afternoon.

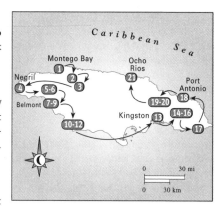

Day 6
Take a trip to **Roaring River** and **Blue Hole Garden** in the morning, followed by lunch in **Little Bay** and a visit to **Bongo's Farm** in the afternoon.

Day 7
Depart for **Belmont** in the morning. Spend the afternoon hiking in the hills and paying respect to Peter Tosh at his memorial garden before returning to Horizon Cottages to enjoy sunset.

Day 8

Go on a **Black River Safari** in the morning, then visit **Y.S. Falls** in the afternoon, with lunch along the way in Middle Quarters. Stop by **Font Hill Beach Park** for an evening swim before returning to Belmont.

Day 9

Head out to **Pelican Bar** in the morning for snorkeling and lunch. Climb up to **Accompong** to meet the colonel and take a short hike with the Maroons to the cave where they signed their treaty with the British. Return to Belmont, stopping in Black River for dinner along the river or at Cloggy's.

Day 10

Depart for **Treasure Beach,** checking in at Mutamba, Ital Rest, or—if you're a baller—at Jake's. Spend the afternoon collecting seashells along lonely stretches of beach. Dine at Jack Sprat.

Day 11

Spend the morning at **Manatee Hole** near **Alligator Pond** followed by a dip at **Guts River.** Dine at Little Ochie in the evening.

Day 12

Depart in the morning for **Mandeville.** Call to arrange a visit at **Marshall's Pen** for early morning birding on the following day. Take a stroll around the historical sites in the square and check out the market before a visit to the Pickapeppa factory and dinner at Bloomfield Great House.

Day 13

Spend the morning birding at **Marshall's Pen,** then depart for **Kingston** in the afternoon. Check in at Country Cottage Inn and head out for dinner and some nightlife.

Day 14

Check out the sights around town in the morning (like Heroes Memorial and the National Gallery) and head into the **Blue Mountains** in the afternoon. Check in at Lime Tree Farm.

Day 15

Rise early for a morning hike up **Blue Mountain Peak.** Spend the afternoon recuperating and birding around the farm.

Day 16

Head out to **Cinchona Gardens,** roads permitting, to take in the historic botanical gardens and birds. Head up to **Strawberry Hill** for dinner with a view.

Day 17

Depart in the morning for **Morant Bay** to take a boat trip through the Morass to the lighthouse. Pass through **Bath** in the early evening for a hot dip before continuing on to **Long Bay** for a night at Yahimba.

Day 18

Enjoy the beach in the morning, then depart after lunch for **Port Antonio.** Stop at **Reach Falls** along the way and have a bite to eat in Boston before checking in at Jamaica Heights Resort.

Day 19

Leave in the morning for a trip up the **Rio Grande Valley** to meet the colonel and try to spot the giant swallowtail butterfly with the help of Maroon guides. Hike to **Nanny Falls** for a swim before returning to Port Antonio for the night.

Day 20

Spend the morning between **Blue Hole** and **Winnifred Beach** before an afternoon departure to **Robin's Bay.** Check in at River Lodge, an old Spanish fort. Take the orchid and tea tour at **Green Castle Estate** before dinner at Sunrise Lawn.

Day 21

Head west in the morning, stopping at Scotchie's near **Ocho Rios** to grab a picnic lunch to enjoy at **Cranbrook Flower Forest.** Continue on to MoBay for an evening departure.

ROOTS AND CULTURE

These are the must-see historical sites and must-do events for those travelers wishing to delve into the pulsating cultural milieu that shapes and defines Jamaican society. Keep tabs on the weekly events calendars in Kingston and Negril to plan your time in these areas. The roots of Jamaican popular music will become vivid with this tour, which touches on the island's evolving music industry.

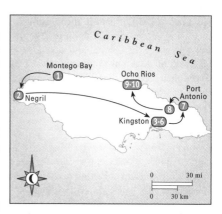

Day 1
Arrive Wednesday in Montego Bay for one night at Richmond Hill. Dine at MoBay Proper before heading over to Wacky Wenzdaze at The Brewery for MoBay's closest approximation to a street dance.

Day 2
Hit Doctors Cave Beach in the morning and then head to Negril in the afternoon. Check out the night's live reggae band on the beach.

Day 3
Leave for Kingston in the morning, stopping at Scott's Pass in Clarendon to meet the Rasta elders at the headquarters of the Nyabinghi House of Rastafari.

Day 4
Hit Kingston's cultural sights, including the Bob Marley Museum, Tuff Gong Studios, Culture Yard, and the National Gallery. Have dinner at Hellshire Beach before a night out on the town at Asylum followed by a street dance.

Day 5
Leave in the morning for Jamnesia in Bull Bay. Spend the day surfing and hanging with Billy Mystic and his family.

Day 6
Spend the day visiting Bobo Hill with Priest Harold. Head into Kingston for Uptown Mondays.

Day 7
Leave in the morning for Port Antonio, checking in at Great Huts or Drapers San. Spend the afternoon at Reach Falls or on the beach with a quick visit to Folly Ruins thrown in.

Day 8
Head up the Rio Grande Valley to Moore Town to hike with the Winward Maroons. Visit Nanny Falls and return to Port Antonio by evening to dine at Dickie's Banana.

Day 9
Depart first thing for Ocho Rios, checking in at Carleen's Villa Guest House or Mahoe Guest House. Visit the Bob Marley Mausoleum or Reggae Xplosion before dinner at Tropical Vibes on Fisherman's Beach.

Day 10
Visit Wassi Art and Coyaba Gardens in the morning before a transfer to Montego Bay for an evening departure. Stop by Time N Place or Culture Restaurant in Falmouth.

KINGSTON AND THE BLUE MOUNTAINS

Kingston is the heartbeat of Jamaica, driving the island's cultural and economic pulse. If the island's major tourist centers of Montego Bay, Ocho Rios, and Negril straddle a surreal world between a party in paradise inside all-inclusive resorts and a meager reality outside, Kingston is refreshing in its raw, real-world atmosphere. Kingston is Jamaica's proud center of business and government and an important transshipment port for Caribbean commerce; the tourist economy on which the country as a whole is dependent takes a back seat in Town, as the capital is known. This is the Jamaica where the daily hustle to make ends meet gives fodder to an ever-growing cadre of young artists following in the footsteps of reggae legend Bob Marley. As such, Kingston is an essential stop for an understanding of the richness on this small island. Jamaica has a diverse historical and cultural heritage, and nowhere is it more boldly revealed than through the country's art, music, dance, and theater. Kingston's vibrant nightlife is a world unto itself with parties and stage shows that never seem to end.

Downtown Kingston is at first sight a case study in urban decay. Blocks upon blocks of buildings haven't seen a paintbrush in decades, and many are collapsed and abandoned. The city became known as a breeding ground for political violence in the 1970s, when area neighborhood dons were put on the payroll of competing political forces to ensure mass support at election time. Downtown neighborhoods like Allman Town, Arnette Gardens, Rima, Tivoli, and Greenwich Town are still explosive politicized communities where gunshots are hardly

KINGSTON

HIGHLIGHTS

◖ **Institute of Jamaica:** The institute and the divisions under its umbrella are the go-to points of record for Jamaica's heritage in all its manifestations (page 39).

◖ **National Heroes Park:** The one-stop-shop to learn about the people whose contributions are paramount to the Jamaican experience from slavery to independence (page 41).

◖ **Emancipation Park:** The most judicious starting point for a walk around New Kingston, the park has an impressive statue sculpted by Laura Facey evoking emancipation (page 43).

◖ **Devon House:** The former house of self-made Jamaican millionaire George Steibel, the museum fronts an array of great shops and restaurants (page 44).

◖ **Bob Marley Museum and Tuff Gong Recording Studio:** Jamaica's most revered son is alive and stronger each day thanks to the music and unstoppable legacy featured at 56 Hope Road (page 45).

◖ **Mutual Gallery:** This is an essential gallery for art enthusiasts keen to get a preview of the up-and-coming in Jamaica's dynamic arts scene (page 48).

◖ **Hellshire:** An assortment of fried fish and lobster shacks crowd this popular weekend spot where Kingstonians relish the epitome of rustic chic (page 78).

◖ **Lime Cay:** Once a haven for buccaneers, this sleepy outpost comes alive on weekends with sound systems, fried fish, and an idyllic beach (page 87).

◖ **Alex Twyman's Old Tavern Coffee Estate:** Worth as much time as you've got, the Blue Mountains have clean air, breathtaking views, and the best coffee in the world (page 92).

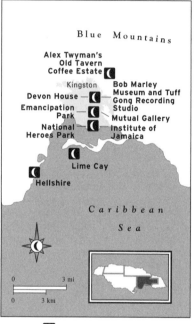

LOOK FOR ◖ TO FIND RECOMMENDED SIGHTS, ACTIVITIES, DINING, AND LODGING.

out of the ordinary. Other communities further out have also gained notoriety, like Riverton City, next to the dump, and Harbour View at the base of the Palisadoes.

Despite the seriousness of crime and violence in these areas, Kingston is not to be feared, as even many Jamaican countryfolk might suggest. With a good dose of common sense and respect, and a feeling for Jamaican "runnings,"

or street smarts, there is little chance of having an altercation of any nature.

The surrounding parish of St. Andrew was at one time a rural area dominated by a handful of estates. Since becoming the nation's capital, however, Kingston has spilled over and engulfed much of the relatively flat land of the parish, its residential neighborhoods creeping ever farther up the sides of the Blue Mountain foothills. At

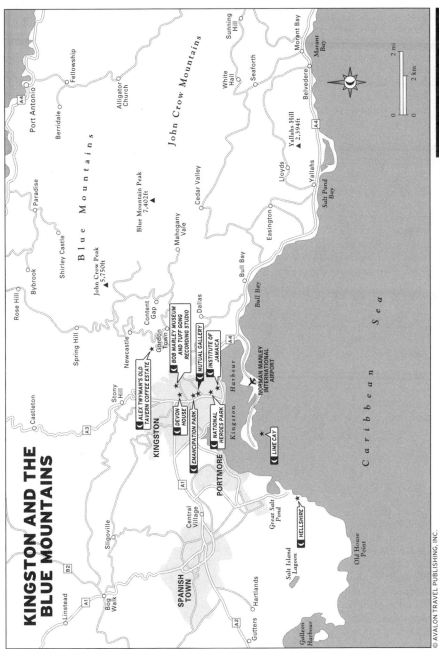

KINGSTON AND THE BLUE MOUNTAINS

the center of St. Andrew is the bustling commercial center of Half Way Tree, where new shopping plazas seem to rise overnight. There are still unpaved patches of St. Andrew, however, like the expansive Hope Botanical Gardens, the Mona campus of the University of the West Indies, and countless well-laid-out properties where it's easy to imagine the days when St. Andrew was truly rural.

Twenty minutes due west is Spanish Town, still seemingly sore about losing its preeminence as Jamaica's capital and business center. Seldom visited by outsiders from Jamaica or abroad, Spanish Town played a central role in the island's early history as a major population center, first for the Tainos, then for the Spanish, and finally for the British. Each group left its mark, a fact recognized by the United Nations when the city was declared a World Heritage Site. Jamaica's second capital city, Spanish Town was founded in 1534 when the Spanish abandoned New Seville on the North Coast. The city lies at the heart of St. Catherine, a parish whose moment of glory has sadly passed in a very tangible sense. Neglect and urban blight permeate Spanish Town. Nevertheless it's littered with fascinating heritage sites, including a few notable churches, memorials, and glimpses of better years. It is a convenient stop as most routes to destinations across the island invariably pass by Spanish Town.

To the north and northeast of Kingston, the Blue Mountains cover portions of four parishes: St. Andrew, St. Mary, St. Thomas, and Portland. All within an hour's drive from Kingston, Irish Town, Hardwar Gap, and Mavis Bank are great for an easy escape from the urban jungle. This is where rural Jamaica is at its coolest. The elevation and lush greenery are a welcome retreat from the often-torturous heat on the plains and foothills around Town. The road up and the rugged terrain are not for the faint of heart, but the prized Blue Mountain coffee, breathtaking views, diverse vegetation, and abundance of native birds are more than adequate rewards, and few are sorry for making the effort.

Together the three parishes containing the greater metropolitan area are home to about 43 percent of the island's 2.8 million residents. Perhaps to a greater extent than in some other developing countries, poverty and excess share an abrasive coexistence in Jamaica, especially in Kingston. This inevitably leads to widespread begging and persistent windshield-washing services at stoplights. Apart from these regular encounters, Kingston is relatively hassle-free compared with major tourist centers on the island, where hustlers tend to be more focused on the tourist trade and are visibly aggressive in their search for a dollar. Kingston is one of the few places in Jamaica where visitors with a light complexion can seemingly blend into the normal fabric of society. People in Kingston have other things occupying their attention, and visitors go almost unnoticed.

PLANNING YOUR TIME

Kingston has a tendency to consume time, so it's perfect for those who like to idle about and soak up local culture. Skylarking is in fact one of Jamaica's favorite pastimes, carefully perfected over many years by some Kingstonians. For visitors looking to hit all the important historical and cultural sites in a rush, at least two nights in a two-week visit to Jamaica should be dedicated to Kingston, and certainly more during a longer stay in order to adopt the local pace and enjoy the sights, food, and nightlife. Most of the historical sights downtown can be seen in one day. Uptown attractions tend to be conveniently concentrated in the Half Way Tree/Hope Road area, and will consume another day's visit to fit in **Devon House, The Bob Marley Museum,** and **Hope Gardens,** with a little shopping and eating in between. One day can easily be spent in and around Spanish Town.

As a place of business, Kingston's inevitable bureaucratic red tape can be frustrating at worst and a challenge to negotiate at best. Most of the island's major music and film studios are located in Kingston, which makes it *the* base for those looking to engage in entertainment production. Kingston's nightlife heats up on the weekends with stage shows and parties held almost weekly at one venue or another, but there are worthwhile events almost any night of the week, and the most popular regular street dances are held on weeknights. Theater performances are held several nights a week, but schedules vary all the time. It is worth calling ahead when planning a visit to Town if you would like to catch a theater performance.

If you can, plan to spend a Sunday at **Lime Cay.** Kingston's most popular beach, just south off the coast from Port Royal, has become a hub for the city's young and hip.

Kingston is not inexpensive by any means in terms of accommodations, and a meal out can match New York City prices if you want to flirt with high society. Still, a night on the town doesn't need to cost more than US$20 and there's always a way to get by regardless of budgetary constraints.

A few days in Kingston perfectly sets the stage for a nice break into the Blue Mountains, within an hour's drive away. Most of the guesthouses in the mountains can arrange transportation to and from Town, and once there, hiking trails abound, and local transport can be easily found with a little patience. Anywhere from three nights to a week should be allowed for a trip into the Blue Mountains, especially for those planning to do some serious hiking or birding. The main draws in the Blue Mountains are relaxation, sipping coffee, and enjoying nature, and therefore the length of stay depends on how much time you want to dedicate to these essential pastimes.

HISTORY

Kingston didn't become an important city, or a city at all for that matter, until well after the British captured Jamaica from Spain in 1655. It wasn't until the great earthquake of 1692 left the nearby boomtown of Port Royal almost entirely underwater that Kingston's population grew to any size—thanks to the survivors fleeing from across the harbor. A subsequent disaster, a devastating fire in 1703, left Port Royal virtually abandoned and sealed the town's fate as a literal backwater. Prior to this, Kingston's downtown area was dominated by a fishing

and pig-farming village known as Colonel Beeston's Hog Crawle.

The well-organized city was built to take advantage of the outstanding natural harbor that had put Port Royal on the map in the first place, and was named in honor of William of Orange, who ruled England from 1689 to 1702. Before long, Kingston became an immigration point for merchants from around the Caribbean seeking fortune from the slave trade and associated commerce. When slavery was finally abolished in 1834, Kingston's population swelled as many former slaves rejected the rural life that reminded them of a not so-distant past. They began coming to Kinston in search of a fresh start.

Thanks to brisk trade that continued along Kingston Harbor, the city soon challenged the capital of Spanish Town in economic importance. In 1872, after what proved to be years of futile resistance, the disgruntled bureaucrats in Spanish Town finally ceded power. Uptown Kingston remained predominantly rural well into the mid-1800s, when wealthier Kingstonians began seeking refuge from the swelling shantytowns that sprang up around Downtown. Most areas of Uptown today still include "manor" or "pen" in reference to the parcels of land that contained the farming estates of yesteryear.

In 1907, a massive earthquake destroyed the majority of buildings along the waterfront, further exacerbating the flight of those with means to Uptown. By the 1930s, prices plunged for the commodities that still formed the base of Jamaica's economy, causing widespread riots around Kingston. This was a time of social and political unrest throughout the African Diaspora, catalyzing the Jamaican labor movement and bringing leaders Marcus Garvey, William Gordon, and Alexander Bustamante to the fore. By the time Jamaica was granted its independence on August 1, 1962 (it technically remains a protectorate of the British crown), redevelopment along the harbor was slated as a priority. Unfortunately for the waterfront area, most of the economic development that ensued took place along the

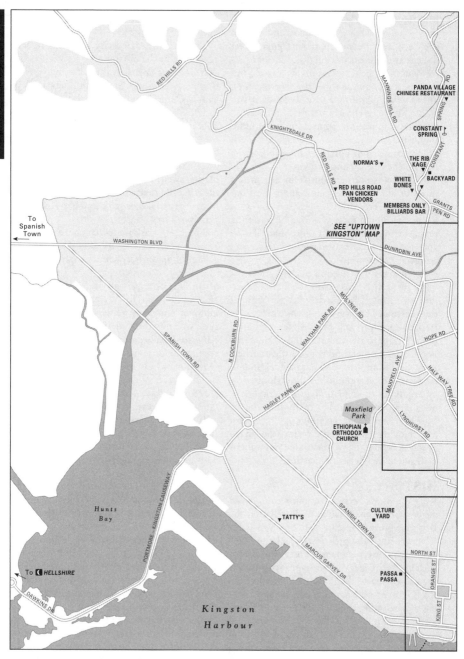

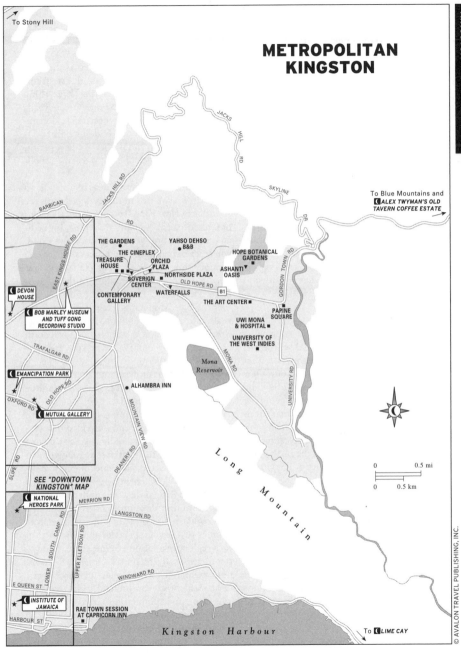

METROPOLITAN KINGSTON

To Stony Hill

JACKS HILL RD

SKYLINE DR

To Blue Mountains and
◖ ALEX TWYMAN'S OLD
TAVERN COFFEE ESTATE

BARBICAN

JACKS HILL RD

RD

EAST KINGS HOUSE RD

THE GARDENS
THE CINEPLEX
TREASURE HOUSE
ORCHID PLAZA
SOVERIGN CENTER
NORTHSIDE PLAZA
CONTEMPORARY GALLERY
WATERFALLS

YAHSO DEHSO B&B

HOPE BOTANICAL GARDENS

ASHANTI OASIS

OLD HOPE RD

B1

THE ART CENTER ■

GORDON TOWN RD

PAPINE SQUARE

◖ DEVON HOUSE

◖ BOB MARLEY MUSEUM AND TUFF GONG RECORDING STUDIO

UWI MONA & HOSPITAL ■

UNIVERSITY OF THE WEST INDIES

TRAFALGAR RD

◖ EMANCIPATION PARK

OLD HOPE RD

OXFORD RD

◖ MUTUAL GALLERY

● ALHAMBRA INN

Mona Reservoir

MONA RD

UNIVERSITY RD

SLIPE RD

MOUNTAIN VIEW RD

SEE "DOWNTOWN KINGSTON" MAP

◖ NATIONAL HEROES PARK

DEANERY RD

MERRION RD

LANGSTON RD

L o n g   M o u n t a i n

0   0.5 mi
0   0.5 km

SOUTH CAMP RD

LOWER

UPPER ELLETSON RD

WINDWARD RD

E QUEEN ST

◖ INSTITUTE OF JAMAICA

RAE TOWN SESSION AT CAPRICORN INN ■

HARBOUR ST

Kingston Harbour

To ◖ LIME CAY

© AVALON TRAVEL PUBLISHING, INC.

city's new hip strip, Knutsford Boulevard, in New Kingston, and further uptown in Half Way Tree and along Hope Road.

Violent political campaigns in the 1970s and 1980s gave Kingston international notoriety, but visitors today rarely, if ever, find themselves subject to or even observers of violent crime. In fact, it would take real effort for a foreigner to get shot in Kingston, perhaps only by making the mistake of wearing an orange People's National Party (PNP) t-shirt while walking through Tivoli Gardens, one of the city's most notorious ghettos and a stronghold for the opposition Jamaica Labor Party (JLP). Generally speaking, the only time foreigners are in the press associated with crime is in cases where they have tried to exit the country carrying drugs. Sticking by the right kind of locals, and hanging in the right places, Kingston is no more dangerous a place than any other big city in the developing world where wealth and poverty coexist.

ORIENTATION

The parish of Kingston encompasses what is today referred to as Downtown as well as the Palisadoes, a 16-kilometer-long stretch that runs from the roundabout at Harbour View to the tip of Port Royal. The city was originally laid out in a grid to house residents fleeing the disappearance of what had been Britain's strongest Jamaican outpost in Port Royal. Kingston developed as Jamaica's economic epicenter following the British takeover and the earthquake of 1692, which left the majority of Port Royal underwater, swallowed by the sea.

Originally laid out in a grid bound by Harbour, North, East, and West Streets, the old city of Kingston soon overstepped these boundaries with residential shantytowns springing up on every side. Over the years, some of these areas have seen simple zinc shacks replaced by homes of slightly better stature. Most of the buildings in the area below the Parade are commercial, while there is an effort underway to bring more middle-income housing to the waterfront area.

Kingston is the capital city as well as Jamai-

ca's smallest parish, engulfed by the parish of St. Andrew, which extends from the causeway traversing Hunt's Bay on the western edge of Town to Castleton, in the parish of St. Mary on the northern border, east across the Blue Mountains to Bull Bay in the southeastern corner, along the St. Thomas border. Everything north of the junction known as Cross Roads (where Caledonia Avenue meets Slipe, Retirement, Half Way Tree, and Old Hope Roads) is considered uptown and is in St. Andrew parish, which contains much of present-day metropolitan Kingston.

Most of the more active areas of Town lie in St. Andrew. The two most developed areas are the hubs of **New Kingston,** immediately north of Cross Roads, and **Half Way Tree,** immediately to the east of New Kingston. **Hope Road,** where several businesses and sites of interest are located, runs northeast from Half Way Tree Square all the way to **Papine** on the edge of town. From there, Highway B1 leads into and over the Blue Mountains. Half Way Tree Road is also a major thoroughfare, starting at Cross Roads, turning into Constant Spring Road north of the Clock Tower in Half Way Tree, and running to the northernmost edge of town where it becomes Stony Hill Road and later turns into Highway A3, which leads to St. Mary and the North Coast via Junction.

Metropolitan Kingston is often referred to as the Corporate Area and is divided into two regions referred to on a daily basis as **Uptown** and **Downtown.** In a spatial sense, Downtown Kingston is the old city, laid out in a well-organized grid, whereas Uptown is an urban sprawl with little order, the result of more recent economic development. Kingstonians also regularly use these neighborhood names to refer to the social classes that live within each region. In a socioeconomic sense, "Downtown" generally refers to Kingston's "have-nots," while "Uptown" refers to the "haves," or at least those who pretend to fit that bill. The city's poor populations are concentrated in tenement yards and shantytowns, most of which are found Downtown. In recent years, however, squatter settlements have sprouted

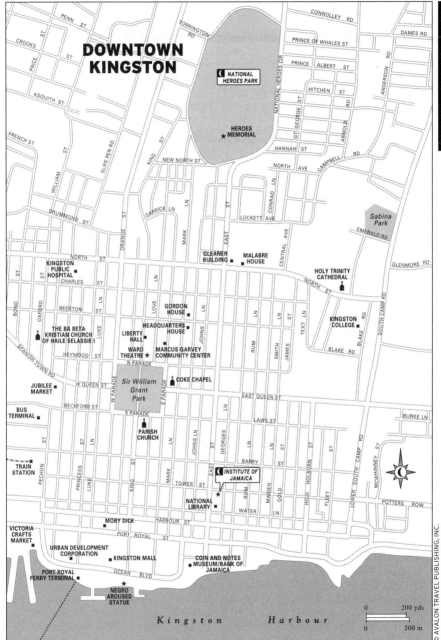

DOWNTOWN KINGSTON

NATIONAL HEROES PARK

HEROES MEMORIAL

Sabina Park

GLEANER BUILDING
MALABRE HOUSE

HOLY TRINITY CATHEDRAL

KINGSTON PUBLIC HOSPITAL

GORDON HOUSE

KINGSTON COLLEGE

THE BA BETA KRISTIAN CHURCH OF HAILE SELASSIE I

HEADQUARTERS HOUSE

LIBERTY HALL

WARD THEATRE
MARCUS GARVEY COMMUNITY CENTER

JUBILEE MARKET

Sir William Grant Park

COKE CHAPEL

BUS TERMINAL

PARISH CHURCH

TRAIN STATION

INSTITUTE OF JAMAICA

NATIONAL LIBRARY

MOBY DICK

VICTORIA CRAFTS MARKET

URBAN DEVELOPMENT CORPORATION

KINGSTON MALL

COIN AND NOTES MUSEUM/BANK OF JAMAICA

PORT ROYAL FERRY TERMINAL

NEGRO AROUSED STATUE

Kingston   Harbour

0   200 yds
0   200 m

© AVALON TRAVEL PUBLISHING, INC.

up throughout the city despite the geographical boundary.

The junction at **Cross Roads** divides Downtown from Uptown. Most of the government buildings that date from colonial days are found south of the line. **New Kingston** technically begins north of the Cross Roads intersection, but the heart of the business district is found north of Oxford Road along Knutsford Boulevard which runs north–south and on the streets parallel to Knutsford to the immediate east and west. Trafalgar Road forms the upper border of New Kingston, with the residential district of Liguanea further to the north.

The **Blue Mountain foothills** flank the entire city, forming a constant backdrop. Along with a handful of high-rises in New Kingston, the hills provide the best natural landmarks for spatial orientation when moving about the city.

Downtown

Kingston boasts the world's seventh largest natural harbor, which helped the city become the most important export center for Europe-bound goods as well as transshipment around the Caribbean. As the nature of trade and commerce changed over the years, the Downtown area has seen less and less direct economic benefit from shipping, which is today centered at the wharfs west of Downtown along Marcus Garvey Drive and along the causeway leading to Portmore. The modern wharfs are unmistakable even from the air, with massive cranes servicing an endless stream of container ships that make Kingston one of the busiest ports in the world today.

Development since independence has been focused almost exclusively above Cross Roads, leaving the Downtown area neglected, with little change in sight. Downtown sees a lot of activity during the day, however, with many government institutions still located there, including the Survey Department, the Urban Development Corporation, the Jamaican Parliament, the Supreme Court, and the Institute of Jamaica.

The Bank of Jamaica, with its Coin and Notes Museum, and Scotia Bank both have

their headquarters along the waterfront. It's not the best place for a lonely stroll at night, however, as the business area becomes desolate and the Parade area tends to be filled with vagrants.

A new wave of Chinese and Indian immigrants have set up a slew of retail outlets along King and Orange Streets, somewhat reviving what was once Kingston's Chinatown.

Jubilee and Coronation Markets more or less fuse together into a seemingly endless array of stalls west of **the Parade,** which marks the heart of Downtown. As the name suggests, the Parade was once used as a marching ground for British troops. Today it is a poorly maintained park where domino games abound. The adjacent market has a distinct buzz and thick air that changes from a mild aroma to an unpleasant stench with little warning. It takes some courage to stroll through the market and navigate the cacophony, but it's worth doing at least once, as it's an experience unto Downtown Kingston alone. The bus terminal just south of the heart of the market is the principal departure point for routes around the country. Expect overpacked and cramped seats and blasting R&B for the entire ride no matter the destination.

Uptown

Until well into the 1800s, St. Andrew parish consisted of a handful of large private estates covering the rolling Blue Mountain foothills. When Downtown began to overcrowd, the land was parceled off and sold to accommodate the overflowing city with new residential neighborhoods. Many areas of greater Kingston still retain the name of the farming estate, or *pen,* they were built on. **Constant Spring, Hope, Mona,** and **Papine** were all rural estates that are now neighborhoods of Uptown.

New Kingston is a hub of business activity and nightlife, and has been the focal point for urban development since independence. Some of the busiest nightclubs, bars, and restaurants are found along or just off of Knutsford Boulevard, as are many hotels catering to business travelers and tourists. New Kingston is a small

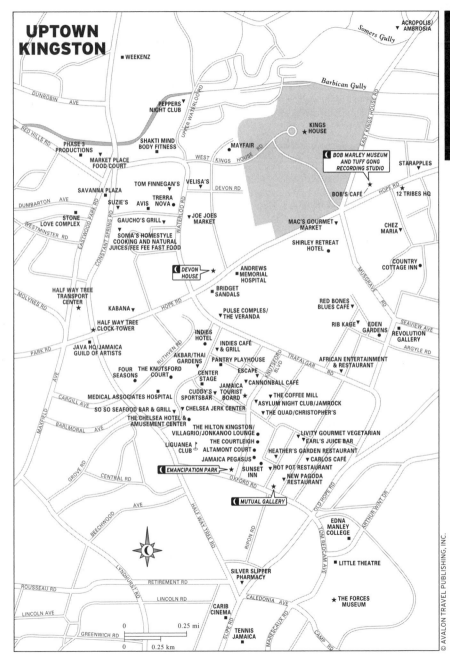

UPTOWN KINGSTON

WEEKENZ

Somers Gully

ACROPOLIS/ AMBROSIA

DUNROBIN AVE

PEPPERS NIGHT CLUB

Barbican Gully

RED HILLS RD

SHAKTI MIND BODY FITNESS

PHASE 3 PRODUCTIONS

MARKET PLACE FOOD COURT

UPPER WATERLOO RD

MAYFAIR

KINGS HOUSE

EAST KINGS HOUSE RD

WEST KINGS HOUSE RD

BOB MARLEY MUSEUM AND TUFF GONG RECORDING STUDIO

STARAPPLES

SAVANNA PLAZA

TOM FINNEGAN'S

VELISA'S

DEVON RD

HOPE RD

DUMBARTON AVE

SUZIE'S

AVIS

TRERRA NOVA

BOB'S CAFÉ

12 TRIBES HQ

STONE LOVE COMPLEX

GAUCHO'S GRILL

JOE JOES MARKET

MAC'S GOURMET MARKET

CHEZ MARIA

WESTMINSTER RD

EASTWOOD PARK RD

CONSTANT SPRING RD

WATERLOO RD

SONIA'S HOMESTYLE COOKING AND NATURAL JUICES/FEE FEE FAST FOOD

SHIRLEY RETREAT HOTEL

COUNTRY COTTAGE INN

DEVON HOUSE

ANDREWS MEMORIAL HOSPITAL

MUSGRAVE

HALF WAY TREE TRANSPORT CENTER

KABANA

HOPE RD

BRIDGET SANDALS

PULSE COMPLES/ THE VERANDA

RED BONES BLUES CAFÉ

MOLYNES RD

HALF WAY TREE CLOCK TOWER

RIB KAGE

EDEN GARDENS

SEAVIEW AVE

REVOLUTION GALLERY

PARK RD

JAVA HQ/JAMAICA GUILD OF ARTISTS

INDIES HOTEL

RUTHVEN RD

INDIES CAFÉ & GRILL

ARGYLE RD

FOUR SEASONS

THE KNUTSFORD COURT

AKBAR/THAI GARDENS

PANTRY PLAYHOUSE

KNUTSFORD BLVD

TRAFALGAR RD

AFRICAN ENTERTAINMENT & RESTAURANT

ESCAPE

CENTER STAGE

CANNONBALL CAFÉ

MEDICAL ASSOCIATES HOSPITAL

CARGILL AVE

CUDDY'S SPORTSBAR

JAMAICA TOURIST BOARD

THE COFFEE MILL

ASYLUM NIGHT CLUB/JAMROCK

SO SO SEAFOOD BAR & GRILL

CHELSEA JERK CENTER

THE QUAD/CHRISTOPHER'S

THE CHELSEA HOTEL & AMUSEMENT CENTER

BARLMORAL AVE

MAYFIELD AVE

THE HILTON KINGSTON/ VILLAGRIO/JONKANOO LOUNGE

LIVITY GOURMET VEGETARIAN

EARL'S JUICE BAR

LIGUANEA CLUB

THE COURTLEIGH

ALTAMONT COURT

HEATHER'S GARDEN RESTAURANT

GROVE RD

JAMAICA PEGASUS

CARLOS CAFÉ

CENTRAL RD

EMANCIPATION PARK

SUNSET INN

HOT POT RESTAURANT

NEW PAGODA RESTAURANT

OXFORD RD

BEECHWOOD

AVE

HALF WAY TREE RD

MUTUAL GALLERY

OLD HOPE RD

ARTHUR WINT DR

RIPON RD

EDNA MANLEY COLLEGE

TOM REDCAM AVE

ROUSSEAU RD

LYNDHURST RD

RETIREMENT RD

SILVER SLIPPER PHARMACY

LITTLE THEATRE

LINCOLN RD

CALEDONIA AVE

THE FORCES MUSEUM

LINCOLN AVE

GREENWICH RD

CARIB CINEMA

SLIPE RD

TENNIS JAMAICA

MARESCAUX RD

CAMP RD

0   0.25 mi

0   0.25 km

© AVALON TRAVEL PUBLISHING, INC.

KINGSTON

area bound by Trafalgar Road and Oxford Road, which run parallel to each other at the northern and southern end respectively.

North of Trafalgar Road, the residential neighborhood of **Trafalgar Park** extends to Hope Road, and from there Liguanea extends west and north to the boarder of Barbican. Barbican is a predominantly residential neighborhood that extends up the slopes toward Jacks Hill.

Directly west of New Kingston is **Half Way Tree** (often pronounced "Half-a-Tree"), the capital of St. Andrew parish and the city's commercial core. Shopping plaza abuts shopping plaza, with the **clock tower,** Half Way Tree's most notable landmark, at the main intersection, and the new Transport Center in between northbound Eastwood Park Road and southbound Constant Spring Road. The new Transport Center is a departure point for public transportation around the city and for major points around the island. Route taxis also leave

© LANCE WATSON

The clock tower in Half Way Tree is at Kingston's busiest intersection and the hub of its principle commercial district.

from Half Way Tree. A few steps west from the heart of Half Way Tree stands the historic St. Andrew Parish Church.

Though 100 years ago St. Andrew was sprinkled with farms and manors, today it is no more than a municipality of the sprawling capital city. The name Half Way Tree apparently refers to a large cotton tree that at one point before the British takeover of 1655 provided shade for resting soldiers traveling between a base in Greenwich, St. Andrew, and a fort in Spanish Town. The tree no longer stands. Plenty of shopping, several restaurants, and a few notable hotels are found in the general area.

The hills around Town are strewn with some of the Island's most excessive concrete homes, where astonishing views and a relatively cool breeze, even in the dead of summer, bless those lucky enough to reside there. The slums of downtown Kingston stand in stark contrast to mansions that dot Uptown areas like Beverly Hills, Jacks Hill, Norbrook, Cherry Gardens, Red Hills, and Stony Hill. Many of these grand homes lay empty, however, while still others were never completed before being abandoned. It is said that many unfinished homes belong to *druggists* (narcotics traffickers) who either fled the country after drawing too much attention with their conspicuous displays of wealth or were nabbed by the authorities.

Along Hope Road

Running from Half Way Tree in the heart of St. Andrew northeast to Papine Square, Hope Road was for a time the quintessential Uptown address, one which marked Bob Marley's rise to fame and fortune when he moved there from the ghetto of Trench Town in the early 1970s. Several noteworthy attractions, a few restaurants, and plenty of shopping line the busy thoroughfare.

Must-see sights including **Devon House,** the **Bob Marley Museum,** and **Hope Gardens** are all along Hope Road. The University of Technology (UTECH) is also located here, and Mona, the main campus for the University of the West Indies (UWI), is a stone's throw away just south of Papine. On Saturdays, **Papine Square** comes alive with drumming and singing when Rastafarians from His Imperial Majesty's School of Bible Study and Sabbath Service, based in a squatter settlement in the hills above Irish Town, descend for their weekly Nyabinghi Sabbath service. Barbican Road winds off Hope Road at Sovereign Centre with a few notable restaurants in Orchid plaza.

DANGERS AND ANNOYANCES

Kingston is a city of nearly one million people, the vast majority of whom live in poverty. It is important to keep in mind that people will say and do just about anything that gives them the opportunity to "nyam food," or eat. While physical intimidation can certainly present itself, a more common occurrence is for someone to yell from across the street, "Come here!" When you get a feeling that this kind of advance may lead to an uncomfortable situation, go with that inclination. It helps to keep petty cash on hand to ease tensions when strategically necessary. If you have a car, someone nearby will invariably help direct you to park it and then volunteer to watch it while you eat or dance in a club. At the end of the night he expects a tip. While you don't need to be intimidated by these everyday occurrences, at times a bit of small change will put you in good for the next time.

For women travelers unaccustomed to aggressive men, Jamaica will most certainly be an eye-opener. Shyness is not a strong part of the Jamaican idiosyncrasy, and Jamaican men will put on all kinds of charm to seduce women with creative and tactful words. While most of these approaches are harmless, it's important to never let down your guard and to maintain a certain degree of aloofness, taking everything with a grain of salt. Standards for what is considered acceptable language are very different in Jamaica from most North American and European countries, and language commonly used for flirtation in Jamaica might be considered sexual harassment in other places.

In club settings, dancing can be very sexual and intimate, with "wining and grinding" a part of normal conduct. Jamaican women are a tough lot, however, and generally run things, or have control over the situation. When a man displeases them, they have no problem making it known. You should feel perfectly comfortable doing the same with a degree of diplomacy.

Sights

DOWNTOWN

Jamaican art pioneer Edna Manley was honored with a re-creation of her sculpture *Negro Aroused* on Ocean Boulevard along the waterfront at the end of King Street. It's as good as any a place to begin a tour of Downtown.

Along Ocean Boulevard, fishermen casually reel in their lines and children jump off big concrete blocks into the choppy waters of Kingston Harbor. It's a great place for an afternoon stroll or to watch sunsets over the Hellshire Hills.

The free **Coin and Notes Museum** (Bank of Jamaica, Nethersole Place, between East and Duke Sts., tel. 876/922-0750, ext. 2110, 9 A.M.–4 P.M. Mon.–Fri.) provides a history of money in Jamaica from the time when goods were bartered to the present. The in-between period saw the circulation of coins from many countries, including Spain and Mexico. Curators Sandra Moody and Elan Edwards have a wealth of knowledge to share with visitors.

For souvenirs, the **Crafts Market** at the junction of Ocean Boulevard and Port Royal Street features some authentic Jamaican crafts, as well as an ever-increasing slew of Chinese-made Jamaican-flag-covered trinkets, t-shirts, and towels.

Culture Yard

Culture Yard (18b Collie Smith Dr. at 3rd St., Trench Town Development Association,

THE LIFE AND LEGACY OF "MISS LOU"

The life of Louise Bennett Coverley (September 7, 1919-July 26, 2006) spanned an evolution in the identity of the Jamaican people. Born in Downtown Kingston at 40 North Street, she was raised during a tumultuous time alongside the growth of Jamaica's Labour Movement, whose leaders were agitating for racial equality. Miss Lou became an outspoken poet, social commentator, and performer at an early age, converting thick Patois – considered at the time the language of the illiterate underclass – into a national art form and a source of pride. Miss Lou began publishing books in Jamaican Creole in the early 1940s, before pursuing opportunities in London to further her performance career. She brought Jamaican folk culture to media and stages around the world, giving presence to a nation yearning for independence. Jamaican folk culture is based overwhelmingly on African traditions, and in bringing her stories and poems into performance and literary forms, Miss Lou validated an integral part of the country's heritage that had for centuries been scorned. While there are still plenty of examples in contemporary Jamaica where shame of an African past is evident, Miss Lou dispelled the taboo associated with this rich heritage with her warmth and lyrical genius. When Jamaica gained its independence in 1962, Miss Lou's popularity was only cemented further as a proven ambassador for the Jamaican identity in the birth of a new era. Miss Lou was a founding member of the Little Theatre Movement.

tel. 876/922-8462, US$7) is a somewhat contrived attraction based around Bob Marley's former home in the ghetto of Rima. It has been deemed a historical site and offers a community tour. Visiting Culture Yard is a decent excuse to see the slums of **Trench Town,** which have certainly retained much of the dire conditions that gave birth to songs like "Concrete Jungle" and "No Woman No Cry," even if the cost for a look-around feels more like charity than value. The area is marked by a large mural of Marley, visible from Spanish Town Road.

A few years ago the Trench Town Development Association was established to carry out projects to benefit the community. One success has been the **Trenchtown Reading Centre** (tel. 876/360-2483 or 876/532-0352, www.trenchtownreadingcentre.com, wgray@airjamaica.com), which was housed in a new building in 2000. The reading center welcomes book donations. Visiting Culture Yard is safe, but the communities in and around Trench Town remain explosive, so it's a good idea not to go wandering on your own. Colin Smikle (tel. 876/370-8243 or 876/978-5833, colinskikle@yahoo.com) can arrange community tours around Kingston, including Culture Yard.

The Parade

The Parade, also known as **St. William Grant Park,** is where a host of labor leaders, including William Grant, Marcus Garvey, and Alexander Bustamante, spoke regularly before large audiences. At one time a parade ground for British soldiers, the park divides King Street into upper and lower regions. The Parade itself is poorly maintained and smells of urine, which doesn't seem to bother the men who sit there playing dominoes all day long. The park was named Victoria Park until it was renamed in 1977 to honor William Grant for his role in Jamaica's labor movement. Grant was a follower of Marcus Garvey and joined forces with Alexander Bustamante in championing workers' rights. In 1938, both he and Bustamante were arrested for fomenting upheavals among the early trade unions. In the early 1940s, Grant broke with Bustamante's Industrial Trade Union and drifted into poverty and obscurity. Nevertheless he was given the Honor of Distinction in 1974 for his contribution to the labor movement, which paved the way for Jamaica's Independence. Three years later Grant died.

Kingston Parish Church stands on the

© OLIVER HILL

Coke Church, on East Parade, was the first Methodist institution on the island.

corner of South Parade and King Street. It was consecrated in 1911 after having been rebuilt following the earthquake of 1907, which virtually flattened all of downtown. The church was constructed as a replica of the original, with the addition of the clock tower. The original church had stood from when the city was planned following the earthquake of 1692. Inside there are several pieces of Jamaican art and a few statues gifted by the Chinese (Our Lady at the High Altar) and Lebanese (St. Thomas) governments.

Coke Church, the most prominent building on East Parade, stands on the site of the first Methodist chapel in Jamaica. The present structure was rebuilt after the 1907 earthquake, replacing the original built in 1840 and named after Thomas Coke, who founded the Methodist missions in the British Caribbean. It is one of the few buildings of brick construction in Kingston.

The **Ward Theatre** facing the park on North Parade was also a regular venue for Garvey speeches. The theatre, like many buildings in town, has gone through many incarnations, the latest being a gift from Colonel Charles Ward, who became wealthy as the "Nephew" in the rum company Wray and Nephew. The rum manufacturer, still among the biggest in Jamaica, started in the Shakespeare Tavern, which once stood beside the theatre. Ward Theatre hosts occasional events, including its famous pantomime performances.

◖ Institute of Jamaica
The Institute of Jamaica (IOJ) (Main Bldg., 14–16 East St., tel. 876/922-0620 or 876/922-0626, ioj.jam@mail.infochan.com, www.instituteofjamaica.org.jm) was founded in 1879 by Governor General Anthony Musgrave to encourage "Literature, Science and Art," as the letters on the main building's facade read. The institute has several divisions: Natural History, National Gallery, National Library, Museum of History and Ethnography, African-Caribbean Institute, and Liberty Hall. It is directed by Vivian Crawford, a multifaceted man who claims Maroon heritage, and

© OLIVER HILL

The Institute of Jamaica on East Street in Downtown Kingston continues to uphold its mandate to support science, literature, and the arts with a museum, library, and numerous exhibits.

chaired by UWI professor Barry Chevannes. The IOJ publishes an excellent series called *Jamaica Journal,* which delves into a range of contemporary topics from dancehall music to sponges off Port Royal to national heroes. It's a great way to get a glimpse at the introspective side of the Jamaican people.

The Natural History Division is the oldest division of the IOJ and is housed adjacent to the Institute's main building on the ground floor. Today the division is led by Tracey Commock, a dedicated naturalist with endless energy with which to explore Jamaica's natural wonders. A Botany Division and a Zoology department are both part of the Natural History division. There is also a science library and a small museum (9:30 A.M.–4:30 P.M. Mon.–Thurs., until 3:30 P.M. Fri., free admission) that features some of the island's wildlife, which have been stuffed for display, as well as a few imported curiosities. The division also has two field stations, one at Green Hills just beyond Hardwar Gap in the Blue Mountains, and the other on the St. Ann–Clarendon border at Mason River. IOJ gallery spaces are on the top floor of

Natural History division, and further south with an entrance on Water Lane.

The **National Gallery** (12 Ocean Blvd., tel. 876/922-1561 or 876/922-1564, tours tel. 876/922-8514, US$1.50 entry) is directed by David Boxer, himself an artist and important figure in the contemporary Jamaican art scene. It has permanent collections showcasing Jamaica's artistic pioneers, while also supporting the country's dynamic contemporary artists with biannual temporary exhibits. The large permanent collection includes extensive works by Edna Manley as well as some of the most important intuitive artists like John Dunkley.

The **National Library** (12 East St., tel. 876/967-1526) was founded in 1979 when it took over the collections of the West India Reference Library, which dates from 1894, when it began as a section of the Institute's public library division. Operations started in 1879 with a small collection of Jamaican and West Indian books before developing into the more comprehensive collection of materials covering Caribbean life that it is today.

The **Museum of History and Ethnography** (10 East St., 8:30 A.M.–5 P.M. Mon.–Thurs., 8:30 A.M.–4 P.M. Fri.) is presided over by curator Wayne Modest, who brings an energetic vibe to the center and keeps exhibits current with colorful examples of present-day Jamaican life. One recent exhibit featured a Nyabinghi drum and a priest's staff from a Rastafarian community above Irish Town.

The **Forces Museum** (Curphy Barracks, Up Park Camp) showcases Jamaica's military past with a few old tanks and uniforms on display. It is also known as the Military Museum.

The **Museum of Jamaican Music** is a new development envisioned as part of the IOJ's museum network and dedicated to conserving Jamaica's musical history. Presided over by the IOJ's Museum of Ethnography, the museum supports research into and documentation of all aspects of Jamaican musical history.

Liberty Hall (76 King St., tel. 876/948-8639, libertyhall@cwjamaica.com, www.garveylibertyhall.com) is the latest addition to the IOJ. The rehabilitated building was Marcus Garvey's base of operations in the 1920s and today has a small reference library with a wealth of knowledge related to the man and his teachings. Liberty Hall houses a museum and resource center as well as sponsoring and endorsing Garvey's vision with programs for local youth.

The **African-Caribbean Institute of Jamaica (ACIJ)** (12 Ocean Blvd., tel. 876/922-4793 or 876/922-7415, acij@anngel.com.jm) has been run under the direction of Bernard Jankee since 1995. The Institute's mandate is to "collect, research, document, analyze and preserve information on Jamaica's cultural heritage, through the exploitation of oral and scribal sources." The ACIJ has a memory-bank program in which oral histories are recorded around the country and then transcribed, as well as an active publications program featuring the ACIJ Research Review. There is a small library at the office where the Institute's top-notch academic publications can be browsed and purchased. The ACIJ also runs an outreach program in schools and does presentations in universities in Jamaica and abroad. The ACIJ has a tradition of collaboration with individual researchers and institutions. Projects have included studies of traditional religions like Kumina and Revival, and research on the Maroons.

National Heroes Park

National Heroes Park, which encompasses **Heroes Memorial,** occupies 30 hectares below Cross Roads on Marescaux Road within the large roundabout known as **Heroes Circle.** The roundabout surrounds what was once the city's main sporting ground, later becoming the Kingston Race Course. The park was also the site of several important historical events, including Emancipation Day celebrations on August 1, 1938; the jubilee celebrating Queen Victoria's reign in 1887; and the free Smile Jamaica concert where a wounded Bob Marley offered the people of Kingston a 90-minute performance in defiance of his would-be assassins in 1976. Heroes Park is also said to have been the battleground where warring factions from East and West Kingston would face-off in organized skirmishes.

The memorial, located at the southern end of the park, commemorates Jamaica's most important historical figures and events. Black Nationalist Marcus Garvey rests there, as does labor leader Alexander Bustamante, who formed the Jamaica Labor Party, and his cousin Norman Manley, who founded the opposition Peoples National Party. Norman's son Michael Manley, who gave the country its biggest communist scare for his closeness with Cuba's Fidel Castro, is also interned here. Paul Bogle and George William Gordon are also honored for their role in the Morant Bay Rebellion, which was at the vanguard of Jamaica's civil rights movement in the post-emancipation period. The most recent icon to be laid to rest at Heroes Memorial is the cultural legend Louise Bennett, referred to lovingly by all Jamaicans as "Miss Lou," who died in June 2006.

Other Sights

Headquarters House (79 Duke St., tel. 876/922-1287, free admission) is home of the

Jamaica National Heritage Trust, which oversees the country's heritage sites; it dates from 1755 and is a good example of Georgian architecture. Merchant Thomas Hibbert built the house in a contest to see who could construct the most ornate edifice with which to impress a local girl. There's a nice gallery on the ground floor with antiquities. It is also called Hibbert House. The Jamaican Parliament was housed at Headquarters House until it outgrew the small confines of the main chamber.

Gordon House was built in 1960 to replace Headquarters House as the meeting place for Jamaica's House of Representatives. There's not much to see, but visitors can drop in and even observe a session in progress. The building is named after labor leader George William Gordon (1815–1865), the son of Scottish planter Joseph Gordon, who owned Cherry Gardens Estate, and a quadroon slave. Young Gordon taught himself to read and write, and became a successful businessman while still in his teens before going into politics. A champion of the underdog, Gordon was not popular with his peers in politics who represented the landed elite. After being elected to the Assembly in 1944, he failed to regain a seat until 19 years later when he was elected to represent St. Thomas-in-the-East, where he owned substantial landholdings. Gordon was a vocal opponent of the Custos as well as the Governor General Edward Eyre. At the same time, he allied himself with Paul Bogle, another champion of the poor, both in politics and in religion. (They were both Native Baptists, seen at the time as a lower-class religion.) When unrest in St. Thomas culminated in the Morant Bay Rebellion, Gordon was held responsible and swiftly court-martialed and hanged. Bogle was hanged shortly thereafter. Both were made national heroes when the Order was established in 1969.

The **Jamaica Gleaner** building (7 North St., tel. 876/922-3400), home to the country's longest-running newspaper, is on North Street, with the cricket grounds of **Sabina Park** a few blocks to the east. Also nearby, on Duke Street, is Jamaica's only synagogue, the United Congregation of Israelites, which dates from 1912.

The Ba Beta Kristian Church of Haile Selassie I, led by the Abuna Ascento Foxe, is located on Oxford Street in front of Coronation Market and is worth a visit for its colorful service on Sunday afternoons. Women must cover their heads, wear dresses, and sit on the right side of the aisle. Men should not cover their heads. The church sponsors community initiatives as well as the Amha Selassie basic school located next door.

Jubilee and Coronation Markets are worth a visit to mosey around and browse through the stalls. Don't expect a lot in terms of interesting buys, but the experience is gritty Jamaica at its best—with all its accompanying smells. While it's most comfortably enjoyed accompanied by a local, there is no danger in going unaccompanied so long as you can handle unsolicited attention from hagglers seeking a sale. If you're a woman, it's guaranteed the market men will display a typical lack of shyness in approaching you with romantic interest.

Marcus Garvey Community Center (69½ Church St.) is the venue for meetings of the Marcus Garvey People's Political Party (MGPPP) (6 P.M.–8 P.M. every Thurs.). The last Friday of every other month (Oct., Dec., Feb., etc.) there is a fish fry held, generally accompanied by a sound system.

Trinity Cathedral (1–3 George Edly Dr., tel. 876/922-3335, 8:30 A.M. Sun. service, weekday mass at 5:30 P.M.), presided over by Father Kenneth Richards, replaced the old cathedral on Duke and Sutton, which was destroyed in the earthquake of 1907. Trinity has been center stage for several important national events. Archbishop Samuel Carter is buried on the site and Norman Manley's funeral—attended by Fidel Castro and Louis Farrakhan, among a host of other dignitaries—was held there. A relatively small-scale earthquake destroyed the stained glass on the cathedral's south face in 1951; it was subsequently replaced with normal, clear glass. In the years since, mischievous children have broken many of the panes by throwing stones. The original mosaic tile on the north wall has been uncovered and a Spanish restoration team is set to restore the rest of the mosaic walls, which were at some point painted over with white. Caretaker Craig Frazer leads tours of the building and points out interesting details. A generous tip is sure to make the pious young man even more devout.

UPTOWN
◖ Emancipation Park

On the corner of Knutsford Boulevard and Oxford Road on the southern edge of New Kingston, Emancipation Park (tel. 876/926-6312 or 876/968-9292, emanpark@cwjamaica .com) boasts a sculpture of two figures. It shows a black man and woman, naked, their heads proudly lifted to the sky as if at once acknowledging the rectitude of their long struggle for freedom and silently praying for guidance in a new era.

The work, titled *Redemption Song,* was the winner of a blind competition commissioned to give the newly constructed Emancipation Park a meaningful headpiece. It was controversial for several reasons. First, its creator, Jamaican sculptor Laura Facey (www.laurafacey. com), has a very fair complexion. Second, the figures are naked, and the man is somewhat well endowed. Some people wanted the sculpture immediately removed, and Facey was the talk of the island for weeks. In the end, artistic freedom prevailed and the sculpture was kept in place, much to its opponents' chagrin.

In late 2006, Facey opened an exhibit at the gallery in the natural history building of the Institute of Jamaica, where the central work was an homage to *Redemption Song:* a multitude of scaled-downed figures—identical to those on the corner of Emancipation Park—packed into a canoe reminiscent of the way they were brought through the Middle Passage. For Facey, the piece was part of a continuum consistent with the earlier work, which sets those captive souls on a new course to freedom. David Boxer, curator of the National Gallery, opened the exhibit by paying tribute to *Redemption Song* with the following words:

"... their heads are raised heavenwards in prayer... yes, this is a prayer – the work is a silent hymn of communion with, and thanksgiving to, the almighty... Their nudity is part of their potency – it is part of the meaning of their emancipation; their rebirth into freedom. They stand there as a symbol of the naked truth of the argument of emancipation; the truth that we are all equal in the eyes of God... "

Redemption Song and the controversy that surrounded it reflect the deep wounds that slavery left on Jamaica and the world at large, wounds that cannot heal without remembering the past. Emancipation Park is perhaps the best-maintained public space in all of Kingston, perfect for reminiscing on the past as well as relaxing on one of many benches and taking a stroll. Events are held frequently on a stage set up at the center of the park.

Half Way Tree

The **clock tower** in Half Way Tree was erected in 1913 as a monument to King Edward VII of England and marks the junction of Kingston's four principal thoroughfares: Half Way Tree Road, Hope Road, Constant Spring Road, and Hagley Park Road.

St. Andrew Parish Church (free) also referred to as Half Way Tree Church, is one of the oldest Anglican churches on the island. The present church has a foundation that dates from 1692, when the previous structure (which had stood only for a decade) was destroyed by the earthquake. One of the first U.S. Consuls to Jamaica, Robert Monroe Harrison, brother of U.S. President Benjamin Harrison, is buried there along with his wife. Philip Livingston, a Jamaica-based merchant and son of one of the founding fathers of the United States, was married in the church. Outside the church is an old cemetery, poorly maintained.

The **Half Way Tree Courthouse** adjacent to the Parish Church is a good example of Georgian architecture dating from 1807. The front of the building is covered with latticework, presumably to keep out the heat as a form of early air conditioning. The building has been repaired and altered several times to fix storm damage, while it miraculously escaped damage during the 1907 earthquake.

The courthouse has seen many uses, from ex-slaves obtaining their certificates of freedom to agricultural society meetings. After the construction of the Resident Magistrates Court on nearby Maxfield Avenue in 1920, court sessions were no longer held at Half Way Tree Courthouse. Up until the mid-1980s, the building was used as a branch of the Institute of Jamaica called the Junior Centre, which held skills-training courses. In 2002, the centre reopened and for a time hosted dance classes of the National Dance Theatre Company under the direction of UWI professor Rex Nettleford. The courthouse was listed as a JNHT site in 1957 and in 1985 the *Jamaica Gazette* declared it a National Monument. Meanwhile the structure suffered neglect and decay.

One important trial held at the Half Way Tree Courthouse was that of Alexander Bedward, a popular folk hero and founder of a Native Free Baptist sect known as Bedwardism. Bedward was an early Black Nationalist who spoke out against the religious and government authorities of the day. For this he was committed to Bellevue asylum until his death in 1930.

The **Ethiopian Orthodox Church** (McDonald Lane) was founded in Jamaica in 1972. This is the original state church of Ethiopia to which Haile Selassie I belonged. The church has an awkward relationship with Rastafarians in Jamaica, many of whom have been baptized as Ethiopian Orthodox, including Bob Marley's children. To this day, the construction remains incomplete with little more than a foundation in place. Its construction has been held up by a lack of cosmic alignment and a lack of togetherness in the Rasta community, according to Rasta elder Kojo and many others who share his view. Meanwhile, many inside the Ethiopian Church scorn Rastas for considering Haile Selassie a God.

Kingston's **Hindu Temple** (139 Maxfield Ave., contact Mrs. Maharaj, tel. 876/927-2105) holds events for all the major Hindu holidays including Ganesh Puja and Diwali. Local Hindus attend in heavy numbers on Sunday mornings.

Devon House

Still one of Kingston's finest homes (26

Devon House was built by George Stiebel, officially Jamaica's first black millionaire, as a showpiece and remains to this day Kingston's most opulent colonial-era mansion.

© OLIVER HILL

Hope Rd., Great House, tel. 876/929-6602, 876/929-0815, or 876/926-0829, devonhouse-jamaica@cw.com, www.devonhousejamaica .com, guided tours 9:30 A.M.–5 P.M. Mon.–Sat., last tour at 4:30 P.M. US$5 for adults, US$1.50 for children under 12), Devon House is a source of pride for the City. The mansion was constructed in 1881 by Jamaica's first black millionaire, George Stiebel, who made his fortune in Venezuelan gold. Some of the city's predominantly white elite of the day were less than happy to be outdone by a black man; it is said that Lady Musgrave—wife of Governor General Lord Musgrave, who founded the Institute of Jamaica—actually had a road built (Lady Musgrave Road) so she wouldn't have to bear the humiliation of passing the spectacular mansion that humbled even her husband's residence. For many years Devon House was home to the National Gallery, before it was relocated to Ocean Boulevard in 1983. Today the inside is furnished and decorated with a range of English, French, and Caribbean antiques, as well as some reproductions. The courtyard behind Devon House is full of boutique shops.

◖ Bob Marley Museum and Tuff Gong Recording Studio

Located in Bob Marley's former residence at 56 Hope Road, just north of New Kingston, the house and museum (tel. 876/927-9152, US$7.50 adults, US$6 children 13–18, US$3 children aged 12 and under, www.bobmarley-foundation .com/museum.html) has been turned into a shrine to the man and his music with rooms full of newspaper clippings and personal effects. One-hour tours run Monday–Saturday; tours start at 9:30 A.M. and the last tour leaves at 4 P.M. Around back, a gallery has transient exhibitions and the very comfortable, albeit small theater is a great place to catch a movie. A presentation on Marley is available as part of the tour, while the theater is also used for occasional touring international film festivals.

Legend Café, on one side of the main gate, has great steamed fish and fresh juices. Marley's Land Rover sits under a protective carport in the other corner of the yard in front of a wall plastered with Wailers photos. It is forbidden to snap photos inside or behind the main building that houses the museum.

Tuff Gong Recording Studio (220 Marcus

© OLIVER HILL

Marley's home at 56 Hope Road became the Bob Marley Museum after his death.

Garvey Dr., tel. 876/937-4216 or 876/923-9383, www.tuffgong.com) operates as living proof that a recording artist can own his music and be in control of his product and legacy. Bob Marley started as a struggling artist much like the one depicted by Jimmy Cliff in Perry Henzell's film *The Harder They Come.* He was subject to the same producer-artist relationship that made voicing the next tune an economic imperative rather than a carefully planned and executed project. When Marley built Tuff Gong Recording Studio he seeded an empire that continues to earn millions of dollars per year. Today the studio operates as Marley's legacy, with his wife Rita and children Ziggy and Cedella in charge. The studio is booked by invitation only, but can be toured provided it is not in use. A small record shop on-site sells CDs and other Tuff Gong paraphernalia.

Along Hope Road

King's House (Hope Rd. at Lady Musgrave Rd., tel. 876/927-6424, fax 876/978-6025, visits can be scheduled by written request) has been the home of the Governor General since the capital was moved from Spanish Town 1872. Jamaica's official head of state is appointed by the Queen of England for six-year terms. King's House was formerly the residence of Jamaica's Anglican Bishop. The original building was destroyed in the 1907 earthquake and rebuilt in 1909. The grounds have nice gardens that can be toured. Jamaica House, just south of King's House on the same grounds, is now the location for the Prime Minister's offices and is closed to the public.

The **Twelve Tribes Headquarters** (81–83 Hope Rd.) is located a bit farther north from the Bob Marley Museum, on the opposite side of Hope Road. Generally there are some members around the yard who will welcome guests, and inside there is a small store selling all the essentials, from roots tonic to Rizzla papers. The Twelve Tribes is one of the most widespread houses of Rastafari, with thousands of members across the globe from every background. The Hope Road HQ is remarkably low-key to be at the center of such a far-reaching network. Dr. Vernon Carrington, also known as the Prophet Gad, was the founder of the Twelve Tribes move-

© OLIVER HILL

Hope Botanical Gardens is the largest park uptown and serves as an oasis from the honking and bustle of Kingston's streets.

ment and died in 2005. The Twelve Tribes advocate strongly for repatriation of Africans from the Diaspora and have made it part of their mandate to facilitate this. They are also commonly recognized as the most devoutly Christian house of Rastafari as they regard Haile Selassie I as an incarnation of the spirit of Jesus.

Hope Botanical Gardens (just below University of Technology on western side of Hope Rd., free admission) managed by the Nature Preservation Foundation (tel. 876/970-3504, npfhopeestate@yahoo.com), is far more pleasant and impressive than the zoo (tel. 876/927-1085, adults US$0.75, children US$0.50), located in the same large park. The zoo is more of a nursing home for a few lost and found animals and a few iguanas waiting to be released into the wild. You won't find leopards or elephants.

The **University of the West Indies** (Mona Rd. and University Rd., www.mona.uwi.edu), in the quiet residential neighborhood of Mona, is worth a visit as the campus sits at the base of the Blue Mountains and has extensive rolling lawns with interesting ruins of the old Mona Estate aqueduct and a beautiful mural created by Belgian artist Claude Rahir with the help of UWI students.

The cut-stone Univeristy Chapel by the main entrance is an excellent example of Georgian architecture. It was transported block by block from Gales Valley Estate in Trelawny at the bidding of Princess Alice, first chancellor of the University. The former sugar warehouse was given a new life at UWI, its interior decorated with materials from all the countries the university has served. The coats of arms of these countries are inlaid in the chapel ceiling.

The yearly **Orchid Show** of the Jamaica Orchid Society is held here, as are numerous other annual functions and occasional parties.

Cherry Gardens Great House

Cherry Gardens Great House (46 Upper Russell Heights) was built by Scottish Planter Joseph Gordon, father of national hero George William Gordon who was born to a quadroon slave in humble quarters next to the main house. George William Gordon went on to become a successful mulatto businessman who agitated

© OLIVER HILL

Cherry Gardens Great House is an architectural gem among Uptown's many mansions.

for civil rights until he was executed for taking a stand. A drive up through Cherry Gardens gives a glimpse into Uptown, with concrete mansions covering the landscape. Cherry Gardens Great House is a breath of fresh air amongst monstrosities that were seemingly built with no regard for the surrounding environment. The great house itself is an architectural masterpiece where louvre windows keep the inside dark and cool while allowing the breeze to move freely through. Though the house is not open to the public, the owners, Oliver Jones and family, are friendly enough and don't mind people stopping by for a look at the outside.

ART GALLERIES

A Touch of Art (19 Willow Way off Barbican Terrace, tel. 876/927-0637, cell 876/789-3076) is a small studio gallery in the home of Peter Peart, a graduate of Edna Manley College. Peart works mainly in acrylic on canvas, doing landscape, abstract, and people studies, as well as some interesting work on tiles and light-switch covers. These latter pieces are small and affordable (US$14–36) and make excellent gift items.

Easel Gallery (134 Old Hope Rd., Liguanea Plaza further up Hope Rd. from Sovereign Centre adjacent to Mothers restaurant, tel. 876/977-2067, 9 A.M.–5 P.M. Mon.–Wed., 10 A.M.–6 P.M. Thurs.–Sat.).

Marso (90 Hope Rd., adjacent to Starapples, tel. 876/978-9720, 10:30 A.M.–5:30 P.M. Tues.–Sat.) is a small shop run by Sophia Rizza and Marie Josephs, selling Jamaican paintings and home items.

Contemporary Gallery (tel. 876/927-9958, cacdian@yahoo.com, 10 A.M.–6 P.M. Mon.–Fri., 10 A.M.–4 P.M. Sat., brunch 11 A.M.–4 P.M. Sun.) is an excellent gallery that displays work by many established Jamaican artists, including Susan Alexander, Beverly Neita Jackson, Viv Logan, Alexander Cooper, Ewan McAnuff, and Winston Clarke. Ceramics work by the Clonmel Potters is also exhibited. Diane Watson is the lovely gallery owner and coordinator. The gallery hosts an excellent Jamaican Sunday brunch offered in a homely setting. Dishes include oxtail, ackee and saltfish, spareribs, vegetables, fish, chicken, and pork. The hominy porridge is a crowd-pleaser.

Revolution Gallery (52 Lady Musgrave Rd., tel. 876/946-0053, 10 A.M.–6 P.M. Mon.–Fri., 10:30 A.M.–3 P.M. Sat.) has some exceptional crafts as well as excellent work by up-and-coming Jamaican painter Natalie Barnes.

Supersad Studios (11 North St., tel. 876/740-1632 or 876/361-6275, supersad_studios@yahoo.com) is run by Phillip Supersad, who makes exquisitely handcrafted ceramics.

Grosvenor Gallery (1 Grosvenor Terrace, Manor Park, tel. 876/924 6684, grosvenorgallery@cwjamaica.com) has contemporary art exhibits and occasional crafts fairs that brings artists and craftspeople from around Jamaica. Call for upcoming events.

The Art Centre (202 Hope Rd., across from UTECH, tel. 876/927-1608, artcentre.ja@gmail.com, 9 A.M.–5 P.M. Mon.–Sat., admission free) is housed in a uniquely designed apartment building commissioned by A. D. Scott in the 1960s. Inside, colorful murals adorn the walls and art is displayed on the upper two levels as part of the building's permanent collection. The gallery uses the ground floor space for its transitory exhibits. Director Rosemarie Thwaites and gallery coordinator Camille Patterson are both lovely people, and the murals are outstanding. Paintings start around US$100–200. On the same compound there is an art supply and framing shop.

◖ Mutual Gallery

The Mutual Gallery (2 Oxford Rd., New Kingston, tel. 876/929-4302, 10 A.M.–6 P.M. Mon.–Fri., 10 A.M.–3 P.M. Sat., free entry), run by curator/director Gilou Bauer, is Kingston's most dynamic venue for new artists. The Mutual Gallery holds a yearly competition looking for trends and upcoming talent; new artists are invited to compete by submitting a catalogue of works and a proposal for what they plan to do in the competition. From the initial submissions, 10 artists are then asked to submit two original pieces created for the competition itself. Then five or six finalists are asked to submit a minimum of three additional works from which the winner is determined. Contestants must be Jamaican or have lived in Jamaica for at least two years. The first-prize winner receives US$1500 and the People's Prize winner receives US$750. The five judges on the selection committee tend to be members of Jamaica's artistic and academic community. The Gallery sells many artists' work, which can be viewed in a storage/viewing room at the back, taking 30 percent gallery commission. Uptown Jamaicans and collectors are the most frequent buyers. Exhibitions are sponsored by local corporations.

Entertainment

Jamaicans love a good party or "session" as they call it, and Kingston has the most consistent and varied nightlife to support partygoers and dance enthusiasts. Don't be alarmed should someone approach to within intimate distance for what is known as a slow *whine* in a club or at a street dance. But it's not just *whining* that Kingston offers. While still less than cosmopolitan in terms of its entertainment offering (you won't find an opera house), the city does support a wide array of cultural and artistic forms from modern dance to art and theater. Of course music touches everybody and Kingston's nightclubs lead to sound systems that deliver a raw celebration of music on dance floors and in the streets.

There's no need to hurry in Jamaica as everything inevitably starts late, certainly true for nightlife. Family-oriented and cultural entertainment generally starts earlier in the evenings around 9–10 P.M. Few people go out to a nightclub before midnight, and the clubs don't really fill up until 2 or 3 A.M. Street dances start particularly late and can be quite boring until a sizeable crowd gathers and people start showing off their moves amidst pan-chicken vendors, enormous speakers, wafting ganja smoke, and a rising sun. All-inclusive parties have also become quite popular, with the Frenchman's parties at the vanguard of Kingston high society chic for its food and select crowd. UWI and University of Technology campuses host parties somewhat regularly.

LIVE MUSIC

Live Music and stage show performances in Kingston are not as frequent or varied as some would expect given the prominent role music plays in Jamaican life. Nonetheless, there are a handful of venues that feature somewhat regular acts. Stage shows are held routinely and there are large events at least once a month at **Mas Camp,** a large outdoor arena just below the center of New Kingston. Neighbors don't appreciate the noise and have challenged use of the area as a concert venue, throwing its future into some uncertainty. But if partygoers get their way, Mas Camp will be around for some time to come. Jokers Wild and other promoters use the popular venue regularly.

Village Café (20 Barbican Rd., tel. 876/970-4861) features live music at least once a week (Tues.). Usually the acts are of the obscure up-and-coming variety and draw a young crowd. The Village Grill upstairs does excellent fish and bammy (US$8.50–14).

Weekenz (80 Constant Spring Rd., tel. 876/755-4091, www.weekenz.com, Tues.–Sat. 6 P.M. until the last customer leaves) is a popular venue that attracts a mostly young crowd. Admission is about US$3–7 depending on the event. Thursday night is dancehall night, Tuesday poetry night, Wednesday live reggae band, Friday club nights, Saturday oldies ('70–80s). Delano Reynolds is the club's owner and manager. Friends Restaurant (contact the manager Donovan, tel. 876/755-4415) is located on the same compound.

Jamaica Association of Vintage Artistes and Affiliates (JAVAA) (7–9 Hagley Park Rd., Oakton Park Entertainment Complex next to York Plaza, tel. 876/908-4464, www .javaa.com.jm) features vintage reggae artists

KINGSTON'S WEEKLY NIGHTLIFE

MONDAYS

Sky Mondays at Indies Cafe & Grill

Uptown Mondays Street Dance in
Savannah Plaza, Half Way Tree

TUESDAYS

Poetry Night at Weekenz

Live music at Village Café

Ladies Night at Asylum

WEDNESDAYS

Heineken Wednesdays at Cuddy'z

Retro Night at the Quad

Live Reggae Night at Weekenz

Wedde Wednesday at Stone Love HQs,
Half Way Tree

Passa Passa Street Dance, Downtown

THURSDAYS

Live Jazz at Christopher's

Dancehall Night at Asylum

Latin Night at the Jonkanoo Lounge in
the Hilton

Fashion Show Session at Village Café

Karaoke Night at Indies

Oldies Night with Merritone Disco Sound
at Waterfalls

Dancehall Night at Weekenz

Energy Thursdays at Stereophonic Lawn

FRIDAYS

Fish Fry and Street Dance in Port Royal

Jamaica German Society social hour, Hotel
Four Seasons

Karaoke Night at Carlos' Café

Wild Coyote Ugly at Indies

Vintage Live Music at JAVAA,
Half Way Tree

Club Night at Weekenz

Something Fishy session at the
Capricorn Inn

SATURDAYS

Fashion Hype at Indies

Latin Mingle at the Courtleigh Hotel

Oldies Night at Weekenz

SUNDAYS

Oldies Street Dance in Rae Town

Culture Alley Sundays at the Chelsea Hotel
with Gabre Selassie spinning roots, culture,
and lover's rock

---

on the last Friday of every month (US$7, doors open at 8:30) for JAVAA Jammin' sessions in an outdoor courtyard in the heart of Half Way Tree. JAVAA carries the torch for Jamaica's early music from the 1950s to the '80s, from lover's rock, to rock steady, ska, and roots reggae. The organization was formed to bring recognition and financial support to these artists, many of whom participated in the formation of Jamaican popular music, as they reach their golden years. Tickets are available from JAVAA members and at the JAVAA office. Food and drinks are sold at the events.

The Villagio (77 Knutsford Blvd., tel. 876/908-2089), a casino at the Hilton, often features low-key solo artists or small jazz bands. Rupert Bent, an accomplished guitarist who's played with countless Jamaican stars—including a longstanding career with Byron Lee—is a regular here on Fridays and Saturdays.

© OLIVER HILL

Ica and Inilek Wilmott, the progeny of reggae legend Billy Mystic, perform at Village Café in Orchid Plaza on a Tuesday night of live music.

Backyaad (126 Constant Spring Rd., call Chris Daly for info, tel. 876/456-5556, link-johnnydaley@yahoo.com) is a spacious outdoor venue that hosts occasional concerts and comedy sessions. Comedy jams are held inconsistently every last Wednesday of the month.

The **Ranny Williams Cultural Centre** (Hope Rd., just above Devon House, tel. 876/926-5726, library@jcdc.org.jm, www.jcdc.org.jm) holds occasional concerts, festivals, and fairs.

Mas Camp (Oxford Rd.) is an enormous walled in venue that holds regular large-scale sessions and stage shows in the heart of New Kingston.

Jam World is a large venue in Portmore that hosts Sting, an annual Boxing Day event.

NIGHTCLUBS AND BARS

Asylum (69 Knutsford Blvd., tel. 876/906-1828 or 876/906-1829, open nightly except Sun., admission US$4) draws a mixed crowd for big events, but generally attracts a very Downtown, or "ghetto," clientele, especially on Ladies Night when flashy hairdos and short skirts compete for patrons' attention. It's the best place to check out the latest hairstyles, street fashions, and dance moves.

The Quad (20–22 Trinidad Terrace, tel. 876/754-7823, www.jamaicanlifestyle.com/quad.htm) is Kingston's Uptown nightclub, with three levels of dance floors and something for everyone. Christopher's Bar and Lounge is on the ground level, Oxygen Nightclub is on the second floor, and Voodoo Lounge is on the top level. Patrons frequently go from one floor to the next throughout the night depending on the genre of music and vibe on each floor.

Waterfalls (160 Hope Rd., tel. 876/977-0652) is a banqueting facility that does functions, and is open to the public as a nightclub on Thursdays (9 P.M.–4 A.M., US$6) for oldies featuring Merritone Disco sound, and a mixture of reggae, Calypso, and hip hop from the '60s, '70s, and '80s. The cover charge includes complementary soup. It's a nice bar known for its mature crowd.

SOUND SYSTEMS AND STREET DANCES

Jamaican sound systems have grown in conjunction with reggae music and dancehall, one giving voice in the street to the other's lyrical genius and social commentary from inside the studio. While a number of different sounds vie for the top ranking at clubs and stage shows, historically they were the voice of the street dance, having replaced the African drums of yesteryear.

A sound is generally comprised of a few individual DJs who form a team to blast the latest dancehall tunes, using equipment that ranges from a home stereo system at max output for those just starting out, to the most sophisticated equipment operated by the more established names. Street dances like Passa Passa foster the development of DJ artistry, providing a venue for the different sound systems to flex and clash, like the ever-popular Stone Love, Renaissance, Black Chiney, or Razz and Biggy. These sounds grew on the coattails of King Tubby's, which remains perhaps the biggest sound system of all time. Sound clashes are held often, during which each sound attempts to outperform the other, with the ultimate judge being the crowd which expresses approval with hands raised in the air as if firing a pistol with the requisite accompanying "braap, braap, braap, braap!" More recently, thanks to the creativity of popular dancehall artist Bounty Killer, many substitute the even more literal "bullet, bullet, bullet!"

Street dances fill an important role in providing entertainment and an expressive outlet for Kingston's poorest citizens. Dances are held for special occasions, including birthdays, funerals and holidays. Many started as one-off parties but were so popular they became established as regular weekly events. Typically a section of street is blocked off to traffic and huge towers of speakers set up. Sometimes the street is not blocked off at all; but the early-morning hours when these dances are held see little traffic, and what does flow is accommodated by the dancers – who sometimes use the passing vehicles to prop up their dance partner for a more dramatic "whine."

While clubs across Uptown Kingston assess an admission fee, which varies depending on the crowd they are looking to attract, the street is a public venue where all are welcome. Up-

Club Escape (24 Knutsford Blvd., tel. 876/960-1856, open 24/7, US$4 on weekends) is an outdoor bar and nightclub that often has heated dominoes games in the early evenings, plus a mix of music that includes hip hop and reggae. Lunch is served daily except Sunday and varies with items like chicken, oxtail, curry goat, pepper steak (US$3.50–5).

The Deck (14 Trafalgar Rd., tel. 876/978-1582, richard@thedeck.biz, open daily from 4:30 P.M. until the last person leaves) is large venue with a boat motif. Fishing nets hang from what was once the roof of an auto garage. There are a few billiards tables and a decent but limited bar food menu (US$3.50–11.50). Tuesdays and weekends are busy nights when music blares and occasionally patrons are inspired to take to the dance floor.

Members Only (120a Constant Spring Rd., no phone) is a flashy rooftop billiards hall with big fish tanks by the bar. It no longer requires membership. The senior bartender is Terri-Anne Rowe (tel. 876/858-2706), and Jeffrey Clarke (tel. 876/873-6755) is a partner.

Villa Ronai (Old Stony Hill Rd., tel. 876/960-0049) in the upscale Stony Hill area is a beautiful mansion owned by Pulse Entertainment that hosts periodic events, including private parties for Fashion Week. The villa is slated for development into a destination resort and spa with an entertainment lifestyle lean.

Stereophonic Lawn (bottom of Mountain View Rd. across from NCB) hosts weekly sessions called Energy Thursdays.

The Veranda (38a Trafalgar Rd., tel. 876/906-3601) at the Pulse Entertainment complex is a favorite place for Uptown Kingstonians to "flex" with their girlfriends. The Pulse model agency, run by Kingsley Cooper and host to the annual Miss Jamaica Universe

town people might have traditionally preferred a bar setting, but Downtown people have resorted to creating the party on their doorstep. Increasingly, Uptown folks venture down to the poor areas on nights when dances are held to partake in a scene that doesn't exist anywhere else and has come to be acknowledged as an invaluable cultural phenomenon where DJs flex their skills to discriminating crowds.

In the past, noise ordinances became the favorite justification for police raids to "lock off di dance," but today the dances are for the most part tolerated by the authorities as harmless entertainment effective in pacifying the city's poor. Intellectuals, like Jamaican poet Mutabaruka who claims "the more dance is the less crime," have come to endorse and encourage these dances as healthy community events. Even though they are often held in areas obviously scarred with urban blight and associated with violence, like Tivoli Gardens and Rae Town, violence is not a part of the street dance. Rather, it is a place where people come to enjoy, decked out in their flashiest clothes (jackets and fancy shoes for men, skimpy skirts and tops for women) to drink a Guinness, smoke a spliff, perhaps, and catch up on the latest dances.

Regular patrons at these events welcome visitors from Uptown and abroad, but care should be taken to show respect and concede that you are clearly not on your turf. Plenty a "bad man" frequent these dances, and even if they are not wanted by the authorities, they tend to like creating the impression that they are and accordingly don't appreciate being photographed without granting their approval first. Parts of Downtown, especially along parts of Spanish Town Road, can be desolate and a bit dodgy at night and many drivers use that as an excuse to proceed with caution at red lights rather than coming to a stop.

Regular street dances in Kingston include Uptown Mondays (Savannah Plaza, Half Way Tree), Wedde Wednesdays (Stone Love HQ, Half Way Tree), Passa Passa (Spanish Town Rd. and Beeston St., Wednesdays starting around 2 A.M.), Port Royal sessions on Friday evenings, and Rae Town (Rae St., Downtown) on Fridays for Something Fishy and Sundays for the regular oldies session by the Capricorn Inn bar.

competition, is located on the same compound. Pulse regularly hosts parties and events at The Veranda, including the after-party for the Miss Jamaica Universe competition and model search events. No food is served.

Heel Bar (behind Treasure House shopping plaza, 96 Hope Rd.) is small and low-key bar in a nice, open-air bamboo structure with a great view of the Blue Mountains. It is a perfect place to have a beer as the sun's rays descend the hills. Heel Bar does not serve food.

SPORTS BARS

Cuddy'z Sportsbar (Shops 4–6, New Kingston Shopping Center, Dominica Dr., tel. 876/920-8019) is owned by Jamaica's favorite cricket star, Courtney "Cuddy" Walsh, the first cricket bowler to take 500 wickets in test cricket. He is also a recipient of the UNESCO award for good sportsmanship and it comes through in his demeanor off the field as proprietor as well. Cuddy'z is flush with TVs at every table and large flat-panels around the bar, making it the best place in town to catch a big game in the presence of a guaranteed raucous crowd. Typical sports-bar fare of burgers and fries (US$6–7) is complemented by Jamaican staples like curry goat and stewed chicken (US$6.50) or ribs, tenderloin, and shrimp (US$17). Cuddy'z is also the new location of Heineken Wednesdays (pay at the door, get Heineken at a discount).

JamRock Sports Bar & Grill (69 Knutsford Blvd., tel. 876/754-4033, 10 A.M.–2 A.M. Fri. & Sat., 10 A.M.–11 P.M. Sun., 10 A.M.–midnight weekdays) is an iconic sports bar where the food has gone steadily downhill over the past few years. Nonetheless, the bar remains a local favorite and there's almost always a raucous crowd watching a game and talking above the din. It's more suitable for a pre-clubbing beer or to emulate the Uptown crowd than for the food. A Red Stripe goes for US$2.75, Guinness US$3, Heineken for US$3.25. The Chicken Nyamwhich (US$4) is the flagship bar snack; other chicken dishes include stewed, jerk, and cordon bleu (US$6–10), with fish dishes being the most expensive on the menu (US$13).

PERFORMING ARTS

Jamaica has a vibrant tradition in theatre, pantomime, and spoken word, with annual shows and competitions sponsored by the **Jamaica Cultural Development Commission** (www .jcdc.org.jm). Events are held throughout the year, but come to a peak during the weeks around Emancipation and Independence.

Little Theatre Movement, the **Little Little Theatre,** and the **National Dance Theatre Company** (4 Tom Redcam Ave., tel. 876/926-6129, www.ltmpantomime.com) share a property on the edge of Downtown. The Xaymaca Dance Theatre also performs here. Plays run throughout the year; call for details on performances. Pantomime performance runs December–May, with school plays after that. The National Dance Theatre performs July–August. Mr. Henry Fowler, Rex Nettleford, Barbara Gloudon, Louise "Miss Lou" Bennett, Oliver Samuels, and Ken Hill are some of the founding members of the Little Theatre Movement.

Center Stage Theatre (Dominica Dr., tel. 876/960-3585) is a small venue where productions tend to be family-oriented musicals in patois.

Louise Bennett Garden Theatre (Hope Rd., tel. 876/926-5726, library@jcdc.org.jm, www.jcdc.org.jm) holds occasional plays and performances.

Phillip Sherlock Centre for the Creative Arts (UWI Mona, tel. 876/927-1047) puts on UWI productions, including those of the student dance society. The building that houses the arts center is impressive architecturally.

Ward Theatre (North Parade, Downtown, tel. 876/922-0360 or 876/922-0453) holds occasional plays, pantomimes, and special events.

Pantry Playhouse (2 Dumfries Rd., tel. 876/960-9845, admission US$11–14) features

different productions throughout the year. Usually plays run for three months and performances are generally held Wednesday–Sunday.

The outdoor amphitheatre at **Edna Manley College of the Visual and Performing Arts** (1 Arthur Winter Dr., tel. 876/929-2350) hosts poetry readings on the last Tuesday of every month starting at 7:30 P.M.; regular dance performances are held in the indoor theatre next door.

Ashe Caribbean Performing Art Ensemble & Academy (call executive director Conroy Wilson for performance dates and location, tel. 876/960-2985 or 876/997-5935, www .asheperforms.com, asheperforms@cwjamaica .com) has regular performances throughout the year. Ashe is a full-time dance company that travels frequently and does "edutainment" projects in schools across the island.

Movements Dance Company (Liguanea, contact director Monica Campbell, tel. 876/ 929-7797 or 876/999-7953, maccsl@cwjamaic a.com) was founded in 1981 by Monica Campbell McFarlane, Pat Grant-Heron, Michelle Tappin-Lee and Denise Desnoes, and has since grown into one of Jamaica's most dynamic and versatile dance companies. Both traditional Jamaican and Caribbean rhythms inform the company's repertoire. The schedule of performances climaxes each year with the annual Season of Dance in November. The company also travels to perform in the United States, the United Kingdom, Canada, and neighboring Caribbean islands.

BETTING AND GAMBLING

Gambling in Jamaica is illegal, while "gaming" is not. Off-track betting is a respectable business supported by nearby Caymanas Park racetrack. Video Gaming Machines (VGMs) are found throughout the island thanks to Supreme Ventures, a company that recently went public with a very poorly received IPO. Nonetheless, there are a few locations in Kingston to play the odds against a machine. Two places include the **Villagio,** behind the Hilton (77 Knutsford Blvd.) next to the pool bar (tel. 876/908-2089, 11:30 A.M.–3 A.M. daily), and **Acropolis** (29 East Kings House Rd., tel. 876/978-1299).

Caymanas Park horse track (racing@cw jamaica.com, www.caymanasracetrack.com) is recognized as one of the best in the Caribbean. Regular races are held Wednesdays and Saturdays (with the occasional Monday race) and are usually well attended. Admission ranges US$0.50–4, depending on seating. Caymanas Track Ltd. (CTL) supports a large network of OTB sites around the corporate area, which offer simulcast races from around the world when races aren't being broadcast from Caymanas Park.

CINEMAS

Carib Cinema (Cross Roads, box office tel. 876/926-6106; movie times, tel. 876/906-1090, www.palaceamusement.com, tickets US$6, typical show times 5 P.M. and 8 P.M. daily) plays Hollywood films.

The Cineplex (shop 47a Sovereign Center, tel. 876/978-3522, movie times tel. 876/978-8286, tickets US$6) is also owned by Palace Amusement and has more of the same Hollywood films.

Shopping

Kingston is full of shopping plazas and strip malls. Half Way Tree easily has the highest concentration of shopping plazas in Jamaica, which include: Lane Plaza, on the eastern side of Hope Road; Pavilion, Central and Savannah Plazas, on the block between Eastwood Park and Constant Spring Roads; and Mall, Tropical, 7th Avenue, Premiere, Twin Gates, and Village Plazas on the north side of Constant Spring Road.

DEVON HOUSE SHOPPES

The famed Devon House I Scream outlet, Café Whatson (tel. 876/929-4490), Rum Roast & Royals gift shop, and a Cooyah outlet make Devon House an essential stop in Kingston. The great house is a worthwhile tour.

Devon House I Scream (tel. 876/929-7028 or 876/908-0346), which some rate as the country's best, has its flagship outlet at Devon House.

Cooyah Designs (96 Hope Rd., tel. 876/946-1930, 10 A.M.–6 P.M. Mon.–Sat.) is the best place to get original Jamaica-inspired roots wear as well as clothes from the Marley family's Zion Roots Wear line. There's another location at Treasure House.

Starfish Oils (tel. 876/908-4763, www.starfishoils.com) is one of Jamaica's best cottage industries. Run by Kynan Cooke, a young and creative entrepreneur, Starfish makes soaps, oils, and candles perfect for compact gift items

and everyday use. These products come standard in the bathrooms at many of Jamaica's best accommodations.

Wassi Art (tel. 876/906-5016, www.wassi art.com) is a highly regarded ceramics studio and gallery in Ocho Rios with a retail gallery at Devon House. The work ranges significantly in price (US$4–480).

Rum Roast & Royals (tel. 876/920-9094, 10 A.M.–7 P.M. Mon.–Thurs., 10 A.M.–8 P.M. Fri. & Sat.) is a great little shop packed with items that include Blue Mountain Coffee, Belcour Blue Mountain Preserves, Cuban cigars, and spices like Walker's Wood jerk seasoning.

Elaine's Elegance (26 Hope Rd., tel. 876/920-0357, eelegance@anngel.com.jm) sells cutwork embroidery dresses, skirts, blouses, and jackets for fashionable ladies—all handmade by Elaine.

TREASURE HOUSE PLAZA

At 96 Hope Road, this plaza has a variety of shops.

SoHo (tel. 876/978-9256) has party-wear for males and females and attracts a primarily Jamaican clientele; the products vary from gaudy to semi-formal elegant.

La Pluma Negra (tel. 876/946-1672) mainly sells casual, going-out wear, mostly t-shirts and accessories.

Heart & Sole (tel. 876/973-5399) carries

CARIBBEAN FASHION WEEK

Jamaica's contribution has been central to a bourgeoning Caribbean fashion industry. **Pulse Entertainment** (38a Trafalgar Rd., tel. 876/960-0049, www.pulsemodels.com, www.caribbeanfashionweek.com), founded by Kingsley Cooper and Hillary Phillips in 1980, started holding Caribbean Fashion Week (CFW) in 2001. CFW has become a wildly successful annual event, described by British *Vogue* as one of the most important fashion trends on the planet. Held during the first half of June, the week is filled with fashion shows, parties, more parties, and some of the world's most striking women clad in creative attire designed by a young cadre of imaginative talent. It's definitely one of the best times of year to be in Kingston.

Pulse Entertainment has found great success in supporting an ever-swelling corps of young model hopefuls, mostly from Jamaica, and giving them a chance on the world stage. Some of the most successful Pulse models have been featured in the world's foremost magazines, like *Sports Illustrated* and *Esquire* (Carla Campbell), *Vogue* (Nadine Willis and Jaunel McKenzie), and *Cosmopolitan* (Sunna Gottshalk). At the same time, CFW has provided a forum for established Caribbean designers like Cooyah's Homer Bair as well as others like Uzuri, Mutamba, and Biggy. Bob's daughter Cedella Marley never fails to create a splash with her proud and tasteful Catch a Fire line.

CFW events are held at numerous venues around the capital, centered on the National Indoor Sports Centre. These typically include the Veranda at the Pulse Entertainment Complex and the stately Villa Ronai in Kingston's uptown suburb of Stony Hill. Fashion Week attendees descend on Kingston amidst a tangible buzz created by an incursion of models, fashion media, and increasingly, designers from the U.S. and Europe, coming to catch a glimpse of the latest unabashed creation with the potential to spur a trend reaching far beyond the little rock of Jamaica.

---

fine shoes for women and men as well as belts, handbags, and other accessories.

OTHER SHOPS

Craft Cottage (Village Plaza, 24C Spring Rd., tel. 876/926-0719) is a good place for authentic Jamaican arts and crafts.

Scents and Sweets (Shop 22, Central Plaza, Constant Spring Rd., north of Half Way Tree, tel. 876/929-4117, 10 A.M.–6 P.M. Mon.–Sat.), owned by Nora Lewis, sells scented candles, incense, coffee, rum and coconut soaps, as well as Cooyah products.

Simiya House Clothing (30 Haining Rd., next to Livity, tel. 876/978-5336, cell 876/373-9150) is a new producer of Rasta gear, from red-, green-, and gold-trimmed skirts to the must-have Jah's army jacket.

Sarai Clothing (Harbour View) has Rasta gear, Ethiopian sharmas, dresses, and men's and children's clothing. Contact Sister May (cell 876/372-6265) for an appointment.

Mutamba, a clothing line developed by the outspoken Jamaican pan-Africanist dub poet Mutabaruka and his wife, Amber, is very popular for its minimalist chic aesthetic. By appointment only (tel. 876/946-0115 or 876/534-2301).

At the Pulse Entertainment Complex, **Melyse Collection** (Patrick and Megan, tel. 876/906-0606) has more classy women's numbers suitable for work or a night on the town. Most are U.S. imports like Ann Taylor, Bebe, and Alyn Page.

J'adore (tel. 876/754-8386), also at Pulse, has clothes imported from Europe, fit for clubbing or going out.

Bling Bling (Shop 5 Mid Spring Plaza, 134 Constant Spring Rd., tel. 876/925-3855, 10 A.M.–8 P.M. Mon.–Sat.) has all the bling you'll need to flex big at Asylum or a street dance. Prices range considerably (US$1.50–357). Sharon Beckford is the friendly proprietor.

Bridget Sandals (1 Abbeydale Rd., opposite the Hope Road entrance to Devon House, tel. 876/968-1913, www.bridgetsandals.com) sells unique and tasteful handcrafted leather footwear for women. Jonathan Buchanan is the manager.

Lee's Fifth Avenue (Tropical Plaza, Half Way Tree, tel. 876/926-8280, www.leesfifth avenue.com, 10 A.M.–7 P.M. Mon.–Sat. and 11 A.M.–4 P.M. Sun.) has good-quality, trendy clothing that includes popular brands like Levi's, Puma, and Hilfiger.

Loran-V Boutique (Shop 2, Northside Plaza, 26 Northside Drive, tel. 876-977-6450, loran_v_swimwear@yahoo.com, 9 A.M.–5 P.M. Mon.–Fri., 10 A.M.–2 P.M. Sat.) is a homegrown boutique and swimsuit and light apparel manufacturer with a handful of women at sewing machines churning out well-designed bikinis and swim trunks.

BOOKSTORES

Kingston Bookshop has several locations around town: 70b King Street, tel. 876/922-4056; 74 King Street, tel. 876/922-7016; Shop 23, 13 Constant Spring Rd.; Lot 1, Springs Plaza, tel. 876/920-1529; Shop 6, Boulevard Super Center, tel. 876/934-0574; Unit 2, 115 Hope Road, tel. 876/978-0615; Shop 6, Oasis Plaza, Spanish Town, tel. 876/749-0466. Kingston Bookshop has Jamaican and Caribbean titles, as well as imports from the United States and Europe covering all kinds of subject matter.

Sangster's Book Stores is another good bookstore with several locations around town: 97 Harbour Street, tel. 876/922-3819; 33 King Street, tel. 876/967-1930; Shop 6, 17 Constant Spring Road, tel. 876/926-1800; 20 Constant Spring Road, tel. 876/926-0710; 28 Barbados Avenue, tel. 876/960-2488; Shop 20, 106 Hope Road, tel. 876/978-3518; 137 Mountain View Avenue, tel. 876/928-3893.

Bolivar Bookshop & Gallery (1D Grove Rd., tel. 876/926-8799) is a nice boutique with a small art gallery and more rare books than can be found at the other bookstores in town.

Headstar Books and Crafts (54 Church St., tel. 876/922-3915, Headstarp@hotmail

.com) is an Afrocentric bookshop operated by brother Miguel.

ANTIQUE FURNITURE

Faith D'Aguilar (26 Gore Terrace, tel. 876/925-8192 or 876/475-7822) refurbishes and sells antique furniture and other oddities.

Books Plus and **The Piano House** (43 Constant Spring Rd., tel. 876/926-8268), located at the same location and both run by Owen Brown, is a used book store where Brown also sells and renovated pianos. In addition, Brown runs a small music school offering piano, flute, and guitar lessons. The shop also holds occasional musical evenings. Call for info on any upcoming performances.

RECORD SHOPS

Techniques Records (99 Orange St., in front of Jamaica Lifestock, tel. 876/967-4367, 9 A.M.–7 P.M. Mon.–Sat.) perhaps has Kingston's best selection for all kinds of traditional music and oldies with LPs (33s and 45s), as well as the latest singles and CDs. Owned by Winston Riley.

Derrick Harriot's One Stop Record Shop (Shop 36, Twin Gates Plaza, Constant Spring, tel. 876/926-8027, 10 A.M.–6:30 P.M. Mon.–Sat.) also has a good selection of oldies as well as the latest LP 45 singles.

Rockers International Records (135 Orange St., tel. 876/922-8015, 9 A.M.–4 P.M. Mon.–Sat.) specializes in reggae, and has CDs and LPs (33s and 45s) with the latest domestic singles and imports.

Record Plaza (Shop 11, Tropical Plaza, tel. 876/926-7645, 10 A.M.–6 P.M. Mon.–Sat.) sells all kinds of domestic and imported CDs. No vinyl.

Sonic Sounds Record Manufacturing Company (25 Retirement Rd., tel. 876/926-1204), run by Jason Lee, sells vintage reggae on vinyl, 45s and 33s. Customers must buy a minimum of three of each item. Sonic doesn't distribute a lot of new stuff. It was founded in 1978 by Jason's father, Neville Lee, the brother of Byron Lee. Byron Lee is the front man for Byron Lee and the Dragonaires, listed in the

Guinness Book of World Records as the longest running band. Neville used to be the manager of Dynamic Sounds before he left and founded Sonic. Among artists represented by Sonic distributions are the Observers and Taxi Gang.

Vynil Records (3 Cassiadene Ave, tel. 876/757-4765, contact Antonio Gessi, aka Billy at 876/849-8404) is a retailer for reggae 33s and 45s.

Dynamic Sounds (15 Bell Rd., tel. 876/923-9138, 9 A.M.–5 P.M. Mon.–Fri.) distributes and retails both vintage and contemporary records and CDs, singles and rhythm tracks on 45s, and complete albums on 33s. Dynamic Sounds also makes samples from DAT or CD. Dynamic Sounds is owned by Byron Lee.

Penthouse Recording Studio (6 Ballater Ave., tel. 876/929-7446) distributes and retails Penthouse label records as well as Flames Productions (Tony Rebel), HMG (Morgan Heritage), Gargamel (Buju Banton), and Ghetto Vibes (Errol Dunkley). Both CDs and records, 45s and 33s. Artists on the Penthouse label include Nadine Sutherland, Daville, Chaka Demus, Tiger, Cutty Ranks, Richie Stephens, Sanchez, Wayne Wonder, Beres Hammond, Marcia Griffiths, and Freddie McGregor, among others. Donovan Germain is CEO of Penthouse.

All Access Entertainment (Shop 24 Central Plaza, tel. 876/908-4948 or 876/908-4949, 9:30 A.M.–5:30 P.M. Mon.–Fri.) is both booking agent for artists like Baby Cham, Spice, Taurus Riley, General Degree, Freddie McGregor, and Gumption Band, as well as one of the island's foremost record distributors. All Access retails both vinyl and CDs with vintage and new artists represented on singles and rhythm tracks on 45 and a smaller selection of complete albums on 33.

ELECTRONICS

Innovative Systems (downstairs in Sovereign Center, tel. 876/978-3512) sells all kinds of electronics goods, from USB cables to headsets.

Photo Express (130 Old Hope Rd., beside Liguanea Plaza, tel. 876/927-0983, 8:30 A.M.

6 P.M. Mon.–Sat.) does one-hour photo developing and sells compact flash cards.

Electro-World, in Mall Plaza (tel. 876/926-5851 or 876/922-4516), has a good selection of electronics, including FireWire cables and earphones.

Watts New is at Tropical Plaza (tel. 876/906-4174).

Speaker Doc (St. Andrew Plaza, tel. 876/931-2627) can fix most any problem with speakers.

HAIRDRESSERS AND BARBERS

At the Pulse Complex on Trafalgar Road, there are three hairdressers. The notable ones, with excellent reputations, are **Angela's** (tel. 876/364-2899) in the front and **Lesma's** (tel. 876/968-5991) at the rear of the complex. For men, there's also **Ian Barracks Barbers** (tel. 876/387-6606) at the back of the complex.

For the best sisterlocks in the Caribbean, contact Natalie Barnes (tel. 876/353-8903, sistergirlnatalie@yahoo.com).

SPECIALTY FOOD STORES AND SUPERMARKETS

Jo Jo's Market (12 Waterloo Rd., in front of Junction with South Ave., tel. 876/906-1509 or 876/906-1612, 8 A.M.–6 P.M. Mon.–Sat., 9:30 A.M.–4:30 P.M. Sun.) is the best place Uptown for fresh produce, including fruits and juices.

Hannah's Fish Market (12 Waterloo Rd., next to Jo Jo's, cell 876/829-7953, 9 A.M.–5 P.M. Mon.–Sat.) is the best place around to get whole or filleted saltwater fish.

Tom Finnegan's (21 Central Ave., tel. 876/960-7799 or cell 876/816-3375, 10 A.M.–5 P.M. Mon.–Fri., 11 A.M.–6 P.M. Sat.) has the best selection of imported cheeses, meats, and wines in Jamaica. Finnegan sees his business as a "supplier of necessities, not luxury goods."

Mac's Gourmet Market (49a Hope Rd., in same parking lot as T.G.I. Friday's, tel. 876/927-3354, 10 A.M.–7 P.M. Mon.–Sat., 10 A.M.–5 P.M. Sun.) opened in January 2006 as a specialty shop selling a mix of imported meats, wines, cheeses, produce, and locally produced cottage-industry products including sauces, salad dressings, and desserts. A prepared-foods section has wraps, and lobster and potato salads, while a hot section at the back serves rotisserie chicken and ribs. Mac's is owned by the Machados, the same family that runs Mac's Chop House (tel. 876/990-3999) in New Kingston.

The Lannaman family owns a small chain of health-food and nutritional products stores throughout the Kingston area. They include **Health & Nutrition** (Sovereign Center, tel. 876/978-3529), **Fit for Life** (South Ave., tel. 876/926-7707; King's Plaza, tel. 876/926-4207), and **Vibrant Health** (Pines Plaza, tel. 876/740-2568), where you can find a few Tom's of Maine products, Knudsen's Spritzers, hemp shampoo, and other granola-lovers' fare.

Chin's Health Products (141 Maxfield Ave., tel. 876/926-2121) sells a selection of natural vitamins (A, B, Omega 3, garlic oil, etc.).

Sovereign Supermarket (1 Barbican Rd., tel. 876/927-5955; Sovereign Manor, 184 Constant Spring Rd., tel. 876/969-5792) is one of the better supermarkets around.

Megamart (29 Upper Waterloo Rd., tel. 876/969-3899, Portmore Mall, tel. 876/988-1172) is one of the bigger supermarkets in town.

SuperPlus Food Stores is a large supermarket chain with a decent selection and locations all over town (11 Hope Rd., tel. 876/926-0108; 121 Old Hope Rd., tel. 876/927-0869; 29 Trafalgar Rd., tel. 876/920-2229; 226 Mountain View Ave., tel. 876/927-3023).

Hi-Lo Food Stores (13 Old Hope Rd., tel. 876/926-6123; 3/4 Barbican Rd., tel. 876/946-3400; Cross Roads Plaza, tel. 876/926-7171; Liguanea Plaza, tel. 876/977-0082; Manor Park Plaza, tel. 876/924-1411) is another basic supermarket.

PriceSmart (111 Red Hills Rd., tel. 876/969-1242) is a wholesale membership supermarket. It can be well worth signing up if you're in town for awhile.

Lee's Food Fair Pharmacy is at 86B Red Hills Road (tel. 876/931-1560).

Sports and Recreation

Kingston is not known for its outdoor recreational opportunities. Nevertheless, there are plenty of options (including diving, hiking, golf, tennis, and surfing) for active visitors.

The **National Stadium** hosts the important sporting events on the island, including the home games of the national soccer team Reggae Boyz (www.thereggaeboyz.com). Next door is the **National Arena** and the **Indoor Sports Centre,** where several trade shows and events are held, including Caribbean Fashion Week. For more information contact the Jamaica Football Federation (20 St. Lucia Crescent, tel. 876/929-0484, 876/929-8036, or 876/926-1182, soccer@thereggaeboyz.com, jamff@hotmail.com) and ask for press officer Garth Williams.

GOLF

Kingston's most reputable golf course is **Caymanas Golf & Country Club** (Mandela Hwy., tel. 876/922-3386, www.caymanasgolfclub.com), west of Town. Designed by Canadian architect Howard Watson in 1958, the course features elevated greens with lush fairways cut through limestone hills. The views from the tees are excellent with Guango trees providing natural obstacles. Non-members pay greens fees of US$37 weekdays, US$43 weekends and holidays, plus US$21 for a cart. The Hilton offers a US$198-per-night golf package with Caymanas.

Constant Spring Golf Club (152 Constant Spring Rd., tel. 876/924-1610, csgc@cwjamaica.com) has a more humble course located in the middle of Uptown Kingston. Built by Scottish architect Stanley Thompson in 1920, the short, tight course is challenging, with an excellent view at the 13th hole. Carts go for US$20, green fees are US$29 on weekdays, US$36 on weekends. Clubs are available for US$17 and a caddy will cost you US$14. Par 70: Blue tees 9,197 yards; White tees 5,866 yards; Red tees 5,205 yards.

Canadian National Railways built a magnificent hotel just below the course, parallel to the 18th hole fairway, which has long since been converted into the Immaculate Conception High School, one of Kingston's most prestigious.

RACQUET SPORTS

Liguanea Club (80 Knutsford Blvd., tel. 876/926-8144, liguaneaclub@cwjamaica.com), across from the Courtleigh Hotel, has squash, billiards, and tennis, plus an outdoor swimming pool. Membership is required to use the facilities. Visitor membership is available for US$86 per month.

Tennis Jamaica (admin offices at 22 Trafalgar Rd., Stes. 14 and 15, tel. 876/978-1521; book a court by calling tel. 876/929-5878 or 876/906-5700, ask for Ms. Davis, 280 Piccadilly Rd., www.tennisjamaica.com, 6 A.M.–6 P.M. daily), formerly the Jamaica Lawn Tennis Association (JLTA), has courts and can set up partners. Non-members pay US$4.50 per hour. Members (US$31/year) pay US$3.50 per hour. The organization sometimes holds events and the administrative offices are best to contact for event information. Heading south on Half Way Tree Road or Oxford Road, take the left on Caledonia Avenue at Cross Roads and then a right onto Marescaux Road. After you pass the National Water Commission on left, take the next right at the back entrance to L.P. Azar, a textile store that serves as a good landmark. The courts are at the end of the road.

The **Constant Spring Golf Club** (see *Golf*) has lit tennis courts for US$7 per hour, open till 10 P.M. nightly (no racquets or balls offered).

The **Jamaica Pegasus** (81 Knutsford Blvd., tel. 876/926-3690, ext. 3023, or ask for the tennis court) has well-maintained, lit courts. Peter Berry and Kevin Riley are the tennis pro coaches and Thilbert Palmer is director of tennis. Court fees are US$14 per hour during the day, US$19 per hour at night, which covers a

lesson for a single player or the court for you and your partner. Racquets are available and included in the lesson fee; otherwise there is a US$10 charge per racquet if you're playing on your own.

POLO

The **Kingston Polo Club** (contact Lesley Masterton-Fong Yee, tel. 876/381 4660 or 876/922 8060, or Shane Chin, tel. 876/952-4370, chinrc polo@yahoo.com) is located on the Caymanas Estate west of town off Mandela Highway. It can be reached by taking the same exit as for the Caymanas Golf & Country Club about 100 meters west of the turnoff for Portmore. The Kinston Polo Club season runs early January–August 7 and is host to some of the highest handicap polo played on the island starting with the ICWI international women's team, ICWI 18 goal, and the NCB High International 15 goal tournament in May. Matches are held on Wednesdays at 4 P.M. and on Sunday mornings at 10 A.M.

WATER SPORTS

Even though Kingston has a lot of waterfront acreage, it's not put to great use; there are no cafés, restaurants, or bars on Ocean Boulevard as one might expect. Nevertheless, there are plenty of places around to have a dip, from Rockfort mineral baths, to the pool at the Mayfair Hotel to Cane River Falls east of Town, to beaches on Lime Cay and west of town at the base of the Hellshire Hills.

Diving

Port Royal Divers (Morgan's Harbour, tel. 876/382-6767, paul@portroyaldivers.com, www.portroyaldivers.com), led by Paul Shoucair aboard his 8.5-meter boat, will take experienced divers to the reefs off Lime Cay to some recent wrecks (US$50 per person for two dives including tanks and weights, gear an additional US$30). Paul also does PADI certification courses for multiple persons: US$450 for Open Water certification, US$350 for Advanced, US$500 for Rescue Diver, and US$500 for Divemaster It is illegal for tourists to dive without a Jamaica Tourist Board–licensed diver like Paul. Diving sites around Kingston include the sunken ship *Edena,* Black Tip, Texas, Winward Edge, and Cayman Trader close to Lime Cay. If you're lucky you may see eagle rays, nurse sharks, and turtles.

Boating

The **Royal Jamaica Yacht Club** (Palisadoes Park, Norman Manley Blvd., tel. 876/924-8685 or 876/924-8686, fax 876/924-8773, rjyc@kasnet.com, www.rjyc.org.jm), located on the eastern side of Kingston Harbor next to Norman Manley International Airport beside the Caribbean Maritime Institute, holds regular regattas: Spring Regatta around the second week in February, RJYC Globe Fishing tournament in March, and Independence Regatta at the end of July or early August. Yachters arriving to Jamaica from overseas should clear Customs in Port Royal before seeking a slip at the yacht club. You can also come directly to the club, which can contact Customs and Immigration. Slips can accommodate vessels up to 50 feet, while the visitors' dock can accommodate larger vessels. Fees are US$1.50 per foot for the first six days, US$1 thereafter; electricity, water, and fuel are also offered. Visitors are welcome to use the restaurant, bar, and pool. Patricia Yap-Chung is the secretary manager, and Richard Jackson is the commodore. If you want to sign on as crew, make your interest known at the club and there's a good chance one of the boats will take you on.

Fishing

Local fishermen go out to the California Banks about 16 kilometers offshore from Port Royal. Nigel Black operates **Why Not Fishing Charters** (tel. 876/995-1142) out of Morgan's Harbour Marina.

Other fishing expeditions can be arranged by inquiring with Anthony DuCasse at **DuRae's Boat Sales** (18 Rosewell Terrace, tel. 876/905-1713, duraes@cwjamaica.com), the best power-boat parts supplier on the island, in business since 1966, or at **E & S Fishing**

Supplies (Harbour View Shopping Center, tel. 876/928-7910, 9 A.M.–6 P.M. Mon.–Sat.), which sells lines, rods, tackle and bait.

SPAS AND FITNESS CENTERS

The Jamaican hospitality industry is making a concerted effort to brand Jamaica as a premiere health and spa tourism destination. In Kingston there are a few good options when it comes to affordable pampering.

Nirvana Day Spa (39 Lady Musgrave Rd., tel. 876/978-1723, 7 A.M.–7 P.M. Mon.–Fri., 8 A.M.–6 P.M. Sat., 10 A.M.–3 P.M. Sun.), owned by Gaudia Aquart, is located at the Eden Gardens complex and offers manicures and pedicures (US$29–41), massages (US$36–56), facials (US$50–71), mud and herb body wraps (US$57–79), body scrubs (US$36–53), and hair removal (US$6–36). All prices do not include tax. Nirvana also offers services at the Jamaica Pegasus Hotel (7 A.M.–11 P.M. Mon.–Sat., 10 A.M.–6 P.M. Sun.).

Jencare Skin Farm (82 Hope Rd., tel. 876/946-3494 or 876/946-3497, jencarejender@yahoo.com) is a slightly more upscale day spa that offers complete bodywork from nails (US$31), to facials (US$43), to massage (US$50). You can also get a haircut (US$7).

Shakti Mind Body Fitness (5 Bedford Park Ave., left before Megamart heading Uptown off Upper Waterloo, tel. 876/906-8403 or 876/920-5868, daily, info@shaktimindbodyfitness.com, www.shaktimindbodyfitness.com) is a full-service fitness center offering cutting-edge classes for body and mind, as well as a spa and fitness-lifestyle store. Choose from over 50 classes including indoor cycling, yoga, body sculpt, Pilates, and Zumba. Shakti often has guest instructors from the United States. Non-members are welcome for drop-in classes (US$11). Call or look online for class schedules as they change frequently. Regular classes run 8:30 A.M.–6:30 P.M. Mon.–Thurs., 8:30–10:30 A.M. Sat., 10 A.M.–noon Sun. Call ahead for spinning, as the classes are often booked. Appointments can also be made for spa treatments such as deep tissue, Swedish, and Thai massage, as well as eyelash tinting and body waxing with qualified therapists. Shakti is owned and operated by certified yoga teacher and aromatherapist Sharon McConnell (sharon@shaktimindbodyfitness.com). Essential oils fill the air and set a relaxing mood. See the website for a full schedule of classes and offerings. Great, healthy food is available, too, including the signature Shakti Granola Bars.

Daling Chinese Acupuncture & Moxibustion (39 Lady Musgrave Rd., tel. 876/978-3838) offers acupuncture service for a variety of ailments.

Rockfort Mineral Spa (Windward Rd., between the Shell gas station and the Carib Cement factory, tel. 876/938-6551, 7 A.M.–5:30 P.M. Tues.–Sun., US$2.50 adults, US$1.50 children) has one of Kingston's few public swimming pools adjoined by a bathhouse. Sitting on the remains of a British Fort from whence it gets its name, the baths are fed by mineral water from the Dallas Mountains. A large swimming pool outside is complemented by enclosed whirlpool tubs that come in different configurations and are available for 45-minute sessions: two-seater (US$14), four-seater (US$17), eight-seater (US$26), 12-seater (US$31). The tubs are heated with electric heaters; by 10 A.M., they're hot and ready for use. Additionally, the spa has a stress-management center offering 45-minute massages (US$35) and reflexology sessions (US$25).

Body Fusion (61 Constant Spring Rd., tel. 876/968-1999, 5:30 A.M.–9 P.M. daily, US$7 per day for non-members, one-month membership costs US$50) has good equipment, including free weights, treadmills, stair-climbers, stationary bikes, and NordicTracks. Aerobics classes are also offered (6 A.M. and hourly 5:30–7:30 P.M. Mon.–Fri., 7:30 A.M. on Sat.). Carolee Samuda is the very sweet manager.

Accommodations

NEW KINGSTON
Under US$75

The **Chelsea Hotel & Amusement Centre** (5 Chelsea Ave., tel. 876/926-5803, US$26 fan, US$29 a/c, US$36 TV), with double beds, is a bit of a dive, but it may well be the cheapest option in New Kingston. No-frills, however, would be an overstatement. Owner Tony Melville is a character and a conversation with him makes a visit worthwhile in itself. The amusement center around back has a bar, billiards hall, and other games, and hosts an open-air roots reggae session on Sundays.

Indies Hotel (5 Holborn Rd., tel. 876/926-2952, indieshotel@hotmail.com, www.indies hotel.com, US$39 s fan & TV, US$47 plus a/c, US$61 plus phone; US$64 d, US$81 t) is a no-frills hotel with basic rooms in a very convenient central location. There is a restaurant and bar in the inner courtyard where meals are served. Continental breakfast is US$2.50 and up and dinner is from US$6.

Country Cottage Inn (5 Upper Montrose, tel. 876/978-4859, US$40–65, 1 room for US$80 has balcony, rooms have a/c or fan, hot water, and some have kitchenettes) is located near the Prime Minister's residence and is an excellent value. Clean foam mattresses, a plant-filled yard, and nice location in a quiet, residential neighborhood within a 10-minute walk of the heart of New Kingston make Country Cottage Inn one of the best budget options in town.

Sunset Inn (1a Altamont Crescent, tel. 876/929-7283, sunsetinn@midspring.com, US$66 d, US$75 king, US$84 for 2 doubles, US$75 suite, US$76 w/ kitchenette) is basic but has all the essentials. Amenities include hot water, cable, air-conditioning, and dressers in all the rooms.

US$75-200

🄲 **Alhambra Inn** (1 Tucker Ave., tel. 876/978-9072, 876/978-9073, or 876/978-4333, alhambra inn@cwjamaica.com, US$85 or US$95–105 for

3 persons) is a very nice boutique hotel with a country feel across Mountain View Road from the National Indoor Stadium and a five-minute drive from New Kingston and Downtown. Twenty spacious rooms with comfortable sheets and a lush courtyard make the inn a cool option where the air-conditioning is barely necessary even in the summer. Bring soap and shampoo, as the soap provided is not high-end. Internet access is available downstairs off the courtyard. The Inn started as a reception center and began offering accommodations in '96. It is owned by the amicable Sonia Gray-Clarke and her husband Trevor Clarke, an antiques collector whose hobby has helped bestow the Alhambra with its distinct character.

Hotel Four Seasons (18 Ruthven Rd., tel. 876/929-7655, hfsres@cwjamaica.com, www .hotel-four-seasons-jam.com) owned by Ms. Helga Stoeckert, offers decent rooms with either two single or two queen beds (US$92 low season, US$106 high season). The hotel complex is large, with newer rooms by the pool in the back. Jamaica's German social club has its weekly meetings at the hotel bar.

The **Knutsford Court** (16 Chelsea Ave., tel. 876/929-1000, sales@knutsfordcourt.com, US$105) is well situated within easy walking distance to the restaurants, bars, and nightclubs on Knutsford Boulevard. The hotel is owned by the Hendricksons, who also operate the Courtleigh and Sunset Resorts on the North and West Coasts. The Knutsford is their most downscale property, but it offers amenities like a 24-hour business center, gym, meeting rooms, two restaurants, and a bar. The rooms are decent with wooden furniture and all the standard amenities like phone and cable TV. Two townhouses in the courtyard have the property's best suites.

Altamont Court (1 Altamont Terrace, tel. 876/929-4497, US$110, altamontcourt@ cwjamaica.com, www.altamontcourt.com) is very well situated on a quiet street in the heart of New Kingston. Many of the city's restaurants and much of its nightlife is centered on Knutsford Boulevard, a five-minute walk away. The Altamont has 57 standard rooms and one large suite. Standards come with two doubles or one king. For US$140 you get a loft with the bedroom upstairs and a living area and pull-out sofa, microwave, and fridge. The Alexander Suite is a spacious and luxurious room with an expansive bathroom that has a tub and a separate shower. Wireless Internet is included in all the rooms, and there is a computer in the business center. Three meeting rooms are also available. A restaurant by the pool and whirlpool tub serves breakfast, lunch, and dinner.

Eden Gardens (39 Lady Musgrave Rd., tel. 876/946-9981, US$120) has large, comfortable suites with broad, functional desks and kitchenettes. Wireless Internet is included and the property has conference facilities, a pool, and a restaurant. While the decor in the rooms is far from fancy, the place is functional and conveniently located in a quiet, well-laid-out compound.

The **Hilton Kingston** (77 Knutsford Blvd., tel. 876/926-5430, US$150 for poolside, US$245 executive) has a large courtyard with a popular poolside bar. The rooms are about what you'd find in a Hilton anywhere in the world, while the pricing fluctuates substantially based on demand. Also on the property are a low-key club, the Jonkanoo Lounge, and the Villagio gaming lounge. Latin Night with salsa classes is on Thursdays.

The **Courtleigh** (85 Knutsford Blvd., tel. 876/929-9000, fax 876/926-7744, US$160–270, US$460 presidential suite, courtleigh@ cwjamaica.com, www.courtleigh.com) is a popular business rest located between the Jamaica Pegasus and the Hilton. Rooms are modern and guests have free wireless Internet throughout the property. Continental breakfast is also included, and there are mini-fridges in rooms, cable TV, air-conditioning, and a 24-hour gym.

Jamaica Pegasus (81 Knutsford Blvd., tel. 876/926-3690, US$171 s/d, US$340 jr. suite) is a government favorite. It's the choice hotel for visiting and local officials, given its status as a joint venture between John Issa's SuperClubs and the Urban Development Corporation (UDC). Rates include buffet breakfast. Government officials from both sides of the aisle

(PNP and JLP) frequent the hotel, but those in power (PNP for the past few decades) seem to dominate. Caribbean ministers and Asian delegations are also frequent guests. A beautiful pool, 24-hour deli, and tennis courts round out this premiere New Kingston property.

HALF WAY TREE, LIGUANEA, AND BARBICAN
Under US$75

Shirley Retreat Hotel (7 Maeven Ave., tel. 876/946-2679, jeshirl@cwjamaica.com, US$65–75 s/d, plus US$10 per extra person) has 13 rooms with either two twins or two doubles. The rate includes continental breakfast and a kitchen on-site does meals to order (US$7–10 for lunch/dinner). There's cable TV, telephones, and refrigerators in the more expensive rooms. The hotel is owned and operated by the United Church in Jamaica and Grand Cayman and managed by executive director Shernette Smith.

C Hope Pastures Great House Bed & Breakfast (40 Charlemont Ave., tel. 876/970-3024, US$75) is located in an old estate house on an acre of land in Hope Pastures with a long wraparound driveway and a wide veranda. The uptown pastoral area was converted to a residential district in the relatively recent past. There are five spacious rooms on two floors with shared bath. Wireless Internet and an expansive yard filled with several mango tree varieties makes up for the basic accommodations and furnishings in a building that, while impressive, remains rough around the edges. Manager Lance Watson is a professional photographer who operates Yahso Dehso Studios out of the same location. The B&B is located two minutes away from a multitude of shopping and dining options along Hope Road and Barbican.

US$75-200

Mayfair Hotel (4 Kings House Close, tel. 876/926-1610 or 876/926-1612, mayfairhotel@cwjamaica.com, US$80 for 2 single or 1 double, with a/c, hot water, cable TV) located next to King's House, the home of the Governor General Kenneth Octavius Hall, has eight houses, each with five medium-size bedrooms. Quilted blankets adorn the beds and recent renovations have added new bathroom tile and split air-conditioned units. On the large lawn there's a decent-size swimming pool, restaurant, and snack shop. There's also a bar in the style of an English pub. Non-guests are welcome to use the pool (US$3.50) and dine at the restaurant.

The Gardens (23 Liguanea Ave., tel. 876/927-8275 or 876/977-8141, mlyn@cwjamaica.com, US$80 for 1BR, US$150 for 2BR) has seven two-bedroom townhouses in a quiet and green setting. The townhouses have spacious living/dining rooms and full kitchens on the ground floor with a master and second bedroom upstairs, each with private bath. Guests can rent out a single bedroom of the two-bedroom units for the lower rate. Wireless Internet reaches much of the property. Owner and manager Jennifer Lyn also operates Forres Park Guest House in Mavis Bank.

The **Terra Nova** (17 Waterloo Rd., tel. 876/926-2211, ext. 217, info@terranovajamaica.com, www.terranovajamaica.com) has comfortable rooms with two double beds (US$160), junior suites with minibar included (US$207), executive suites with whirlpool tubs and a bit more space (US$332), and three royalty suites each have balconies (US$568 Blue Mountain and Darby suites, US$688 Terra Nova suite). DSL in the rooms costs an additional US$15 per day. A highlight is the Sunday brunch buffet (US$21) with its wide assortment of great food, including imported lox and meats, as well as more typical Jamaican items like ackee and saltfish, fried dumpling, and callaloo.

Food

DOWNTOWN AND NEW KINGSTON
Breakfast and Cafés

Cannonball Café (three locations: 20–24 Barbados Ave. behind Pan Caribbean Bank, tel. 876/754-4486; lower Manor Centre, Manor Park, tel. 876/969-3399; Loshusan Plaza, 29 East King's House Rd., Barbican, tel. 876/946-0983; all locations 7 A.M.–7 P.M. daily) has sandwiches (US$4.50), beef lasagna (US$9), quiches (US$9), Greek salad (US$7), in addition to coffee (US$3), pastries, scones (US$3.50), and juices. The atmosphere is relaxing and cozy with 15 seats; wireless Internet is offered free for customers at all locations. Karen Lee is a very pleasant attendant at the New Kingston location.

The Coffee Mill (17 Barbados Ave., tel. 876/929-2227, 7 A.M.–8 P.M. Mon.–Fri., 10 A.M.–6 P.M. Sat.) part of Jamaican coffee wholesaler Coffee Industries, is a cozy hideout with six tables and five stools at the bar. It serves coffee (US$1) and sandwiches (US$4.50; ham and cheese, smoked marlin, pastrami), chicken (US$3.50), cheesecake (US$4), chocolate (US$2.50), and pastries (US$0.50–1) such as donuts, cinnamon rolls, cupcakes, and carrot and banana muffins. Breakfast (US$5) comes with eggs, bagel, and a juice or coffee. Frappes (US$2) and lattes (US$2.50) are also for sale. Eileen Thompson is one of the very sweet and helpful employees. There are branches at both international airports as well, and one in China. Jamaica Blue Mountain coffee is sold by the pound (US$20).

Earl's Juice Garden (28 Haining Rd., tel. 876/920-7009; 6 Red Hills Rd., tel. 876/754-2425; 16 Derrymore Rd., tel. 876/920-7009; delivery tel. 876/929-3275; earlsgarden@hotmail.com) makes excellent juices and baked goods (US$2–5). Events are sometimes held in the courtyard next to the Haining Road location.

Jamaican

Tatty's (29 4th St., Greenwich Town, no phone) is open for lunch only. Tatty's makes a trip into one of Kingston's most notorious shantytowns worth it for the peanut juice alone (US$3 for a bottle), not to mention the delicious steamed fish (US$4.50–7).

Up on the Roof (73 Knutsford Blvd., tel. 876/929-8033, 10 A.M.–midnight Mon. and Wed., 10 A.M.–2 A.M. Tues. and Thurs., 5 P.M. until last person leaves the bar Sat., kitchen closes at midnight every night) found by climbing up a narrow staircase through an unassuming entrance next to JamRock, has a great location that gives the feeling of sitting on top of New Kingston. The food is dependably good and moderately priced. Appetizers include crab backs (US$8.50), tropical salad (US$9), and peppered shrimp (US$13), or try chicken (US$11), shrimp (US$13), or marlin salad (US$13). Entrees include stewed conch (US$12), Virginia Calypso chicken (US$13), Cuban shrimp or ackee shrimp (US$14), Boston jerk pork (US$14), and, the most expensive dish, surf and turf (US$36; shrimp and lobster, or steak and lobster). The bar serves beer (US$3) and a range of cocktails.

Christopher's bar/lounge on the ground floor of the Quad (see *Entertainment*) has a pleasant, upscale atmosphere and decent bar food: battered jumbo shrimp, crab cakes, and two beers goes for US$25. Free wireless Internet is available.

Indies Cafe & Grill (8 Holborn Rd., tel. 876/920-5913) is a popular local hangout with decent food. Entrees range from roast chicken (US$7) to steamed fish (US$16). The menu also includes pita pockets (US$8.50 chicken, US$10 veg) and pizzas (US$6–9.50 plain, plus US$2–3 for toppings). The supervisor, Yaquema, is friendly and very pleasant. Indies hosts events during most nights of the week. Call for a schedule.

Carlos' Café (22 Belmont Rd., tel. 876/926-4186) is a Cuban-inspired bar with Martini Mondays (two for one 6–9 P.M.) and karaoke on Fridays (9:30 P.M.–1 A.M.). Prices range from US$1.50 for garlic bread to US$18.50 for lobster or filet mignon.

African Entertainment & Restaurant (94n Old Hope Rd., between Commissioners office and the Texaco station, tel. 876/946-0996, 7:30 A.M.–9 P.M. daily) serves rice and peas, pot roast pork, BBQ chicken, sweet and sour chicken, jerk chicken, jerk pork, steamed fish, curry goat, brown stew fish/chicken, okra and saltfish, ackee and saltfish, calaloo and saltfish, fried chicken, dumpling, banana, yam, green and ripe fried plantain (US$2.50 small, US$3.25 large), as well as peanut porridge for breakfast (US$1). African dishes are prepared to order or for special events. Dances and cultural events are sometimes held. Call to inquire.

Hot Pot Restaurant (2 Altamont Terrace, tel. 876/929-3906, 7 A.M.–6 P.M. daily) serves items like red pea soup (US$1.50–3), stew peas and pigs tail (US$5), ackee and saltfish (US$5), pigs feet (US$4.50), and tripe and beans (US$5).

Chelsea Jerk Center (7 Chelsea Ave., tel. 876/926-6322) has decent fast-food-style jerk at affordable prices (US$3.50–6) and much better prepared than at Jamaican fast-food chain Island Grill.

Gwong Wo (12 Trinidad Terrace, tel. 876/906-1288 or 876/906-1388, 11 A.M.–9 P.M. Mon.–Sat., noon–9 P.M. Sun.) has excellent fried chicken and rice (US$3.50–7).

Le Barons Restaurant & Lounge (13 Barbados Ave., tel. 876/929-3872, 11 A.M.–6 P.M. Mon.–Thurs., Fri. till late) is a nice spot on the roof of the First Union Financial building with affordable food and an inviting, inconspicuous ambiance. A balcony fills up with dominos players, especially on Domino Thursdays. Lyming Fridays includes a happy hour. Dishes include lobster, shrimp, pork chops and steaks.

Vegetarian

⦗ **Livity Gourmet Vegetarian** (30 Haigning Rd. in New Kingston, tel. 876/906-5618, US$2–6) recently reopened in New Kingston after this vegetarian favorite relocated from its previous Old Hope Road address. The menu continues to be filled with Ital favorites like pepperpot soup and brown lentil rice as well as more innovative dishes like raw veggie fajita, veggie wraps, veggie burgers, and tofu burgers. A wide variety of juices are on sale, including June Plum, Mango Pine (pineapple), Guinep Pine, Tamarind Moss, cherry, and limeade. Events are sometimes held in the outdoor bar area around back.

Indian, Thai, and Chinese

⦗ **Moby Dick Restaurant** (3 Orange St. at the corner of Port Royal, tel. 876/922-4468, 9 A.M.–7 P.M. Mon.–Sat.) is a landmark establishment owned by the McBeans since 1985. The restaurant dates from the early 1900s when it was opened by a Mr. Masterton to service his workers at the port. Moby Dick specializes in curry dishes accompanied by roti with an ambiance reminiscent of India: The cashier sits on a raised structure by the entrance with an overseer's view of the dining area. Some of the best curried dishes anywhere in Jamaica are offered, both seafood (shrimp/conch, US$14) and landed staples (goat, oxtail; US$8.50–11.50) with good fresh fruit juices (US$1.50).

Akbar and Thai Gardens Restaurant (11 Holborn Rd., tel. 876/906-3237, noon–3:30 P.M.and 6–10:30 P.M. daily) has decent Indian and Thai food with staples like chicken or shrimp pad thai (US$10/17) on the Thai side, and on the Indian food side items ranging from chicken tikka masala (US$11) to lobster bhuna (US$24).

New Pagoda Restaurant (5 Belmont Rd., tel. 876/926-2561) has decent Chinese for US$4–17.

Steak and Seafood

⦗ **So So Seafood Bar & Grill** (4 Chelsea Ave., tel. 876/906-1085, 10:30 A.M.–1 A.M. Mon.–Sat., 3 P.M.–midnight Sun.) is a nice seafood joint owned by Michael Forrest. It serves excellent steamed/fried fish (US$9–11/lb), various shrimp dishes (US$11), curry or stewed conch (US$10), and lobster in season (US$20–23). Finger food is also served, including crab back, bammy, fries, fish tea, and mannish water, a broth made of all sorts of animal parts said to promote virility. The pleasant ambiance with Christmas lights and a little waterfall, reggae in the speakers, and good food make So So a definite misnomer.

Heather's Garden Restaurant (9 Haining Rd., tel. 876/926-2826) is owned by Meleta Touzalin, who bought the business when Heather went off to fly airplanes. The food is very good and moderately priced (US$11–31 for entrees).

Red Bones Blues Café (21 Braemar Ave., tel. 876/978-6091) has decent food (ranging US$14 for linguine to US$36 for grilled lobster) and a nice ambiance with regular low-key events like fashion shows, poetry readings, and cabaret performances. There are usually shows on weekends, and poetry on some Wednesday nights.

Mac's Chop House (adjacent to The Quad at 24–26 Trinidad Terrace, tel. 876/960-6328, 6:00 P.M.–9:15 P.M. Mon.–Sat., reservations recommended) is Kingston's only veritable steakhouse; be prepared to shell out cash (US$50) for a well-prepared NY strip or lobster (US$40). Mostly Californian and Australian wines are served with a few French (US$30–550) as well. Mario and Fiona Machado, and son David, who is the manager, run the place.

HALF WAY TREE AND CONSTANT SPRING ROAD
Jamaican

◖ **Sonia's Homestyle Cooking & Natural Juices** (Shop 9, Lane Plaza, Constant Spring Rd., tel. 876/968-6267, 7 A.M.–5:30 P.M. Mon.–Fri., 7:30 A.M.–5 P.M. Sat., 8 A.M.–5 P.M. Sun., US$5–7.50) is Half Way Tree's best and most authentic sit-down eatery for Jamaican dishes like fried chicken, curry goat, and oxtail. Natural juices (US$1–2; June plum, Otaheite apple, soursop) are different every day based on seasonal availability. The menu changes daily. Tamra is the lovely assistant manager, and owner Sonia's daughter.

© OLIVER HILL

Sonia's Homestyle Cooking & Natural Juices in Half Way Tree is one of the best places uptown for authentic, affordable eats.

Gaucho's Grill (20A South Ave., tel. 876/754-1380) serves a blend of Jamaican and American food with an alleged Italian touch. The ambiance is relaxing with open-air seating by a reflecting pool. The bar makes a decent margarita. Prices range from inexpensive for a quarter chicken (US$6.50) to a bit pricey for steak or lobster (US$26).

◖ **Boon Hall Oasis** (4 River Rd., Stony Hill, tel. 876/942-3064, lunch 12:30 P.M.–3 P.M. Wed.–Sat., brunch 10 A.M.–3 P.M. Sun., and dinner by reservation) is a beautiful rainforest-like garden venue in the Stony Hill area of St. Andrew. The all-inclusive brunch buffet (US$17) is excellent, with typical Jamaican fare like ackee and saltfish, liver, mackerel, boiled banana, and dumpling. Take a right on Eerie Castle road in Stony Hill square and a left at Roti Bar onto River Road. A steep decline leads off River Road to the left to the parking area. Lunch (US$13.50) dishes include fish, chicken, and curry goat, while dinners (US$21 and up) involve shrimp, chicken, and lobster. Steven Jones owns the place.

Country Style Restaurant (Stony Hill Square, tel. 876/942-2506, 7:30 A.M.–9 P.M. daily) serves typical Jamaican and Chinese dishes ranging from curry mutton, stew pork or escoveitch fish (US$4) to curried shrimp (US$10.50). Georgianna's, based at the same location, offers catering.

Pepper's Night Club (Upper Waterloo Rd., tel. 876/969-2421 or 876/905-3831), set on a big open-air compound next to Megamart, has very decent food (US$4–14), the pepper shrimp being the highlight. The bar can be lively and has plenty of billiard tables.

Indian, Japanese, and Chinese

Just west of the Junction of South Avenue and Constant Spring Road, the **Courtyard at Market Place** shopping plaza (67 Constant Spring Rd.) has become the premiere international food court in Kingston.

◖ **Taka's East Japanese Restaurant** (Shop 50 & 51, tel. 876/960-3962, noon–10 P.M. Wed.–Sun., 5–10 P.M. Tues., closed Mon.) has the best sushi in Jamaica at

competitive prices (US$25 per person for a full meal) and a very convincing ambiance. Taka Utoguchi opened the restaurant in 2005.

Jewel of India (Shop 37, tel. 876/906-3983, noon–10 P.M. daily, reservations recommended) serves North Indian cuisine in an upscale South Beach contemporary atmosphere with Indian Buddha bar music. Dishes range from chicken shorba and tomato soup (US$5), to lamb (US$13), lobster (US$30), tandoori filet mignon (US$28), and masala lamb chops (US$23). The bar has a nice range of liquor and an extensive cocktail menu, including house items Kama Sutra, Indian Sunrise, Indian Smooch, and Vindaloo Margarita. The food can be hit or miss and quickly adds up.

China Express (Shop 53, Market Place, tel. 876/906-9158 or 876/906-9159, noon–9:30 P.M. Sun.–Thurs., noon–10 P.M. Fri.–Sat.) has decent Chinese food in a nice setting. Items on the menu range from wonton soup to Cantonese lobster (US$34). It's a popular lunch location.

Panda Village Chinese Restaurant (Shop 21, Manor Park Plaza, 184 Constant Spring Rd., tel. 876/941-0833, 11:30 A.M.–9 P.M. Mon.–Thurs., 11:30 A.M.–10 P.M. Fri. and Sat., US$5–8) has dependable Chinese food with chicken, fish, and shrimp dishes.

Restaurant Cocoro (Mayfair Hotel, 4 West Kings House Close, tel. 876/929-0970, noon–10 P.M. Tues.–Sun.) is a Japanese restaurant opened in late 2006 by Takahiro Sawada. The restaurant offers some of the most attentive service in all of Kingston, with traditional Japanese dishes like shrimp shumai (US$6), edamame (US$3), and seaweed salad (US$4), as well as creative dishes that incorporate typical Jamaican cuisine like the Cocoroll, a deep fried pork and tomato roll, or the Pirates Roll with jerk chicken and tomato (US$7). While Taka's East Japanese Restaurant takes the prize for most authentic Japanese cuisine, Cocoro is an excellent option in a nice quiet setting on the veranda of the Mayfair.

Dragon Court (6 South Ave., tel. 876/920-8506, 11:30 A.M.–9:30 P.M., till 10 P.M. for takeout daily) serves decent Chinese food ranging from chicken dishes (US$7) to lobster (US$28.50).

C Tropical Chinese (Mid Spring Plaza, 134 Constant Spring Rd., tel. 876/941-0520, noon–10 P.M. daily, closed only on Christmas and Good Friday) serves entrées like chicken (US$8.50), shrimp with cashew nuts (US$16), steam whole fish (US$28.50), lobster dishes (US$23.50), and eggplant (US$7), seafood (US$17), and stewed duck (US$14). Brothers Chris and Fred Chai run the place.

Steak and Seafood

White Bones (1 Mannings Hill Rd., where it branches off Constant Spring Rd., tel. 876/925-9502, 11:30 A.M.–11 P.M. Mon.–Sat., 2–10 P.M. Sun.) has a great setting and excellent seafood. Appetizers (starting at US$8.50) include raw or grilled oysters, soup du jour, and salads. Entrées include snapper fillet (US$20) and grilled snapper burger (US$11.50).

C The Rib Kage Bar & Grill (149 Constant Spring Rd., tel. 876/905-1858 or 876/931-8129; 12 Braemar Ave., tel. 876/978-6272; 11 A.M.–10:30 P.M. Mon.–Thurs., 11 A.M.–11:30 P.M. Fri. and Sat., 1–9 P.M. Sun., US$6–30) is the best place in town for ribs: fingers, tips, spare, and baby back. They also serve chicken, fish, and lobster. The outdoor setting is worth hanging out for, but delivery is also available. A new branch opened in late 2006 on Braemar Avenue in New Kingston.

Fusion

C Habibi Latino Restaurant (Shop 35, Market Place, tel. 876/968-9296, 11 A.M.–11 P.M. Mon.–Sat., 3–11 P.M. Sun.) is easily one of Kingston's finest eats. Co-owners Abdul El Khalili and Yani Machado, of Lebanese and Cuban origin respectively, bring together their native cuisines as if they were created for each other, delivering tasty combinations of hummus appetizers, rosemary-seasoned steak, and *tostones* (fried plantains). A meal for two costs around US$50.

Cafe Aubergine (noon–10:30 P.M. daily, tel. 876/754-1865, cafe_aubergine@mail .infochan.com, www.cafeaubergine.com) opened a branch at Market Place in July 2006, giving Kingston-based fans of the original location in Moneague, St. Ann, a closer alternative. Owned by partners Neville Anderson and Rudolf Gschloessl, Cafe Aubergine features a mix of Caribbean and Mediterranean cuisine. Entrees include from pork tenderloin (US$12), lamb chops (US$32), and grilled loup de mer (US$40).

HOPE ROAD, LIGUANEA, AND BARBICAN
Bakeries and Pastry Shops

Susie's Bakery & Coffee Bar (Shop 1, Southdale Plaza, behind Popeyes on Constant Spring Rd., tel. 876/968-5030, 9 A.M.–6 P.M. Mon.–Sat.) has prepared foods like lasagna and sandwiches, as well as some of the best Otaheite juice around.

Blessed Delights (tel. 876/899-6332), run by Ngozi, makes delicious baked goods, many of which are vegan, and supplies Bob's Café and other outlets around Town. Call for the real goods.

Brick Oven (Devon House, tel. 876/968-2153) sells delicious pastries and cakes.

Elaine's Bakery (30 Slipe Rd., tel. 876/968-4966) makes whole wheat, raisin, and corn bread.

Captain's Bakery (100 Orange St,, tel. 876/922-2022; New Kingston Shopping Center, tel. 876/926-3891; 25 Dominica Dr., tel. 876/929-6571; 16 Half Way Tree Rd., tel. 876/906-5875) makes regular white bread, buns, cake, and patties.

All Fresh Bakery (42 Shortwood Rd. tel. 876/924-0957) bakes bread and pastries and cake. Sub rolls, sandwich and fancy bread.

Sugar and Spice Pastry has four locations in Kingston (1–3 Red Hills Rd., tel. 876/906-7011 or 876/906-7013).

Jamaican

Kabana (12 Hope Rd., tel. 876/908-4005, noon–11 P.M. Mon.–Thurs., noon–midnight Fri. & Sat., 10 A.M.–11 P.M. Sun., US$10–34) serves mostly Jamaican food ranging from curry goat to lobster, as well as shrimp, ribs, salmon, and steak . Appetizers include fritters, spring rolls, and spicy shrimp. It serves Jamaican brunch (US$14) on Sundays, which includes dishes like ackee and saltfish, mackerel rundown, steamed calaloo, roast breadfruit, boiled banana, yam, jerk chicken, and rice and peas.

The Grog Shoppe Restaurant and Pub (Devon House, 26 Hope Rd., tel. 876/926-3512, noon–midnight Mon.–Thurs.; Fri. and Sat.: noon until you say when; 11 A.M.–midnight Sun.) serves Jamaican staples like stewed oxtail, curry goat, ackee and saltfish. Prices range from US$7 for curried chicken to US$29 for steak.

Norma's on the Terrace (Devon House, 26 Hope Rd., tel. 876/968-5488, normasjamaica@kasnet.com) is the first restaurant founded by Norma Shirley, one of the Caribbean's most revered chefs for her innovative cuisine founded on the island's culinary heritage. Norma's is in a beautiful setting overlooking the central courtyard at Devon House. The food is pricey, second only to Mac's Chop House, with entrees like stuffed chicken breast (US$14), lamb chops (US$40) and lobster (US$43). Appetizers include ackee with salt fish (US$11), marlin salad (US$13), and crab back (US$14).

Velisa's (11a Devon Rd., tel. 876/754-0749 or 876/906-3574, 10 A.M. to 10:30 P.M. Mon.–Fri., 1–11 P.M. Sat.) has a wide variety of creative vegetarian and non-vegetarian fare. Appetizers (US$5–6.50) include ackee bami, dulse (seaweed) salsa with pita triangles, lean green soup, and Velisa's salad. For entrees (US$8–40), try the lentil nutloaf, mock chicken, grilled tofu with Thai curry sauce and vegetable, lobster Chardonnay, seafood fetuccine, or grilled salmon. Chef Damian Thorpe also makes a mean chicken breast stuffed with calaloo and mushroom with three cheeses. At the cocktail bar, Mr. Winter makes an excellent lychee martini (US$5), the house specialty.

Ambrosia (29 East Kings House Rd., 11:30 A.M.–midnight daily, US$5.50–24), inside the gaming lounge of Acropolis, specializes in Jamaican dishes like oxtail, peppered shrimp, and fish and bammy. International food is also served, including rack of lamb, ribs, eight- and 16-ounce steaks, burgers, and club sandwiches. Ambrosia has a casino vibe with gaming machines ringing rather loudly, adding to the general bar and restaurant din.

Legend Café (56 Hope Rd., at the Bob Marley Museum) is open during museum hours (9 A.M.–5 P.M. daily). It serves escoveitched fish (US$17) and fresh juices (US$2), is a great place to hang out and get some Ital food. You're likely to see any number of reggae icons passing through.

Starapples (94 Hope Rd., tel. 876/927-9019, fax 876/946-1833, starapples@cwjamaica.com, 11:30 A.M.–9 P.M. Mon.–Thurs., 11:30 A.M.–10 P.M. Fri., 9 A.M.–10 P.M. Sat., 9 A.M.–6 P.M. Sun.) serves excellent dishes, from appetizers (US$2–4) like saltfish fritters, pepper shrimp, and crab cakes to entrees (US$5–16) like escoveitched fish, curried shrimp, and reggae lobster in coconut curry. More typical Jamaican fare is also served, including roast yam and saltfish, jerk chicken, and curried goat, as well as creative vegetarian dishes like vegetable lasagna and callaloo quiche. The setting is nice with indoor and outdoor seating with a view of busy Hope Road.

Vegetarian

Ashanti Oasis (Hope Botanical Gardens, Hope Rd., tel. 876/970-2079, noon–6 P.M. Mon.–Sat. dining in, take-out till 6:30 P.M., 12:30–5:30 P.M. Sun.), owned by Yvonne Hope, has some of the best and most reasonably priced vegetarian food in Kingston—in what must be the most natural setting on the manicured grounds of Hope Gardens. Combo meals are the best value, giving a taste of everything for US$4, or US$3.50 per single serving of any one dish. The menu changed daily and includes items like chile tofu in smoked sauce. Juices (US$1.50) are the best in town. The menu changes daily. Call the day before to know what will be served on the following day.

Lebanese

Chez Maria (7 Hillcrest Ave., tel. 876/927-

8078 or 876/978-7833, chezmaria@cwjamaica .com, 11:30 A.M.–3 P.M. Mon.–Sat., 6–10 P.M. Sun.) is an excellent Lebanese restaurant that makes its own pita bread and often has fresh fish caught by the owners, who are expert free divers. All the typical Lebanese favorites are covered on the menu, from tabouleh salad to hummus to grape leaf mehsheh, as well as good-value main dishes (US$9–18) like kafta kabab, shawarma, filet mignon, shrimp, and lobster.

Sovereign Food Court

Located downstairs at Sovereign Center at 106 Hope Road and Barbican, the food court has several options for a quick bite. A purchase of US$3.50 at many of the participating shops comes with a half-hour of wireless Internet access.

Kibby Korner (Shop 10, Sovereign Mall, tel. 876/978-3762, US$2.75–6.50) has affordable Lebanese food, including falafel, kibby, and kebabs. A grape leaf combo gives you a mix of dishes and an assortment of sides is also available.

Jamaica Juice (tel. 876/978-9756, US$3.50) is perhaps the best shop in Sovereign's food court, with fresh juices, smoothies, as well as food items, most notably chicken or chickpea roti. The mango smoothie is highly recommended.

Bucks and Johnny (US$1.75–4.25) specializes in fruit and vegetable salads. A grilled fish salad can come with a variety of sauces. The chef's special comes topped with fruit. Cane and other natural juices are also served.

Other Sovereign food court restaurants include **Kowloon** (tel. 876/978-3472, 11 A.M.–9 P.M. Mon.–Thurs., 11 A.M.–9:30 P.M. Fri. and Sat., 12:30–7 P.M. Sun.), serving passable Chinese fast food.

Orchid Plaza

Orchid Plaza, on the right going up Barbican Road, has three good places to eat across from Burger King: **Daily Bread** (20 Barbican Rd., tel. 876/970-4571, 9 A.M.–10 P.M. Mon.–Sat.), a branch outlet of Susie's, has a great hot lunch buffet (US$10–24) with items like fried

Ashanti Oasis at Hope Botanical Gardens cooks up some of Kingston's best vegetarian fare and serves excellent natural juices.

or BBQ chicken, rice and peas, shrimp with a fresh salad bar, delicious pastries, and the best Otaheite apple juice in town. **Guilt Trip** (20 Barbican Rd., tel. 876/977-5130, 10 A.M.–11 P.M. Tues.–Sat., 6 P.M.–10 P.M. Sun.) is well known for its desserts, and also has an innovative and well-executed dinner menu that includes beef tenderloin, shrimp, soups, and salads. It's reasonably priced, with most entrees around US$11–21.

Village Café (20 Barbican Rd., tel. 876/970-4861) does excellent fried fish and bammy for a reasonable US$8.50 plus sides.

Village Grill (tel. 876/451-2229 or 876/390-7218, 6 P.M. until closing Tues., Thurs., and Fri.) is located at Village Café in Orchid Plaza on Barbican Road. The grill is run by Tiny and Nadine who prepare excellent steamed and fried fish with bammy or festival as a side (US$10–20).

Takeout, Fast Food, and Delivery

While it is sometimes said that Jamaica's national dish is KFC's fried chicken, there are also a host of Jamaican-style fast-food joints, like Tastee Patties, Juici Patties, and Island Grill to compete with ackee and saltfish for that title. In fact, only select international franchises have been able to survive in Jamaica; notably, both McDonald's and Taco Bell were forced to close their doors. Others, like Domino's, Pizza Hut, Popeyes, and Subway do extremely well, but have not been included in these restaurant listings. Pan chicken, along with beef patties, comprise the real Jamaican fast food.

Pan chicken vendors set up all over town from evening until the early morning. Some of the best spots in town for real, hot-off-the-street pan chicken include the line of vendors next to one another on Red Hills Road just beyond Red Hills Plaza heading towards Meadowbrook and Red Hills.

A few **jerk vendors** hawk their goods in the evenings on the corner of Northside Drive and Hope Road by Pizza Hut; they have a devoted following. Jerk pork (US$8.50/lb) is sold on one side of the plaza with chicken (US$3.50/quarter) on the other.

Just above the Sovereign Center intersection on Hope Road there are a few plazas, namely Lane Plaza with a SuperPlus supermarket, a Juici Patties outlet, Vegas Gaming Lounge, and Liguanea Lane Pharmacy; above that on Hope Road is Northside Plaza, which holds Kingston's closest approximation to a Chinatown, with three Chinese restaurants right next to one another: **Golden State** (tel. 876/977-9213), **Dragon City** (tel. 876/927-0939), and **Dragon Heights.** All three keep similar hours (11:30 A.M.–9 P.M. Mon.–Sat., 2–9 P.M. Sun.), though Dragon Heights open a few hours earlier on Sundays (10 A.M.). Of the lot, Golden State has especially good service and decent food.

Pushpa's (Northside Plaza, tel. 876/977-5454 or 876/977-5858, 11 A.M.–10 P.M. daily, US$4–6.50) is by far the best restaurant in the complex and likely the best Indian food on the island, serving a mix of North and South Indian dishes, including dosas and idli on Sundays. Lunch specials include chicken dishes like moghlai, vindaloo, and kurma; vegetarian dishes like aloo mutter, paneer mutter, and eggplant curry; with mutton, shrimp, and fish also served either curried, fried, or vindaloo.

Food for Life (corner of Standpipe Ln. and Hope Rd., cell 876/878-6267, Osta cell 876/848-7572, 6 A.M.–10 P.M. Mon.–Sat.) serves Ital dishes and natural juices (US$1–3.50) out of a rustic roadside stall that contrasts nicely with the behemoth U.S. Embassy just down the road.

Norma's (31 Whitehall Ave., tel. 876/931-0064) takeaway is the best home cooking in town for Jamaican staples like curry goat, oxtail, and stewed chicken—and you won't find better value; at times fish and shrimp are also available. Call in advance to know what's on the menu and to make sure it "nah sell-off" yet. Ask Norma if you can view the kitchen around back with its industrial-size pots and flurry of activity. Lunches come in small (US$2.50) or large (US$3). Oxtail is US$6.50, and juices are US$1.

Fee Fee Fast Food (Shop 7 Lane Plaza, Half Way Tree, tel. 876/929-5465, 7 A.M.–6:30 P.M. daily, US$2–6) has Indian-Caribbean dishes like roti and curries, rice and peas, and oxtail. Fee Fee delivers all over Kingston down to Cross Roads and up to Constant Spring. The breakfast menu changes daily, with porridge and hearty Jamaican breakfasts like ackee and saltfish, calaloo and cabbage, and stew chicken.

925-JERK is a decent, fairly rapid, delivery jerk service. The name of the place is the number to call.

Eden Vegetarian Restaurant (24 Central Plaza, tel. 876/926-3051, entrées US$3.50– 8.50) has excellent vegetarian fare at a good value and delivers relatively quickly.

Information and Services

GOVERNMENT INFORMATION OFFICES

The **Jamaica Tourist Board** (64 Knutsford Blvd., tel. 876/929-9200 fax. tel. 876/929-9375, info@visitjamaica.com, www.visitjamaica .com, 8:30 A.M.–4:30 P.M. Mon.–Fri.) has a small library with staffers available to assist visitors with information on Jamaica's more popular attractions.

The **Jamaica National Heritage Trust** (79 Duke St., tel. 876/922-1287, www.jnht.com) is located Downtown in the historic Headquarters House. The Trust can provide information on Heritage sights across the island.

The **Survey Department** (23½ Charles St., tel. 876/922-6630 or 876/922-6635, ext. 264, patricia.davis@nla.gov.jm) sells all kinds of maps. Contact Patricia Davis in the business office. The Survey Department is a division of the National Land Agency, based on Ardenne Road.

The **Urban Development Corporation,** sometimes referred to as the "Utterly Destructive Corporation," has extended its reach far beyond urban centers to own tourism assets like Reach Falls and Two Sisters Caves. The UDC has often had problems integrating locals into its projects.

The Tax Office (Constant Spring Rd., tel. 876/969-0000, Cross Roads tel. 876/960-0097, Kingston tel. 876/922-7919) is a trying but essential stop for any paperwork related to motor vehicles, like registrations, titles, and plates. Most transactions require a Taxpayer Registration Number (TRN), which is obtained by standing in line at the small building around back. A TRN can also be used to demonstrate

residence in Jamaica, which is grounds for a 20 percent discount at hotels across the island.

POLICE AND IMMIGRATION

Police stations are located at Half Way Tree (142 Maxfield Ave., Half Way Tree, tel. 876/926-8184), Downtown Kingston Central (East Queen St., tel. 876/922-0308), and Constant Spring (2–3 Casava Piece Rd., tel. 876/924-1421).

Immigration is located at 25 Constant Spring Road (tel. 876/906-4402, tel. 876/906-1304).

HOSPITALS AND MEDICAL FACILITIES

UWI's **University Hospital** (Papine Rd., Mona, tel. 876/927-1620) has a good reputation and is probably the best public hospital in Jamaica. Tony Thwaites is UWI's private facility (University Hospital, Mona, tel. 876/977-2607).

Andrews Memorial Hospital is located at 27 Hope Road (tel. 876/926-7401, emergency tel. 876/926-7403).

Medical Associates Hospital and Medical Center (18 Tangerine Place, tel. 876/926-1400) is a private clinic with a good reputation. It also has a pharmacy at the same location.

Imperial Optical Jamaica has eye-care services (Kingston Mall, 8 Ocean Blvd., tel. 876/922-0991 or 876/922-0992).

Pharmacies

Silver Slipper Pharmacy (9 Old Hope Rd., tel. 876/926-4365) in Silver Plaza makes excellent fresh juice blends and whole wheat patties.

Liguanea Drugs and Garden is at 134 Old

Hope Rd. (tel. 876/977-0066), while **Lee's Family Pharmacy** is at 86B Red Hills Rd. (tel. 876/931-1877).

Andrews Memorial Hospital Pharmacy (27 Hope Rd., tel. 876/926-7401) is open 8 A.M.–10 P.M. Mon.–Thurs., 8 A.M.–3:30 P.M. Fri., 9:30 A.M.–3:30 P.M. Sun.

COMMUNICATIONS AND MEDIA

Jamaica Information Service (JIS HQ, 58A Half Way Tree Rd., tel. 876/926-3590; TV Div. 37 Arnold Rd., tel. 876/922-3317) accumulates all kind of data and statistics as well as archival television footage.

The **Public Library** (Main Branch, 2 Tom Redcam Rd., tel. 876/928-7975 or 876/926-3315, ksapl@cwjamaica.com, jamlib.org.jm, free) has a decent collection and allows visitors to check out books by leaving a deposit.

Music and Film Studios

Phase Three Production (30 Red Hills Rd., tel. 876/929-5975) has the best equipment for rent, from tripods, to cameras, to flat-screen TVs. Phase Three also does music videos and event production.

Caveman Studio (cell 876/774-5217, simone mc2003@yahoo.com) has a Mackie 24-track together with Nuendo and access to numerous contemporary artists and live studio musicians. Bargain rates for recording (US$215/hr) and mixing (US$70/mix) make Caveman a top choice in Kingston for streamlined production. Dub plates vary in price depending on the artists, but generally for a big name like Richie Spice or Warrior King it'll run around US$500, with bigger artists like Sizzla charging at least double that.

Anchor Studios (7 Windsor Ave., tel. 876/978-2711, www.anchorstudios.com), run by Gussie Clarke, has reel-to-reel as well as Protools. Rates are US$215 and US$260 per hour, respectively.

Newspapers

Kingston is home to two well-established newspapers, the *Jamaica Gleaner* (www.jamaica-gleaner.com) and the *Jamaica Observer* (www.jamaicaobserver.com), both of which are distributed island-wide. The *Gleaner* was the island's first daily news publication and considered the paper of record; it also owns *Jamaica Star*, the entertainment daily where you'll find the latest gossip on feuds between recording artists. The Star also publishes the advice column "Dear Pastor" and photos of partygoers from Kingston's happening nightlife scene.

Local Societies and Organizations

The **Jamaica Orchid Society** (contact secretary Violet Barber tel. 876/977-1130, jaos@hamlynorchids.com, or president Jeremy Whyte, tel. 876/946-8356, www.hamlynorchids.com/jaos.htm) holds its annual impressive Spring Show the last weekend in March at the assembly hall at UWI. The society meets on the first Saturday of each month at the Joint Trades Unions Research and Development Centre Visitors (1 Hope Blvd.) at 4 P.M.; visitors are welcome. Members bring plants to discuss, and they hold short lectures and a judging session, where members learn about orchids and how to judge shows.

Claude Hamilton, an accredited judge of the **American Orchid Society** (tel. 876/927-6713) is the largest commercial grower in Kingston and the number one expert in Jamaica. He has large nursery in Kingston. Call him to set up an organized visit. The society also holds an autumn show between October and November. See website for complete details on events.

The **Georgian Society of Jamaica** (Richmond Park Great House, 58 Half Way Tree Rd., tel. 876/754-5261, www.georgianjamaica.org) is a private society dedicated to the appreciation of Jamaica's architectural heritage from the Georgian period, and dedicated to the restoration and preservation of Georgian buildings. Geoffrey Pinto is the society's founder, honorary secretary is Pauline Simmonds. They have a list of sights where they visit on four or five annual private tours to public and private buildings. Richmond Park Great House is now headquarters for Xerox Jamaica.

The Department of Life Sciences at UWI has a **Natural History Society of Jamaica** (tel. 876/977-6938, naturalhistory@hotmail.com), which holds regular meetings to discuss and explore the country's natural endowment.

Post Offices and Parcel Services

Post Offices are located Downtown at 13 King Street (tel. 876/922-2120), Cross Roads (tel. 876/968-0948), and Half Way Tree (118 Hagley Park Rd., tel. 876/923-8665 or 876/926-6803).

Shipping services are available through **DHL** (19 Haining Rd., tel. 876/920-0010) and **FedEx** (40 Half Way Tree Rd. and 75 Knutsford Blvd, 888/GO-FEDEX).

Telephone, Internet, and Fax

A few locations around Kingston offer free wireless access to customers. These include **Cannonball Cafe, Christopher's Bar** (tel. 876/754-7823) and **Cafe Whatson.**

Logic Microsystems Internet Cafe (32 Hagley Park Rd., tel. 876/920-3791, 9 A.M.–5 P.M. Mon.–Fri., 10 A.M.–3 P.M. Sat., info@logicmicrosystems.com, www.logicmicro systems.com), very close to Half Way Tree, has the best rate in town for Internet usage (US$1.40/hour). Fax service is also available.

Liguanea Cybercentre is also good (above Half Way Tree post office, tel. 876/968-0323).

Indies Cafe & Grill has a few computers available (US$4.25/hr).

Café Whatson (26 Hope Rd., tel. 876/929-4490) offers free wireless at Devon House for customers; they charge US$3.50 per hour to use their PC.

Anbell (51 Knutsford Blvd., tel. 876/906-8479, www.anbell.net) provides pricey wireless access across New Kingston. Turn on your device, connect, and pay online with a credit card.

NetKyaad (tel. 876/755-1342, www.net kyaad.com) offers prepaid dial-up Internet cards for access over a phone line using a modem.

Digicel (10 Grenada Way, tel. 876/511-5000) offers island-wide wireless cards for lap-tops. GSM chips can be bought at the Digicel outlet on Knutsford Bloulevard and across the street behind the Tourist Board at Digicel headquarters.

MONEY

It's generally best to carry an ATM card and draw money at local ATMs. Foreign charges are the only drawback, but generally a few dollars in fees is worth the convenience. All the major banks can change travelers checks, but lines are typically long, slow-moving, and over-whelmingly frustrating.

Western Union (main office at 2 Trafford Place, tel. 876/926-2454) has offices all over the island including in Kingston at Cross Roads, 20 Tobago in New Kingston, Hi-Lo in Liguanea Plaza, at Blue Menthal in Lower Manor Park Plaza, and in Pavillion Mall on Constant Spring in Half Way Tree (shop 30 upstairs, and Super Plus downstairs).

Banks

Scotiabank has several branches at the following locations: Downtown (35–45 King St., tel. 876/922-1420), Cross Roads (86 Slipe Rd., tel. 876/926-1530 or 876/926-1532), Liguanea (125–127 Old Hope Rd., tel. 876/970-4371), New Kingston (2 Knutsford Blvd., tel. 876/926-8034), Portmore (Lot 2, Cookson Pen), Bushy Park (tel. 876/949-4837), and UWI (tel. 876/702-2518 or 876/702-2519).

RBTT has branches at the following locations: Downtown (134 Tower St., tel. 876/922-8195), Cross Roads (15 A Old Hope Rd., tel. 876/926-5492), New Kingston (17 Dominica Dr., tel. 876/960-2340), and Half Way Tree (6C Constant Spring Rd., tel. 876/968-4193).

NCB has branches at the following locations: Downtown (37 Duke St., tel. 876/922-6710), Cross Roads (90–94 Slipe Rd., tel. 876/926-7420), New Kingston (32 Trafalgar Rd., tel. 876/929-9050), and Half Way Tree (Half Way Tree Rd., tel. 876/920-8313).

Dehring Bunting and Golding (7 Holborn Rd., tel. 876/960-6700, 8:30 A.M.–5 P.M. Mon.–Fri.) has the best **currency exchange** rates in town.

LAUNDRY

Bogues Brothers runs three laundry facilities in Kingston: **Spic 'n' Span** (26 Lady Musgrave Rd., on corner of Trafalgar, tel. 876/978-7711, 7 A.M.–6 P.M. Mon.–Sat., 9 A.M.–4 P.M. Sun.), **Molynes Fabricare** (55 Molynes, tel. 876/923-4234), and **Liguanea Fabricare** (144 Old Hope Rd., tel. 876/977-4900). All have dry cleaning, drop-off laundry service, and self-service.

Supercleaners Dry Cleaners & Launderers (25 Connolley Ave., tel. 876/922-6075, 7 A.M.–5 P.M. Mon.–Sat.) has a plant Downtown behind Sabina Cricket Grounds where the drop-off service can get your clothes back the same day.

Getting There and Around

GETTING THERE
By Air

Norman Manley Airport (tel. 876/924-8546 for arrival and departure information) is located on the Palisadoes heading towards Port Royal east of Downtown.

Regular domestic flights depart from Tinson Pen for Montego Bay (approximately US$60 per person one way) with Air Jamaica Express and AirLink. Charters depart for smaller aerodromes in Oracabessa, Port Antonio, and Negril with TimAir and AirLink.

By Ground Transportation

Buses ply routes between Kinston and major towns around the island. The main bus terminal for getting in and out of Kingston is the new Transportation Centre in the heart of Half Way Tree. There is also a terminal downtown below crossroads by the market, west of the Parade. **Route taxis** depart from Cross Roads, Half Way Tree, and by the roundabout on upper Constant Spring Road for destinations due north. Route taxis depart for Kingston from virtually every city or town in the surrounding parishes and from parish capitals further afield.

Knutsford Express (tel. 876/960-5499 or 876/971-1822, www.knutsfordexpress.com) offers the most comfortable bus service between Kingston, Ocho Rios, and Montego Bay, with two daily departures from each city. New Kingston–Montego Bay departs 6 A.M. and 4:30 P.M. daily; Montego Bay–New Kingston departs 5 A.M. and 4:30 P.M. daily. Buses run between 24 Haining Road in New Kingston and Pier 1 in Montego Bay. The trip lasts between three-and-a-half and four hours depending on traffic.

GETTING AROUND
On Foot

The Jamaicans who walk around Kingston generally don't choose to, by day or night. It's mainly because of the heat that they would prefer not to walk, however, because the dangers of Town are generally exaggerated. There is really no better way to get to know the layout of some of the more congested areas like Downtown around the Parade, Knutsford Boulevard's Hip Strip, and around the center of Half Way Tree than to go on foot. Beyond that, route taxis and public buses are the best way to move about for those without a car.

By Bus

Jamaica Urban Transit Company (www.jutc .com, US$0.75) operates buses in and around the Corporate Area. Routes are extensive, but service and schedules can by daunting. Covered street-side bus stops are scattered along all the major thoroughfares throughout the city, and the more people gathered there, the sooner you're likely to see a bus. This is definitely the most economical way to move about.

By Taxi

Taxis are relatively safe off the street, but it's always best to call a dispatch to ensure accountability. Fares are assessed by distance rather than with a meter, and you may want to haggle if it seems too high. Downtown to New Kingston should cost around US$4.25, New Kingston to Half Way Tree around US$3.50, Half Way Tree to Papine about US$4.25. **City Guide Taxi** (tel. 876/969-5458) is a decent and dependable service, as are **Safe Travel Taxi Service** (tel. 876/901-5510) and **El-Shaddai** (tel. 876/969-7633). All the taxis in Jamaica tend to use white Toyota Corolla station wagons, and when you see one of these, chances are it's a taxi and can be waved down.

By Car

Rental cars tend to be very expensive across the island, but unfortunately indispensable when it comes to independently moving about and exploring remote areas. For the upper reaches of the Blue and John Crow Mountains a four-wheel-drive vehicle is indispensable. Pervasive potholes in town don't really warrant a 4x4. Check with the rental agency to see if your credit card covers insurance.

Scams in Jamaica infiltrate every line of business, including rental cars. A case was recently reported whereby a rental car was stolen by the employees of an international franchise. The client was charged the deductible and the agency claimed the insurance while the car was sold. To be safe, it might be better to put an alternate address on the rental form rather than where you will actually be staying when using a franchise where there could be a lack of direct oversight.

Unlicensed rental operators abound. While they may be cheaper (US$50/day) than more reputable agencies, there is less accountability in the event that anything should go less-than-planned. These private rentals don't take credit cards, often want a wad of cash up front, and usually don't offer insurance. These informal agencies are best avoided.

Listed rates do not include insurance or the 16.5 percent GCT. Insurance is typically US$15–40, depending on coverage. A deposit is taken for a deductible when customers opt for anything less than full coverage. The use of select gold and platinum credit cards obviates the need to purchase insurance from the rental agency. Check with each individual establishment for their particular policies.

Compact Car Rentals (94N Old Hope Rd., tel. 876/978-4914, compactcarrental@yahoo.com) rents Toyota Yaris (US$50), Corolla (US$65), Camry (US$80), Honda Civic (US$75), Accord (US$100), and CR-V (US$100). MasterCard, Visa Platinum or Gold, and and American Express Platinum or Gold cover insurance. Marjorie Lue is the cordial manager. Compact does free pickups and delivery from Norman Manley.

Island Car Rentals (17 Antigua Ave., tel. 876/926-5991 or Norman Manley tel. 876/924-8075, icar@cwjamaica.com, www.islandcarrentals.com) has a wide range of vehicles from the Toyota Yaris (US$44 low season/$55 high season) and Camry (US$99 low/$109 high) to Honda Civic (US$58 low/$59 high) and Accord (US$78 low/$87 high), Suzuki Grand Vitara (US$99 low/$109 high) to Space Wagon (US$83 low/$90 high).

Fiesta Car Rental (14 Waterloo Rd., tel. 876/926-0133, fiesta@kasnet.com, www.fiestacarrentals.com) has fairly new Japanese vehicles, including Hyundai Accents and Honda Accords (US$92) and Honda CR-Vs (US$105).

Budget (53 South Camp Rd., US tel. 877/825-2953, UK tel. 800/731-0125 direct to HQ, tel. 876/759-1793, 8 A.M.–4:30 P.M. Mon.–Fri., Norman Manley tel. 876/924-8762, 8 A.M.–10 P.M. daily, budget@jamweb.net, www.budgetjamaica.com) has a range of vehicles from Toyota Yaris (US$60 low season/$75 high season) and Daihatsu Terios (US$75 low/$100 high) to VW Passats (US$95 low/$120 high).

Bargain Rent-A-Car (1 Merrick Ave., tel. 876/926-1909; Norman Manley Airport, tel. 876/924-8293, info@avis.com.jm, www.avis.com.jm) is the Avis franchise in Jamaica, with a range of vehicles from Hyundai Accent, Mitsubishi Lancer, Toyota Yaris/Corolla/Camry, Subaru Forrester, and vans. Prices range between the Yaris (US$74 low season/$114 high season) and the Nissan Urvan minibus (US$125 low/$166 high).

Ideal Car Rentals (43 Burlington Ave., tel. 876/926-2980) has a decent selection of Japanese models including a few 4x4s.

Spanish Town and St. Catherine

With over a million people, St. Catherine parish has the largest share of Jamaica's population. Spanish Town, the sedate parish capital, was the nation's capital until it was moved to Kingston in 1872. Today the city is a UN World Heritage Site with the national archives and the oldest Anglican Church outside of England.

PORTMORE VICINITY

Immediately west of Kingston, past the wharfs and across the causeway is Portmore, a bedroom community supporting the overflow from burgeoning Kingston. As the causeway meets land on the St. Catherine side of the water, **Fort Augusta** sits on a point overlooking the harbor.

Portmore consists mainly of private and government-sponsored housing schemes, with **Jamworld Entertainment Centre** and **Caymanas Park** horsetrack on its northern side, reached by taking a right on the Portmore Parkway when coming off the bridge. Jamworld is the site for **Reggae Sting,** an annual show held on Boxing Day that never ceases to cause a stir. Accommodations in Portmore consist exclusively of hourly-rate joints, some of them dodgier than others.

Fort Augusta

Named after the mother of King George III, the fort was completed in the 1750s after an arduous construction process during which many workers suffered sickness and fevers. The area on which it was built was known as Mosquito Point. The fort was the sentinel on the harbor during a time when Spanish Reprisals were still a tangible fear, and it also served as a well-stocked arsenal. Ships coming into Kingston Harbour would unload their ammunition at the fort as a safety measure, but fewer precautions were taken at the fort itself, and in 1782 the magazine containing 300 barrels of gunpowder was struck by lightning. The resulting explosion destroyed the building,

killed 300 people, and broke windows as far as 27 kilometers away. Today the Fort is the site of Jamaica's only female prison. The St. Catherine Parish Council has made overtures towards demolishing the prison to allow for restoration of the fort, but the issue has gained little traction.

Port Henderson

Once a busy entry port for new arrivals to Spanish Town, Port Henderson today is little more than an extension of Portmore. There are several budget hotels like **Casablanca** (2–4 Port Henderson Rd., tel. 876/939-6999, US$44–51), which has air-conditioning, cable, and hot water, and even includes complimentary breakfast for two, but it sees few tourists, if any.

Fort Clarence (admission US$1.50) is the nicest beach in the greater Kingston area. It is usually well maintained, but where it's not it can accumulate seaweed and trash as it does the further away you go from the main area where the admission fee is charged. It is just east around the bend from Hellshire.

◖ Hellshire

Once a quiet fisherman's beach, Hellshire has become the quintessential rustic chic weekend hangout, with prices varying widely depending on the appearance of customers at many of the beach shack restaurants. There are a handful of dependable and honest shacks including Shorty's, the most highly recommended, Aunt May's, Aunt Merl's, and Prendy's where you can get a good fried fish with accompanying *festival.* There are several other beach shack restaurant besides, many of which will have your wallet if you're not careful. Be sure to come to an agreement as to what you'll be charged when selecting a fish from the cooler, and don't allow any generous add-ons, as these will certainly not come as a gift. A snapper large enough for one person shouldn't cost more than US$10.50.

Fishermen clean snapper on Hellshire Beach.

Hellshire Beach itself can be a bit littered, but the water is generally clean enough to swim in spite of the fisherman scaling snapper at the water's edge. The sand gets a bit cleaner as you walk east along the beach past the multitude of fried fish stands. There are peddlers and hustlers of all kinds at Hellshire, and it can be a bit dodgy at night. Horseback rides are offered by Damian (tel. 876/479-3250, US$14/hr). Don't be alarmed by constant solicitations from vendors and beggars; it's the basis of their livelihood and can be considered part of Hellshire's color.

Two Sisters Cave

Recently reopened by the Urban Development Corporation, Two Sisters Cave was a regular hangout for the first Jamaicans centuries ago. Two cavernous caves, one with a deep pool suitable for swimming, lie about 100 meters apart down a series of newly constructed steps. Security personnel at the recently reopened attraction have indicated that swimming at Two Sisters Cave may not be permitted in the future.

For a less-developed option, where there are no security guards, there's another cave about 100 meters before reaching Two Sisters, accessed by a footpath descending from the road.

SPANISH TOWN

Originally founded as Villa de la Vega by the Spanish, the city was named Spanish Town after the British takeover in 1655. The old part of the city is well organized in a grid with Spanish Town Square at its center. There is little activity in the old city, with most activity in modern Spanish Town centered around the commercial areas along Bourkes Road.

Sights

White Marl Taino Museum (call caretaker Tyrone to schedule a visit, cell 876/384-2803) is reached by taking a left immediately after a blue bus stop about three kilometers from the roundabout on the eastern edge of Spanish Town heading towards Kingston. The turnoff is marked by a vendor selling chairs by the side of

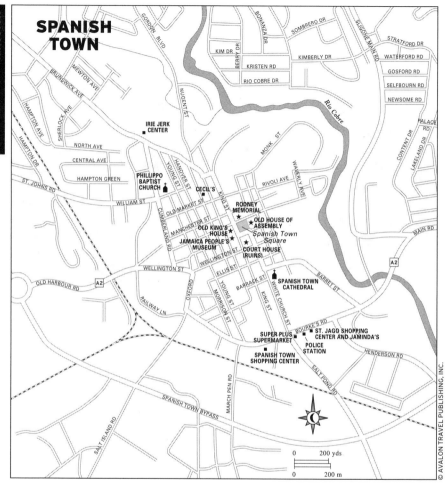

the highway immediately after the blue bus stop. Just before the bus stop the road passes through high rock embankments. From Kingston it is best to go to the first Spanish Town roundabout and switch directions as the two-lane highway is usually full of traffic and crossing dangerous. The museum is located on the site of what was once the largest Taino settlements in Jamaica. Recently reopened, the small museum features artifacts and displays locating Taino archeological sites across the island and providing infor-

mation on the lifestyle and practices of these first Jamaicans.

The **Iron Bridge** over the Rio Cobre on the eastern edge of Spanish Town was erected in 1801 and shipped in prefabricated segments from where it was cast in England by Walkers of Rotherham. Today it is used as a pedestrian crossing and is in a poor state of preservation. Designed by English engineer Thomas Wilson, it was the first prefab cast-iron bridge erected in the Western Hemisphere.

© OLIVER HILL

historic cast-iron bridge in Spanish Town

Spanish Town Cathedral, or the Anglican Cathedral Church of St. James, stands on the site of the Roman Catholic Red Cross Spanish Chapel, originally built in 1525 and run by Franciscans. Cromwell's Puritan soldiers destroyed the Spanish chapel along with another on the northern end of town known as White Cross, run by Dominicans. The church has been destroyed and rebuilt several times in a series of earthquakes and hurricanes. It became the first Anglican cathedral outside England in 1843, representing the Jamaican diocese. It's also the oldest English-built foundation on the island, after Fort Charles in Port Royal. Several monuments of historical figures are found inside and in the walled churchyard.

Spanish Town Square was laid out by Jamaica's first colonial rulers as their Plaza Mayor. It is surrounded by the burnt remains of the old courthouse on its southern side, Old King's House on the west, the Rodney Memorial, and behind it the National Archives on the north side; the Old House of Assembly, now parish administration offices, on its east-

ern side, is the only building facing the square that's still in use.

The People's Museum of Craft and Technology (call caretaker Tyrone to schedule a visit, cell 876/384-2803, tel. 876/907-0322, 9 A.M. to 4 P.M. Mon.–Thurs., till 3 P.M. Fri., admission US$1.50 adults, US$0.50 children) located in the Old King's House complex on Spanish Town Square, began as a Folk Museum in 1961 and was refurbished in 1997 when Emancipation Day was declared a national holiday. The exhibit has indoor and outdoor sections with carriages, early sugar and coffee processing machinery, and a variety of other colonial-period implements.

The **Rodney Memorial,** on the northern side of Spanish Town Square, was erected in homage to Admiral George Rodney, a British naval officer who prevented what was seen as imminent conquest by an invading French and Spanish naval fleet led by Admiral de Grasse in 1782. The memorial is housed in a spectacular structure for its European palatial look and gives a nice facade to the National Archives

© OLIVER HILL

Spanish Town Square is surrounded by reminders of past glory from when the city was the nation's capital.

housed just behind. The statue of Rodney was contracted to one of the most respected sculptors of the day, Englishman John Bacon (1740–1799) who reportedly made two trips to Italy before finding the right block of marble for the job. A panel inside Rodney's octagonal "temple" is written in Latin and tells of Rodney's victorious sea battle, which restored some dignity to Britain, badly defeated by the French-American allies in the American War of Independence. Rodney was duly lauded as a national hero and £1,000 was allocated for the monument, which would eventually cost nearly £31,000. The two brass cannons displayed just outside the statue enclosure were taken from defeated Admiral de Grasse's flagship, *Ville de Paris.*

Spanish Town Baptist Church, or Phillippo Baptist Church as it is better known (at the junction of Cumberland Rd. and Williams St.), is located a few blocks northwest of the square. The church was built in 1827 on an old artillery ground before playing an active role in the abolition movement. Abolitionist Reverend James Murcell Phillippo arrived in Jamaica in 1823, and went on to establish the church with help from freed slaves. On the night of emancipation in 1838 when Jamaica's slave population was granted full freedom by local authorities, 2000 freed slaves were baptized in the church. There is a tablet in the churchyard commemorating the act of emancipation, which was celebrated there after the proclamation was read in front of Old King's House.

Mountain River Cave (caretaker Monica Wright, tel. 876/705-2790) with its Taino wall paintings first uncovered in 1897, is located 21 kilometers due northwest from the roundabout at the beginning of St. John's Road on the western edge of Spanish Town. After leaving an Uptown suburb area, St. John's becomes Cudjoe's Hill Road as you pass through red earth hills on the way to **Kitson** and then Guanaboa Vale, the stomping ground of Juan de Bolas. A few kilometers beyond a beautiful old church pull over at Joan's Bar & Grocery Shop, marked by a painted facade reading Cudjoe's Cavern. Monica will indicate the trailhead that leads down a steep hill across the meandering Thompson's River and up the facing bank through cacao and passion-fruit stands to where the small cave is caged in against vandals. The cave itself is shallow and unspectacular, but the paintings themselves are interesting and it's easy to make out a man with a spear, a turtle, some fish, and a few women. The paintings are said to be authentic, given the ash and bat guano mix used, supposedly a typical medium for the earliest Jamaican artists. The highlight of this attraction, apart from the well-preserved petroglyphs, is the beautiful walk through lush forests and the Thompson's River, which has a large pool upstream and a waterfall downstream from the crossing fitting for a cool dip.

Food

In **St. Jago Shopping Centre,** a small food court has some good options. **La Cocina for Mom's Cooking** (St. Jago Plaza, shop 31, 876/943-9355) serves Spanish-inspired Jamaican fare like brown stew chicken/fish, fried fish/chicken, curry mutton, stew pork, stew peas and chicken soup (US$2.50–3.50). **Tastebuds Delight** (tel. 876/907-5024, US$2–4) also has Jamaican dishes ranging from chicken to oxtail. **Natural Vitamins Herbs & Vegetarian Place** (tel. 876/984-1305) is the best place around to get vegetarian dishes and urban Ital cuisine.

Irie Jerk Center (21 Brunswick St., tel. 876/749-5375, 9 A.M. until early morning daily, most dishes US$1–4) has jerk pork (US$7/lb) and chicken (US$2.50/lb) and also serves fried chicken, curry goat, porridge, and soup.

Cecil's (35 Martin St., tel. 876/984-2986 or 876/984-2404, US$3–11) is easily Spanish Town's most-lauded restaurant. Cecil Reid was a chef at a number of other restaurants for years before opening his own place in 1983. Menu items have a decidedly Asian lean, with more sueys than you've ever heard of including chop suey, chow mein, fried rice, choy fan, ham choy, suey mein, as well as more typical curry dishes, beef, chicken, and lobster. A beer costs US$1.50 and fresh juices are US$1.

© OLIVER HILL

Cecil hangs out with his crew across from his restaurant, considered by many the best in Spanish Town.

Getting There and Around

Spanish Town is served by Kingston's JUTC with buses from Half Way Tree Transport Centre and the Downtown bus terminals departing every 10 minutes on the 21 and 22 series routes. A private taxi will need to be negotiated. A reasonable rate would be US$50 round-trip from Kingston for a half-day outing.

Route taxis ply all major roads in Spanish Town and can be flagged down if need be. It's best to come with your own transportation however.

The best way to reach Spanish Town with a private vehicle is by heading west on Mandela Highway. At the first roundabout, after passing the turnoff for Portmore, stay to the right. The Old Iron Bridge marks the entrance to town. Take a right at the stop light immediately thereafter to reach the historical sites surrounding Spanish Town Square. Keeping straight at the stop light leads to the commercial district and the Prison Oval.

WEST OF SPANISH TOWN

Out of Spanish Town, take a left following well-marked signs at the second roundabout off the Spanish Town bypass to head southwest along Old Harbour Road, passing through vast tracts of sugar cane towards the town of **Old Harbour.**

On the way, **Serenity Fishing and Wildlife Sanctuary** (708/5515-17, www.serenitypark jamaica.com, serenitypark@cwjamaica.com, email for groups, 10 A.M.–5 P.M. Thurs. and Fri., 10 A.M.–6 P.M. Sat., Sun., and public holidays, US$2 children 4–12, US$3.50 adults) is reached by taking a right turn in front of Buds Service Station. Set among well-manicured lawns and ponds stocked with tilapia, the park features a modest petting zoo with macaw, ostrich, emus, llamas, a monkey, a crocodile, iguanas, and several turkeys. Brief horse and pony rides are offered (US$1.50) as well as paddle boating (US$3 per four-person boat). Fishing rods and bait are included with admission.

The "clean and eat" service lets you give your fresh-caught fish to staff members who will prepare it for lunch (US$1.85/lb carry-away, US$2 cleaned, US$5 prepared). The park does not allow you to bring in your own food to compete with what is on sale. Beyond fish, local Jamaican dishes (US$3.50–5.75) include oxtail, curry goat, and fried chicken.

Serenity is managed by John Bennett and owned by Guardsman Group, which uses the site to breed and train its guard dogs.

Old Harbour

Continuing on Old Harbour Road 18 kilometers southwest of Spanish Town, you arrive at the town of Old Harbour. Old Harbour is a congested little backwater full of storefronts and food vendors next to the square. A clock tower dating from the 17th century is the town's centerpiece.

Old Harbour was the disembarkation point for the first Indian indentured laborers arriving in 1845, who were brought to Jamaica following emancipation by plantation owners who suddenly found themselves lacking willing workers. A century later the bay was used as a U.S. Naval anchorage during World War II, with bases set up on Little Goat Island and at Salt Creek and Sandy Gully nearby on the mainland. The Americans didn't depart until 1949.

Old Harbour Bay, 4.8 kilometers south of town, is significant historically as the place where Columbus met with the preeminent Taino leader referred to as the cacique of Xamayca in 1494. It was an important port serving Spanish Town under the Spanish and later under early British rule it was the principal port for the area, until Port Royal and later Kingston took over in imports. Originally called Puerto de Vaca, or Cow Bay, by Columbus in reference to the manatees, or sea cows, that once flourished there, today the town is little more than a fishing village. Fish stalls along the waterfront peddle fried fish, conch soup, and lobster. **Cheryl's** (cell 876/410-3299), serving exquisite fried fish, bammy, and veggies right on the water with a sea breeze, is highly recommended.

Old Harbour Bay has a few islands, including Little Goat Island and Great Goat Island. A trip to the islands for a picnic can be arranged with local fishermen, some of whom live in ramshackle huts there.

Colbeck Castle is located just over three kilometers northwest of Old Harbour near the Clarendon border. To get to the abandoned ruins take a right heading inland by the clock tower and keep straight ahead rather than right at the Y. After passing a large farm with five buildings perpendicular to the road, you will soon cross a bridge over a small river. Take the first left after the bridge. Within 1.5 kilometers you will arrive at the ruins.

Built by Colonel John Colbeck, who came with the English to take Jamaica from the Spanish in 1655, mystery shrouds the building's past; its date of construction is thought to have been somewhere around 1680. In its day, it was the biggest great-house structure of its kind, obviously built with defense from the Spanish and Maroon insurgents in mind. Its present appearance suggests it fell victim to fire in slave revolts. Designed in the style of a 17th-century Italian mansion, with ornate arches and a 12-meter-high tower in each corner, Colbeck Castle was the epicenter for a strategically located immense landholding in close vicinity to Spanish Town and Old Harbour.

NORTH OF SPANISH TOWN

The first free village for ex-slaves was established at **Sligoville,** just north of Spanish Town, when Jamaica's pro-abolition transition period governor Howe Peter Browne, known as the Marquis of Sligo, granted land to Baptist missionary James Phillippo. Browne's former summer residence, **Highgate House,** now a JNHT site, can be reached by taking a left heading east off the main road to the north coast from Spanish Town (A1).

Nearby, the father of the Rastafarian movement, Leonard Howell, fled persecution on the North Coast to establish the Rasta commune of **Pinnacle.** Eventually, Pinnacle was smothered and Howell committed to a mental institution by the authorities, who would have none of his reverence for Ethiopian Emperor Haile Selassie I.

Bog Walk, derived from Boca de Agua in Spanish, is a gorge prone to flooding that is entered by traversing **Flat Bridge.** Horrendous traffic tends to accumulate on either side of the old stone single-lane bridge, especially as the weekend begins and comes to a close. Midway through the gorge on the west flank of the gorge you can see the Pum Pum Rock, named as such because it bears a remarkable resemblance to part of a woman's anatomy.

Linstead, celebrated in the folk song *Linstead Market,* still has a busy market on Saturdays. Also in this small inland town, the island's public records were kept under guard at the Anglican Church when the French threatened invasion in 1805. The church has been destroyed and rebuilt several times.

On the border with St. Ann, **Ewarton** is noticeable from kilometers away by the stench created by aluminum processing. It's not a place you'll want to spend too much time.

East of Kingston

The areas along the coast east of Kingston include the communities of Harbour View, Seven Mile, Palm Beach, and Bull Bay. The Palisadoes, a 16-kilometer-long stretch that runs from the roundabout at Harbour View to the tip of Port Royal, is home to the Kingston Yacht Club and Marina, the Marine Research Institute, Norman Manley International Airport, Plumb Point Lighthouse, Port Royal, and just offshore, the Kingston area's most popular beach on the small island of Lime Cay.

The community of **Harbour View** surrounding the roundabout at the base of the Palisadoes was built on the site of **Fort Nugent,** originally constructed by a Spanish slave, James Castillo, and later fortified by Governor Nugent in 1806 to protect the eastern approach to Kingston Harbour. Today all that remains of the fort is the Martello tower, which takes its name from

the first such tower built in Corsica and popularized throughout England.

PORT ROYAL AND THE PALISADOES

Part of Kingston parish, the Palisadoes is 16-kilometer-long thin stretch of barren sand, scrub brush, and mangroves; it acts as a natural barrier protecting Kingston Harbour with Port Royal at its western point. History has not smiled on this corner of Jamaica, perhaps due to some divine justice aimed at washing clean the sins and abuses that made Port Royal Britain's first commercial stronghold in Jamaica. After Lord Cromwell seized Jamaica for Britain from the Spanish in 1655, Port Royal grew in importance as the town's strategic location brought prosperity to merchants who based themselves there. The merchants were joined by pirates and buccaneers, who together through their commerce, pillaging, and looting created one of the busiest and most successful trading posts in the New World. Imports included slaves, silks, silver, gold, wine, and salmon, while exports consisted mostly of rum, sugar, and wood. The British collaborated with the pirates as an insurance policy against the Spanish, who were thought to be seeking revenge on the island's new colonial masters. Port Royal flourished with a local service economy growing alongside its bustling maritime commerce until June 7, 1692, when a massive earthquake left 60 percent of Port Royal underwater, immediately killing 2,000 people. Eight hectares supporting the principal public buildings, the wharfs, merchant shops, and two of the town's four forts disappeared into the sea. Aftershocks rocked the rattled city for months. In 1703 a fire devastated what little remained of Port Royal, sending most survivors across the harbor to what soon grew into the city of Kingston. The town also sustained significant damage in the earthquake of 1907, and then again during Hurricane Charlie in 1951.

Sleepy Port Royal is well worth a visit. The village is hassle-free and small enough to stroll leisurely around in a few hours. Scuba trips can be arranged through Port Royal Divers based out of Morgan's Harbour Marina. On weekends the square comes alive with a sound system and an invasion of Kingstonians who come for the fish and beach just offshore at Lime Cay.

Plumb Point Lighthouse

Protecting the approach to Kingston Harbour, Plumb Point Lighthouse was built in 1853 and has gone out only once since, during the earthquake of 1907. Sitting on a point named Cayo de los Icacos, or Plumb Tree Cay (a reference to the coco plum by the Spanish), it is constructed of stone and cast iron and stands 21 meters high. Its light is visible from 40 kilometers out at sea. The beach immediately to the west is known for its occasional good surf, as is the shoreline between Plumb Point and Little Plumb Point. The area is also known for its strong currents, however, and surfers should use precaution.

Fort Charles

Fort Charles (tel. 876/967-8438, 9 A.M.–4:45 P.M. daily, US$3 admission/tour) is the most prominent historical attraction in town, and is the most impressive, well-restored fort in Jamaica. Built in 1656 immediately following the British takeover, it is the oldest fort on the island from the British colonial period, and one of the oldest in the New World. Originally it was named Fort Cromwell on Cagway after Lord Protector of England Oliver Cromwell (ruled 1653–1658), who was responsible for designing the strategic takeover of the island meant to give Britain control over the Caribbean basin. The fort was renamed in 1662 when the monarchy was reinstated in England with Charles II as King. Fort Charles sank a meter during the earthquake of 1692.

Admiral Horatio Nelson (1758–1805), lauded as Britain's all-time greatest naval hero for his victorious role in the Battle of Trafalgar, spent 30 months in Jamaica, much of it at Fort Charles. Nelson was given charge of the Fort while the island was under fear of a French invasion, and spent the tense period pacing and nervously scanning the horizon from what's now referred to as Nelson's Quarterdeck, a raised platform along the southern battlement. On the inside wall of the fort there is a plaque commanding those who tread Nelson's footprints to remember his glory.

Also within Fort Charles walls, there is the grogge shop and a very nice little museum managed by the Museum of History and Ethnography with period artifacts and old maps and information about Port Royal and its glorious and notorious inhabitants.

Other Attractions

St. Peter's Church, built in 1725, replaced earlier churches on the site destroyed by the 1692 earthquake and then the 1703 fire that again ravaged Port Royal. Inside there are several period items on display. In the churchyard is the tomb of Lewis Galdy. One of the founders of St. Peter's, Galdy miraculously survived the 1692 earthquake after being swallowed by the earth and spit out by the sea, where he was rescued. The tomb is inscribed with the complete legend of Galdy, who went on to become a local hero.

McFarlene's Bar is the oldest tavern in Port Royal, constructed in the 1800s, and one of the few buildings to withstand Hurricane Charlie in 1951. Unfortunately the pub no longer serves pints.

The **Old Gaol** (jail, Gaol Street) was once a female prison.

Giddy House sits half-submerged at an awkward angle in the earth behind Fort Charles. It was built in 1888 as an artillery store by the British Navy, but the earthquake of 1907 left the building skewed as a reminder of how dramatic seismic events can humble the most vicious buccaneers as much as the world's foremost navy.

The **Old Naval Hospital** is the oldest prefabricated cast-iron structure in the Western Hemisphere. The hospital was built in 1818 with slave labor under the direction of the Royal Engineers of the British Army on the foundation of an earlier hospital destroyed by fire a few years prior. The hospital went out of use in 1905 before getting a new lease on life as the Port Royal Centre for Archaeological and Conservation Research in 1968. Seventeen hurricanes have not fazed the structure, nor did the earthquake of 1907 do it any harm.

🔆 Lime Cay

Lime Cay is a paradisiacal islet, just barely big enough to sustain some vegetation. The beach gets crowded on weekends, especially on Sunday, but is worth a visit. Launches leave for Lime Cay on weekends from Y-Knot Bar, or at Morgan's Harbour (US$7 per person round-trip) and on any other day as well for a slightly higher price. At times there are launches from the old Ferry Dock area that will do the trip for a bit less, especially for small groups.

Accommodations

Morgan's Harbour (1 Port Royal Rd., US$120 d, includes tax and Jamaican breakfast, tel. 876/967-8040, fax 876/967-8873, info@morgans harbour.com, www.morgansharbour.com) is the best bet in Port Royal, having been recently

© OLIVER HILL

Giddy House behind Fort Charles

refurbished. Slip fees, as all over Jamaica, are very reasonable, at US$1 per foot per day plus 16.5 percent tax. Water, electricity, and laundry services are available at per-use cost. Morgan's Harbour was built on the former naval shipyard (US$7 adults, US$3.50 children for the launch to Lime Cay).

Food

ⓒ Gloria's Seafood Restaurant has two well-heeled locations ("Bottom," managed by Cecil, 1 High St., tel. 876/967-8066; and "Top" on the beach side, managed by Angela, 15 Foreshore Rd., tel. 876/967-8220) and is a must for anyone who appreciates seafood (US$9.50 for a fried fish and bammy). Gloria died a few years ago, but her legacy lives strong with her children doing an excellent job running the business. Service can be slow owing to the crowds that swarm in, especially on Friday evenings and after church on Sundays.

Y-Knot (tel. 876/967-8448 or 876/967-8449, 9 A.M.–7 P.M., 9 A.M. till you say when Fri., Sat., and Sun.), at Port Royal Slip Way, is an excellent bar that serves food (US$3.50–11; chicken, fish, shrimp) on weekends. Y-Knot is the home of Lime Cay Tours, where launches leave daily for Lime Cay (US$10 Mon.–Fri., US$7 Sat.–Sun.).

Fisherman's Cabin (4 P.M.–midnight Mon.–Wed., 10 A.M.–2 A.M. Thurs.–Sun., tel. 876/967-8800, US$7–14) has tables right on a dock overlooking the harbor down in a corner by Port Royal Square. The place is very popular on weekends when Kingstonians flock for all kinds of fish, lobster, and seafood platters.

Getting There

JUTC buses leave from the downtown bus terminal (Route 98, US$1) or hire a taxi (US$25). Route taxis between Downtown and Port Royal run sporadically, leaving once filled with passengers.

The ferry service, which once brought passengers between downtown Kingston and Port Royal, has unfortunately been indefinitely discontinued (call Mr. Val Meeks, Manager of Harbour Department, at tel. 876/922-2216 to voice your alarm or discontent).

BULL BAY

Bull Bay is a quiet fishing community along the A3, 15 minutes east of Kingston. It has a long beach that lacks fine sand, but also crowds. It is a nice place for a dip, and the surf is decent for sport at times. The community is perhaps best known for the Bobo Shanti (Ashanti) Rasta, who have their base nearby on Bobo Hill.

Sights

About 1.5 kilometers before reaching Bull Bay, a sign for **Cane River Falls** marks a left off the main onto Greendale Road by Nine Mile Square. The attraction is on the right just before a bridge and cannot be missed. The "falls" are nothing to write home about compared to other more spectacular falls across Jamaica and hardly justify the US$3 entrance fee. Nevertheless it's a nice place to relax and get some food to the sound of the passing water, which varies from a bubble to a roar depending on recent rainfall.

Cane River meets the sea just before Bull Bay at Seven Mile on the main road east of Kingston heading towards St. Thomas. The river is formed by the Barbeque and Mammee Rivers among smaller tributaries that run down the northern slopes of the Dallas Mountains. The falls were once the stomping ground of Three Finger Jack, a legendary Robin Hood–like cult figure who terrorized the planter class with kidnappings for ransom and murder. Later they became a favorite cool off spot for Bob Marley, who immortalized the spot with his lyrics, "uppa Cane River to wash my dread… " on the "Trench Town" track of his *Confrontation* album.

Bobo Hill (Wise Rd., call Priest Harold cell 876/843-9749) is home to the Bobo Shanti, or Bobo Ashanti, house of Rastafari. Known for their peaceably militant interpretation of Marcus Garvey's teachings, the Bobo have been popularized by many dancehall artists who proclaim an affiliation. Paramount to Bobo philosophy and lifestyle are the ever-present themes of self-confidence, self-reliance, and self-respect. The Bobo can often be seen around Kingston, their locks carefully wrapped with a turban, peddling natural fiber brooms, one of their signature crafts. At the center of the Bobo philosophy is the holy trinity between Bobo Shanti founder Prince Emmanuel Charles Edwards, who is said to have carried the spirit of Christ, Marcus Garvey, the prophet of the Rastafari Movement, and Haile Selassie I, the late Ethiopian emperor who is their King of Kings.

Leonard Howell, recognized as the first Jamaican to proclaim the divinity of Haile Selassie I, founded a commune at the inception of the movement in Pinnacle, St. Catherine, similar to the community found today at Bobo Hill. Despite much popular belief to the contrary, the Bobo are among the most open and welcoming of the various houses of Rastafari. While it might not be appreciated should you just turn up to sight-see at their commune unannounced, sincere interest is well received and they routinely open their home and hearth to visitors from around the world. Some visitors stay several days with them to share food and partake in their ritualized lifestyle. While there is no fee assessed to enter their commune, it is customary to bring a contribution, which should be offered based on your means and the degree of hospitality you have enjoyed at their cost. Call Priest Harold to organize a visit. To reach the camp turn left on Wise Road right after a bridge about 1.5 kilometers past Shenique's Hair Salon in the center of Bull Bay. If you plan on staying at the camp, Priest Harold advises you bring a cup for porridge as well as a sleeping bag or blanket, as beds may not be available.

Entertainment

On Tuesday nights, check out the street dance at **Shooter's Hill,** an outdoor space easily located by the booming bass when heading east out of Bull Bay.

Little Copa (Nine Mile, along the main road between Kingston and Yallahs, no phone) has karaoke on Thursdays and ladies' night on Fridays. The club has a large indoor dance floor that gets packed for the occasional live performance.

Accommodations

Jamnesia (in the community of Eight Mile, just before reaching Bull Bay adjacent to Cave Hut Beach, immediately after Shenique's Hair Salon turn right into the driveway, tel. 876/750-0103, jamnesiasurf@yahoo .com, www.geocities.com/jamnesiasurfclub/ surfcamp.html) is Jamaica's number-one surfing destination. It's run by Billy "Mystic" Wilmot, of Mystic Revealers fame, his wife Maggie, sons Icah, Inilek, Ivah, and Ishack, and daughter Imani. They are great hosts for a surf vacation and offer the widest variety of boards for rental, as well as complete surf vacation packages. Rates vary from US$7.50 per person to camp with your own tent, to US$10 for use of their tents and linen, to US$30 for a simple double room. Week-long packages include a tent and two meals daily, available from US$178.50 per person. Larger bungalow rooms and a cottage are also available for a bit more.

There are two good surf seasons, one during the summer (June–Sept.), the other in winter (Dec.– March). The fall and spring seasons can be more of gamble as far as surf is concerned, but the accommodation rates are lower off-season and open to negotiation. The property also features a skateboard bowl for when the water is flat.

The Blue Mountains

The highest mountain range in Jamaica, the Blue Mountains have a rich history in providing refuge to runaway slaves, runaway French-Haitian coffee planters, and even Bob Marley, when he sought safety and seclusion at Strawberry Hill following the attempt on his life in 1976. Blue Mountain Peak, the highest point in Jamaica at 2,256 meters, offers a stunning view of five parishes: Kingston, St. Andrew, St. Thomas, Portland, and St. Mary. The Blue Mountain range forms a physical barrier for the northeasterly weather fronts that frequently descend on the island, giving Portland and St. Thomas especially copious amounts of rainfall compared to the southern coastal plains of Jamaica where drought is common.

During the rainy season (Oct. and Nov.) the mountain peaks often cloud over by midmorning. Skies are clearest June–August and December–March.

MARYLAND TO HARDWAR GAP

Turning left at the Cooperage onto the B3 leads up a series of 365 turns that can leave unaccustomed passengers with an upset stomach. The windy road first passes through the lower hills and valleys of Maryland before reaching the principal hamlet along the route, Irish Town. **Irish Town** has as its centerpiece St. Mark's Chapel, a quaint little church reached by a 15-minute walk along a footpath.

Sights and Recreation

Belcour Lodge (left at a white milestone marker below Maryland, call Robin at least 24 hours in advance to schedule a visit, tel. 876/927-2448, limlums@cwjamaica.com) is a beautiful private, colonial-era home set in a lovely little valley amidst expansive gardens, where Robin and Michael Lumsden have a bee farm with 100 colonies. Robin markets honey as well as jellies and sauces on a cottage-industry scale.

The house is open to visitors (US$10) for a tour that includes a visit with the bees and a stroll around the beautifully planted yard. Citrus trees, orchids, and a host of other flowers attract a wide variety of birds, most notably the beautiful hummingbirds that seem born to enthrall. A small river meandering alongside the property is quite suitable for a dip. You'll want to take home some honey and sauces; they're outstanding, especially the scotch-bonnet-pepper honey-mustard sauce.

The Observation Deck, Fine Art & Tings (just below Irish Town, tel. 876/944-8592, 10 A.M.–6 P.M. Thurs.–Sun., call for other days, observe@cwjamaica.com), run by Tiffany Recas, has a range of arts and crafts from high-end contemporary paintings, sculpture, and photography to local crafts made in the Blue Mountains area. Prices range US$1–1,000.

St. Mark's Chapel is a beautiful old church that sits up on a hilltop in Irish Town and is a great destination for a short hike. As you arrive in Irish Town the junction looms up ahead. Anyone in Irish Town can indicate where the trail begins to reach the chapel.

Mount Zion Hill (call Priest Dermot Fagan to request a visit, cell 876/868-9636) is a Rastafarian farming community based in a squatter settlement known as Mt. Zion Hill. The carefully maintained trail and fence along the path up the hill demonstrates the respect given to Priest Dermot Fagan, referred to simply as "the priest" by his following, who rank in the range of 50-odd adults and children living at Zion Hill. Fagan has established His Imperial Majesty School of Bible Study and Sabbath Service with a small yurt-like structure at the entrance to the community serving as its chapel. The small community follows primarily an agrarian life, growing food and herbs and selling roots wine around town to bring in a little cash. There are several people who espouse the School's teaching that do not live on Zion Hill but rather in town. It becomes evident when the group descends on Papine Square every Saturday for a Nyabinghi Sabbath Service of singing and drumming that the following is significant indeed. Fagan advocates a total rejection of and distancing from the Babylonian system that has separated humankind from direct reliance on our labor and the food we can provide for ourselves. He warns of an even greater divide between man and his sustenance through the impending mass implantation of micro-biochips. He sees the use of implantable homing devices in soldiers in Iraq or in medical patients, or their common use in wildlife management, as a precursor to more universal implantations, which he says will result in the consolidation of the global labor force and a new kind of slavery. The Mt. Zion Hill community has established itself as one of the more colorful, albeit apocalyptic, Houses of Rastafari.

Holywell National Park

Holywell National Park (entry US$5, or

US$1.50 for residents) sits atop Hardwar Gap affording a view of St. Andrew Parish to the south and St. Mary and Portland to the north. The birding is excellent in the 50-hectare park that borders Twyman's Old Tavern Coffee Estate on the north side and is a haven for migratory birds in the winter months. Hiking trails lead to a few peaks and there's also a loop trail.

The **Oatley Mountain Loop Trail** is paved with gravel and about 1.2 kilometers long, with a steep ascent to Oatley Mountain Peak at 1,400 meters. Three lookout points along the way offer great views of St. Andrew, St. Mary, and Portland.

The **Waterfall Trail** is also about 1.2 kilometers long, meandering along the mountain edge and then following a stream with a small waterfall at the end.

Shorter and less strenuous trails include the **Shelter Trail** (600m), the **Blue Mahoe Trail** (350m), and the **Wag Water/Dick's Pond Trail** (630m).

Rustic accommodations in cabins at the

© OLIVER HILL

one of the rustic hilltop cabins at Holywell National Park just below Hardwar Gap in the Blue Mountains park are available through the **Jamaica Conservation and Development Trust (JCDT)** (29 Dumbarton Ave., tel. 876/920-8278 or 876/920-8279, jcdt@cybervale.com, www.greenjamaica.org.jm). Book at least two weeks in advance for a weekend stays in one of three self-contained cabins (two one-bedroom units with open layout US$50, one two-bedroom unit US$66; resident rate US$39 for 1BR, US$55 for 2BR). Camping is also available with shower stall, toilets, and BBQ pits on-site (US$5, or US$1.50 residents).

◖ Alex Twyman's Old Tavern Coffee Estate

The Twymans (call Kingston office to arrange visit, tel. 876/924-2785, farm tel. 876/399-1222, dtwyman@colis.com, www.export jamaica.org/oldtavern, www.oldtaverncoffee .com) grow some of the best—if not *the* best—Blue Mountain Coffee. Operations on the es-

tate are slowly being taken over by David, the son of owners Dorothy and Alex Twyman.

The Twymans bought their property in 1968 and persevered through extreme challenges in obtaining a Coffee Board License, which allows them to sell directly to their customers and market their beans as "Blue Mountain Coffee," a coveted trademark belonging to Jamaica just as "Champagne" does to France. The Twymans' use a natural approach on their farm with limited use of chemical fertilizers and pesticides, and a traditional fermentation and sun-drying process. The unique climatic condition found at the Twymans' Estate requires a longer maturation period—the berries remain on the trees for 10 months due to the near constant cloudy mist blanketing the mountains around Hardwar Gap.

Three different roasts are produced from the Twymans' beans: medium, medium dark (Proprietors Choice), and dark roast. Pea-

© OLIVER HILL

The Twyman family's Old Tavern Coffee Estate benefits from ideal misty cloud-covered growing conditions that extend the maturation period, giving the sought-after coffee a distinct rich, smooth flavor.

berry beans produce an additional variety. Peaberry is an unusual bean, where one side of the normally paired beans does not develop. As a result, a smaller bean with a unique mild flavor develops. It is not fully understood what causes peaberry beans to grow this way. The peaberry beans are carefully separated and sold as a distinct variety that is prized by many coffee connoisseurs.

The Twymans' choice beans are served at Norma's on the Terrace, Suzie's, Cannonball Café and Strawberry Hill. Rum, Roast & Royals at Devon House and Kraft Cottage in Village Plaza retail Twyman's coffee, and of course it is sold directly on the farm and online at the best rate of US$30/lb. plus shipping (for orders write to oldtaverncoffee@kasnet.com).

"Never put coffee in the freezer because it will take on flavor of anything that's in there," advises Alex Twyman, who has a wealth of information on anything to do with the precious bean. There is no charge for a guided tour of the gorgeous estate. Instead, guests are encouraged to show their appreciation by buying a pound or two before departing.

Accommodations

Strawberry Hill (tel. 876/944-8400, www .islandoutpost.com) was once the site of a British naval hospital and remains a place where people seek health and refuge from the heat and dusty air on the plains below. Chris Blackwell, founder of Island Records and Bob Marley's first international producer, bought the property in 1972. Shortly thereafter, Marley took a retreat here after an attempt on his life during a spell of particularly heated political violence in 1976. Strawberry Hill is the highest of St. Andrew's limited high-end market, both in ambiance and elevation (945 meters). Rates start at US$385 for a deluxe one-bedroom villa, and climb to US$515 for a studio with a veranda overlooking Kingston.

© OLIVER HILL

The Main House at Strawberry Hill is an architectural masterpiece with wide verandas that take advantage of stunning views.

The hotel boasts an Aveda concept spa and wellness centre with a holistic approach to rejuvenation dubbed Strawberry Hill Living. Views from the well-appointed villas are spectacular. The restaurant serves some of the best food around and is a popular spot among high-society locals, many of whom make a habit of driving up for Sunday brunch. The smoked marlin eggs Benedict should not be missed. The winding ride up that takes guests to Irish Town is not for the weak of heart. A helicopter pad is located on-site adjacent to Blackwell's private cottage, and transfers can be arranged from Norman Manley (US$600) or from any other part of the island.

Mount Edge Guesthouse (just before the 17 mile marker approaching Newcastle, call Michael Fox, tel. 876/944-8151 or 876/351-5083, jamaicaeu@kasnet.com, www.jamaicaeu.com, US$20–40 per person) has three simple cottages hanging on the edge of a cliff, plus a main building containing two private rooms with a shared bathroom, living and dining room, in addition to the three cottages with double beds and private baths. A third building has bunk beds for four with an adjoining bathroom. Amenities include hot water, Internet, a small roadside bar, a trail to the river, and a hot tub in the garden. Mountain bikes are available.

(**Woodside** (contact Robin Lumsden, tel. 876/927-2448 or cell 876/383-8942, or Carolyn Barrett, tel. 876/382-6384, for bookings; US$100 per room, or US$300 for the entire house) is a beautiful, staffed colonial house on a 12-hectare coffee farm located about 1.5 kilometers past Newcastle just below Hardwar Gap and Holywell National Park. Minutes from the Gap Café and Twyman's Estate, Woodside is a stylish base for hiking in the park and exploring the western Blue Mountains. The three-bedroom house is impeccable in its old-Jamaica feel and boasts spectacular views, gardens, and a spring-fed pool. There is no better place to escape mid-summer heat on the plains below.

Starlight Chalet & Health Spa (Silver Hill Gap, tel. 876/969-3070 or 876/924-3075, sales@starlightchalet.com, www.starlightchalet.com, US$66) is a quaint retreat past Hardwar Gap. Heading north from Hardwar Gap, where the road forks keep to your right and straight ahead until you reach Section. Turn right at Section and travel until you reach Starlight Chalet & Health Spa at Silver Hill Gap.

Food

Blue Cafe (tel. 876/944-8918) and **Crystal Edge** (Winsome Hall, tel. 876/944-8053) have good Jamaican dishes at Jamaican prices. The owners of Blue Cafe are the Sharps, who own Coffee Traders and run tours. The restaurants are located just before reaching Irish Town where the road levels out and the sharp curves in the roads become less pronounced.

(**The Gap Café B&B** (cell 876/997-3032, admin@uniquejamaica.com), owned by Gloria Palomino, has a spectacular view, good food, and a cool breeze. It's minutes away from Holywell Park, and the Twyman's Coffee Estate is just over the hill. The well-prepared food includes oxtail, curry goat, chicken, fish, and pork chops starting from US$11. Basic but well-maintained rooms are available for US$70.

MAVIS BANK

Mavis Bank is a sleepy village. Its principal economic foundation for the past century has been the Mavis Bank Coffee Factory, which keeps many of the area's residents employed. The area is the best base for exploring the upper reaches of the Blue Mountains.

Sights

Mavis Bank Coffee Factory (MBCF) (right off the Main Road at entrance to Mavis Bank heading towards Mavis Bank from Gordon Town, 8:30 A.M.–noon and 1 P.M.–3:30 P.M. Mon.–Fri., tel. 876/977-8005, 876/977-8013, or 876/977-8015, fax 876/977-8014, tour reservations recommended, admin@mbcfcoffee.com, US$8 adults, US$3.50 children) was established in 1923 by an English planter,

© OLIVER HILL

Coffee put out to dry sits in the rain at Mavis Bank Coffee Factory in the Blue Mountains.

Victor Munn, and as the biggest coffee factory in Jamaica has been the economic foundation for the area since. The company is currently owned by the National Investment Bank of Jamaica (NIJB) and the founding Munn family, who share 70/30-percent stakes. Today, operations at the 327-worker factory are overseen by local PNP politician Senator Norman Grant, who holds the position of managing director.

Mavis Bank Coffee Factory is supplied by six of its own plantations, including Abbey, St. Thomas, and Orchard Rest, and around 5,000 independent farms. Most of the picking is done by local women, who receive about US$50 per box full of berries. From this, the lion's share goes to the farm owner where the berries were picked. The coffee is then left outside to dry for 5–7 days, weather permitting, or dried in a giant tumbler for two days if it's too rainy outside. Once dry, the coffee is aged in big sacks for 4–6 weeks before the outer parchment, or hull, is removed and the beans are cleaned and roasted. The whole process takes 3–4 months

from bush to mug. Four grades (peaberry, 1, 2, and 3) are produced at MBCF, around 75–80 percent of which is consumed in Japan, with 5 percent going to the United States and 4 percent to Europe and the rest of the world. The remainder goes to local markets. MBCF processes 1.4 million pounds of green beans per year from 6,000 farmers.

The best tours of the factory are led by Doreen "Barbara" Johnson (tel. 876/895-3437), who has worked at MBCF for the past 18 years.

Cinchona Gardens, while not the best-maintained botanical gardens, have a spectacular variety of plants, including many orchid species, making it a magical place with an incredible view.

Flamstead (left up hill at Guava Ridge when heading down from Mavis Bank toward Gordon Town) is the site where Horatio Nelson used to stay before he was killed in the battle of Trafalgar. More than a century later, Peter King, who was killed in 2006, built an interesting building that still stands.

The Blue and John Crow Mountains National Park

Consisting of nearly 81,000 hectares in the parishes of St. Andrew, St. Mary, St. Thomas, and Portland, the Blue and John Crow Mountains National Park (BJCMNP, tel. 876/920-8278, jcdt@cybervale.com, www.greenjamaica.org.jm) covers the highest and steepest terrain in Jamaica. This alpine terrain is the last-known habitat for the endangered giant swallowtail butterfly, the second-largest butterfly in the world, which makes its home especially on the northern flanks of the range. Several endemic plant and bird species reside in the park as well, and many migratory birds from northern regions winter there. Among the most impressive of the native birds are the streamertail hummingbird, know locally as doctor bird, the Jamaican tody, the Jamaican black bird, and the yellow-billed parrot. The Blue Mountains generally are the source of water for the greater Kingston area and for this reason, among others, it is important to tread lightly and disturb the environment as little as possible. The BJCMNP has the largest unaltered swath of natural forest in Jamaica, with upper montane rainforest and elfin woodland at its upper reaches.

Blue Mountain Peak can be reached by a variety of means depending on the level of exhaustion you are willing to endure. Generally people leave from Whitfield Hall at Penlyne, St. Thomas, after having arrived there by four-wheel-drive. For more ambitious hikers, however, there's also a 4.5-kilometer trail from Mavis Bank to Penlyne Castle, which is pleasant and covers several farms and streams. This option also obviates the need to send for a four-wheel-drive vehicle. From Penlyne Castle, you follow the road to Abbey Green (3.2 km), and then from there to Portland Gap (3.7 km). At Portland Gap there is a ranger station, sometimes unmanned, with bunks, toilets, showers, and campsites. These facilities can be used for US$5 by contacting the JCDT, which asks that visitors register at the ranger station. From Portland Gap

to the peak is the most arduous leg, covering 5.6 kilometers. Warm clothes, light rain gear, and comfortable, supportive footwear are recommended.

Blue Mountain Peak is a mildly challenging four-hour hike from **Whitfield Hall,** a rustic farmhouse with a great fireplace. Trips to overnight at the farm and climb Blue Mountain by sunrise can be arranged through **Barrett Adventures** (contact Carolyn Barrett, tel. 876/382-6384, info@barrettadventures.com, www.barrettadventures.com).

From Portland Gap westward along the Blue Mountain range there are several other important peaks along the ridge, which are hiked to a far lesser extent. These include Sir John's Peak, John Crow Peak, and Catherine's Peak. Get your hands on a copy of *Guide to the Blue and John Crow Mountains;* it has the most thorough coverage of hiking trails throughout the national park. Otherwise locals are the best resource.

Accommodations

Lime Tree Farm (Tower Hill, www.limetreefarm.com, tel. 876/881-8788, US$100 per person per night, inclusive of three meals per day; alcohol served at an additional cost) overlooking Mavis Bank, and with a spectacular view of Portland Gap, Blue Mountain Peak, and the Yallahs River Valley, is a small coffee farm with tastefully decorated concrete cabins owned by partners Charles Burberry, Rodger Bolton, and Oliver Foot. The property is run as an all-inclusive and the hosts prepare excellent meals that make Lime Tree Farm one of the best values in Jamaica. Meals are shared in the open-air communal kitchen/lounge/dining area, which gives the place a warm, family vibe. Charlie gained notoriety as the clown in a recent Cable & Wireless ad campaign, but his heritage is far more distinguished than Irish impersonations would imply. His grandfather, and Oliver Foot's father, Hugh Foot, was colonial secretary of Jamaica from 1945 to 1947. He later became governor general from 1951 to 1957, during which time he oversaw moves leading up to

© RODGER BOLTON

The cabins at Lime Tree Farm sit amongst flowers and a small coffee plantation.

independence in 1962. Foot, also known as Lord Caradon, marveled in the "the charm and strength of Jamaica in her variety," a commentary brought to life by his heirs at Lime Tree Farm. A 4x4 is needed to reach the property, and can be obtained in Kingston or Mavis Bank as required.

Forres Park Guest House (reservations office tel. 876/927-8275, in Mavis Bank tel. 876/977-8141, mlyn@cwjamaica.com, www .forrespark.com, US$75) is the best option for bird-watchers and hikers, especially for groups. A two-story main house and four cabins are surrounded by a small coffee farm that attracts many endemic and migratory bird species. The large veranda is a great vantage point, as all three of Jamaica's hummingbirds—vervain, Jamaica mango, and streamertail—frequent the bushes all around the chalet-style main house. Rooms are basic with a true mountain cabin feel. You won't miss the lack of air-conditioning as nights are pleasantly cool. Hot water on the other hand comes well appreciated. Ca-

rissa Sterling and Sharla Valentine manage the day-to-day operations on-site and will prepare meals.

Whitfield Hall (Penlyne, St. Thomas, tel. 876/927-0986, bookings@whitfieldhall.com, www.whitfieldhall.com, dorm bunks US$15, room in main house US$40) a few kilometers Past Hagley Gap, lies just over the border in the highest reaches of the parish of St. Thomas. It is a beautiful old house and coffee farm that offers rustic accommodation in a grand setting with a well-appreciated fireplace to fend off the night chill. Whitfield is the most common starting point for expeditions up to Blue Mountain Peak via Portland Gap, which generally start in the early morning hours to arrive at the summit for sunrise and the surest chance of a crisp view. As the morning progresses, the clouds tend to roll in, often obscuring the peaks and valleys. A guide to the peak is offered from Whitfield Hall for US$36 per party. Penlyne is only accessible by 4x4 from Mavis Bank. Transportation can be arranged from any point

KINGSTON

© OLIVER HILL

Forres Park Guest House is a birder's paradise set on a small coffee farm in Mavis Bank.

in Kingston or Mavis Bank, with the cost depending on distance (US$40 from Mavis Bank, US$65 from Papine Square, US$100 from Kingston).

Services

Mavis Bank is not the place to go for culinary delights or nightlife of any kind. Nonetheless, **Karen's Container Bar** (tel. 876/872-4320), around the corner from Forres Park, is open whenever there are customers to serve.

In Mavis Bank square, **By-Way Bar** is a livelier local hangout. Also in the square is the post office (tel. 876/977-8047) and police station (tel. 876/977-8004).

To venture further into the mountains, a four-wheel-drive vehicle is necessary. There's a local Mavis Bank Land Rover (tel. 876/881-8135), or if you're heading up to Blue Mountain Peak you can call Whitfield Hall (tel. 876/364-0722) for their vehicle to meet you at the constabulary, which is a good place to leave your two-wheel-drive if you have one.

GETTING THERE AND AROUND

The Blue Mountains are accessible from three points of entry: from Kingston via Papine; from Yallahs, St. Thomas via Cedar Valley; and from Buff Bay, St. Mary on the North Coast via the B1, which runs alongside the Buff Bay River. The latter route is subject to landslides and has been impassable for the past few years but is expected to re-open in late 2007. Local citizens have cut a bypass around the washed out road through a coffee plantation. It is sometimes possible to get through with four-wheel-drive, and if you're lucky, in dry weather with a regular vehicle.

There are two main routes into the southern slopes on the southern side of the Blue Mountain range. The first, accessed by taking a left onto the B1 at the Cooperage leads through Maryland to Irish Town, Redlight, Newcastle, and Hardwar Gap before the Buff Bay River Valley opens up overlooking Portland and St. Mary on the other side of the range.

The second route, straight ahead at the Cooperage along Gordon Town Road leads to Gordon Town, and then taking a right in the town square over the bridge, to Mavis Bank. Continuing beyond Mavis Bank requires a four-wheel-drive vehicle and can either take you left at Hagley Gap to Penlyne, or straight down to Cedar Valley and along the Yallahs River to the town of Yallahs.

Getting to and around the Blue Mountains can be a challenge, even if keeping lunch down on the way isn't. Only for the upper reaches, namely beyond Mavis Bank, is it really necessary to have a 4x4; otherwise the abundant potholes and washed-out road is only mildly more challenging to navigate than in any other part of Jamaica because of its sharp turns.

A hired taxi into the Blue Mountains will cost from US$25 for a drop-off at Strawberry Hill, to $100 for the day to be chauffeured around. Route taxis travel between Papine Square and Gordon Town throughout the day (US$2), as well as to Irish Town (US$3.50), but you must wait for the car to fill up before heading out.

To reach Whitfield Hall, the most common starting point for hiking Blue Mountain, four-wheel-drive taxis can be called from Mavis Bank or arranged by Whitfield Hall.

Many travelers find letting a tour operator take care of the driving is the easiest, most hassle-free way to get around the island. One of the most dependable and versatile tour companies on the island is Barrett Adventures (contact Carolyn Barrett cell 876/382-6384). Barrett can do pick ups from any point on the island,

getting off the beaten path more often than any other tour company in Jamaica. Carolyn Barrett also books many of the best budget accommodation options across the island, including a few spots in the Blue Mountains.

Colin Smikle (cell 876/370-8243 or 876/978-5833, colinskikle@yahoo.com) offers a tour he dubs "Blue Mountain in a Hurry" ($150 for one or two persons with their own vehicle) where he'll guide hikers up and down within a day.

PORT ANTONIO AND THE EAST COAST

The parishes of Portland and St. Thomas form Jamaica's easternmost region and contain the island's least exploited natural treasures. A quiet town in the center of Portland's coast, Port Antonio boasts some of Jamaica's most secluded beaches among a handful of other stunning natural wonders. The world-famous Blue Hole, or Blue Lagoon, where ice-cold spring water mixes with the warm waves lapping in from the sea, is surreal beyond measure, and reason in itself to visit the region.

Navy Island, an abandoned little paradise in the middle of Port Antonio's twin harbors, is surrounded by coral reefs and sand bars. Steep, lush hills rise from a coastline dotted with beaches, inlets, and mangroves. Reach Falls is a nature lover's paradise, where local guides take visitors by the hand along trails that only they can see through the middle of the river. In Bath, natural hot springs have a mineral composition that is said to cure almost any ailment. When one of these destinations occupies top priority on your daily agenda, life just seems to flow at the right speed. Perhaps the languid pace of this side of the island is just meant to be, and as a visitor you won't be sorry for the lack of crowds.

Located about 65 kilometers from Morant Bay around the eastern flank of the John Crow Mountains and about 95 kilometers east of Port Maria, Port Antonio is the largest town in Portland, and the parish capital. The fact that the area attracts only a minute fraction of the three million or so visitors Jamaica gets each year is either the way it should be or a crying shame, depending on whom you ask. Those

HIGHLIGHTS

◖ **Errol Flynn Marina:** This world-class facility in the heart of Port Antonio has a sea wall lined with flowers and benches (page 105).

◖ **Bonnie View:** No degree of dilapidation to the remains of one of Errol Flynn's grand hotels can take away its view (page 106).

◖ **Folly Mansion:** A perfect metaphor for the state of Portland's boom-to-bust tradition, Folly is still impressive even as it lies in ruins (page 109).

◖ **Blue Hole:** Popularly known as the Blue Lagoon, a 55-meter-deep freshwater spring wells up in a protected cove to mix with the warm tide (page 110).

◖ **Reach Falls:** Dotted with caves and crystal-clear pools, the island's most exciting waterfalls carve through a lush valley (page 110).

◖ **Winnifred Beach:** One of Portland's finest beaches, also has great seafood at Cynthia's. Winnifred is a popular gathering place for locals and is especially crowded on Sundays (page 111).

◖ **Upper Rio Grande Valley:** Home base for the Winward Maroons, the wide river valley has a rich history and some of the island's most intact wilderness (page 126).

◖ **Bath Hot Springs:** Said to cure all manner of diseases, the hot springs and baths are never crowded and provide rejuvenating relaxation (page 136).

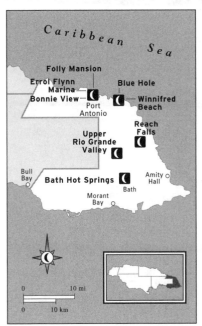

LOOK FOR ◖ TO FIND RECOMMENDED SIGHTS, ACTIVITIES, DINING, AND LODGING.

PORT ANTONIO

who depend on the tourist trade complain the area is not marketed to its potential, while it is said those who own the area's most extravagant private homes prefer it just the way it is.

PLANNING YOUR TIME

Some say Port Antonio is a place time forgot. What's clear is it's an easy place to fall in love with, and despite the languid pace, it's impossible to get bored. You'll want to give the area no less than three days to get in all the main sights without feeling rushed, but if you get there at the beginning of a trip to Jamaica, it's possible you won't want to see anything else.

Port Antonio is small enough to fit in two main activities in a day. Folly Mansion is a good morning activity when the sun lights up the side facing the sea, and is nicely complemented with an afternoon at the beach. The dusk hours are best spent from a bench at the marina with a Devon House I Scream in hand.

If you're planning on heading into the higher reaches of the Rio Grande Valley it will take up at least a day there and back if you're

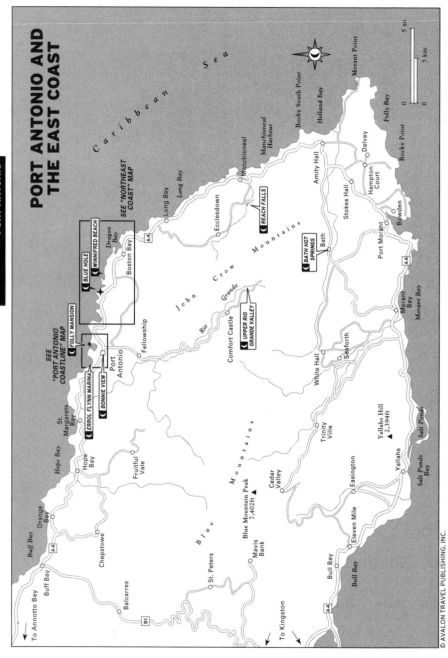

PORT ANTONIO AND THE EAST COAST

Caribbean Sea

5 mi

5 km

Morant Point

Booby South Point
Holland Bay

Folly Bay

Rocky Point

Morant Point

Dalvey

Hampton Court

Bowden

Amity Hall

Stokes Hall

BATH HOT SPRINGS

Bath

Port Morant

Manchioneal

Manchioneal Harbour

REACH FALLS

Ecclesdown

Long Bay

Long Bay

SEE "NORTHEAST COAST" MAP

Dragon Bay

Boston Bay

BLUE HOLE

WINNIFRED BEACH

John   Crow   Mountains

Morant Bay

Morant Bay

Seaforth

White Hall

Trinity Ville

Yallahs Hill
▲ 2,394ft

Salt Ponds

Salt Ponds Bay

Yallahs

Easington

Eleven Mile

Bull Bay

Bull Bay

FOLLY MANSION

SEE "PORT ANTONIO COASTLINE" MAP

Fellowship

Port Antonio

BONNIE VIEW

ERROL FLYNN MARINA

St. Margarets Bay

Hope Bay

Fruitful Vale

Rio   Grande

Comfort Castle

UPPER RIO GRANDE VALLEY

Blue   Mountains

Blue Mountain Peak
▲ 7,402ft

Cedar Valley

Mavis Bank

St. Peters

Chepstowe

Buff Bay

Orange Bay

To Annotto Bay

Buff Bay

Balcarres

To Kingston

© AVALON TRAVEL PUBLISHING, INC.

to fit in a hike to the falls and at least three days round-trip to hike with Maroon guides to the site of Nanny Town higher up in the Blue Mountains.

HISTORY

Port Antonio did not develop until Portland was established as a parish in 1723. Originally called Titchfield, the town was concentrated on the peninsular hill dividing the twin harbors that still retain the town's original name. Port Antonio, like much of the eastern side of the island was not developed in the early colonial period thanks to the rough terrain not suitable for sugar, the principal cash crop during the slavery period. To further dissuade European settlers, the Maroons had their eastern stronghold inland from Port Antonio up the Rio Grande Valley.

Port Antonio was completely transformed, starting in 1876, by the banana trade, which turned the hills into lucrative plantations in a way sugar never could; the area grew further in recognition when the empty banana steamers returned with New Englanders who'd heard about paradise in Portland, Jamaica. Steamer captains George Busch and later Lorenzo Dow Baker basically invented the lucrative banana trade by encouraging local farmers to plant the "green gold" as they fed an exploding, almost accidental demand in the northeastern United States. Jamaica dominated world banana production until 1929, when Honduras took over as top producer after blight destroyed Jamaica's crop. But this was not before Baker was able to invent a new trade in tourism, building the Titchfield Hotel, one of the most extravagant hotels in the Caribbean, which enticed the world's early steam-set to discover Port Antonio. After tourism dropped off during the Great Depression, the area experienced a brief resurgence in the 1950s and 1960s when it became a chic destination for Hollywood stars, with the likes of Errol Flynn and Ian Fleming making it their preferred stomping ground. Some of the world's wealthiest people visited and bought property in the area. Since then Portland has been somewhat overshadowed in promotional efforts by tourism developments in Ocho Rios, Montego Bay, and Negril.

ORIENTATION

The town of Port Antonio is easy to get around on foot or bicycle, with the furthest attractions being no more than a few kilometers apart. For all nature attractions you will need a ride. While the main road (A4) along the north coast passes through Port Antonio, it follows many different streets before coming out again on the other side of town. Approaching from the east, the A4 first becomes West Palm Avenue, then West Street going through the center of town, before joining Harbour Street in front of the Village of St. George, which later becomes Folly Road and then finally once again simply the main road (A4). Harbour Street and William Street together form a one-way roundabout circling the Court House and the Parish Council.

Titchfield Hill, the old part of town, sits on a protrusion next to Navy Island, which divides the East and West Harbours. Titchfield has several interesting gingerbread-style buildings and a few guesthouses, with Fort George Street, King Street, and Queen Street running the length of the peninsula parallel to one another. In town itself, most of the action is on Harbour and West Streets, where the banks, a few restaurants, the town's two nightclubs, and Musgrave Market are located. From Harbour Road, West Avenue starts up again, wrapping around a residential district and becoming East Avenue before reuniting with the Main Road, at this point called Allen. Red Hassell Road, which is the delineator between East and West Palm Avenues, is the route to the Rio Grande Valley.

East of Port Antonio along the coast are a series of hills dropping gently down to coves and bays, which help delineate the districts of Anchovy, Drapers, San San, and Fairy Hill. Farther east lies Boston and then Long Bay. The main beaches including San San, Frenchman's Cove, Dragon's Bay, and Winnifred are all located on this stretch of coast east of town, as is the Blue Lagoon and Reach Falls just past Manchioneel.

Port Antonio

Sheer wealth is readily apparent everywhere east of Port Antonio along the coast, sometimes to an astonishing degree; however, the town's over-the-top grandeur has been fading for decades, leaving in its place potholed roads, dilapidated historical sites, and an increasingly desperate dependence on a barely trickling tourism trade. Some of the most beautiful real estate in Jamaica—and perhaps in the entire world—can be found in the vicinity, much of it overgrown and conspicuously neglected. The restaurant and bar on Navy Island, a two-hectare piece of land that protects Port Antonio's West Harbour, has trees growing up through the rotting floorboards with little remaining in reminder of the island's more glamorous days. Efforts to return Navy Island to its former glory have apparently stifled. Similarly, the restaurant at Blue Hole, or Blue Lagoon, as it was popularized in the movie of the same name, was closed from 2003 to 2007. Michael Lee Chin, one of Jamaica's wealthiest

businessmen, recently bought the lease on the Lagoon, in addition to buying Trident Castle and the Trident Hotel from Earl Levy.

Many residents ask themselves why such unique and marketable natural assets are being so poorly managed. Some blame the area's remoteness, exacerbated by windy potholed roads and say the new North Coast Highway is key to turning the area around; some blame Jamaica's promotional institutions like the Jamaica Tourism Board or the Urban Development Corporation for mishandling resources and retarding the development process; and still others blame the landed elite, many of whom are absentee and when they do return prefer the quiet, old world character emanating from the land and its history, preserved in time perhaps in part thanks to crippled infrastructure.

Despite the seemingly stagnant pace of development, efforts have been made and are underway to return Port Antonio to its former glory

PORTLAND'S BANANA BOOM

The global banana trade, currently a multi-billion dollar industry, has its roots in Portland and St. Thomas. The originators of the banana trade were American sea captains George Busch and later Lorenzo Dow Baker of the 85-ton *Telegraph*, who arrived in 1870. These two established a lucrative two-way trade bringing salt fish (cod), shoes, and textiles from New England, where they found the bananas sold at a handsome profit. Baker was the most successful of the early banana shippers and eventually formed the Boston Fruit Company in 1899, which later became the United Fruit Company of New Jersey and went on to control much of the fruit's production in the Americas. As refrigerated ships came into operation in the early 1900s, England slowly took over from the United States as the primary destination, thanks to tariff protection that was only recently

phased out. With the establishment of the Jamaica Banana Producers' Association in 1929, smallholder production was organized, a cooperative shipping line established, and the virtual monopoly held by United Fruit was somewhat broken. In 1936 the association became a shareholder-based company rather than a cooperative due to near-bankruptcy and pressure from United Fruit. It was perhaps this example of organized labor that gave Marcus Garvey the inspiration for a shipping line to serve the black population in the diaspora and bring commerce into its hands. In the 1930s, Panama disease virtually wiped out the Jamaican banana crop, hitting small producers especially hard. Banana carriers and dock workers were at the fore of the labor movements of 1937-1938, which led to trade unions and eventually the establishment of Jamaica's political parties.

and jumpstart the economy of what should be one of the Caribbean's most popular, exclusive tourist destinations. The new Errol Flynn Marina on the West Harbour in the heart of Port Antonio was inaugurated in 2004 and has world-class facilities, low docking fees, and an outpost of the acclaimed Kingston-based chef Norma Shirley. Never mind that the aforementioned Navy Island development was slated for inclusion in the Marina project before funds disappeared. Other recent developments have seen Butch Stewart, who owns the Sandals and Beaches all-inclusive resorts, buy Dragon Bay, formerly one of the area's top resorts made famous as a set for the movie *Cocktail*. Apparently Stewart is waiting on the government, which has promised to extend the runway at Port Antonio's Ken Jones Aerodrome to allow for the arrival of large aircraft before refurbishing and opening Dragon's Bay.

What is certain is that the present trickle of visitors who come through Port Antonio do not constitute a strong enough driving force to support a healthy economy, leaving crumbling Folly Mansion, its enormous structure built in the Roaring Twenties with a cement–salt water mix, an ironic symbol of stagnation. But few who visit can help but comment on the area's tremendous natural beauty. Secluded white-sand beaches, extravagant villas, plentiful rivers, and strikingly unique topography where the hills fall gently to the sea make Port Antonio and the northeast coast an immediate favorite.

The reality is that any hope of a new economic boom may have faded alongside the memory of Portland as the Caribbean's first tourist destination as a result of the banana trade in the early 19th century. Port Antonio saw a brief comeback in the 1960s and 1970s when it became the playground of choice for the rich and famous from around the world, many of whom left grand mansions seemingly transplanted from old world Europe to the lush green hills of Portland. These past luminaries include the film star Errol Flynn, who left an important legacy in Port Antonio when he died in 1959. Many of Flynn's former properties lie in ruins today.

SIGHTS

The heart of historic Port Antonio, known as **Titchfield Hill,** is best visited by strolling around the peninsula—consuming little more than an hour at a leisurely pace. Titchfield Hill is today a run-down neighborhood dotted with several buildings that hint of more prosperous times with decorative latticework and wide front steps leading up to wraparound verandas. The **Demontevin Lodge** (21 Fort George St., tel. 876/993-2604) is a case in point. It was once the private home of David Gideon, who became Custos of Port Antonio in 1923. Today it is a tired hotel operated under unenthusiastic management and not recommended for lodging, but its decorative gingerbread house ironwork reminiscent of old sea captains' homes on the Massachusetts coast is striking and worth a look.

The foundation and scattered ruins of the **Titchfield Hotel,** built by banana boat captain Lorenzo Dow Baker of the Boston Fruit Company, stand across Queen Street from Ocean Crest Guest House and are now occupied by the Jamaica Defense Force that patrols Navy Island across the water. At its peak the Titchfield was the favored watering hole for luminaries like Bette Davis, J. P. Morgan, and Errol Flynn, who ended up buying the place in addition to Navy Island and the Bonnie View Hotel overlooking the town from the best perch around. The Titchfield was destroyed and rebuilt several times before it was gutted and abandoned after Flynn's death.

At the tip of the Titchfield peninsula stands **Titchfield School,** constructed on the ruins of **Fort George.** Built by the English to defend against Spanish reprisals that never came, Fort George never really saw any action but operated nonetheless until World War I and had walls three meters thick and embrasures for 22 cannons, a few of which are still present. Nobody manages this historic sight, making it free and accessible anytime.

◖ Errol Flynn Marina

Errol Flynn Marina (tel. 876/993-3209 or 876/715-6044, fax 876/715-6033 info@errol flynnmarina.com, www.themarinaatport

antonio.com, 8 A.M.–5 P.M. daily) has slips for 32 boats. Vessels under 50 feet are charged US$0.75 per foot per day, over 50 feet US$1.25 per foot per day; electricity and water are also available at metered rates (US$0.24/kWhr for electricity and US$0.09/gallon of water) and a well-laid-out and planted promenade along the waterfront has benches. Wireless Internet is included for marina guests, and there is an Internet cafe open to non-guests (US$4/hour). **Devon House I Scream** and **Norma's at the Marina** are both located within the gated complex (complete listings under *Food*) and the scenic waterfront makes a romantic spot to let evening drift into night. A private beach faces Navy Island just beyond Norma's. The **park along the waterfront** is open to the public (7 A.M.–11 P.M. Mon.–Fri., 7 A.M.–midnight Sat. and Sun.), as is the marina and restaurant, the docks and pool being reserved for marina guests. The beach is open to customers of Norma's. The Errol Flynn Marina is owned by the Port Authority of Jamaica and managed by Westrec Marina. The marina opened in September 2002 and was renamed the Errol Flynn Marina in 2006.

Port Antonio Marina, also under the control of the Port Authority of Jamaica, also offers docking ($0.35/foot) with water, electricity, and showers, but no security after 4 P.M. By car, access the Port Antonio Marina down the road next to the old train station across from CC Bakery. There is walking access between the two marinas. The difference between them comes down to security, proximity to the bar and restaurant, and complimentary wireless Internet.

Navy Island

Navy Island, originally called Lynch's Island, is a landmass slightly larger than Titchfield Hill about 0.75 kilometer long with an area of about two hectares. It protects Port Antonio's West Harbour with a large sand bar extending off its western side. The island was at one point sited for construction of the town, but the British Navy acquired it instead as a place to beach ships for cleaning and repairs. A naval station was eventually built there and

later Errol Flynn bought the island and turned it into an exclusive resort. Today Navy Island is owned by the Port Authority; it's meant to be developed at some undetermined point down the road. A private bid for the land put together by a consortium of local landowners was blocked by the Authority, which seems wary to cede control in spite of doing nothing with the land for the moment, to the dismay of many local residents.

The island is not serviced by any official tourist operation, but it's a great place to tromp around and explore, and the Jamaica Defense Force Officers there on patrol are friendly enough to visitors. Dennis Butler (cell 876/809-6276) will take visitors over (US$10 per person, US$20 with lunch) from Shan Shy fisherman's beach just west of Port Antonio, adjacent to his father's restaurant, Dickie's Banana.

◖ Bonnie View

The Bonnie View Hotel (Bonnie View Rd.) is another dilapidated former Errol Flynn property no longer in operation as a hotel. The view remains the best in town, or at least in close competition with Helmut Steiner's Jamaica Heights Resort. To get there, take the washed-out Richmond Hill Road directly across from the Anglican Church on the corner of West Palm and Bridge Streets. Bonnie View is not an organized attraction and there is no cost to have a look around so long as no one is around to make reference to the sign on property that states all sightseers must pay US$3 (J$150), which doesn't compute for today's exchange rate and dates the effort. Bonnie View makes a good early-morning walk from town for some aerobic exercise, and if someone asks for money to look at the view, perhaps offering to buy a drink from the nonexistent bar would provide adequate incentive for someone to establish a legitimate business there once again. The hill is passable by taking endless potholes at a snail's pace by car.

Other Sights

Musgrave Market (6 A.M.–6 P.M. Mon.–Sat.) is located across from the square in the heart of

Port Antonio. The market sells fresh produce towards the front and down a lane on one side. The deeper in you go towards the waterfront, the more the market tends towards crafts, "Jamaica no problem" t-shirts, and Bob Marley plaques. The most authentic artistry can be found at the very back where Rockbottom (cell 876/844-9946), a woodcarver since 1980, has his setup. His pet name comes from his sales approach, he says, referring to his pricing. For jewelry, clothing, and other Rasta-inspired crafts, check out Sister Dawn's (Shop 21, cell 876/486-7516, portlandcraftproducers@yahoo.com).

Boundbrook Wharf is the old banana-loading wharf just west of town behind the old railway station that now serves as the Portland Art Gallery. While not as busy as in the banana-boom days, the wharf continues to be used on occasion. The wharf makes a good 20-minute walk from town. Just north from the entrance to the wharf, a sandy lane leads off the main road to the beach where fishing boats are tethered in front of the small fishermen's community.

Beaches

Shan Shy Beach is located just west of town. This is principally a fisherman's beach. It's the best departure point for trips to Navy Island and local reefs.

One of the less-frequented beaches in Port Antonio, Shan Shy is a good place to take off on snorkeling or fishing excursions, which can be arranged through Dennis Butler (cell 876/854-4763) of Dickie's Banana. The beach is located five minutes west of town at a sharp curve in the main road.

Errol Flynn Marina has a well-maintained, free private beach for guests of the Marina and patrons of Norma's restaurant.

Directly in front of the crumbling Folly Mansion, **Folly Beach** is a small beach with a narrow strip of sand. It has coral and a rough floor and sees few visitors.

Frenchman's Cove (entrance fee US$5) is one of the most picturesque coves in Jamaica. The beach here is well protected and drops off steeply after the first 30 meters.

Dragon Bay is a private beach protected by

© OLIVER HILL

Frenchman's Cove is a romantic inlet with a wide sandy beach and a river meandering down to meet the sea on one side.

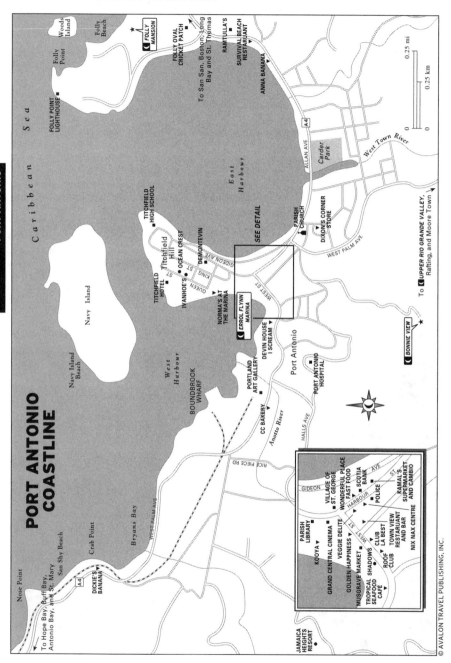

PORT ANTONIO COASTLINE

Woods Island

Folly Beach

Folly Point

★ ◖ FOLLY MANSION

FOLLY OVAL CRICKET PATCH ■

To San San, Boston, Long Bay and St. Thomas

RAMTULLA'S ■

SURVIVAL BEACH RESTAURANT ■

ANNA BANANA ▼

Caribbean Sea

FOLLY POINT LIGHTHOUSE ■

A4

ALLAN AVE

Carder Park

West Town River

East Harbour

WEST TOWN RIVER

TITCHFIELD HIGH SCHOOL ■

Titchfield Hill

SEE DETAIL

PARISH CHURCH ◖ ◄

DIXON'S CORNER STORE ◄

WEST PALM AVE

Navy Island

OCEAN CREST ●
DEMONTEVIN ◄
KING ST
TITCHFIELD HOTEL ■
QUEEN ST
IVANHOE'S ■
GIDEON AVE
WEST ST

To ◖ UPPER RIO GRANDE VALLEY, Rafting, and Moore Town

NORMA'S AT THE MARINA ◄

◖ ERROL FLYNN MARINA

DEVIN HOUSE I SCREAM ▼

◖ BONNIE VIEW ★

Navy Island Beach

West Harbour

Port Antonio

PORT ANTONIO HOSPITAL ■

BOUNDBROOK WHARF ■

PORTLAND ART GALLERY ■

CC BAKERY ■

Anuto River

HALLS AVE

WEST PALM AVE

RICE PIECE RD

Bryans Bay

Caribbean Sea

Crab Point

San Shy Beach

Nose Point

To Hope Bay, Buff Bay, Antonio Bay, and St. Mary

A4

DICKIE'S BANANA ▼

JAMAICA HEIGHTS RESORT ◖ ●

0   0.25 mi
0   0.25 km

[Detail inset]

VILLAGE OF ST. GEORGE ■
WONDERFUL PLACE FAST FOOD ■
SCOTIA BANK ■
HARBOUR AVE
S... ST
GIDEON
POLICE ■
KAMAL'S SUPERMARKET AND CAMBIO ■

PARISH LIBRARY ■
KGOYA ▼
GRAND CENTRAL CINEMA ■
VEGGIE DELITE ▼
GOLDEN HAPPINESS ▼
MUSGRAVE MARKET ■
WEST ST
CLUB LA BEST ▼
ROOF CLUB ▼
TROPICAL SHADOWS SEAFOOD CAFE ▼
TOWN VIEW RESTARUANT AND BAR ■
NIX NAX CENTRE ■

© AVALON TRAVEL PUBLISHING, INC.

guards. In the near future, however, visitors may be able to gain access from Butch Stewart's at Dragon Bay Resort.

Known as the people's beach, **Winnifred** lies in a wide, shallow, white-sand cove. It's a local favorite and the best place for conch soup and fried fish.

Boston Beach consistently get the best swells in the area and has a surf shop to match.

San San Beach (10 A.M.–4 P.M. daily, US$5) is the most exclusive beach in Port Antonio. It's located at the base of San San hill, where many of the area's nicer villas are. The fine-sand beach hugs a cove next to Alligator Head and overlooks Pellew Island from where a protective reef extends eastward to the mouth of Blue Hole.

C Folly Mansion

Just east of Port Antonio along Alan Avenue, a left onto a dirt road before the cricket pitch follows the edge of East Harbour out to Folly Point Lighthouse. A right turn after the cricket pitch

along a grassy vehicle track through low-lying scrub forest leads to Folly Mansion, which is an unmanaged attraction (free, always accessible) on government-owned land. Folly was for a few years after its construction the most ostentatious building in Jamaica, before it started to crumble and fall apart. Built by Connecticut millionaire Alfred Mitchell in 1905, the mansion had 60 rooms, with an indoor swimming pool, and was made almost entirely of cement. Apparently the cement was mixed with saltwater, which quickly proved a bad combination. The salt not only weakened the cement but rusted the steel framework, causing almost immediate deterioration. Nonetheless, Mitchell lived in the mansion with his wife, a Tiffany heiress, and their family on and off until his death in 1912, and it wasn't until 1936 that the house was abandoned. On the waterfront in front of the pillared mansion is the humble little **Folly Beach,** which faces small Wood Island—where Mitchell apparently kept monkeys and other exotic animals. The beach isn't bad for a swim, but care should be taken

© OLIVER HILL

The steadfast pillars of Folly Mansion have withstood the ravages of time while the rest of the mansion deteriorated rapidly following its construction in 1905.

as the sea floor is not even and there are parts covered with sharp reef. The area is also known to have a strong current at times.

The name "Folly" predates Mitchell and his ill-fated mansion as made clear by **Folly Point Lighthouse** which was built and named in 1888. Apparently the name refers to Baptist minister James Service, who once owned the property, having acquired it piece by piece. For this he was lauded with a playful expression extolling his frugal ways, which were *not,* in fact, based in folly. Many legends surround the mansion, the most popular story being that the mansion was built as a wedding gift. It is said that the bride ran off in tears when her new dream home began to crumble as soon as she was carried across the threshold.

Folly Point Lighthouse stands on a point extending along the windward shore of East Harbour. The lighthouse is not generally open to the public, but the property manager is known to let visitors in on occasion. A track usually too rutted and muddy for a vehicle runs between the lighthouse and the mansion along the water's edge.

◖ Blue Hole

Blue Hole is also commonly known as the **Blue Lagoon** thanks to a 1980 Randal Kleiser adventure film of the same name shot there starring a teenage Brooke Shields. Portland's Blue Hole is Jamaica's largest underground spring-fed lagoon, of which there are many smaller ones scattered across the island. The Blue Lagoon is made all the more unique by its location in a 55-meter-deep protected cove along the coast, where warm tidal waters gently mix with fresh water welling up from the depths. Some claim Blue Hole has no bottom. At one time, Robin Moore, the author of *The French Connection,* owned much of the land surrounding the lagoon; today his cottages lie in ruins. A restaurant and bar with a deck overhanging the lagoon has been closed for several years. In 2006 Michael Lee Chin, National Commercial Bank (NCB) chairman and one of Jamaica's richest men, took over the lease for the land bordering the western edge of the lagoon; he is

expected to manage the attraction and reopen the restaurant and bar in late 2007. A handful of craft vendors line the fisherman beach waiting patiently to make a sale. Someone will likely volunteer to watch your vehicle, or ask for an entrance fee, but there is noone officially sanctioned to conduct these functions as the place has been left unmanaged. Many fishermen here offer rides on their boats out snorkeling or to Pellew Island. Rates are negotiable. The Blue Lagoon is a great place to cool off even when the sea is lukewarm; the spring water remains icy cold year-round, making for a stimulating mix.

Blue Hole is located east of San San Beach and Pellew Island just past the well-marked turnoff for Goblin Hill heading east. Turn onto the lane off the main road along the Blue Lagoon Villas and continue down to a small parking area along the beach.

◖ Reach Falls

Reach, or Reich Falls (contact property manager Renee Radcliffe, tel. 876/993-6606 or 876/993-6683, 8:30 a.m.–4:30 p.m. Wed.–Sun., US$10 adults, US$5 children under 12, US$4.25 residents), as it's sometimes spelled, is located in a beautiful river valley among the lower northeast foothills of the John Crow Mountains. The river cascades down a long series of falls which can be climbed from the base far below the main pool where the attraction, which is managed by Jamaica's Urban Development Corporation (UDC), is based. You will want to start at the bottom and continue far above the main pool to get the full exhilarating experience. To climb the full length of the cataracts requires about two hours, but if you stop to enjoy each little pool it could easily consume all day. Before reaching the dedicated parking area there is a dirt road just before a wooden shack that leads down to the base of the falls.

To get to Reach Falls, head inland by a set of shacks just east of Manchioneel up a picturesque windy road. The turnoff is marked by a large sign for Reach Falls. Unofficial guides made their services mandatory for years when

© OLIVER HILL

climbing Reach Falls

the falls were officially closed as a managed attraction. These guides often congregate at a fork in the road where you turn left to get to the falls. The guides still offer their services on days when the UDC-managed sight is closed. The guides are in fact indispensable when it comes to climbing the falls, as they know every rock along the riverbed, which is very slippery in certain places. As always get a sense for what your guide will expect for the service up front (US$5–10 is reasonable) to avoid the discomfort associated with unmet expectations when you leave. Leonard Welsh ("Sendon") (cell 876/540-7358) and Byron (tel. 876/868-3549 or 876/871-3745) are recommended guides on days when the UDC-managed sight is closed (Mondays and Tuesdays); contact Rugy ("Taliban") at the Look In Lookout bar (cell 876/538-6667) to arrange for a guided visit. Rene is a charismatic local craftsman who makes lung exercisers, which he claims enhance breathing ability and lung capacity. A few other craftsmen have stands along the road selling wood carvings.

Two local guides/lifeguards have been employed by the UDC since it opened the attraction officially in early 2007. The UDC's lease on the property extends from a little below the main pool to a little above it, and unofficial guides will be turned away from the main waterfalls area on either side of the leased land. **Mandingo Cave,** which is found further up the river, is not currently part of the official tour offered but can be reached by going with the local guides.

◖ Winnifred Beach

Winnifred is a beautiful, free public beach in the Fairy Hill district just east of San San and the Blue Lagoon. Food and beverages are sold by a slew of vendors and there's a nice restaurant. Named after the daughter of Quaker minister F. B. Brown as a rest place for missionaries, teachers, and the respectable poor, Winnifred has remained decidedly local thanks perhaps to the trust that once managed the area and had provisions ensuring that locals could access and enjoy the beach.

PORT ANTONIO

© OLIVER HILL

Winnifred is Port Antonio's most popular public beach.

The Urban Development Corporation now controls the land, but local resistance to its being developed has ensured that it remains a local hot spot.

Cynthia's on the western end of the beach serves excellent fried fish with rice and peas (US$10). Undoubtedly someone will ask for a "contribution," but it's not necessary. Instead support the vendors. The rocky road down to the beach has two access points from the main road. The best route goes through the housing scheme on the sea side of the road less than 0.75 kilometer east of Dragon Bay. A turn into a housing scheme across the road from Jamaica Crest, followed by a quick right in front of the Neighborhood Watch sign allows you avoid the worst part of the road that descends off the main next to Mikuzi.

Arts and Crafts

The **Portland Art Gallery** (9 A.M.–6 P.M. Mon.–Sat.) is located inside the old Railway Station by the Banana Docks on West Street, about a 10 minutes' walk from the Main Square. Hopeton Cargill (cell 876/882-7732 or 876/913-3418), whose work includes landscape paintings, portraits, and commercial signs, is the gallery director.

At the **Jamaica Palace Hotel** (tel. 876/993-7720, 7 A.M.–9 P.M. daily, US$150L/170H), Fahmi Sigi keeps a large collection of Ken Abendana Spencer paintings for sale. A Portland native, the late Ken Spencer was one of, if not the most prolific artists in the country's history. He captured scenes from Jamaican life with quick, effortless strokes that allowed him to become well recognized for selling his paintings very cheaply and distributing them widely. The hotel lobby, while far from inviting, is filled with kitsch art by the owner herself. Other artists whose work is represented at the hotel include John Campbell and Ann-Marie Korti. A walk around the hotel is a real trip.

Philip Henry (tel. 876/993-3162, philartambokle@hotmail.com) is a talented artist who has prints, portraits, and sculpture that can be purchased from his small home studio. Call or email to set up an appointment.

Michael Layne (19 Sommers Town Rd., tel. 876/993-3813, cell 876/784-0288, miclayne@ cw.jamaica.com) is considered by many the top ceramist in the parish and has exhibited at galleries in Kingston countless times. Layne was born and raised in Portland, studying at Titchfield High School and then going on to Edna Manley College in Kingston to concentrate in ceramics. Today Layne teaches art at Titchfield High School and works out of his home studio (open by appointment) where he creates works that include large bottles, bowls, and vases that are assembled with clay slabs, decorated with oxides, and single fired.

Marcia Henry (Lot 5, Red Hassell Lane, tel. 876/993-3162) is a talented local artist with a home studio.

Carriacou Gallery (tel. 876/993-7134, 9 A.M.– 5 P.M., daily) located at Hotel Mocking Bird Hill, features work of co-owner Barbara Walker in addition to many other local artists.

ENTERTAINMENT AND EVENTS

Port Antonio is not a haven for club-goers by any means, but there are two good venues that hold regular theme nights throughout the week, as well as occasional live performances. Several times a year, stage shows are set up around the area, Somerset Falls being a favorite venue for concerts and Boston and Long Bay also hosting occasional events. Many of the area's more upscale villa owners and visitors prefer to entertain with dinner parties, which can be quite lavish.

Nightclubs

Club La Best (5 West St., contact club manager/owner Chris, cell 876/896-9024) does Ladies Night on Wednesdays (US$2, ladies free) with a disco, R&B, reggae mix; after-work jams that stretch into long club hours on Fridays (free) with mostly dancehall; and Smart Casual Sundays (US$2) with reggae and R&B vintage music. Wednesday is a slower night. Live shows, when they happen, are held on Saturday nights. Club La Best opens at 9:30 P.M. and closes when the last person leaves. The club holds around 800 people, who crowd in

for occasional radio DJs and performers. Club La Best opened in April 2006.

Roof Club (11 West St., managed by Shawn "Blue" Rankine, cell 876/449-0852, 10 P.M. until the last person leaves, US$3) is open for Ladies Night on Thursdays, Crazy Saturdays, and occasional special events on Fridays. It's the longest-standing nightclub in Port Antonio, open for the past 33 years. It generally plays dancehall, reggae, and R&B—in other words the perfect mix for bumping and grinding, or "whining," in local parlance. It's an earthy, at times seedy, place with old wooden floors, a DJ booth on one side, and the bar opposite with neon lights and a disco ball hanging from the ceiling. Don't be surprised if a patron approaches and uses a forward introduction by commanding, "buy mi a drink nuh."

Town Talk (next to the Parish Library in Clock Tower Square, contact owner Owen Robinson tel. 876/993-2903, or bartender Tenisha Donaldson, cell 876/384-0825) has a clothing store on the ground floor, a bar on the second floor called **Grand Central Cinema,** and another bar on the roof called **Baldi's,** along with a restaurant called **Kooya** (see *Food*). Grand Central has a small stage and hosts occasional performances and dances.

Festivals and Events

Fi Wi Sinting (Contact founder Sister P, cell 876/426-1957, www.fiwisinting.com) is a must-see festival celebrating Jamaica's African heritage. It's held the third Sunday in February. (See sidebar, *Fi Wi Sinting,* for a complete description.)

Portland All Fest (contact Somerset Falls, held mid-March, tel. 876/913-0046, info@somersetfallsjamaica.com, www .somersetfallsjamaica) is a family fun-day with food, swimming, and concerts at the open-air venue at the base of Somerset Falls.

Bling Dawg Summer Jam (www.visit jamaica.com, held July) is one of several annual events held at Somerset Falls. Bling Dawg is a well-recognized promoter who brings together an array of dancehall artists for the event. Contact Somerset Falls for more information.

PORT ANTONIO

FI WI SINTING

Translated into English as "something for us," Fi Wi Sinting (contact Pauline Petinaud, "Sister P," cell 876/426-1957, www.fiwisinting.com) is an Afro-centric family fun day held on the third Sunday of February (President's Weekend in the United States). The event began in 1991 as a fundraiser for a local school and has grown in popularity each year as more and more Jamaicans and foreign visitors arrive in Nature's Way, Portland to celebrate Jamaica's African heritage. African dance and drumming, Mento sessions, Kumina and Jonkunnu performances, crafts, and food are the main draws. The event is a draw for Rastafarians who maintain African heritage as a central pillar of their philosophy and lifestyle, and Rasta dub poet Mutabaruka is a regular selector.

Most Jamaicans find the idea of Black History Month absurd, given that black history is something black people should live with and recall every day, week, and month of the year. Nonetheless, February is chock full of events celebrating the country's African heritage, and Fi Wi Sinting is the largest grassroots event of its kind, where it's most evident that the country's traditions haven't disappeared.

Swift River Bussu Festival (contact Patrick Montaque, aka Sergeant Baker, cell 876/318-8858 or 876/359-0405, mcsgt baker@yahoo.com, held sometime in June or July) along the banks of the Swift River 15 minutes' drive west of Port Antonio, celebrates the Jamaican version of escargot, Bussu, which is prepared in every way possible for this family-oriented event. Music, crafts, and cultural items complement the river snails, which are found only in Portland and considered a delicacy.

Portland Jerk Festival (Jerk Festival office, shop 33, Village of St. George, 2–4 Fort George St., contact the sweet and helpful secretary Dahlia Minott, tel. 876/715-6553,

or chair person Sybil Rendle, cell 876/389-1601, or vice-chair and regional manager for JTB Cynthia Perry, www.visitjamaica.com) is held on the first Sunday in July and admission tends to be around US$10. Local arts, crafts, and concerts complement every kind of jerk imaginable. The venue was once in Boston, but has been relocated to Folly Oval as of 2007.

The **International Blue Marlin Tournament** (contact Ron DuQuesnay, chair of the Sir Henry Morgan Angling Association, rondq@mail.infochan.com, cell 876/909-8818) is held out of the Port Antonio Marina each October (US$170 registration). The event draws anglers from far and wide and also runs a concurrent 35-canoe folk fishing tournament for local fishermen who fight the billfish with hand-held lines.

SHOPPING

The **Village of St. George,** a surreal building with a mosaic of facades built by Jamaica Palace Hotel owner Fahmi Sigi as if transplanted from an assortment of European buildings, has a number of shops, a few of them worthwhile checking out. The building itself took years to complete, combining a variety of architectural styles to comply with the childhood vision of its creator.

Cooyah Designs (Shop 12, tel. 876/993-4207, cell 876/410-4746, 10 A.M.–6 P.M. Mon.–Sat.), on the second floor, has a good selection of original Cooyah and Zion Roots Wear clothing. The shop is supervised by Kemeisha Johnson and Shelly Johnson.

Sportsman's Toy Box (Shop 28, tel. 876/715-4542, 9 A.M.–5 P.M. Mon.–Fri.) sells diving and fishing equipment.

Portland Jerk Festival Office offers fax and photocopy services.

Hamilton's Bookstore (24 West St., contact co-owner Avarine Moore, tel. 876/993-9634, 9 A.M.–7 P.M. Mon.–Sat.) has a small but decent selection of Jamaican folk books and cookbooks.

Town Talk (2a Harbour St., tel. 876/993-2563) has a little clothing store.

Little Steve has a small shop at the end of Winnifred Beach where he sells bracelets and other souvenir items.

SPORTS AND RECREATION

Carder Park is the community football field across the road from East Harbour that comes alive for several family-fun events throughout the year, like the dominos championship.

Folly Oval is the town's cricket pitch and where the schools practice sports; it extends along the edge of East Harbour. The large field comes alive annually for the Portland Jerk Festival.

Island Massage Therapy & Yoga (cell 876/818-4771, Portland tel. 876/993-7605, Kingston tel. 876/924-5503, namaste_ja@ hotmail.com, US$90/per hour for massage) is led by Barbara Gingerich who, as the name implies, is both a certified massage therapist and yoga instructor. Barbara holds sessions in a studio at her house and on her large veranda, which has a stunning view of the sea and gardens. You can also have Barbara come to you for an additional charge if you're staying in the area. She works between Kingston and Port Antonio and yoga classes are priced based on group size.

Water Sports

Pellew Island is a private island given, as the legend has it, by industrial magnate and famed art collector Baron Von Thyssen to super-model Nina Dyer, one of his many brides, as a wedding gift in 1957. Nina Dyer committed suicide some five years later, and Von Thyssen himself died in 2002. The island is now slated for development of four villas which are up for sale. While there are no organized tours of the private island, fishermen from the small beach adjacent to Blue Hole can take visitors over for excellent snorkeling along the reefs around the island.

Lady G'Diver (Errol Flynn Marina, contact Steve or Jan Lee Widner, office tel. 876/715-5957, cell 876/995-0246 or 876/452-8241, ladygdiver@cwjamaica.com, www.ladygdiver .com) runs diving excursions from the Marina. Port Antonio's waters are quieter than those off Ocho Rios or Montego Bay and are less over-fished. Wall diving is especially popular. Lady G'Diver offers a wide range of packages and programs, from basic PADI certification to Master courses. The most basic is the two-dive package (US$84 plus US$7 per person for equipment rental).

Jamaica Deep-Sea Adventures (tel. 772/475-3555, local cell 876/909-9552, CaribbeCapt@aol.com, www.themarinaatport antonio.com) offers charters skippered by Captain Paul Bohnenkamper on *La Nadine,* a 40-foot, 2000-model, tournament-edition Luhrs sportfisher with the latest equipment. Inside the air-conditioned cabin you'll find two staterooms, leather sofas, a DVD player, VCR, two televisions, a stereo system, and a well-equipped galley. Rates vary for half-/full-day trips: US$750/US$1,200 (5 or 6 people), US$700/US$1,100 (for 3 or 4 people), or US$650/1,000 (for 1 or 2 people). The rate includes bait, tournament tackle, soft drinks, bottled water, beer, sandwiches, snacks, towels, and anything else you could need.

Captain Paul skippers the most well-equipped fishing vessel in Jamaica's best fishing grounds around the island's eastern banks in pursuit of blue marlin, wahoo, tuna, and dolphin fish. Anglers practice tag and release of all billfish. Port Antonio is home to an annual International Marlin tournament. Spring brings great wahoo fishing—10–15 fish per trip sometimes. The summer has excellent yellowfin tuna, as well as wahoo, blackfin tuna, dorado, and a shot at a blue marlin. September–November is peak blue marlin season, but they can be caught any time.

Paul is a U.S. Coast Guard–licensed 100-Ton Master, an IGFA certified observer, and the only IGFA Certified Captain in Jamaica with over 40,000 kilometers of experience fishing the northeast coast. Both Captain Paul and his excellent crew are all licensed lifeguards with CPR and first-aid certification. The boat has been inspected and licensed by the Maritime Authority and Tourist Board of Jamaica. Transportation can be arranged from other parts of the island.

Barrett Adventures Sailing Charters (contact Captain Carolyn Barrett, Barrett Adventures, cell 876/382-6384, info@barrett adventures.com, www.barrettadventures.

com) operates two cruises out of Port Antonio, a roundtrip to Cuba, and a Pirates of the Caribbean cruise to Port Royal (US$1000 per person per week for 2–6 persons, US$900 for 7–8 persons). Other destinations are also possible to arrange. If the 40-foot Jeanneau is in the area, day cruises can be arranged (US$125 per person for 2–6 persons, US$100 per person for 7–10 persons). Otherwise, day cruises are generally based out of Montego Bay. Provisioning is at the passenger's expense, while the captain and cook are included. Shorter charters for less than a week are also offered (US$150 per person per day).

Bicycling

Pro Bicycles (3 Love Lane, contact Rohan who runs the shop, cell 876/838-2399 or 876/993-2341, 9 A.M.–5:30 P.M. daily) has a few basic all-terrain 18-speed bicycles (US$10/day). They're not in the best shape, but you can't beat the price.

Blue Mountain Bicycle Tours (121 Main St., Ocho Rios, tel. 876/974-7075, info@bmtoursja.com, www.bmtoursja.com) runs a popular downhill biking tour that has been somewhat truncated over the past few years due to landslides that blocked the upper reaches of the route. While the operation is based in Ocho Rios, people staying in Portland can link up with the bus in Buff Bay before it leaves the coast to ascend the B1 into the Blue Mountains to where the lazy downhill ride starts.

Horseback Riding

Riding is offered by Delroy Course (cell 876/383-1588, Winston (brother) cell 876/485-1773), who hangs out by the driveway to Frenchman's Cove across from San San Golf waiting on potential customers. Delroy takes groups of up to four persons on a 1.5-hour trip around to San San beach, or 4–5 hour trip to Nonesuch Caves, starting at US$20 per person and going up to US$30 for longer trips. A small sign with red letters hangs across from the gate at Frenchman's Cove marking Delroy's outdoor "office."

Golf and Tennis

The **San San Golf & Country Club** (tel. 876/993-7644) located across the street from Frenchman's Cove, gets very little use nowadays and is officially closed, but people with their own clubs often sneak in to use the driving range or play a few holes—to the chagrin of owner Ernie Smatt.

Goblin Hill (San San, tel. 876/993-7537) allows non-guests to use the hotel's hardtop **tennis courts** (US$15/hr, US$12 for racquets per pair).

ACCOMMODATIONS

Port Antonio has a wide range of accommodation options with a notable concentration of high-end villas. Nonetheless, budget hotels and guesthouses dot the coast from town all the way to Long Bay. As in many parts of Jamaica, there are no street numbers and roads are often referred to as the "main." Refer to the maps in this book for exact locations.

Under $75

There are a two recommended, well-maintained guesthouses among the general dilapidation on Titchfield Hill. Both are owner-managed. **Ivanhoes** (9 Queen St., tel. 876/993-3043, US$30–60, ivanhoesja@hotmail.com, lornacamburke@hotmail.com) is a classic Jamaican wooden house with a red painted zinc roof surrounded by a white picket fence. In the center of the compound is a small courtyard with vines and flowers all about. The rooms are comfortable and airy, and the better ones have good views over the East Harbour. A combination of rooms with queen and single beds all have private baths with hot water and TV. Breakfast and dinner are available to order.

Ocean Crest (7 Queen St., tel. 876/993-4024, lydia.j@cwjamaica.com) is located next door to Ivanhoe's and owned by Lydia Jones, a friendly and warm woman who takes pride in being attentive with her guests. The building is a more typical concrete construction, with tiled floors in the rooms. Ocean Crest rooms range from basic interior (US$35) to two top-floor balcony rooms (US$50 fan, US$60 fan a/c)

with a view over the East Harbour. There is an open kitchen (with stove, refrigerator, pots, and utensils) for use by the guests and Ms. Jones can also prepare breakfast on request (US$5). Ocean Crest is near to all the useful conveniences such as ATMs, banks, supermarkets, craft market, restaurants, nightclubs, and public transportation. All the rooms have private bathroom, ceiling fan, hot water, and cable TV. There's a living and dining room and an open porch. The living room can be used for small conferences or meetings up to 20 people.

Shadows (West St., cell 876/828-2285, US$40) is a guesthouse and restaurant/bar in the heart of town owned and managed by the amicable Barrington Hamilton. The five small rooms have double beds, cable TV, air-conditioning, and private baths with hot water.

❰ Drapers San Guest House (Drapers, tel. 876/993-7118, carla-51@cwjamaica.com) sits oceanside toward the easternmost end of Drapers district; it's an excellent budget option. A few rooms have shared baths (US$50, incl. breakfast and GCT) and a few have private baths (US$60). Two newer rooms offer a step up: Rasta Cottage (US$70) is self-contained with a private bath and veranda; the other "high-end" room is in the main building with its own bath and shared veranda (US$60). Drapers San owner Carla Gullotta is an avid reggae fan and can help arrange trips to stage shows and cultural heritage sights and events. She is also a good contact for travelers interested in visiting Culture Yard in Trench Town, Kingston.

Wright's Guest House (Tipperaire Rd., cell 876/838-2399, US$40) managed by Rohan Lawrance (nephew of the Wrights) has five basic double-occupancy rooms with full-size beds, fans, hot water, and TV. To get there head east of Blue Lagoon 1.2 kilometers, and take the next left after Dragon Bay into the development signed Lower Zion Hill Fairy Hill Gardens; go left again, you'll see two apartment buildings in one lot. Winnifred Beach is 20 minutes' away on foot.

Search Me Heart (Drapers, cell 876/882-8747 or 876/353-9217, info@searchmeheart.com, www.searchmeheart.com, US$55 per room, including breakfast) is a comfortable and clean two-bedroom cottage run as a guesthouse by Culture and his wife Roseanna. Amenities include hot water in private bathrooms and standing fans. The cottage is about a five-minute walk to Frenchman's Cove, one of Port Antonio's best beaches. Culture offers tours for guests and non-guests to area attractions.

Mikuzi (Fairy Hill, Kingston office tel. 876/978-4859, Steve cell 876/329-8589, Ms. Deans cell 876/813-0098, info@mikuziresorts .com, www.mikuziresorts.com, US$30–90) located in the Fairy Hill district across from Jamaica Crest is a great budget option within a few minutes walk of Port Antonio's best public beach, Winnifred. Mikuzi bills itself as a typical Jamaican yard, and indeed, it's not far off. Four cottages have either two singles or one queen bed, bedside fans, and private baths with hot water. A few rooms have TV. A kitchen is available for shared use in the larger two-bedroom house.

$75-200

The Fan (overlooking Drapers, tel. 876/993-7915, book through Carla Gulotta from Drapers San, tel. 876/993-7118 or 876/362-4771, carla-51@cwjamaica.com, US$150 incl. breakfast and GCT) is a modest private villa in the hills above Drapers with a breathtaking view of Dolphin Bay, Trident Castle, and Blue Mountain Peak. The villa rents a guest apartment with one king bed, a large living room, dining room, bathroom, kitchen, and balcony. A couch can be turned into an extra bed if needed. Meals are prepared to order (at additional cost) by the housekeeper. The Fan's owner, Mrs. Palomino, also owns The Gap café, a small bed-and-breakfast near Hardwar Gap in the Blue Mountains.

Bay View Villas (Anchovy, tel. 876/993-3118, info@bayviewvillas-ja.com, www.bay viewvillas-ja.com, US$90) has 21 rooms in a large building with a variety of room arrangements. The hotel sits above Turtle Crawle Bay just east of Trident Castle. Food is available and a B&B (US$102) as well as all-inclusive (US$126) packages are also offered. Rooms are

basic with TV, air-conditioning, balconies, and private bathrooms with hot water.

San San Tropez (San San, tel. 876/993-7213, info@sansantropez.com, www.sansan tropez.com, US$75–250) is an Italian restaurant and five-bedroom accommodation just east of the San San police station. Rooms are comfortable with cable TV, air-conditioning, ceiling fans, and private bathrooms with hot water. There is a swimming pool on the property. Fabio Federico Favalli is the owner and managing director. The restaurant has eastern Jamaica's most authentic Italian cuisine, serving freshly prepared pizza and spaghetti, as well as fish, lobster and meat dishes (US$10–30).

Fern Hill Club (tel. 876/993-7374 or 876/ 993-7375, fernhill@cwjamaica.com, www.fern hillclubhotel.com, US$80 and up) began as a 31-unit timeshare complex. Owners Carol and Vincent Holgate have been consolidating the rooms over the past decade. There are a handful of villas separate from the main building, some one-bedroom, some two-, which are a good value, while not by any means state of the art. The property itself covers a hillside and has great views at every elevation level, especially from the open-air dining room and bar area.

Frenchman's Cove (tel. 876/993-7270, fax 876/993-7404, flawrence@cwjamaica.com, www.frenchmans-cove-resort.com, US$146 s, US$202 d, US$221 t, inclusive of tax and continental breakfast) remains one of Jamaica's prime properties, considered by some to have the best beach on the island. The cove itself is small with a short, wide beach and fine white sand. Fifteen villas are scattered about a large property. The three villas in use and the 12 rooms in the main house are not sparkling by any means and could certainly use more attention than they get, but for its proximity to an excellent beach, Frenchman's is still a good accommodation option, especially for a family that is more interested in affordability and convenience than shiny shower rods.

Jerk lunch is cooked every afternoon on the beach, which is open to non-guests as well (9 A.M.–5 P.M. daily, admission US$5). Manager Frank Lawrence has worked on the property since 1959, when he started on the construction work and then worked as a waiter during the height of Port Antonio's glamorous tourism boom. After its opening in 1961, Frenchman's Cove quickly became one of the most exclusive resorts around. Formerly a part of Cold Harbour Estate—which encompassed all of San San, Frenchman's, and Drapers Harbour—Frenchman's Cove is today owned by the Weston family, who run several international business ventures. Frenchman's Cove Villas have suffered repeated hurricane damage, especially during Gilbert in 1988, but according to Mr. Lawrence, the main house has remained in operation since opening.

Moon San Villa (tel. 876/993-7600 or 876/993-7777, Sansan1999@hotmail.com, www.moonsanvilla.com) is run as a bed-and-breakfast and is the most affordable way to stay next to the Blue Lagoon. The villa has four double-occupancy rooms (US$145 low season, US$155 high season) that rent individually. While not on the water, Moon San overlooks the Blue Lagoon strip of villas that are among the most luxurious in Jamaica and guests have easy water access as well as access to the beach at Frenchman's Cove. Breakfasts are communal around a large table with a view out to sea. It's not a place for exclusive privacy, but Moon San makes a good base for excursions and frequent dips in Blue Hole. Owner Greg Naldrett also operates Blue Mountain Bicycle Tours and Riverwalk at Mayfield Falls.

(Goblin Hill (tel. 876/993-7537, reservations office tel. 876/925-8108, reservations@goblinhill.com, www.goblinhillvillas.com) further up the hill in the San San district is an excellent option for families or couples. The spacious rooms and self-contained duplex suites (US$115–195 low season to US$125–265 high) are a great value, especially for a family. The two-bedroom duplex suites have large master rooms with a second bedroom on the opposite end upstairs, and a living area and kitchen downstairs. The living rooms have sliding doors that open onto a beautiful lawn rolling down and exposing a view of San San Bay, also visible from the master bedroom. Goblin Hill is well situated for all the best attractions on one of Port Antonio's most grandiose hillsides. While its interiors may be less extravagant than at some of its neighboring villa properties, Port Antonio is much more than art on the walls, and Goblin Hill boasts a large swimming pool, tennis courts, and comfortable digs within easy walking distance of San San Beach and the Blue Lagoon. Guests get complimentary use of the beach at Frenchmen's Cove.

Trident Hotel and Villas (tel. 876/993-2602, trident@infochan.com, www.tridentvillas.netfirms.com, US$129/229 low/high) has 14 villas and 11 rooms in the main building. Inside the rooms the decor ranges from classy to gaudy, but luckily what could be considered excessive showiness works perfectly with the peacock walking across the manicured lawn just outside the open French doors. Wireless Internet is available in the lobby and bar area. All-inclusive packages are also an option.

Trident Castle (www.tridentcastle.com) built by Earl Levy next door, is also available for rent (US$5,500/7,500 nightly low/high) and sleeps 16–18 people. The castle has a full-time staff of three housekeepers, three waiters, one bartender, one chef, and three gardeners. Many celebrities and nobility have found Trident Castle adequately grandiose for their time in Jamaica.

Jamaica Palace Hotel (tel. 876/993-7720, pal.hotel@cwjamaica.com, www.jamaicapalacehotel.com) just across Turtle Crawle Bay from Trident, is an enormous concrete compound with giant checkerboard-tiled courtyards, a gallery that defines kitsch in the lobby, a swimming pool in the shape of Jamaica surrounded by hot black surface, and stale bedrooms that make you jump for their total lack of regard for the verdant surroundings outside.

Jamaica Palace was built by Sigi Fahmi, the baroness who began building Trident Castle before running out of funds and selling it to the architect Earl Levy. Jamaica Palace was obviously constructed in an attempt to one-up Trident with enormous columns out front that boast of excess. Clearly Ms. Fahmi is a dear customer of Carib Cement, as the hotel's

© OLIVER HILL

Trident Castle was built to be the most ostentatious private residence in Jamaica, and remains so today.

construction gave them plenty of business. Definitely not an eco-tourism lodge, rooms at the Palace all have air-conditioning, private baths with hot water, and TV. It's the only place in Jamaica that offers a room with a round bed in the middle. The ceiling are very high, the walls whitewashed concrete and covered in art. Several large caged birds are on the property and it's a great place get a Ken Spencer painting and to catch a glimpse of the bold creations of the Baroness herself.

(Jamaica Heights Resort (tel. 876/993-3305, www.jahsresort.com) remains the choice property in the town area. Its views are spectacular. The buildings, while primarily made of concrete, were tastefully designed with simple columns and banisters along the verandas complementing the well-conceived layout around the property. The large pool is set among columns reminiscent of a Roman bath, while the dining room and bar area farther up the hill adjacent to the main house is the perfect spot to hang out. From every vantage point you get a proper view of Port Antonio's twin harbors with

Navy island smack in the center. There are two rooms by the pool (US$75), and four rooms at the property's highest heights, two downstairs (US$95) and two upstairs (US$125). Helmut also offers more humble quarters for backpackers and students in the gatehouse (US$45), making Jamaica Heights the most reasonable and accommodating hotels in Port Antonio for the value. The rooms are unpretentious, spacious, and inviting with poster beds and comfortable linens. French doors open onto verandas with the best view in town. Sitting there watching the light change across the hills is entertainment in itself, and sunrise is a special treat. But you'll want to do other things as well, and there's a nice trail leading down to a brook running through the property.

The staff at the hotel are outstanding, and owner Helmut Steiner, a German-born Jamaican, lives on property with his wife Charmaine and children Marcus and Zora.

Over US$200
Hotel Mocking Bird Hill (Drapers, tel. 876/

993-7134 or 876/993-7267, info@hotel
mockingbirdhill.com, www.hotelmocking-
birdhill.com) has nicely decorated garden
view (US$180/245 low/high) and sea view
(US$235/295 low/high) rooms with ceiling
fans and mosquito nets. Wireless Internet is
available in the lounge where a computer is set
up for guest use. Solar hot-water systems, locally minded purchasing practices, and mini-
mal-waste policies have earned Mocking Bird
Hill an eco-friendly reputation. With stunning
views of both the Blue Mountains and Portland's coast, it's hard not to love the place. The
owners, Barbara Walker and Shireen Aga, keep
five large dogs that can often be seen tagging
along behind their masters. The hotel is closed
every year in September.

To get to the hotel, take the first right after
Jamaica Palace and climb straight up the hill
for about 200 meters.

Sanwood Villas (San San, tel. 876/993-
7000 or 876/383-7921, rose@geejam.com,
www.geejam.com), home of GeeJam Studios
is a recording artist's paradise where the likes of
Les Nubians, No Doubt, and India.Arie have
preferred to take their working vacations. Sitting on a low hill overlooking San San Bay,
Sanwood Villas consist of the main house with
three bedrooms plus an adjoining guestroom,
and three eco-huts dispersed across the property. Inside the huts, more than the basic amenities are covered: TV, DVD, Wi-Fi, minibar.
More importantly the mattresses are comfortable, the linens soft and clean, and there's hot
water in the showers. The main house, more
of a bona fide villa, is decorated with contemporary Jamaican art and has a stylish pool out
front. At the bottom of the property is the
recording studio, a deck with whirlpool tub
crowning its roof. The studio has all the latest
gear and oversized windows overlooking the
water. While the property is specifically designed as the ideal recording retreat for a band-
sized group (US$3,000/day), it is also ideal for
couples or other kinds of retreats. Couples can
stay in the huts without meals (US$400) or
on an all-inclusive plan (US$600). Within a
five-minute walk you are on San San Beach,

with the Blue Lagoon also a stone's throw away.
Rates include a full staff.

☎ Tiamo Spa Villas (tel. 876/993-7745,
fax 954/364-7655, info@tiamospavillas.com,
www.tiamospavillas.com, US$495 and up) is
one of the area's most chic boutique hotels,
with four sleek villas dotting a gorgeous property covered with flowers overlooking San San
on one side of the hill and the mouth of the
Blue Lagoon on the other. A recently refurbished Caribbean Spa with all the modern features has been established and is the only one
of its kind in the northeast. The spa treatments
are done in a lush outdoor setting using the recently launched natural Jamaican Starfish Oils
spa products line. The rooms have all the modern amenities like flat panel TVs and DVD
players, split system AC, and ceiling fans. The
Royal Palm Master Villa evokes pure ecstasy
with one of the best views from bed available
anywhere and an adjoining sitting room with a
fireplace to take off the evening chill.

Kanopi House (contact Michael Fox, tel.
876/993-8509, cell 876/351-5083, info@kanopi
house.com, www.kanopihouse.com) is the latest addition to Port Antonio's high-end market
(US$600–1000 all-inclusive). Four self-con-
tained wooden cottages stand on stilts along
the jungle-covered slope rising from the eastern bank of the Blue Lagoon. For a Medicine
Man rush or even a spoiled-Tarzan kind of feel,
there's no place like Kanopi, and it's the only
accommodation option that actually sits on
the lagoon. The most tasteful and simple decor
adorns the cottages' exposed wood interiors.
The cottages are naturally cool in the shade
of the forest, with ceiling fans rather than air-
conditioning, and do not have TV. The bathrooms are well laid-out, and each cottage has
a wide veranda with an outdoor grill. Elaine
Williams Galimore is the sweet housekeeper
and cook. Kanopi's entrance branches off the
driveway to Dragon Bay. When the project is
complete, Kanopi is slated to have 14 one- and
two-bedroom cottages with king beds.

Villas

Port Antonio's villas are definitely some of the

nicest in Jamaica, and far less pricey than those in Ocho Rios and MoBay. Typically these villas either have breathtaking hilltop views over mountains and out to sea, or are directly on the water, like the famous Blue Lagoon Villas which comprise the most coveted real estate in Jamaica, perfectly placed between San San Bay and the Blue Lagoon. Blue Marlin, Nautilus, and Bonne Amie are among the crème de la crème. A full staff and all the amenities of home come standard in all these villas; the main difference in prices reflect principally the level of opulence you should expect. The best way to book most of the area's villas is through **Villa Vacation** (2 West St., tel. 876/993-2668, cell 876/778-3241 or 876/420-9376, yvonne. blakey@cwjamaica.com, www.villavacation. net), run by Yvonne Blakey. Yvonne lives in Port Antonio and represents many of the area owners, and can perfectly tailor your interests with a villa to put you in paradise. Most of the villas are also members of the Jamaica Association of Villas and Apartments (JAVA). The following are a few highlights from the lot rented by Villa Vacation.

Panorama (US$2,800/4,000 weekly low/ high) is the ideal vacation house for families, especially those who like deep-sea fishing. Situated at the top of a hill overlooking the most beautiful stretch of coastline in Jamaica, Panorama has an enormous barbeque grill, an open clubhouse-style living and dining area, and a pool through sliding glass doors set in the middle of a manicured lawn. Absent from Panorama is the Old World white-glove pretension present at the more over-the-top villas. The service remains impeccable with a focus on casual and efficient.

The owners of Panorama also own *La Nadine,* the best deep-sea fishing vessel in Port Antonio, and quite possibly in all of Jamaica. While not included in the price of the villa rental, a day out to sea on *La Nadine* with Captain Paul as your skipper could land you a week's worth of fish to come back and cook up on the grill. Of course, there's always a master chef on call, Timmy, who can handle any number of complexities when it comes to matters

of the palate. If you're lucky enough to taste the pumpkin soup with smoked marlin, you'll know there is a God.

Norse Hill (www.norsevillas.com, US$3,500/$4,000 weekly low/high) was built by Iris and Reidar Johanssen as their winter home. The Johanssens lived amazing lives jumping across the globe before their time in Hong Kong during the 1930s. The Norwegian-style chalet is accordingly grand and filled with art and antiques from China. Norse Hill is a steadfast, gorgeous, stately structure, with an industrial-size kitchen, three bedrooms, and a loving and dedicated staff. The master bedroom and the slightly less opulent room on the other end of the chateau both have large tiled bathrooms and oversized mirrors. Verandas look out over the pool and gardens and beyond that the wide, open sea. All the amenities are there, including DSL. The property itself is arguably the best endowed in Port Antonio. Hectares of botanical gardens sit on top of a hill looking over San San Bay. An enormous ficus tree shades the best seat in town, a real contender against Henry Morgan's Lookout, which later became Noel Coward's Firefly. The gardens have extensive pathways through lush flowerbeds.

Norse Point (US$1,400/1,750 low/high weekly) is the only one-bedroom villa in Port Antonio. The little sister property to Norse Hill, this quaint cottage lies directly across a short stretch of water from Pellew Island, between San San Beach and Blue Hole. There's no better spot in Port Antonio, nor is there a more-secluded honeymoon cottage in all of Jamaica.

Gremlin Hill (contact owner Gaia Budhai, tel. 305/534-9807, gaiamylove@yahoo .com, www.gremlinhill.com, US$2,500/3,400 weekly low/high, two-night minimum stay) has a great vantage point over Pellew Island. The artfully decorated villa has accommodations for eight. Master Chef Linette Bernard has a reputation that precedes her. The villa is a popular venue for intimate yoga and other retreats. Bookings can be made either through the owner or locally through Yvonne Blakey's Villa Vacation.

Birdie Hill (US$4,000/6,680 weekly low/high) also in the San San district, was built by the Woolworth family as Pixie Hill and given its new name under the present ownership of Lord and Lady Neidpath. The property has four bedrooms.

FOOD

Town View Restaurant & Bar (rooftop overlooking Market Square in front of Musgrave Market) serves typical dishes like curry goat, chicken foot soup, and fried chicken accompanied by rice and peas served at local rates (US$2–5).

Tropical Seafood Café (28a West St., tel. 876/715-5367, 11 a.m.–11 p.m. Mon.–Sat., US$3–14), a nice bar and grill overlooking West Harbour, is run by Michael Badarie "Mikey" (cell 876/364-5833). Fresh juices are excellent, while lunch and dinner dishes include Jamaican staples like fried and stewed chicken, curry goat, and seafood items like bussu and shrimp soup (made with river snails), steamed fish, and a seafood platter.

Nix Nax Centre (16 Harbour St., across from Texaco, tel. 876/993-2081, 8 a.m.–10 p.m. Mon.–Sat., late in morning on Sun., US$2.50–3.50) serves Jamaican favorites like fried chicken and curried goat and stewed pork. Ackee and saltfish and stewed chicken is served for breakfast daily.

Trident Restaurant (at the Trident Hotel and Villas, open to non-guests) serves international cuisine with dishes starting around US$16. It's open 8–11 a.m., noon–4 p.m., and 7–9 p.m.

The restaurant, **Mille Fleurs,** is open daily for breakfast (8–10:30 a.m.), lunch (noon–2:30 p.m.), and dinner (7–9:30 p.m.) and serves guests and non-guests alike with an alternating menu every day (chicken US$24, fish US$26).

Woody's Low Bridge Place (Drapers, tel. 876/993-7888, 10 a.m.–10 p.m. daily), run by Charles "Woody" Cousins and his charismatic wife Cherry, is definitively the coolest snack bar and restaurant in Port Antonio; it serves what is quite possibly the best burger (US$2.50) in Jamaica. Woody's Low Bridge Place opened in 1986 but Woody has been in the tourism business since '63.

Norma's at the Marina (tel. 876/993-9510, 10 a.m.–6 p.m. Tues.–Sat. and 11 a.m.–8 p.m. Sun. by beach, 4 p.m.–9:30 p.m. daily upstairs, www.normasatthemarina.com, US$10–27) is the latest of Norma Shirley's reputable establishments. This is Port Antonio's only bona fide high-end restaurant, serving dishes like lamb, steak, lobster, pork chops, shrimp, chicken, and pan-seared fish. The food at Norma's is dependably good, smoked marlin being the famous specialty appetizer.

Devon House I Scream (Errol Flynn Marina, tel. 876/993-3825) serves the best ice cream for kilometers around, but avoid the tubs that have thawed and refrozen.

Dickie's Banana (Byron's Bay, about 1.5 km west of town center, cell 876/809-6276, reservations required, hours based on demand, US$18 per person) is also known as "Best Kept Secret" since it was the winner of the Jamaica Observer's best kept secret award in 2002. It has wonderful food at a great value and even better service. Five courses are served up based on Dickie's creative culinary magic, with no ordering necessary. Just let him know if there's something you'd prefer or something you don't eat and he'll take care of the rest. For main course there's a choice of fish, chicken, goat, lobster, or vegetarian. Dickie Alvin Butler is assisted by his wife Marjorie Edwards and their son Dennis. In 2006 the restaurant underwent a substantial expansion and now the cozy room up top is complemented by a much larger space downstairs where the restaurant can now sit up to 60 people.

Dixon's Corner Store (12 Bridge St., tel. 876/993-3840, 8:30 a.m.–6:30 p.m. Mon.–Fri.) is an Ital restaurant serving excellent vegetarian dishes (US$3) like veggie chunks, veggie steak, fried whole-wheat dumplings, steamed cabbage, and saltfish. Excellent fresh juices (US$1) like sorrel and ginger are also served. Mr. and Mrs. Dixon run the place.

PORT ANTONIO

© OLIVER HILL

Dorine Simpson makes spinners, rolled pieces of dough added to the corn soup she sells on Winnifred Beach.

Veggie Delite (Clock Tower Square, tel. 876/993-3265, 8 A.M.–7:30 P.M. Mon.–Thurs., 8 A.M.–5:30 P.M. Fri., US$1.50–2.50) serves faux hot dogs, homemade veggie burgers, stew peas, pizza, tuna fish sandwiches, and veggie steaks. The restaurant opened in August 2006 with Sharon Larson as supervisor and Ernie McKenzie as cook.

Anna Banana Restaurant, Sports Bar & Grill (7 Folly Rd., tel. 876/715-6533 or contact manager Richard Titus, cell 876/352-1992) re-opened as of May 2007. Anna's serves items like club sandwiches and egg sandwiches as well as cheese omelets, and Jamaican continental breakfasts with dumpling and boiled banana, ackee and salt fish, egg and bacon (US$2–6). For lunch, fish fillet sandwich (US$8.50), shrimp salad sandwich (US$10), or chicken salad sandwich (US$6.50). Dinner items range from grilled pork chops (US$10) to a seafood platter combo with lobster, shrimp and fish (US$23). Anna Banana reopened with several new activities and services, including aerobics classes, poetry jams, free wireless Internet, disco nights, karaoke, and membership discount cards.

◖ Survival Beach Restaurant (Allan Ave., Oliver Weir cell 876/384-4730, son Everton cell 876/442-5181) is an Ital shack on the beachfront marked by yellow picket fence on East Harbour. Vegetarian food, jelly coconut, and Ital juices are served at reasonable prices (US$5–10).

Golden Happiness (2 West, tel. 876/993-2329, 10:30 A.M.–10 P.M. Mon.–Sat., 2–9 P.M. Sun.) is the best Chinese food in town, but the place lacks ambiance and is best for takeout. The food is good value (US$4–7).

Wonderful Palace Fast Food (9 Harbour St., tel. 876/993-2169, 9 A.M.–9 P.M. Mon.–Sat., 3–9 P.M. Sun., US$3–8) also has decent Chinese and Jamaican staples.

Kooya (Town Talk, Clock Tower Square, tel. 876/715-5827, contact owner/manager Stephanie, cell 876/369-9535, or Junior, the chef, cell 876/865-3911; 8 A.M.–8 P.M. daily, US$1–5.75) is a rooftop restaurant serving a mix of Jamaican and international dishes like chicken wings, pasta, fresh juices, and pastries. Tex manages Baldi's Bar, which shares the roof. Kooya offers free delivery.

Groceries

Chucky's Wholesale (21a West St., tel. 876/715-4769, 7:30 A.M.–8 P.M. Mon.–Sat.) has groceries.

Ramtulla's Supercenter (Folly Rd., tel. 876/715-5132) is the most modern supermarket in Port Antonio with the largest selection of groceries.

For groceries, also head to **Kamlyn's Supermarket and Cambio** (19 Harbour St., tel. 876/993-2140; 12 West St., tel. 876/993-4292; cambio 8:30 A.M.–5P.M. Mon.–Thurs., 8:30 A.M.–6 P.M. Fri., 8:30 A.M.–5 P.M. Sat., closed Sun.; supermarket 8:30 A.M.–7 P.M. Mon.–Thurs., 8:30 A.M.–8:30 P.M. Fri., 8:30 A.M.–9 P.M. Sat.).

Kamal's (12 West St., tel. 876/993-4292, 8:30 A.M.–8 P.M. Mon.–Sat., 9 A.M.–4 P.M. Sun.) is a grocery and cambio owned by Mr. Sinclair, who also owns Kamlyn's.

CC Bakery is at 1 West Palm Avenue (tel. 876/993-2528).

INFORMATION AND SERVICES

Don J's Computer Center (Shop 10, tel. 876/715-5559, 9 A.M.–7 P.M. Mon.–Sat.) has Internet access (US$1.50/hr). Faxing and telephone services are also offered.

Tourist Organizations

At the **Jamaica Tourist Board** (City Centre Plaza, tel. 876/993-3051 or 876/993-2117) if you're lucky you'll catch Cynthia Perry, the regional manager.

The **Jamaica Agricultural Society** (JAS, 11 Harbour St., tel. 876/993-3743, jas1@cw jamaica.com), a member of the Rural Agricultural Development Authority (RADA), has a small farmers market in the office that sells local coffee, fruit, jams, liquor, and honey. On April 20, the JAS holds an agricultural expo at the old marina by the banana wharf. The JAS motto is, "Grow what we eat, eat what we grow." Hilma Wedderburn is the parish man-ager while Keisha Campbell is the secretary. At times volunteers have come to work with the group from abroad.

Banks, Laundry, and Car Rental

ScotiaBank is located at 3 Harbour Street (tel. 876/993-2523).

For shipping services, **DHL** operates through local agent, **Port Antonio Company** (City Centre Plaza, tel. 876/993-9401 or 876/993-3617, 9 A.M.–5 P.M. Mon.–Sat.).

Ever-Brite Cleaners and Laundromat (17 West Palm, tel. 876/993-4071, 9 A.M.–8 P.M. daily.) can take care of your dirty clothes for US$5 per load.

Police and Medical Emergencies

Port Antonio Police is located at 10 Harbor Street (tel. 876/993-2546), whereas **San San Police** is at the base of San San Hill (tel. 876/993-7315).

Police advice in Port Antonio includes all the typical warnings (like don't sleep with the door wide open, watch your belongings on the beach, don't use drugs in public, and be wary of thieving prostitutes). Petty theft incidents are reported regularly, but on a whole Port Antonio is relatively crime-free compared to other areas of the island. Constable Brown and Superintendent Bowen are in charge at the Port Antonio constabulary.

Port Antonio Hospital (Naylor's Hill, tel. 876/993-2426,) is run by doctors Terry Hall and Jeremy Knight, who have a very good reputation.

Modern Dentistry's Eric Hudecek (9 West Harbour St., cell 876/860-3860 or 876/371-2068, info@modern-dentistry.de) is a highly regarded dentist with a smart, well-equipped office overlooking Navy Island. He is sought out by patients from abroad who come to Jamaica specifically to see him.

Dr. Lynvale Bloomfield (32 Harbour St., tel. 876/993-2338) has a private practice in town and also owns the **City Plaza Pharmacy** (City Center Plaza, Harbour St., tel. 876/993-2620).

PORT ANTONIO

GETTING THERE

Port Antonio is served by route taxis from Buff Bay (US$1.50) from the west and Boston (US$1.50) and Morant Bay (US$4.50) from the east. Minibuses leave twice daily for these areas from Market Square. Taxis gather in Market Square and in front of the Texaco station on Harbour Street. Most guesthouses and hotels arrange transportation from Kingston or Montego Bay airports, Kingston being the closer international airport at about 2.5 hours away.

Driving from Kingston, the shortest route (B1) passes over Hardwar Gap in the Blue Mountains before descending to the coast in Buff Bay. From Buff Bay head east along the coast until reaching Port Antonio. The road over Hardwar Gap is regularly blocked by landslides and is at times impassible for years on end. This route takes about two hours.

The alternate route from Kingston (A3) passes over Stony Hill and then through Castleton, St. Mary, and Junction before hitting the coast around Annotto Bay. When the road through the Blue Mountains is blocked, this is the quickest route between Kingston and Port Antonio, taking about two and a half hours.

A third route (A4) every bit as scenic, follows the coast east of Kingston along the southern flanks of the Blue Mountains through Morant Bay turning west at Hector's River. This route takes 2–3 hours on decent roads.

The Ken Jones Aerodrome, 10 minutes west, of Port Antonio receives flights from Kingston, Oracabessa, MoBay, and Negril with charter operators International Airlink (tel. 876/940-6660, res@intlairlink.com, www.intl airlink.com) and TimAir (tel. 876/952-2516, timair@usa.net, www.timair.net, Kingston US$642, MoBay US$537, Boscobel US$549, and Negril US$697).

GETTING AROUND

The town of Port Antonio is compact enough to get around comfortably on foot. For any of the attractions east, west, and south of town however, it is necessary to jump in a route taxi or hire a private charter. If you're feeling ener-

getic, traveling along the coast between town and Winnifred Beach or even Boston by bicycle is very feasible. Route taxis congregate by the Texaco station on Harbour Street for points east, and in Market Square for points west and south. It's easy to flag down route taxis along the main road. Expect to pay around US$1.50 for a ride a few kilometers down the coast as far as Boston.

Richard Dixon (cell 876/312-4743) is a dependable taxi man for charters, as are Indian (cell 876/866-6920); William Reid, aka Busout (cell 876/849-0867); and Aldwyne (cell 876/358-8086).

Eastern Rent-A-Car (16 West St., manager Kevin Sudeall tel. 876/993-2562 or cell 876/850-2449, www.lugan.com/east.html, eastcar@cw jamaica.com) has Toyota Yaris (US$85)/Corolla (US$75), Mitsubishi Gallant/Honda Accord (US$120), Mitsubishi Lancer (US$90), Space Wagon (US$120), and Toyota RAV4 (US$120). Longer rentals will be discounted.

Derron's Car Rental (Drapers, contact proprietor Derron Wood, tel. 876/993-7253 or cell 876/423-2449, 9 A.M.–5 P.M. Mon.–Sat.) has a small fleet of fairly new vehicles that include a Honda Civic or Toyota Corolla (US$60/day) and a Toyota Land Cruiser (US$200/day).

◖ UPPER RIO GRANDE VALLEY

Nestled between the Blue Mountains and the John Crow Mountains are the culturally rich communities of the Upper Rio Grande Valley. These include the farming communities of Millbank and Bowden Pen and the Maroon community of Moore Town. Trails including Cunha Cunha Pass lead into the lush rain forest of the Park and provide an opportunity to see the endangered Giant Swallowtail, the largest butterfly in the Western Hemisphere. The best way to get to know this area is by contacting the Maroon Council to learn from the people who have staked out this land as their own for centuries.

Nonesuch Cave and Athenry Gardens (contact site manager, Erma Wright, cell 876/425-6390, or proprietor Robert Toby, cell

PORT ANTONIO

© OLIVER HILL

The Rio Grande Valley is home to the Winward Maroons, the Giant Swallowtail Butterfly, and most of the island's endemic birds.

876/919-6656; admission US$7.50, opens on occasion) in the hills just south of Port Antonio, are on private land generally only open for group visits, which means essentially when a cruise ship is in town. The small caverns are well shy of spectacular, being filled mainly with stalactites and bats while easy-to-spot fossils recall a time when Jamaica was entirely under water. Perhaps more of an attraction is the garden surrounding the caves for its beautiful flowers and spectacular view. To get there from the east, turn inland just east of Dragon Bay, turning right at principal intersection in the small community of Sherwood Forest, and staying straight along the main road until seeing a sign for Nonesuch. From Port Antonio, head up the Rio Grande Valley and take a left at the fork in Breastworks over the bridge.

Rio Grande Rafting (tel. 876/993-5778, US$50/raft, riogranderafting@yahoo.com) is a much-touted attraction controlled by the Jamaica Tourism Board and the Tourism Product Development Corporation that operates along the banks of the wide and gentle Rio Grande River. Ninety-eight raft captains compete fiercely for clients, who once secured enjoy a sedate relaxation for a 2.5 hour ride down the river on long bamboo rafts. The captains are consistently lobbying parliament, which controls such matters, to increase the rate for the trip. To reach the start of the ride, take Breastworks Road from Port Antonio, keep right on Wayne Road in Breastworks past fellowship, and keep right following the signs to Berridale. The raft ride ends in St. Margaret's Bay by the mouth of the river. At Fellowship Crossing take a left over the bridge to Moore Town, a right for Rio Grand Rafting.

MOORE TOWN

The stronghold of Jamaica's Winward Maroons led by Colonel Wallace Sterling since 1995, Moore Town is a quiet community located along the banks of the Rio Grande about an hour's drive south of Port Antonio. Prior to the election of Colonel Sterling, the Moore Town Maroons were led by Colonel C.L.G. Harris (from 1964), and before him, it was Colonel Ernest Downer (from 1952).

Colonel Wallace Sterling can organize B&B-style home stays (cell 876/898-5714, US$30/person) in the community, as well as hikes to Nanny Town farther up into the mountains. It's a two- to three-day hike round-trip that will cost US$100 per person for guides, food, and shelter. If you don't bring your own tent, guides will use materials from the bush to make shelter at night. Along the way you're likely to pick up a few basic Maroon words like "Medysie," meaning "thank you." If you are unable to reach Colonel Sterling, Moore Town Maroon Council Secretary Charmaine Shackleford (cell 876/867-6939) can also help arrange home stay visits and guides and ensure someone will be able to open the gate at Bump Grave.

The Maroons have maintained their customs throughout the years, as well as their language, a mix of West African tongues brought by captured slaves who belonged to the Ahanti, Fanti, Akan, Ibo, Yoruba, and Congo peoples, among others.

Sights

Bump Grave (admission based on donation) is the final resting place of Nanny, the legendary Maroon leader and Jamaica's only national heroine. It's the principal attraction in Moore Town; a plaque and monument recall her glorious leadership and victory over British forces who tried unsuccessfully to conquer the Maroons. Bump Grave is fenced off, but the gate can be opened by the caretaker of the school located across the road. Call to alert the Colonel or Maroon Council Secretary of your arrival to ensure someone is around to open the gate.

Nanny Falls is a small waterfall within an easy hour's walk from Moore Town. Ask any local to indicate where the trail starts just above Nanny's grave. There is also an alternate, longer route, about three hours round-trip, if you're looking for more of a workout. The Colonel can help arrange a guide (US$10).

The **Moore Town Maroon Cultural Center** is at time of writing still in the conceptual stages,

while there is adequate momentum from the Maroon Council and the Institute of Jamaica to guarantee that the project will develop over the coming years. The concept is to establish a museum and cultural center for the exhibition and preservation of Maroon heritage. Young people will be taught to make and play drums and the *abeng*, a traditional Maroon horn used to communicate over great distances. The *abeng* is said to have struck fear into the hearts of the British, who were never able to conquer the Maroons. Craft items, toys, and a whole range of items considered to be the rudiments of the Maroon culture are also to be produced, and the center will have an adjoining gift shop and restaurant to accommodate visitors. "We are looking at a living thing rather than strictly an exhibition of the past," Colonel Sterling said about the project. The Maroon Council is currently working with UNESCO and the IOJ in developing the plans and securing funding.

Accommodations

Ambassabeth Cabins (Bowden Pen, Lennette Wilks, cell 876/395-5351 or 876/381-1528, US$50 per cabin, sleeps 2–4; US$25 for a tent that can sleep eight) is the most remote accommodation option in the Rio Grande Valley, located above Millbank at the uppermost reaches. The famous Cunha Cunha Pass Trail leaves from there, as does the White River Trail leading to a series of cascades. There is an unmanned ranger station maintained by Ms. Wilks in Millbank, just over the border into St. Thomas two miles before reaching Bowden Pen. The Quack River and White River Falls are both nearby. Ms. Wilks can arrange trail guides and meals, as well as cultural entertainment. There are a total of eight cabins, which can house up to 20 people. Cabins have beds with sheets and blankets; towels and bug dope should be brought along. One cabin has private shower bath and the others share common facilities. There's also an indoor dining and recreation area. Cabins come with breakfast, rundung with fish or vegetables.

Millbank is 17 miles up the river valley from Port Antonio; as an alternative to the route from the Rio Grande Valley, there is a well-established 5.5-mile trail from Hayfield, St. Thomas. Trained guides at Ambassabeth are knowledgeable in biodiversity and local cultural history. The Cunha Cunha Pass Trail connects Portland and St. Thomas over the Blue Mountains, where a lookout point at Cunha Cunha gives spectacular views.

Getting There and Around

Barrett Adventures (contact Captain Carolyn Barrett, Barrett Adventures, cell 876/382-6384, info@barrettadventures.com, www.barrett adventures.com) offers transportation to and from the Blue and John Crow Mountains well as a hiking expedition, both from the Portland side as well as from Kingston.

East of Port Antonio

The region east of Port Antonio is dominated by the John Crow Mountains, which run northwest to southeast and butt up against the Blue Mountains, where they meet with steep slopes falling down to the sea near Hector's River. The John Crow Mountains are some of the less-traversed territory on the island, and even the coast in the area, which varies from fine sandy beaches to windswept bluffs, sees few visitors. A few minutes' drive east of Port Antonio, Boston is a quiet community that is said to be the original home of jerk. Long Bay is the area's predominant tourist strip, though it only has a handful of budget accommodations serving a trickle of backpackers and adventurous travelers.

BOSTON

Boston was bustling in the early years of the banana trade when it took the name of the North American city that made it prosperous for a brief period. Boston is the so-called origin of jerk seasoning, but the **Boston Jerk Center** that claims this fame has become overrun with hustlers unmindful of the fact that their harassment has damaged the area's reputation. The jerk center is easily recognizable on the western edge of the community of Boston Bay just before crossing a bridge and going over a rise in the road heading toward Port Antonio. Max (cell 876/435-3013) operates one of the newer stalls and may just be a good bet where integrity is concerned. Many will insist you buy their "noni juice," said to have aphrodisiacal properties and to improve

overall performance; others will simply beg for money. Beyond the annoyance, there are also serious inconsistencies in the quality and pricing of food at Boston Jerk Center. Weekends when it gets busier are the best time to take a stab if you must eat where jerk is said to have originated, as during the week the meat can sit on the grill until it goes cold before someone comes along to eat it. Fish is also served, but this is not the best place for it. If you do order fish, size it and understand what you will pay before it gets cooked. The best time to eat jerk in is during the annual Portland Jerk Festival (July) when the multitudes don't let the meat sit around for long before eating it up. Based in Boston in years past, the festival has been relocated recently to Port Antonio's Folly Oval.

Boston Beach (free) is on a picturesque cove with turquoise waters that sees more local than foreign visitors, especially on weekends. Boston Bay can have a decent swell suitable for surfing and is the only place around where you can rent boogie-boards and surfboards.

Accommodations and Food

Great Huts (overlooking the water near the Jerk Center, cell 876/353-3388 or 876/993-8888, drpaulshalom@yahoo.com, www.great huts.com) is a stylishly rustic accommodation in the heart of Boston, offering Bedouin-style tents (US$25/person) and tree houses (US$115) with meals served to order. The place was developed by Paul Rhodes, an American doctor who has practiced extensively in Jamaica.

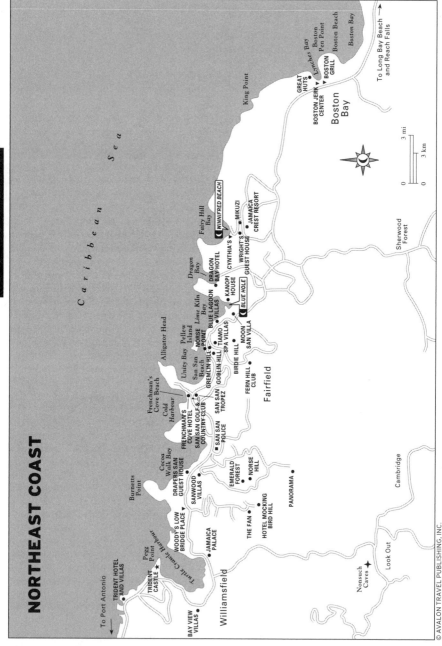

NORTHEAST COAST

Caribbean Sea

To Port Antonio

TRIDENT HOTEL AND VILLAS

TRIDENT CASTLE

Pegg Point

Turtle Crawle Harbour

BAY VIEW VILLAS

WOODY'S LOW BRIDGE PLACE

JAMAICA PALACE

Williamsfield

Burnetts Point

Cocoa Walk Bay

DRAPERS SAN GUEST HOUSE

SANWOOD VILLAS

THE FAN

HOTEL MOCKING BIRD HILL

PANORAMA

Look Out

Nonsuch Caves

Cambridge

EMERALD FOREST

NORSE HILL

SAN SAN POLICE

Frenchman's Cove Beach

Cold Harbour

FRENCHMAN'S COVE HOTEL

SAN SAN GOLF & COUNTRY CLUB

SAN SAN TROPEZ

Alligator Head

Unity Bay

San San Beach

Pellew Island

Lime Kiln Bay

NORSE POINT

GREMLIN HILL

GOBLIN HILL

TIAMO VILLAS

SPA VILLAS

BIRDIE HILL

MOON SAN VILLA

FERN HILL CLUB

Fairfield

BLUE LAGOON VILLAS

BLUE HOLE

KANOPI HOUSE

Dragon Bay

DRAGON BAY HOTEL

WRIGHT'S GUEST HOUSE

CYNTHIA'S

Fairy Hill Bay

WINNIFRED BEACH

MIKUZI

JAMAICA CREST RESORT

Sherwood Forest

King Point

Boston Bay

GREAT HUTS

BOSTON JERK CENTER

BOSTON GRILL

Lynches Bay

Boston Pen Point

Boston Beach

Long Bay

To Long Bay Beach and Reach Falls

3 mi

3 km

0

0

© AVALON TRAVEL PUBLISHING, INC.

Charles Town Maroons led by Frank Lumsden are known to make an appearance on Friday evenings for drumming sessions.

Boston Jerk Grill (cell 876/878-5015 or 876/993-8093, garnetk13@hotmail.com, open from 10 A.M.–late, restaurant closed on Sun.) may be a better option than the neighboring Jerk Center. It's also a good place for local dishes, with friendly management under Garnet King. King can arrange catering as well. Fried chicken, brown-stewed pork (US$5), and grilled lobster (US$10) represent the range of items on the menu. The bar is open daily.

LONG BAY

Long Bay is a sleepy fishing village with one of the most picturesque and unspoiled beaches in Jamaica. A few low-key accommodation spots have sprung up over the past decade serving a trickle of off-the-beaten track travelers. Long Bay's beach is also known for having a decent swell on occasion and draws surfers from nearby Boston Bay as well as the die-hard Mystic crew from Jamnesia in Bull Bay, St. Andrew. At times the current can be quite strong; precaution is always advised.

One of the most curious attractions, if it can be called that, in Long Bay is the home of the late Ken Abendana Spencer, one of Jamaica's most prolific and noted painters of the 20th century. The building, located on Pen Lane a few hundred meters inland from Fisherman's Park, resembles a science fiction scene from Batman or Mad Max, with a 10-meter-high wall built to keep out thieves, according to Spencer's common-law wife, Charming (cell 876/412-4116). Charming resides in the first floor of the immense structure built in the vein of a castle, but never completed. Charming's two sons, Ken Abendana Spencer Jr. ("Jr.," cell 876/448-7374) and Kensington Spencer ("Hopie," cell 876/429-7380) also live on the property and receive guests, who can tour the surreal building and purchase Spencer' paintings created by both father, and son Jr., also an artist who inherited his father's style.

Accommodations

Blue Heaven Resort (tel. 876/913-7014, cell.

tel. 876/420-5970, www.blueheavenjamaica .com, info@blueheavenjamaica.com) has two very basic cottages for a total of three rooms on a private cove just west of Long Bay Beach. The two adjoining rooms rent for US$30 per night, while the stand-alone "Sunrise Cottage," which sits closest to the water's edge, goes for US$60 (all are double occupancy). A kitchen and bathroom adjoin the rooms. Owner/manager Natasha Duncan includes hot breakfast in the nightly rate, and longer stays are open to some price negotiation.

Seascape (near the gas station, David is the manager, tel. 876/913-7762 or 876/913-7808, cell 876/890-7661, www.jamaica-beachvillas .com, US$60) has six basic but comfortable rooms in two beachfront houses with double and queen beds, fans, and hot water. The lounge has a TV and CD player.

Yahimba (tel. 876/402-4101, info@ yahimba.com, www.yahimba.com, US$75/ night), owned by Rasta-inspired Lizzy Bentley, has three thatch-roofed wooden cottages directly on the sand. It's the best place to stay in Long Bay for its cleanliness, charm and the attention paid to maintenance and service. Nonetheless, it is closer to rustic than Ritz, but glamour won't be missed when you're steps from the lapping sea. Erica McDonald, the housekeeper, and Shellica Green, assistant property manager, are always nearby.

Likkle Paradise (tel. 876/913-7702 or 876/ 913-7475, US$30), marked by a small sign across the road from Yahimba, is run by Ms. Herlette and is the best deal in Long Bay, with clean and proper bedding in its one bedroom with a queen bed, verandah, kitchen, and bathroom.

Morgan's Glass House Guest House (across from the Texaco gas station on the beach, contact Letecia Cunningham, aka Mama Lue, tel. 876/913-7475, cell 876/891-0516, US$40–50) is a basic guest house with two rooms downstairs, each with two twin beds and a shared bath and a big kitchen and living room, and three rooms upstairs, two with one double bed each, and one with two

© OLIVER HILL

Chill Out Beach Bar & Restaurant on the eastern end of Long Bay is the best spot around for a drink or a meal.

twin beds. There is a kitchen upstairs with living room and shared bath. The bigger rooms go for the higher rate.

Food

The **Glass House,** owned by the Morgan's and managed by Mama Lou, and **Sweet Daddy** next door are the best places for typical Jamaican dishes at local rates (US$3–5).

Chill Out Beach Bar & Restaurant (tel. 876/931-7171, cell tel. 876/471-4722, 10 A.M.–10 P.M. daily) is the number one spot on the beach for a bite or a drink. Chill Out hosts dances on special occasions. Local dishes and excellent seafood is served.

Fisherman's Park (corner of Pen Lane and the main road, contact manager Wayne, cell 876/350-4815, 7 A.M.–9 P.M. daily, US$3–8.50) is an open-air bar and restaurant on the west side of town that serves fish when available in addition to Jamaican staples.

❰ **Sweet Daddy** (next to Morgan's Glass House, contact Mama Lue, tel. 876/913-7475, cell 876/891-0516, US$2–5, 7–11 A.M. Mon.–Sat., 7 A.M.–9 P.M. Sun.) serves baked or fried chicken, and curry goat with rice and peas. Fish is served based on availability.

MANCHIONEEL

Portland's most quintessentially authentic seaside village, Manchioneel sees few visitors; a small fisherman's beach known as Sandshore, on the east end of the community, is the main attraction.

Accommodations and Food

Uncle Lenny's (Castle, tel. 876/913-1680, 8:30 A.M.–9 P.M. Mon.–Fri., US$2.50–3) serves tasty local dishes like stew beef, stew peas, and fried chicken.

Hotel Jamaican Colors (Ross Craig district, cell 876/893-5185, 876/407-4412, or 876/916-7713, jamaican@anbell.net, www.hotel jamaicancolors.com, US$65) is run by a nice French couple Martine and Robert Bourseguin who live on property with their son Romain. Rooms are basic but comfortable, with fans and TV. A nice pool and hot tub are located in front of the dining area. There is one larger cottage that holds six (US$135).

Ras Johnson's Christmas River Ranch and Bar (contact property managers "16," cell 876/362-3049, or Paul, cell 876/449-7593) has a rustic cottage (the "ranch") that can be rented (US$30 for up to 3 persons) with food prepared on request (fish US$6, chicken US$5). The cottage is located in a picturesque little clearing along the banks of the Christmas River on a curve in the road known as See-Me-No-More near the hamlet of Kensington. A driveway leads down the nice, flat grassy area by the river's mouth just before crossing a bridge over the river heading east. Ras Johnson, 16's brother, owns the property and lives with his wife in Germany. The property is also known as "Zimmerfrei," which means "ranch" in German.

Zion Country (just east of Manchioneel, Free-I, cell 876/871-3623, US$42) has four basic rooms that have a sea-view balcony, fan, and hammock. Each room has two single beds with shared bathrooms. To get there keep straight at the sharp bend in the main road following the signs on the eastern end of Manchioneel.

Morant Bay

St. Thomas parish holds an important place in Jamaican history. In the early colonial period, its mountainous terrain played an important role in providing sanctuary to the runaway slaves who formed the Maroon settlements of eastern Jamaica. Later, it became an important sugar- and banana-producing region under British rule. And finally, with the slaves freed but not being permitted advancement in society, the parish erupted in a rebellion that gave birth to Jamaica's labor rights movement.

At the center of what was once some of Jamaica's prime sugarcane land, Morant Bay is a laid-back town with little action beyond the central market. Between Morant Bay and Port Morant, 11 kilometers to the east, there are a couple of basic accommodation options which make a convenient base for exploring the rivers and valleys that cut across the southern slopes of the Blue Mountains as well as the isolated beaches and Great Morass on Jamaica's easternmost tip.

SIGHTS

The burning **Morant Bay Courthouse** played a central role in spurring the Morant Bay Rebellion of 1865, in which disenfranchised poor led by Paul Bogle revolted against the local government and the white planters—sending tremors through the British Empire. A **statue of Paul Bogle** created by Jamaican art pioneer

Edna Manley, wife of Peoples National Party founder Norman Manley, stands in front of the courthouse. The building was in use until early 2007 as the St. Thomas Parish Council offices before it was, once again, gutted by fire. A historic marker by the statue honors the many patriots buried behind the building "whose sacrifice paved the way for the independence of Jamaica."

The **Morant Bay Market** on the main road has an excellent stock of produce and a fish market in the back that rivals that of Downtown Kingston. It is a great place to stop for a stroll around to take in a bustling market.

Lorna's Crafts (cell 876/396-9337) has some nice Jamaican crafts, jewelry, and Rastafarian motif goods in the Old Arcade.

East Fest (Goodyear Oval, Springfield, St. Thomas) is held annually on Boxing Day (December 24). The event is organized and hosted by the cultural reggae group Morgan Heritage (www.morganheritagemusic.com).

PRACTICALITIES

Dave's Place (cell 876/461-3103) just past Scotia serves good chicken.

ScotiaBank is located at 23 Queen Street (tel. 876/982-2310), and **NCB** is at 39 Queen Street (tel. 876/982-2225).

The Morant Bay **Police Station** (guard office tel. 876/982-2233, for the crime office

PAUL BOGLE AND THE MORANT BAY REBELLION

Paul Bogle was the founding deacon at the Native Baptist Church in Stony Gut, St. Thomas, a village at the base of the Blue Mountains about five miles inland from Morant Bay. Bogle founded a church where African elements similar to those found in Revival were strong and a black pride ethos was a central doctrine. Baptist churches throughout Jamaica provided an alternate philosophy to the Anglican church, which had descended from the Church of England and for the most part represented the suppressive mandate of the white planter class and government. Bogle used the church as a base to gather support for a militant resistance movement, similar to that envisioned by Sam Sharpe in the Christmas rebellion 34 years earlier in that violence was not the intended means.

Bogle lived in the post-emancipation period during which the vast majority of his fellow men were denied suffrage, justice, and equal rights, while he, a mulatto landowner, was one of 106 persons in the parish allowed a vote. The five years leading up to the Morant Bay Rebellion coincided with the American Civil War (1861-1865), which complicated the economy of Jamaica. Local food shortages owing to floods and drought, combined with a slump in imports from the fragmented United States, created a mood in Jamaica rife with discontent. While the white ruling class controlled both the legislature and the economy, the poor

felt subjugated and left to fend for themselves in difficult times. Petty crimes rooted in widespread poverty and social decay were dealt with by severe punishment by local authorities responding to the landowners.

Meanwhile, Governor Eyre blamed the condition of poor on laziness and apathy, while Baptist Missionary Society secretary Edward Underhill sent a letter to British Secretary of State for the Colonies outlining concerns about poverty and distress among the poor black population. The so-called Underhill Letter spurred a series of civic meetings known as the Underhill Meetings, which provided a public forum for the poor to voice their discontent. Mulatto legislator George William Gordon, Bogle's comrade both in the church and in politics, led several such well-attended meetings in Kingston and elsewhere in which he criticized the colonial government.

On October 7, 1865, Bogle and some followers staged a protest at the Morant Bay courthouse disputing severe judgments made on that particular day. When a standoff with the police came to blows, arrest warrants were issued against 28 of the protesters, including Paul Bogle. After the police were deterred from arresting Bogle by a large crowd of his followers in Stony Gut, they returned to Morant Bay and told the Custos of Bogle's plans to disrupt a meeting of the Vestry on

876/734-7111) is located just off the main road through town at 7 South Street.

EAST OF MORANT BAY

In **Stony Gut,** eight kilometers north of Morant Bay, a marker placed by the JNHT indicates Paul Bogle's birthplace and the place where his Revival Baptist church once stood. To get there, head inland at the center of town to Morant where a right turn leads to the nondescript hamlet of Stony Gut.

Heading straight in Morant leads to Seaforth, a small community along the Morant River. North of the main intersection you

soon come to a bridge across the river where the road forks. A right leads further up the river to **Sunny Hill,** an important Rastafarian center in St. Thomas where occasional Groundations are held. It is said one of the first Rasta communes was formed in Trinity Ville, near Sunny Hill as early as 1934. For info on upcoming Rasta-related events contact St. Thomas native Karl Wilson (cell 876/439-1471). Alternatively, for Rasta events island-wide, including those at Sunny Hill, contact Paul Reid, known as Iyatolah (cell 876/850-3469) or Charlena McKenzie, known as Daughter Dunan (cell 876/843-

October 11. The Custos sent an appeal to the Governor for assistance and called out the local volunteer militia. The next day Bogle and 400 followers confronted the militia in Morant Bay; during the ensuing violence, the courthouse was burned and the Custos killed along with 18 deputies and militiamen. Seven of Bogle's men were also killed in the fighting, which quickly spread throughout the parish. Several white planters were killed, kidnapped, or hurt and, as the news spread throughout the island, fear of a more generalized uprising and race war grew, prompting Governor Eyre to declare martial law and dispatch soldiers from Kingston and Newcastle. The Winward Maroons were also armed after offering their services, and it was they who ultimately captured Bogle, bringing him to a swift trial and ensuing death sentence in Morant Bay. George William Gordon was also implicated in the Rebellion, taken to Morant Bay, and hanged. Martial law lasted for over a month following the rebellion, during which time hundreds were killed by soldiers or executed by court martial while over 1,000 houses were burned by government forces. Little regard was taken for differentiating innocent from guilty, augmenting a general sense of fear in St. Thomas and around the island.

The Morant Bay Rebellion pushed Britain to discuss the blatant injustices in its colony asset in the West Indies. Governor Eyre was ultimately removed from his post for excessive use of force while English Parliament debated whether he was a murderer or hero. Many sought to indict him on murder charges for the execution of George William Gordon, but others, including the Anglican clergy, supported his actions as a necessary means to uphold the control of the Crown.

Meanwhile, the Jamaica House of Assembly, which had operated as an independent legislative body since 1655, was dissolved and Jamaica became a Crown Colony under the direct rule of England. In the following years, the colonial power ushered in more egalitarian measures that lessened the power that had been exerted by the landed elite for centuries.

Paul Bogle and George William Gordon were considered troublemakers and virtually expelled from the national psyche through the remainder of the colonial period. At independence their memory was rekindled as Jamaica began to come to terms with its past and contemplate its identity and future. At the 100th anniversary of the Morant Bay Rebellion, Bogle and Gordon were featured prominently and were declared national heroes in 1969 when the order was created. Today the rebellion is remembered during National Heritage Week and Heroes Weekend, which coincides with the anniversary of the uprising the second week in October.

3227) at Jamaica's Nyabinghi headquarters in Scott's Pass, Clarendon.

Reggae Falls is a popular spot for locals to come splash around and jump off the large rocks along the river. There is a hut nearby where drinks and food are served.

A left across the bridge at the intersection in Seaforth leads to Mt. Lebanus, a picturesque district with fruit trees growing along the river, which has lots of pools suitable for swimming.

Port Morant

Overgrown and noticeably forgotten today, Port Morant was at one time very busy exporting barrels of sugar, rum, and bananas. Today there is an oyster operation on the eastern side of the harbor bordering the mangroves that reaches down to Bowden across the bay. The oyster growing area is protected from fishing and serves as a spawning area as well. Several fishermen keep their boats on the waterfront and can be contracted to tour the mangroves and visit the lighthouse on Point Morant. Karl Wilson (cell 876/439-1471), director of the St. Thomas Environmental Protection Agency, has been working with fishermen and other local groups to encourage sustainable use of the vast mangrove reserve, one of Jamaica's last untouched marine wilderness areas. Karl can arrange marine tours as well as mountain tours to the best sights in the area.

The **Morant Point Lighthouse** sits on Jamaica's easternmost point. Cast of iron in London, the 30-meter tall lighthouse was erected in 1841 by Kru indentured Africans brought in the post-emancipation period. There is a beautiful, desolate beach along Holland Bay just north of Morant Point. To get there, head east from the village of Golden Grove through the Duckenfield Sugar Plantation. Four-wheel-drive is essential in the rainy season, but otherwise it is possible to get through without it.

Stokes Hall Great House, located in the parish of St. Thomas near Golden Grove, was built by Luke Stokes. A former governor of the island of Nevis, he came to Jamaica shortly after the conquest of the island by the British. Like many of the early houses it was built in a strategic location and was securely fortified.

Stokes Hall Great House was destroyed by the 1907 earthquake and today stands in ruin. The house is currently owned by the Jamaica National Heritage Trust but not managed by anyone.

◖ Bath Hot Springs

The town of Bath was erected using government resources and had a brief history of glamour as a fashionable second-home community for the island's elite. The splendor was short-lived, however, and the town quickly declined to become a backwater—as it remains today.

Bath Mineral Spring or "The Bath of St. Thomas the Apostle" as it is properly called, was discovered by the runaway slave Jacob in 1695 on the estate of his master, Colonel Stanton. Jacob found that the warm waters of the spring healed leg ulcers that had plagued him for years and he braved possible punishment to return to the plantation to relate his discovery to Stanton. In 1699 the spring and surrounding land was sold to the government for £400. In 1731 the government allocated £500 to develop the bath and a road to the spring, and a small town was built.

The hot springs are located 180 meters north of the **Bath Hotel and Spa,** itself located about three kilometers on a precariously narrow, windy road north of the town of Bath. An easy-to-follow path leads to the source, where water comes out from the rocks piping hot on one side and cold on the other. There are massage therapists on hand who use wet towels to give an exhilarating treatment, albeit exorbitantly priced (typically around US$14). These masseurs are either lauded or despised by visitors and can be quite aggressive in offering their services from below the gate of the hotel. Some visitors swear by their technique, however, which involves slopping hot towels over the backs of their subjects.

For a more institutional bath, the **Bath Hotel and Spa** (tel. 876/703-4345, US$50 private bath, US$33 shared bath) has traditional Turkish-style tiled tubs, as well as more modern whirlpool tubs. There are three rates for a dip, depending on how many are enjoying the tub: US$6 for one person, US$8.50 for two, or US$11 for three. The water at bath is mineral-heavy. It is suggested that bathers stay in the water for 15–20 minutes to derive full benefit.

Basic rooms in the hotel have either private bath or shared bath. Meals (US$8.50–10) are served throughout the day and range from rotisserie chicken to curried shrimp.

Bath Botanical Garden

Bath Botanical Garden was established by the government in 1779, and is the second-oldest garden of its kind in the Western Hemisphere (one in St. Vincent dates from 1765). The garden retains little of its former glory as a propagation site for many of Jamaica's most important introduced plants including jackfruit, breadfruit, cinnamon, bougainvillea, and croton. A stand of royal palms lines the road by its entrance, and a two-century-old Barringtonia graces the derelict grounds.

From the western side of Bath, a road runs north to Hayfield, where an 8.8-kilometer well-maintained trail provides an alternate route over the Blue Mountains to the Rio Grande

Valley. If you're heading to Portland, head east along the Plaintain Garden River to where the main road east of Bath hits the A4 a few miles west of Amity Hall.

Accommodations
Whispering Bamboo Cove Resort (105 Crystal Dr. retreat, just east of Morant Bay, tel. 876/982-2912 or 876/982-1788, US $75/80 mountain view/ocean view) is a decent accommodations option with 15 rooms run by Marcia Bennet. Rooms have TV, hot water, and air-conditioning, except one mountain view room which has a fan instead of a/c (US$60).

Brown's Guesthouse (tel. 876/982-6205, cable, a/c, hot water, US$40) is a basic rest with six rooms owned by Neason Brown. Food can be prepared to order. To get there, follow the main road towards Prospect and look out for a sign just east of Whispering Bamboo on the ocean side of the road.

WEST OF MORANT BAY
The road west of Morant Bay towards Kingston hugs the coast, passing through dusty communities where jerk vendors and a few shops mark the centers of the action. This is an area most people just pass through. There are a few notable stops, however, but few accommodation options beyond a few quickie joints before reaching Bull Bay in St. Andrew.

White Horses
Just east of White Horses you arrive at **Rozelle Falls,** where locals often congregate to wash or cool off. The falls are visible from the main road (A4).

The **Ethiopian Zion Coptic Church** (service on Sat.) has its headquarters at Crighton Hall in White Horses just before reaching Yallahs, where it sits on more than 600 hectares of land. To get there turn inland off the main road (A4) by a set of fruit vendors in the middle of White Horses. Coptic Road is on the left marked with a sign. Said to be 20 million strong, the Ethiopian Zion Coptic Church is led by Everton Shand, chief elder, and spiritual

leader Brother Shine. Niah Keith and Brother Love were the founders of the original Coptic Church in Jamaica, while the institution originates in Ethiopia where it was the official Imperial church for ages from ancient Egypt. A large tablet that dates from 1738 written in Old English was found during excavations and is on display. Many of Jamaica's roots reggae artists have attended the Ethiopian Zion Coptic Church. The White Horses Kumina Group, Upliftment hosts cultural and sports events in the community on a regular basis.

Yallahs
Sixteen kilometers west of Morant Bay, large **salt ponds** can be seen along the coast marking the approach to Yallahs. These ponds were once used as a source for salt and are home to brine shrimp and yellow butterflies. The name Yallahs is derived from the surname of a Spanish family that settled there to raise cattle on a ranch known as **Hato de Ayala.** The road inland from the center of Yallahs leads up along the river to Bethel Gap and from there deeper into the mountains ultimately reaching Hagley Gap on a poor road traversable only by four-wheel-drive vehicles. Eleven kilometers north of Yallahs across the river from Easington is Judgment Cliff, which collapsed during the earthquake of 1692—burying an entire valley in judgment, it is said, of the Dutchman who maltreated slaves on his plantation. Nevertheless, judgment was not justice and most of his slaves died alongside him under the weight of a small mountain.

About 1.5 kilometers west of Yallahs, the broad washed-out **Yallahs River** overflows during periods of heavy rain, and dries completely for much of the year near its mouth due to dry, pebbly soil along its bed. At 37 kilometers from its source to the sea, it's one of Jamaica's longest rivers, starting 1,371 meters up and running down the principal trough along the base of the southern slopes of the Blue Mountains. Along the way, it is fed by several tributaries. Bridges built across the Yallahs have a tendency to disappear during hurricanes and are replaced routinely. For most of the year the riverbed near its mouth can be forded with no sign of water. The Yallahs River feeds the Mona Reservoir next to UWI via an above-ground pipe. Along with the Hope River, it is a major water source for the metropolitan area. There are decent beaches around Yallahs: Bailey's Beach to the east and Flemarie Beach just west of town.

Links Seafood Restaurant & Lounge (cell 876/703-3927, 10 A.M.–10 P.M. Mon.–Sat.) on Fleming Beach is a nice chill-out spot to get some grub on the waterfront.

West of Yallahs just shy of the St. Andrew border, Eleven Mile is a small community known as the old stomping ground of legendary Jack Mansong, aka "Three-Finger Jack." A runaway slave, Three-Finger Jack became a bandit who took justice into his own hands in the vein of a Jamaican Robin Hood. He wreaked terror on the plantocracy and tried to kill a slave trader before ultimately being captured by Maroon leader Quashie, who carried his head to Spanish Town to collect the £300 reward.

West of Port Antonio

The road west of Port Antonio runs along the coast cutting inland occasionally through several small towns including St. Margaret's Bay, Hope Bay, and Buff Bay before reaching the border with St. Mary just east of Annotto Bay. The region is characteristically lush with fruit vendors and roadside shops intermittently along the road. Apart from Somerset Falls on the eastern edge of Hope Bay, the area is void of developed tourist attractions, but the sparsely populated coastline is in itself enticing and for the adventurous looking for secluded beaches, there are great opportunities for exploring around Orange Bay.

From Buff Bay, the B1 heads inland climbing past Charles Town into the Blue Mountains and affording great views. This is the route on which Blue Mountain Bicycle Tours operates.

ST. MARGARET'S BAY

The quiet seaside village of St. Margaret's Bay is notable principally as the end point for the rafts coming down the Rio Grande. There are a few accommodation options and a notable craft shop, **Jah Tobs Crafts** (tel. 876/913-3242) making Rasta-style knits and other craft items including tams, belts, swimsuits, bags, chains, calabash purses, and much more.

Accommodations and Food

Paradise Inn (tel. 876/993-5169, paradiseinn295@hotmail.com, US$35–60) located along the main road (A4), has nine rooms, some with two double beds, others with one double. Rooms have balconies, some of which face the road, others face the sea, while some rooms have both. Cable TV, ceiling fans, and hot water come standard. Four rooms have kitchenettes.

◖ **Rio Vista Resort Villas** (on the eastern banks of the Rio Grande, tel. 876/993-5444, fax 876/993-5445, riovistavillaja@jamweb .net, www.riovistajamaica.com, US$75–115) has 12 rooms in total, with one-bedroom cottages (US$155) suitable for a couple and two-bedroom cottages that sleep four (US$185). To get there, turn right up the hill just around the corner after crossing the Rio Grande heading east. The "room with a view" is perhaps the nicest cottage, with a private balcony overlooking the river, which can also be seen from the inviting king bed. Henry and Sharon Miller own Rio Vista and live on-property. Some of the rooms have a view up the Rio Grande towards the Blue Mountains.

Rafter's Rest (tel. 876/993-5778) is where the bamboo rafts pull in at the end of the 2.5-hour journey. There is a restaurant serving Jamaican staples (US$5–15) and bar overlooking the river. The river is fit for swimming and there is a beach where the river meets the sea.

HOPE BAY
Sights
Somerset Falls (about 3 km east of Hope Bay,

tel. 876/913-0046, info@somersetfallsjamaica
.com, www.somersetfallsjamaica.com, 9 A.M.–
5 P.M. daily, US$7 adults, US$3.50 children)
is a great place to stop for a dip. The falls are
reached by rowboat through cavernous cliffs
surrounding a narrow inlet. Rocky is one of the
more talented boatmen you'll find. There is a
bar and restaurant (US$5–11) and occasionally
large events are staged. The park has a number
of caged birds, and once had deer that escaped
in a hurricane. Mark (tel. 876/853-3498) is a
Somerset Falls guide.

Pauline Petinaud, aka "Sister P" (cell 876/
426-1957) recently moved her African-Jamai-
can **crafts shop** and guest house from Port
Antonio to Hope Bay, where she rents two
basic rooms with common kitchen and bath
for budget-minded travelers (US$30). Sister
P, not to be confused with PNP politician
Portia Simpson-Miller of the same pet name,
is an important figure behind the movement
to celebrate in a more concerted manner the
African heritage inherent in Jamaican culture. Her craft shop sells African-inspired
Jamaican items as well as a variety of African imports, but perhaps she is best known
for her founding role in the annual African-
heritage festival, Fi Wi Sinting, which translates as "something for us." (See sidebar, *Fi
Wi Sinting*.)

I-tal Village (cell 876/898-5323, info@ital
village.com, www.italvillage.com, US$30/40
low/high season) is a mellow Rasta-inspired
simplistic living retreat about three kilometers
off the main road near Orange Bay. The retreat
is near 6.5 kilometers of volcanic beaches that
see virtually no outside visitors. Ital (natural)
food is served to order.

BUFF BAY AND CHARLES TOWN

Buff Bay is a dusty coastal town along the route
between Port Antonio and points west. There
is little to keep visitors in the area and few accommodation options. In the hills a few minutes inland along the B1, Charles Town is a
Maroon community where a cultural heritage
tour with the local Maroon Colonel Frank

Lumsden makes a detour away from the coast
worth it for a few hours' visit.

The most impressive structures in Buff
Bay are the **courthouse** and the **St. George
Anglican Church** located across the street. St.
George was the official church for the parish
of St. George before it became part of Portland
in 1867. The present cut-stone structure dates
from 1814, but the foundation is much older.
Both the church and the courthouse, which
is still in use, can be accessed during business
hours, and service is held on Sundays.

Three kilometers above Buff Bay along
what used to be an old Maroon bridal path
up the Buff Bay River (now known as the B1)
is the Maroon community of Charles Town.
There is a **museum** (free admission) of Maroon
heritage and a refreshment stop by the river.
Charles Town Maroon Colonel Frank Lumsden (cell 876/445-2861) or Ken Douglass (cell
876/427-1303) will lead visitors on community
tours and on one-hour hikes (US$10) to the
ruins of an 18th-century coffee plantation. A
traditional country-style lunch (US$12) can
be arranged at Quaco Village to try traditional
dishes like rundown, saltfish, green sweet potato, and pumpkin. There is an area where you
can pitch a tent in Charleston, but guest rooms
are not available.

Practicalities

Blueberry Hill Guest House (Kildare district,
near the Digicel phone tower, contact Devon or
Doris Williams, cell 876/913-6814, US$40–50)
has seven rooms with private bath, standing
fans, and cable TV. Some rooms have a nice
view overlooking the sea; otherwise, the common verandah is great for enjoying the breeze.

Crystal Springs (contact Jackie Stuart, tel.
876/942-2411, jstuart@cwjamaiac.com, www
.jamaicariddim.com) just east of Buff Bay, is
a fenced-off nature park that offers camping
(US$5 per person) with fresh water, bathrooms,
and a common kitchen area. Rustic one- and
two-bedroom cottages are slated for refurbishment while the concert ground and camping
facilities are occasionally used for events like
drumming and stage shows. The grounds are

© OLIVER HILL

St. George Anglican Church is one of the most impressive structures in the seaside town of Buff Bay.

looking good after years of neglect. A natural amphitheatre on the 63-hectare property is sometimes used for stage shows; artists like Capleton and Ninja Man are regular performers. Drumming sessions are held often with the Hurricane Turbo drummers, who play a mix of mento and revival rhythms.

B&G Jerk Centre (contact owner Glen Ford, cell 876/859-5107) on the east side of town is the best spot for a roadside bite of jerk pork or chicken (US$3.50/quarter pound).

Hibiscus Restaurant (adjacent to courthouse, cell 876/466-0946, 9 A.M.–11 P.M. Mon.–Sat., 5 P.M.–11 P.M. Sun., US$2–3) serves Jamaican staples like fried chicken, curried goat, and stew peas.

Kildare Villa (22 Victoria Rd., tel. 876/996-1240, 8 A.M.–7 P.M. daily, contact business partner Earle Brown who can be helpful, especially to give a heads up if groups are expecting to pass through, tel. 876/996-1498) serves seafood and local cuisine (US$5–15) and sells souvenirs in the gift shop. The restaurant boasts clean bathrooms, making it a popular stopover point.

Pace Setters Cafe (6 Russell Ave., tel. 876/996-1498, 8 A.M.–10 P.M. daily, (US$1–10)) serves pastries, ice cream, and snacks as well hot meals.

Buff Bay Police Station (9 First Ave., tel. 876/996-1497) is located opposite the Adventist Church.

OCHO RIOS AND THE CENTRAL NORTH COAST

St. Ann is full of rivers and gardens, having earned it the well-deserved nickname of "the garden parish." Ocho Rios, or "Ochi" as the community is commonly referred to, is the biggest town in St. Ann; its name is a creative derivation of the Spanish name for the area, Las Chorreras (Cascades), in reference to the abundance of waterfalls. Before the Spanish conquest, the area was known as Maguana by the Tainos. There are indeed several rivers in the vicinity, but not necessarily eight as the name suggests. Four major waterways flow through the town area of Ocho Rios: Turtle River, Milford River, Russell Hall River, and Dairy Spring River. Just east of town are Salt River and the White River, forming the border with St. Mary, and to the west is the famous Dunn's River.

Tourism became important in Ocho Rios in the late 1970s, taking over as the area's chief earner from bauxite, which is still exported from the pier just west of town. The cruise ship industry has been a key component of the city's tourism boom, bringing mixed results. The steady income is appreciated by many businesses, especially those concentrated around the terminal, but the enormous volume of passengers flowing through each day has created a huge demand for services that has not been met with adequate housing for the thousands who have arrived to work in the sector over the past few decades. Many of these arrivals are professionals who have been given little choice but to resort to living in squatter settlements. Still others come to Ochi with little credentials and earn their living hustling

© OLIVER HILL

HIGHLIGHTS

◖ Coyaba Gardens and Mahoe Falls: The most well-maintained waterfalls and garden combo in Ocho Rios handsomely exemplifies St. Ann's motto of "The Garden Parish" (page 149).

◖ Wassi Art: Jamaica's most commercially successful ceramics studio uses both local terra-cotta and imported white clay to create exceptional works (page 150).

◖ Walkerswood: This world-renowned jerk-sauce manufacturer is a great success story in community development and offers an entertaining and tasty family-oriented tour (page 173).

◖ Bob Marley Mausoleum: Seeing the humble roots of Jamaica's greatest prodigal son goes miles towards cultivating *overstanding* (page 174).

◖ James Bond Beach: Jutting out from the mainland near Goldeneye, this beach park holds popular events and visitors swim at Stingray City (page 177).

◖ Firefly: Noel Coward's "room with a view" is easily one of the best in Jamaica, if not the Caribbean (page 179).

◖ Green Castle Estate: There is no better way to immerse yourself in Jamaica's languid country life than with the orchid tour and high tea in Robin's Bay (page 184).

◖ Sunrise Lawn: A quintessential St. Mary hangout, Sunrise Lawn is *the* spot in Robin's Bay for relaxed evenings by the water with thumping music accompanied by a cup of conch soup (page 185).

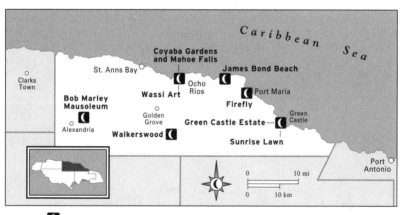

LOOK FOR ◖ TO FIND RECOMMENDED SIGHTS, ACTIVITIES, DINING, AND LODGING.

any way they can, making harassment of tourists a widespread problem.

Just west of Ocho Rios is St. Ann's Bay, on whose outskirts the first Spanish capital was established at Sevilla la Nueva (New Seville). Today Seville is an archeological site and Great House complex where several heritage events are held throughout the year. Farther west along the coast are the communities of Run-

away Bay and Discovery Bay. Runaway Bay is a small town with a golf course, a few resorts, and a small commercial strip along the highway, whereas Discovery Bay is likely Jamaica's most exclusive villa enclave—where rentals go for upwards of US$10,000 per week.

Neighboring St. Mary has in recent years gained the reputation of Jamaica's best-kept secret, a place where hustlers are few and far between and the vast majority carry on with their lives oblivious to the tourism trade. The parish has a beautiful rocky coastline punctuated with beaches of all kinds, with forested hills dropping down rapidly to the sea in places like Oracabessa and the wilderness area between Robin's Bay and Port Maria. Boscobel, 15 minutes east of Ochi, has a small aerodrome with somewhat regular flights. The town is a bedroom community for many workers in Ochi, and has developed as a result of overflow to the point where several destination resorts and villas line the coast between Ochi and Oracabessa. Oracabessa has become known as an artist community and produces some of Jamaica's most unique crafts (items you won't find at the markets in Ocho Rios or Kingston). Further east past Galina Point is Port Maria, a sleepy fishing and market town whose days of glory are long gone. Nonetheless it's worth a stop to stroll around a picturesque port town far removed from the country's mainstay tourism economy. St. Mary lacks a tourism hub, which is perhaps central to its charm. Instead, its principle town of Port Maria caters to the parish's predominantly rural population with a few banks and markets. Still farther east is Robin's Bay, an off-the-beaten-track destination populated by fisherfolk and a strong Rastafarian community. The port town of Annotto Bay is quieter yet than Port Maria, but still an active transportation hub. The St. Mary interior is some of the prettiest countryside in Jamaica, with areas like Islington covered in rolling hills with spectacular views of the coastline. In Annotto Bay, the main road splits, continuing eastward toward Portland along the coast (A4), and heading south towards Kingston via Junction and Castleton (A3).

PLANNING YOUR TIME

Unless your goal is to simply loaf on the beach, or you happen to be staying in a destination resort or villa that's too comfortable to leave, Ocho Rios is not a place to spend more than a few days if you're trying to see other parts of the island in a short period of time. It's the most practical

base, however, for a number of key attractions, including Dunn's River Falls, Dolphin Cove, Nine Mile, Walkerswood, Seville Great House, White River Valley, Prospect Plantation, and the Rio Nuevo battle sight. Oracabessa is only a half-hour away, and there are a couple of good farm tours in that vicinity, in addition to James Bond Beach and Stingray City, which are popular attractions in themselves.

Most of these sights are serviced by organized tours that generally consume the better part of a day. If you're driving yourself or have chartered a taxi, however, there's far more flexibility to fit in a string of activities in a day, and there's no reason you can't spend the morning horseback riding at Seville Heritage park and then stop by Dunn's River to cool off and climb the falls on the way back to Ochi. Most developed attractions have factored transportation into their formula, and while they certainly profit by it, it's often worth letting someone else do the driving given the potholed roads and the lack of clear signage. Car rentals in Jamaica are typically very expensive, as is fuel.

Several annual events make a stay in Ocho Rios all the more worthwhile. During Easter, Jamaica's carnival season is in full force with events east and west of Ocho Rios along the coast. (For a full listing of annual festivals, see *Entertainment and Events*.)

HISTORY

St. Ann figures strongly in Jamaica's early colonial history. Italian explorer Christopher Columbus landed on the shore near Discovery Bay in 1492 while under contract from the Spanish Crown to find a shorter passage to the Far East. Within a few years, the Spanish began to inhabit the island as they systematically wiped out the native Taino population, establishing their capital at Sevilla la Nueva, or New Seville, just west of St. Ann's Bay. Later, after the British seized the island in a carefully executed attack on Santiago de la Vega, or what's now known as Spanish Town, most of the Spaniards who were determined to stay in Jamaica fled to the North Coast where they regrouped and continued to carry out guerrilla reprisal attacks on the

British with the help of Maroon loyalists. But the British had exploited a clear lack of organization that had its roots in a lack of commitment on the part of the Spanish to develop the island as it had done in many other colonies, a neglect many scholars attribute to a lack of gold in Jamaica. The decisive battle that ended any lingering doubt about the fate of Jamaica occurred at the mouth of the Rio Nuevo, just east of present day Ocho Rios. The town was later at the center of Jamaica's slave economy and sugar boom, with vast plantations around the area. Later, Ocho Rios played an important role in the development of Jamaica's chief mineral export, bauxite, and remains an import shipment point today. When tourism grew to overtake bauxite as the country's chief earner of foreign currency, Ocho Rios was again at the center of this trans-

formation, building the cruise ship terminal to attract massive flows of capital that continue to play a vital role in the local economy.

DANGERS AND ANNOYANCES

Corporal Roger Williams of the Ocho Rios Police Department gives sound advice regarding delinquency in Ocho Rios. According to Williams, harassment in Ocho Rios is higher than in other places due to the large squatter settlements around town that support thousands of people from neighboring parishes. St. Ann is the poorest parish, even though you wouldn't necessarily notice because it is well developed, and many come to Ochi in search of opportunity that doesn't always surface in the formal economy.

Hustlers tend to be more aggressive here than in other parishes, and Williams recom-

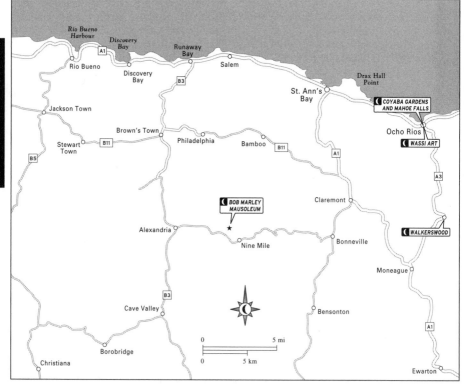

mends greeting advances with a smile, followed by clear communication demonstrating your lack of interest. Ignoring advances is not wise, he says, as it can make the hustler upset. It is not uncommon for people to follow tourists touting any and every kind of service, tour, or drug. According to Williams, crack use is generally confined to street people, while tourists are often offered cocaine and, most frequently, marijuana. Williams reminds that all drugs are illegal in Jamaica. Prostitution is very apparent in Ocho Rios, and it's not uncommon for women to solicit cruise ship passengers in full view of the police. Williams noted that while prostitution is illegal in Jamaica, it is rarely prosecuted. Many parts of Ocho Rios can feel unsafe at night, and it is indeed best not to go out alone—parts of downtown, like James Av-

enue, can be desolate late at night. Petty theft is common, and it's not unheard of for tourists to feel threatened. Women especially should be accompanied walking around town at night.

Behind the inevitable theatrics used by hustlers to get the attention of unassuming visitors, there is a down-to-earth Jamaican sincerity that will often surface by entertaining advances with a "no, thank you," or "I'm all set, thanks, bredren…" Should undesired suitors not be placated with that, or should they react in a less-than-honorable form, it's important to remember they are only self-appointed representatives—or not representative at all of the majority of Jamaicans, who understand the value of hospitality as a cultural and economic virtue central to the Jamaican idiosyncrasy and the tourism industry alike.

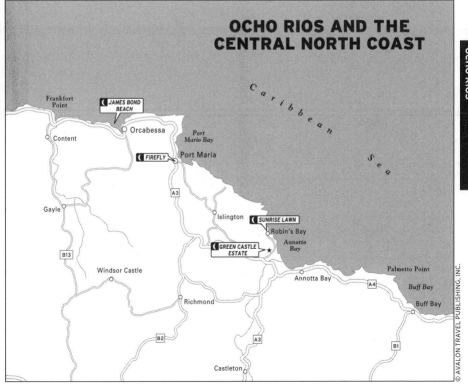

OCHO RIOS

© AVALON TRAVEL PUBLISHING, INC.

Ocho Rios

Hustling and bustling Ocho Rios can feel stifling at times, with the incessant solicitations and persistent attempts by hopeful locals to sell you something or take you somewhere. But seasoned visitors are hardly troubled once they learn to walk with confidence like they know where they're going and take the attention with a grain of salt. In spite of the chaos and confusion that has become a permanent fixture in the central square by the clock tower, there are still places within a 15-minute walk or five-minute cab ride where natural beauty reigns. Natura Falls, Shaw Park Botanical Garden, White River Valley, and Reggae Beach are a few examples.

The rivers in and around Ochi are also an important draw for the beautiful gardens they sustain and the recreation they provide for swimming and cooling off in the shade. The town of Ocho Rios spills over into the bordering parish of St. Mary, just across the White River.

Much of the North Coast is within easy reach of Ocho Rios, as are several attractions in the interior. Bob Marley's birthplace and mausoleum at Nine Mile is within an hour's

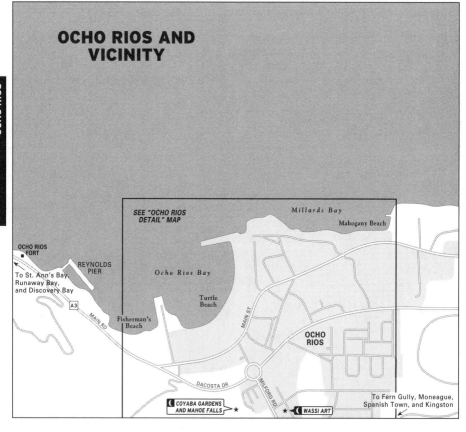

OCHO RIOS AND VICINITY

drive into the hills, and the birthplace of one of Jamaica's foremost national heroes, Marcus Garvey, is located in nearby St. Ann's Bay, marked by a statue in front of the parish library; it's worth stopping to ponder. Several other great beaches dot the coast to the east and west.

The nicest part of Ocho Rios proper, and perhaps one of the nicest developed waterfront areas in all Jamaica, is the stretch of coastline between Mahogany Beach and the White River, which separates St. Ann from St. Mary. Here, along what could be considered St. Ann's Riviera, Royal Plantation and Jamaica Inn share a stretch of spectacular ledged coral shoreline interspersed with small, private beaches. One of Jamaica's finest villas, Scotch on the Rocks, is nestled between the two up-market hotels.

SIGHTS
Beaches

Most of the resorts in town and along the coast have cordoned off their seafront areas. Despite the fact that all beaches in Jamaica fall under the public domain, private landowners along the coast can apply for exclusivity permits, a clause in the law most hotels take advantage of.

Turtle Beach (admission US$3) in the heart of Ochi is popular among tourists; several hotels claim large pieces on either side of the public area at the center of the bay.

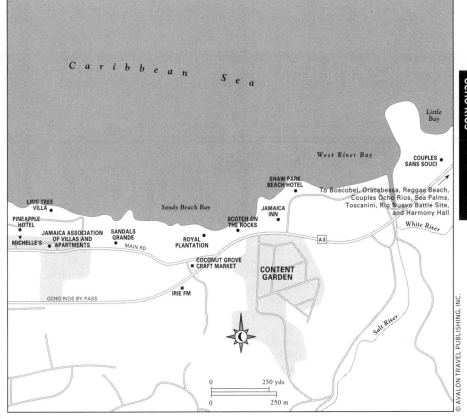

OCHO RIOS

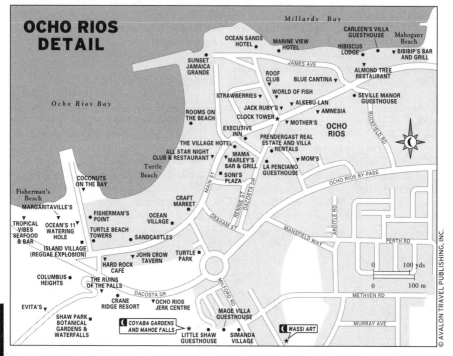

© AVALON TRAVEL PUBLISHING, INC.

Mahogany Beach (free) is the most popular beach among locals and heats up on weekends with music blasting and youth playing soccer and splashing around. The beach is located east of the town center off Main Street just past Bibibip's. It's the best place to soak up the local scene and is also the departure point for Five Star Watersports' cruises.

Fisherman's Beach (free), adjacent to Island Village, is one of the best spots around to get fresh seafood—at Tropical Vibes restaurant or the other fish shacks set up there. This is not a beach for swimming, but rather for chilling out with some food and a beer.

Irie Beach (free) is small beach on the banks of the White River east of Ochi where locals go to cool off and enjoy picnics. The beach hosts occasional events. To get there head east out of town, taking a right off the highway opposite the entrance to Jamaica Inn just past the Texaco gas station, following the White River inland until you reach the beach.

Reggae Beach (admission US$5) is a picturesque stretch of sand on an unspoiled cove a few minutes east of Ocho Rios. The beach hosts excellent annual events like Luau and Frenchman's Parties.

Laughing Waters (free), probably the nicest beach in Jamaica and the original beach from the James Bond movie *Dr. No,* is located in Mammee Bay, just east of Dunn's River Falls. The property facing the beach is a prime minister's residence that comes with the post. To get there, park along the seaward side of the highway on the broad shoulder just east of a JPS electrical substation that sits adjacent to the dirt road entrance. The road leads down to the seaside, where a breathtaking waterfall meets the sea. The beach sees few visitors and remains almost a state secret.

River Parks and Gardens

Ocho Rios is known for its lush gardens, though some are far better maintained than

© OLIVER HILL

Ocho Rios, one of Jamaica's most developed tourism destinations, appears less chaotic from the surounding hills.

others. One of the nicest free waterfalls in Ochi, known as **Nature Falls,** is frequented mostly by locals who come for picnics and to wash off their vehicles in the shade. The river and falls are located just off Shaw Park Road along a dirt road that branches off the road to Perry Town just past the Y where it splits from Shaw Park Road.

Shaw Park Botanical Garden and Waterfalls (DaCosta Dr., tel. 876/974-2723, 8 A.M.–5 P.M. daily, US$10) is a nice river garden full of ginger lilies and little cascades. There is a rear entrance accessible from Shaw Park Road when the front entrance is closed. This is a great shady and scenic place to get some natural air conditioning when it's hot. The back entrance to the park can be accessed from the end of Shaw Park Road where a little bridge leads from a parking lot by some abandoned apartment buildings into the park.

Turtle River Park (tel. 876/795-0078, 7 A.M.–8 P.M. Mon.–Fri., 8 A.M.–9 P.M. Sat. and Sun., contact Ms. Newman, park supervisor, free) borders the bypass, located straight ahead as you descend from Fern Gully at the junction of Milford, Main Street, and DaCosta Drive. Turtle Park was inaugurated on June 18, 2004. Koi fish, butterfly koi, tilapia, and some turtles in a cage populate the small park.

Fern Gully is a former underground riverbed that was planted with ferns in the 1880s and later paved over to create the main highway (A1) between Spanish Town and the North Coast. Arts-and-crafts stands line a few of the less precarious curves along the steep, lush, and shady road.

◖ Coyaba Gardens and Mahoe Falls

Coyaba Gardens and Mahoe Falls (Shaw Park Rd., tel. 876/974-6235, coyaba@hotmail.com, www.coyabagardens.com, 8 A.M.–5 P.M. daily, admission US$10 for waterfalls and gardens, US$5 for gardens alone) are the most well-maintained gardens in Ochi, with a small waterfall fit for swimming and climbing, and a nice museum featuring a history of Jamaica's earliest inhabitants and a display covering the local watershed. There is also a snack bar on-site, and a Romanesque pavilion above the falls used for events and weddings. Mahoe Falls is on the Milford River, which flows through Coyaba Gardens before descending through town and out the storm gulley by Sunset Jamaica Grande. Owner Simon Stuart's grandmother built the first resort in Ochi at Shaw Park Gardens farther down the hill in 1923. Coyaba was a banana walk, or gully, on Shaw Park Estate until the gardens and waterfall were developed in the early 1990s. To get to Coyaba, turn right opposite the Anglican church heading up towards Fern Gully on Milford Road (A3) and follow the signs off of Shaw Park Road.

(Wassi Art

Wassi Art (tel. 876/974-5044, info@wassiart .com, www.wassiart.com, 9 A.M.–5 P.M. Mon.–Sat., 10 A.M.–4 P.M. Sun. and holidays) is easily the highest commercial quality and most productive ceramics studio and gallery in Jamaica. A complimentary tour of the ceramics studio is offered, showing visitors the complete cycle of creativity, from processing of clay to the throwing and firing. The raw, red terracotta clay used in much of the work is brought from Castleton, St. Mary, before being processed at Wassi. The studio also works with imported white clay.

There are 20 full-time artists on salary, many self-taught who start at Wassi through an apprenticeship program where they develop their skills. The name Wassi is from Jamaican slang, meaning anything terrific, or something sharp like the sting of a wasp that would create an impression. Lovely general manager Sylvie Henry oversees the day-to-day operations, while the company is owned by Robert and Teresa Lee. Wassi Art began as a hobby of Mrs. Lee's in 1982. The company gets a discount with FedEx based on volume, savings it passes on to customers who wish to ship pieces abroad. There is a wide range of pottery on display and for sale at Wassi Art, from small souvenir items to huge display pieces (US$5–5000).

Get there by taking the A3 in the direction

of Fern Gully; take a left on Great Pond, and then another left on Bougainvillea Drive.

Museums and Galleries

Reggae Xplosion (Island Village Plaza, tel. 876/675-8895, 9 A.M.–5 P.M. Mon.–Fri., 10 A.M.–5 P.M. Sat., US$7 or US$3.50 for locals) is a museum offering an interactive history of reggae music with punch buttons to listen to tracks at each booth. Along with the shopping center itself, Reggae Xplosion is owned by Island Jamaica, Chris Blackwell's Jamaican venture.

Harmony Hall (Tower Isle, tel. 876/975-4222, 10 A.M.–6 P.M. Tues.–Sun.) is a beautiful old great house with a gallery on the second floor run by Peter and Anabella Proudlock. It features works by the likes of Susan Shirley and Graham Davis and several other contemporary painters. There is also a nice bookshop in the gallery with cookbooks and works by local authors. A crafts fair is held on Easter weekend in the yard out front, with regular exhibitions during the winter season. Downstairs is Toscanini, the area's best Italian restaurant. The colonial-era building is located five minutes' east of Ochi along the main road.

Historical Sights

Rio Nuevo Battle Site, just east of Harmony Hall, is the location of the decisive battle that left Jamaica in English hands. After three years of guerrilla warfare and harassment of the British, the last Spanish governor, Don Cristobal de Ysassi, finally received reinforcements from Cuba to help retake the island. The first set of troops arriving from Spain landed at Ocho Rios, where they were soon discovered by the British and quickly defeated. The second detail of 557 men was sent from Cuba and landed at the mouth of the Rio Nuevo. They too were soon discovered by British warships, and the battle that ensued left 300 Spanish soldiers dead for Britain's 50. Ysassi miraculously escaped and continued to wage guerilla attack with a few remaining loyal bands of Maroons on his side until the treaty of Madrid was signed, officially conceding defeat and leaving Jamaica in British hands. Ysassi finally fled the island in handmade dugout canoes from Don Christopher's Point in Robin's Bay. A plaque mounted by the JNHT at the Rio Nuevo battle site reads: "The stockade that once stood here was captured on the 17th June 1658 by Colonel Edward D'oyley and the English forces under his command after a gallant defense by Don Cristobal de Ysassi the last Spanish governor of Jamaica."

Ocho Rios Fort is located beside the Reynolds bauxite installation and the helicopter pad for Island Hoppers. The fort was built in the late 17th century. Like many other forts on the island, it was strengthened in 1780 when a French attack was feared imminent. In 1795, an enemy vessel appeared off Ocho Rios harbor but, fearing the guns there, it made an attack at Mammee Bay. The Ocho Rios Fort was recently rebuilt by Reynolds Jamaica and contains two of the original guns from Ocho Rios and two of the guns that defended the town of Mammee Bay. The fort is not a managed attraction, but is worth a quick stop to have a look around.

Sights East of Ochi

White River Valley runs along the St. Ann–St. Mary border, where the White River was an important feature for the Spaniards, who built the first thoroughfare from the South to North Coasts along its banks. The oldest **Spanish bridge** on the island can still be seen at the river's upper reaches, just above Chukka Caribbean's kayaking and tubing site. A new arrival on the river is the competing and slightly more edgy Caliche River Rafting operation.

Prospect Plantation (contact property operator Dolphin Cove, tel. 876/994-1058, 8 A.M.–4 P.M. Mon.–Sat.) is a 405-hectare working plantation bought by Sir Harold Mitchell in 1936. Mitchell entertained all manner of dignitary in his vast property, which beyond the great house has some of the area's most luxurious villas. A tradition was established whereby all his guests would plant a tree on the grounds to mark their visit. The most notable of these tokens of remembrance is the giant mahogany planted by Winston Churchill in 1953 that stands in the driveway behind the great house.

Prospect Plantation offers rides on camel, horse, or jitney with a tour of the great house included. The basic plantation tour (US$32 per adult, free for children under 7) includes a jitney ride, a great house tour, and a stop to pet the camels and see the ostriches. The tour can be upgraded (US$89) to include a 20-minute camel trek. The plantation tour can also be done on horseback (US$58). Nestled among the groves of tropical hardwoods below the great house is a beautiful non-denominational chapel built by Mitchell to mark the passing of his wife, Mary Jane Mitchell Greene, known as Lady Mitchell. The chapel was constructed completely with hardwoods and stone found on the plantation.

ENTERTAINMENT AND EVENTS

Margaritaville (Island Village, tel. 876/675-8800, Mon., Wed., and Sat. are club nights (9 A.M.–4 A.M. those nights) and 9 A.M.–midnight on Sun., Tues., Thurs., and Fri.) is Ochi's most popular club with the tourist crowd. This is one of Jimmy Buffet's chain, and it sees a lot of debauchery—the pool party on Wednesdays attracts a large crowd. On Sundays, parties are held geared towards cruise ship passengers.

Amnesia (70 Main St., tel. 876/974-2633, US$3–7) is Ochi's most authentic Jamaican nightclub. Thursday is Ladies Night and gets quite busy, with a regular after-work jam and occasional deejay performances on Fridays.

Roof Club (James Ave., no phone) is another typical Jamaican club with a bar and plenty of wining to go around. The club gets busy on weekends.

Spinning Wheel Club (James Ave., no phone) is a local hangout where men gather any time of day for dominoes. There is no bar; it's basically just a hangout spot where you may be able to get in on a game.

Strawberries Night Club (James Ave., no phone) is another earthy Jamaican club where blasting music competes with Roof Club across the street.

Festivals and Events

While several events in Ocho Rios don't seem to persist, several more get stronger with each passing year. In 2007, the **Fat Tire Festival** (Feb. 8–11), created specifically for mountain biking enthusiasts, resumed its ninth season after having skipped a year and relocated from Negril. While the Fat Tire Festival is now based in Ochi, daily excursions shuttle riders as far away as Robin's Bay in the middle of the St. Mary coast.

Ocho Rios sees its share of excitement during carnival season in April with **Bacchanal** hosting a mad soca bashment at Chukka Cove. Bacchanal Jamaica is a series of events during Jamaica's carnival season, which begins in mid-January and lasts through Easter. Bacchanal events are put on by an organization called **Revelers, Inc.** (contact Charmaine Franklin, revelersinc@hotmail.com, www.bacchanal jamaica.com). While Soca music is not Jamaica's most popular, being more indigenous to Trinidad and Tobago or even Barbados, during Jamaica's carnival season it takes center stage at events produced by Revelers, Inc. **Luau** is held at Reggae Beach also around Easter. **Beach J'ouvert,** part of the carnival month festivities, takes place at James Bond Beach in Oracabessa, with after-parties spilling over into Ocho Rios at places like The Ruins.

In July 2006, Reggae Sunsplash resumed for its 14th season after a hiatus, taking place in an immense field adjacent to Chukka Cove. A poor turnout and huge financial losses have once again put the festival's future in question, however, even while organizers are confident the show will go on. Reggae Sunsplash was not held in 2007 in Jamaica. Keep your eyes and ears open for a potential comeback in the future.

Seville Heritage Park hosts a number of excellent events throughout the year, including a **Kite Festival** on Easter Monday and, the main event of the year, the **Emancipation Jubilee** held on July 31.

Further inland in St. Ann parish, the Marley family hosts an annual concert on the weekend before or after Bob's February 6 birthday, and nearby the **Claremont Kite Festival** is held on Easter weekend a few months later.

St. Mary hosts a few notable events and music festivals that are not to be missed should they coincide with a sojourn in the area. These include Capleton's **St. Mary Mi Come From** held in Anotto Bay, **Beach J'ouvert** and **Follow Di Arrow,** both held at James Bond Beach in Oracabessa.

SHOPPING

Chris Blackwell's **Island Village** is a large, smartly laid-out shopping complex next to the cruise ship terminal. It rakes in the lion's share of the money flowing from passengers, who generally spend only a few hours off the boat. **Margaritaville** shares the complex with several duty-free, but nonetheless overpriced, jewelry and gift shops. **Reggae Xplosion** and the **Blue Mountain Cafe** are also located here, and charge exclusively in dollars. Nevertheless, it's a decent place to get some real Blue Mountain coffee. **Shade Shack** (shop k4, tel. 876/675-8965) is one of the best places in Ochi to get brand-name sunglasses; it's staffed by owner Jackie Dodson.

Countless smaller shopping centers vie for the cruise ship dollars farther into the heart of Ochi, most notably in the Taj Mahal complex behind Hard Rock. The crafts market on Main Street across from Scotia Bank is definitely worth a visit. There's also another crafts center at Pineapple Place, and a third in Coconut Grove at the eastern junction of Main Street and the Ocho Rios Bypass, across from Royal Plantation, where the best deals can be found.

For clothes and shoes, there are several stores in the downtown area; haute couture will not be featured anywhere. **Deals,** in Soni's Plaza, is the best place for tight-fitting clothes for clubbing in Jamaican style.

Classic Footwear (20 Main St., tel. 876/974-4815) has shoes for both men and women.

The Shoe Works (Shop #6, Ocean Village Plaza, tel. 876/974-5415, 9 A.M.–7 P.M. Mon.–Sat.) has the best service in town for fairly-priced name-brand footwear. Claudette Matthews is the owner and manager, while Antony Pinnock is often supervising.

Scent of Incense & Things (79 Main St., tel. 876/795-0047), run by Janet Gallimore, is a nice shop selling incense, oils, herbs, spiritual products, and a variety of small gift items.

SPORTS AND RECREATION

Sandals Golf and Country Club (tel. 876/975-0119, www.sandals.com, 7 A.M.–5 P.M. daily, US$100 green fees, US$45 for locals) is a *Golf Digest* 3.5-star-rated course in the hills above Ochi. The course is compact and very walkable, but carts are also available (US$40). Clubs are also rented (US$30 Wllson/US$45 Calloway) and players are obliged to use a caddy (US$17, min US$10 tip/person).

A patio restaurant and bar serves burgers, hot dogs, and chicken sandwiches (US$7). The driving range offers baskets of 40 balls for US$4. Tony Ebanks is the golf course manager and Laura Chin is the helpful and charming cashier and telephone operator. Sandals guests don't pay green fees and special rates apply for several other area accommodations.

Water Sports

From the Marina at Fisherman's Point there are several outfits that offer sailing, snorkeling, and water sports.

Margarita (contact Paul Dadd, cell 876/381-4357, pdadd@cwjamaica.com) is a 12-meter sloop that can be rented for sailboat charters ranging from day-sails to multiple-night trips around the island or to neighboring islands. The boat is chartered with a captain and can accommodate up to 15 people for day sails (US$50/person or US$400 for half day, US$800 full day). For overnight charters (US$1000/day), the boat can sleep 8 passengers.

Fun Seekers Watersports (Patrick Buley cell 876/468-9950 or 876/859-5000) offers a variety of activities like snorkeling, glass-bottom boat tours, and fishing trips.

Gary Boating (cell 876/310-9840) is the best option for fishing or snorkeling excursions on a typical Jamaican fisherman's boat

(snorkeling US$25 per person, fishing US$50 per hour).

Resort Divers is based in a Runaway Bay five-star PADI dive facility, newly opened in 2007 (Bamboo Beach, previously known as Salem Beach, contact Laura or Everett Heron, tel. 876/973-7876 or cell 876/881-5760, resort divers@cwjamaica.com, www.resortdivers .com). Resort Divers also operates out of Rose Hall Resort and Country Club (Rose Hall, Montego Bay, tel. 876/953-2650) and Tropical Beach (cell 876/878-3483), just north of the airport. Tropical Beach is the gateway to Montego Bay's Marine Park. Resort Divers offers snorkeling, glass-bottom-boat reef-viewing, banana boat and water skiing, drop-line and deep sea fishing and parasailing, in addition to its core dive services. Runaway Bay dive highlights include canyons, crevices, and flats, with popular sites being Ricky's Reef, Pocket's Reef, a Spanish Anchor, and wreckages like Reggae Queen, a 100-foot freighter, two airplanes, and a Mercedes Benz car.

At the new base in Runaway Bay, Resort Divers will also coordinate traditional drop-line fishing excursions with local fishermen. Resort Divers also operates Sharkey's seafood restaurant at Bamboo Beach. Other beach toys at Bamboo Beach include a trampoline, kayaks, water bicycles, and a climbing wall. Resort Divers has been in operation since 1986 with a five-star PADI rating since 1992. Call or visit the website for pricing specific to each water sport.

Five Star Watersports (U.S. tel. 877/316-6257 or 876/974-2446, redstripecruises@cw jamaica.com, www.fivestarwatersports.com) operates two catamarans and a trimaran named some rendition of *Cool Runnings*. Daily cruises to Dunn's River Falls (US$69, 12:30–4 P.M.) include an open bar, snorkeling gear, and the entrance fee to the falls. A **Taste of Jamaica** evening cruise (US $59/person, 5–8 P.M. Fri.) offers an open bar and Jamaican food like jerk pork, chicken, steak, rice and peas, festival, and bammy. Other cruises offered are the **Carnival Party Cruise** (US$49, 9 P.M.– midnight Thurs., min 20 persons) and the

OCHO RIOS

© OLIVER HILL

Mahogany Beach is the most popular local beach in Ocho Rios, where kids play soccer and show off their dance skills on weekends.

Wet and Wild clothing-optional cruise (US$59, 2:30–5 P.M. Thurs., min 15 persons). The boats depart from Mahogany Beach and leave passengers at Turtle Beach. The Taste of Jamaica tour departs from Turtle Beach. Drinks at the bar include Red Stripe, rum punch, rum and Coke, fruit punch, Pepsi, and water. Fiona Anglin is the sweet and helpful reservationist.

Organized Tours

Blue Mountain Bicycle Tours (121 Main St., tel. 876/974-7075, info@bmtoursja.com, www .bmtoursja.com) runs a popular downhill biking tour which has been somewhat truncated over the past few years due to landslides that blocked the upper reaches of the route.

Chukka Caribbean Adventures (tel. 876/ 972-2506, ochorios@chukkacaribbean.com, www.chukkacaribbean.com) offers a host of organized tours, from horseback riding to ATV tours, to canopy tours with ziplines through the forest, to tubing and kayaking on the White River, the Irie Bus Ride to Nine Mile, and Stingray City at James Bond Beach. This is

one of the island's most successful operations; it sees almost as many cruise ship passengers as Dunn's River. Chukka Cove, 15 minutes west of Ocho Rios, is the original flagship base for Chukka Caribbean Adventures, which now has operations all over the island.

Caliche Rainforest Whitewater Rafting (tel. 876/940-1745, calicheadventuretours@ yahoo.com, www.whitewaterraftingmontego bay.com) recently opened an operation on the White River in the canyon below the Chukka operation. Rafting excursions cost slightly more when departing from MoBay, but the new location gives Caliche Class III rapids during the dry season (Feb.–Apr.) when it's no longer possible to navigate the upper reaches of the Great River in St. James where the original Caliche operation was based. Children under 12 do the amateur rafting ride (US$50–70) on the Great River year-round.

H'Evans Scent (Free Hill, cell 876/847-5592 or 876/427-4866, info@hevansscent .com, www.mrmotivator.com, www.hevans scent.com, US$85/person) is an ecotourism outfit run by Derrick Evans offering ziplines, ATV tours, nature tours, and an experience where visitors get to mingle with locals 610 meters up in the hills of St. Ann. To get to H'Evans Scent, turn inland along the Bamboo Road in Priory for seven kilometers up the hill. The operation offers transportation from nearby accommodations in Ocho Rios, Runaway Bay, and Discovery Bay.

Lee's Elite Travel and Tours (54 Main St., tel. 876/974-6234, cell 876/487-6793, leestrs@ yahoo.ca, www.leestours.com; in Toronto book through Imagine Holidays, tel. 866/881-8233 or 905/881-0800) at Village Hotel has an Internet café (US$6/hr, 9 A.M.–5 P.M. Mon.–Fri., 10 A.M.–4 P.M. Sat.) and offers tours to Nine Mile, Dunn's River Falls, Dolphin Cove, H'Evans Scent, Hooves, and Green Grotto. Lee's arranges transportation and entrance fees at discounted rates for families, groups, and customized packages that include an airport transfer. Transfers are offered to Kingston (US$150 per couple) and MoBay (US$80) airports. Leroy Villiers and Norma Lee-Villiers run the travel and tours operation.

Spas

The best spas in town are the **Kiyara Spa** at the Jamaica Inn and the **Red Lane Spa** at Royal Plantation. Both spas are open to non-guests. (See hotel listings in *Accommodations*.)

Veronica's Day Spa (54–56 Main St. at the Village Hotel, tel. 876/795-3425) offers aromatherapy massages, reflexology, mani/pedi, and waxing. Carmelita is the sweet and helpful receptionist.

ACCOMMODATIONS

Ocho Rios has developed a wide array of accommodation options thanks to its place as one of the original resort towns in Jamaica. Nevertheless, at the lower end, conditions tend to be consistently on the shabby side with few exceptions, while there are several good midrange and high-end options.

Under US$75

Simanda Villa (1 Shaw Park Rd., tel. 876/974-0708, simi@cwjamaica.com) may just have the cheapest rooms in Ochi. The accommodations are basic with air-conditioning (US$25) or fan (US$20). Sun Flower Restaurant on the property serves good local dishes like chicken with rice and peas (US$5).

Mahoe Villa Guest House (11 Shaw Park Rd., tel. 876/974-6613, jahwanzariley@yahoo .com) is a cozy and private guesthouse run by Michael Riley and his son Wanza. There are seven basic rooms (US$20/30 depending on size) with two single beds, fan, TV, and shared bath; plus two slightly larger rooms (US$40) with private bath and private entrance; as well as a master suite (US$75) with standing fan, a component stereo, TV, a whirlpool bath, two walk-in closets, and a private balcony with a sea view.

La Penciano Guest House (3 Short Lane, tel. 876/974-5472), run by Kenneth Thomas, is a relatively decent dive right in the center of town. The rooms are clean with fans, twin beds, TV, and hot water. The more expensive rooms (US$35) have private baths. Meals can be prepared to order. Longer stays can be negotiated. It should be noted La Penciano also gets its share of short-term guests.

Carleen's Villa Guest House (85a Main St., tel. 876/974-5431) is well situated, with a common balcony overlooking the water. It has seven no-frills rooms (US$40) equipped with ceiling fans, two twin beds, TV, and hot water in private baths. There's no pool on property, and no food, but it's located five minutes away from Mahogany Beach, Ochi's most popular with locals. It has a convenient location between downtown Ochi and Mahogany Beach and is reasonably priced for what you get.

Seville Manor Guest House (84 Main St., tel. 876/795-2900) is a basic but comfortable guesthouse with queen beds in double-occupancy rooms (US$55), as well as triple rooms (US$64) that have a queen and a twin. Amenities include air-conditioning and hot water.

Marine View Hotel (9 James Ave., tel. 876/974-5753) has rooms with either king or two double beds with air-conditioning and TV (US$65), one double with air-conditioning

(US$45, with TV US$50), or one double bed with ceiling fan (US$35). There is a pool and restaurant at this ocean-view accommodation. Credit cards are accepted.

Little Shaw Park Guest House (21 Shaw Park Rd., tel. 876/974-2177, littleshawpark@ yahoo.com, www.littleshawparkguesthouse .com) is the only place in Ochi to offer camping (US$20) in addition to its basic rooms (US$50 fan, US$60 a/c). The property has been owned and managed since 1977 by Deborah and Trevor Mitchell, who have maintained a laid-back, quiet garden setting in spite of the development boom outside the compound walls. The furnishings inside the rooms have apparently changed little since the era when the guesthouse was opened. There is one triple-occupancy room (US$75).

Pineapple Hotel (Pineapple Place, Main St., tel. 876/974-2727, fax 876/974-1706, US$60) has 18 basic rooms with hot water, air-conditioning, housekeeping, security, and pool access. Pineapple is the closest hotel to Mahogany Beach. The manager is Anthony Thompson and Heneesah is the lovely front desk clerk.

Ocean Sands Hotel (14 James Ave., tel. 876/974-2605, (US$50/60 low/high season) is a decent hotel right on the waterfront. All room have two double beds, air-conditioning, hot water, and fans. There is a pool and beach area but no food on the premises. Nevertheless, the hotel is within five minutes walking distance from the heart of Ocho Rios where food options abound.

US$75-200

The Village Hotel (54–56 Main St., tel. 876/974-9193, villagehtl@cwjamaica.com, www.villagehoteljamaica.com, US$90 includes breakfast) has standard, deluxe, and suite rooms. All rooms have air-conditioning, kitchenette, cable TV, and ceiling fans. The Village Hotel has a swimming pool on property and The Village Grill serves a mix of international and Jamaican cuisine (US$10–25).

Turtle Beach Towers (Main St., tel. 876/974-2381 turtlebeachtowers@cwjamaica .com, www.turtlebeachvacations.com, US$65–

160) is one of the original and less-attractive apartment-style accommodation options, with its cluster of grey towers at the base of Fisherman's Point resembling government housing projects. Do not book here without first seeing the room in person as individual owners appoint the apartments according to taste, or neglect as the case may be, and the decor and amenities varies greatly from unit to unit. Reduced rates can be negotiated for longer stays.

Executive Inn (60 Main St., tel. 876/795-4070, US$100/person) has 20 rooms with one, two, or three beds, and TV, air-conditioning, and private baths with hot water. It includes continental breakfast in its per night rate. The Executive Inn also runs Carlitos Cafe, located around back on DaCosta serving typical Jamaican dishes.

Columbus Heights Apartments (tel. 876/974-9057 or 876/974-2940 for manager Mr. Jackson, www.columbusheights.com, US$100/120 low/high) has studios with air-conditioning and hot water. Longer stays get reduced rates.

Fisherman's Point (Cruise Ship Wharf, tel. 876/974-5317, fishermanspoint@ cwjamaica.com, www.fishermanspoint.net, (US$100/125 low/high) is run as a strata with individual apartment owners pooling their units. These are some of the nicer self-contained units available in Ocho Rios, and while decor and furnishings vary somewhat between the apartments, there is much better oversight of the conditions than at neighboring Turtle Towers. All units are fully furnished with hot water, living rooms, equipped kitchens, TV, air-conditioning, and telephones. There is a nice pool at the center of the complex, with Turtle Beach access two minutes away.

ROOMS on the Beach (Turtle Beach, Main St., tel. 876/925-0925, U.S. 800/GO-ROOMS, www.roomsresort.com, www.superclubs.com , US$99 ocean view, US$105 ocean view with balcony, US$111 ocean view jr. suite; the first two room categories can accommodate up to four, the suite can accommodate up six at an additional charge of US$25 per adult, US$13 per child) is SuperClubs' answer to the demand for a dependable European-plan option on the beachfront in Ochi. Located in the heart of Ochi, ROOMS is a beachfront property with a pool and all the fixtures of an all-inclusive without the all-inclusive. The rooms are clean, with TV, air-conditioning, telephones, and hot water. Previously the property was called Inn On The Beach and then Club Jamaica before being refurbished and reopened as ROOMS in 2004. The property is a short walk from all the restaurants and nightlife in downtown Ocho Rios.

Crane Ridge Resort (17 DaCosta Dr., 876/974-8051 or U.S. tel. 888/790-5264, craneridge@craneridge.net, www.craneridge .net) has 90 units perched on a hill overlooking Ocho Rios off the bypass above Ruins at the Falls. Standard rooms (US$81/133 low/high) have private bathrooms with hot water and share a balcony. The two-bedroom suites (US$175/210 low/high) have a private balcony, whirlpool tub, kitchenette, and living room. The nine three-story buildings surround a large pool with a swim-up bar. Complimentary wireless Internet is accessible from the lobby and dining room area.

Hibiscus Lodge (83 Main St., tel. 876/974-2676, info@hibiscusjamaica.com, www.hibis cusjamaica.com, (US$130/140 low/high) has comfortable rooms with air-conditioning, TV, and private baths with hot water. Rooms come with two twins or one queen, suites have ocean views. The hotel is within easy walking distance to the heart of Ochi and Mahogany Beach.

US$200 and Up

 Jamaica Inn (tel. 876/974-2514 or U.S. tel. 800/837-4608, fax 876/974-2449, reservations@jamaicainn.com) is one of the classiest hotels on the island, and it's little wonder it maintains a high rate of repeat guests (60 percent), among them many national and foreign dignitaries. Winston Churchill stayed in the signature White Suite years ago, and Marilyn Monroe was also a guest. Since these luminaries were at the hotel, the amenities have only improved.

You won't find clocks, TVs, or Internet access in your room at the Jamaica Inn; these items are seen as distractions from what is designed to be the primary activity at this stately accommodation: relaxation. For those who need to stay connected, however, there is wireless Internet in the library, and a computer for guest use. What you will find in the rooms is the classiest and most tastefully soothing color scheme and decor anywhere, with open living rooms just off the bedrooms—literally on the beach, and complete with a foot pan to wash off the sand before stepping inside.

Three room categories are differentiated principally by their proximity to the beach and the size of the room: second-floor balcony suites (US$290/550 low/high), deluxe suites (US$340/670 low/high), and premiere suites (US$420/825 low/high). The Jamaica Inn sits on one of the nicest private beaches in Jamaica, on Ocho Rios' equivalent of the Italian Riviera.

More exclusive rooms include the White Suite (US$820/1,760 low/high), and the Cowdray Suite (US$435/860 low/high), a more humble high-end room. Two spectacular one-bedroom cottages, Cottages 3 and 4 (US$820/1,760 low/high), have private plunge pools, decks and outside showers. The six Jamaica Inn cottages were refurbished in 2006 and come in two categories, one-bedroom (US$630/1,170 low/high) and two-bedroom (US$740/1,340 low/high).

The Kiyara Spa, run by Carolyn Jobson, sits beside the cottages along the waterfront, and specializes in freshly mixed treatments using all-natural ingredients, many of which are grown on the premises.

Royal Plantation (tel. 876/974-5601 or U.S. tel. 305/284-1300, rpres@jm.royalplantation .com, www.royalplantation.com, US$450–935 low season, US$605–1245 high season, including tax) is the brainchild of Sandals-owner Butch Stewart's daughter Jamie Stewart-McConnell. The upscale property is her father's Sandals on champagne and caviar, and the extra amenities are well appreciated by guests. Offering both all-inclusive and European plans gives guests the opportunity to get off the premises and taste a bit of local cuisine if they so choose. Executive chef Basil Dean comes from a background at other world-class hotels, having competed in the Culinary Olympics. Royal Plantation has three restaurants: One features "Nouveau Caribbean Fusion,", Le Papillon is a French restaurant, and La Terrazza has Italian cuisine.

There are six room categories: deluxe; premium oceanfront junior suite; luxury oceanfront junior suite, with whirlpool tub, French balcony; the honeymoon grand luxe, with a walkout balcony and larger whirlpool bath with separate shower; the honeymoon plantation one-bedroom suite adds a living and a whirlpool area with separate standing shower; and the sixth category, the one-bedroom suites, have two walkout balconies with lounge chairs for two, and a huge living room area with one and a half baths. The Royal Plan incurs an additional charge (US$215 per person) for unlimited food and drink. Royal Plan guests have green fees and transportation to the Sandals Golf Course included, while non-guests pay standard fees (US$70) in addition to clubs, cart, and caddy fees (US$25, US$25/40, US$12/17 for 9/18 holes).

In addition to the rooms in the main building, there is also a three-bedroom villa with a private pool. The top of the villa has two bedrooms (US$1,355/1,940 low/high, sleeping 2–4 persons) with a third bedroom downstairs that can added (US$495/655 low/high, sleeping 1 or 2 persons). All bedrooms have king beds.

Red Lane Spa (www.redlanespa.com) is one of the most comprehensive spas on the island with 14 full-time employees and eight full-time therapists specializing in different treatments. Under the expert direction of Tanya Vassel, the spa offers a wide variety of services, from hot stone massage, to nails and facials. Specially built for the grand opening of Royal Plantation Inn, the European-inspired spa is open to non-guests as well.

Sun Cuisine Retreat and Detox Centre (Upton, Ocho Rios, www.suncuisine.com, www.sunfirefoods.com, www.vegsoul.com, tel. 876/441-0124 or 876/975-0134) has a two-bedroom villa and two one-bedroom cottages

(US$300 per day per person with meals and therapy, half-price for couples sharing a bed). Yoga, massage, tai chi, and a mud tub exfoliation process are all included in the experience. There is a nice swimming pool on the three-acre garden estate.

Raw foods guru Aris LaTham offers a variety of alternative health retreat and workshop options in the area. Namely, LaTham's **Sunfired Culinary Institute** (www.sunfiredfood.com) offers weeklong raw food training programs (US$3000 including accommodations, meals, and certification) whereby LaTham certifies up to three students at a time to absorb the knowledge behind his raw food diet and lifestyle.

Villas

Scotch on the Rocks (Pineapple Grove, just east of the junction of Main St. and the Ocho Rios bypass, contact Alan Marlor, SunVillas, U.S. tel. 888/625-6007, alan@sunvillas .com, www.sunvillas.com; or rent locally through owner tel. 876/927-2448, www.scotch ontherocksja.com) is one of Jamaica's top five villas in terms of elegance, luxury, and an all-permeating sense of class, while still remaining unpretentious and full of vibes. The five-bedroom house (US$5,500/7,000 low/high per week) is well laid-out for privacy, but still spacious enough for the whole family. Each bedroom has a private bath and a large balcony overlooking the sea. You won't find more soothing rooms anywhere with soft linens and delicate white curtains that catch the evening breeze to blur the line between heaven and earth. A large pool deck out front overlooks the sea at the top of a staircase down to the picture-perfect dock with a gazebo on its tip. The exquisite meals are taken either in the large indoor dining room, or more often outside. Scotchie, as the villa is known by those who have become its intimate guests, is situated on Sandy Bay, the equivalent of Ocho Rios' Riviera. The neighbors on either side are the most upscale hotels in town, Jamaica Inn and Royal Plantation. Villa membership at the latter offers tennis courts and spa discounts within a few minutes' walk. The staff at Scotchie is top-notch, from Bryan the Rasta butler, Henry the gardener, Elvis the caretaker, Cherry the cook, to Pauline the housekeeper. By the end of a stay, these exemplary Jamaicans will be family, and if you're so lucky as to taste Cherry's pineapple cake, you'll make every effort to take her with you when you leave.

Prendergast Real Estate and Villa Rentals (7 DaCosta Dr., tel. 876/974-2670, pren@cwjamaica.com) run by Clinese Prendergast, books a large selection of villas, some in the hills overlooking Ochi and others directly on the water in town and along the coast to the east. One of the nicer waterfront properties is **Lime Tree,** an expansive four-bedroom in the heart of Ocho Rios along a choice stretch of coastline just off Main Street. Other highlights are Edgewater, adjacent to Couples Ocho Rios, and Stonaway in the hills, which commands a gorgeous view of Ochi.

SunVillas (contact Alan Marlor, SunVillas, U.S. tel. 888/625-6007, alan@sunvillas.com, www.sunvillas.com) rents a nice assortment of villas on the North Coast between Ocho Rios and Galina, which vary considerably in price while all having much more than the basic amenities. Scotch on the Rocks in Ocho Rios, and Golden Clouds in Oracabessa are definite highlights.

Prospect Villas (tel. 876/994-1373, ian@prospect-villas.com, www.prospect-villas.com) rents five of the nicest villas in Ocho Rios, in addition to the Prospect Plantation great house. The villas (US$2,500–14,000 low season, US$3,500–16,500 high season for a weeklong stay) have three or four bedrooms, with a minimum two-night stay (from US$360/500 low/high per night). Part of the Prospect Plantation Estate, formerly owned by Sir Harold Mitchell, Prospect Villas have hosted some of the most important political and entertainment figures of the 20th century, including Charlie Chaplin and Henry Kissinger, to name a few. The villas have every amenity imaginable from DSL to iPod docks to satellite TV, not to mention the private waterfront and full staff.

Jamaica Association of Villas and Apartments (JAVA) has its headquarters in Ocho Rios (Pineapple Pl., tel. 876/974-2763, java-jam-villas@cwjamaica.com, www.villas injamaica.com) under the direction of Carmen McNight and offers booking services for its members.

All-Inclusive Resorts

Sunset Jamaica Grande (tel. 876/974-2200, reservations@sunsetochorios.com www.sunset jamaicagrande.com, from US$325/370 low/high) is the most prominent hotel on Turtle Beach, occupying the prime piece of real estate on the point of the bay. Refurbished in 2004, Sunset Jamaica Grande boasts the biggest conference facilities in Jamaica, with 3,066 square meters of meeting room space. The hotel has a total of five restaurants, five swimming pools, and the longest private beach in Ochi. The rooms are clean and well appointed, with full amenities. The Cabana Beachfront rooms on the two-story wing are especially nice, overlooking the lawn and beach area from their low balconies. Free wireless Internet is available to guests in the lobby. Food and beverages at the Sunset are not luxurious by any means, the hotel catering to more of a budget all-inclusive tourist focused on family fun rather than classy meals. Nonetheless, the specialty restaurants, which include Ginger Lily and LaDiva, are markedly better than the buffets and serve high-quality dishes. Liquor is not premium brand. The average stay is four nights. It's one of the most cost-effective places to get married (US$700), with a constant stream of fiancées.

Sandals has two properties in the area: **Sandals Dunn's River Villagio** and **Sandals Grande Ocho Rios Beach and Villa Resort** (Main St., tel. 876/974-5691, US$2590 weekly rate, www.sandals.com). The latter is a 529-room property covering land on both sides of the bypass.

Both properties are for couples only, but Sandals Dunn's River was recently refurbished and reinvented as an Italian Renaissance theme resort complete with imported Italian food and beverages. The recent overhaul has left the rooms smartly appointed with mass-produced furnishings consistent with the mass-market formula. The staff wear jester hats and greet guests with *"buon giorno!"*

Riu Ocho Rios is the latest all-inclusive, built right next to Sandals Dunn's River. Rooms at Riu are clean and appointed in replica furniture that makes an attempt to create a classy feel. Riu is easily the least expensive of the all-inclusive hotels, but it's hard to see the value when reservations in one of the three "premiere dining" restaurants requires standing in a long line 10 A.M.–noon. To make matters worse, the attempt at sushi in the Japanese-inspired restaurant falls terribly short. In the buffet dining room, where thankfully no reservations are required, the food quality is decent, while overwhelmingly imported. There is little inside the purple-painted buildings to remind guests that they are in Jamaica. Internet access is offered in the café off the lobby (US$18/hr).

◖ Couples (from US$507/551 low/high) has two all-inclusive resorts just east of town across the border in Tower Isle, St. Mary: **Couples San Souci** (White River, tel. 876/994-1353) and **Couples Ocho Rios** (Tower Isle, tel. 876/975-4271).

Couples Resorts are easily at the top of the all-inclusive ranking, firstly for the quality of food and beverages, which include items like fresh-squeezed juices for breakfast and premium liquor at 24-hour bars. The rooms at Sans Souci, which means "worry free" in French, are tasteful with simple decor and balconies overlooking a private beach. Couples Ocho Rios boasts a private island within swimming distance from the beach where nudists are welcome to hang loose.

FOOD
Seafood
◖ Tropical Vibes Seafood and Bar (contact Garwin Davis, tel. 876/392-8287 or 876/386-0858, 8 A.M.–11 P.M. daily, US$6.50–21) is a great breezy bar serving the best fresh escoveitched fish and bammy in town, as well as lobster, conch, and shrimp.

Jack Ruby's (1 James Ave., contact Peter Turner, cell 876/381-3794 or 876/974-7289, 11 A.M.–11 P.M. daily, US$5–13) serves local fare, such as fried chicken with rice and peas, as well as seafood.

World of Fish (3 James Ave., tel. 876/974-1863 8 A.M.–1 A.M. daily) serves fish, chicken (US$3.50) rice and peas, curry goat (US$5), stew chicken, fried, roast, or steam fish with bammy or festival.

Jerk
◖ Scotchies (Jack's Hall Fair Ground, beside the Epping gas station, tel. 876/794-9457, 11 A.M.–11 P.M. daily, A.M.–9 P.M. Sun., US$4–11) is Jamaica's famous jerk center and has its home base in Montego Bay; it recently opened a branch just west of Dunn's River.

Ocho Rios Jerk Centre (tel. 876/974-2549, 10 A.M.–11 P.M. daily, US$6–13) serves pork, whole and half chickens, ribs and fish by the pound, and conch. It's located between Cane Ridge and the stop light at the junction of DaCosta and the road to Fern Gulley.

John Crow's Tavern (10 Main St., tel. 876/974-5895, 9:30 A.M.–12:30 A.M. daily, later on Fri. and Sat.; US$7–12) is a small restaurant and bar on Ochi's main drag a few steps from the Hard Rock Café. Dishes include club sandwiches, oxtail, escoveitch fish, curry conch, curry chicken, jerk chicken, and pasta alfredo and marinara. The mixed vegetables and dip is very popular, as is the coconut jumbo shrimp. Friday is jerk night, with a sound system and a mixed crowd of locals and tourists. There are three 42-inch flat-screen TVs. Sahai Ruddock, the lovely operations manager, is a pleasure to deal with. Ravi Chatani owns the joint.

International
The Ruins at the Falls (17 DaCosta Dr., tel. 876/974-8888, noon–10 P.M. daily, www.ruinsjamaica.com) has an extensive menu with buffet lunch (US$15) that includes jerk chicken/pork, chicken, and escoveitched fish. Dinner items include Chinese roasted chicken (US$14), grilled lamb chops (US$28), Jamaican-style oxtail, curry goat (US$20) to Jamaican Red Stripe butterfly shrimp (US$28), and grilled lobster lobster thermador (US$35).

An American doctor, Robert Page, created

The Ruins in 1960s with bricks brought from a great house in Trelawny. The restaurant is one of the most scenic in Ocho Rios, with its dining room overlooking a natural 12-meter waterfall. The Ruins was once part of a larger property called Eden Bower which covered much of the hill behind the restaurant, including the plot on which Evita's Italian restaurant sits today. Eden Bower was owned by the Geddes family, one of the founding partners of Red Stripe beer. In 1907 the property was parceled off and sold.

🄲 **Blue Cantina** (first left when entering the eastern entrance of 81 Main St., entrance is around the corner on James Ave.; contact owner Cecile Henry, tel. 876/974-2430, 9 A.M.–8 P.M. daily, US$3–6) is not to be confused with the restaurant of the same name at 102 Main Street. Apparently Ms. Henry previously rented that space with much success before the property owners kicked her out—keeping the name in an effort to maintain her loyal clientele. The local Jamaican dishes (curry goat and chicken) are excellent, and the tacos, the cantina's specialty, are the best on the island. Ms. Henry bought the business from a man who bought the business from its original Mexican owner, and the culinary knowledge was thus passed down.

Almond Tree Restaurant (83 Main St., tel. 876/974-2676, 7:30 A.M.–10:30 A.M., noon–2:30 P.M., 6–9:30 P.M. daily) serves a mix of Jamaican and international dishes like lobster (US$24), a variety of chicken (US$14), and fish (US$21), pork chops (US$15), lamb chops (US$17), and butterfly shrimp (US$30). A full bar in the restaurant serves the typical Heineken, Guinness, and Red Stripe (US$2.50), as well as mixed drinks. Indoor and outdoor dining areas overlook the water.

Michelle's Pizzeria (tel. 876/974-4322 or 876/974-9484, 11 A.M.–11 P.M. daily) is located at the Pineapple Hotel and has a nice outdoor dining area. Four specialty pizzas are served (10–16-inch, US$6–25): Hawaiian delight, seafood sensation, meat lovers, and conscious decision. Other dishes (US$7–8) include lasagna, spaghetti and Bolognese sauce, and

vegetarian Rasta penne with traditional Jamaican ingredients. Subs are also prepared with smoked ham, jerk pork, fish, or plain cheese.

Evita's (Eden Bower Rd, reached by turning up the hill next to The Ruins; tel. 876/974-2333, 11 A.M.–10 P.M. Mon.–Sat., till 4 A.M. Sun. morning, US$11–30) is an Italian restaurant serving seafood, including lobster, steak, and pasta dishes . While Evita's might lack the upscale edge of Toscanini, the view is excellent and worth a trip.

Passage to India Restaurant & Bar (Sonis Plaza, 50 Main St., tel. 876/795-3182, 10 A.M.–10 P.M. Tues.–Sun., Mon till 3 P.M., US$11–26) serves very authentic North Indian cuisine with dishes like palak paneer, mala costa, chicken vindaloo, lamb, lobster, and shrimp.

Hong Kong International Restaurant (Soni Plaza, 50 Main St., tel. 876/974-0588, 10 A.M.–10 P.M. daily, from US$8.50) is one of the better places for Chinese food in Ochi, serving chicken, beef, shrimp, seafood, and pork, with noodles and rice. Hong Kong is a bit dodgy in its ambiance, making takeout a good option.

Bibibip's Bar & Grill (93 Main St., tel. 876/974-7438, 9 A.M.–1 A.M. daily, US$7–34) is a nice spot overlooking the water near Mahogany Beach. It features a wide range of seafood, as well as Jamaican and international dishes.

Food at **Coconuts** (Fisherman's Point, opposite Cruise Ship Pier, tel. 876/795-0064, 8 A.M.–10 P.M. daily, US$7–25) ranges from the ménage à trois appetizer (coconut shrimp, chicken samosa, and conch fritters); to chicken quesadillas made with jerk chicken; to jerk chicken wings; to a medley of shrimp, conch, and chicken; to grilled sirloin strip steak. Coconuts has an all-you-can-drink special (9 A.M.–4 P.M., US$20) that includes house-brand vodka, gin, and Appleton Special rum.

Toscanini Italian Restaurant & Bar (Harmony Hall, tel. 876/975-4785, US$10.50–24) is the most high-end and best-quality Italian restaurant in town with tables on the ground floor of a beautifully renovated great house and outside on the patio. Dishes include appetizers like marinated marlin, prosciutto and papaya, and yellowfin tuna tartare and entrées like spaghetti ciopinno di mar; the menu changes daily. The food is excellent, but be prepared to pay for it. Toscanini is run by congenial Lella, who is always around the place chatting with customers. Toscanini has been in operation since 1998.

Hard Rock Café (4 Main St., tel. 876/974-3333, hrsales@cwjamaica.com, 11 A.M.–11 P.M. Sun.–Thurs., 11 A.M.–midnight Fri. & Sat., , US$10–30) opened in November 2006 in Ocho Rios, bringing the world's greatest tourist trap to one of the Caribbean's foremost tourist towns. Dishes are essentially what is served at any other Hard Rock, from club sandwiches to burgers to steak. Local memorabilia adorning the walls includes Junior Murvin's guitar used by Bob Marley for recording of the *Kaya* album, as well as the original handwritten lyrics to "Jammin'." Also on display are a suede jacket worn by Jimi Hendrix and a cap worn by John Lennon.

Ocean's 11 Watering Hole (Cruise Ship Pier, tel. 876/974-8444, manbowen@cwjamaica .com, open when ship in town, closes at midnight at Tues. & Fri.) is a bar and restaurant opened in 2004 on the wharf that services the cruise ships. Open primarily when the ship is in port (8 A.M. at 1 A.M.). When there's no ship in (4 P.M. to 1 A.M.). Much business in Ochi resolves around cruise ship schedules, which tend to change. Call ahead if you're not within sight of the pier to be sure. You can get Red Stripe (US$3) at the bar downstairs; upstairs there's a snack bar, coffee shop, and seafood restaurant with some nice antique coffee equipment that was at one time part of the small coffee museum on-site. Coffee is sold by the cup and by the pound (US$18–26/lb).

Golden Crust Baking Company (72 Main St., tel. 876/974-2635, 8 A.M.–8:30 P.M. Mon.–Sat.) makes bread and pastries.

Three Star Restaurant (Rexo Plaza, tel. 876/795-1320, 10 A.M.–9 P.M. Mon.–Sat., 1–9 P.M. Sun., US$2–19) serves Chinese food, with dishes like chop suey, sweet and sour chicken, and shrimp fried rice.

Jamaican

My Favorite Place Restaurant (Shop 7, Ocean Village, tel. 876/795-0480, 8 A.M.–5 P.M. Mon.–Sat., breakfast only on Sun., US$2–6) serves typical Jamaican dishes like fried chicken, curry goat, escoveitched fish, brown stew, baked chicken; the menu changes daily, apart from the Jamaican staples. Paulette Garvey is the helpful proprietor and manager.

San-Mar Cafe (Shop 8, Ocean Village Shopping Centre, tel. 876/795-1024, US$2–6) serves local staples and Chinese dishes.

Healthy Way Vegetarian Kitchen (Shop 54 Ocean Village, tel. 876/974-9229, 8 A.M.–6 P.M. Mon.–Sat., US$1.50–5) serves escoveitched tofu, hominy or peanut, plantain carrot, bulgar porridge, steam cabbage with banana, and fried dumpling. Paula is the wonderful cashier of eight years.

Alkebu-Lan (Main St. across from the clock tower, US$3–4) is an excellent vegetarian health food restaurant serving Ital food in well-rounded meals. An irie Afro-centric ambiance complements roots music in the speakers.

◖ Mom's (7 Evenly St., tel. 876/974-2811, 8 A.M.–11 P.M. Mon.–Sat., US$4–6.50) not to be confused with Mother's on Main Street, is located in a blue building across from the police station towards the clock tower. It's a local favorite, with oxtail, brown stewed fish, baked chicken, fried chicken, curry goat, stew peas, and stewed beef.

Lion's Den (2.4 km west of cruise ship terminal; Joseph Morrison, supervisor, cell 876/896-1352; US$4–8.50) serves some of the best Jamaican home cooking in the Ocho Rios area, with dishes like fried chicken, curried goat, and stew pork. It makes a great stop for lunch on the way in or out of Ochi.

Mama Marley's Bar & Grill (50 Main St., tel. 876/795-4803) serves mediocre Jamaican and international dishes. The restaurant is owned by Cedella Marley, Bob's mother, commonly known as Mama B.

All Star Night Club and Restaurant (47 Main St., tel. 876/795-2547) is more dive bar than night club or restaurant, but an interesting local hang nonetheless.

Caribbean Sun Freeze (19 Main St., next to Burger King and NCB, contact proprietor Mr. Millot cell 876/384-1580, 8 A.M.–8 P.M. Mon.–Sat., noon–8 P.M. Sun., caribsunfreeze1@cw jamaica.com) owns the **Bella Italia** franchise in Ocho Rios and also serves a variety of fresh and frozen fruits and juice blends.

Sun Juice Cafe & Market (1 Main St., Sandcastles Hotel, tel. 876/441-0124, 9 A.M.–midnight daily), located across from Hard Rock Café, is a juice bar and café run by Sun-fired Foods master Aris LaTham serving the proprietary juice line, Jungle Juice, as well as the naturalist delight, Paradise Pies. The market specializes in exotic local fruits, with 80 percent of its products being raw foods and 20 percent cooked.

Coco Browns (Island Village, tel. 876/675-8991, cell 876/329-0597, coco_browns@yahoo.com, 9 A.M.–8 P.M. Mon.–Sat., 10 A.M.–8 P.M. Sun.) serves sandwiches, salads, pasta, coffee, tea, and natural juices. Jennifer and Michael Movery opened the business at Island Village in December 2006.

Scoops Unlimited (Island Village, tel. 876/675-8776, 9 A.M.–8:30 P.M. Mon.–Thurs., 9 A.M.–10 P.M. Fri. and Sat., 10 A.M.–9:30 P.M. Sun.) is one of the local Devon House I Scream franchises.

Groceries

Coconut Grove Supermarket and Wholesale (188 Main St., tel. 876/974-3049) is the best wholesale liquor store in Ochi, also selling a limited range of grocery items.

Liu's Rexo Supermarket is located at New Ocho Rios Plaza (tel. 876/974-2328).

DJ Supermarket & Wholesale (80a Main St., tel. 876/974-3462, 9 A.M.–9 P.M. Mon.–Sat.) sells groceries and liquor.

Money's Worth Meat Mart (128 Main, tel. 876/974-2917) is the best place for fresh meat and imported frozen fish if you have trouble finding the local, fresh variety. Items include beef, chicken, local pork, snapper, Cornish hens, and imported turkey.

Willy's Variety (130 Main St., tel. 876/974-5175, 9 A.M.–8 P.M. Mon.–Sat.) sells groceries, liquor, and hardware.

Park 'N' Shop Wholesale Supermarket is at 20 Main Street (tel. 876/795-4718).

Tropical Oven (Shop 2, Ocean Village, tel. 876/795-4970) is a bakery selling pastries and breads.

INFORMATION AND SERVICES

The **St. Ann Chamber of Commerce** (tel. 876/974-2629) has tourist booklets that advertise the area's tourism businesses and attractions.

Car Rentals

Freehill Car Rental (Coconut Grove beside Petcom gas station, manager Cecil Subaran, cell 876/865-3704, tel. 876/795-4966, www.freehillcarrental.com, 8 A.M.–8 P.M. Mon.–Sat., till 5 P.M. Sun.,) rents Corolla, RAV-4, Nissan Cube/March (US$60–110/day, US$500–650/week), as well as scooters. The company also offers airport transfers and tours.

Villa Car Rentals (Shop 7, Coconut Grove shopping centre, tel. 876/974-2474, villacar rentalscoltd@msn.com, 8 A.M.–5 P.M. Mon.–Sat., 9 A.M.–2 P.M. Sun.) has 2006 Toyota Corolla (US$420/week) and 2005 Yaris (US$320/week) plus tax and optional insurance ($50). Linda Mash and Harry Chung are co-owners.

Budget (15 Milford Rd. on bypass across from Turtle Park, tel. 876/974-1288, 8 A.M.–4:30 P.M. daily) has cars for rent.

Sunshine Car Rentals (154 Main St., Pineapple Place, tel. 876/974-2980 or 876/974-5025, 8 A.M. 5 P.M. Mon.–Fri., 9 A.M.–2 P.M. Sat.) has 2004 Suzuki Grand Vitara (US$125/day, US$582/weeky) and Mitsubishi Lancers (US$149/day, US$700/week).

SunSpree Car Rental (tel. 876/974-6258, cell 876/378-5682, fax 876/974-2652) rents Lancers and Corollas (US$70/day, US$378/week).

Caribbean Car Rentals (99a Main St., tel. 876/974-2513, 8:30 A.M.–5 P.M. Mon.–Fri., 9 A.M.–2 P.M. Sat., 9 A.M.–noon Sun.) has 2004 Mitsubishi Lancer, 2005 Suzuki Liana

(US$82/day, US$492/week) and 2006 Toyota Corollas (US$97/day, US$571/week).

Internet
Jerkin' @ Taj Internet Cafe (Taj Mahal Centre, tel. 876/795-0862, 9 A.M.–5 P.M. Mon.–Sat.) has access for US$8 per hour. The restaurant section (10 A.M.–7 P.M.) serves decent jerk: quarter chicken (US$15), jerk (US$13).

Power Plus Computers (Rexo Plaza, Main St., tel. 876/795-4664, 9:30 A.M.–5:30 P.M. Mon.–Sat.) sells and repairs computers and basic accessories and also offers Internet access (US$3.50/hr).

Cable and Wireless Communications Center (Shop 13–15, Island Plaza, Main St., tel. 876/974-0996 or 876/926-9700) managed by Core Communications sells prepaid cellular phones, phone cards, and accessories and has the best rates in town on broadband Internet access (US$2.50/hr) and phone-card calling.

Banks
NCB Bank is at 40 Main Street next to Island Plaza/BK and across from the craft market (tel. 876/974-2522).

Scotia Bank is also on Main Street, three buildings west of NCB (tel. 876/974-2311).

Nancy's Cambio (Taj Mahal, 4 Main St., tel. 876/974-2414; 50 Main St., tel. 876/795-4285; St. Ann's Bay, tel. 876/972-8842, 9 A.M.–5 P.M. Mon.–Sat.) offers slightly better exchange rates than the banks. Travelers checks are accepted with two forms of ID. Money transfers are also possible at the St. Ann's Bay Moneygram outlet.

Healthcare and Pharmacies
Kulkarni Medical Clinic (16 Rennie Rd., tel. 876/974-3357, cell 876/990-7726) has a well-respected private practice used by many of the area's better hotel. It's located between RBTT bank and Jamaica National.

St. Ann's Bay Hospital (Seville Road, tel. 876/972-2272) is the most important in the region, with people coming from kilometers around. Better service can be obtained at private health centers in Ocho Rios, however.

Ocho Rios Pharmacy is in Ocean Village Shopping Centre (Shop 67a, tel. 876/974-2398, 8 A.M.–8 P.M. daily).

Pinegrove Pharmacy is east of the clock tower on Main Street (Shop 5, Ocho Rios Mall, tel. 876/974-5586, 9 A.M.–8 P.M. Mon.–Sat., 10 A.M.–3 P.M. Sun.).

Photo
Quick Shots Imaging Labs (4 DaCosta Dr., tel. 876/974-8498 or 876/974-8498, 9 A.M.–6 P.M. Mon.–Sat.) offers one-hour processing and sells film and memory cards.

Bailey's Photo Studio & Colour Lab (2 Rennie Rd,, tel. 876/974-2711) offers photo processing and sells a limited range of digital camera products.

Laundry
Carib Laundro-Mat (Shop 6, Carib Arcade opposite of 112 Main St., tel. 876/974-7631, 7 A.M.–6:30 P.M. Mon.–Sat.) and **Express Laundromat** (18–20 Pineapple Place, Main St., tel. 876/795-0720 or 876/795-0721, 7 A.M.–7 P.M. Mon.–Sat., 9 A.M.–4 P.M. Sun.) both offer laundry services.

Communications and Media
DHL is at Ocean Village Plaza (Shop 3, tel. 876/974-8001, 9 A.M.–5 P.M. Mon.–Sat.).

Studio Tokyo (Coconut Grove, cell 876/864-3640) offers music recording, mastering, and video production services in a modest studio near Irie FM.

GETTING THERE
Route taxis and buses leave for Kingston and points east and west along the coast from the lot just south of the clock tower in downtown Ocho Rios. Buses go between Ochi and Downtown Kingston (US$4) as well as to Montego Bay (US$4), while route taxis ply every other route imaginable to Brown's Town (US$3), Moneague (US$1), and east and west along the coast to Oracabessa (US$2) and St. Ann's Bay (US$1.50).

Flights into the Oracabessa Aerodrome, 15 minutes east of Ochi, can be booked with any of the island's charter operators from Kingston,

MoBay, Negril, or Port Antonio. All the fixed-wing operators are based in MoBay and offer better rates when departing from there.

International Airlink (tel. 876/940-6660, res@intlairlink.com, www.intlairlink.com) offers service from MoBay (US$302 one-way paid in cash for two persons), Kingston (US$1,324) and from Port Antonio (US$1,575). Airlink passes on bank charges of an additional 5 percent when paying with a credit card.

TimAir (tel. 876/952-2516, timair@usa.net, www.timair.net) also offers service from MoBay (US$316 for up to four persons plus tax), Kingston (US$579), Port Antonio (US$549), and Negril (US$566).

Island Hoppers (tel. 876/974-1285, www.jamaicahelicoptertours.com, helicopter@mail.infochan.com, 8 A.M.–5 P.M.) offers helicopter airport transfers for up to four passengers from MoBay (US$889), Kingston (US$747), and to and from virtually any other points on the island.

GETTING AROUND

Route taxis are the most economical way of getting around if you don't mind squeezing in with several other people. Taxis leave from the rank by the clock tower and can also be flagged down by the roadside if there is any room. Route taxis display their destination and origin in painted letters on the side of the cars and are typically white Toyota Corollas. Overcrowding has been somewhat reduced in recent years with increased oversight from the authorities. It is impossible to walk the streets of Ocho Rios without being offered a chartered taxi; bear in mind that these drivers will quote any figure that comes to mind. Haggling is very much a part of hiring a local charter, and be sure not to pay everything in advance if you hope to see your driver stick around. (See *Information and Services* for car rental listings.)

West of Ocho Rios

As you head west from Ocho Rios, the North Coast Highway hugs the waterfront passing Dolphin Cove, Dunn's River Falls, and Laughing Waters before reaching a cluster of villas and the Sandals and Riu resorts that front Mammee Bay. Just past the entrance to the resorts, an Epping gas station marks the junction where Scotchie's Jerk Centre occupies one corner across the highway from the Drax Hall Polo Club.

Continuing west, the next community is St. Ann's Bay, a busy town with one of the better hospitals on the North Coast and a few attractions worth stopping for, including Seville Great House and Heritage Park and the Marcus Garvey Statue by the Parish Library.

Still further west, the small community of Priory sits along a dusty stretch of highway with few passersby stopping there, except on Sundays when the community's public beach comes alive for dance parties.

From Priory westward the highway becomes lonely, passing Chukka Cove and a few ill-conceived housing schemes that barely made it past the conceptual stages. The next community of any size is Runaway Bay, where several hotels hug the highway or the beach. From Runaway Bay the highway continues westward to Discovery Bay, the last settlement of any size before the Trelawny border. Discovery Bay is one of Jamaica's most exclusive villa communities; the eastern side of the bay is dotted with luxury homes. Meanwhile the center of the bay is dominated by an immense domed bauxite facility.

SIGHTS

Dolphin Cove (tel. 876/974-5335, info@dolphincovejamaica.com, www.dolphincovejamaica.com, 8:30 A.M.–5:30 daily, reservations required for encounters) is located just around the corner from Dunn's River Falls and offers a variety of programs where visitors interact with dolphins to a varying degree

OCHO RIOS

of intimacy, depending on the price—starting with a Touch Encounter (US$67), where you get to touch the dolphins' snout in knee-high water, to the Swim Encounter (US$129), where you get to touch the dolphins while swimming in an enclosed area of the ocean, to Swim with Dolphins (US$195), where visitors actually do a dorsal pull and a foot push with two dolphins.

In the shark program (US$119), there is a feeding show and petting and snorkeling session with six nurse sharks, ranging 0.6 meter to up to three meters long.

The basic admission (US$45) includes kayaking, snorkeling, mini motor-boat rides, and glass-bottom boat tours. Listed prices reflect direct booking through Dolphin Cove.

Dunn's River Falls

Dunn's River Falls (tel. 876/974-4767 or 876/974-5944, www.dunnsriverfallsja.com, 8:30 A.M.–4 P.M. daily, US$15 adult, US$12 children 2–11) is the most highly visited tourist attraction in Jamaica, if not the Caribbean. The site is owned by the Urban Development Corporation (UDC) and receives over 300,000 visitors a year who come to climb the steps up the falls. There is a small beach by the mouth of the river and two restaurants serving local dishes and beer. Patricia Parkins manages the attraction.

Dunn's River Falls is best visited on days when there are no cruise ships in Ocho Rios, which is easy to determine by taking a look at the pier. Every all-inclusive resort offers tour packages to the falls, however, so it's hard to avoid the crowds on any day. While it's a worthwhile attraction, there are several other falls in the area that see fewer visitors and offer a more serene experience even if they aren't as spectacular for their size.

Dunn's River is located a few minutes' drive west of Ocho Rios. Route taxis pass by the falls on their way to St. Ann's Bay and will stop at Dunn's River by request. A private taxi charter from Ocho Rios shouldn't cost more than US$10, though the hard-hustling Ochi cabbies will likely start at a much higher price. Don't be afraid to haggle and remind the driver it's only a few kilometers.

Drax Hall Polo Club

Located across the highway from Scotchie's and the Epping gas station just west of Sandals Dunn's River, Drax Hall Polo Club has one of the oldest polo fields in the world, and certainly in the Caribbean. Home to the St. Ann Polo Club (Contact Shane Chin, tel. 876/952-4370, cell 876/383-5586, chinrcpolo@yahoo.com; or Lesley Masterton-Fong Yee, cell 876/681-4660), the fields have been in continual use since 1905. Polo has been in Jamaica since 1800 when it was introduced by the British army. The game is played strictly on an amateur level in Jamaica, with approximately 40 playing members spread over two clubs: the Drax Hall Polo Club in St. Ann and the Kingston Polo Club. There are three other privately owned fields on the island.

The St. Ann Polo Club originated in Orange Hall in 1882 and today has a casual ambiance where members hang out to enjoy English tea or a beer after matches. In addition to the polo grounds, the facilities at the club include a full-size dressage ring and jumping ring, stable, turn-out paddocks, and, of course, the Polo Bar. The polo season at Drax Hall starts in late January with practice matches on Thursday afternoons and matches on Saturdays at 4P.M. The club is host to many international players and riders from the United States, Colombia, Costa Rica, England, Guatemala, Scotland, India, Barbados, and Argentina. The players on the island are handicapped international from -2 to 4 goals. The Association can host tournaments from 1-goal to 14-goal polo. The Jamaica Polo Tournament is played at the St. Ann Polo Club and starts in March and goes through the end of May.

Fire River

Fire River is found in a park area a few hundred meters off the highway about 1.5 kilometers before the main junction to turn off into St. Ann's Bay. The river is so named thanks to flammable gas that rises from a pool in the river and can be lit in a curious mixing of the elements. While locals will tell legends of the history and significance of the spot, a large housing subdivision just through the trees prompts the question of whether the gas is actually methane derived from the area's septic systems. Still, claims are made that the phenomenon predates the bordering urbanization. The attraction is not managed and can be reached by turning off the highway by the easternmost entrance to St. Ann's Bay and taking an immediate left after the dog clinic off the road along a dirt track leading to the river.

MAMMEE BAY

Mammee Bay is located a few minutes' west of Dunn's River and is home to two large all-inclusive resorts, Sandal's Dunn's River and Riu Ocho Rios. The beach in front of the hotels is cordoned off with security guards, preventing non-guests from entering. Just west of the hotels there are a number of lovely private villas that face the beach, which that can be accessed through the subdivision adjacent to the entrance to Riu. The beautiful beach goes undiscovered by most visitors to Jamaica. The lucky few who reside on the bay might prefer it that way, but the beach is public.

ST. ANN'S BAY

The parish capital, St. Ann's Bay is a small bustling town at the base of the hills that leads into the interior along rough potholed roads. Originally called Santa Gloria by Columbus, St. Ann's Bay was the site for the earliest Spanish settlement of Sevilla La Nueva, or New Seville, which became the colony's first capital. Santa Ana, as the area was named by the Spanish, was where they formed a cultural mix with the native Taino population and imported enslaved Africans. From the Spanish arrival straight through to the emancipation of slavery the area was an epicenter of conflict between the violent anti-missionary Colonial Church Union and the Baptist abolitionists. It was these struggles for liberation that inspired St. Ann's most renowned son, pan-Africanist Marcus Garvey.

Sights

Marcus Garvey Statue in St. Ann's Bay is located in front of the St. Ann parish library just above the center of town. Garvey's bust stands in remembrance of a man whose ideas were suppressed by the powers of his day, but whose teachings have made serious ripples around the globe inspiring black power movements in a number of countries.

Seville Heritage Park (tel. 876/972-2191 or 876/972-0665, seville@anbell.net, 9 A.M.–5 P.M. daily, US$5 adults, US$2 children) is an estate great house with a museum where a historical tour covers artifacts on display.

Cultural Treasures is a very nice gift shop located in the great house complex with authentic Jamaican preserves and crafts.

Hooves (Seville Heritage Park, tel. 876/972-0905, hooves@cwjamaica.com, www.hooves jamaica.com) offers 2.5-hour horseback rides (9 A.M. and 2 P.M. daily) from Seville Great House to the beach (US$65/person; with transport, US$70/person from Ochi, US$75/person from Runaway), as well as a bush doctor ride in the hills (US$60 with transport from Ochi, US$65 from Runaway Bay). The bush doctor ride is offered during the week only.

Accommodations

High Hope Estate (Priory, tel. 876/972-2277, reservations@highhopeestate.com, www.high hopeestate.com, US$95–165) is a lovely B&B-style accommodation. Lunch and dinner are served, but the kitchen is closed on Sundays. Rooms have ceiling fans, a nice breeze to keep things cool, coffee pots, and mini-fridges, radio and CD player, and cable in many of the rooms with TVs on request. The property has beautiful gardens and a large swimming pool. Dennis Donald is the on-site owner/manager.

Seacrest Beach Hotel (Richmond Cove, Priory, tel. 876/972-1594 or 876/972-1547, seacrestresort@cwjamaica.com, www.seacrest resorts.com, from US$80) is a 35-room property with standard rooms that have air-conditioning, private baths with hot water, cable TV, and private balcony with sea view. There is also a pool and juice bar on property.

MARCUS MOSIAH GARVEY

Marcus Mosiah Garvey was born in St. Ann's Bay in 1887 to humble but educated parents. After completing elementary school, he moved to Kingston where he worked in a print shop and became increasingly interested and engaged in organized movements aimed at improving conditions for black Jamaicans. Black Jamaicans, while free from the bonds of slavery since 1838, were far from equal to their white counterparts and denied suffrage, among other basic rights. In 1907 Garvey was elected vice president of the Kingston Union, a charge which would cost him his job at the printer's when he became involved in a strike. At the age of 23 Garvey left the island to work in Central America, as many Jamaicans in search of opportunity did at the time. His travels around the region gave Garvey an awareness of the common plight faced by the black race, seeding in him what would become a lifelong struggle to unite Africans of all nations under one common aim. In 1912 Garvey traveled to England where he became engaged with black Africans and further broadened his vision of seeing black people take control of their destiny across the globe. In 1914 Garvey returned to Jamaica and founded the first chapter of the United Negro Improvement Association (UNIA) whose motto, "One God! One Aim! One Destiny!" summed up the broad goal of the organization to improve the lot of black people through solidarity and self-determination.

While Garvey's message was well received by his followers in Jamaica, it was in the midst of the Harlem Renaissance in New York City that he was first lauded as a prophet. Garvey is credited as the father of the Black Power movement, which would take Harlem, and ultimately the entire U.S., by storm and eventually lead to the Civil Rights Movement of the 1960s. Garvey sought to enfranchise black people by fomenting black-owned businesses that would be linked on an international level. To facilitate this project he established the Black Star Line, an international shipping company that was to promote commerce.

Garvey's following numbered four million members worldwide in 1920, a movement large enough to catch the attention of both the U.S. and British governments. When Garvey began to sell the notion of a mass return to Africa however, he met resistance at the highest level of government. Garvey was convicted of mail fraud and imprisoned for a five-year term on what his followers considered trumped-up charges. After two years, he was released on an executive pardon and deported back to Jamaica. Local authorities were none too happy to see Garvey continue agitating for wider rights by forming the People's Political Party (PPP) in an effort to bring reform to Jamaica's colonial system. Garvey ran for a seat in Parliament, and after losing, won a seat on the Kingston and St. Andrew Corporation from a jail cell where he'd been placed for contempt of court. At the time, suffrage was limited to land owners, a class to which many of Garvey's followers did not belong, and his political support was accordingly stifled. Frustrated by the slow pace of change in Kinston, Garvey returned to London in 1935 where he would remain until his death in 1940. In 1964 Garvey was declared a national hero in Jamaica, and his remains were reinterned at Heroes Memorial in Kingston.

Garvey's legacy has been mixed in Jamaica to say the least. Perhaps the greatest disservice to his teachings lies in the fact that his pleas for universal education have never been met at an institutional level. At the same time, there is no doubting the impact he has made in certain circles. Rastafarians claim Garvey repeatedly iterated the call, "Look to the east for the crowning of a black king." It was one of Garvey's followers, Leonard Howell, who first cited the crowning of Ethiopian Emperor Haile Selassie on November 2, 1930, as a fulfillment of that prophecy, leading to the birth of the Rastafarian movement. Even today, it is the Rastafarian community both in Jamaica and abroad that has embraced Garvey's teachings to the greatest extent, often comparing him to John the Baptist.

Honeymoon suites and one- and two-bedroom cottages are a bit more spacious and separate from the main building.

Seascape Hotel (876/972-2753, cell 876/335-5195, or U.S. tel. 866/879-9292, seascape@seascapejamaica.com, www.seascapejamaica.com, US$45/50) has 10 basic rooms in three separate cottages centered around a common living area run under a hostel concept. Amenities include hot water, fans, air-conditioning, and a common kitchen facility is available for guest use. Seascape caters to budget travelers offering dorm room accommodations (US$25/person). The seafront property has 6.5 hectares. Lloyd Chen is the helpful owner/manager. Cell phone rentals are also offered for a nominal charge (US$10). The property has a swimming pool and access to a craggy beach.

Priory

Just east of the stoplight in Priory a turnoff leads down to **Priory Beach.** There are several small cook shops, pan chicken vendors, a pudding shop, and a billiard hall along the stretch of highway running through the hamlet.

Cranbrook Flower Forest and River Head Adventure Trail (tel. 876/770-8071, www.cranbrookff.com, US$10 adults, US$5 children 12 and under, 9 A.M.–5 P.M. daily) is one of Jamaica's best-maintained and most highly acclaimed gardens. The nature trail follows the Little River to its source. The park is located 29 kilometers west of Ocho Rios and 6.5 kilometers east of Runaway Bay. A large sign 1.5 kilometers west of Chukka Cove indicates where to turn inland off the main road.

RUNAWAY BAY

Runaway Bay is lined with a strip of fine sand with all-inclusive resorts like SuperClubs' Breezes and Hedonism commanding the choice properties at the center and eastern tip of the Bay, respectively. The center of the Runaway Bay community consists of a few strips of buildings that include hole-in-the-wall restaurants, grocery stores, and a multitude of small dive bars with colored Christmas lights strung around.

While many would suggest the bay was named after the flight of Don Cristobal Arnaldo de Ysassi, Spanish Governor of Jamaica at the time of the British takeover, Ysassi actually fled from Christopher's Point in St. Mary, and the more likely story involves the flight of runaway slaves to Cuba to seek their freedom.

Sights

Runaway Bay Public Beach has Flavors Grill, which serves fried chicken and beer and is a popular hangout that attracts throngs on weekends with loud music. The beach itself has clean, fine sand with a reef just offshore. To get to the beach, turn off the main highway in the center of town by The Runaway's Sports Bar.

Green Grotto Caves (tel. 876/973-2841 or 876/973-3217, 9 A.M.–4 P.M. daily) is Jamaica's most commercially successful cave attraction, located on a 26-hectare property between Runaway and Discovery Bays. While tamer than the experiences you can have in the heart of Trelawny's Cockpit Country a bit further west, Green Grotto, also known as Runaway Cave or Hopewell Cave, is nonetheless a well-conceived organized tour, especially considering it is owned and operated by Jamaica's Urban Development Corporation. During the 45-minute tour that descends to an underground lake, well-rehearsed guides give a history of the caves, their formations, and their importance to the Taino and Spanish. A drink is included in the price of admission (US$20 adults, US$10 children). The caves are located 2.5 kilometers west of Runaway Bay off the North Coast Highway, where a big yellow sign indicates the turnoff heading inland.

Shopping

Earth Kloz & Tingz (adjacent to Hedonism III and the Baptist church, contact Worknesh, cell 876/880-5859) sells Afro-centric clothing, tie-dye, and African fabrics.

Stop & Shop (Salem, tel. 876/973-7168, 9 A.M.–8 P.M.) has a good selection of supplies and groceries.

Sports and Recreation

Breezes Golf Club (Runaway Bay, tel. 876/973-7319, greens fees US$80 or $US25 JGA

OCHO RIOS

members, US$16 for caddy, US$35 for cart, US$20/30 clubs) has an 18-hole championship course. The course recommends gratuity of US$10+ per person. Consecutive days pay less, down to US$40 on the third day and thereafter, which comes with rate reductions. Guests at Breezes Runaway Bay have green fees waived, and Hedonism guests get reduced rates.

Accommodations
UNDER US$75
Lazy Day Cottages (tel. 876/973-4318, cell 876/357-2608) has basic rooms (US$13) with double beds, fans, and cold water in private bathrooms. Three rooms have kitchenettes (US$21), while one two-bedroom cottage separate from the rest known as the Bob Marley Cottage (US$33) is more tasteful, in a rustic sense, with simple wood construction and a lovers' loft. Lazy Day Cottages are frequently used in three-hour intervals (US$8.50) but also get their share of foreign guests on a shoestring budget. You may find Mistress Campbell, the sweet, enterprising #2 to owner Ms. Marlene Taylor, who lives abroad. Security at Lazy Day is dubious with threats and break-ins having been reported by management.

The Runaway's (Bryan Wards, cell 876/412-1454; US$70) has basic rooms with tiled floors, air-conditioning, and hot water. While not the most charming accommodations, rates are reasonable and the hotel is situated centrally along the highway with food upstairs and the beach five minutes away.

Salem Resort (Salem, tel. 876/973-4256, salemresort@yahoo.com, www.salemresort .com, US$35–60) is a basic accommodation with rooms ranging from basic with standing fan, to suites with ceiling fan, air-conditioning, and kitchenette.

US$75-200
Runaway Heart Hotel (tel. 876/973-6671, runaway.heart@cwjamaica.com, www.run awayheart.com.jm, US$83/90 low/high) is a hotel run by Jamaica's HEART training institute in close proximity to the golf course. The hotel has 56 rooms, which are well maintained

with tiled floors and floral bed-covers on king or two double beds, balconies overlooking the bay, TV, air-conditioning, and private baths with hot water. A computer in the office is available for guests to browse the Web and is included in the rate. There is a pool and small fitness center at the hotel as well.

Club Ambiance (tel. 876/973-4705, info@ clubambiancejamaica.com, www.clubambiance .com/villa.htm, US$95/105 low/high) is a 90-room 18+ property billed as an alternative to the mega resorts. Rooms have king beds, air-conditioning, hot water, and TV, with basic wooden furniture and tiled floors. Decor is definitely early '90s, with loud colored bedspreads and cheap art on the walls. There is one villa on property with a private pool that can accommodate up to six (US$570/630 low/high). The hotel has a lively activities schedule.

ALL-INCLUSIVE RESORTS
Franklyn D. Resort (FDR) (876-973-4591, reservations@fdrholidays.com, www.fdrholi days.com, US$250/375 low/high per person) is a family-oriented all-inclusive that differentiates itself by offering each family a dedicated nanny (US$4/hr).

Royal DeCameron Club Caribbean (tel. 876/973-4802, ventas.jam@decameron.com, US$94/110 low/high per person) is the second hotel of the DeCameron group in Jamaica. There are 183 pleasant rooms, some in a main block, others are either beachfront or garden cottages with king beds, air-conditioning, TV, hot water. The property has two pools and a private beach.

Hedonism III (tel. 876/973-4100 or U.S. tel. 877-GO-SUPER,, www.superclubs.com) is the second such establishment on the island, after Negril's Hedonism II. The resort bills itself as a place to escape inhibitions and worries and focus on guilty pleasures. All the features of SuperClubs all-inclusive are present, from the trapeze on the beach to swim-up bars. Of course Hedonism sets itself apart with whirlpool tubs in every room, mirrors over the bed, and nude beaches outside. With the exception of sex out in the open, everything else goes.

Several organized events are held throughout the year used to market vacation packages, and porn stars like Devin Lane have been invited guests in the past to help cement the resort's risqué reputation.

Breezes Runaway Bay (tel. 876/973-4820 or 876/973-6099, www.superclubs.com) was closed for six months in 2006, during which time the resort underwent a massive refurbishment that gave the entire property a facelift. The renovations have left the flagship Breezes Resort with five restaurants, including the SuperClubs signature Japanese-inspired Munasan, and culturally inspired Reggae Café, three swimming pools, 40 suites with private plunge pools, and a total of 266 rooms. A new three-story block on the western beach has 30 oceanfront rooms and suites, 14 of which have private plunge pools. In the eastern courtyard, 30 garden-view rooms were converted into verandah suites, also with private plunge pools. Rooms at Breezes are spacious with complete amenities.

Food

The Runaway's Sports Bar and Grill (cell 876/407-1293, owner Bryan Wards cell 876/412-1454, 11 A.M.–2 A.M. Mon.–Fri., 10 A.M.–2 A.M. Sat. & Sun., US$9–36) is a cool spot on top of a four-story building in the easternmost of Runaway Bay's little shopping plazas. The roof has a small swimming pool, a billiards table, and flat-screen TVs linked into a satellite connection. The bar serves domestic beers and mixed drinks, with the kitchen serving items like fried chicken, crab backs, tacos, with sides of fried plantain. Fresh juices are also served (US$2).

Northern Jerk, across from Royal DeCameron Club Caribbean, has good food and a clean environment for a jerk center.

There is a **Devon House I Scream** franchise along the main strip by Tek It Easy.

Sharkey's (Bamboo Beach, cell 876/881-5760, 8 A.M.–10 P.M. daily) is a seafood restaurant serving items like fried, roasted, and steamed fish (US$7–10), conch (fritters, stewed, curried, US$5–7) and lobster (US$15).

DISCOVERY BAY

Originally named Puerto Seco, or Dry Harbour, by Christopher Columbus, Discovery Bay was renamed to reflect the debated assertion that this was the first point in Jamaica where the explorer made landfall. Many experts believe that the actual first point of entry was in Rio Bueno, a few kilometers farther west, where Columbus would have sought fresh water.

Sights

Puerto Seco Beach (tel. 876/973-2660 or 876/973-2944, cell 876/325-7520 or 876/450-8529, 9 A.M.–5 P.M. daily, US$3.50 adults, US$2 children 7–12, US$1.50 children under 7), pronounced "seeko," can be accessed by turning in across from the Texaco station in Discovery Bay. The public beach has some of the cleanest bathrooms at any public beach in Jamaica, Jupsy's Snack Bar, and Puerto Seco Beach Bar. Isolyn Walters is the sweet property manager.

Columbus Park (free) located on the western side of the bay, is a little roadside park and open-air museum wedged between the highway and the slope descending to the water, with a mural depicting the arrival of Italian explorer Christopher Columbus and several relics from the colonial period scattered about the well-kept park.

Accommodations

Many of Jamaica's most wealthy families have weekend homes on Discovery Bay, making it one of the island's most exclusives villa enclaves. Many of these homes rent, either through the owners or through **Villas by Linda Smith** (U.S. tel. 301/229-4300, linda@jamaicavillas.com, www.jamaicavillas.com).

Discovery Bay Villa (tel. 876/973-2836 or 876/973-2663) is a convenient and affordable rest a three-minute walk from Puerto Seco Beach across the highway. The spacious two-story house has a downstairs bedroom with queen-size bed, TV and fan (US$36), as well as two rooms upstairs: one with queen bed, air-conditioning, and TV (US$50); the other

Columbus Park in Discovery Bay displays a number of colonial-era instruments like a Spanish-era water filter, a dugout canoe replica, and a water wheel.

with a king bed, air-conditioning, TV, and a whirlpool tub in the bathroom.

Sugar Bay (Peter McConnell, tel. 876/903-6125, pmcconnell@worthyparkestate.com, www.jamaicavillas.com, US$11,900/14,400 low/high weekly) is one of the nicest villas on Discover Bay.

Amanaoka, rented through Linda Smith (U.S. tel. 301/229-4300, linda@jamaicavillas .com, www.jamaicavillas.com), also on D-Bay, is perhaps the most over-the-top-luxurious villa in Jamaica.

Food

Bigga (Portland's Point Road before reaching the villas) does the best jerk around on weekends.

Ultimate Jerk Center (10 min west of Breezes approaching Discovery Bay, tel. 876/973-2054, 10 A.M.–10 P.M. daily, US$1–5) does chicken, pork, stewed pork, curry goat, stewed chicken, stewed conch, potato, festival, bammy and fritter, rice and peas, and french fries. Stephanie and Marcia are the sweet bartenders. The bar serves a variety of liquor and every last Saturday of the month an oldies party is held.

Mackie's Jerk Centre (on the eastern edge of town, no phone, 9 A.M.–9 P.M. daily), around the bend from Ultimate on the way to Discovery Bay, was at one time the number one jerk center in the area. The quality has fallen off and the product tends to sit out in the display case for extended periods before anybody buys it. The business changed hands in 2006 and reopened under the new management of Michael Thompson, the same owner of Yow's (tel. 876/954-0366). Live music on weekends tends to be uncharacteristically sedate coming from the synth keyboard of their regular musician. A small gift shop (Lorraine, cell 876/458-0728) sells the ubiquitous "Jamaica no problem" t-shirts.

Grill 3000 (contact proprietor Lindel Lawrence, tel. 876/973-3000, 9 A.M.–until the last person leaves, US$1–3.50) serves steam fish and fish soup accompanied by cornmeal dumplings (complimentary), as well as cappuccino to wash it down.

PSSL Supermarket (Philmore Mall, tel. 876/670-0327) is a good bet for groceries and supplies.

South of Ocho Rios

From Ocho Rios, Milford Road (A2) heads south from the main intersection by Turtle Park and uphill along the steep windy route through Fern Gully. A few roadside vendors sell crafts in the cool shade of a few of the wider corners. The road exits in Colgate and continues on to Bromley, Walker's Wood, and then Moneague before reaching Faith Pen just before the border with Clarendon. From the main intersection in Moneague, the A1 heads to St. Ann's Bay passing through Claremont. A left at the intersection in Claremont leads to Nine Mile. Staying on the A1 past Claremont will take you through Green Park where the road splits. By taking a left at the Y intersection you reach Brown's Town where the road meets the B3, which runs from May Pen through Cave Valley, Alexandria, and Brown's Town to Runaway Bay on the North Coast. The region is known as the Dry Harbour Mountains. Brown's Town is the closest town of any size to the Bob Marley Mausoleum in Nine Mile and is famous for its bustling market. Cave Valley is a small community along the Clarendon border, which has a bustling Saturday market where livestock is sold.

Bromley (alexsale@usa.net, annedwards@furrowsworks.com, www.bromleyjamaica.com) is a stately great house owned by the founding family of Walkerswood jerk sauces; it's today rented out for groups and retreats.

Art Beat Studio (Bromley, tel. 876/917-2530 or 876/350-6193, inansi@cwjamaica.com, open by appointment) is a beautiful little craft studio run by Inansi (Nancy Burke) and located next to one of Jamaica's most beautiful functioning great houses. Inansi creates a variety of artistic crafts items from masks to pillows.

💶 WALKERSWOOD

Walkerswood (located between Fern Gully and Moneague just past Bromley Great House heading south, contact tour coordinators Denyse Perkins and Kemisha Stevens, tel. 876/917-2318, denyseperkins@walkerswood.com, www.walkerswood.com, 8 A.M.–4:30 P.M. Mon.–Sat., US$15 adults, US$7.50 children 3–12) is

home of a farmers' co-op that has grown into makers of some of the finest and most successful barbecue sauces, marinades, curry seasonings, and fruit pickles exported from Jamaica. A factory tour is offered where visitors see how the products are made and get to sample jerk pork or chicken made with Walkerswood products. Large groups should call in advance to schedule a tour. Walkerswood is a success story as a community-based cottage industry that has gained a global presence while staying true to its roots. The company currently employs 150 full-time staff at the factory.

MONEAGUE

Moneague is small community along the main road between Spanish Town and the North Coast notable for the Moneague Teacher Training College, the Jamaica Defense Force Training Camp, the mysterious rising lake, and the Café Aubergine, one of the most charming restaurants on the island.

Gloster Hall Resort (Blackstoneedge, tel. 876/983-0217, Sun.–Fri. by reservation) is a day resort for family outings located on the old Gloster Hall estate. There are three swimming pools, tropical oriental and European-themed pavilion areas, lawn tennis, table tennis, horseback riding for children, mini-golf comes with entry (US$12). Food is served chicken and fish with rice and peas (US$4). Rooms are planned; call Robert Ffrench for more info. To get there take the Old Bauxite Road from Faith's Pen, east towards Middlesex and then continue straight at the intersection to Blackstonedge. Ffrench's brother runs a similar resort in Lodge, near Port Esquivel St. Catherine, with a swimming pool, tennis courts, and eating area.

Moneague's curious **rising lake** has been steadily claiming house after house for the past few years, and many local residents must now take a ferry to get home where once they could simply walk. A popular local dance is held on its shores on Sundays.

OCHO RIOS

Food

⟨ Café Aubergine (tel. 876/973-0527, noon–8:30 P.M. Wed.–Sun., US$12–28) had the first tavern license to sell booze to the carriage men taking the two-day journey over the mountains to the North Coast from Kingston and Spanish Town. Today it is a well-recognized local favorite with old world charm, serving a mix of Caribbean and Mediterranean cuisine. Owners Neville Anderson and Rudolf Gschloessl bring European haute cuisine to a Caribbean sensibility with starters that include french onion soup, escargot provencales, conch in lemon vinaigrette, and pate de la maison. Main courses include pork tenderloin medallions in sherry mushroom sauce, grilled lamb chops, grilled filet mignon, and lobster in tarragon wine sauce. Top it off with an apple pie à la mode or chocolate mousse and you're good to go.

Faith's Pen, a few kilometers south of Moneague, has a famous rest stop lined with shacks dishing out jerk and conch soup at the best local prices. Fruit stands also appear sporadically along the road north and south of Faith's Pen.

BROWN'S TOWN

A large inland town named after Hamilton Brown, who represented the parish for 22 years, Brown's Town was a center of the Baptist-fueled abolitionist movement before the Colonial Church Union destroyed the Baptist chapel following the Christmas Rebellion. Brown was a colonel in the militia that saw the chapel torn to the ground. If you're heading to Nine Mile via route taxi, Brown's town is the connection point from St. Ann's Bay.

NINE MILE
⟨ Bob Marley Mausoleum

The Bob Marley Mausoleum (call mausoleum manager Harry Shivnani for booking at cell 876/843-0498, info@ninemilejamaica.com, www.ninemilejamaica.com, open 9 A.M.– 5 P.M., admission US$15) was built next to the humble country house where the world's foremost reggae superstar was born. Today

© OLIVER HILL

A guide at the Bob Marley Mausoleum rests his head on the rock pillow mentioned in "Talkin' Blues."

it's part of a complex that draws fans from around the world to experience the humble beginnings of a man many consider prophetic. Arriving at the hillside hamlet of Nine Mile, the Cedella Marley basic school looms up in its full red, gold, and green splendor just before reaching the Marley family home. In a large parking area, countless Rastas offer guide services and other paraphernalia, all of which will require compensation at the end of the tour. The tour (US$15) starts at the gift shop, where visitors pay an entry fee and from there are led up to the mausoleum and Bob's small house. In and around the house are countless details the Rasta guides make note of as inspiration for a multitude of songs from Marley's discography, including the single bed and the rock pillow from "Talkin' Blues." Below the mausoleum a club house–style building with contemporary, sleek Rasta styling has a restaurant and lounge on the second floor and great views from the balcony over the quiet hills of the St. Ann interior. A bus requiring a day's advance reservation departs Mama Marley's (tel. 876/795-4803), Cedella Marley's restaurant on Main Street in Ocho Rios, usually around 10 A.M. daily, contingent upon adequate bookings (US$55 including entry, transport, and lunch).

Claremont
Home of an annual kite festival held on the Saturday before Easter, this small hilltop village draws thousands of people who come out for the competitive event and an evening stage show.

St. Mary

One of the most under-visited corners of Jamaica, St. Mary is considered by many the most attractive parish for its proximity to Kingston, Ocho Rios, and Portland; for its vast wilderness areas; and for its people, who don't exhibit the same hustle mentality rampant in more urbanized areas of the island. St. Mary is one of the best places in Jamaica for birding and farm tours, with Green Castle Estate standing out clearly among the large plantations of the area that are still active in agricultural production.

White River is a slow-moving river that has figured prominently in the history of the North Coast; the first Spanish road to the North Coast from Spanish Town followed its banks. The Spanish Bridge that still stands at the upper reaches of the White River is the oldest on the island. Near its mouth, the White River is a home and business place for fishermen in the area who bring in their catch under the bridge early in the morning. To get down to the banks take a right immediately after the Texaco station across from Jamaica Inn when heading east out of town, and then take the first left. A few bars and fish spots make a decent hangout while fresh fish can be hard to get as the day goes on. To reach the upper Irie Beach, the Prospect Plantation Great House, and the Chukka's White River Park, take a right after leaving the main road at the Texaco gas station and follow the river upstream.

TOWER ISLE AND BOSCOBEL
Basically a suburban outskirt of Ocho Rios today, Boscobel has the only regularly serviced airstrip in the area with the Boscobel Aerodrome (tel. 876/726-1344).

Villa Viento (tel. 876/975-4395, US$125 per night per room, US$4,800/6,800 low/high weekly for the whole house) has seven bedrooms in a large seaside ranch-style house two minutes down the road from Reggae Beach. This is one of the few villas that will rent out individual rooms.

Sea Palms Resort (Robert Cartade, tel. 876/926-4000, cartade@cwjamaica.com, www.seapalmsjamaica.com) is a seafront property with a handful of buildings containing condo-style rooms and suites (from US$105/145 low/high) that all have balconies, kitchens, air-conditioning, washer and dryer, and TV. A beach has been created on the waterfront complete with two levies that create a small protective cove. Next to the beach is a clubhouse and pool.

Heaven's Wynter Lodge (Tower Isle, tel. 876/975-5886, 7:30 A.M.–11:P.M.) serves typical Jamaican dishes like curry goat and fried chicken (US$3.50–6), as a vegetarian restaurant on the premises serves tofu chunks, vegetables, and sip (US$4). All-you-can-eat dinner buffet every Friday (6 P.M.–10 P.M., US$7) serves shrimp, fish, jerk pork, jerk chicken, fried chicken.

Rooms (US$43) on the premises have air-conditioning, ceiling fans, TV, private bath, with a recently opened swimming pool free of charge.

Beaches Boscobel (tel. 876/975-7777, US$420/night for double in high season) dominates the waterfront just west of the airfield, and with 323 rooms it's easily the largest hotel on the North Coast east of Ocho Rios. Like all Beaches resorts, Boscobel is a family-oriented all-inclusive.

OCHO RIOS

CHRIS BLACKWELL

One of the world's foremost music producers and founder of Island Records, London-born Chris Blackwell is credited with having introduced reggae music to the world. He built his early career first by selling record imports to the Jamaican market and then by bringing international attention to the budding careers of artists like Millie Small whose "My Boy, Lollipop" topped the charts in England in 1964, giving Island its first hit. Blackwell signed a slew of early English rock artists like Jethro Tull, King Crimson, Robert Palmer, and Cat Stevens. Then came Bob Marley, whose 1973 *Catch a Fire* album would be the first of many for Bob on the Island label. The deal was a huge hit and brought world recognition to a genre that was gaining popularity in Jamaica but unheard of elsewhere.

While Blackwell was scoping the world for new talent, Jamaica was never far from his mind, and he cultivated his love for the country by buying some of the island's most beautiful properties, including Strawberry Hill and Goldeneye, eventually forming Island Outpost to market them to discerning travelers seeking luxury without hype. His grand vision has set in motion a transformation in Oracabessa with the new villa development on a private island next to Ian Fleming's Goldeneye. The 80-villa development was designed as an exclusive community where those lucky enough to get their hands on a piece of Goldeneye have access to all the amenities and services the resort offers, with a private villa they can call home.

Blackwell was inducted into the Rock and Roll Hall of Fame in 2001 for his contribution to the world music industry as we know it. Blackwell sold Island Records to PolyGram UK Group in 1989, staying on at the head of the Island division. Blackwell left the company in 1997 just before PolyGram was acquired by Seagram and merged into Universal Music Group. A year later Blackwell established Palm Pictures, a film production and distribution company based in New York. Palm sources films from across the world and produced the touring film festival RESFEST for a decade. Palm Pictures was by no means Blackwell's first foray into film however. He first entered the film industry by backing Perry Henzell's cult hit *The Harder They Come* in 1971, before going on to produce other Jamaican classics like *Country Man*, as well as successful Hollywood films.

In Jamaica Chris Blackwell receives a mix of admiration from his peers and disciples, and resentment from those who jealously allege he made his millions on the back of Bob Marley. Some who are bitter refer to him as "Whitewell." What is indisputable is that his business acumen and eye for talent and opportunity have made Blackwell one of the world's most creative and successful businessmen. Beyond Island Outpost, Blackwell maintains other business interests that include Island Village in Ocho Rios and recording studios in Miami, and at Compass Point, Bahamas.

ORACABESSA

Oracabessa is yet another bastardized Spanish name whose derivative, Oro Cabeza, translates as "gold head." A half-hour's drive east of Ocho Rios, Oracabessa is a secluded enclave of high-end tourism where Ian Fleming's Goldeneye has become the benchmark for sophisticated, hip luxury tourism in Jamaica. Oracabessa has fostered a number of artists whose crafts show more originality while being far less expensive than what is offered in the markets of Ochi, Montego Bay, or Negril. The small community offers some decent beaches and picturesque countryside for those looking to get off the beaten track. Oracabessa experienced a brief boom as an important banana port in the early 1900s. Today the community is experiencing a different kind of boom, with entrepreneur Chris Blackwell building a luxury villa development at Goldeneye that will cement the area's reputation for exclusivity.

The area from Oracabessa to Port Maria has one of the nicest stretches of coast in all of Jamaica, where cliff-side villas were built by the likes of Ian Fleming, Noel Coward, and in more recent times, record magnate Chris Blackwell. The districts of Race Course, Galina, and Little Bay have small, quiet communities where discreet tourism accommodations blend with the surrounding landscape to the point that they're easy to miss.

◖ James Bond Beach

James Bond Beach (US$5) is a private beach park in Oracabessa that holds several annual events, including Follow Di Arrow, a popular stage show held in February, and Beach J'ouvert, held Easter weekend. The park extends from the roundabout at the junction of the main road and Jack's River Road to the edge of Goldeneye. Events are held on the beach park jutting out into the sea, as well as at a venue closer to the main road. There is a restaurant and bar, as well as beach chairs.

Stingray City (www.stingraycityjamaica .com, tel. 876/726-1630, 9 A.M.–5 P.M. daily) is the main attraction, where visitors swim with the pet fish (US$55 adult, US$25 children; locals pay US$25adults, US$8.50 children) on James Bond Beach when there isn't an event being held. Anyka Fray is the spectacular office manager.

Annual events held include **Follow Di Arrow** (mid-Feb.), Beach J'ouvert (early Apr.), **Fully Loaded** (third week in Aug.), and **Pepsi Teen Splash** (Boxing Day, December 26).

The entrance to James Bond Beach is located right by the roundabout on the western end of Oracabessa.

Sights

Sun Valley Plantation (sunvalleyjamaica@ yahoo.com, cell 876/995-3075 or 876/446-2026, 9 A.M.–2 P.M. daily, US$12) offers an excellent guided farm tour that includes a welcome drink, and a drink and snack at end of the tour. The educational stroll about the farm familiarizes visitors with native crops like sugar cane and banana that have played important roles in Jamaica's economy and in the history of the area. Sun Valley is owned by Lorna and Nolly Binns, who live on the property with their son Bryan. Nolly's father bought the property in 1966 to grow bananas for export. Today the farm produces mainly coconuts for the local market. To get to Sun Valley, head inland at the roundabout in Oracabessa, passing through Jack's River, and stay straight rather than left at the Epping gas station for about 1.5 kilometers farther.

Brimmer Hall (tel. 876/994-2309, 9 A.M.–4 P.M. Mon.–Fri.) offers tractor-drawn jitney tours around the plantation, where there's also a pool for swimming and a lunch area. Guides teach visitors about the fruit trees and give a bit of history of the estate. Brimmer Hall great house dates to the 1700s when the farm was a slave plantation owned by Zachary Bailey. The house is full of period furnishing and antiques. To get to Brimmer Hall, head east from Port Maria and turn right three kilometers past Trinity on the road towards Bailey Town, continuing about 1.5 kilometers past there.

Asset Recording Studio (Race Course, tel. 876/726-2362) run by Lawrence Londal "Jah Vibes" Oliver (cell 876/990-0378) and Kenya (cell 876/440-4087) is owned by Germany-based Papa Curvin (cell 876/389-0508, papacurvin@ gmx.d), who runs back and forth between Europe and Jamaica. The studio has digital audio mixing, dub cutting, and live recording facilities. Asset Recording recently put out an album: *Asset Vol. 1,* with 13 tracks on their Wan-T Wan-T rhythm. This is a cool spot to stop.

Entertainment and Food

In the center of Oracabessa there is a covered open-air produce market as well as a supermarket. Across from the police station there is also a produce stand, and up a lane by the school a bit farther east there's a shop that sells the basics like eggs, bread, and jam that opens around 7 A.M.

Chicken Hut (Center of Oracabessa, cell 876/485-8217), operated by Kerri and Yhan Chinloy, is the best spot for a quick bite to go, with the house specialty being Chinese-style fried chicken, of course with the requisite rice and peas.

◖ **Tropical Hut** (Race Course, cell 876/818-8376 or 876/434-5155, US$2.50–5)

OCHO RIOS

is a very mellow local bar, restaurant, and jerk center owned by Ciyon Gray with chef Clinton Clarke making excellent local dishes.

Dor's Fish Pot (Race Course, US$4.50–8.50) is a local favorite for all manner of fish from steamed to fried.

The **Galina Sports Bar** (Galina, US$5) sells local dishes like fried chicken with rice and peas.

Feeling Night Club (Wharf Road, tel. 876/726-1499) has music on weekends.

Shopping

Exotic Jewelry by Jasazii (Jasazii and Maji McKenzie, cell 876/726-0013 or 876/909-8403, jasazii@gmail.com, www.exoticjewelry byjasazii.com) is based in Gibraltar Heights, where Jasazii and Maji have their Sacred Healing Artz Sanctuary.

Jamma Design by Marie Smith (Galina, tel. 876/431-8122, caryl_smith2005@yahoo .com) is a funky apparel shop specializing in handmade African-inspired rootsy designs, with excellent children's clothes and stylish dresses (from US$25).

Wilderness House of Art (Idlewhile Road between Galina y Oracabessa between Galina and Race Course, across from a yellow house, cell 876/462-8849 or 876/994-0578, babai reko@yahoo.com) is the home and studio of Ireko "Baba" Baker, who is a member of A Yard We Deh artist collective together with Tukula N'Tama and Orah El. Ireko does excellent screen printing work and gourd art and has several good value items of practical art for sale. Ireko takes his work to various crafts fairs, on occasion to Harmony Hall in Ocho Rios or to the Grosvener Gallery in Manor Park, Kingston. Ireko's work can also be seen displayed in the foyer and rooms at Couples Negril.

Accommodations

Executive Inn (tel. 876/975-3540, info@golden seas.com, www.goldenseas.com, US$115) was recently bought by the management of the other Executive Inns in Ochi and MoBay. It was formerly called Golden Seas. At time of writing rooms were decent but outdated, with all the basic amenities including hot water, TV, and air-conditioning. The real draw, however, is the nicest natural beach for kilometers around that's right outside the door. Rates include full Jamaican breakfast.

Sagaree (Race Course, between Dor's Fish Hut and Tropical Huts) run by Walton Gordon, aka "Sparrow" (cell 876/379-6089), is a seafront property with six rustic cabins (US$60) that have private baths. There are also a few permanent tents (US$45) set on raised wooden platforms that have use of common bathrooms. Sparrow lives on property with his family in true Ital style. Rates include breakfast.

◖ **High View Cottages,** (Gibraltar Heights, tel. 876/975-3210, cell 876/831-1975, U.S. tel. 718/878-5351, fax 876/726-4199, keelie07@ hotmail.com, US$60) is owned by the amiable Colleen Pottinger, who lives in the main house on the property. There are two one-bedroom self-contained cottages with kitchens, private bathrooms with hot water, access to the swimming pool, and wireless Internet. There is one queen in one, and two twin beds in the second cottage. There are also inflatable mattresses for extra persons. The nightly rate includes breakfast, and additional meals can be arranged.

Tamarind Great House (cell 876/995-3252, tamarind@mailja.com, tamarindgreat house@yahoo.com, www.jamaica-gleaner .com/gleaner/tamarind, US$85) on Crecent Estate was destroyed by fire in 1987, and then was rebuilt and restored to a 10-bedroom colonial-style great house by English couple Gillian and Barry Chambers, who live on the property with their son Gary. Nine attractive rooms have fans and private bath with hot water. Some rooms have private balconies. The house was completely rebuilt on the foundation of the original, while furnishings and decor reflect the colonial period. To get to Tamarind House, head inland at the roundabout in Oracabessa along Jack's River Road, keeping straight ahead at the Epping gas station; continue for about 0.8 kilometer past Sun Valley Plantation, keeping left at the broken bridge and continuing up the hill.

Villas

Goldenfoot (Gibraltar Heights, tel. 876/842-1237 or U.S. tel. 650/941-1760, agoldenfoot .villa@yahoo.com, www.agoldenfootvilla.com, US$600) is a spectacular two-bedroom villa owned by Joel Goldfus. You won't find a place with more privacy, and caretaker Godfrey is a phone call away to ensure every need is attended to.

The villa features a master bedroom with a canopy queen bed, and across the living room/dining room area the second bedroom has two twin beds. The ceiling of the living room is detailed with bamboo work to match the bamboo construction throughout the property. Wicker furniture sits on a large veranda overlooking the pool (which is imprinted with golden feet along its edges), Oracabessa, and out to sea.

(C Goldeneye (tel. 876/975-3354, Kingston office tel. 876/960-8134, goldeneye@ cwjamaica.com, www.islandoutpost.com/ goldeneye) the former home of *007* author Ian Fleming is today the most exclusive resort in Jamaica. From the moment the gates swing open off the main road, you know you have arrived at a place unlike any other. No large sign announces the property's presence from the road, a reflection of the understated grandeur that lies within.

Ian Fleming's villa boasts enormous bamboo-framed canopy beds, which beg to be slept on, but there is too much competition to stay there long. Deluxe indoor master bathrooms are complemented by an outdoor bath area that resembles paradise, and are surrounded by a wooden fence to ensure privacy. The villa lacks nothing, from its spacious living area to the pool outside, to the lawns overlooking Fleming's private beach. Adjacent to the pool, an enclosed lounge features a projection screen and bar.

On the opposite side of the vast property, Royal Palm sits on the tranquil lagoon surrounding a private island. It's the kind of place that makes you grateful to be alive. Downstairs, a living area with windows on all sides opens out to the front veranda, where you can step into the lagoon.

Meals are offered in a casual setting in a centrally located gazebo overlooking the water. The food is delicious and generally features the best local cuisine. It is also possible to arrange meals in your villa.

If you can drag yourself away from your villa, Nico is ready to take you on a Jet Skiing adventure to remote waterfalls for a hike and swim. Otherwise, there's always windsurfing, kayaking, or simply lazing on the beach of your private island.

Goldeneye is currently undergoing a transformation to become the island's most exclusive resort community. Eighty private villas, whose owners will have been invited to buy, will sit on the private island. A spa is also in the works.

This is not a resort for those with shallow pockets. Nightly rates per couple range based on the villa; the least expensive is Honey Chile Villa (US$750/950 nightly low/high), and the most expensive is Ian Fleming's Villa (US$2,800/3,800 nightly low/high), also known as the main house. While you can certainly spend a fortune staying at Goldeneye, especially since leaving is quite difficult, the service and general value for your money is excellent and you're highly unlikely to experience the slightest feeling of regret.

Bolt House (tel. 876/975-3354, www.island outpost.com) is a hilltop property owned by the founder of Fila sportswear; it overlooks Port Maria. The property was previously built and occupied by Blanche Blackwell, mother of Island Records founder Chris Blackwell, whose Island Outpost boutique hotel group currently books the property. It was recently refurbished in impeccable style. This and Goldeneye are the most high-end accommodations in the area.

LITTLE BAY
(C Firefly

Firefly (tel. 876/974-8354 or 876/974-8356, US$10 admission includes guided tour and refreshment, 9 A.M.–5 P.M., closed Fri. and Sun.) is easily one of Jamaica's most beautiful properties with the most magnificent view of the St. Mary and Portland coast. The property has had a glamorous past, first as the home of the pirate Henry Morgan, and centuries later as a playground for playwright Noel Coward, both of whom were captivated by the stunning view that graces the small plateau. Henry Morgan's house, which dates from the 17th century, has been rebuilt and is now used as the visitors center and has a small bar and several tables. Across the lawn, Noel Coward's house remains preserved as a museum essentially as he left it. Downstairs in his studio an incomplete painting stands on the easel as if Coward was interrupted in mid-stroke. His famous "room with a view" was inspiration for several works completed in there, and the piano where he entertained his famous Hollywood guests remains the centerpiece in the study. On the lawn outside a statue of Coward immortalizes his fascination with the view as he holds his cigarette and ponders the northeast coastline. Coward's tomb is in a corner of the lawn.

At the time of Coward's death the property was left to Graham Payne, who in turn gave it to the Jamaican government, which today leases it to Chris Blackwell, whose Island Outpost manages the attraction. Up to 120 people visit Firefly daily in the high season, while the visits can drop to a trickle during the slower months.

Kokomo Beach

Kokomo Beach is a decent free public beach across the road from Casa Maria frequented mostly by locals. The beach is small and not particularly noteworthy, but good enough for a dip or to cool out with the locals.

Accommodations

Little Bay Inn (Little Bay, tel. 876/994-2721, US$20–25) opened in 2005 as a basic and clean guesthouse overlooking Little Bay just west of Port Maria. Nine bedroom suites have private baths with hot water, fans, double beds, and simple furnishings. The more expensive rooms have TV. A small jerk center in the yard serves food and beverages on occasion. Downstairs in the same building is Cribs Disco, where music at times blasts into the wee hours.

Casa Maria Hotel (Castle Gardens, tel.

876/725-0156, fax 876/725-0157, emaxwell@ cwjamaica.com, www.nwas.com/casamaria, US$50 standards, US$75 suites) is a massive concrete hotel with 18 rooms, which range from standard with ocean view, double bed, shared bed, private bath to the suites, which have private balcony with oceanview king beds and cable TV. A restaurant (7 A.M.–10 P.M. daily) and bar on the premises is open to non-guests.

Galina Breeze (Galina, tel. 876/994-0537, www.galinabreeze.com, office@galinabreeze .com, US$75) is a small property of 14 rooms in a basic concrete structure overlooking the pool and an excellent view of the northeastern coast; plus there's one stand-alone villa. Standard rooms (single or double occupancy) have air-conditioning, king beds, cable TV, and hot water. The property is geared towards accommodating special-interest groups and the management helps in engaging guests with the community, whether for educational, church, or outreach programs.

Blue Harbour (Galina Point, Galina, tel. 505/586-1244, cell 876/725-0281 or 876/994-2262, blueharb@aol.com, www.blueharb.com, US$100/person all-inclusive) is a bit rundown and under-maintained, with tired linens and cracked walkways. Still, the property is an unmistakable gem, and it's easy to imagine famous playwright Noel Coward, the builder of the three villas, entertaining his distinguished guests, who included, among many others, Winston Churchill, Errol Flynn, Marlene Dietrich, Katharine Hepburn, and Sean Connery. With such a spectacular view to the east from each of the many verandas, entertaining came easy, so much so that Coward soon bought a retreat from his retreat called Lookout, a property perched high on the hill above Blue Harbour owned by the pirate Captain Morgan in earlier days. Now known as Firefly, Lookout had been Morgan's vantage point from where he would target approaching ships for hijack before going on to become Jamaica's governor. Blue Harbour is an enticing property, but at this point the hammock may be a cozier alternative to the beds.

Dowling House (Galina, call Nancy or Steven Sicher, tel. 876/725-1004 or U.S. tel. 309/693-2830; ssicher@insightbb.com, www .dowlinghouse.com, not available Oct., Nov., Jan., and Feb.) is a three-bedroom seafront cottage (US$800/1,200 per week low/high) with king beds in two rooms, and two twins in the third. The cottage can accommodate up to six people (US$1,400/week), comes with a caretaker and cook, and is tastefully decorated with a pool and large lawn overlooking Blue Harbour and Port Maria. A land line, an iPod docking station, a gas stove, hot water, DSL, and a washer/dryer make up for the lack of TV.

PORT MARIA

One of the most picturesque towns in Jamaica, Port Maria has a large protected harbor with the small Cabarita Island, also known as Treasure Island, in the center. Originally inhabited by the Tainos and later by the Spanish, the island was vulnerable to pirate attacks and warring colonial powers and fell into the hands of the pirate Henry Morgan before he lost it in a gamble. By the late 1700s a village began to take shape on the harbor shores on land owned by Zachary Bailey. The parish vestry acquired land for the growing village from Bailey's nephew in

TACKY'S WAR

On the morning after Easter Sunday in 1760, a slave known as Tacky led a revolt in St. Mary that would reverberate around northeastern Jamaica until September of that year. The uprising became known as Tacky's Rebellion or Tacky's War.

Tacky was an overseer on Frontier Plantation outside Port Maria, giving him the limited freedom necessary to strategize and organize the rebellion at both Frontier and bordering Trinity plantations. A former chief in his homeland of Ghana, Tacky had the confidence and clout to amass wide support for what was meant to be an island-wide overthrow of the British colonial masters.

Tacky and about 50 of his followers awoke before dawn that morning and easily killed the master of Frontier Plantation before raiding the armory at nearby Fort Haldane, where they took guns and ammo, killing the storekeeper in the process. The owner of Trinity Plantation had escaped on horseback to warn the surrounding estates. But with newfound artillery, the ranks of the rebel army began to swell, and they quickly took nearby Haywood and Esher Plantations and began to celebrate their early success. A slave from Esher plantation, however, slipped away to call in the authorities, and before long a militia of soldiers from Spanish Town and Maroons from Scott's Hall was sent to quell the uprising.

The rebels' confidence had been bolstered by Obeah men (witch doctors) among their ranks who spread incantations and claimed the army would be protected and that Obeah men could not be killed. This confidence took a blow when the militia, learning of these claims, captured and killed one of the Obeah men. Nonetheless the fighting would last months and take the lives of some 60 whites and 300 rebels before it was diffused. Tacky himself was captured and beheaded by the Maroons from Scott's Hall, who took his head to Spanish Town on a pole to be displayed as dissuasion for any further resistance of the sort.

The legend of Tacky spread across the island giving inspiration to other resistance movements that would come in the later years of slavery and after emancipation. Many of Tacky's followers committed suicide rather than surrendering, while those who were captured were either executed or sold and shipped off the island. Ringleaders were either burned alive or starved in cages in the Parade in Kingston. It was during Tacky's War that the British authorities first learned of the role African religion played behind the scenes in these uprisings, and Obeah thus became part of the official record with a 1970 law passed to punish its practitioners by death or transportation at the court's discretion.

OCHO RIOS

1816 and by 1821 public buildings including the parish council offices and the courthouse were built. Port Maria boomed with exports that included sugar, rum, indigo, pimento, tropical hardwoods, and coffee. Port Maria has long since passed its prime. Nevertheless, it still has a strong fishing community and is a commercial center for the people of the surrounding rural districts. Several infrastructure improvements associated with the North Coast Highway project have recently given the town a bit of a facelift. The Outram River forms the eastern border of town, beyond which begins a vast wilderness area wrapping around the hilly coastline all the way to Robin's Bay.

Sights

St. Mary Craft Market (Port Maria Civic Center, by appointment cell 876/373-7575) is one of the island's most eclectic, featuring work exclusively from artists residing in the parish. If you're planning a stop to check out the old Court House and Anglican Church, call in advance to arrange to see the crafts.

Pagee Beach is where Port Maria's fishermen keep their boats and bring in their catch. Outings to Cabarita Island, a great place to explore in true Robinson Crusoe fashion, can be arranged from here by negotiating with the fishermen (US$10 per person is a reasonable round-trip fare). Pagee is not an ideal place for swimming.

Fort Haldane, or sparse and scattered remains of it, are located on a road that cuts across the point jutting into the sea forming the western flank of Port Maria's harbor. The road runs between the Anglican Church and the middle of the bend on the other side of the hill on Little Bay. Two cannons overgrown with bush aim out to sea just past the oldest structure on the premises, a low brick building sitting alongside discarded car parts. The Fort was built in 1759 for coastal defense during the seven years war and named after the then governor, George Haldane. The property was later an home for the elderly, called Gray's Charity, but has since fallen

© OLIVER HILL

The royal seal adorns a cannon at Fort Haldane, which is less a fort and more a pair of cannons and an old brick storeroom today.

into disuse. The gates to this seldom-visited historical site are typically left ajar and are otherwise unlocked.

The old **Courthouse and Police Station** (across from the Anglican church on east side of town), originally built in 1821 is one of the nicest examples of Georgian architecture in Port Maria after its recent restoration. Much of the original building was destroyed by fire in 1988 before being marked for restoration by the Urban Development Commission in 2000. The partial restoration was completed in 2002 with funds from the Jamaican and Venezuelan governments and the building is now in use as the Port Maria Civic Center. A plaque by the main entrance dedicates the premises to labor leader and Jamaica Labour Party (JLP) founder Alexander Bustamante. A second plaque recognizes former Prime Minister P. J. Patterson, who attended the official opening in 2002.

St. Mary Parish Church was built in 1861 and has an adjoining cemetery with an epitaph dedicated to the Jamaicans who fought

The St. Mary Parish Church stands along the waterfront across from the civic center with a small cemetery beside it.

OCHO RIOS

in World War I. The **Tacky Memorial** is also located in the church cemetery.

Practicalities

 Almond Tree Club Restaurant (56 Warner St., tel. 876/994-2379, 9 A.M.–11 P.M. daily, US$2–6) is the best bet in Port Maria, serving typical Jamaican dishes like curry goat, fried chicken, oxtail, stew peas, stew pork. Other dishes like chicken chop suey and shrimp fried rice are cooked to order. This Almond Tree claims to be the original, predating the one in Ocho Rios. Donna Gibson is the sweet and helpful manager.

Uncle B's Miracle Jerk Center on the road east of out town has great jerk and an irie roadside atmosphere.

Most country folk arriving in Port Maria come for the market or to stock up at the **Hi-Lo** supermarket (7–11 Stennett St., tel. 876/994-9878) or do their business at **NCB** (8 Main St., tel. 876/994-2219) or **ScotiaBank** (57 Warner St., tel. 876/994-2265).

Port Maria is serviced by regular route taxis from Ocho Rios (US$3), Oracabessa (US$1.50), and Annotto Bay (US$1.50) that leave the square as they fill up.

The **Port Maria Police Station** (tel. 876/994-2223) is located at the plaza by the bus park.

Islington

Islington is a small community 20 minutes further east of Port Maria, which sits atop a hill and offers great views eastward along the coast towards Buff Bay and Port Antonio from some of its lookout points along the road. Islington is of little importance as a tourist destination, but is the proud hometown of dancehall deejay Capleton, who organizes an annual festival called A St. Mary Mi Come From. The agricultural community is also known for its pimento (allspice) crop, as well as for growing some of Jamaica's most potent illicit weed.

ROBIN'S BAY

One of the most laid-back and picturesque corners of Jamaica, Robin's Bay is entirely apart from what is marketed on JTB posters. Robin's Bay is the Treasure Beach of yesteryear, remaining a quiet fishing and subsistence agricultural community with a few accommodation options catering to those looking for a laid-back retreat or the experience of enjoying an intimacy with nature. Beginning with Green Castle Estate, a working farm that commands a large swath of land fronting the bay, the area has a delectable, charming pace found nowhere else on the island.

Green Castle Estate

Green Castle Estate (contact property manager Angie Dickson for reservations, cell 876/881-6293, angiedickson@cyou.com, www.greencastleja.com, www.greencastletropicalstudycenter.org) is a 650-hectare farm producing a mix of fruit and—above all in terms of revenue—orchids, which today fill two large shade houses. Named after the Irish holdings of one of its earlier owners, several archaeological finds on the property indicate it has been continuously lived on since the time of the Tainos. Spanish settlement at Green Castle left the iconic windmill that still stands today. Land use has changed from cassava cultivation under the Tainos and Spanish, to orange, cotton, pimiento, cacao, indigo, sugarcane, and then bananas. For centuries the estate was connected with the rest of Jamaica only by sea. After years of British and then American ownership fraught with frequent mortgage defaults and border disputes, the property ended up in the hands of one of the world's foremost agricultural families and majority-share owners of Cargill, still the largest private company in the United States. Since the 1950s the farm has grown an increasingly diverse mix of fruit crops, and more recently went into organic fruit production and became one of Jamaica's foremost orchid farms, now supplying a large portion of domestic demand. Historical sites on the expansive estate include excavated Taino middens (1300), a militia barracks (1834), and the signature coral stone windmill tower (1700).

A variety of tours are offered on Green Castle Estate, all of them excellent values. Children are always half-price. The **Orchids and Organics** (US$20) tour introduces visitors to some of the 120 hectares of certified-organic tree crops planted on the farm. No other farm in Jamaica has more certified organic hectares under cultivation, and the organic coconut oil operation is one of the farm's more important products and a central focus of the tour. Visitors also learn about the 12 hectares of papaya and roughly 2,000 pimento (allspice) trees grown on the farm. Pedigree beef production is also a major activity, with hundreds of head roaming around the rolling grassy hills. The tour concludes with a visit to the orchid propagation shade houses where visitor are dazzled with 50,000 orchid plants of several varieties and taught the basics of one of the islands most important orchid operations.

The **Green Castle Garden Tour and Tea** (US$40) is highly recommended, not least for the great company of one Mrs. Susan Crum Ewing, who has impeccable knowledge of the history and plant life of the farm. The tour starts in the orchid shade houses before continuing on to the grounds of the great house, planted with gorgeous flower specimens, which are visited throughout the day by countless birds. The tour ends with high tea where guests sample delectable finger sandwiches, cake, and, of course, tea. You'll also get to sample some of the best seasonal juices in Jamaica, made from fruit grown on the property. Mrs. Crum Ewing together with her husband, who manages the beef operations, have lived on the farm for decades and share a wealth of knowledge on its history, as well as having an enlightened perspective on Jamaica's socioeconomic development since independence.

Another option offered, best for more dedicated birding and exploring, is a **Day at Green Castle** (US$50), where visitors are allowed to roam the vast estate to count bird species, visit the orchid houses, or just relax and enjoy nature along the many hiking trails

© OLIVER HILL

The iconic windmill at Green Castle Estate dates to the early 1700s.

OCHO RIOS

and coastline. The birds that frequent Green Castle Estate are as spectacular as the orchids and include 18 of the countries 30 endemic species: the chestnut-bellied cuckoo, Jamaican owl, yellow-billed parrot, red-billed stream-ertail, Jamaican mango, Jamaican tody, Jamaican woodpecker, rufous-tailed flycatcher, sad flycatcher, Jamaican becard, Jamaican elania, Jamaican pewee, Jamaican crow, white-chinned thrush, Jamaican vireo, Jamaican euphonia, orangequit, yellow-shouldered grassquit, and the Jamaican stripe-headed tanager. In total 100 species have been sighted at Green Castle Estate including the native and visiting birds.

Perhaps the best option is to **rent the great house** and stay at Green Castle Estate (US$2,600/3,600 low/high weekly for up to four people, inclusive of meals, or US$2,900/3,900 low/high for up to six). While a weekly rental is preferred, it is also possible to rent the great house for as little as three nights (US$370 nightly for up to four people). For those who enjoy nature and an alternative idea of tourism but don't want to sacrifice the utmost in elegance and comfort, there is probably no better accommodation option in Jamaica. The great house has classy colonial furnishings in three spacious bedrooms with private baths, and a fourth room with two twin beds. The swimming pool overlooks the gardens with a spectacular view of the coast and Blue Mountains from almost every window and veranda. There are also tennis courts on the property. All tours are included with the great house rental. There are also opportunities for farm volunteer work and outreach work in the neighboring community of Robin's Bay.

🅒 Sunrise Lawn

Sunrise Lawn (contact the proprietor Sanchez, cell 876/436-1223, noon till the last customer leaves, daily) is the coolest chill-out spot in Robin's Bay. with its picket-fenced east-facing lawn overlooking the sea. There are benches fit for enjoying the view on the lawn. A cook shop prepares steamed and

A fishing boat idles in Robin's Bay.

fried fish and conch soup, based on demand throughout day (US$5–10). There is also a bar area with stacks of speakers waiting for a proper occasion to hold a session. Try the house drink, "Smooth Sunrise," made with Guinness, Suplogen, and Wray & Nephew white rum. It allegedly improves stamina and enhances libido.

Accommodations and Food

Robin's Bay Village and Beach Resort (cell 876/361-2144, US$75–135) has 43 rooms designed mainly for retreats or romantic getaways. The lower-priced rooms have mountain views with ceiling fans; the more expensive rooms have sea views and air-conditioning. All rooms have private bathrooms and hot water. There is a pool on the roof as well as restaurant serving Jamaican dishes open to non-guests (US$6.50–21).

Sonrise Retreat (cell 876/999-7169, sonrise@cwjamaica.com, www.in-site.com/sonrise, US$60–90) is a seven-hectare property with a handful of cabins that have a varying degree of amenities, from rustic to more comfortable. There are two small sandy beaches and an outdoor dining area.

River Lodge (tel. 876/995-3003, riverlodge@cwjamaica.com, www.river-lodge.com, US$32–50 per person including breakfast and dinner) is located on the site of a refurbished 400-year-old Spanish fort owned by Brigitta Fuchslocher. Rooms inside the fort complement a pair of cottages. From River Lodge there are hectares and hectares of unspoiled wilderness reaching almost all the way along the coast to Port Maria, where waterfalls and black-sand beaches are best reached by boat with the local fishermen.

Getting There and Around

The best way to reach Robin's Bay is by route taxi (US0.75) or private taxi charter (US$7) from Annotto Bay. Getting around in Robin's Bay often requires long waits before a car passes, but the road is only a few kilometers long before it becomes a dirt track and disappears in the wilderness to the west.

ANNOTTO BAY

At one time an important port town for export of the area's annatto crop, from whence it get its name, Annotto Bay is today bustling only by the busy taxi stand in the center of town. Otherwise, sleepy is a good description. Two notable attractions are the unique **Baptist Chapel** on the main road through town, and the **Human Service Station** (Emmannuel "Irie" Johnson, cell 876/843-1640), an excellent pit stop on the east side of town that serves great fresh seafood and some of the best fish tea and conch soup in Jamaica.

Accommodations

RiverEdge (contact Cavell Chuck tel. 876/944-2673, cell 876/461-8154, riveredge99@hotmail.com, by reservation required) is a camping facility nestled on the banks of the Pencar River in Fort George, about five kilometers inland from Annotto Bay. In addition to campsites there are furnished dorms (US$20 per person) and two self-contained units (US$45) with kitchenettes and private bathrooms. Tents are also available to rent (US$15). A kitchen is available for campers' use and a cook can also be available (US$10) with meals prepared by arrangement. The owner can facilitate transfers as well as overnights in Kingston. The river is excellent for swimming and cooling off. RiverEdge also allows entry of non-guests during the day (US$3).

Services

Annotto Bay Hospital (tel. 876/996-2742 or 876/996-9004) is the largest and most well-equipped medical facility in St. Mary, while still miles behind institutions in Kingston or Montego Bay.

Getting There and Around

Annotto Bay is major transfer point for route taxis and minibuses. The major destinations serviced from Annotto Bay include Constant Spring (US$3) in Kingston, Port Maria (US$1.50) to the east along the coast, Buff Bay (US$1.50) across the border in Portland, and Port Antonio (US$3) farther east into Portland. Route taxis also go to Islington and Robin's Bay (US$0.75), but at times it will take a while before the car fills up. To charter a route taxi in the Annotto Bay area, call Aldene "Ansel" Fairclough (cell 876/477-0544) who can take you up to Fort George or to Robin's Bay (US$7) or to any other destination for a negotiable price.

ST. MARY INTERIOR

Castleton Botanical Gardens (Castleton, tel. 876/942-0717, free) along the main Kingston to Annotto Bay road (A3) just over the border from St. Andrew, is still one of the nicest parks in Jamaica despite having suffered years of neglect and recurring hurricane damage. Castleton was established in the 1860s and planted with 400 species from Kew Gardens in England. It remained an important introduction point for ornamental and economically important species, including scores of palms as well as Poincianas and the large Bombay Mango variety. One of the most interesting specimens in the gardens is the Scew Palm (*Pandanus tectorius*) which sends down aerial, or stilt, roots, and another notable tree is the Poor Man's Orchid (not a true orchid), which has become ubiquitous around the island. Other economically important tree species still growing at the gardens are the Burma Teak and West Indian Mahogany.

Scott's Hall is one of the less-well-known, but every bit as strong communities of the Winward Maroons presided over by Colonel Noel Prehay (cell 876/533-5325). Prehay is St. Mary's top Maroon representative.

Clonmel Potters (Arthur's Ridge, east of Highgate on the B2, tel. 876/992-4495, clonmelpotters@hotmail.com, www.theclonmelpotters.net, call to arrange visit 9 A.M.–5 P.M. Mon.–Sat.), established by Donald and Belva Johnson in 1976, work in a variety of local media from porcelain to terra-cotta. Like many Jamaican men, Donald's favorite subject is the female nude, which is countered by his wife's concentration in organic forms. Works are thrown on the wheel and made from rolled slab and include both artistic pieces as well as practical vessels. Both Donald and Belva continue to be involved with the Edna Manley School of Visual Arts, Jamaica's foremost art college, located in Kingston.

Accommodations and Food

Tapioca Village (6.5 kilometers north of Castleton, tel. 876/472-5255, tapioca_retreat@ yahoo.com, US$50 includes breakfast, US$64 for three-meal package) just over the border from St. Andrew in Devon Pen, St. Mary, has simple, respectable rooms; a large lawn in a lush river valley; and a nice swimming pool. Rooms can be rented without meals (US$38) and bunks (US$7) are also available in the peaceful river valley. Breakfast, lunch, and dinner are cooked to order (US$3–5).

MONTEGO BAY AND THE NORTHWEST

Montego Bay is the capital of St. James parish. Commonly referred to by locals as "MoBay," it's a place buzzing with cruise ships and international flights brimming with tourists. Many of these tourists spend barely a day on land before climbing aboard to depart for the next port. Others stay with their families in private villas for months of the year. MoBay's bustling service economy serves a large middle class, many of whom spend much of the year abroad. This contrasts with large squatter settlements and an urban squalor that permeates the downtown area. On the quiet peninsula of Freeport the city has an active yacht club, whose members partake in exciting events throughout the year; golf courses competitive with any in the world lie east and west of the city. It's little wonder that many hotels register high occupancy throughout much of the year. Yet because the economy is overwhelmingly dependent on tourism, there arises at times a tangible resentment between the local population, a proud lot with fiery roots steeped in a not-so-distant, brutal history, and the endless flow of transient visitors, often perceived as cogs in the local economic machinery. But the congested angst of downtown MoBay quickly dissipates beyond the city limits, where the landscape of rural St. James quickly transforms into forested hills traversed by the occasional river.

The bordering parish to the east along the North Coast is Trelawny, seemingly still reminiscing a glorious but languished past when Falmouth, its ornate capital, had money and class. As sugar lost importance to the island's economy in the late 1800s, Falmouth faded

© OLIVER HILL

HIGHLIGHTS

Richmond Hill: With the best view over MoBay – and a hotel, bar, and restaurant rich in history and ambiance – this is a choice spot for a sunset cocktail (page 195).

Gallery of West Indian Art: Not only does it have an excellent collection of Jamaican work, but there are Cuban and Haitian paintings as well (page 196).

Rose Hall Great House: There's perhaps no great house as ominous and grand, and the spirit of White Witch Annie Palmer can still be felt (page 196).

Greenwood Great House: One of the most beautiful and true-to-its-day estate

houses in Jamaica, it also played a central role in the island's sugar history (page 197).

Doctors Cave Beach: Center stage on MoBay's Hip Strip, this is the best spot to see and be seen on weekends. It's also the site of monthly full-moon parties (page 200).

Falmouth: Considered to be one of the world's best examples of a Georgian town, it's changed little from its boom years at the height of the island's sugar trade (page 215).

Queen of Spain Valley: Home to a 810-hectare citrus plantation, ceramics studio, and luxury retreat, it's worth every bit of bad road covered on the way (page 221).

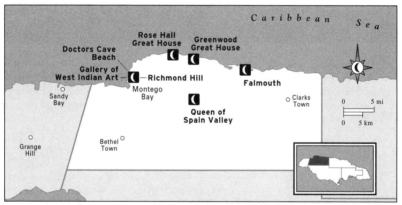

LOOK FOR **(** TO FIND RECOMMENDED SIGHTS, ACTIVITIES, DINING, AND LODGING.

from preeminent port to sleepy backwater. Today the parish is slowly showing signs of rejuvenation as the world begins to acknowledge its architectural treasures, with international funding being successfully sourced and funneled by local NGO Falmouth Heritage Renewal. Trelawny boomed during the years of the sugar trade, but was an important strategic area even before parishes—going back to when the Spaniards used the Martha Brae River as a thoroughfare to traverse the island from the South to North Coasts. Their first major settle-

ment of Melilla is said to have been near the mouth of the river. Before the Spaniards, the Martha Brae was the lifeblood for the area's Taino population, whose surviving legends are evidence of the river's importance to them.

Cockpit Country occupies the interior between the North and South Coasts, covering some of the most rugged terrain in the world, where limestone sinkholes, craggy hillocks, countless caves, and underground rivers made pursuit of Jamaica's Maroons a difficult task for the British colonists attempting to establish

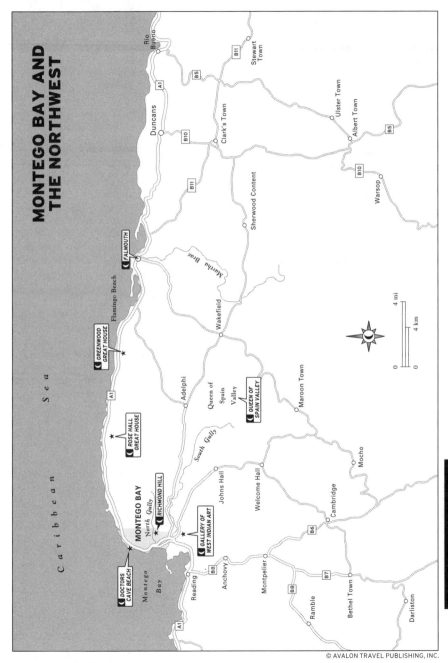

MONTEGO BAY AND
THE NORTHWEST

Caribbean Sea

Montego Bay

DOCTORS CAVE BEACH

MONTEGO BAY

North Gully

RICHMOND HILL

GALLERY OF WEST INDIAN ART

ROSE HALL GREAT HOUSE

South Gully

Johns Hall

Reading

Anchovy

B8

Montpelier

B6

Ramble

Bethel Town

B7

Darliston

Welcome Hall

Cambridge

B6

Mocho

Maroon Town

Queen of Spain Valley

QUEEN OF SPAIN VALLEY

Adelphi

A1

GREENWOOD GREAT HOUSE

Flamingo Beach

FALMOUTH

Martha Brae

Wakefield

Sherwood Content

B11

Duncans

A1

B5

B10

Clark's Town

Rio Bueno

B11

Stewart Town

Ulster Town

Albert Town

B5

B10

Warsop

4 mi

4 km

0

0

© AVALON TRAVEL PUBLISHING, INC.

order and dominion. Together with the island's mountainous northeast, Trelawny gave respite to the indomitable Maroons and the parish remains a Maroon stronghold and adventurers' paradise. At the same time the parish has the most peaceful and romantic farmlands in Jamaica, the Queen of Spain Valley being a particularly beautiful crown jewel amidst rough, rounded hilltops, where a citrus plantation today stands on the sugar estate of yesteryear. Cruising on horseback through this part of Jamaica is exhilarating and timelessly romantic, with orange and coconut groves and picturesque misty hills making for breathtaking scenery. This parish is rarely explored by tourists beyond the coastal areas of Falmouth, the Luminous Lagoon, and the Martha Brae River. As remote as Trelawny may seem when deep inside a cave or otherwise immersed in the bush, you are never more than a couple hours from civilization, or some semblance of it, in Montego Bay.

PLANNING YOUR TIME

Given the proximity of Negril, Jamaica's most developed beach town, as well as the mountains of the Dolphin Head range in Hanover, the interior and South Coast of neighboring Westmoreland and Cockpit Country in St. James and Trelawny, there are plenty of opportunities for recreation and relaxation from a base in Montego Bay without being on the road for more than a couple hours. Closer to town there several estate great house tours and plantation tours that make excellent half-day outings. Should you wish to hit the beach, there are plenty of options right in town while Trelawny also has its share of good beaches.

MoBay makes a convenient base thanks to Sangster International Airport on the east-

ern side of town. As a point of entry, MoBay is probably the best option, and a night or two in the city, especially if you arrive on the weekend, can be a good way to catch the Jamaican vibe before heading off to a more tranquil corner of the island. But MoBay shouldn't be the only area you visit on a trip to Jamaica. Ideally the area deserves around five days, splitting your time between the beach or another natural attraction and a visit to a historical site, with some fine dining around the city.

Historical places of interest include Sam Sharpe Square in downtown MoBay, Bellefield, Rose Hall and Greenwood Great Houses, of which at least one should be seen on a trip to Jamaica, and the Georgian town of Falmouth. All of these make good half-day visits, while Falmouth can easily consume the better part of an unhurried day strolling around. Natural attractions in the region include the Martha Brae River, Cockpit Country caves, Mayfield Falls, the Great River, and a handful of working plantations that offer tours. Organized tour operators on the western side of Jamaica usually include transportation to and from Montego Bay or Negril hotels. A few decent beaches along the Hip Strip, on Dead End Road, and at the resorts further east along the coast make MoBay a good place to hang out and catch some sun, but the city is by no means the place to go for secluded stretches of sand or unspoiled wilderness.

A few times a year, MoBay comes alive for music festivals that are for many people reason enough to travel to Jamaica. These include the island's premiere music festival, Reggae Sumfest, held in July, and Jazz and Blues Festival, held in January.

Montego Bay

Jamaica's "vibes city," MoBay has been the principal hub of the island's tourism industry since the 1950s, with the country's most well-heeled duty-free shops and beaches. The close proximity of the area's hotels to the Montego Bay airport makes it a convenient destination for long-weekenders visiting from the United States and those looking to take advantage of the proximity of destinations on the western side of the island. Sangster International Airport receives most of Jamaica's three million annual tourists, and the surrounding region offers plenty of activities for day trips out of town, making the MoBay area the most popular place to find lodging for visitors to Jamaica. But the picture is not entirely pretty, and plenty of strife plagues the city, not least of which derives from growing squatter communities in and around town. Many visitors find in Montegonians, also known as "bawn a bays," a hard-edged matter-of-fact idiosyncrasy that reflects the dual worlds coexisting in the energetic city. Perhaps a tumultuous history kept fresh by perpetuating injustices leads the city's inhabitants to despise the subservience inherent in a tourism-based economy out of pride, even if it is tourism that sustains the town. Montego Bay has been at the center of the island's economic movements since the days of the Spanish, and it is not lost on the local population that the city remains an economic powerhouse with its booming service economy.

Old timers recall the golden years of 1960s MoBay, when clubs like the Yellow Bird on Church Street, and Club 35 on Union Street and Cats Corner were brimming with tourists and locals alike. Taxis would carry guests from the hotels to the city center, where they would await patrons into the early morning hours to emerge from smoky cabarets bursting with live music. The Michael Manley era, which began in 1972, ushered in a socialism scare that destabilized Jamaica, affecting the tourism market directly with travel advisories warning would-be visitors to stay away. Nowhere was the impact more severe than in Montego Bay,

which was the most-developed resort destination in Jamaica at the time. It was during the 1970s too that all-inclusive tourism became a phenomenon and gated resorts became the norm. The overwhelming dominance of all-inclusive hotels in recent years has led fewer visitors to leave the hotel compounds to explore the city, stifling business for restaurants and bars, the more successful of which cater as much to the local market as to tourists. Today MoBay comes alive on certain nights of the week, and gets especially lively for several notable annual festivals, like Jazz and Blues Festival and Reggae Sumfest.

Commercially Montego Bay is organized like many U.S. cities. Large shopping centers dot the urban landscape, with KFC and Burger King dominating two strong poles of the quasi-modern city; Quasi-modern because in a small space, MoBay contains some of Jamaica's roughest areas (there have been weeks in recent memory that saw several police-inflicted killings in some of MoBay's worse districts), living in close proximity to Doctors Cave Beach, where the mood is as outwardly genteel as during the early British colonial period.

MoBay has been crucial to the island since the arrival of the Spanish conquistadores. The name Montego is said to have its origin in the Spanish word, *manteca,* meaning lard and referring to the use of the bay as an export center for wild hog products, namely lard. The city was previously named Golfo de Buen Tiempo (Bay of Good Weather) by Christopher Columbus.

Orientation

Montego Bay has distinct tourist zones well separated from the bustling and raucous downtown area. The main tourist area is the **Hip Strip** along Gloucester Avenue, where most of the bars, restaurants, and hotels catering to tourists are located. Extending off the strip is **Kent Avenue,** aka Dead End Road, which terminates at the end of the airport runway.

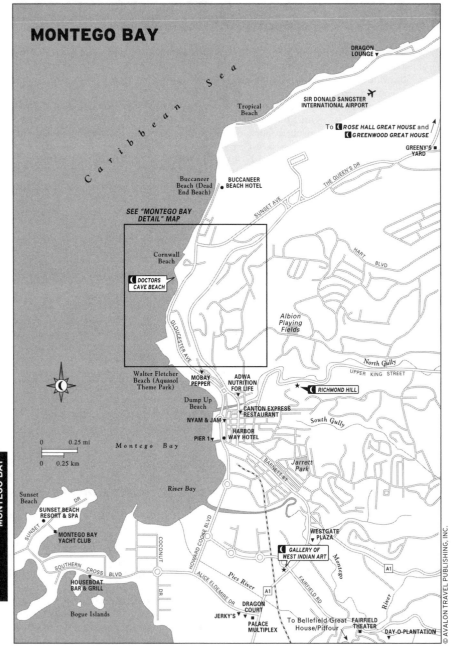

MONTEGO BAY

DRAGON LOUNGE ▼

Caribbean Sea

Tropical Beach

SIR DONALD SANGSTER INTERNATIONAL AIRPORT ✈

To ☾ROSE HALL GREAT HOUSE and ☾GREENWOOD GREAT HOUSE

GREENY'S YARD ■

THE QUEEN'S DR

Buccaneer Beach (Dead End Beach) ●

BUCCANEER BEACH HOTEL

SUNSET AVE

HART BLVD

SEE "MONTEGO BAY DETAIL" MAP

Cornwall Beach

☾DOCTORS CAVE BEACH

Albion Playing Fields

GLOUCESTER AVE

North Gully

UPPER KING STREET

Walter Fletcher Beach (Aquasol Theme Park)

MOBAY PEPPER

ADWA NUTRITION FOR LIFE

★ ☾RICHMOND HILL

Dump Up Beach

CANTON EXPRESS RESTAURANT

NYAM & JAM ▼

South Gully

PIER 1 ▼

HARBOR WAY HOTEL

Montego Bay

BARNETT ST

Jarrett Park

0   0.25 mi
0   0.25 km

River Bay

Sunset Beach

SUNSET BEACH RESORT & SPA

SUNSET DR

■ MONTEGO BAY YACHT CLUB

COCONUT DR

HOWARD COOKE BLVD

WESTGATE PLAZA ■

GALLERY OF WEST INDIAN ART

A1

Montego

SOUTHERN CROSS BLVD

ALICE ELDEMIRE DR

Pies River

FAIRFIELD RD

A1

River

HOUSEBOAT BAR & GRILL ■

A1

Bogue Islands

JERKY'S ▼

DRAGON COURT

PALACE MULTIPLEX

To Bellefield Great House/Pitfour

FAIRFIELD THEATER

DAY-O-PLANTATION

Queens Drive passes along the hill above the Hip Strip with several budget hotels, many of them frequented by locals seeking privacy with their special someone.

Downtown Montego Bay is centered around **Sam Sharpe Square,** where a statue of the slave rebellion leader stands in one corner. The peninsula of **Freeport** sticks out into the Bogue Lagoon and the Montego Bay Marine Park just west of downtown, with the cruise ship terminal, the yacht club, and Sunset Beach Resort located there.

East of the airport, Ironshore is a middle class area that covers a large swath of hill in subdivisions. East of Ironshore is Rose Hall, the location for many of the area's all-inclusive resorts that are wedged between the main road and the sea. The Ritz Carlton is the most high-end resort along this strip with new developments neighboring to the east including a luxury condominium complex, Palmyra, and farther east, a new Iberostar all-inclusive resort. Also in this neighborhood bordering the sea is the old Windham Resort, now under new management as Rose Hall Resort, and farther east still is Sea Castles.

SIGHTS
◖ Richmond Hill

Whether or not you choose to stay at this gorgeous hilltop property, a sunset cocktail from the beautiful poolside terrace will remain a romantic memory indefinitely.

The hotel has an illustrious history. Columbus apparently stayed here for a year while he was stranded in Jamaica, and it was once part of Annie Palmer's Rose Hall Estate. Later, in 1838, the property was acquired and built into a palatial abode by the Dewar family of Scotch whisky fame. Today the hotel is owned and operated with charm by Stefanie Chin and her daughter Gracie, Austrian expatriates in Jamaica since 1968.

An interesting time to be at Richmond Hill is 5 A.M. on Thursday mornings when Royal Caribbean's newest and biggest floating city, the *Freedom of the Seas,* comes into port with its glimmering lights set against the breaking

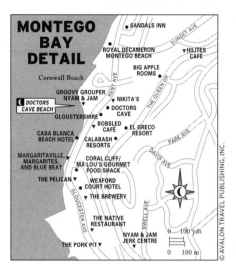

dawn. The hotel restaurant hosts occasional parties, which shouldn't be missed.

Montego Bay Marine Park

Montego Bay Marine Park (tel. 876/952-5619, contact@mbmp.org, www.mbmp.org) consists of the entire bay from high-tide mark on land to 100-meter depth from Reading on MoBay's western edge, to just east of the airport on the eastern side. The marine park encompasses diverse ecosystems that include mangrove forests, islands, beaches, estuaries, sea-grass beds, and corals. The best way to see the marine park is with a licensed tour operator for a snorkeling trip or with a glass-bottom boat tour. Tropical Beach and Aquasol both operate glass-bottom tours, with the former including snorkeling.

Pitfour Rasta Settlement

Pitfour (contact Ras Junior Manning, cell 876/433-2582) is a Rastafarian settlement in the Granville district in the hills above Montego Bay. A Nyabinghi ceremony lasting more than a week begins every November 1 to celebrate the coronation of His Imperial Majesty Haile Selassie I, revered by Rastafarians as their God. On Good Friday of every year, a Nyabinghi vigil known as the

Coral Gardens Groundation is held to commemorate the murder of Rastafarians by the Jamaican authorities in the early years of the movement. When events are held, Rastas come from across Jamaica to participate. Otherwise the settlement is very sleepy with little happening beyond perhaps a reasoning between bredren over a burning chalice. To get to Pitfour head inland from Catherine Hall along Fairfield Road taking a right after the Fairfield Theatre passing Day-O Plantation. Take the first right after the police station in the square and then continue straight and then take the first left in Granville. By the gate to Pitfour you will see Bongo Manny and Daughter Norma Ital food shop.

Montego Bay Civic Centre and Museum

MoBay's Civic Center (Sam Sharpe Square, tel. 876/971-9417, 9 A.M.–5 P.M. Mon.–Fri., US$2 adults, US$0.75 children) houses a museum featuring a history of St. James. The small collection of artifacts spans the Taino period to the present day. The museum is under the management of the Institute of Jamaica, with assistant curator Leanne Rodney offering 30-minute tours throughout the day. Arrangements can be made for the museum to be open on weekends for 10 or more visitors by calling during the week to make a request.

The Cage, also in Sam Sharpe Square, was once used to lock up misbehaving slaves and sailors.

St. James Parish Church (Church St., tel. 876/971-2564) is one of the most attractive buildings in town. It's set amongst large grounds that house a small cemetery.

Burchell Baptist Church (Market St., tel. 876/971-9141) is a more humble church where Sam Sharpe used to preach. His remains are interred there.

【 Gallery of West Indian Art

The Gallery of West Indian Art (11 Fairfield Rd., Catherine Hall, tel. 876/952-4547, nikola@cwjamaica.com, www.galleryofwest indianart.com) is one of the most diverse galleries in Jamaica—as far as carrying both Jamaican art and pieces from neighboring islands, especially Haiti and Cuba. The gallery is owned and operated by Nicki and Steffan, who make quality pieces accessible with very reasonable pricing. Look out for work by Jamaican artists Delores Anglin and Gene Pearson, a sculptor specializing in bronze heads.

ESTATE GREAT HOUSES

Each of the area's estate great houses are worth visiting and quite unique from one another. A visit to one or all of these historic properties is like traveling back in time and is a great way to catch a glimpse of the island's glorious and tumultuous past.

Bellefield Great House

Bellefield Great House (tel. 876/952-2382, www.bellefieldgreathouse.com), five minutes from MoBay at Barnett Estate, offers a lunch tour Wednesdays and Thursdays (10:30 A.M.–2 P.M., US$40). It consists of a 45-minute visit through the great house and gardens, and a one-hour lunch serving well-prepared Jamaican dishes. The tour can be arranged on any day of the week for parties of 10 people or more. A basic tour, without the delicious lunch, is also offered (US$20). Bellefield belongs to the Kerr-Jarretts, a family that at one point controlled much of the land in and around MoBay as part of Fairfield Estate. The tour is operated by Nicky and David Farquharson, who are also behind the production of the exquisite meal. To get to Bellefield, take Fairfield Road from Catherine Hall, staying right where the road splits on to Chambers Drive until you reach the Granville Police Station. Take a right on Bellefield Road at the police station until you see the great house on the left.

【 Rose Hall Great House

Rose Hall Great House (tel. 876/953-2323, greathouse@rosehall.com, www.rosehall .com, US$20 adults, US$10 children) is the former home of Annie Palmer remembered as the White Witch of Rose Hall in Herbert De

© OLIVER HILL

Rose Hall Great House is the most foreboding estate house in Jamaica, with a palpably ominous mood that evokes the brutal past associated with its most infamous mistress, Annie Palmer.

Lisser's novel of the same name. It's the most formidable and foreboding estate great house on the island today, with a bone-chilling history behind its grandeur. The tour through the impeccably refurbished mansion is excellent. Rose Hall was built in 1770 by John Palmer, who ruled the estate with his wife, Rosa. The property passed through many hands before ending up in possession of John Rose Palmer, who married the infamous Annie in 1820. A slight woman not more than five feet tall, Annie is said to have practiced voodoo, or black magic, and would eventually kill several husbands and lovers, starting with Mr. John Rose. Annie ruled the plantation brutally and was much feared by the estate's slaves. She would ultimately taste her own medicine, as she was killed during the Christmas Rebellion of 1831 (which pushed England one step further towards the abolition of slavery).

Rose Hall was virtually abandoned with the decline in the sugar economy until an American rags-to-riches businessman, John Rollins, bought the estate in the 1960s and restored

the great house to its old grandeur. Today the estate is governed by Mrs. Rollins, who has upheld the ambitious development ethic of her late husband. Rose Hall Great House forms the historic centerpiece of the vast Rose Hall Estate, which encompasses three 18-hole golf courses, the Ritz Carlton, Half Moon and Rose Hall resorts, and the most desirable residential district of Montego Bay, Spring Farms. Also on the Rose Hall Estate, Cinnamon Hill Great House was the home of the late Johnny Cash. Cinnamon Hill is not currently open to the public except for special events.

Greenwood Great House

Greenwood Great House (tel. 876/953-1077, greenwoodgreathouse@cwjamaica.com, www .greenwoodgreathouse.com, 9 A.M.–6 P.M. daily, US$12) is the best example of a great house kept alive by the owners, Bob and Ann Betton, who live on property and manage the low-key tour operation. It's said that when the Barretts built the great house in the late 1600s, the drive up from Falmouth was the best in Jamaica. Today the 1.5-kilometer-long road requires slow going, but the panoramic view from the great house and grounds are still as good as ever.

Interesting relics like hand-pump fire carts and old wagon wheels adorn the outside of the building. Inside the great house is the best collection of colonial-era antiques to be found in Jamaica, from obscure musical instruments to Flemish thrones, and desks from the 17th century with secret compartments. An inlaid rosewood piano belonged to King Edward VII, and a portrait Elizabeth Barrett Browning's cousin hangs on the wall. In its heyday the Barretts' estate had 2,000 slaves and nearly 34,000 hectares. The Barretts used a gryphon on the family seal. Another historical treasure at the great house is the will of reverend Thomas Burchell, who was arrested for his alleged role in the Christmas Rebellion.

Farther inland from Greenwood lie the ruins of Barrett Hall, the estate family's primary residence.

Plantation Tours

Several plantations in the area offer visitors a chance to learn about Jamaica's principal agricultural products—from those that were important historically to crops adapted to the modern economy. These include **Kew Park** and **Hilton High Day Tour** in Westmoreland (see *Negril and the West* chapter), as well as Croydon, John's Hall, and Mountain Valley Rafting, which offers a basic banana plantation tour.

Croydon Plantation (tel. 876/979-8267, tlhenry20@hotmail.com, www.croydonplantation.com, open Tues., Thurs., and Fri.) is a pineapple and coffee plantation located at the base of the Catadupa Mountains and was the birthplace of slave rebellion leader and national hero Sam Sharpe. The walking tour takes visitors through a working section of the plantation with an accompanying narrative, with three refreshment stops allowing visitors to sample different kinds of pineapple of the 12 grown on the estate, in addition to other crops like jackfruit, sugarcane, and Otaheite

Greenwood Great House is the most authentic colonial-era estate house in Jamaica that's still in use today as a residence.

© OLIVER HILL

apple based on what's in season. The tour includes a typical Jamaican country lunch. Total tour time from pickup to return is six hours (contact Tony Henry, tel. 876/979-8267, tlhenry20@hotmail.com, www.croydonplantation.com, open Tues., Thurs., and Fri., as well as other days when cruise ships are in port). Cost of the guided tour (US$65 per person) is inclusive of transportation, refreshments, and lunch. Croydon Plantation has the only privately owned forest reserve in the country. The 53-hectare estate is owned by Dalkeith Hanna, with Tony Henry, a partner in the tour operation.

John's Hall Adventure Tour (tel. 876/971-7776, relax.resort@cwjamaica.com, www.johnshalladventuretour.com) offers a plantation tour (US$60 per person inclusive of jerk lunch and fruits) with a historical and contextual commentary by the guides. Stops along the way include the Parish Church, Sam Sharpe Square, and Mt. Olive Basic School. John's Hall Adventure Tour also operates the **Jamaica Rhythm Tour** (6–9 P.M. Wed. and Sun., US$69 inclusive of dinner), a musical show held at John's Hall operated and featuring old-time heritage (from Maypole dancing and limbo to mento). Both tours include transportation from MoBay area hotels.

OTHER SIGHTS

Mount Zion is a quaint community that overlooks Rose Hall with excellent panoramic views of the coast northeast of MoBay. A small church forms the centerpiece of the village, where views over Cinnamon Hill Golf Course and along the coast of Iron Shore and Rose Hall are unmatched. To get to Mount Zion, turn inland on an uncommonly well-paved road (no name) just past the small bridge that crosses Little River heading east from the Ritz Carlton. The road heads up a steep hill toward the community of Cornwall. As the hill tapers off toward the top, a right turn leads further up to the community of Zion Hill. Heading straight at the junction leads to Cornwall.

BEACHES

Walter Fletcher Beach is the location of **Aquasol Theme Park,** where two tennis courts, go-carts, bumper boats, and water sports heighten the entertainment inherent in

---

SAM SHARPE, NATIONAL HERO

Sam Sharpe was the central figure of the Christmas Rebellion of 1831-1832, which many point to as the beginning of the end of slavery in Jamaica (officially granted in 1838). Sharpe was a Baptist deacon, well respected across the deep societal divides. Sharpe was ultimately executed in a public hanging, in what is now Sam Sharpe Square in the heart of Montego Bay, along with over 300 other slaves for their role in the rebellion. Only 16 white people were killed during the rebellion, but around 20 large estates were torched and the rebellion struck fear into the heart of the "plantocracy." Sharpe had originally envisioned and promoted a peaceful rebellion of passive resistance whereby the slaves would stage a sit-down strike until the planters agreed to pay them for their labor in accordance with what was perceived as a royal decree from England being withheld in Jamaica. The rebelling slaves were swept up in the excitement of the hour, however, as Sharpe's lieutenants swept across the western parishes to the sound of war drums belting out from the slave villages. Sharpe was hanged on May 23, 1832, in the last of the executions – after taking responsibility for the rebellion and relieving the white missionaries of blame that was focused on them by the established powers of the day, including the Anglican Church (which with few isolated and notable exceptions backed the landed elite, even organizing terror squads to target the Baptist missionaries who had made it their charge to foment discontent among the slaves). The Christmas Rebellion was consequently also known as the Baptist War.

the small strip of sand facing MoBay's harbor. The beach is located on the Hip Strip across from The Pork Pit.

Dead End Beach is the best free public beach in close proximity to the Hip Strip at the heart of MoBay's tourism scene. Several mid-range hotels face the beach, which borders the end of the runway at Donald Sangster International Airport. The beach is located on Kent Avenue, better known as Dead End Road.

Tropical Beach is a decent, narrow strip of sand on the far side of the airport with the best windsurfing and Jet Ski rental outfit in MoBay. The beach isn't a bad spot for a dip, but it's not a destination for spending the whole day unless you're there for the water sports. To get to Tropical Beach turn left after the airport heading east towards Ironshore and Rose Hall.

Sunset Beach (US$60 adult, US$40 children, all-inclusive day pass, 10 A.M.–6 P.M.) is the private beach for Sunset Beach Resort (tel. 876/979-8800 or U.S. tel 800/234-1707, www.sunsetbeachresort.com), which occupies the tip of the peninsula known as Freeport. The resort has a small water park with large pools and slides, as well as excellent tennis facilities. The day pass includes food and drink at the main buffet-style restaurant and several bars scattered throughout the property. To get to Sunset Beach continue past the cruise ship terminal on Southern Cross Boulevard. The hotel is the largest complex on the peninsula located opposite the Yacht Club.

One Man Beach and Dump-Up Beach across from KFC and MoBay's central roundabout is a venue for occasional events and horse grazing. The beach is no good for swimming however, as the city's effluent emerges from a neighboring gulley.

Cornwall is a private beach marked for development adjacent to Doctors Cave that has been closed for the past several years.

Old Steamer Beach is located 100 yards past the Shell gas station heading west out of Hopewell, Hanover. An embankment leads down to the skeleton of the U.S.S. *Caribou*, a steamer dating from 1887 which washed off its mooring from MoBay. You can hang your towel on the skeleton ship and take a swim at one of the nicest beaches around, which only gets busy on weekends when locals come down in droves to stir the crystal clear waters.

◖ Doctors Cave Beach

Doctors Cave Beach (US$5) is the see-and-be-seen Hip Strip beach that is always happening. The beach is a favorite for the area's uptown youth on weekends. Breezes Montego Bay faces the beach as does the Groovy Grouper Restaurant, with Casa Blanca Hotel on the other side. Chukka Caribbean Adventures uses a pier on Doctors Cave Beach for its Underwater Sea Trek tour.

ENTERTAINMENT AND EVENTS
Bars and Clubs

For an early evening drink, the **Montego Bay Yacht Club** (10 A.M.–10 P.M. daily) is a popular spot among the uptown crowd, especially on Fridays. The **Houseboat Bar** is also a popular early evening spot, while **MoBay Proper** has the most consistently happening local scene in town every night of the week. (See *Food* for location information.)

Hilites Cafe, Bar and Gift Shop (19 Queens Dr., tel. 876/979-9157, jamaica_flamingo_ltd@hotmail.com, 8:30 A.M.–6 P.M. daily) has a great view over the harbor and airport and is another great spot for an early evening drink or to watch the planes take off and land from Sangster Airport.

Margaritaville (Gloucester Ave., tel. 876/952-4777, 11 A.M.–you say when daily; US$5 Sun.–Wed., US$10 Thurs.–Sat. starting at 10 P.M.) is a wildly popular restaurant and bar with a water slide dropping off into the sea and giant trampoline inner tubes just offshore for use by its customers. The restaurant serves dishes like cheeseburgers, jerk chicken and pork, and lobster (US$9–28) while almost every night of the week has a different theme: Tuesdays is 2-for-1 special on margaritas; Wednesdays is the Threesome Party, where three patrons enter for the price of one and select drinks are also three for one; Thursdays is Latin Night, where ladies enter free till midnight; on Fridays there is a rotating guest selector; and Saturdays is World Beat Night with a live sound system.

Margaritaville is the brainchild of a Jamaican partnership between Ian Dear and Brian Jardim, who struck a deal with Jimmy Buffet to carry his franchise in the Caribbean. In 10 years the pair has grown a business venture that is today a fixture in the three major tourism hubs: Ocho Rios, Negril, and MoBay, with a branch at Sangster Airport now as well.

Blue Beat (Gloucester Ave., tel. 876/952-4777, 6 P.M.–2 A.M. daily, free entry) is Margaritaville's more sophisticated and upscale cousin, located at the same property under the same ownership. The laidback club features an in-house jazz band every night.

Jamaican Bobsled Cafe (69 Gloucester Ave., tel. 876/940-7009) serves pricey drinks and bar food at the center of the action on the Hip Strip.

Royal Stocks (Half Moon Shopping Village, tel. 876/953-9770) is an English pub–style bar and restaurant, serving pricey international cuisine. The air-conditioned bar is a great place to go when missing the cool of England, though the beer selection is not the same as back home: Guinness, Red Stripe, and Heineken are the only brews on offer.

The Keg (across from fire station, no phone) is a local dive bar and a good place to soak up the local scene and listen to oldies.

Greeny's is a Rasta yard located across from the airport on the main road east of MoBay. While Greeny was murdered in early 2006, sessions are still often held there and natural food is served.

Wacky Wenzdaze (US$4, ladies free before 10 P.M.) is held at The Brewery with a different selector every week and occasional performances by big-name artists like Bounty Killer. Wacky Wenzdaze is organized by promoter Junior Barnes of Flette Promotions (tel. 876/971-2889, cell 876/377-0217, gangreenjb@hotmail.com).

Live Music

Unfortunately, live music in MoBay is hard to come by—in sharp contrast to decades past when there was an active regular music scene. Today, the all-inclusive resorts have their house bands that entertain the hotel guests, who are often discouraged from leaving the compound. Nevertheless, there is often live jazz at Day-O Plantation, as well as at Blue Beat, and Margaritaville hosts occasional live performances, as does The Bowery. Of course if you want world-class music the best time to visit is during Reggae Sumfest (July) or during the Jazz and Blues Festival (January). Catherine Hall Entertainment Center, the main venue for Sumfest, also holds occasional stage show concerts throughout the year.

Festivals

Several annual festivals draw thousands from around the island and abroad, chief among them being **Air Jamaica Jazz and Blues** (www.airjamaicajazzandblues.com) and **Reggae Sumfest** (www.reggaesumfest.com), sponsored by Red Stripe beer. The Montego Bay Yacht Club has its share of events, including annual and biannual yacht races and a **Marlin Festival.** In Albert Town, Trelawny, the highlight of the year is the **Yam Festival** (www.stea.net/yam.htm), which is a family fun day centered around one of the island's most important staple foods, with tugs of war, beauty competitions, and, of course, music. Jamaica's **Carnival** season also brings at least one night of events to MoBay, with a free concert at Dump-Up Beach.

In the hills above MoBay, the Rastafarian community of Pitfour hosts annual **Nyabinghi sessions** lasting for days to commemorate the coronation of the late Ethiopian Emperor Haile Selassie I, as well as to commemorate the Coral Gardens Massacre on Good Friday.

Art and Theater

Alpha Arts (tel. 876/979-3479, cell 876/605-9130, alphaarts@hotmail.com, www.alphaarts.com), adjacent to Sahara de la Mar resort in Reading, produces and sells on-site a variety of colorful ceramics.

Fairfield Theatre (Fairfield Rd., tel. 876/ 952-0182, US$10) is the only venue in the MoBay area for small, amateur theatrical productions that strive to uphold professional standards. Performances are generally held on weekends. Fairfield Theatre was originally founded as Montego Bay Little Theatre Movement in 1975 by Paul Methuen and Henry and Greta Fowler. The theatrical company was named after the Little Theatre Movement in Kingston, which was formed by Jamaican cultural icons like Louise Bennett. Contact theater chairman Douglas Prout (cell 876/909-9364, dprout@globeins.com, d_freezing@hotmail .com) for more information or call the theater directly for performance schedules.

Mostly contemporary works from the best Jamaican and Caribbean writers are performed at the Fairfield Theatre, but the company produces works from a wide range of playwrights from Shakespeare to Noel Coward Peter Schaeffer, Lorraine Hansbury, and Neil Simon. Caribbean writers such as Derek Walcott, Errol Hill, and Douglas Archibald have been produced to critical acclaim, but greater audience appeal has been found with the current crop of Jamaican playwrights that include Basil Dawkins, Trevor Rhone, Patrick Brown, and David Heron.

Palace Multiplex (tel. 876/971-5550, movie times 876/979-8624) is a cinema showing standard Hollywood films next to Jerky's on Eldemire Drive.

The Montego Bay Yacht Club holds several annual events that are worth participating in whenever possible. These events can be found with the Yacht Club listing under *Sports and Recreation.*

SHOPPING

Montego Bay is full of duty-free stores and gift shops. **Klass Traders** (tel. 876/952-5782) produces attractive hand-made leather sandals from a workshop adjacent to MoBay Proper on Fort Street. Leroy Thompson (cell 876/546-8657) is the head craftsman.

Rastafari Art (42 Hart St., tel. 876/885-7674 or 876/771-7533) has a variety of red, gold, and green items, including flags, belts, t-shirts, bags, and friendship bands that make

inexpensive, authentic, and light-weight gifts and souvenirs.

For clothes, try **Lloyd's** (26 St. James St., tel. 876/952-3172) or **Payless Bargain Centre** (Bayest Centre, Harbour St., tel. 876/971-0017).

Craft centers abound in MoBay, from Harbour Street to Kent Avenue to Charles Gordon Market and Montego Bay Craft Market. A discriminating eye is required at all these markets to sift out the junk from the quality Jamaica-produced crafts.

Freeport Cruise Ship Terminal has several shops, most of which carry overpriced souvenir and mass-produced crafts items of little inherent value.

Dutyfree shops are found anywhere you glance in MoBay, concentrated around City Centre Complex, the Hip Strip, and at the Half Moon Shopping Village east of town. The new Rose Hall Shopping Complex also has its share of dutyfree items.

Sangster's Book Stores is at 2 St. James Street (tel. 876/952-0319).

SPORTS AND RECREATION
Water Sports

The **Montego Bay Yacht Club** (tel. 876/979-8038, fax 876/979-8262, mbyc@cwjamaica .com, www.montego-bay-jamaica.com/mbyc/) was refurbished in 2006 with a new building, landscaped grounds, and a small swimming pool. The club is a warm and friendly family environment with a great bar and restaurant, making it the place in western Jamaica for sailing, fishing, or just to hang out and make friends. Entertainment at the club is facilitated by pool tables, foosball, and table tennis. Every Friday, the club hosts a buffet dinner. Social and sailing membership is available by the day (US$5) or by the year (US$150).

The MoBay Yacht Club is home of the famous Pineapple Cup Race, 1,305 kilometers of blue water from Fort Lauderdale to Montego Bay. This classic race—a beat, a reach, and a run—is held in February of every odd year. Other events include the annual J-22 International Regatta held every December, and the Great Yacht Race, which precedes every

Easter Regatta, a fun-filled and friendly competitive multi-class regatta. The International Marlin Fishing Tournament is held every fall with sailing camps held for children during the summer and courses offered to adults based on demand.

If you arrive in Jamaica on a private vessel, the MoBay Yacht Club has some of the lowest docking fees anywhere (US$0.87 per foot 1–7 days) which are greatly reduced for longer stays (US$0.50 per foot for 8–30 days). Utilities are metered and charged accordingly, while boats at anchor can use the club facilities for the regular daily membership fee (US$5 per person). MoBay's mangrove areas in the Bogue Lagoon are often used as a hurricane hole for small vessels. All charges carry 16.50 percent tax.

Aquasol Theme Park (Gloucester Ave., tel. 876/979-9447 or 876/940-1344, aquasol@ cwjamaica.com, www.aquasoljamaica.com, 9 A.M.–7 P.M. Mon.–Thurs., till midnight Fri.– Sun., US$3.50 adults, US$2 children under 12) is a small theme park located on Walter Fletcher Beach, with go carts (US$4 single-seated, US$7 double), bumper boats (US$3 single, US$4 double), two tennis courts (operated by Steve Nolan cell 876/364-9293, 6:30 A.M.–10 P.M. daily, US$5.75/hr), billiard tables (US$0.75 per game), a video games room, kayaking (US$17 for 10 min), glass-bottom boat excursions to see coral reef (US$21 for 30 min), Jet Skis ($64 for 30 min), waterskiing (US$47 for 10 min), and tube rides (US$21 for 15 min). There's also a sports bar with satellite TV and the Voyage restaurant (US$4–8), serving fried chicken, fried fish, and jerk, fried fish. A gym on property, Mighty Moves (tel. 876/952-8608, 7 A.M.–8 P.M. daily, US$5.75 daily), has free weights, machine weights, and aerobics classes included with the day pass. Joan Grant is the wonderful receptionist.

Tropical Beach Water Sports (tel. 876/940-0836, 9 A.M.–5 P.M. daily) is run by Chaka Brown with professional-quality equipment, including wind surfers (US$45) and Jet Skis (US$65/half-hour, US$120/hour). Bogue Lagoon excursions are also offered (US$180/ hour for up to six people).

Chukka Sea Trek (www.chukkacaribbean .com, US$60) is like scuba diving without the tanks. Sea Trek leads 25-minute tours of the reef just off Doctors Cave Beach (must be age 12 or older). The underwater experience facilitated by oxygen helmets, is billed as the closest thing to walking in space.

Freestyle Sailing (Denise Taylor, cell 876/381-3229) operates private catamaran charters (minimum US$400/2 hours for up to 10 people) with a 51-foot catamaran and a 51-foot trimaran out of the Yacht Club with a capacity of up to 60 people. Denise can make catering arrangements upon request.

Ezee Fishing (Denise Taylor, cell 876/ 381-3229, chokey@reggaefemi.com, dptgone fishing@hotmail.com, www.montego-bay-jamaica.com/ajal/noproblem, US$400 half-day, US$750 full day) operates a 39-foot Phoenix Sport Fisher for big deep-sea expeditions, offering a good chance of catching big game like wahoo, blue marlin, or dorado (depending on time of year).

Dreamer Catamaran Cruises (Donna Lee, tel. 876/979-0102, 10 A.M.–1 P.M., 3 P.M.– 6 P.M. Mon.–Sat., US$60, reservation required) operates two daily three-hour cruises on its two 53-foot catamarans. The catamarans depart from Sandals Montego Bay or Doctors Cave Beach. The excursion includes an open bar and use of snorkeling gear.

Tropical Beach Fitness (tel. 876/952-6510, tropicalfitness@hotmail.com, 6 A.M.– 9 P.M. Mon.–Thurs., 9 A.M.–5 P.M. Sat., 9 A.M.–2 P.M. Sun.) is a decent beachfront gym with free weights, treadmills, bicycles, steppers, and bench-press equipment. Membership is offered for a day (US$3), a month (US$30), three months (US$70), six months (US$100) or a year (US$170). The club has about 200 local members, with two trainers available for an extra fee.

Calico Pirate Cruises and Undersea Tours (tel. 876/940-2493, david@calicopirate cruises.com, www.calicopiratecruises.com, 10 A.M.–1 P.M. Tues.–Sun., US$60, US$30 children 3–11) offers sailing excursions on a pirate-style sailboat for a three-hour cruise around the harbor, with a stop at Margaritaville to use the slide and whirlpool tub. Drinks are included.

The **Undersea Tours** (tel. 876/940-4465, www.mobayunderseatours.com, 11 A.M.–1 P.M. Tues., Thurs.–Sun.) operates out of a semi-submersible glass-bottom boat that offers a view of the reefs without getting wet. Snorkeling equipment is available on both tours. Both tours depart from Pier 1 but bus transport is included for passengers staying at hotels along the coast between Sunset Beach and Sea Castles.

Two-hour **Calico Sunset Cruises** (5 P.M.–7 P.M. Tues.–Sun., US$40, US$20 children 3–11) are offered on the same Calico sailboat with an optional dinner package (US$65) that includes a four-course meal at the Town House Restaurant following the sail.

Barrett Sailboat Charters (contact Captain Carolyn Barrett, Barrett Adventures, cell 876/382-6384, info@barrettadventures.com, www.barrettadventures.com) operates luxury day cruises with snorkeling and a gourmet Jamaican lunch included out of MoBay (US$125 per person for 2–6 persons, US$100 per person for 7–10 persons).

Multi-day charters are also offered (US$1000 per week per person for 2–6 persons, US$900 for 7–8 persons). Provisioning is at passenger expense while the captain and cook are included. Shorter charters of less than a week are also offered (US$150 per person per day).

Charter cruise options include Port Antonio to Cuba, Pirates of the Caribbean Cruise from Port Antonio to Port Royal, as well as a cruise to any destination around Jamaica of your choosing.

Golf

Montego Bay is the best base for golfing in Jamaica, with the highest concentration of courses on a nice variety of terrains, some with gorgeous rolling hills, others seaside, all within the immediate vicinity.

White Witch Golf Course (Rose Hall, tel. 876/953-2800 or 876/518-0174, www.rosehall .com, 6:30 A.M.–9 P.M. daily) is the most spectacular course in Jamaica, for its views and rolling greens. The course has a special for Ritz guests (US$180 per person includes green fees, cart, and caddy, not including US$20 recommended gratuity per player). The course is also open to non-guests (US$200 includes cart caddy and 18 holes, but not gratuity). White Witch offers a Twilight Golf Special (US$99 per person, inclusive of cart, caddy, and green fee, after 2:30 P.M.). The last tee time is at 4:30 P.M.

A gorgeous clubhouse features beautiful views and the **White Witch Restaurant** (noon–9 P.M.), open to non-golfers as well, and a pro shop. The restaurant serves sandwiches, soups, and salads for lunch and fish and steak for dinner.

Cinnamon Hill Golf Course (Rose Hall, tel. 876/953-2650) is operated by Rose Hall Resort, and offers special rates to in-house guests (US$141, inclusive of cart, caddy, and green fees—extended to Half Moon and Sandals guests). The club also offers a Twilight Special (US$99 after 1:30 P.M.), in addition to the standard rack rate (US$160 inclusive of cart, caddy, and green fees) with clubs an additional charge (US$40/50). Recommended caddy tip is US$10–15 per player. Cinnamon Hill is the only course in Jamaica that's on the coast. Holes five and six are directly at the water's edge. There is a gorgeous waterfall at foot of Cinnamon Hill great house, which was owned by the late Johnny Cash until his death.

Half Moon Golf Course (Rose Hall, tel. 876/953-2560, www.halfmoongolf.com) is a Robert Trent Jones Jr.–designed course, with reduced rates for Half Moon Guests (US$75 for nine holes, US$105 for 18 holes). Rates for non-guests are US$90/150 for 9/18 holes, US$12/20 for caddy, US$40/50 for club rental, US$25/35 for cart. Half Moon is a walkable course. Nadine Powell manages the pro shop, while Ian Smith manages the course itself.

SuperClubs Golf Course at Iron Shore (tel. 876/953-3682) is a very respectable 18-hole course with regular green fees (US$50) waived for SuperClubs hotel guests. Caddy (US$11/16 for 9/18 holes) and cart (US$17/35 for 9/18 holes) fees are the lowest in MoBay; many prefer the course, in spite of it never having hosted a PGA tournament. Shelly Clifford is the sweet and amiable golf course manager.

ACCOMMODATIONS

Accommodation options vary widely from cheap dives to inexpensive guest houses, to luxury villas and world-class hotels. In the center of town, on Queens Drive (Top Road), and to the west in Reading there are several low-cost options, while the mid-range hotels are concentrated around the Hip Strip along Gloucester Avenue (Bottom Road) and just east of the airport. Rose Hall is the area's most glamorous address, both for its private villas and mansions surrounding the White Witch Golf Course, and for the Ritz Carlton and neighboring Half Moon, the most exclusive resorts in town. Also on the eastern side of town is Sandals Royal Caribbean, easily the chain's most luxurious property complete with a private island.

Along the Hip Strip several mid-range hotels provide direct access to MoBay's nightlife, a mix of bars and a few clubs, and guesthouses farther afield offer great rates.

MoBay is the principal entry point for most tourists arriving on the island, many of whom stay at one of the multitude of hotels in the immediate vicinity. The old Ironshore and Rose Hall estates east along the coast are covered in luxury and mid-range hotels.

Under US$75

Palm Bay Guest House (Reading Rd., Bogue, tel. 876/952-2274) has decent, basic rooms (US$45) with air-conditioning and hot water in private bathrooms. While not the most glamorous location in town opposite MoBay's biggest government housing project—Bogue Village, built to formalize the squatters of Canterbury—Palm Bay is quiet and safe and appreciably well removed from the hustle and bustle along the Hip Strip.

Harbour Way Hotel (1 Harbour St., tel. 876/952-6560, US$55) is a bit of a dive but well situated in the center of MoBay within easy walking distance to the heart of town right across from Pier 1. Rooms have air-conditioning, carpets, hot water, and king beds. About 70 percent of guests are locals.

Big Apple Rooms (18 Queens Dr., tel. 876/952-7240, bigapple1@yahoo.com, www .bigapplejamaica.com, US$56) is a no-frills hotel perched on the hill above the airport. The basic rooms have private baths with hot water, air-conditioning, and cable TV. There is a pool deck with a view of the ocean.

Sahara de la Mar (Reading, tel. 876/952-2366, sahara.hotels@yahoo.com, www.sahara hotels.com, US$60) is a 24-room oceanfront property nicely designed to hug the coast and provide a central protected swimming area. Amenities include hot water in private bathrooms, fans, air-conditioning, and TV. Food is prepared to order in the restaurant on the ground level.

Calabash Resorts (5 Queens Dr., tel. 876/952-3999 or 876/952-3890, www.calabash resorts.com, US$50–99) has a variety of basic rooms with air-conditioning and hot water. Some rooms command a view of the bay. A nice pool has a great view as well.

$75-200

Buccaneer Beach Hotel (7 Kent Ave., tel. 876/952-9200, info_2@buccaneerjamaica .com, www.buccaneerbeachjamaica.com, US$75 pool view, US$84 ocean view, US$100 during local music festivals) has 42 rooms and suites all with air-conditioning, private baths with hot water, and cable TV. The decor adheres to the tired, colored floral bedcover aesthetic with white tiled floors. The hotel sits on MoBay's popular public Dead End Beach on Kent Ave, aka Dead End Road.

Emerald Escape Beach Resort (tel. 876/952-6133, info@emeraldescape.com, www.emeraldescape.com, US$65/85 low/ high) has 21 basic, no-frills, waterfront rooms with air-conditioning, cable TV, and hot water in private bathrooms. The hotel faces MoBay's lagoon from its location west of town in Reading.

Villa Nia (cell 876/382-6384, info@barrett adventures.com, www.carolynscaribbean cottages.com/VillaNia/indexnia.htm, US$85–

95 per room) is a four-bedroom duplex property owned by Ron Hagler, located right on the water adjacent to Sandals Montego Bay on the opposite side of the airport from the Hip Strip. The rooms rent independently and feature either queen or king beds with sitting areas, small kitchens, and balconies. Each room has a private bath with hot water.

Richmond Hill (tel. 876/952-3859, www.richmond-hill-inn.com, info@richmond-hill-inn.com, US$70/115 low/high) is located at the highest point in the vicinity of downtown MoBay with what is easily the best view in town from a large terraced swimming pool area and open-air dining room. While the accommodations fall short of luxurious, the sheets are clean, the restaurant excellent, and the pool area, with its unmatched view and free wireless Internet access, make Richmond Hill one of the best values in town.

Gloustershire Hotel (Gloucester Ave., or 876/952-4420 or U.S. tel. 877/574-8497, res@gloustershire.com, www.gloustershire.com, US$100/120 low/high) is well situated across from Doctor's Cave Beach on the Hip Strip. It has a total of 88 rooms, many with balconies with a view of the bay. Other amenities include 27-inch TVs, hot water, and air-conditioning.

El Greco Resort (Queens Dr., 876/940-6116 or U.S. tel. 888/354-7326, elgreco4@cwjamaica.com, www.elgrecojamaica.com, US$125/134 low/high) is a large complex of suites overlooking the bay with a long stairway down to Doctors Cave beach across Gloucester Avenue. Suites feature living areas with ceiling fans, air-conditioning in the bedrooms, and private baths with hot water. Many of the suites have balconies with sea views.

At the **Wexford Hotel** (Gloucester Ave., tel. 876/952-2854, wexford@cwjamaica.com, www.thewexfordhotel.com, US$135/136 low/high), most rooms have two double beds, all with private baths and full amenities. Two rooms have king beds that can be requested. The hotel has a restaurant, The Wexford Grill (7 A.M.–11 P.M. daily) that does an excellent Sunday Jamaican brunch buffet (US$10) well attended by locals and tourists alike.

Casa Blanca Beach Hotel (Gloucester Ave, tel. 876/952-0720, info@casablancajamaica.com, www.casablancajamaica.com, US$148, cash only) was in its heyday one of MoBay's most glamorous hotels. Only around 20 of the hotel's 72-rooms have been in operation over the past years, however, with a construction effort brought underway more recently. The rooms all overlook the water along the prime strip of Gloucester Avenue adjacent to Doctors Cave Beach. Unfortunately poor maintenance and signs of neglect abound. Nonetheless the hotel sits on the best location in town for bars and nightlife. Norman Pushell is owner/manager. Amenities are private bath with hot water, air-conditioning, waterfront balconies, and cable TV. Guests get free entry to Doctors Cave Beach.

Doctors Cave Beach Hotel (Gloucester Ave, tel. 876/952-4355, info@doctorscave.com, www.doctorscave.com, from US$140/190 low/high) is a no-frills hotel catering to those looking for direct, easy access to Doctors Cave Bathing Club across the street. Amenities include cable TV, air-conditioning, and hot water. Rooms are spacious with either a garden or poolside view.

Over $200

🄲 **Coyaba Beach Resort** (Rose Hall, tel. 876/953-9150, www.coyabaresortjamaica.com, US$210/320 low/high) is one of the most professionally run hotels in MoBay, with impeccably clean and well-appointed rooms with all the amenities of home and pleasantly unobtrusive decor. The hotel grounds are also attractive, with a pool and private beach area. The only drawback to the property is its proximity to the airport and the occasional roar of a departing flight. On the other hand the proximity is also an advantage for the majority of guests, who tend to be weekend getaway visitors to Jamaica who stay three or four nights on average. Coyaba is located 10 minutes east of the airport and 15 minutes from MoBay's Hip Strip. The beachfront resort was built 15 years ago and has developed a niche in the three-to-four night weekend getaway market.

☾ Ritz Carlton Rose Hall (Rose Hall, tel. 876/953-2800 or U.S. tel. 800/241-3333, rc.mbjrz.concierge@ritzcarlton.com, www.ritz carlton.com, US$229/429 low/high room-only, US$379/699 low/high all-inclusive) is a 427-room, AAA Five-Diamond golf and spa resort with the Rose Hall Estate Great House as its historical centerpiece.

Rose Hall is easily one of the nicest Ritz properties in the world, with a private beach and two world-class golf courses right next door. A 1,003-square-meter ballroom and meeting space for up to 700 people make the Ritz one of the most popular corporate retreat destinations in the Caribbean, with on-site spa facilities and Jamaican touches to help ease any work-related tension. The property also boasts a state-of-the-art fitness center. The rooms at the Ritz uphold the highest standards of the brand, with attractive art depicting Jamaican flora and fauna throughout.

Half Moon Resort (Rose Hall, tel. 876/953-2211 or U.S. tel. 866/648-6951, reservations@halfmoonclub.com, www.halfmoon.com, US$250–900 low season, US$400–1,360 high season) is one of the most exclusive resorts in MoBay, second only to the Ritz. There are villa-style rooms with either garden or ocean view, many of them with private pools. Half Moon accommodations come with full amenities and balconies.

All-Inclusive Resorts

Sunset Beach (US tel. 800/234-1707, tel. 876/979-8800, reservations@sunsetmobay.com, www.sunsetbeachresort.com, US$280/320 low/high) occupies the choice property on the Freeport Peninsula, which is also home to the Yacht Club and the cruise ship terminal. Sunset Beach is a 430-room mass-tourism venture and part of the Sunset Resorts group. It is very comparable to the group's property in Ocho Rios in catering to everyone with its motto, "Always for Everyone, Uniquely Jamaican," but especially popular among families on a budget. The rooms are divided between a main building and smaller structures on the other side of a large pool area. Rooms either face out to sea, or towards downtown Montego Bay. The hotel has excellent tennis facilities, a great beach, and spa facilities. Food is mass-market American fare with large buffet spreads at Banana Walk, complemented by Italian Botticelli, and pan-Asian Silk Road. Several bars dot the property offering unlimited bottom-shelf product. This is a convenient place to stay for Reggae Sumfest with a shuttle provided by the hotel to the Catherine Hall Entertainment Center a few minutes away. It is not centrally located for walking the Hip Strip, however, while still within 10 minutes by cab.

Royal DeCameron Montego Beach (2 Gloucester Ave. tel. 876/952-4340 or 876/952-4346, ventas.jam@decameron.com, www.decameron.com, US$116/132 low/high per person) is a budget-minded all-inclusive recently opened as the chain's second property in Jamaica. At times it can be hard to get through for a reservation, but otherwise the property could be a good value when compared to the other all-inclusive prices.

Holiday Inn Sunspree (Rose Hall, tel. 876/953-2485, www.montegobayjam.sunspreeresorts.com, US$315/535 low/high) has the most decidedly mass-market ambiance of all the all-inclusive resorts. Large groups arrive from the airport to be corralled through the check-in process, which generally means standing in long lines. Guests are not encouraged to leave the walled compound, which has all the over-energetic entertainment and cheap alcohol you could want. The hotel has 524 rooms, some with sea view, others with garden view. The property has two swimming pools, one with a swim-up bar, and four restaurants and snack bars. Fine dining restaurants serve Italian and Mexican-inspired food in a commendable attempt at authenticity.

Rose Hall Resort (Rose Hall, tel. 876/953-2650, www.rosehallresort.com, US$99 room only, US$199 double all-inclusive rate, up to US$349 high season) is a 488-room property built in 1974. The hotel was formerly the Wyndham and recently underwent extensive interior renovations after changing ownership. Both room-only and all-inclusive options are offered.

Sandals (tel. 800/sandals) has three properties in MoBay, Sandals Inn, Sandals Montego Bay, and Sandals Royal Caribbean, in order of increasing luxury. Sandals Inn faces the public Dead End Beach, Sandals Montego Bay is located on the other side of the airport on the continuation of Kent Avenue with a private beach, and Sandals Royal Caribbean is also located on a private beach further east in Rose Hall facing a private island. Sandals Royal Caribbean is easily the nicest property belonging to the group in Jamaica.

Breezes Montego Bay (tel. 876/940-1150, US$129/154 low/high per person) is the most toned-down Breezes property, with the best feature being its location on Doctors Cave Beach. Rooms are comfortable while less showy than other SuperClubs properties around the island. The food is decent and served buffet-style.

Villas

Villas by Linda Smith (U.S. tel. 301/229-4300, linda@jamaicavillas.com, www.jamaicavillas.com, US$3,000/3,450 low/high weekly for 3BR, US$16,450/19,600 low/high weekly for 4BR) rents several of the classiest villas in the Montego Bay area, in addition to villas in Hanover Trelawny and St. Ann. The villas typically have a one-week minimum while rates and stay-length are more negotiable in the low season. Goat Hill has perhaps the best view of Montego Bay from its east-facing perch, which juts out into the sea overlooking the mouth of the Great River just across the border in Hanover; in Trelawny, Good Hope Plantation is the most romantic and luxurious time warp. Amanaoka is the prize property in Discovery Bay, with Sugar Bay another favorite.

Sunny Villa Holidays (U.S. tel. 815/308-7604, Canada tel. 416/848-6049, UK tel. 0844 562 0583, info@sunnyvillaholidays.com, www.sunnyvillaholidays.com, room range from US$470 per week to US$5000 per day) is a family-operated agency in operation since 1988 that keeps tabs on each villa offered in Jamaica. Sunny Villa offers a range of villas from basic to luxurious, three to 15 bedrooms, representing properties in Spring Farms, Unity Hall,

Iron Shore, and on the Bogue Lagoon, some of MoBay's most desirable residential areas. All villas represented by Sunny Villa Holidays have private pools, ocean views, and full staff.

FOOD
Jamaican

Dragon Lounge (Whitehouse, tel. 876/952-1578, 7 A.M.–11 P.M. daily, US$8.50–14), run by Sebil and Peter Tebert, serves excellent seafood dishes, including shrimp, conch, and lobster in a gritty and rootsy Jamaican bar environment with a dining room out back by the kitchen.

Nyam & Jam (17 Harbour St., tel. 876/952-1922, 7 A.M.–11 P.M. daily, US$3–4.50) has a variety of Jamaican staples like fried chicken, curry goat, and oxtail. Breakfast items include ackee and saltfish, calaloo and saltfish, brown stew chicken, yam, boiled bananas, and fried dumpling.

Nyam 'N' Jam Jerk Centre (just before descending the hill into MoBay from "top road," aka Queens Dr., tel. 876/952-1713, 7 A.M.–11 P.M.) has local dishes as well as decent jerk under the same ownership. The jerk center offers delivery as well as having a small dining area.

Adwa Nutrition for Life is the best place in town for natural food. It has three locations, including one full-service sit-down restaurant (Shops 158–160, City Center, tel. 876/940-7618) and two stores (Shop 7, West F&S Complex, 29–31 Union St., tel. 876/952-2161; and Shop 2, West Gate Plaza, tel. 876/952-6554) with imported and domestic products and delis serving freshly made foods and juice blends. Dishes (US$1–4.50) include curried tofu, peppered veggie steak, red pea sip, with beverages like cane juice, fruit smoothies, and carrot juice also served.

Ruby Restaurant (Shop 3, Westgate shopping centre, tel. 876/952-3199, 8 A.M.–8:30 P.M. Mon.–Sat., US$3.50–11) has Jamaican breakfast dishes like callaloo and codfish, ackee and saltfish, kidney and onion, brown stew chicken, as well as more international standards like eggs and bacon, French toast, and ham and bacon omelette. The lunch menu ranges from curried goat to escoveitch fish. More expensive dishes include shrimp plates and steamed fish. Sui mein, foo yong, and chow mein are also available.

〖 MoBay Proper (44 Fort St., tel. 876/940-1233, noon–2 A.M. daily, US$3.50–14) is the in spot for MoBay's party-hearty youth and fashionable business people alike. The food is excellent and a great value, with dishes like fried or jerk chicken, fish done to order, curry goat, roast beef, plus steam, escoveitch, or brown stew fish. This is the best place to get a beer (US$1.75) and play some billiards (US$0.75 per game).

The Pelican (Gloucester Ave., tel. 876/952-3171, 7 A.M.–11 P.M. daily, US$10–40) serves a mix of local and international dishes at international prices. Jamaican favorites like stew peas (US$8), curry goat (US$12), steam or brown stew fish (US$11), and lobster (US$40) complement international staples like cordon bleu (US$17) and hamburgers (US$9).

The Brewery (Miranda Ridge, Gloucester Ave., tel. 876/940-2433, 11 A.M.–2 A.M. daily, US$6–27) has American fare ranging from hamburgers, to meat lasagna, chicken pesto penne, to New York sirloin. Unfortunately the brewery doesn't brew its own beer and instead serves the usual staples (Guinness, Red Stripe, and Heineken), in addition to other drinks from the bar. Wednesday is lobster special with the second half-price. Thursday is karaoke night, Friday is happy hour after 5 P.M. and Saturday is Sizzling Saturday.

The **Montego Bay Yacht Club** (Freeport, tel. 876/979-8038, 10 A.M.–10 P.M. daily, US$6–25) has a good menu with burgers, sandwiches, salads, and entrées like lobster and shrimp thermador, snapper, lamb chops, seafood pasta, coconut curry chicken, zucchini and bowties in a pleasant waterfront setting. A popular buffet dinner (US$14) with a rotating menu is served on Fridays.

Jerk

〖 Scotchie's (Carol Gardens, tel. 876/953-3301, 11 A.M.–11 P.M. daily, US$4–11) is easily

Shorty, the pork man at Scotchie's in MoBay, lifts the zinc to show off the smoked meat underneath.

the best jerk in Jamaica serving pork, chicken, and steam fish. Sides include breadfruit, festival, and yam. Scotchies was forced to move back from the expanded highway and took the opportunity to redesign the dining area, adding a nice bar in the open-air courtyard.

The Pork Pit (27 Gloucester Ave., tel. 876/940-3008 (US$5–11)) has jerk by the pound: pork, chicken, ribs, and shrimp.

Jerky's (29 Alice Eldemire Dr., tel. 876/684-9101 or 876/684-9102, 11 A.M.–midnight Sun.–Fri., open later on Sat. for karaoke, US$3–10) has jerk chicken, steamed fish, escovitch fish, ribs, conch, shrimp, and fried fish. There is a large bar where a beer costs US$1.75.

Palm Bay Guest House (Bogue Main Rd., 7 A.M.–10 P.M., US$4–6.50) has a small restaurant serving local dishes like curry goat, stew pork, fried chicken, and oxtail, as well as an outdoor jerk center (noon–midnight daily) that serves decent Boston-style jerk.

The Road House (Reading Rd., cell 876/446-2125, 10 A.M.–7 P.M. Mon.–Sat., US$3–9)

© OLIVER HILL

MONTEGO BAY

is a new jerk and Jamaican food joint just past Bogue in Reading heading west out of town. Original Jamaican dishes include curry goat, steam fish, fried chicken, and stew pea with pig tail, fish, and shrimp.

Chinese

Dragon Court (Fairview Shopping Center, Alice Eldemire Dr., Bogue, tel. 876/979-8822 or 876/979-8824, fax 876/979-8825, 11:30 A.M.–10 P.M. Mon.–Sat., US$5–18) has good dim sum every day. The shrimp dumplings are a favorite.

Canton Express Restaurant (43 St. James St., tel. 876/952-6173, 10:30 A.M.–7 P.M. Mon.–Sat., US$3.50–7.50) has roast chicken, oxtail, shrimp, chicken chow mein, and shrimp fried rice.

Fine Dining

◖ **The Houseboat Grill** (Southern Cross Blvd., Freeport, tel. 876/979-8845, house boat@cwjamaica.com, www.montego-bay-jamaica.com/houseboat/index.html, 6–11 P.M. Tues.–Sun., bar open from 4:30 P.M., happy hour 5:30–7 P.M., US$12–26), run by Scott Stanley, on Montego Bay's Marine Park is an unparalleled setting for a romantic dinner, and the food is excellent. Reservations are recommended. Dishes range from chicken and fish to lobster.

Ma Lou's Gourmet Food Shack (tel. 876/952-4130, www.coralcliffjamaica.com, 6–11 P.M. daily, US$23–30) serves fish, lobster, shrimp, and steak in a pleasant indoor setting. The restaurant is located in the Coral Cliff entertainment complex on the Hip Strip.

Akbar and Thai Cuisine (tel. 876/953-8240, Half Moon Shopping Village, noon–3:30 P.M., 6–10:30 P.M. daily, US$10–24) is a decent, dependable Thai restaurant with Akbar, a North Indian place in the same venue. Staples like chicken or shrimp pad thai on the Thai side complement items like chicken tikka masala and lobster bhuna from the Indian kitchen. This is MoBay's branch of the same restaurant found on Holborn Avenue in Kingston.

You won't find a more picturesque setting for a romantic sunset dinner than at the Houseboat Grill, which sits on Bogue Lagoon.

◖ **The Groovy Grouper Bar & Grill**
(Doctors Cave Beach, tel. 876/952-8287,
fax 876/940-3784, mtulloch@margaritaville
caribbean.com, www.groovygrouper.com,
9:30 A.M.–10 P.M. daily, US$10–24) serves ex-
cellent food ranging from fish tea, to steam
fish and bammy, to steak and lobster tail. The
setting on Doctors Cave beach is unbeatable
in Montego Bay and is popular with locals
and tourists alike. The restaurant holds regular events like its seafood buffet every Friday
(7–10 P.M., US$20) and full-moon party every
month (on select Sat.).

Nikita's (Gloucester Ave., tel. 876/979-
6473, 6–midnight daily, US$28–50) bills it-
self as the crossroads of international cuisine
with a French lean. The food is consistently
good, though it's a bit pricey. Dishes include
cashew-crusted chicken breast, beef dishes,
and a host of seafood: pan-spiced salmon; fried
grouper fillet; Caribbean Snapper Fiesta; Sun
Fest Mahi Mahi; Seafood Curry Nikata's with
lobster, shrimp, mussels, and scallops; broiled
lobster Tropicana; and baked lobster Santa
Cruz (US$50).

◖ **The Native Restaurant** (29 Glocester
Ave., tel. 876/979-2769, reservations recommended, US$9–12) is easily one of MoBay's
best, with an extensive menu including items
like smoked marlin appetizer or Caesar salad
with spicy shrimp to entrées like Yard Man
steamed or escoveitch fish (or gingered plan-
tain-stuffed chicken). Vegetarian options garlic
char-grilled vegetables and green vegetable coconut curry. The Boonoonoonos Native sam-
pler platter is a good way to get a taste for a
variety of Jamaican dishes in a single sitting.
Other creations bring an international flair
to traditional cuisine with dishes like ackee
and codfish quesadillas, and lobster roll-ups.
The restaurant has an in-house band perform
smooth, live music Tuesday–Saturday for dinner. Dinner is served starting at 5:30 P.M. with
the last order taken at 10:30 P.M. Families are
always welcome. Reservations are strongly suggested. Free door-to-door transport is provided
to many hotels and villas in the area.

Margarites (Gloucester Ave., adjacent to

Margaritaville, tel. 876/952-4777, 6–10:30 P.M.
daily, US$20–50) is the fine dining wing of
MoBay's popular Margaritaville, serving dishes
ranging from the Caribbean-style chicken to
seafood penne, to sugarcane-seared drunken
lobster tail.

◖ **Day-O Plantation** (Fairfield Rd.,
tel. 876/952-1825, cell 876/877-1884, day
orest@yahoo.com, www.dayorestaurant.com,
US$16–35) was formerly part of the Fairfield
Estate, which at one time encompassed much
of MoBay. It is perhaps the most laid-back
and classy place to enjoy a delicious dinner.
Entrées range from typical chicken dishes
to lobster. A beer costs US$3–5. Day-O is a
favorite for weddings and other events that
require the finest setting around a gorgeous
pool. Owners Jennifer and Paul Hurlock are
the most gracious hosts, and on a good day
Paul will bring out his guitar and bless din-
ers with his talent. Other professional musicians who have played at the restaurant's
dinner shows include guitar legend Ernest
Ranglin, jazzist Martin Hand, and steel pan
artist Othello Molineaux.

Pier 1 Restaurant and Marina (tel. 876/952-
2452, 9 A.M.–11 P.M. daily, later on weekends)
is an excellent restaurant and entertainment
venue run by Anna-Kay Russell. The Sunday
seafood buffet starting at 3 P.M. is a must. Pier
1 hosts a Pier Pressure party on Fridays, and
a fashion and talent show on Wednesdays as
well as occasional large events. The grounds
just outside the restaurant are a venue for a few
nights of Reggae Sumfest. Dishes include appetizers like crunchy conch (US$4.50), chicken
wings (US$6.25), shrimp cocktail (US$7.50),
while entrées include chicken and mushrooms
(US$10), bracelet steak (US$18), whole snapper (US$16/lb), and lobster (US$28).

Town House by the Sea (at Casa Blanca
Hotel, Gloucester Ave., tel. 876/952-2660,
townhouser@cwjamaica.com, www.townhouse
bythesea.com, reservations recommended,
10 A.M.–10:30 P.M. daily, no lunch Sat. or
Sun., US$14–35) serves items ranging from
appetizers like escoveitch fish, cream of mushroom phylo pastry, and smoked marlin, to

entrées like crispy duck breast, filet mignon, and chicken kebab. Seafood entrées include a mixed seafood platter, sautéed snapper, and stuffed lobster.

INFORMATION AND SERVICES
Parcel Services
Both **DHL** (34 Queens Dr., tel. 888/225-5345) and **FedEx** (Queens Dr., tel. 888-GO-FEDEX) have operations near the airport. Domestic carrier AirPak Express (tel. 876/952-8647) is located at the domestic airport terminal.

Banks and Money
As elsewhere in Jamaica, the easiest way to get funds is from an ATM with your regular bankcard. Nevertheless, you can get slightly better rates in the cambios, or currency trading houses, that can be found all over town.

NCB has locations at 93 Barnett Street (tel. 876/952-6539); 41 St. James Street (tel. 876/952-6540), Harbour Street (tel. 876/952-0077); ATMs at Sangster Airport and at the junction of 92 Kent and Gloucester Avenues.

ScotiaBank is at 6–7 Sam Sharpe Square (tel. 876/952-4440), 51 Barnett Street (tel. 876/952-5539), and Westgate shopping plaza (tel. 876/952-5545).

Cambios abound virtually everywhere you look in MoBay, from the duty free areas at City Centre Plaza, to the Hip Strip, to the Plazas east of the Airport heading toward Iron Shore.

Government Offices
Jamaica Tourist Board has an office at the Cornwall Beach Complex (Gloucester Ave., tel. 876/952-4425) on the Hip Strip. Clive Taffe is the regional manager.

Internet Access
The best place in MoBay to get online if you have a laptop is **Richmond Hill,** where there is no charge to use the Wi-Fi, which reaches from the open-air lounge across the verandah and pool area. Richmond Hill has the best view of MoBay's harbor in town. Buy a

drink from the bar or a snack for good measure in exchange for the service. Otherwise the **Parish Library** (Fort St., tel. 876/952-4185, 9 A.M.–5 P.M. Mon.–Sat.) offers Internet access as well (US$1.50/hour.)

Medical Services
MoBay Hope Medical Center (Half Moon, Rose Hall, tel. 876/953-3981) is considered by many the best private hospital in Jamaica.

Soe Htwe Medicare (14 Market St., tel. 876/979-3444) is the best private clinic in town.

Supermarkets
Adwa (West Gate Plaza) has a wide array of natural foodstuffs like imported organic grains as well as cosmetics products by Tom's of Maine.

Little Jack Horner Health Food Store (2 Barnett St., tel. 876/952-4952) has nice baked goods and pastries.

Devon House I Scream (Bay West Center, tel. 876/940-4060) is open 11 A.M.–11 P.M. daily.

Organized Tours
Most of the major organized tours to attractions across the island run out of Montego Bay and/or Negril with transportation included as a package with entry and sometimes a meal. These include Mayfield Falls, Chukka Cove, Rhodes Hall, and Caliche White River Rafting. The farm and plantation tours operate similarly including transport and food.

The best and most versatile tour operator running with transport to even the most remote and unheard-of interesting corners of Jamaica is **Barrett Adventures** (contact Carolyn Barrett, cell 876/382-6384, info@barrettadventures.com, www.barrettadventures.com). With personalized service, Barrett Adventures tailors an excursion or even an entire vacation precisely to your interests and likings. Whether it's climbing Blue Mountain Peak, more humbly climbing Reach Falls in Portland, tubing down the YS, or getting a historical tour of Falmouth, veteran adventurer Carolyn Barrett will get you there and ensure that anything you could want to do gets done in the allotted timeframe, which, if you're lucky, won't be less than a week.

GETTING THERE AND AROUND
Airlines
Donald Sangster International Airport (Jamaica Tourist Board information desk, 876/952-2462, airport managers MBJ Ltd. tel. 876/952-3133) is the primary point of entry for most tourists visiting Jamaica. The airport is located by Flankers district a few minutes east of the Hip Strip and about 10 minutes from Downtown or from Rose Hall.

Beyond the national airline, Air Jamaica, Sangster airport is served by many North American and European carriers including US Air, Delta, United, Air Canada, Northwest, American, Spirit, Continental, Cayman Airways, and Virgin.

The domestic terminal is located separately from the international terminal. To get to the domestic terminal turn left from the main entrance before reaching the gas station just after coming off the roundabout.

International Airlink (tel. 876/940-6660, res@intlairlink.com, www.intlairlink.com) offers service from Negril (US$134 one way paid in cash for two persons), Kingston (US$134), and Port Antonio (US$1,575). Airlink passes on bank charges of an additional 5 percent when paying with a credit card.

TimAir (Sangster International Airport, MoBay, tel. 876/952-2516, www.timair.net, timair@usa.net) has charter flights to and from all Jamaica's aerodromes: Norman Manley (US$512 for two), Tinson Pen (US$466), Negril (US$172) Boscobel (US$316), Port Antonio (US$537).

Buses and Route Taxis
Buses and route taxis run between MoBay and virtually every other major town in the neighboring parishes, most notably Sav-la-Mar in Westmoreland, Hopewell in Hanover, Falmouth in Trelawny, and Runaway Bay in

St. Ann. The bus terminal on Market Street is a dusty and bustling place where it pays to keep your sensibilities about you. Buses to any point on the island, including Kingston, never exceed US$7. Time schedules are not adhered to but you can generally count on a bus moving out to the main destinations at least every 45 minutes.

Real Deal Taxi Service and Tours (Curtis cell 876/436-5727, tel. 876/971-8212) will take you wherever you want to go in a comfortable van holding up to eight passengers.

Car Rentals
Foreign-owned car rental outfits can be less dependable and more prone to scams than their local counterparts in Jamaica. Customers have reported cases where employees stole vehicles from clients in order to resell the cars while securing the deposit. When renting from a foreign-owned franchise, especially in Kingston, it's advisable to use secure parking facilities that issue receipts for the parked vehicle, and/or use a third address in the paperwork if you're staying at a private residence. Vehicle theft is common in Jamaica, with the most common vehicle on the island, the Toyota Corolla, being the preferred target (its parts are in high demand). Most rental agencies offer airport and hotel pick-ups.

Dhana Car Rental & Tours (4 Holiday Village Shopping Centre, tel. 876/953-9555) has vehicles ranging from Toyota Starlets to Toyota Noah minivans and gives heavy discounts for reserving a month (US$75) or week (US$50) in advance on the walk-in weekly rates (from US$250).

Sunsational Car Rental & Tours (Suite 206, Chatwick Centre, 10 Queens Dr., tel. 876/952-1212, fax 876/952-5555, sensational@cwjamaica.com, www.sensationalcarrentals.com) is located across from the airport and has decent rates on a variety of Japanese cars (from US$40/55 per day low/high season for a Corolla). The company also offers free cell phones with a minimum two-day rental. The minimum age is 21, with a young driver surcharge until age 25. Max age for drivers is 68.

Alex's Car Rental (1 Claude Clarke Ave., Karen Fletcher, tel. 876/940-6260 alexrental@ hotmail.com, www.alexrental.com) has vehicles ranging from 2001–2005 Corolla, Nissan Suzuki Vitara, Nissan Xtrail, Honda CR-Vs (US$40/50 per day low/high plus tax and insurance).

Thrifty Car Rental (28 Queens Dr., tel. 876/952-1126, 7 A.M.–9 P.M. daily) has 2003/2004 Toyota Corollas (US$92 per day including insurance and tax).

Prospective Car Rentals (2 Federal Ave. at Hotel Montego, across from the airport, tel. 876/952-3524, fax 876/952-0112, reservations@jamaicacar.com, 8 A.M.–5 P.M. Mon.–Fri., till 4 P.M. Sat.) rents 2004 Toyota Yaris, Nissan Sunny, Toyota Corolla, and RAV4 (US$45–85 per day plus tax and insurance).

ST. JAMES INTERIOR

The St. James Interior extends from the coast inland as far as the Trelawny border where Cockpit Country begins. The interior can be accessed from Montego Bay along three main thoroughfares, one extending up Long Hill from Reading west of MoBay, the next heading inland from Catherine Hall along the continuation of Fairfield Road ultimately skirting the western end of Cockpit Country leading into St. Elizabeth, and the third road heading inland due east into Trelawny along the northern flanks of Cockpit Country. This latter road (B15) is an alternate scenic route leading to Windsor Caves, even if it does take a few extra hours due to the road's poor quality.

From the western side of town Long Hill extends from Reading up along the Great River to where it meets the Westmoreland border. Developed tourist attractions in this area consist mainly in a few low-key river rafting operations, Rocklands Bird Sanctuary, and a few plantation tours.

Sights and Recreation

Caliche Rainforest Whitewater Rafting (tel. 876/940-1745, calicheadventuretours@yahoo .com, www.whitewaterraftingmontegobay .com) is one of two true white-water river

St. James Parish Church

MONTEGO BAY

rafting tours in Jamaica located on the upper reaches of the Great River, which divides St. James from Hanover. Rafting excursions (1.5–2 hrs) depart daily at 10 A.M. and 1 P.M. (US$80 with transport from Negril or MoBay included in the cost). Children under 12 do the amateur rafting ride (US$50–70). For those with their own transportation, park at the Caliche office (first building on left above the post office at the base of Long Hill) and ride up with the group that was picked up from hotels in MoBay or Negril.

To reach **Mountain Valley Rafting** (Lethe, tel. 876/956-4920 or 876/956-4947, 8:30 A.M.–4:30 P.M. daily, US$45 per raft), go up Long Hill, take the second right turn at Cross Roads at the small Les Supermarket, and continue nearly five kilometers from the intersection until you cross the bridge into Hanover. Pick-ups from hotels in Montego Bay are offered (US$20 per person), as is a tractor-drawn banana plantation tour (US$15).

Great River Rafting (US$20) is offered on long bamboo rafts along the lower reaches of the great river and out onto the tranquil bay where it exits into the sea. Immediately after crossing the Great River turn inland and back to the river's edge where several rafts are tied up under the bridge. Ask for Hugh.

Rocklands Bird Sanctuary and Feeding Station (Anchovy, tel. 876/952-2009, noon–5:30 P.M. daily, US$10 per person) was created by the late Lisa Sammons, popularly known as "the bird lady," who died in 2000 at age 96. Sammons had a way with birds, to say the least, summoning them to daily feeding sessions even after going partially blind during the last years of her life. Since her death these feeding sessions have been upheld and the sanctuary maintained by Fritz, his wife Cynthia, and their son Damian. Visitors are instructed to sit on the patio and hold hummingbird feeders, which entice the birds to come perch on their fingers. There is also a nature trail where the property's 17 species can be sighted. To get to Rocklands, head up long hill from Reading, and turn left off the main road as indicated by a big green sign that says Rocklands Bird Sanctuary. Follow one abominable road to the top of the mountain and down the other side, about 100 meters, turning right at the first driveway on the downhill.

Rocklands Cottage (US$150–200 for up to six people) is a cute three-bedroom on the property that has one king, one queen, two twin beds, two bathrooms, and a kitchen with a big living and dining room. The cottage has air-conditioning and hot water.

East of Montego Bay

East of Montego Bay proper, Ironshore and Rose Hall cover the coast with hotels and housing schemes that range from middle-class to super-luxury before reaching Greenwood, a small community once part of the Barrett estate that sits beside the sea bordering the parish of Trelawny. The Trelawny coast has a smattering of tourism development concentrated in the area just east of Falmouth along the bay, while the inhabited parts of Trelawny's interior are covered in farming country where yam, sugarcane, and citrus fruit are major crops. The early morning mist that rises from dew-covered cane fields makes a trip through the interior from Rock, Trelawny to St. Ann a magical alternative to the coastal route at this time of day.

◖ FALMOUTH
Trelawny's capital, Falmouth, is today a run-down shadow of its short-lived former Georgian prime. Nevertheless, noble and much-appreciated efforts are underway to dust off years of neglect and shed favor on the town's glorious past by restoring its architectural gems. Falmouth was formed in 1790 when the port of the former capital Martha Brae silted up and shippers needed an export base. The town was laid out in a well-organized grid and named

© OLIVER HILL

Trelawny Parish Church is the oldest house of worship in the parish and the oldest public building in Falmouth.

after Falmouth, England, birthplace of the governor at the time, William Trelawny, who lent his name to the parish. The land for the town was acquired from Edward Barrett, who owned Greenwood Estate a few kilometers west. For the town's first 40 years during the height of Jamaica's sugar production, Falmouth experienced a housing boom and was fashionable amongst the island's planter class. But as the sugar industry faded in importance, so too did Falmouth, leaving a virtual ghost town by the late 1800s.

Today, with somewhat decent roads and its close proximity to resort areas in Montego Bay and Trelawny Beach, the town is attracting a growing population once more. Thanks to the efforts of an NGO known as **Falmouth Heritage Renewal** (4 Lower Harbour St., tel. 876/617-1060, jmparrent@yahoo.com, www.falmouth-jamaica.org) the town has become a laboratory for architectural restoration. Falmouth Heritage Renewal, directed by James Parrent, has been working for several years to revitalize the architectural heritage of Jamaica's most impressive Georgian town by training local youth in restoration work. The Georgian Society in Kingston has a wealth of information on Falmouth, which can be acquired by contacting their office (tel. 876/754-5261).

Falmouth is famous for its **Bend Down Market** held every Wednesday since the town's founding.

Sights

The **Baptist Manse** (Market St., cell 876/617-1060) was originally constructed as the town's Masonic Temple in 1780. The building was sold to the Baptist Missionary Society in 1832 after it had lost many buildings in raids of terror and reprisal following the slave rebellion of 1831 that the Baptists were credited with having fueled with their fiery abolitionist rhetoric. The building was home to several Baptist missionaries before it was destroyed by fire in the 1950s to be reconstructed as the William Knibb School in 1961. Today the building serves as headquarters for the Falmouth Heritage Renewal.

Falmouth Courthouse was built in 1815 in classic Georgian style, destroyed by fire and re-

© OLIVER HILL

The courthouse in Falmouth is a classic example of Georgian architecture.

built in 1926. The building stands prominently on a little square facing the water just off the main square at the center of town.

Trelawny Parish Church of St. Peter the Apostle (Duke St.) is one of the most impressive Anglican structures in Jamaica, built in typical Georgian style. It was constructed in 1795 on land donated by rich estate owner Edward Barrett, whose descendent, Elizabeth Barrett Browning, would later go on to become a well-recognized feminist poet of the Romantic movement. The parish church is the oldest public building in town and the oldest house of worship in the parish.

Other historic churches in Falmouth include the **Knibb Memorial Baptist Church** (King and George Sts.) named after abolitionist missionary William Knibb, who came to Jamaica in 1825 and established his first chapel on the site of the existing structure, which was erected in 1926, and the **Falmouth Presbyterian Church** (Rodney and Princess Sts.), which was built by the Scots of the parish in 1832. Knibb's first chapel was destroyed by the non-conformist militia after the Baptist War, aka Christmas Rebellion of 1831–832. Later structures were destroyed by hurricanes. A sculpture relief inside Knibb Memorial depicts a scene (repeated at several Baptist churches across the island) of a congregation of slaves awaiting the dawn that granted full freedom in 1838.

Falmouth All Age School sits on the waterfront in an historic building and makes a good destination for a stroll down Queens Street from the square.

Shopping

Falmouth is by no means a shopping destination. Nevertheless there is a small mall on Water Square with a few crafts shops to poke around.

For more original crafts, call **Isha Tafara** (cell 876/610-3292, cell 876/377-0505) an artist and craft producer who lives in Wakefield near Falmouth farther inland from Martha Brae. Tafara makes red, green, and gold crochet hats, Egyptian-style crafts, handbags, belts, and jewelry with a lot of crochet and fabric-based items. Tafara works from home, which can be visited by appointment, and supplies Things Jamaican, among other retailers.

Services

For groceries and supplies, try **T&W Supermarket** by the Texaco station.

Next to the courthouse there is new **ScotiaBank** branch built in replica Georgian style, with a **ScotiaBank ATM** also by the Shell station.

Trelawny Parish Library (Rodney St., with entrance on Pitt St., tel. 876/954-3306, 9 A.M.–6 P.M. Mon.–Fri., till 4 P.M. Sat.) offers DSL Internet service (US$1.50).

The **Falmouth Police** are based along the waterfront on Rodney Street (tel. 876/954-5700). The **Montego Bay Police** department has offices at 14 Barnett Street (tel. 876/952-2333).

MARTHA BRAE

The town of Martha Brae was Trelawny's first parish capital, before the mouth of the river silted up and forced the relocation of the port from Rock to Falmouth. Along with several other locations in Jamaica, Martha Brae is thought to have been the location of the first Spanish settlement of Melilla. Until 1790 when the first bridge was constructed across the river, a ferry was in service. Today with the North Coast Highway, it's possible to speed past without noticing the river at all. Martha Brae is a literal backwater, with little to distract tourists as they pass through on their way to start the rafting trip or to Good Hope Plantation in the Queen of Spain Valley.

The **Martha Brae River** is one of Jamaica's longest rivers and is navigable for much of its 32 kilometers extending to the deep interior of Trelawny, from where it wells up out of the earth at Windsor Cave. The river's name is an awkward derivation of "Para Matar Tiburon Rio," which translates literally as "to kill shark river." Legends surround the Martha Brae, likely owing to its important role in the early colonial years when the Spanish used the river to reach the North Coast from their major settlement of Oristan, around present-day Bluefields. The first commercial rafting tour began in 1970.

Martha Brae Rafting

Martha Brae Rafting (tel. 876/940-6398 or 876/940-7018 or 876/952-0889, info@jamaica rafting.com, www.jamaicarafting.com, 9 A.M.–4 P.M. daily) is the most developed bamboo rafting attraction in western Jamaica. Rafts hold two passengers in addition to the raft man, who guides the vessel down the lazy Martha Brae. The tour (US$55) includes a welcome drink, and round-trip transport can be arranged from MoBay (US$15 per person). To reach the departure point on the Martha Brae River, exit left off the highway ramp after passing the first turnoff for Falmouth heading east. Turn inland (right) through the underpass, continuing into the small village of Martha Brae. At the intersection in the town, turn left and then right after the second bridge. The five-kilometer raft ride takes about 90 minutes. The excursion will not get the adrenaline pumping, but it's a relaxing and romantic experience.

The Luminous Lagoon

The Luminous Lagoon is one of Jamaica's favorite natural phenomena, created from a unicellular dinoflagellate less than 1⁄500th of an inch in diameter, *Pyridium bahamense,* that glows when the water is agitated. The organism photosynthesizes sunlight using chlorophyll during the day and then emits the energy at night. Tours of the Luminous Lagoon are offered by two operators, **Glistening Waters Restaurant & Marina** (tel. 876/954-3229, info@glisteningwaters.com, www.glisteningwaters.com) and **Fisherman's Inn** (tel. 876/954-4078 or 876/954-3427, fishermansinn@cwjamaica.com). The Glistening Waters tour (US$17/person) lasts for half an hour, with boats leaving each the marina every half-hour from 7–9 P.M. nightly. Fisherman's Inn organizes virtually identical outings (US$15/person) every evening at 7 P.M.

Glistening Waters also offers fishing charters from the Marina (US$600) on a 46-foot sport fisher with a capacity of eight people. A smaller, 32-foot boat (US$400/four hours) carries five people. Two complimentary drinks per person are included on fishing excursions. The marina also welcomes visiting yachts (US$1/foot/day) and can accommodate boats of up to 86 feet. Boaters should call ahead for special instructions on entering the lagoon. Longer stays can be negotiated.

Accommodations

Bougain Villa (Queens St., contact Klaes Secher tel. 416/491-4655, cell 876/427-7996, klaes@secher.ca, www.villa-jamaica.com, US$800 weekly, minimum stay) sits on the edge of the Luminous Lagoon in the heart of Falmouth. It's the best accommodation around (the only good one near the heart of town) and an excellent value. The rental includes a cook and housekeeper. There is also a small one-bedroom self-contained studio (US$400 weekly) on the same property. Amenities include ceiling fans, hot water, full kitchen, and DSL Internet connection.

Fisherman's Inn (tel. 876/954-4078 or 876/954-3427, fishermansinn@cwjamaica .com, from US$75) is a hotel and restaurant on the Luminous Lagoon with clean, spacious rooms overlooking the lagoon and a small marina with private baths and hot water, TV, and either fans or air-conditioning. Jean Lewis is the very helpful and accommodating manager.

The inn organizes outings every evening (US$15 per person) at 7 P.M. on the lagoon to see the phosphorescent microbes light up the agitated water.

Food

In the center of Falmouth on the square there is a small Juici Patties kiosk, as well as **Spicy Nice** (Water Square, tel. 876/954-3197), a bakery that sells patties, breads, pastries, and other baked goods.

There are two main roads leading off the highway into Falmouth. Along the easternmost road, two restaurants sit adjacent to one another on the Luminous Lagoon. **Fisherman's Inn** (tel. 876/954-4078, fishermansinn@cwjamaica .com) is a hotel and restaurant on the Lumi-

nous Lagoon. The restaurant serves items like callaloo-stuffed chicken breast and stuffed jerk chicken, lobster and surf and turf (US$13–30).

Glistening Waters Restaurant & Marina (tel. 876/954-3229, info@glisteningwaters.com, www.glisteningwaters.com) has food ranging from oyster bay seafood chowder (US$3.45) to the Falmouth Seafood Platter (US$31.05), which comes with grilled lobster, shrimp, and snapper.

Farther toward Falmouth, there is a jerk center that keeps irregular hours, mostly opening on weekends.

On Foreshore Road, the western entrance to Falmouth with the ramped exit off the highway, **Culture Restaurant** (Foreshore Road, contact proprietor Pablo Plummer, cell 876/781-7339 or 876/362-4495, 8 A.M.–8 P.M. daily, US$4–8) represents with a decidedly Rasta experience and takes the cake for original roots value. It's a small restaurant and cultural center where Ital food and juices are served in an atmosphere brimming with black pride and Rastafarian symbolism. Owner Pablo Plummer is as conscious as they come, and also incidentally runs independent PADI diving courses with full equipment provided after spending years as a dive instructor at Half Moon in Montego Bay.

Aunt Gloria's (Rock district, cell 876/353-1301, 6 A.M.–8:30 P.M. Mon.–Sat., US$3–4.50) serves brown stew fish, fried chicken, curry goat, and brown stew pork. Gloria opens her jerk center on Fridays and sometimes on Saturdays for the best jerk pork and chicken in town. Breakfast items include ackee and saltfish, kidney, dumpling, yam, and banana.

EAST OF FALMOUTH
Duncans

Silver Sands Beach is an excellent beach virtually unvisited by tourists. It's located 15 minutes east of Falmouth just before reaching Duncans. A sign from the main indicates the left turn, which descends a few kilometers to a fork in the road. Take the road to the right.

The **Bob Marley School of the Arts Institute** (Flamingo Beach, Ras Astor Black,

C&W tel. 876/327-9991, Digicel tel. 876/861-5233, astor@bobartsinstitute.com, www.bobartsinstitute.edu) is a bold project dreamt up by Ras Astor Black to draw Jamaica's youth into a technically savvy education in the arts, with music and production courses. As an annex to the school the vision includes a **Reggae Walk of Fame,** where artists deemed honorable will be inducted once per month. Black lives up on a hill between Falmouth and Greenwood where he has created the Reggae Village. He intends to host regular live concerts to appeal to the masses of tourists who arrive expecting to see more in the way of live reggae music, like they are accustomed to seeing in the United States and Europe.

Accommodations and Food

Natural Vibes Gift Shop Bar & Restaurant (Long Bay, Greenwood, tel. 876/953-1833, 8 A.M.–10:30 P.M. daily) has a mix of seafood and Jamaican favorites like curry lobster (US$25), curried shrimp (US$20), escoveitch fish (US$15), jerk chicken (US$10), and jerk pork (US$12–13). The waterfront property is a favorite chill-out spot for Montegonians and tourists alike.

Time N Place (adjacent to Pebbles, call owner Tony Moncrieffe, tel. 876/954-4371, cell 876/843-3625, timenplace@cwjamaica.com, www.timenplace.net) is the quintessential laid-back rustic beach spot with an open-air seafood restaurant and beach bar and four cottages planted in the sand (US$65–90). The spot has been a local favorite since it opened in 1988. The cottages are comfortably rustic, with front porches, basic foam queen beds, fans or air-conditioning, Jamaican art on the walls, and private bathrooms sectioned off with hot water. Tony offers coffee, fruit, and toast for breakfast. The restaurant (8 A.M.–8 P.M.) prepares excellent seafood and Jamaican favorites as well as burgers and fries.

FDR Pebbles (next to Time 'N' Place along the old main road, tel. 876/973-5657 or 876/617-2500, US$250) bills itself as an eco-

Time N Place is a timeless bit of the old laid-back Jamaica that drew tourists seeking simplicity on the beach during the 1970s and '80s.

friendly, family-oriented resort. The hotel is by no means exemplary in the environmental department, however, with clear signs of dumping of grey water into the bay and a generally untidy backyard. Pebbles, along with its sister property in Runaway Bay, has created the family-friendly niche by proving nannies for guests. Pebbles' private beach has been sectioned off from the expanse with a pair of stone piers. Nevertheless, guests often hop the fence to get a taste for the authentic Jamaica vibe found next door at Time N Place. All rooms at Pebbles have air-conditioning, ceiling fans, and hot water.

Excellence Resorts (www.excellence-resorts.com) is building a 450-room, adult-only luxury all-inclusive resort on five kilometers of beach adjacent to Time N Place. The resort is expected to open in December 2008.

TRELAWNY INTERIOR

Some of the most gorgeous and unexplored countryside in Jamaica lies in the interior of Trelawny where **Cockpit Country,** with its myriad caves, sink holes, and springs, stretches from the border of St. James in the west to St. Ann at the heart of the island. Hiking and exploring in this region is unparalleled, while adequate supplies and a good guide are essential. Meanwhile, the Queen of Spain Valley only a few minutes drive inland is one of the most lush and picturesque farming zones in Jamaica, where the morning mist lifts to reveal stunning countryside of magical, lush pitted hills.

Cockpit Country has some of the most unique landscape on earth, where porous limestone geology created what is known as Karst topography molded by water and the weathering of time. Cockpit Country extends all the way to Accompong, St. Elizabeth, to the south and Albert Town, Trelawny, to the east. Similar topography continues over the inhospitable interior as far as Cave Valley, St. Ann, even farther east.

There are three principal routes leading into Trelawny's interior and providing access to the northern border of the impassible Cockpit Country. The first few routes lead inland from Martha Brae. To get to Good Hope Plantation, bypass the town of Martha Brae to the

right when heading inland from the highway, and take a left less than 1.5 kilometers past the town following well-marked signs. Continuing on the road past the turnoff to Good Hope ultimately leads to Wakefield, where the B15 heads back west to Montego Bay.

By taking a left at the stop sign in Martha Brae, and then a right after crossing the river, the road leads inland to past Perth, Reserve, and Sherwood Content, to where it ultimately peters out near Windsor Caves.

🄲 Queen of Spain Valley

Good Hope Plantation (cell 876/469-3443, goodhope1@cwjamaica.com, www.goodhope jamaica.com, starting at US$3,500/4,400 low/high weekly for 3BR River Cottage) located in the Queen of Spain Valley, is one of the most picturesque working estates on the island. Citrus has today replaced the cane of yesteryear, while the plantation's great house and a collection of its historic buildings have been converted into the most luxurious countryside villas, with a total of 10 bedrooms between the main house, the carriage house, and the river cottage. Good Hope features old-world luxury that sets itself apart from any other accommodation option on the island, with authentic antique furniture decorating every room, while not skipping the modern luxuries like iPods and air conditioning. The villas are fully staffed with the most professional chefs, housekeepers, and gardeners to be found anywhere.

Good Hope is the ideal place for family retreats, birding, hiking, and mountain biking. There is no better place for horseback riding, which is still the best means of exploring the surrounding countryside. Of course, the inviting swimming pools and a brimming river make relaxation a favorite pastime for guests as well. From the United States, Good Hope is rented through Linda Smith (www.jamaicavillas.com), while the property can also be rented locally direct from the owners.

David Pinto's Ceramic Studio (8 km north of Falmouth, dpinto@cwjamaica.com, www.jamaicaclay.com, cell 876/886-2866, 8 A.M.–4 P.M. Mon.–Fri. or by appointment)

© OLIVER HILL

The estate house and surrounging buildings at Good Hope Plantation have been impeccably restored with antiques and tastefully redesigned interiors.

is run by a Jamaican-born potter who studied ceramics during high school in the UK and later at Rhode Island School of Design before practicing in New York City. He returned to Jamaica in 1992 to establish his present studio in the Queen of Spain Valley on Good Hope Plantation, where he runs retreats led by internationally acclaimed guest master potters. Pinto's work ranges from functional to decorative pieces and is on display in the permanent collection at the National Gallery in Kingston. A stop by Pinto's bustling studio with its five kilns is a great excuse to visit the spectacular grounds of Good Hope, a working citrus plantation.

Albert Town

A small hamlet at the edge of Cockpit Country, Albert Town is the center of Trelawny's yam-growing region, which celebrates the crop each year with the **Trelawny Yam Festival.** Albert Town is the base for the **South Trelawny Environmental Agency (STEA)** (tel. 876/610-0818, www.stea.net), which organizes the yam festival and also offers guided excursions with

its **Cockpit Country Adventure Tours** outfit in the surrounding area. They offer four different tours that cover caving and hiking. STEA is one of the most well-organized environmental advocacy organizations in the country, which has recently taken up the cause of protecting the area from an intended incursion by bauxite mining interests which appear to have government backing.

Windsor

Located at the farthest accessible point into Cockpit Country, Windsor is a small community. **Windsor Great Caves** is its main draw. Franklyn (Dango) Taylor is the sanctioned warden for the Jamaica Conservation and Development Trust (JCDT) and the official guide for Windsor Great Caves. The caves are best visited with Dango (US$20), though experienced cavers may prefer to go it alone. All visitors should check in with Dango, and sign the guestbook at the very least, which serves to both monitor efforts and provide some degree of accountability in the case of emergencies. Dango runs a little shop selling drinks and snacks. The Martha Brae River source is nearby, affording a great spot to cool off.

The Windsor caverns are rich in both geological history and animal life, with up to 11 bat species emerging to feed in the evenings in large swarms. The geological formations should not be touched inside the caves, and a minimal-impact policy should be generally observed, which starts with visitors staying on the established path. Shining flashlights on the ceiling is also not advisable since it is a good way to disturb the resting bats.

For more in-depth spelunking of lesser-developed attractions, **Jamaica Caves Organization (JCO)** (info@jamaicancaves .org, www.jamaicancaves.org) is a useful group that knows Cockpit Country literally inside and out. They can arrange guides for hiking as well as caving. There is also a good circuit mapped out on their website to take a driving tour of Cockpit Country for those not interested in exercise. For those with a serious interest in hiking, the **Troy Trail** is one of the most interesting and arduous hikes in western Jamaica, traversing Cockpit Country from Windsor to Troy. Again, the JCO can provide guides and maps for a reasonable fee that goes toward helping to maintain the organization.

Accommodations

The Last Resort (Ivor Conolley tel. 876/931-6070 or cell 876/700-7128, iscapc@cwjamaica .com) is the most remote accommodation option in Cockpit Country. It's the headquarters for Jamaica Caves Organization, led by chairman Stefan Stewart. The facilities were recently renovated but remain rustic with 20 bunk beds (US$15 per person) and a common bath. One private room has a queen bed. Although recently renovated, Last Resort remains rustic, which makes for a pleasant intimacy with the surrounding environment. Bug repellent is an essential item.

Windsor Great House (cell 876/997-3832, windsor@cwjamaica.com, www.cockpit country.com) was built by John Tharp in 1795 to oversee his vast cattle estate, which included most of the land bordering the Martha Brae River. Today the great house is operated by Michael Schwartz and Susan Koenig, who offer rustic accommodation and a weekly "Meet the Scientists" dinner (US$25 for the dinner).

Getting There

To get to Windsor, head inland from Falmouth to Martha Brae crossing the bridge to the east and turning right to follow the valley south into the hills. On the way, the road passes through the small farming communities of Perth Town and Reserve. Once the road leaves the riverbanks, it heads to Sherwood Content, Coxheath, and finally Windsor. To get to Last Resort, turn right at Dango's shop continuing on for about 0.75 kilometers. A four-wheel-drive vehicle with clearance is recommended, but the route is also traveled frequently by low-lying Toyota Corollas.

BURWOOD BEACH

The small community neighboring Super-Clubs' Starfish Trelawny Resort has the spectacular Burwood Beach in Bounty Bay, which is also called Mutiny Bay. It's the best spot in Jamaica for **windsurfing** and **kite surfing** thanks to its gradual slope and lack of reefs that make these sports perilous in most other areas of the island. Brian Schurton (cell 876/586-0900, U.S. tel. 541/490-2047) runs an informal windsurfing and kite-surfing school on the beach. His coworker Andrew (cell 876/543-0169 or 876/873-4991) is usually the one on the ground attending to students and rentals. With essential equipment like harnesses lacking in most of the all-inclusive resorts, wind-surfers will find a better bet at Burwood Beach. To get to there, turn off the highway toward the sea about 1.5 kilometers east of Starfish Trelawny next to a sign for Bounty Bay.

Accommodations

Starfish Trelawny (Coopers Pen, Falmouth on Burwood Beach, tel. 876/954-2450 or U.S. tel. 800-GO-SUPER, www.superclubs.com, US$99/139 low/high per person) is the place to go if you love water slides, video gaming, trapeze acrobatics, and water sports. Rooms come with a stocked fridge, TV, air-conditioning, and CD player, but with all the activities in store, you won't be there much. Starfish is the SuperClubs brand's most budget-friendly and family-oriented property, with the food and service reflecting a more lean approach than at the other properties like Breezes, with a noticeably different caliber than the high-end Grand Lido resorts.

Grand Lido Braco (tel. 876/954-0000 or U.S. tel. 800-GO-SUPER, glbreservations@ superclubs.com, www.superclubs.com, US$224/349 low/high per person) is the second Lido all-inclusive in Jamaica, centered around a recreated and much-tamer-than-typical Jamaican village courtyard area where dinners are served under the stars. Braco rooms are luxurious by American standards, with spacious suites that have balconies and large sitting areas. All the amenities of home are there, and the fridge is stocked daily with beer and soft drinks. Braco has a decent beach and large swimming pool areas with the best food of the SuperClubs properties and premium liquors. The hotel sits on a 34-hectare estate. Horseback riding and tennis are some of the more popular activities at the resort, while water sports like scuba, snorkeling, and sailing are also offered.

For horseback riding, **Braco Stables** (tel. 876/954-0185, bracostables@cwjamaica.com, www.bracostables.com, US$65 with transportation from MoBay or Runaway Bay, US$55 without transport) offers very tame tours where riders traverse the Braco estate in single file. Experienced riders may be disappointed as there is little freedom to roam about and leaving the group is not a real option.

RIO BUENO

The first community in Trelawny across the border from St. Ann, Rio Bueno is considered by many experts to have been the actual landing point for Christopher Columbus, on his second voyage, while the claim is also made for Discovery Bay. The port at Rio Bueno was an important export point as can still be seen by the dilapidated warehouses and wharfs along the waterfront beside the community's only accommodation, the **Rio Bueno Hotel.**

The small village is today undergoing somewhat of a renewal, with the new North Coast Highway bypassing the town entirely, which could ultimately enhance its picturesque appeal even while the busy Rio Braco rest stop will be less relevant. A new dock is being built, apparently with the idea of attracting cruise ship stops.

The riverbank along the Rio Bueno is great for a stroll where visitors can see ruins of the **Baptist Theological College.** The college was the first of its kind in the hemisphere. Other ruins in town include those of **Fort Dundas** behind the school. The **Rio Bueno Baptist Church** was originally built in 1832 before being destroyed by the Colonial Church Union, whose mostly Anglican members organized militias to terrorize the abolitionist Baptists who were upsetting the status quo. The church was quickly rebuilt twice as large in 1834, and the present structure was built in 1901. While the roof is largely missing, services are still held downstairs.

The **Rio Bueno Anglican Chuch** was built at the water's edge in 1833 and remains there today. The church was petitioned by the community after years of attending service in a rented space.

The extensive **Gallery Joe James,** on the grounds of the Lobster Bowl and Rio Bueno Hotel, displays artwork by proprietor Joe James, among other selected Jamaican Artists. The gallery extends throughout the restaurant, bar, and hotel and makes for a surreal waterfront setting. The restaurant itself is enormous, with outside seating extending out on a dock along the waterfront, as well as inside a large dining hall.

The Rio Bueno Primary School up the road is sometimes used for entertainment and events.

Accommodations and Food

Rio Bueno Hotel (tel. 876/954-0048, gallery joejames40@hotmail.com, US$100) is a 20-room rustic accommodation with balconies

© OLIVER HILL

Dilapidated wharves and warehouses along the waterfront are all that remain of the days when Rio Bueno was an important port.

overlooking the sea, ceiling fans, TV, and hot water in private baths. The ground floor rooms are larger with three double beds geared towards families.

The Lobster Bowl Restaurant (tel. 876/954-0048, 8 A.M.–10 P.M. daily, US$18–40) serves excellent shrimp, chicken, fish, and lobster. The restaurant was founded by Joe James and his wife, Joyce Burke James, over 40 years ago.

Yow's Restaurant and Beach Bar (on the western side of the village, tel. 876/954-0366, 7:30 A.M.–6 P.M. daily, US$5–14) is a popular pit stop for typical Jamaican fare with dishes like jerk, fried chicken, fish (steam/escoveitch), curry goat, lobster, shrimp, and conch.

NEGRIL AND THE WEST

Hanover and Westmoreland are Jamaica's westernmost parishes. Hanover wraps around from Montego Bay on its northeastern edge to where Negril's large hotel strip overflows from Westmoreland along its western border. It is a picturesque parish with small mountains tapering down to the coast with rivers, deep, navigable coves, and lush valleys. Caves dot the landscape of some of Jamaica's most biologically diverse ecosystems in the shadow of the Dolphin Head range.

Negril, which straddles the Hanover-Westmoreland border, has become a mass-market destination popular among Jamaicans and foreign visitors alike. The Kingstonian phenomenon of a weekend escape to "country" often implies a trip west to kick back and adopt the beach life, which necessarily involves taking in

spectacular sunsets and the enviable slow pace evoked in Tyrone Taylor's 1983 hit, "Cottage in Negril." A constant stream of new visitors also gives hustlers a chance to do their thing, and Negril has gained a reputation as a mecca for sinful indulgence as a result.

While Negril is the region's most well-known draw, there are several low-key communities farther east that are just as easily accessible from Montego Bay's international airport and worthy coastal destinations in themselves, namely Little Bay, Bluefields, Belmont, and Whitehouse. The Westmoreland interior consists of vast alluvial plains on either side of Cabarita River, still some of Jamaica's most productive sugarcane territory. The plains extend from the base of the Orange Hills just east of Negril to where the Roaring River rises

© OLIVER HILL

HIGHLIGHTS

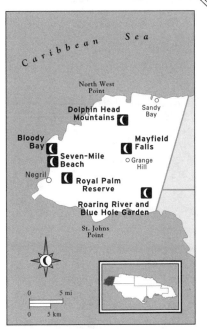

Bloody Bay: Negril's most tranquil beach is also the location of the Office of Nature, a seaside lobster and fish grill (page 229).

Seven-Mile Beach: Seven-Mile Beach is great for long walks into the sunset (page 230).

Royal Palm Reserve: Home to a species of palm found nowhere else, the reserve is also an important habitat for a slew of domestic and migratory birds (page 230).

Dolphin Head Mountains: The small mountain range near Lucea claims some of Jamaica's highest rates of biodiversity and endemic species (page 254).

Roaring River and Blue Hole Garden: One of Jamaica's most picturesque blue holes sits in a lush garden near the source of Roaring River (page 256).

Mayfield Falls: The best developed waterfalls attraction in Westmoreland parish, Mayfield is easily accessible and a good day's fun (page 257).

LOOK FOR (TO FIND RECOMMENDED SIGHTS, ACTIVITIES, DINING, AND LODGING.

out of the earth from its underground source in the hills above Blue Hole Garden.

PLANNING YOUR TIME

Negril is the ultimate place to kick back on the beach and forget what day of the week it is. The general area has other worthwhile sights, however, which can help avoid sunburn and provide a glimpse of the "true" Jamaica—with all the allure of its countryside lifestyle and lush scenery. Most visitors to Negril come specifically to laze on the beach in the dead of winter, but there are special events throughout the year to be considered if you're planning a trip with some flexibility.

Negril is invaded each year March–April by American college kids on all-inclusive spring break vacation packages. The spring breakers come from different institutions for about a month, but mostly during the first and second weeks of March. Recent years have been disappointing from an economic standpoint, with fewer visitors than years past. Still, you will want to keep this in mind when planning your trip to Negril to either avoid the spring break crowd or coincide with it, depending on what you hope to get out of your beach vacation.

HISTORY

Negril's natural beauty has been appreciated for centuries, first by the Tainos, Jamaica's first inhabitants; later by pirates and fishermen; and, finally, after a road was built connecting Negril to Green Island in 1959, by the

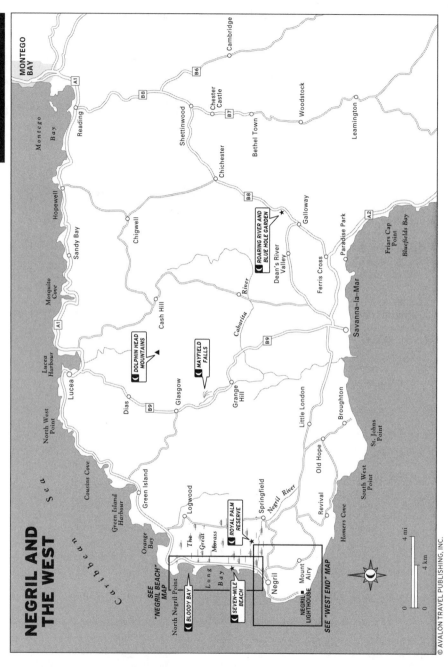

NEGRIL

NEGRIL AND THE WEST

MONTEGO BAY

Caribbean Sea

Montego Bay

Reading

Hopewell

Sandy Bay

Chigwell

Mosquito Cove

A1

Lucea Harbour

Lucea

North West Point

Cousins Cove

Dias

B9

Glasgow

Green Island Harbour

Green Island

Logwood

Orange Bay

North Negril Point

SEE "NEGRIL BEACH" MAP

BLOODY BAY

SEVEN-MILE BEACH

Long Bay

The Great Morass

ROYAL PALM RESERVE

Negril

NEGRIL LIGHTHOUSE

SEE "WEST END" MAP

Mount Airy

Springfield

Negril River

Revival

Old Hope

Homers Cove

Shettlewood

Chichester

B8

Cash Hill

DOLPHIN HEAD MOUNTAINS

MAYFIELD FALLS

Grange Hill

Cabarita River

B9

Little London

Broughton

South West Point

St. Johns Point

B6

Cambridge

Chester Castle

B7

Woodstock

Bethel Town

Leamington

B8

ROARING RIVER AND BLUE HOLE GARDEN

Galloway

A2

Dean's River Valley

Ferris Cross

Paradise Park

Friars Cup Point

Bluefields Bay

Savanna-la-Mar

0   4 mi

0   4 km

© AVALON TRAVEL PUBLISHING, INC.

rest of Jamaica and the world at large. Negril Harbor, or Bloody Bay as it is more commonly known, got its name from the whales slaughtered there whose blood turned the water red. Today the water is crystal clear. The bay was a favorite hangout for the pirate Calico Jack Rackham and his consort piratesses Mary Read and Anne Bonney, all of whom were captured drunk and partying in Bloody Bay. Calico Jack was hanged in Kingston, while his female counterparts were pardoned. Bloody Bay was also a regular departure point for ships heading to Europe who would go in fleets to ensure their survival on the high seas. The Bay also provided a hiding place from which ambushes were launched on Spanish ships. It was also the departure point for the British naval mission, which saw 50 British ships launch a failed attempt to capture Louisiana, which culminated in the Battle of New Orleans during the American War of Independence.

Negril

Negril has become Jamaica's foremost beach town, evolving over the past decade along with the changing nature of the tourists who come to bask in the sun and adopt the island's pace. Today, world-class restaurants and lodging provide an alternative to the low-key guest houses and seafood stalls that became the norm during Negril's transition from fishing village to tourist boom-town in the 1970s. What was once Jamaica's secret paradise is today the heart of the island's diversified tourist economy.

Orientation
Life in Negril is focused on the west-facing coastline, which is divided between Seven-Mile Beach and the West End, or the Cliffs. Seven-Mile Beach runs from Bloody Bay in Hanover on its northern end to the mouth of the Negril River in Westmoreland on the southern end of Long Bay. There are three principal roads that meet at the roundabout in the center of the Negril: Norman Manley Boulevard, which turns into the A1 as it leaves town heading northeast towards MoBay; West End Road, which continues along the coast from the roundabout hugging the cliffs well past the lighthouse until it eventually turns inland, rejoining the main south coast road (A2) in the community of Negril Spots; and Whitehall Road, which extends inland from the roundabout towards the golf course, becoming the A2 at some point with no warning before continuing on towards Sav-la-Mar.

Negril is too informal a place to have been founded as a careful community. As a consequence there are no street numbers—the best way to orient yourself is with a map showing the relative locations of the listings, which primarily span Norman Manley Boulevard along the beach and West End Road.

The A2 starts at the roundabout in Negril where the A1 ends, but none of these "highways" are marked, and as in the rest of Jamaica, everybody simply refers to these principal roads as "the main."

A left turn off the main road in the little settlement of Sheffield leads towards Royal Palm Reserve and Springfield after that. The reserve is sited in the middle of Negril's Great Morass, which backs the developed dry strip of land along Norman Manley Boulevard. Most of the nightlife is based along the beach, while restaurants and bars are found everywhere you look, both on West End Road and on either side of Norman Manley Boulevard along Seven-Mile Beach. The cliffs are the most popular place for sunsets and provide a great setting for some of the better bars and restaurants overlooking the water.

SIGHTS
◖ Bloody Bay
Bloody Bay is located just north of the piece of land jutting out towards Booby Cay that is home to Hedonism II, Point Village, and Grand

Lido Negril. Bloody Bay is currently dominated by all-inclusive hotels, including two relatively new Riu Hotels, SuperClub's flagship Grand Lido Negril, Couples Negril, and the private beach for Sunset at the Palms, located across the road. The beach on Bloody Bay is accessible to non-guests at several points along the road, most easily at the **Office of Nature** (contact PR agent Jospeh Reid, cell 876/369-0395), which is just past the fenced-off private beach of Sunset at the Palms. Here you can chill out and get lobster and fish (11 A.M.–sunset, US$10–30) from the outdoor grill manned by Robert, Symore, and Binghi. Next door, Johnny P's Jamaican Kitchen (cell 876/999-6325, US$2–3) serves up staples like chicken with rice and peas. On the same little stretch of beach, Ackee (Roydel Reid, cell 876/868-7312) and Andy (Conrad Getten, cell 876/894-3042) take visitors out for snorkeling excursions (1.5 hrs, US$20/person with 2-person minimum) and glass-bottom boat tours.

Seven-Mile Beach

Jamaica's longest beach is no longer the undisturbed keep of fishermen as it was in the 1960s, but there are plenty of benefits that have come as a result of the virtually uncurbed development of the last 30 years. The sand remains a beautiful golden color, and the waters, while increasingly over-fished, remain crystal clear. A bar is never more than an arm's length away, and every kind of water sport is available. Expect advances from all manner of peddler and hustler until your face becomes known and your reaction time to these calls for attention slows. The northern end of the beach is cordoned off by security in front of the all-inclusive resorts, while at the southern end the Negril River forms a natural border by the fishermen's village and crafts market. Also on the southern end is Negril's community park, where dances and daytime events are sometimes held.

Royal Palm Reserve

Managed by the Negril Area Environmental Protection Trust (NAEPT) and located 1.5

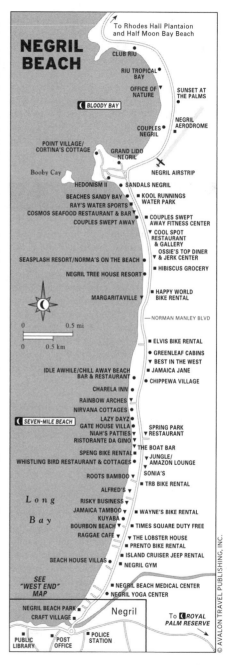

kilometers into the middle of the Great Morass from Sheffield, the 121-hectare Royal Palm Reserve (cell 876/364-7407 info@royal palmreserve.com, www.royalpalmreserve.com, 9 A.M.–6 P.M. daily) is home to 114 plant species, including the endemic Morass royal palms found only in western Jamaica. It's also home to over 300 animal species, including insects, reptiles (including two species of American crocodile), and birds. The 26 resident bird species, which include the Jamaican woodpecker, Jamaican oriole, Jamaican euphonia, Jamaican parakeet, and the endemic endangered West Indian whistling duck, are joined by 16 migratory species that arrive at different times of the year. Admission for a guided or unguided tour around 0.75 kilometers of boardwalk is US$10 and the ponds are open for sportfishing (US$5); you are almost guaranteed to catch African perch, tilapia, or tarpon. Shuttle service can be arranged (US$20 per person) from Ne-

gril. Royal Palm Reserve was leased by NAEPT from the Petroleum Corporation of Jamaica (PCJ) as an alternative to a peat-mining project that had been planned. In the environmental impact study, it was found the project would have destroyed the beach and reef ecosystems. The present facilities were completed in 1989. Bird-watchers should make reservations with the NAEPT office (tel. 876/957-3736) to get in earlier than normal opening hours. There is a nice bar area overlooking the water where drinks are served.

Other Sights
Whitehall Great House is yet another great house in ruins located on the old Whitehall Estate on the ascent to Mount Airy. To get there, take a right immediately before the Texaco Station on Good Hope Road heading east from the Negril roundabout towards Sav-la-Mar. The ruins are about a mile up the hill on the

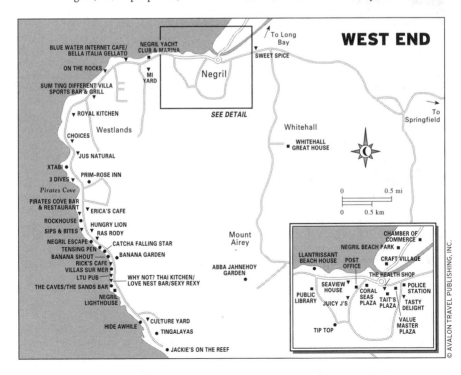

© OLIVER HILL

Negril's Seven-Mile Beach is a seemingly endless strip of fine golden sand, extending from the Negril River to Bloody Bay.

left and command an excellent view of Negril Beach and the morass. One of the largest cotton trees in Jamaica stands on the property.

Bongo's Farm, owned by Bongo and Fanette Johnson, hosts visitors for hikes over gorgeous terrain with great views of Negril's coastline. This is the best place within 10 minutes from the beach to kick back and unwind in a truly Jamaican rural setting; the lush vegetation and laid-back company make for a great attraction. Jelly coconuts are served fresh from the tree, and visitors are shown a variety of botanical specimens cultivated on the farm. Contact Fanette to arrange a visit (tel. 876/957-4694, cell 876/897-9492, fanette@ mail.infochan.com).

Negril Lighthouse is located at the westernmost point of Jamaica on West End Road just past The Caves. The lighthouse dates from 1894 and stands 30 meters above the sea.

ENTERTAINMENT

The great thing about Negril is the fact that no matter the season, you can forget what day of the week it is in a hurry. While weekends remain "going-out nights," and important acts that draw large Jamaican audiences will perform generally on a Friday or Saturday, big artists also perform on Monday, Wednesday, and Thursday nights. Because Negril is so small, the handful of clubs that monopolize the regular live entertainment market have made a tacit pact whereby each takes a night, or two, of the week. This way, the main clubs are guaranteed a weekly following, and Negril's transient crowd can somewhat keep tabs on where to go on any particular evening.

Bars and Clubs

Negril has an overwhelming number of bars and grills; those that are especially recommended for dining are covered under *Food.* This section covers establishments that can be considered more as nightlife draws, rather than for their food.

The Jungle (tel. 876/954-4005 or 876/954-4819, info@junglenegril.com, www.jungle negril.com) is Negril's only off-the-water club,

NEGRIL WEEKLY NIGHTLIFE SCHEDULE

Note that the slash marks in cover fees indicate the charges for a regular night with a local group versus a big-name act.

MONDAY
Live Reggae at Bourbon Beach (US$5/10)

TUESDAY
Live Reggae Beach Party at Alfred's (US$4)

WEDNESDAY
Live Music at Roots Bamboo (from US$5)

THURSDAY
Live Reggae at Bourbon Beach (US$5/10)
Ladies Night at The Jungle (US$6/7)

FRIDAY
Live Reggae Beach Party at Alfred's (US$4)

SATURDAY
Live Reggae at Bourbon Beach (US$5/10)
Party Night at The Jungle (US$6/7)

SUNDAY
Jazz at Roots Bamboo (free)
Live Reggae Beach Party at Alfred's (US$4)

headquarters for spring break activities for a number of years, and is one of the most successful bar chains on the island. Villa Negril, as the Negril branch is called, is a more laid-back version of the Jimmy Buffet franchise than its MoBay or Ochi counterparts. When it isn't peak party season, it's mostly known for its giveaways and beach parties on Tuesdays and Wednesdays in the early evening. Margaritaville is also one of the venues frequently used for ATI around Emancipation weekend.

Risky Business (tel. 876/957-3008) has live reggae three nights a week and is a bar and grill daily. Monday is Appleton's Ladies Nite, on Thursdays all local liquor is US$2. Saturday it's a bottomless mug 8 P.M.–1 A.M. (US$12).

Roots Bamboo (tel. 876/957-4479) is run by the congenial Ted Plumber. It's been in business since 1979, when Ted bought the property and constructed bamboo bungalows. Ted was inspired by camping communities he saw along lakes in Canada. When Hurricane Gilbert destroyed the bungalows in 1988, he built the current concrete-and-wood houses. Care should be taken with securing belongings should you stay at Roots Bamboo. Security has been an issue in the past as the bar hosts live music a few nights per week when non-guests take over the property. Roots Bamboo has been an entertainment venue since 1985 and recently started free live jazz on Sundays 6–10 P.M., in addition to its longstanding live performances on Wednesdays.

Bourbon Beach (tel. 876/957-4405, www.bourbonbeachnegril.com) took over from Debuss and is owned by four brothers and managed by Jimmy Morrell. Monday features big acts like Gregory Isaacs, John Holt, and Yellowman, who are all regulars. Thursdays and Saturdays are usually reserved for a live local act.

Alfred's Ocean Palace (tel. 876/957-4669, info@alfreds.com, www.alfreds.com) has been in operation since 1982. Jamaican and international cuisine with chicken, shrimp, and fish dishes (US$10–15) is served daily 8 A.M.–10:30 P.M. in season; the kitchen closes at 9 P.M. in the low season. Alfred's also

located in an old bank towards the middle of the beach on the Morass side of Norman Manley Boulevard. It has regular theme nights throughout the week, as well as special events, normally held on weekends. Ladies Night on Thursdays gets packed, and Saturdays generally see a good crowd dancing well into the morning. The Amazon Lounge at Jungle is open daily (4 P.M. to midnight).

Margaritaville (tel. 876/957-4467) has been

NEGRIL

has eight double- and triple-occupancy rooms (US$40–50). Sundays, Tuesdays, and Fridays are Live Reggae Beach Party nights, which typically feature local acts (US$4) with occasional big-name international acts like Toots and Capleton (US$10–15).

Jamaica Tamboo (tel. 876/957-4282,) is perhaps best known as the location for some of the parties during ATI weekend around Independence Day. Occasional events are held at other times throughout the year as well, while it functions day-to-day as a restaurant and sports bar. The beachfront property has decent rooms and wireless Internet at a good value (US$60).

Wavz (cell 876/881-9289, www.wavzevents .com) is a seasonal venue and promotions company that hosts occasional parties throughout the year.

Sexy Rexy is a funky little bar just past Rick's Cafe overlooking the cliffs near The Caves.

Festivals and Events

The weekends around Emancipation Day (August 1, 1838) and Independence Day (August 6, 1962) are filled with parties in Negril as **Absolute Temptation Isle,** (www.atiweekend. com) and competing event **Appleton Treasure Island** (contact Appleton's Kingston office, tel. 876/923-6141, appleton@infochan.com) try to outdo each other by throwing the hottest and most back-to-back parties. Big-time promoters from Kingston and Miami draw Jamaica's uptown party youth from across the globe, who arrive to indulge in booze, ganja, general debauchery, and a few stage shows. ATI Weekend is well worthwhile as a more genuinely Jamaican party scene and it's the only time of year when

---

NEGRIL'S EMANCIPATION-INDEPENDENCE PARTIES

Every summer at the end of July, masses of Jamaican youth descend on Negril and book virtually every room in town for what's known as ATI Weekend (www.atiweekend.com), or simply ATI. All-inclusive parties go virtually non-stop for three or four days straight. ATI stands for Absolute Temptation Isle, but in 2006, Appleton's Rum, a sponsor in previous years, formed its own competing ATI the following weekend – adopting the same acronym, which in this case stands for Appleton Treasure Island.

The original ATI, organized by Alex Chin, promoter and founder of Absolute Entertainment, began in Negril in 2000 as Stages, bringing to Jamaica a regular party held in Miami a few times per year. The idea was to replicate the mood of Trinidad's or Brazil's Carnival, with crowds moving from party to party for days on end. The event has grown steadily, and in 2006, for the biggest ATI Weekend yet, nine promoters were brought together to organize 12 different parties at venues around Negril that included Wavz, Tamboo, Margaritaville, and Chances, each with a different theme – from foam parties

to stage shows. A host of selectors were brought in, as well as many of Jamaica's most popular contemporary dancehall artists. Selectors included Black Chiney from Miami, Xcaliber from Trinidad, Jamaica's top sound, Renaissance, and DJ Chrome from Zip FM. There is no better week to be in Negril for those seeking an overwhelming dose of booze, flesh, and sound.

Even though Appleton's pulled its sponsorship of the original ATI, other sponsors stepped in readily, including Digicel, Bacardi, and Smirnoff Ice. The Jamaica Tourist Board also endorsed the event for the first time in 2006. Appleton's competing event now bookends the festivities held to coincide with Jamaica's Emancipation and Independence celebrations. Spring break pales in comparison.

All-inclusive parties in Jamaica have been around since the early 1990s, when the famous Frenchman's Parties, organized by Ian Wong as Jamaica's most exclusive regular all-inclusive soiree, began. Frenchman's parties are held a few times annually, the main "sell-off" events being staged for New Year's and Heroes Weekend.

Negril is decidedly taken over by Jamaicans, making spring break look like child's play.

Other notable annual festivals include the **Negril Reggae Marathon** (www.reggae marathon.com) held in December and the **Negril Jerk Festival** (contact 3 Dives Jerk Centre owner Lyndon Myrie, aka Lloydie, tel. 876/957-0845 or 876/782-9990) held on the last Sunday of November, where different jerk vendors from across the island are invited to set up stalls by 3 Dives Jerk Center on the West End.

SHOPPING

Jamaica Jane (opposite Idle Awhile, tel. 876/957-9079, www.jamaicajane.com) has a range of products from local crafts to silver jewelry to imports.

Devon's Custom Design Jewelry (White Swan Plaza, tel. 876/957-3228) makes custom-designed jewelry of silver, gold, and platinum.

Bongo Johnson (tel. 876/486-0006) makes beautiful art sculptures, which can be seen by special arrangement. Johnson's delicate lignum vitae sculptures are on exhibit at the National Gallery in Kingston. He could be convinced to sell a piece if the price is right.

Abdel, based on the beachfront at Wavz Entertainment Centre (8 A.M.– 8 P.M. daily), is one of the most talented wood carvers around and also retails for several less-accomplished woodworkers in his little shop.

Errol Allen (cell 876/453-4952) is a talented local artist who makes unique silhouette sculptures and oil paintings. Allen's sculptures can be seen on the grounds of Whistling Bird.

Cooyah Negril (at Bar-B-Barn, tel. 876/957-3972) has Cooyah brand roots wear as well as the Bob Marley Family's Zion Roots Wear.

Mary Wonson sells her excellent Flower Hill Oil and Soap Company products at the Swept Away Gift Shop and at Jamaica Jane. Extra virgin coconut oil is used as a base in lip balms and soaps and rejuvenating oils and restorative hair oil products are in the pipeline.

Cigar King (on beach next to Chances, tel. 876/957-3177; and shop #7 in Times Square, 876/957-9064) has all the Cubans you could smuggle in your suitcase home. Manager Martin is a pleasant chap and not overly pushy. The air-conditioning and smell of fresh tobacco is a good reason to stop in and browse.

Negril Crafts Market (between the Negril Beach Park and the river) has a wide variety of crafts, some better and more authentic than others. Sadly an increasing proportion of the products on sale are made in China rather than locally produced.

Rutland Point Craft Center is located next to the aerodrome just before the Petcom gas station heading northeast towards MoBay.

A Fi Wi Plaza, next to Scotia Bank by the roundabout has crafts and t-shirts from Sun Island.

There is a **fruit and produce market** (open daily) by Devon House Ice Cream in the plaza, which is set to move to the taxi stand.

Time Square Mall Plaza (tel. 876/957-9263, 9–7 P.M. daily, duty-free closed on Sun.) is located on Norman Manley Boulevard across from Bourbon Beach. The duty-free shopping centre has several shops selling jewelry, Cuban cigars, crafts, liquor, watches, and trinkets.

SPORTS AND RECREATION

Opportunities for outdoor recreation are everywhere in Negril, from mountain biking and hiking to windsurfing and scuba diving.

Biking

Speng Bike Rental (across from Jungle next to Westlea Cabins, tel. 876/414-5189) rents scooters (US$30) and dirt bikes (US$40), negotiable for multiple-day rental. Proprietor Tony Hilton also does airport transfers (US$60), as well as private tours.

Elvis Bike Rental (in front of Coco la Palm, tel. 876/848-9081) rents scooters (US$30/day, $140/wk), dirt bikes (US$40/day, US $210/wk) as well as cars (US$60/day, $250/wk)

Tykes Motorcycle and Bike Rental (West End Rd., tel. 876/957-0388)

Kool Bike Rental at Negril Yacht Club (tel. 876/957-4992, cell 876/782-3661, info@ negrilyacht.com, www.negrilyacht.com) has a variety of two-wheeled rentals from bicycles (US$10) to scooters (US$30) to trail bikes

(US$40) to larger 500 and 600cc road bikes (US$50–60).

Rusty's X-cellent Adventures (left on Hylton Ave. just past the lighthouse on West End Road, cell 876/781-8161, www.rusty.nyws .com, rustynegril@hotmail.com) organizes two-hour mountain biking tours for any experience level at US$25 with your own bike, US$40 with one of theirs. Rusty can also organize occasional in-depth excursions into the interior for camping, hiking, and biking. Rusty also rents rooms with common bath and ceiling fans for US$40 in a jungle setting. Rusty heads up the Jamaica Mountain Bike Association and knows the best rides across the island.

Water Sports

Negril is overflowing with water sports opportunities. From excursions in glass-bottom boats, to parasailing, Jet Skiing, windsurfing, scuba, snorkeling, and catamaran cruises, there is something for every level of enthusiasm and interest.

Ray's Water Sports (tel. 876/957-5349, info@rayswatersportsnegril.com, www.raywater sportsnegril.com) is one of the more successful outfits on the beach, impossible to miss with the parasail chutes plastered with his name.

Negril Treehouse has a water sports center managed by Ron Mirey, which offers parasailing (US$40), Jet Skis (US$50/half-hour) and fishing trips (US$150 up to four people)

Aqua Nova Water Sports (Mariners Beach Club, tel. 876/957-4323 or 876/957-4754) offers Jet Skis (by Coral Seas) and parasailing (US$50/person or US$80/couple) from its office at Mariners Negril Beach Club. Aqua Nova also runs regular three-hour catamaran and trimaran cruises, one leaving at 10:30 A.M. (US$60 includes lunch and open bar), the other at 3:30 P.M. (US$50 includes snack and open bar). Boats pick up guests from hotels along the beach. Private charters are also offered for US$250 for three hours.

Negril Escape, formerly Mariner's Inn, was recently renovated under the supervision of Cary Wallace and is now home to the **Negril**

Scuba Centre (Negril Escape and Spa, West End Road, 876/957-4425, neg.scuba.centre@ cwjamaica.com, www.negrilscuba.com). The scuba center offers dive packages that include accommodations at Negril Escape and Spa where the centre is based, or at other participating hotels, namely Xtabi, Catch a Falling Star, LTU and Mariners Negril Beach Club. Popular dive sites include Booby Cay Island, The Arches, Ballard's Reef, a Deep Plane, Gallery, King Fish Point, the Throne Room and Blue Castle Ship Wreck among several others. PADI courses range from a beginner three-hour Discover Diving session (US$80) to Advanced Open Water (US$300), Rescue Diver (US$350) and Scuba Master (US$600) courses. Those already certified can rent tanks (US$40) and shortie wetsuits (US$6/ day). Several other water sports activities are offered besides.

The decor in the newly refurbished hotel rooms is straight out of 1970s Bombay—with matching blue plastic beaded curtains on the windows and lamp shades, bright blue painted walls sponge-washed with a bit of gold, and artificial yellow orchids. The colored plywood headboard is the icing on the cake. The basic amenities are all there however: hot water, air-conditioning, cable, clean sheets and towels, and Internet in the main office; and if diving is the main objective, it's a great base. One of the classic-style rooms is probably best unless you're on a honeymoon with the girl or guy you picked up last weekend in Vegas.

Negril Yacht Club & Marina (tel. 876/957-4992, cell 876/782-3661, info@negrilyacht .com, www.negrilyacht.com) offers motor yacht cruises on the 60-foot Willow Dean (US$50), and glass-bottom boat tours (US$20). Dock space is limited, but gas is now sold at the marina. Slips (US$1/foot/day) and moorings are available, while the fuel dock can handle boats that draft up to eight feet (about US$3/gallon gas or diesel). Chuck Birkestrand runs the marina.

Kool Runnings is (tel. 876/957-5400, info@koolrunnings.com, 11 A.M.–7 P.M. daily, US$28 adults, US$19 four feet and under, free two years and under) is a new water park with several slides and a re-created flowing river for gentle tubing. It's located across from Beaches Sandy Bay. There is food and a bar on the property, as well as a juice bar and coffee shop.

Golf

Negril Hills Golf Club (Sheffield, east of the roundabout on the A2, tel. 876/957-4638, www.negrilhillsgolfclub.com, 7:30 A.M.–3 P.M.) has very reasonable rates for non-members: for 9 holes: greens fee (US$28.75), cart (US$17.25), caddy (US$7); for 18 holes: greens fee (US$57.50), cart (US$34.50), caddy (US$14); clubs can also be rented (US$18 for older, US$20 for newer).

Horseback Riding

Mountainview Horseback Riding Stables offers two-hour tours (US$30) around the Negril Hills; booking is through the Yacht Club (tel. 876/957-4992, cell 876/782-3661, info@negril yacht.com, www.negrilyacht.com).

Paradise Park (tel. 876/955-2675, cell 876/543-2221 paradise1@cwjamaica.com, US$30) is one of the best places in Jamaica for down-to-earth small-group rides in an expansive seaside park located a few kilometers east of Savanna-la-Mar in Ferris Cross.

Chukka's Horseback Ride 'N Swim (tel. 876/953-5619, montegobay@chukkacaribbean .com, US$76) offers three-hour rides through forest and along the shoreline before swimming on horseback. The tour is located halfway between Negril and MoBay in the fishing village of Sandy Bay.

Rhodes Hall Plantation (tel. 876/957-6883 or 876/957-6422, rhodesresort@comcast.net, www.rhodesresort.com) also has good horseback riding with an expansive seaside property five minutes northeast of Negril.

Aqua Nova (tel. 876/957-4323) books horseback riding through all the outfits as well as with Negril Country and Western (US$40), one of the oldest horseback riding ventures on the island; it's owned by Mr. Washington and based between Sheffield and Little London just east of Negril.

Fishing

The waters just off Negril's shoreline are severely over-fished, with very low counts found in surveys conducted by the Negril Area Environmental Protection Trust. Nevertheless, a bit farther offshore in deeper waters it's possible to catch plenty of wahoo and even marlin.

Stanley's Deep Sea Fishing (www.stanleys deepseafishing.com, tel. 876/957-6341) is the most professional outfit in Negril. It's run by Captain Stanley Carvalho and offers a good mix of options from half-day (US$400) to three-quarter day (US$600) to full-day trips (US$800) for up to four people. Additionall persons can be added up to a total of eight passengers (additional person US$50/75/100 for different length trips). An excellent option offered is charter sharing, where individuals can team up with others to fill up the boat (US$100).

Fitness Centers

Couples Swept Away (7:30 A.M.–9 P.M.) has the best sports complex in Negril and offers a day pass (US$20/per person), which includes access to tennis, squash, and racketball courts, a sauna, steam room, whirlpool tub, and a lap pool. Racquets are available for rent (US$10 each). Yoga and pilates classes are offered daily and included. Tennis clinics are also included (Mon.–Fri.), while private lessons incur an additional charge.

Negril Fitness Center (US$5/day, US$25/week, US$45/month) next to the Café Taino, has basic equipment like dumbbells, Stairmasters and treadmills and serves a mostly Jamaican clientele.

Yoga and Massage

Fanette Johnson (cell 876/897-9492, fanette@ mail.infochan.com) leads Iyengar-style yoga sessions at Tensing Pen and Rockhouse and will also do private sessions. She has 20 years' experience teaching yoga around the globe.

Oya Oezcan (cell 876/440-7071) offers therapeutic body massage.

Jackie's on the Reef (tel. 876/957-4997 or 718/469-2785, jackiesonthereef@rcn.com, www.jackiesonthereef.com) accepts non-guests for daily yoga sessions. (See *Accommodations on the Cliffs* for more information).

ACCOMMODATIONS ON THE BEACH

Negril definitely has something for everyone when it comes to finding the ideal place to stay. From couples-only all-inclusive resorts, to hip, inexpensive independent cottages by the sea and exclusive villas, there's an option for every taste and budget. Low-season and high-season rates apply here as much as, if not more than, the other tourism centers on the island. Some establishments increase rates in the middle of the low season for special events like Independence weekend at the beginning of August when Jamaicans from "yard" and "abroad" flock for a torrent of non-stop parties that last for days on end.

Accommodations and food have been divided geographically by Negril's roundabout which is used to distinguish between the properties on either side of Norman Manley Boulevard ("on the beach") from those on the either side of West End Road ("on the cliffs"). Within each price category, the accommodations are organized from north to south.

Seven-Mile Beach starts at the mouth of Negril River and stretches the length of Long Bay as well as Bloody Bay farther north. Long Bay is fronted by a multitude of small hotels as well as large all-inclusive resorts on its northern end. It is no longer possible to walk the continuous length of the beach, as the all-inclusive resorts don't permit non-guests to traverse the now "private" sections of beach in their front yards.

Under US$75

Cortina's Cottage (tel. 876/382-6384, www.carolynscaribbeancottages.com, US$75) is actually a studio apartment located in the Point Village complex at the end of Seven-Mile Beach. It's a good option for those looking for all the amenities normally associated with a large resort at an affordable price. Swimming pool access and a private beach reserved for Point Village and nearby restaurants make

Cortina's an excellent option on the beach. The apartment is tastefully decorated with plenty of curtains.

Greenleaf Cabins (Marni cell 617/448-5180, info@indikanegril.com, www.indika negril.com) next to Jamaica Jane on the Morass side of Norman Manley Boulevard, has a spacious four-bedroom main building called Devon House, which sleeps up to seven people, and a next large structure, Dolton House with three bedrooms which also sleeps seven (US$150 each building). Also on the property is a self-contained cottage with a full kitchen and two beds (US$60), as well as two rustic cabins (US$35), each with two beds, a small fridge, shower, and floor fan. The Dolton House bedrooms all have exterior entrances and can rent separately (US$50) and share the kitchen and living area. Airport transfers are offered with Devon (US$110 round-trip).

Chippewa Village (tel. 876/957-4676, cell 876/885-7676 or 877/670-8426 chippewavillage@hotmail.com, www.chippewa villageresort.com) is a comfortable assortment of seven cottages on the Morass side of Norman Manley Boulevard tastefully decorated with a Sioux motif. Owner John Babcook is a leather designer whose great-grandfather Red Shirt was chief of the Dakota Sioux and represented his nation at the 1906 World's Fair.

Three yurt-like stand-alone cottages rent for US$60 per night (double occupancy), while the larger house can sleep up to six people for US$220 per night. Add US$20 per head for stragglers. Some of the bedrooms at Chippewa Village look out over Negril's Great Morass, a savanna-like wetlands area that runs behind the dry stretch of land backing the beach. The beach is an easy two-minute walk.

The Buddha Groove restaurant by the main road serves good pizza when it's open. Wireless Internet (included) reaches many of the cottages on the property, and there is a pool and deck on the Morass to lounge around with a beer. Chippewa Village is one of the few places that retains the original Negril vibe, where the main objective was communing with nature and getting back to basics.

Negril Yoga Center (tel. 876/957-4397, info@negrilyoga.com, www.negrilyoga.com, from US$30/35 low/high), also known as The Little Oasis, has simple, clean, and nicely decorated rooms with single and double beds. The center is tasteful and secure with a very good restaurant that specializes in vegetarian curries and Thai food cooked to order. The property boasts, "There is no bar, no pool, and no dance club at the Centre which keeps our prices low, and our ambience low-key."

US$75-200

Lazy Dayz (tel. 876/957-3571, U.S tel 905/826-2079, negril@passport.ca, www.lazydayz negril.com, US$80–250) has a variety of cabins and beach-front cottages. They stay true to the original Negril vibe with their rustic styling, while still covering all the basic amenities like fans and hot water.

 Kuyaba (tel. 876/957-4318 or 876/957-9815, kuyaba@cwjamaica.com, www.kuyaba.com) is one of the longest-standing rental options on the beach and has developed into a handful of tasteful cottages. The more rustic cottages (US$56–64 low, US$70–77 high) hold true to Negril's original rustic hippy vibe, while newer, more elegant cottages (US$77–85 low, US$97–106 high) have been added in recent years to round out the mix. All cottages have ceiling fans, air-conditioning, and private baths with hot water. A restaurant on the property has good, albeit pricey, food.

Charela Inn (tel. 876/957-4277, fax 876/957-4414, info@charela.com, www.charela.com) is a medium-size hacienda-style property with deluxe suites facing the beach (US$155/221 low/high) as well as more humble garden-view rooms (US$114/166 low/high). Charela is one of the more tasteful large properties on Seven-Mile Beach, with well-designed and lushly planted grounds.

Beach House Villas (tel. 876/957-4731, U.S. tel. 801/363-3529, contact@negril jamaicavillas.com, www.negril-hotels.com, from US$141/201 low/high) are an assortment of self-contained units which are well maintained, clean, and command good views of the sea. All rooms have air-conditioning, TV, and hot water. The property has a total of 21 bedrooms for a maximum of 62 guests. An Internet connection is available in the common living area.

Gate House Villa (call Ali Provines to book, U.S. tel. 435/615-7474 or 888/595-1579; info@gatehousevilla.com, www.gatehousevilla.com) is a comfortable and stylish house with four rooms and a fully equipped kitchen. This is an ideal place for a medium-size group of up to eight people. The rooms, each with one king or two twin beds, rent individually for rates ranging US$89–109 in low season, and US$139–159 in high season. (The most-expensive room is the large upstairs suite, which has a verandah overlooking the sea and a large open shower.) There is a bar, Tony's Hut, on the property right on the beach. The whole property can also be rented (US$400/550 low/high) and can sleep up to 10 people.

Seasplash Resort (tel. 876/957-4041, sea splash@cwjamaica.com, www.seasplash.com, US$96/146 low/high) is a large concrete structure with little to distinguish it from many other like-hotels that crowd Seven-Mile Beach, the suites are nonetheless spacious, clean, and well appointed with complete amenities. It's also home to Norma's on the Beach (see *Food on the Beach*).

Whistling Bird Restaurant & Cottages (tel. 876/957-4403, whistlingbird@negril jamaica.com, from US$98/140 low/high)) has been operated by proprietor Jim Boydston since 1978, when Negril's tourism boom was in its infancy. The property consists of 12 cottages with a total of 20 rooms spread over lush tropical gardens that attract many birds, including Jamaica's national bird, the red-billed streamertail. The cottages have simple, tasteful rooms with an open layout. Half the rooms have air-conditioning, and TV is available on request. Whistling Bird has an excellent restaurant that prides itself on its "fancy Jamaican" cooking and offers five-course dinners (US$35). A variety of inclusive packages are available.

Negril Tree House Resort (tel. 876/957-4287, info@negril-treehouse.com, www.negril-treehouse.com, US$100–200 low, US$145–340 high) has reasonable rates that vary depending on the size of the room and the view out the window (garden or sea). Manager Gail Jackson and her husband Jimmy Jackson had the first two buildings built in 1982 and have expanded the property successively to its current 70 units. Most rooms have king beds or two twins. Wireless Internet is available in the lobby and beach areas. There is also a water sports shop on the property. Jimmy Jackson runs Negril Spots Farm, which provides all the meat served at Negril Tree House. He was named farmer of the year in 2005 and 2006. Negril Tree House is moving towards 100 percent solar-powered hot water, with 25 percent of the hot-water systems already converted to solar.

Negril Escape and Spa (tel. 876/957-0392, info@negrilescape.com, www.negrilescape.com, US$90L/180H) offers a variety of themed accommodations, from the Oriental Express, to Passage to India, to Romancing the Kasba, to Back to Africa, to Atlantis, to Negril Cottage and Coconut Grove. Some of these are more tasteful than others, but the fact that a variety of options are offered is well appreciated by its returning guests who found the recent renovations a welcome infusion of color. Rooms come with all the basic amenities including hot water, air-conditioning, cable TV, clean sheets and towels, and Internet in the main office. If diving is the main objective, it's a great base.

Over US$200

[Idle Awhile Resort (tel. 876/957-3303, U.S tel. 877/243-5352, fax 876/957-9567, stay@idleawhile.com www.idleawhile.com, from US$120/305 low/high) opened in 1999, immediately establishing itself as one of the finest properties on Seven-Mile Beach. The rooms are beautifully decorated with louvre windows, minimalist designs, wooden furniture, ceiling fans, and air-conditioning. Idle Awhile guest have access to Negril's best sports complex at Couples Swept Away. Wireless Internet is included. An excellent restaurant, Chill Awhile, faces the beach serving Jamaican dishes and fresh juices.

All-Inclusive Resorts

[Sunset at the Palms (www.sunsetatthepalms.com, resort tel. 876/957-5350, reservations tel. 876/979-8870 or U.S. tel. 800/234-1707) is the most alluring of athe Sunset Resorts' all-inclusive properties. It features small one-bedroom bungalows spread out across lush, well-manicured grounds. The food, with a mix of buffet style and à la carte meals, is markedly better than at the other Sunset properties, as is the level of service; but prices are also higher: US$325/400 low/high per couple for a deluxe bungalow (US$75 extra per child), and US$500/575 low/high for a one-bedroom suite.

Inside the bungalow-style cottages, a pleasant natural design with wooden furniture, Bali-esque detailing, and plush bedding are overwhelmingly inviting. The bathrooms are sleek and modern with shower fixtures suitable for two.

While Sunset at the Palms is set back from the beach across Norman Manley Boulevard, it has a private beach with bar and grill right in the middle of Bloody Bay, a two-minute walk from the lobby. There is a tennis court and weight room on the property as well a beautiful whirlpool tub and pool with the bar at arm's length. Internet is available off the lobby.

Grand Lido Negril (www.superclubs.com/brand_grandlido/resort_negril, from US$224/389 low/high) is the top-end SuperClubs flagship resort. One of the first SuperClubs properties, Grand Lido Negril has a dramatic entrance corridor surrounded by fountains and reflecting pools that lead into the lobby and dining room areas. Grand Lido Negril has 210 junior and full suites, each equipped with full amenities including air-conditioning, satellite TV, direct-dial telephone,s and CD player. One of the best and most distinguishing features of SuperClubs' crème de la crème is the 24-hour room service. Laundry and dry-cleaning service are also included.

Several restaurants on the property give guests a lot of options. Piacere serves Nouvelle French–inspired cuisine in an elegant candlelit setting that requires formal attire (jackets, slacks, and shoes for men). Cafe Lido serves continental cuisine and is a bit more toned down on the dress, with a no-shorts rule. La Pasta is a more casual Italian-inspired pasta bar open daily 3–10 P.M. Breakfast and lunch are served at Gran Terraza, the open-air buffet area between the beach and the lobby; dinner is also served there 7:30–10 P.M. on Mondays and Fridays evenings. RASTAurant serves Jamaican favorites like jerk chicken and rotti. Munasan is the newest restaurant on the property, serving very convincing sushi and teppanyaki. The specialty restaurants are open 6:30–9:30 P.M. except Mondays and Fridays, and reservations may be required. Cafe Lido is also closed on Mondays. Guests from other hotels must purchase a pass to dine at the restaurants (day pass US$79 per person, evening pass US$99 per person).

Grand Lido Negril occupies the choice property on Bloody Bay, where calm inviting waters gently lap the shore. There is an *au naturale* beach on one end of the property reserved for nature lovers, with the main expanse of beach open to those who can keep their bathing suit on. The highlight of the nine-hectare gardens is a centuries old cotton tree that stands between the 24-hour bar and the spa.

Couples has two properties in Negril: Couples Negril (tel. 876/957-5960, U.S. tel. 800/COUPLES, US$408/590 low/high per couple per night), which is actually just across the border into Hanover, and Couples Swept Away (tel. 876/957-4061, US$413/US$602 low/high per couple per night), at the north end of Long Bay. For proximity to off-site activities and an easy walk to Negril's nightlife, Couples Swept Away has clear advantages. On the other hand, for couples looking to get away from it all, including adjacent public beaches and other reminders of the existence of outside civilization, Couples Negril could be a better option.

Couples Swept Away is an exceptional all-inclusive with a new wing on the south end of the compound that has a wet bar, grill, and beautiful lounge tastefully decorated by Jane Issa, wife of Couples owner Lee Issa. Mr. Issa can often be found around the property checking in with his guests and making sure everything is running smoothly. The gym facilities and tennis courts at Couples are top-notch. Day passes, offered for eight-hour periods (US$75), entitles pass-holders complete access to everything on the property.

Hedonism II (tel. 876/957-5200, www.super clubs.com, US$135–215 low season, US$175–285 high season) is the original and notorious all-inclusive resort where anything goes. Situated at the northern end of Negril's Long Bay, Hedonism II has 280 rooms and 15 suites, all with tiled floors, air-conditioning, TV, and, of course, mirrored ceilings. Many of the suites have private whirlpool tubs right on the beach. It's a great place for couples and singles looking to unwind and let go, and potentially do things they would never do at home—or alternatively, do exactly what's done at home whenever, wherever, and with whomever they see fit.

Two private beaches (one nude, one not) offer plenty of activities from water sports to volleyball to acrobatics. The main terrace dining area is complemented by Italian-inspired Pastafari, Japanese-inspired Munasan, and Reggae Cafe, as well as beach grills. The food is very good. Many premium-brand liquors are served at several bars throughout the property, which also has excellent spa, fitness, and tennis court facilities. There is also an underwater disco where "nuff debauchery a gwaan."

It's important to be aware of any special theme weeks being held at Hedo when booking, lest you should arrive and be expected to swap spouses with one of your fellow guests during swingers' week.

ACCOMMODATIONS ON THE CLIFFS
Under US$75

Tip Top (turn inland on Red Ground Rd. at Scotia Bank, cell 876/360-4857 or 876/435-7222) sits at the top of a hill in an area known as Red Ground. It's a popular spot for budget travelers from Europe, as well as for long-term stays. Rates start at US$25 for simple rooms with private bath and fan. For US$35 you get a kitchenette. Clean sheets and towels are provided. Marva Mathe manages the guesthouse, which has been in business for 30 years.

(Xtabi (tel. 876/957-0121, fax 876/957-0827, xtabiresort@cwjamaica.com, www.xtabi-negril.com) is one of the most accommodating properties in Negril in terms of the price range for the rooms on offer and value for your money. From economy rooms (US$49/65 low/high) with fans, to spacious suites (US$59/90 low/high) with air-conditioning and TV, to stylish cliff top cottages (US$120/210 low/high), there is something for every budget. The restaurant and bar, also on the cliffs, serve up some of the best lobster (US$25) in Negril, and the conch burger is highly acclaimed. Xtabi is the most unpretentious, well situated hotel on the West End. The name Xtabi is Greek for "meeting place of the gods."

Prim-Rose Inn (tel. 876/771-0069 or 876/640-2029, US$20/35 low/high) is a real shoestring joint run by Gasnel Hylton. It has five basic rooms featuring fans, hot water, and hammocks on a porch. The inn is set back on the bush side of West End Road. The driveway is marked by a sign for Haciender Inn. Prim-Rose will be about 100 meters from the main road on the left.

US$75-200

Catch a Falling Star (tel. 876/957-0390, stay@catchajamaica.com, www.catchajamaica.com, US$95–175 low, US$120–250 high) has five one-bedroom cottages, two two-bedroom cottages and a recently completed thatch-roofed building on the cliffs with six units. One of the choice properties on the West End, the cliff-top grounds are well maintained with neat walkways and verdant gardens.

Banana Shout (tel. 876/957-0384, cell 876/350-7272, reservations@bananashout resort.com, www.bananashoutresort.com, from US$80/120 low/high) is owned by author Mark Conklin, who wrote a novel of the same name about Jamaica. It's a beautifully deco-

rated property on one of the West End's most gorgeous stretches of cliffs. Four one- and two-bedroom cottages adorn the cliffs with nice furniture and an artsy vibe. A live band performs oldie reggae covers every evening from Rick's Cafe next door for an earful of music to set the mood for sunset.

(Banana Garden (across West End Road from Rick's Cafe, www.bananasgarden.com, bgnegril@hotmail.com, tel. 876/957-0909, cell 876/429-1655) is a tasteful retreat with four quaint, self-contained cottages surrounded by lush vegetation. The cottages range from US$90 for the smaller units to US$135 for the bigger cottages (US$75–110 low season). Each has unique, hand-carved wood trim detailing, ceiling fans, louvre windows, hot water, and kitchenettes, making the property ideal for those looking for independence and the modest, back-to-basics vibe that put Negril on the map. The pool is beautiful. Food is not generally prepared for guests. Owners Caroline and Gilles are some of the nicest people and can arrange outings to nearby destinations and concerts. Banana Garden is ideal for small groups looking to book the entire property.

Villas Sur Mer (tel. 876/371-2927, villassurmer@yahoo.com, www.villassurmer.com) started as two well-equipped, self-contained duplex villas, each with a one-bedroom and a two-bedroom unit on the cliffs with Rick's Café and The Caves as neighbors. The one-bedroom units go for US$185 per night, the two-bedrooms for US$280, and the whole six-bedroom property can be rented for US$880 per night in high season (US$170/225/750 low season). Amenities include fully equipped kitchen, air-conditioning, housekeeping and cook, cable TV, wireless Internet, and CD player. A hot tub and pool on the deck overlook the most azure waters beckoning from below. In 2006, a massive expansion took place in which 12 new villas were added on a deep and narrow property on the "bush" side of the road. A tunnel under the road connects these adjoining villas to a stone deck at the water's edge. The new villas combine the best in classic Jamaican design with wooden louvre windows and wood detailing surrounded by lush gardens. The rooms are well appointed, with wireless Internet covering the property. The one-bedroom bush-side units will go for slightly less than their counterparts across West End Road.

Over US$200

Rockhouse (tel. 876/957-4373, fax. 876/957-0557, info@rockhouse.com, www.rockhouse hotel.com) is a favorite for hip New York weekenders looking to get away in style. The hotel is always booked, testament to good marketing, quality service, well-maintained grounds, competent management under Matt Marzouca, and beautiful villas (US$225–275 low, US$295–375 high) perched on the cliffs. A total of 34 rooms also include standards (US$95/125 low/high) and studios (US$125/150 low/high). The restaurant has a nice evening ambiance and the coconut-battered shrimp are a must. The pool is also notable for its assimilation with the cliffs.

The Caves (tel. 876/957-0270, fax 876/957-4930, thecaves@cwjamaica.com, www.islandoutpost.com) is Negril's most vibesy upscale hotel. Thatch-roofed, contoured cottages are seamlessly integrated with the cliffs. The property is perfectly conducive to spiritual relaxation, with its sophisticated Africa-inspired motif, soft music floating on the breeze, and hot tubs carved into the cliffs like they belong there. At the same time, you're never far from the greatest adrenaline rush of your life, thanks to the many cliff-tops from which to vault into the crystal-clear waters—as much as 18 meters below. Everywhere you turn there are platforms for sunbathing or for diving. At night, a large grotto just above water level is strewn with flowers and set up as the most romantic dining room imaginable, lit with hundreds of candles.

Bertram and Greer-Ann Saulter teamed up with Island Records magnate Chris Blackwell to create their idea of paradise at The Caves. The rooms are all unique with king beds, African batik pillow covers, classic louvre windows and well-appointed baths. Cozy wooden ceilings and

© OLIVER HILL

One of four quaint cottages for rent at Banana Garden on Negril's West End.

© OLIVER HILL

Negril Lighthouse stands on Jamaica's westernmost point. Its next-door neighbor, Moon Shadow, is one of the nicest cottages at The Caves.

whitewashed walls create a soothing ambiance, and love seats are nestled into the surroundings. The cottages are decorated with an assortment of Jamaican carvings and paintings. Every detail at The Caves is deliberately skewed toward setting guests in relaxed mode—to the point of entrancement. Open bars (some manned, some self-serve) dot the property and a snack bar has gourmet food whenever you're hungry.

Rooms range from one-bedroom suites (US$615/800 low/high) to two-bedroom cottages (US$720/915 low/high). Perhaps the nicest two-bedroom cottage, Moon Shadow, is separated from the rest by The Sands bar, which is open to the public for sunset and features a balcony overlooking the lighthouse and an azure cove below. All suites have king beds, while the two-bedroom cottages have queen beds downstairs.

Tensing Pen (tel. 876/957-0387, fax 876/957-0161, tensingpen@cwjamaica.com, www.tensingpen.com) is the West End's crown gem. Luxurious, thatch-roofed, bungalow-style cottages adorn the cliffs above lapping turquoise waters. The absence of TVs in the cottages is very deliberate, as is every other meticulous detail that makes Tensing Pen so hard to leave. The staff at Tensing Pen exhibit the epitome of Jamaican warmth, from Daisy, Sandra, and Sonia at the front desk, to Errol the bartender, to Judith the cook and Peggy the housekeeper, at Tensing Pen since the early '80s. They all conspire to make guests feel a deep sense of belonging. Resident manager Timothy Blake and general manager Courtney Miller treat guests with the utmost attentiveness and with the highest regard for those minute details that create the most pleasant and relaxing environment on earth, from the hibiscus flowers on your pillow to cool water at the bedside. An infinity-edge 16x30-foot saltwater pool was recently installed in front of the dining area and is fed by a rock fountain.

Jackie's on the Reef (tel. 876/957-4997 or 718/469-2785, jackiesonthereef@rcn.com, www.jackiesonthereef.com) is the place to go for a nature, yoga, or tai chi retreat. At US$150 for double occupancy in high season (US$125 low season), including morning activity ses-

© OLIVER HILL

The coastline of Tensing Pen is dotted with tasteful and luxurious wooded cottages perched on low cliffs over the turquoise Caribbean waters.

sions, it's great value. The hotel is one of the farthest out along West End Road, where there's less development and it's easy to meditate undisturbed.

Cottages and Villas

Llantrissant Beach House (tel. 876/957-4259, U.S. tel. 305/668-9877, cell 305/467-0331, info@beachcliff.com www.beachcliff.com), owned by Dr. and Mrs. Travis, is a truly unique property in that it is extremely proximate to everything in Negril. It sits out on a point just west of the roundabout with a perfect view over Long Bay and Seven-Mile Beach. Rates are reasonable, given the luxury of having a tennis court and two private beaches (ranging US$320/400 low/high for two persons to US$530/660 low/high for up to the maximum occupancy of 11 people). Three meals per day cost an extra US$30 per person. A friendly and committed staff include housekeepers Rose and Dela, and groundskeeper Otis Colquhoun.

◖ Hide Awhile (three-minute drive west of the lighthouse, tel. 876/957-9079, www

.jamaicajane.com, www.idleawhile.com) is Negril's most exclusive and luxurious private villa complex. Best for those looking for independence away from the hustle and bustle, the three villas feature a duplex layout with a spacious master bedroom upstairs. Amenities include all the details expected in a top-end property, from flat-panel televisions to a fully equipped kitchen, to plush bedding and a porch that puts all worries to rest. The property is ideally suited for those with a car and provides guests with a remote control to open the gate, giving the feel of a 007 retreat. Wireless Internet is available. Chisty (cell 876/841-5696) is the Rastafarian caretaker who serves up excellent cooking.

Tingalayas (reservations@tingalayasretreat.com, tel. 876/957-0126) is named after a donkey, Tingalaya, that lives on the property. It has two independent cottages plus five rooms in two bigger cottages with a big communal kitchen. Owned by David Rosenstein, Tingalayas is a good place for a group or family, with accommodations for up to 14 people. Amenities include ceiling fans, hot water, wireless Internet, and a combination of queen and bunk beds. Breakfast is included and resident Rasta cook Jubey does excellent lobster, jerk chicken, and rice and peas to order.

FOOD ON THE BEACH
Ital/Vegetarian

Aris LaTham (cell 876/441-0124, aris@sun firedfood.com, www.sunfiredfood.com) takes vegetarian to a new level with his scientifically focused preparation of raw food. The founder of Sunfired Foods, Aris LaTham leads workshops, seminars, and retreats, and is a sought-after lecturer and pioneer in the field.

Jamaican

Best in ihe West is Negril's favorite jerk chicken spot; it's located directly across the road from Idle Awhile.

Rainbow Arches (Joy James, tel. 876/957-4745) has an excellent curry shrimp and curry goat to order. The James family is one of oldest Jamaican families in Negril.

◖ Niah's Patties (10 A.M.–8 P.M. daily) at Wavz entertainment center, makes the best patties in Negril (US$3), and perhaps in all of Jamaica.

Spring Park Restaurant (across from Mariposa, cell 876/373-8060 or 876/401-5162, 8 A.M.–10 P.M. daily, US$4.50–8.50), is run by Henry Gardener, a pig farmer who makes the best roast pork around, as well as fried and grilled chicken. Henry also does Jamaican breakfast every day.

Ozzie's Top Diner & Jerk Center (10 A.M.–10 P.M. daily), across the road from the Tree House, has the best steam fish on the beach (US$4.25).

Sonia's (across from Roots Bamboo, 8 A.M.–9 P.M. daily, US$5–10) is well recognized for her delicious Jamaican cuisine and homemade patties.

Sweet Spice (Whitehall Rd., tel. 876/957-4621, 8:30 A.M.–10:30 P.M. daily, US$3–8) is the best place along the main road heading towards Sav for typical Jamaican fare.

Peppa Pot (Whitehall Rd., tel. 876/957-3388, 9 A.M.–8 P.M. Mon.–Sat., US$4–10)

is located a bit farther down Whitehall Road heading east out of Negril. It's a popular local joint for jerk, as well as steam fish with the requisite sides of breadfruit and festival.

Tasty Delight (Fire Station Rd., no phone) is the favorite restaurant of local taxi drivers with typical Jamaican dishes at local rates.

Fine Dining and International

Charela Inn (tel. 876/957-4277, 7:30 A.M.–9:30 P.M. daily), serves dinner entrées like vegetarian, chicken, fish, steak, lobster, and shrimp dishes (US$20–48) has good Jamaican and international dishes with a large selection of wines.

◖ Kuyaba (tel. 876/957-4318, 7 A.M.–11 P.M. daily, main courses include pork kebab, brown stew conch, peppered steak, and seafood linguine lobster, US$12–27) has consistently decent, but pricey international and Jamaican fusion cuisine.

Whistling Bird Private Club for Fine Dining (at Whistling Bird villas, 7 A.M.–7P.M., by reservation only, tel. 876/957-4403) specializes in gourmet five-course meals (US$35) that offer a choice of dishes that include "Grandma's Favourite" pepperpot soup, pineapple chicken, escovitched fish, stuffed grouper, and bourbon rock lobster.

The Lobster House (at Sunrise Club, beside Coral Seas Garden, tel. 876/957-4293, noon–11 P.M. daily) serves Italian and Jamaican food: Dishes range from pasta with tomato sauce (US$8), to gnocchi (US$12), to pizza baked in a wood-fired brick oven (US$10–16), to grilled lobster (US$26). Wines are about US$24–26, and great coffee is served.

The Boat Bar (between Rondel Village and Mariposa, tel. 876/957-4746, 8 A.M.–10 P.M. daily, US$10–30) is a favorite that has been serving chicken, fish, shrimp, goat, pork, and steak since 1983. The garlic lobster gets rave reviews. Bunny and Angie are the proprietors. A webcam is set up on Fridays, viewable at www .realnegril.com, to allow fans to keep in touch.

Ristorante da Gino (at Mariposa Hideaway, tel. 876/957-4918, 7 A.M.–11 P.M. daily) is a good Italian restaurant managed by Vivian Reid, the wife of the late Gino. He was killed in 2005, allegedly by Italian thugs. The menu includes mixed salad (US$5), spaghetti alioli (US$10), linguine lobster (US$20), grilled lobster (US$25), and mixed grilled fish (US$30). A complete breakfast (US$10) comes with eggs and bacon, toast, fruit plate, juice, and coffee. Gino's also has a decent selection of Italian wines.

Seaview House Chinese Restaurant (Cotton Tree Place, tel. 876/957-4925, 10 A.M.– 10 P.M. daily) has decent, albeit heavily greasy, Chinese food. They serve vegetable dishes (US$5), chicken (US$7), seafood (US$8), roast duck (US$17).

Cosmos Seafood Restaurant and Bar (Next door to Beaches Negril, tel. 876/957-4330, 9 A.M.–10 P.M. daily, US$5–43) serves good Jamaican seafood dishes, including conch soup, shrimp, and fried fish—in addition to other local dishes like curry goat, stew pork, fried chicken, and oxtail.

Chill Awhile (at Idle Awhile Resort, tel. 876/957-3303,7 A.M.–9 P.M. daily) offers free lounge chairs and wireless Internet for its customers, with a charming beachfront deck restaurant serving a variety of light food items for lunch including club sandwiches, burgers, fish and chips (US$6–8), and jerk chicken (US$10). For dinner, international and Jamaican-style entrées are served ranging from grilled chicken breast with peanut or Jamaican sauce (US$8.50), coconut-breaded snapper with tartar sauce (US$12.50) to lobster thermidor (US$23.50), or seafood platter, grilled lobster and coconut shrimp (US$25). There is also a full bar next to the restaurant.

Norma's on the Beach (at Sea Splash Resort, tel. 876/957-4041, 7:30 A.M.–10 P.M. daily), of the legendary Jamaican culinary dynamo Norma Shirley, who has compiled the recipe and menus at numerous fine dining locales in Jamaica, such as Devon House, with her unique Caribbean fusion cuisine. Norma's gives the feel of being served straight out of her own kitchen. Entrées range from fillet of snapper (US$17) to salmon fillet (US$27), to lamb chops (US$29) and lobster (US$33).

FOOD ON THE CLIFFS

Jus Natural Restaurant Seafood and Vegetarian (Across from Blue Castle Hotel, tel. 876/957-0235, US$3.50–12, 8 A.M.–9 P.M. daily, sometimes half days on Sundays in low season) serves breakfast, lunch, and dinner with items like callaloo or ackee omelets and fresh juices. Vegetarian dishes and seafood items are served for lunch and dinner.

3 Dives Jerk Center (contact owner Lyndon Myrie, aka Lloydie, 876/957-0845 or 876/782-9990, noon–midnight daily, US$3.50 per quarter chicken with bread, US$4.50 per quarter chicken with rice and peas and vegetables, US$8 for half chicken with rice and peas and veggies, steamed or curried shrimp (US$17), and grilled lobster (US$34)) is *the* place to get jerk on the West End. Located right on the cliffs, the open-air restaurant has a outdoor nice barbeque vibe. 3 Dives hosts the Negril Jerk Festival every November.

Ras Rody (across from Tensing Pen, 10 A.M.–6 P.M.) is an Ital food shop that specializes in soups, normally red pea soup (US$8–10).

The Health Shop (Tait's Plaza, tel. 876/957-4274, cell 876/427-1253, 10 A.M.–6 P.M. Mon.–Thurs., 10 A.M.–4:30 P.M. Fri.) sells whole-wheat vegetarian patties, hearty juice blends, and other natural foods at local prices.

The Hungry Lion (West End, tel. 876/957-4486, 4 P.M.–10:30 P.M. daily, US$8–24), under the ownership of Bertram Saulter who also owns The Caves, is an excellent dinner spot with healthy-sized entrées. The lobster burritos are delicious. A pleasant atmosphere is created with irie music, carved faces, and mellow tones covering the walls. The Hungry Lion is good value for the money, and the drink special—the Lion Heart, made with mango, ginger, and rum—shouldn't be missed. Closed in October.

The Sands is the best place to experience the West End's cliffs away from gawking crowds that convene at Rick's each evening. It is a great bar right next to the nicest and most secluded villa at Negril's top resort, and therefore a great way to experience The Caves' vibe short of staying there. There is a challenging-enough spot to jump into the water approximately 12 meters below—with the best view of Negril's lighthouse right next door. Professional jumpers come show off on Wednesdays and Saturdays when jerk is served.

Mi Yard (located across from the Houseboat, tel. 876/957-4442, www.miyard.com) serves snack items like fish, egg, cheese, or ham and cheese sandwiches, as well as Jamaica's favorite starchy food snacks or accompaniments like plantain, festival, breadfruit, and bammy. Meals are done to order, and include items like cabbage and carrot cooked down, curry chicken, brown stew chicken and fish (US$3–4). Eight computers are available for web browsing by purchasing a card (US$3.50 per hour). It is a 24-hour restaurant and an especially convenient and popular spot for a late-night bite.

◖ Blue Water Internet Cafe (contact propietor Randy cell 876/884-6030, randys bluewater@yahoo.com, US$1.50 per 20 min, 8 A.M.–11 P.M. daily) serves Jamaica's best ice cream, La Bella Italia, founded by Valerio Ferrari who opened a factory in Mandeville and teamed up with Randy who runs the Negril operation. The Internet café has the best equipment in Negril with CD burning, fax, webcam, and inexpensive VoIP telephony. Pizza is made from scratch daily (US$2 per slice, US$12.50 for a large pie) and is some of the best in Negril.

Sum Ting Different Villa Sports Bar & Grill (tel. 876/957-0015, sumtingdifferent@ excite.com, www.sumtingdifferent.com), in the heart of the West End, has a late-night menu that lasts until 2 A.M. serving fried chicken and fish, The property also has a small hotel with basic rooms for US$50–75, the difference being air-conditioning and TV, or lack thereof. There's nothing especially charming about the concrete accommodations, but the pool hall and bar upstairs can be a lively local hangout.

Erica's Cafe (5–10 P.M. daily) has excellent Jamaican staples. Many locals consider Erica's the best stewed chicken (US$5) on the island.

Sips & Bites (adjacent to Rock House, tel.

The Sands bar is a more relaxed venue for sunsets than nearby Rick's Café, while also having respectable cliffs of its own for jumping into the azure waters below.

876/957-0188, 7 A.M.–10:30 P.M. Sun.–Thurs., 7 A.M.–5:30 P.M. Fri., closed Sat., US$5–10) is a good spot for breakfast and has good Jamaican dishes like fried chicken, curry goat, and oxtail.

◖ Why Not? Thai Kitchen (woowar@ hotmail.com, tel. 876/891-0628, open for dinner daily, closed in the low season) adjoining Love Nest bar between Sexy Rexy and the Caves is easily the best Thai cuisine in Jamaica. The small restaurant is run by Gillian and Brian and open only during high season. Starting with the delicious ginger-and-scallion-laced fish cakes, this joint serves up a rootsy and non-formulaic approach that goes way beyond pad Thai. Brian spent years in Thailand learning his culinary art before becoming a migratory Jamaican. The restaurant was closed for the 2006 season but is expected to reopen for the 2007–2008 winter season. Keep your eyes peeled for any activity at this excellent little restaurant.

Choices (tel. 876/957-4841, 7 A.M.–11 P.M., US$4–8) is an earthy restaurant on the West End serving Jamaican fare at moderate prices.

Juicy J's (behind ScotiaBank, tel. 876/957-4213, 7 A.M.–10 P.M. daily, US$4–15) is a popular local joint serving typical Jamaican dishes at low cost.

Royal Kitchen (Chef Errold Chambers, cell 876/406-5196, 8 A.M.–11 P.M. daily, US$3–5) is one of the best spots in Negril for Ital vegetarian food prepared Rasta style with excellent fresh juices to accompany the meal.

LTU Pub & Restaurant (tel. 876/957-0382, 7 A.M.–11 P.M. daily, US$10–25) has decent, but pricey international food in a great, laidback setting perched on the cliffs. The name apparently is derived from the Germany-based airline Lufthansa Transport United.

On The Rocks (noon–midnight daily) is an interesting bar with what looks like a drive-in movie theatre in its parking lot. Movies are played nightly (free admission) and popcorn and ice cream is served. Inexpensive drinks in a vibesy setting close to the waters edge make this a good place to down a mid-evening drink before hitting the clubs.

Rick's Café (tel. 876/957-0380, noon–10 P.M. daily, serves chicken, shrimp, fish and lobster with rice and peas, french fries or sweet potato sides, US$18–28; a beer cost US$4) is a moneymaker that has other business owners in Negril envious. It's worth stopping by for a look at the immense crowd that is bussed in each evening, making it one of Negril's most successful commercial ventures. The property was renovated in the recent past after a large chunk of cliff fell into the sea during a hurricane. A huge boom was erected for a rope swing, and there are plenty of platforms to jump off for all levels of adrenaline junkies. A diver in a Speedo climbs to the top of a tree for the highest dive of all, waiting for enough tips to be collected by his cohort before tucking into a cannonball for the 80 or so foot drop. Meanwhile, a live band belts out reggae classics throughout the evening, some of them coming across more true to the originals than others. Food and beer at Rick's is mediocre and outrageously expensive, but nobody seems to mind. If you don't want to pay the cover (US$5) to get in Rick's but still want to partake in the action, you can enjoy the same scene with a more local perspective from the outcropping next door behind an artist's shack, Jah Creation, where kids beg two dollars from the tourists to jump off the cliffs. There are plenty of better, more tranquil, and less hyped spots for cliff-jumping, including Pirates Cave, and The Sands, both of which are recommended.

Pirates Cave Bar & Restaurant (tel. 876/957-0925, www.piratescavenegril.com, 11 A.M.–11 P.M. daily, entrées range from jerk chicken, to fillet of red snapper, to T-bone steaks, US$10–18) is a pleasant bar on the cliffs with stairs into the large cave underneath leading to the water. The place was used as a set in *20,000 Leagues Under The Sea* and in *Papillon*. Cliff-jumping and snorkeling are a great way to build up an appetite, and with food and drink at arms length you can't go wrong.

Ackee Tree Restaurant (Whitehall Road, cell 876/871-2524, 8 A.M.–10 P.M. daily) serves the best Ital stew and local dishes, and is frequented by popular artists in the know. Noel Masters, aka Wall, runs the joint.

INFORMATION AND SERVICES

Negril has a very active online community (www.negril.com) where message boards, news, and events are posted, as well as advertising for hotels in Negril and beyond. Other relevant organizations include the Negril Resort Association (www.negriljamaica.com), which has special offers among select hotels.

NCB is at Sunshine Village (tel. 876/957-4117) with ATMs at Plaza Negril and Petcom). Scotiabank is at Negril Square (tel. 876/957-4236).

The Negril **police station** (tel. 876/957-4268, emergency dial 119) is located just beyond the roundabout on Nompriel Road.

Negril police officer Dwayne advises to stay away from dark, secluded areas at night as people have had bags grabbed. Don't leave valuables on the beach while swimming, and take care not to get robbed by prostitutes. Prostitution is illegal, but common and not prosecuted, the penalty being nominal in court.

The Negril **post office** (tel. 876/957-9654, 8 A.M.–5 P.M. Mon.–Fri.) is located on West End Road near to the plazas by the roundabout next to Samuel's Hardware.

The **Negril Chamber of Commerce** (Vendors Plaza, West End Rd., tel. 876/957-4067, www.negrilchamberofcommerce.com) has tourist information, including a regularly updated brochure full of ads for hotels and attractions.

Long Bay Medical & Wellness Center (Norman Manley Blvd., tel. 876/957-9028) is run by Dr. David Stair.

Negril Beach Medical Center (Norman Manley Blvd., tel. 876/957-4888) is run by Dr. Witold Radomski.

Omega Medical Center (White Swan Plaza, Sunshine Plaza, tel. 876/957-9307 or 876/957-4697) has two branches run by husband and wife team Dr. King and Dr. Foster.

Dr. Grant (Sunshine Plaza, West End, tel. 876/957-3770) runs a private clinic.

Internet Access

Mi Yard (West End) is the best option around with food and free wireless 24 hours.

Café Taino (US$2/30 min) is located across the road from the beach next to Negril Fitness Center.

Lynks Internet Café & Gift Shop (US$2/20 min) is located beside Sips and Bites.

GETTING THERE
Air

Negril's Aerodrome has private charter operators that fly to destinations across the island. **International Airlink** (www.intlairlink.com) offers service between Sangster International Airport in MoBay and Negril's Aerodrome for US$130 for up to two passengers each way, or US$65 per person for three or more, plus tax.

Both carriers also offer charter service to Boscobel near Ocho Rios, Port Antonio, and Kingston. Daily flights are not on regular schedules and the prop planes are small, so it's essential to book in advance. Airlink and Tim Air both use Cessna propeller planes.

Ground

Negril can be reached by several means, depending on your budget and comfort requirements. Most accommodations offer airport transfers, and a host of private taxi operators generally charge around US$60 per couple, with an additional US$20 added for extra passengers.

For airport transfers and personalized taxi and tour service, two dependable options are **Sydney Taxis & Tours** (cell 876/371-8845, US$60 per couple), which has a spacious van, and **Alfred's Taxi and Tour Company** (tel. 876/854-8016 or 876/817-0671, or U.S. tel. 212/380-1650, alfredstaxi@aol.com, negriltracy@aol.com, US $50) with "Irie Airport Rides and Vibes" in Mr. Barrett's standard tinted Toyota Corolla wagon.

For those with less money and more time, there are buses from MoBay to Sav (US$2) and then from Sav to Negril (US$1.50), mainly serviced by route taxis. It is also possible to take a route taxi from MoBay to Hopewell (US$1.50), and then another from Hopewell to Lucea (US$1.50), and then a third from Lucea to Negril US$1.50), but these cars leave when full and won't have much room for luggage.

Negril has two main taxi stands: one next to Scotia in Negril Square, where taxis depart to West End along the coast; and the other in the main park next to the police station on Whitehall Road, where taxis depart for points along Norman Manley Boulevard and east towards Sav-la-Mar.

GETTING AROUND

Route taxis run up and down the coast from the Beach to the West End, generally using the plaza across from Burger King by the roundabout as a connection point. Some negotiating will generally be required, as the route taxis always try to get a higher fare from tourists, especially at night when everyone is charged extra. From anywhere on the West End to the roundabout should never be more than US$1.50 during the day, and as much as double at night. From there to the beach should also not cost more than US$1.50. Excursions beyond the beach and the West End can be arranged with private taxi and tour operators.

Hanover

Hanover is Jamaica's third-smallest parish after Kingston and St. Andrew, with roughly 451 square kilometers of land. It has six major rivers, two of which flow into Lucea Harbour. The Great River, along the border with St. James, has Jamaica's most heart-thumping navigable rapids in the hills of the interior, as well as serene bamboo rafting where it lazily meets the sea.

Lucea, Hanover's capital, sits on an idyllic horseshoe-shaped harbor a few kilometers from Dolphin Head Mountain. Dolphin Head is a small limestone peak at 545 meters, which overlooks some of the most biologically diverse forest land in Jamaica, with the island's highest concentration of endemic species managed by an environmental group, the Dolphin Head Trust (www.dolphinhead.org). A few kilometers away, Birch Hill—at 552 meters—is the highest point in the Parish. Together the small range protect Lucea harbor from the dominant easterly winds. Both Lucea and Mosquito Cove are well-regarded hurricane holes for small yachts. Hanover is the only parish without a KFC.

HISTORY

Hanover exists as a parish since it was portioned off from Westmoreland in 1723 and given the name of English monarch George I of the House of Hanover. The Spanish first settled the area when New Seville was abandoned in 1534 and the capital moved to Spanish Town. Lucea became prosperous with a busier port than Montego Bay in its heyday, which served 16 large sugar estates in the area. Remnants of many estate great houses dot the landscape to the east and west of Lucea, their ruins showing evidence of having been torched and destroyed during slave riots and then abandoned. Kennilworth, Barbican, and Tryall are a few of the old estates that have visible ruins; although they have been declared national heritage sights, they are not maintained.

HOPEWELL TO TRYALL

Just west of Montego Bay, the Great River marks the border of St. James and Hanover, which represents Jamaica's high-end tourism. Before arriving at Round Hill, one of Jamaica's most exclusive club hotels, Tamarind Hill and its surrounding coastline are strewn with luxurious villas, most of which fetch upwards of US$10,000 per week during the high season.

The town of Hopewell is not especially remarkable beyond its present status as a somewhat active fishing community. There's a ScotiaBank ATM, a small grocery store, and a few hole-in-the-wall restaurants for typical Jamaican fare in the heart of town. There is generally a sound system slowing traffic through town on Friday evenings, which precedes a busy market day on Saturday; if you're staying in the vicinity, it's worth a stop.

A few kilometers farther west of Round Hill and Hopewell is Tryall, a former sugarcane plantation destroyed during the Christmas Rebellion of 1831–1832. The old water wheel fed by an aqueduct from the Flint River can be seen as you round the bend approaching Tryall from the east, but little else remains as a reminder of its past as a sugar estate. Today the hotel and villa complex, which fans out from the historic great house, sits on one of the Caribbean's premiere golf courses; its winter residents include boxing champion Lennox Lewis.

Bordering Tryall to the west is a burgeoning bedroom community, Sandy Bay, where new housing developments are rapidly springing up. Still farther west, the highway wraps around Mosquito Cove, where sailboats create a flotilla to party the night away before Easter weekend in preparation for a morning race back to MoBay every year.

Accommodations

Round Hill Hotel and Villas (tel. 876/956-7050, fax 876/956-7505, suites from US$350–590 low, US$600–1,180 high nightly, reservations@roundhilljamaica.com, www .roundhilljamaica.com), just over the Great River, is an exclusive hotel and club on meticulously manicured grounds. The hotel's main Pineapple Suites were recently redesigned by Ralph Lauren, giving the airy rooms an atmosphere of plush, stately, oceanfront elegance. A host of returning guest luminaries has sealed Round Hill's well-deserved reputation for opulence.

In the Pineapple Suites, a series of hinged windows open onto verandas overlooking an infinity pool and the sea beyond, perfectly aligned for dreamy sunsets. The bathrooms feature rainwater showerheads above glass enclosures and large bathtubs. Just above the hotel suites, villas are strewn across the hillside, each surrounded by a maze of shrubs and flowers ensuring the utmost privacy. Next to the small, calm beach there's a charming library with a huge TV (to make up for their absence in the suites) and an open-air dining area; a short walk down the coast is the spa, based in a renovated plantation great house. Villas at Round Hill (US$780–2,350 low, US$1,250–4,100 high nightly) can be booked through the hotel, as well as through the owners, some of whom are represented by Linda Smith.

Tryall Club (tel. 876/956-5660, U.S. tel. 800/238-5290, reservation@tryallclub.com, www.tryallclub.com) has private and club-owned suites adjoining the main house, as well as villas scattered throughout the property that are rented through the club reservation offices. Rates for hotel suites start at US$275/440 low/ high. Most villas have minimum stays during the high season, reduced to three days during the low season.

Tryall has one of the top golf courses in the Caribbean; it sits on a 890-hectare estate that extends several kilometers into the Hanover interior. Tennis and golf are offered to nonmembers (greens fees US$125 daily, carts are US$30 after tax, and a caddy is US$30, plus a customary US$20 tip), while Tryall Guests pay substantially less (greens fees US$40/US$85 low/high). There are nine tennis courts, two

with lights. The cushioned courts are less slippery than the faux clay. Courts are for members and guests only and included in the stay. Related fees include US$23/hr for hitting partner, US$45 to play with a club pro, and US$7 per hour for a ball boy. At night, courts costs US$20 per hour for the lights.

The food at Tryall is excellent value, while far from inexpensive, with Master Chef Herbert Baur clearly demonstrating his wealth of experience in overseeing day-to-day operations. Meals are kept interesting with the Jamaican barbeque dinner on Wednesdays and seafood dinner on Fridays held on the beach and open-air à la carte dining on the verandah of the main house on other evenings.

Tryall villas come fully staffed with excellent cooks who prepare the most delectable Jamaican favorites, as well as being adept in international cuisine. Anthony Darling has been restaurant manager at Tryall for 20 years and maintains excellent service. Tryall sources 95 percent of the produce it serves locally, as well as 100 percent of the chicken and pork it serves.

Food

(**S&D Sports Club Bar & Restaurant** (just before the entrance to Round Hill heading west, 7:30 A.M.–6 P.M. daily, US$3–15) serves brown stew pork, stew beef, curried goat, curried chicken, baked chicken and fish soup. Conch and lobster is served when it's in season. Steamed and fried fish is done to order. S&D stands for Scottie and Dulcy, the husband and wife who run the business.

Sea Shells (cell 876/436-9175,9 A.M.–9 P.M. daily, US$7–21), just west of Hopewell, is run by Lorna Williams and serves chicken, pork, fish, and lobster dishes. The restaurant has a rootsy vibe, with the dining area right next to the water. There is a bar on the roadside with the very pleasant Elaine Gray as bartender.

(**Dervy's Lobster Trap** (cell 876/783-5046, open by reservation daily, US$8–20), owned by the charismatic Dervent Wright, has some of the island's best lobster—plus a great view of Round Hill from its vantage point on the water. Be sure to call ahead to make reser-

Dervy's Lobster Trap is a funky waterfront restaurant serving fish and, of course, lobster.

vations. Reach it by taking the second right in Hopewell heading west down Sawyer's Road to the sea's edge. A Saratans Mood Mark sign marks the road.

LUCEA TO GREEN ISLAND

Hanover's capital, Lucea is a quiet town that occasionally comes alive for a special events like Independence Day, when the town hosts a talent show. Lucea's **Fort Charlotte,** which sits at the mouth of the harbor, was never used. The town was busier than Montego Bay at the height of the colonial period following emancipation and would become important for the export of molasses, bananas, and yams. The large Lucea yam, exported to Jamaican laborers in Cuba and Panama during the construction of railroads and the canal, is still an important product from the area today. The clock tower atop the historic 19th-century courthouse was originally destined for St. Lucia, but was liked so much by the town's residents, they refused to give it up in favor of the less ornate version they had commissioned by the same manufacturer in Great Britain.

Sights

Fort Charlotte, located on the point of Lucea Harbor, is the most intact fort in western Jamaica, with three cannons in good condition sitting on the battlements. It was built by the British in 1756 with 23 cannon openings to defend their colony from any challenge from the sea. Originally named Fort Lucea, it was renamed during the reign of King George III after his queen Charlotte. The **Barracks,** a large rectangular Georgian building next to the fort, was built in 1843 to house soldiers stationed at Fort Charlotte. It was given to the people of Jamaica in 1862 by the English War Office; it became the town's education center and is now part of the town's high school complex.

Hanover Historical Museum (US$1.50 adults, US$0.50 children) is housed in the old police barracks and *gaol* (jail). It opened in 1989, and was at one point expanded to include artifacts from excavated Arawak middens (refuse piles) found in Hanover. The community museum has displays covering the history of Hanover from the Tainos to the present.

Kenilworth is one of Jamaica's most impressive great houses, located on the former Maggoty Estate. Currently the property is home to the HEART Academy, a training skills institute. To get there, pass Tryall and then Sandy Bay, then Chukka Blue; turn right after crossing a bridge over the Maggoty River in the community of Barbican, and look out for the sign for HEART Trust NTA Kenilworth on the left. Turn in and look for the ruins behind the institute, which is painted in blue and white.

◖ Dolphin Head Mountains

Dolphin Head Mountain and the **Dolphin Head Forest Reserve** (call Paula Hurlock tel. 876/382-4678 or 876/307-9591, director@ dophinhead.org, www.dolphinhead.org) was spearheaded by the Dolphin Head Trust, which brought the government, NGOs, and local farmers together to push for sustainable use of one of Jamaica's few remaining pockets of biodiversity and high endemism. A **Nature Trail** and **Living Botanical Museum** has been developed as part of the initiative. To reach the Dolphin Head Nature Trail and Live Botanical Museum, take the B9 inland from Lucea towards Glasgow. The trail starts in Riverside on the east side of the road a few kilometers before reaching Glagow. The well-maintained trail was opened in February 2007 and leads along Retirement and Rugland Mountains on the western flank of the Dolphin Head range.

One especially successful initiative led by the trust has been the Bliss Bamboo project, whereby the sustainable management of bamboo groves is providing the resources for high-end furniture and accessories with 10 full-time staff employed. The studio is in Eaton just above Riley Ridge on the Lucea West River along the road to Askenish where the trail starts up **Dolphin Head Peak.**

Accommodations and Food

The **Fiesta Group,** a Mexico-based hotel chain, recently began construction of a 2,000-room all-inclusive hotel just west of Lucea on Molasses beach.

Tapa Top Food Hut is located on the south side of the main road just east of the town center, with **Vital Ital** on the harbor side of the road a few meters farther east. Neither of these places have a dedicated land line for the business. Both places serve decent, cheap Ital, while the food is generally available based on availability. Otherwise, you can always count on a patty from **Juici Beef** (Mid Town Mall, tel. 876/956-3657) in the heart of Lucea on the west-bound circuit.

Services

NCB has a branch (tel. 876/956-2204) as well as an ATM location at Haughton Court.

ScotiaBank (tel. 876/956-2235) has a branch on Willie Delisser Boulevard facing the main intersection by the courthouse on the western side of town.

Lailian Wholesale Supermarket is at Shop #14, Mid Town Mall (tel. 876/956-9712).

Family Care Pharmacy is at Shop #1, Mid Town Mall (tel. 876/956-2685).

Shoppers' Choice Supermarket is located in Green Island (tel. 876/955-2369).

BLENHEIM

Just before the one-way circuit around Lucea reaches the courthouse heading west, the B9 leads inland through Middlesex to Dias, where a right-hand turn leads back towards the coast and Davis Cove. About five kilometers west of Dias is Blenheim, the birthplace of Jamaica Labour Party founder William Alexander Clarke, who later took the name Bustamante after traveling and living in several Latin American countries. Blenheim is a quiet village with a simple museum devoted to the national hero popularly known as "Busta." The museum in located inside a re-created house, which was built by the National Heritage Trust after Busta's original house was destroyed by fire. More of a thatch-roofed hut, inside newspaper clippings and pictures of Sir Alexander adorn the walls.

GREEN ISLAND TO NEGRIL

An interesting development to keep an eye on is Palma Taylor's studio and concert venue in Green Island (cell 876/609-6266). Taylor is a studio musician based just outside Hopewell where he lives adjacent to the beautiful villa, Spyglass Hill. His studio is located down a lane toward the water in the middle of the small Green Island community. The compound is an interesting place, its interior walls painted with portraits of artists and heroes in typical Rasta style. According to Taylor, the place *buss*, or gave a career break, to many an up-and-coming deejays. The concert space has been out of use for years, but Taylor began renovations in 2006 to rehabilitate the recording studio, and in the near future perhaps stage shows will be held there again.

Orange Bay, just west of Green Island, is a peaceful little cove with the idyllic **Half Moon Beach** just east of Rhodes Hall Plantation. Half Moon is a great place to come for a more low-key change to Negril's often-crowded Seven-Mile Beach.

❰ Half Moon Beach Bar & Grill (Amanda Mackay, cell 876/347-1498, half moonbeach1@hotmail.com, www.abingdon estate.com) is a laid-back restaurant serving typical Jamaican favorites as well as creative international fusion like shrimp with pineapple, sweet pepper kebab, and seafood crepes. There are five rustic cabins (US$40) on the property, one of them a two-room (US$60) where extra persons can be squeezed in (US$25).

Rhodes Hall Plantation (tel. 876/957-6883 or 876/957-6422, rhodesresort@comcast.net, www.rhodesresort.com, US$95–340) sits on a 223-hectare estate adjacent to Orange Bay. Far enough removed from the hustle and bustle of Negril to feel neither the bass thumping at night nor the harassment during the day, Rhodes Hall has enough outdoor activities to not feel like you're missing anything either. The most recent addition to the list is the rhino safari, inflatable speedboats that will take you to cruise Seven-Mile Beach in no time. Other activities include horseback riding, hiking, and birding. A variety of modern, comfortable rooms, suites, and villas all have verandas with views out to sea. Satellite TV, air-conditioning, cell phones, queen beds, and hot water are standard. Never mind the floral bedcovers, much of the woodwork and bamboo detailing was hand-crafted from materials sourced on the property. Rates vary depending on size and amenities, which include three bathrooms, full kitchen, dining room, and whirlpool tub in the largest villa.

Savanna-la-Mar

Along the route from Negril to Savanna-la-Mar, the Orange Hills open up a few kilometers east from the beach to vast alluvial plains along Cabarita River that sustain Jamaica's largest sugarcane crop, processed at Frome. Small communities like Negril Spots and Little London dot the route and offer little excuse to stop. A turn off the main road in Little London leads to Little Bay, one of Jamaica's most laid-back beach towns, which is predominantly the keep of small-scale fishermen.

LITTLE BAY AND HOMERS COVE

About 1.5 kilometers farther east from Homers Cove is Little Bay, another rootsy fishing vil- lage relatively untouched by the outside world. Little Bay was a cherished retreat for Bob Marley, who would come to escape the pressures of Kingston and his burgeoning career.

Accommodations

Purple Rain Guest House (call Cug, pronounced "Cudge," at cell 876/425-5386; or book through Donna Gill Colestock at U.S. tel. 508/816-6923, greenbiscuit03@hotmail.com) is a small cottage set back from the beach owned by Livingston "Cug" Drummond. It's a basic cottage with two rooms in the downstairs and a loft with ceiling fans and water at air temperature. Rates are US$60 per person or US$400 per week, which includes two meals a day.

NEGRIL

◖ **Tansobak Seaside Cottage** (U.S. tel. 608/873-9391 or 608/873-8195, mmous hey55@aol.com, www.littlebaycottages.com) is a tastefully appointed accommodation a few meters from the water's edge in Little Bay. It has simple but comfortable decor, louvre windows, tiled floors, and hot water. Air-conditioning is available by request. Denis and Michelle Dale have owned the property since the mid-1990s. Rates run US$665, per person per week, which includes two meals a day. There is a minimum three-night stay for double occupancy.

Dreamcatchers (contact proprietors Woody or Greg, tel. 876/374-8988, U.S. tel. 800/485-8470, gregnhski@yahoo.com, info@dream catchersjamaica.com, www.dreamcatchers jamaica.com, US$68 per person, reduced rates apply for longer stays) has six one-bedroom suites, two two-bedroom suites and two one-bedroom suites, all with queen beds and private baths. The property overlooks a coral-lined seashore with a nice beach that's only a few minutes away.

Food

Tiki's Guinep Tree Restaurant & Bar (in front of Uncle Sam's, tel. 876/438-3496, 10 A.M.–9 P.M., US$3.50–5), run by Vernon "Tiki" Johnson, is a favorite with locals. It serves dishes like stewed conch, fried fish, fried chicken, and jerk pork, accompanied with rice and peas or french fries.

Uncle Sam's Garden Park (next to sea, tel. 876/867-2897, US$1–3), run by Tiki's uncle, Samuel "Uncle Sam" Clayton, serves fried chicken, fried fish, and conch soup.

BRIGHTON BEACH

Brighton Beach is a secluded eight-kilometer-long beach reached by taking a right at the gas station in Little London followed by a left at the T junction. Keep left at the Y junction and you will come to the parking lot of the Lost Beach Hotel on Brighton Beach. It is principally a fishermen's beach, but it has nice fine, white sand and an open expanse free of peddlers and hustlers.

Lost Beach Hotel (876/957-4041, reservations@lostbeach.com, www.lostbeach .com) is a large hotel on Broughton Beach, not to be confused with Brighton, which is west of Little Bay. The hotel has basic one-, two-, and three-bedroom apartments that more than suffice for a beach bum. At US$39–69 in low season and US$49–99 in high (a bit more with air-conditioning), it's not a bad deal. Long-term rentals start at US$500 per month.

SAVANNA-LA-MAR AND VICINITY

Savanna-la-Mar, or simply Sav, as it is commonly referred to by locals, is one of the most subdued parish capitals in Jamaica in terms of attractions, with a few notable exceptions—namely the annual Curry Festival held in July behind Manning's School, and Western Consciousness, held in April at the Landilo Cultural Center on the western edge of town (see sidebar *Western Consciousness*). A free concert and symposium are also held in Sav every year in October to commemorate the life of the late Peter Tosh, who was born a few kilometers away in Grange Hill.

Sights

Manning's School, the most architecturally appealing building in town, is one of Jamaica's oldest schools, established in 1738 after local proprietor Thomas Manning left 13 slaves with land and what it could offer as the endowment for a free school. Now serving as a high school, the attractive wooden structure (built in late-colonial style in 1910 on the site of the original school) is backed by newer, less stylish concrete buildings set around a large field.

◖ Roaring River and Blue Hole Garden

Ten minutes from Savanna-la-Mar off of the B8, Roaring River and Blue Hole Garden (tel. 876/446-1997, 8 A.M.–5 P.M. daily) make for a good day trip from Negril or Bluefields. The Roaring River cave guided tour is run by the Tourism Product Development Company (TPDCo) and costs US$10 per person. Expect to be aggressively approached as soon as you near the main building for the site. Tipping the guide is also expected.

If you are headed for the Blue Hole, the real highlight of the park, continue farther up the road where Angel manages the Lover's cafe and guest cottages and provides access to Blue Hole Garden (US$7). The Blue Hole is one of Jamaica's most spectacular subterranean springs, and wells up in a refreshing turquoise pool.

Mayfield Falls

Located in Flower Hill near the Hanover border, Mayfield Falls are some of the most gentle and entertaining in all of Jamaica. It's a great place to spend an afternoon, regardless of the competing interests that have laid claim to either side of the river. Both Original Mayfield, run by Sarah Willis, and Riverwalk, operated by Greg Naldrett, offer a similar guided tour on the same river.

Original Mayfield (tel. 876/957-4864, info@ mayfieldfalls.com, www.mayfieldfalls.com) runs the show along the west bank of the river, with Lester among the best guides on that side.

The entry fee is significantly lower (US$15) for those with their own transportation.

Based along the east bank, Riverwalk (www .riverwalkatmayfield.com, tel. 876/957-3444, theriverwalk@hotmail.com) offers a package that includes transportation from Negril, a guide, and lunch after the walk up the falls for US$69 per head. The entry-only rate for locals is US$3.

Mayfield is accessible from both the North and the South Coasts. From the North Coast, turn inland at Flint River on the eastern edge of Tryall Estate and follow signs for "Orginal Mayfield." From the South Coast, turn inland in Sav, keeping straight ahead at the gas station on the east side of town rather than turning right towards Ferris Cross. In Torrington take a left and follow the road through to Flower Hill.

Paradise Park

Paradise Park (tel. 876/955-2675, cell 876/543-2221 paradise1@cwjamaica.com, admission US$5), 1.5 kilometers west of Ferris Cross,

© OLIVER HILL

Manning's School is based in the most attractive building in Savanna-la-Mar.

offers a 1.5-hour tour on horseback (US$30) around a 809-hectare estate along the waterfront. It's also a great place for independent exploring, picnics, and general relaxation. There's a river running through the property suitable for swimming.

Accommodations and Food

Blue Hole Garden (contact property manager Empress Angel, cell 876/446-1997) has a handful of basic cottages (US$40–50), the nicest of which, Lover's Nest, sits right over Roaring River. There is also a large house

---

WESTERN CONSCIOUSNESS

Conscious Reggae is back in the limelight after nearly 20 years in the backseat – thanks to steadfast artists and promoters like Worrel King who have stood by the principles established by the genre's early pioneers. Starting around the time of Bob Marley's death in 1981, the reggae industry was taken over by dancehall artists like Shabba Ranks and Yellowman. The style of these artists' lyrics signified a departure from roots reggae, with its messages of truth and progress, to an often violent and sexually explicit form of music that became known as "slackness." When Peter Tosh was killed six years later in 1987, dancehall had taken over, and conscious reggae music was like yesterday's news. It was around that time that Worrel King founded King of Kings Promotions to try to rescue the truth from the mire.

King of Kings hit the ground running in 1988, organizing a very successful event at Titchfield High School in Port Antonio dubbed Eastern Consciousness, which showcased several artists, all of whom displayed some conscious leaning. "It was to attract people who needed to be uplifted, rather than just wasting away gyrating," King says. After a second successful Eastern Consciousness the following year, King took the event to Westmoreland, the parish of his birth, where he says the people were yearning for it. King describes his work as being guided by the hand of the Most High Jah, but says it has not been an easy road as consciousness is not something that sells easily. Nevertheless, the success of these early conscious stage shows has been mirrored in a multitude of other annual events inspired directly or indirectly by Eastern Consciousness. These include East Fest, held in Morant Bay and organized by Morgan Heritage, and

Rebel Salute, held at the Port Kaiser sports ground in Saint Elizabeth and organized by Tony Rebel. Both events have a decidedly "conscious" theme rarely challenged by the invited performers. "I look at artists that have been depicting consciousness," King says, "I don't look only at the hardcore consciousness, but at those who have the repertoire of conscious songs – even Beenie Man has a good 40-minute set that depicts consciousness – he performed at Western Consciousness as Ras Moses – it's not just those artists that are hardcore roots."

In 2006, King succeeded in bringing producer/performer extraordinaire Lee Scratch Perry back to Jamaica to perform for the first time in decades. King says he was termed a madman when he first suggested bringing Scratch home to perform, not any less given that many consider Scratch himself mad. After meeting with Scratch and his manager wife however, King said, "If he was mad that was the kind of madness I wanted to work with."

King has also created other concert events, including Tribute, dedicated to Peter Tosh. The free event held yearly in Sav's Independence Park is meant to showcase reggae sanity. In addition to the concert there is a Peter Tosh Symposium at the University of Westmoreland, which looks at the intellectual side of Peter Tosh and also highlights the work of other artists such as Burning Spear and Lee Scratch Perry. The event has drawn attendees from the highest levels, including finance minister Omar Davis, a self-proclaimed Tosh scholar. The Tribute concert is held on the Saturday closest to Peter Tosh's October 19 birthday, with the symposium held the previous Saturday.

(US$80) up on the hill, which has a full kitchen and TV.

The Ranch Jerk Center cooks up Boston-style jerk on the western side of Sav.

Sweet Spice (Barracks Rd., beside new bus park, tel. 876/955-3232, US$4.50–7.50) serves fried chicken, curry goat, oxtail, and fish fillet.

Devon House I Scream is at 104 Great George Street, across from the post office (tel. 876/918-1287, daily 11 A.M.–9 P.M. Mon.–Thurs., 11 A.M.–11 P.M. Fri.–Sun.s).

Services

Shopper's Choice Wholesales & Retail has three locations in Sav (Queen St., tel. 876/955-2702 or 876/955-9645; 12 Brooks Plaza, tel. 876/955-2936; and Llandilo Rd., tel. 876/918-0620 or 876/918-1482).

Del-Mar Laundromat is at 2 Queen Street (tel. 876/918-2105).

WESTMORELAND INTERIOR

Beyond Mayfield Falls, which has grown into a favorite eco-tourism attraction, the interior of Westmoreland sees few visitors. Nevertheless, there are a few notable cultural and agricultural attractions, namely Seaford Town and Key Park Coffee Estate, both within close proximity of one another and reached via the South Coast from Ferris Cross.

Sights

Kew Park Estate Coffee Tour (tel. 876/957-1108 or 876/957-1109, ann@kewpark.com) is run by Peter and Gina Williams. It's well worth a trip into the hills of Westmoreland if you find yourself longing for a hometown coffeeshop. The tour covers every stage of the coffee process, from berries on the bush to the steaming cup and includes a walk through the plantation, where you will see a tropical hardwood forest, many native and migratory birds, and a cave. A ride up to the Copse great house takes visitors to where the coffee is roasted, bagged, and brewed. A comfortable verandah is where the tour ends, with a fresh cup in hand and a view of the whole Great River Valley. All

tours must be arranged in advance by phone or email.

From Montego Bay, turn left at the stoplight in Reading up Long Hill to Shettlewood (where the big orange groves are). Take the left fork in the road that is marked to Bethel Town. Travel on that road through Chester Castle and Bethel Town. About five kilometers past Bethel Town is the village of Struie. Turn left and go 1.5 kilometers to Kew coffee farm on right.

From Negril, take the A2 east through Sav-La-Mar to Ferris Cross. Turn left up the hill to Whithorn. Turn right and follow the road (not going into Darliston). Stay to the left and go to Woodstock and turn left at the stop sign. Follow the road to Struie and turn right. The coffee farm is 1.5 kilometers on that road on the right.

From Mandeville and the east, follow the A2 to Middle Quarters, St. Elizabeth. Take the right off the roundabout, following the signs to Newmarket along the B7 passing through Newmarket, New Roads, Leamington, and Woodstock. Turn right at Struie and go 1.5 kilometers to Kew coffee farm on the right.

Hilton High Day Tour (St. Leonard, tel. 876/952-5642, normastanley@cwjamaica.com, www.jamaicahiltontour.com, US$64 per person, halfprice children 5–12, free for children under 5) includes a Jamaican country-style breakfast before a tour of a coffee, banana, and pineapple plantation. Transportation is provided from hotels in Montego Bay and Negril.

Seaford Town is a cultural anomaly deep in the hills of Westmoreland. Founded in 1835 under a township act aimed at populating Jamaica's interior with Europeans, Seaford Town became the isolated home for 249 individuals transplanted from Germany. Jamaica's landed elite had feared land in Jamaica's interior would be captured by slaves who were to be given full freedom in 1838. Baron Seaford thus allocated 202 hectares of his Montpelier Mountain Estate to the cause, and Jamaica's first German township was formed. The immigrants didn't find in Jamaica exactly what they had expected, however, and many died within the first weeks due to food shortages and their vulnerability to tropical diseases. The majority survived nonetheless, adopting Jamaican food and customs and all but losing their connection to their homeland.

To this day many residents in Seaford Town have a light complexion, Catholicism is still an important religion, and a some residents can still recall a few words of German. A small museum in the center of town features the area's unique history. The African Caribbean Institute recently launched a project called The Seaford Town Community History Project with support from the German Embassy to produce comprehensive history of the community from 1835 to the present, including an audio documentation as part of the Jamaica Memory Bank (JMB).

Bluefields, Belmont, and Whitehouse

This stretch of Westmoreland coast is as laid-back and "country" as Jamaica gets, with excellent accommodation options and plenty of seafood. Bluefields public beach has more locals on it than tourists, with shacks selling fried fish, beer, and the ubiquitous herb. The windfall that Butch Stewart and the Jamaican government were to bring the area in terms of jobs and revenue from the opening of another monstrous all-inclusive resort, Sandals Whitehouse, has hardly materialized as the guests are not encouraged to venture off the compound and rarely do so.

History
The stretch of coast around Bluefields has a rich history. One of the three earliest Spanish settlements, named Oristan, which was initially based in Parottee, St. Elizabeth later

Sunsets on Bluefields Bay are quite possibly the most colorful and languid anywhere.

© OLIVER HILL

© OLIVER HILL

the Peter Tosh Memorial Garden in Belmont, where the body of the late reggae legend and Wailers co-founder was laid to rest

moved to present-day Bluefields. Oristan was connected by road to Sevilla la Nueva, the Spanish capital just west of present-day St. Ann's Bay, as well as to Santiago de la Vega, in present-day Spanish Town. The area was favored by the Spanish under early colonial rule, and later, the pirate Henry Morgan departed from Bluefields Bay to sack Panama in 1670. Still later, it was the spot Captain Bligh landed after finally successfully completing his charge of bringing breadfruit to the island from Tahiti. What is said to be the original breadfruit tree in Jamaica was taken down by Hurricane Ivan and sits in a pile of cut up pieces on one side of the lawn at **Bluefields Great House.** Pimento, or allspice as it's known in many places, was an important cash crop in the area, at some point having been replaced by marijuana in importance for the local economy.

SIGHTS

Bluefields Beach is a popular local hangout and sees very few tourists. It has fine white sand and is lined with vendors. Music is often blasted on weekends when the beach fills up.

Bluefields Great House, located about 0.4 kilometer inland from the police station, on the road to Brighton, was the home of many of the area's most distinguished temporary inhabitants, including Philip Henry Goss, an English ornithologist who resided in Jamaica from 1844–1846 subsequently completing the work *Birds of Jamaica, a Naturalist's Sojourn in Jamaica.*

The **Peter Tosh Memorial Garden,** where the remains of this original Wailer lie, is worth a quick stop, if only to pause amid the ganja seedlings to remember one of the world's greatest reggae artists. An entrance fee is assessed (US$5) when there's someone around to collect it. Otherwise the gate is unlocked and a quick visit usually goes unnoticed. In mango season the yard is full of locals fighting over the heavily laden branches. Peter Tosh was born in nearby Grange Hill before making his way to Kingston, where he became one of the original three Wailers along with Bob Marley and Bunny Livingston. His mother still lives in Belmont.

RECREATION

The Bluefields area is the perfect place for activities like hiking and swimming, snorkeling and relaxing. Nobody is touting parasailing or Jet Skiing, and the most activity you will see on the water are catamarans crossing Parker's Bay off the Culloden shoreline. There are two good horseback opportunities within a 15-minute drive in either direction, one at **Paradise Park** to the west in Ferris Cross, the other at **Font Hill** just across the St. Elizabeth border to the east.

ACCOMMODATIONS

Brian Wedderburn has a few **Roots Cottages** (cell 876/384-6610, US$25) at his yard in Belmont that each have a little fridge, fan, and attached bath.

Belmont Garden Cottages (contact Juicy, cell 876/425-2387 or 876/955-8143, US$21) has inexpensive cottages, with private baths, ceiling fans and standing fans, TV, stove fridge, and microwaves.

Shafston Great House (call Frank, cell 876/869-9212, mail@shafston.com, www .shafston.com) is one of the few plantation great houses that you can actually stay in. Set on a hill overlooking Bluefields Bay, Shafston has a large pool and rooms that range from basic with shared bath (US$90) in the side building, to suites in the Great House with hot water in private baths (US$160). Rates include meals and drinks. Four-wheel-drive is needed to reach Shafston as the road is in bad shape; Frank, who also offers transfers from the airport in MoBay (US$60), will come down from the hill in his SUV to meet guests.

Rainbow Villas (tel. 876/955-8078, cell 876/872-9080 or 876/378-7853, rainbowvilla@ anbell.com, US$55), owned and managed by the stunning and ever-helpful Carlene, is located across the road from the water along a little lane adjacent to Sunset Paradise Bar & Grill. The spacious, clean rooms have ceiling fans and kitchenette, hot water, and air-con-

PEDRO BANK AND PEDRO CAYS

Nearly 100 kilometers offshore south of Bluefields Bay, the Pedro Cays form the surface of the Pedro Bank, one of Jamaica's few remaining unspoiled marine ecosystems. The Pedro Bank is a submerged mass about three quarters the size of mainland Jamaica, one of the largest banks in the Caribbean Basin, and provides a habitat for queen conch, which has historically been one of Jamaica's most important exports. Increased fishing is threatening the bank however, and an international conservation effort is underway to protect the unique marine habitat. Fishermen leave from points all along the South Coast for extended periods on the cays, usually returning with a lucrative catch to bring to market.

ditioning. Carlene is setting up a spa on the property and has trained in massage therapy. She also recommends local massage therapist Cindy Wimsatt.

Reef Carlton (cell 876/382-6384, info@ barrettadventures.com, www.carolynscaribbean cottages.com, US$60) is a one-bedroom cottage that can accommodate up to six people. The self-contained cottage is owned by Susie Watkins and rented by Carolyn Barrett. Located up a little lane from the main road in Belmont Reef Carlton is furnished with a stylish rustic motif. It's a great place for a small group looking to adopt the simple country lifestyle a short walk down to the water's edge, where there are plenty of fishermen's beaches to choose from.

Horizon Cottages (cell 876/382-6384, info@barrettadventures.com, www.carolyns caribbeancottages.com, US$115 with three-night minimum stay) define rustic elegance, with two perfectly situated wooden cottages on Bluefields Bay. Each cottage is tastefully decorated with local artwork and has classic louvre windows, queen beds, soft linens, attached bath with private outdoor showers, and cute, functional kitchens. The porch steps of **Sea Ranch,** descend onto the small but beautiful white-sand private beach and a pier off the manicured lawn makes the perfect dining room and cocktail bar. **Rasta Ranch** is a slightly larger cottage set farther back in the yard. Kayaks and snorkeling gear are on-hand for excursions to the reef just offshore. Property manager Carolyn Barrett is a seasoned tour operator who runs Barrett Adventures, one of the island's best outfits, and can accommodate the interests of every kind of adventure seeker. Horizon's main house was the first built on the waterfront in the area. Wireless Internet, hot water, and gentle lapping waves make Horizon a very hard place to leave. The property owners also own Blue Hole Garden on Roaring River 20 minutes to the west.

Bluefields Villas (tel. 202/232-4010, fax 703/549-6517, vacations@bluefieldsvillas.com, www.bluefieldsvillas.com) are easily the area's most luxurious accommodation option, and perhaps the most scrupulously maintained villas in Jamaica. If you've ever had the desire to feel like royalty, there is no better place than **The Hermitage** (US$5,600/8,400 low/high weekly). Antique furniture and four-poster beds, seamlessly integrated with the classic design of the spacious villa, seem to have been specially created for a neocolonialist emperor. A large sundeck off the dining room looks over the sea, while the next dining room door opens over a tiled pool. The "silent butler" is never far off to deliver what you might require, and delicious food is served at mealtimes with the utmost attention to presentation and form.

San Michele (one of the Bluefields Villas properties), 1.5 kilometers down the coast, is another gorgeous villa from the set. It has a small island perfect for enjoying the area's spectacular sunsets with cocktail in hand, connected to the lawn by a narrow bridge.

Sandals Whitehouse (tel. 876/640-3000, dhibbert@swh.sandals.com, US$790) is the newest Sandals property in Jamaica. It took about 15 years to complete at a total cost of around US$110 million. At the high end of Sandals' many properties island-wide, the four-star Sandals Whitehouse features premium drinks, a variety of dining options, and a beautiful cabaret bar. Rooms have all the amenities you could ask for. The property is stunningly grand, designed like a European village with a large central courtyard and enormous pool with a wet bar. The beach is one of the best in the area. Day passes (US$85, leave by 6 P.M.) and evening passes (US$80, 6 P.M.–2 A.M.) are also available, and the hotel also offers a full-day pass (US$130, 10 A.M.–2 A.M.). There's a two-night minimum stay.

The Sandals Whitehouse project turned into one of the biggest scandals in the history of the Urban Development Corporation, which conceived of the project and was also project manager. Clear favoritism in selecting the contractors, together with obvious mismanagement and misappropriation of funds, forced the resignation of UDC head Vincent Lawrence in 2006 when details came to light resulting in high-profile discussions in the parliament and national press. The project had originally been budgeted at US$40 million and a 373-page Forensic Audit Report delved into the numerous serious deficiencies found in the development process, not least of which saw the Minister of Tourism Aloun Assamba's brother Charles Wood of Charsal Marketing hand-picked by the UDC and awarded contracts for procuring furniture and fittings without having to go through a competitive bidding process—in clear violation of the Government of Jamaica's policies. Aloun Assamba remains Minister of Tourism, unfazed by the scandal.

In spite of the scandalous construction process, and a few engineering problems like a sewage treatment plant that required an overhaul and other flaws that should have been noted during and not after completion, the audit found Sandals Whitehouse to be well designed compared to other benchmark properties and of an overall high standard.

Natania's (tel. 876/963-5349, cell 876/883-3009, info@natanias.com, Nataniasjamaica@yahoo.com, www.natanias.com, US$75–80) is run as B&B-style with eight double-occupancy rooms, some facing inland, the others out to sea. Rooms have either two single beds or one king. Owner Veronica Probst took the name Natania from the names of her two daughters, Natalie and Tania. Veronica has run the place since 1983. The property sits on the waterfront overlooking Parkers Bay.

Culloden by the Sea is a large subdivision development just west of Whitehouse. Several repatriated Jamaicans have built houses there to retire to and a few of them rent as nice, low-key guesthouses.

Sierra-la-Mar Villa (call Garth Lee at tel. 876/963-5922, cell 876/841-2299, garthlee@ sierralamar.com, www.sierralamar.com, US$1,250/1,450 low/high weekly) is a nice three-bedroom villa perched high on the hill overlooking Whitehouse. Sierra-la-Mar has a five-day minimum in winter, three-day minimum in the summer. Amenities include satellite TV, washer/drier, fully equipped kitchen, air-conditioning in bedrooms, pool deck with a beautiful view, and Wi-Fi.

Jim's Place (tel. 876/894-9933 or 416/260-5306, jmplax@interlog.com, jplaxton@cw jamaica.com) is a unique, owner-designed and -built guesthouse in a lush, hillside garden setting a short walk down across the main road from a private beach. Accommodations include a rustic, poolside cottage for two with separate kitchen and bathroom cabana (US$30); a double suite with kitchen, bathroom, and verandah (US$40); and a spacious, two-bedroom villa featuring one of the best sunset views to be had in Jamaica (US$70). Meals, car rentals, tours, Montego Bay airport pick-ups, cell phones, and Internet are available on request. Breakfast can be included for an additional US$5.

Just east of Whitehouse, **South Sea Park** is an unspectacular subdivision where several repatriating Jamaicans have constructed large concrete homes. There are a few guesthouses, which are decent, budget options. The large concrete structures in this development are a bit cold and imposing, and the guesthouses see little traffic from international visitors.

Ocean Air Guest House (call owner/manager Mrs. Palmer at tel. 876/963-5788, oceanairguesthouse@yahoo.com, US$43–71) is the better of the few options in South Sea

Park. Rooms have queen or double beds, air-conditioning, and local TV. The pool overlooks the waterfront, and there is a small beach below the house. Meals can be arranged.

FOOD

(Box Video Rental and Cook Shop (Whitehouse Square, cell 876/363-0091 or 876/963-5330, 9 A.M.–3 P.M. daily, rent videos until 8 P.M.; food US$1.50–3) is a great food joint run out of a shipping container by enterprising Raquel "Keisha" Smith and her lovely auntie Christine "Tina" Clarke. Chicken and pork dishes come in three sizes small, medium, and large. Fish is also available contingent upon availability.

Ruby's 24/7, located in Whitehouse Square, serves typical Jamaican dishes around the clock in a box to go or to stay.

Becky's (tel. 876/963-5247, 8:30 A.M.– 11 P.M. Mon.–Sat., US$2–5) serves typical Jamaican dishes like oxtail, fish, pork, curry goat, and fried chicken, as well as burgers and fries.

Judge Beer Joint, run by Eugene "Judge" Stephenson (just west of Kd's, tel. 876/385-5184) serves steam fish (US$6/lb) steam roast, and fish tea (US$1 per cup).

Sunset Paradise Bar & Grill (across from Kd's, tel. 876/955-8164) is owned by Quashi and serves drinks around a nice rustic bar as well as Jamaican staples like stewed chicken (US$3). Quashi's cousin Patrice can usually be found behind the bar.

Kd's Fish Pot (on the water 50 meters east of the Peter Tosh Memorial Garden) has been in business since 1973, but opening hours are not regular. Kd generally cooks in the afternoons, depending on supply of fish and demand from customers. A small stage setup on the waterfront is sometimes used for events.

Fresh Touch Restaurant (Bluefields Beach Park, 6:30 A.M.–10 P.M. daily, tel. 876/955-8088) serves steamed, roasted, and fried fish as well as other coastal staples like fish tea, lobster, fried chicken, curry goat, all served with a side of rice and peas. The establishment is owned by Otis Wright. On Sundays and holidays Bluefields Beach Park is the most happening scene on the South Coast.

PRACTICALITIES
Services
Woodies Grocery (tel. 876/963-5413) across from Natania's has basic food goods and sells the paper.

Cindy Wimsatt is a recommended masseuse (cell 876/889-3087) based in Belmont.

Brian "Bush Doctor" Wedderburn (cell 876/384-6610), also known locally as Rasta Brian, leads hikes (US$10 per person) into the hills and to learn about local flora and fauna.

Fishing excursions can be organized by Lagga or Trevor who can be contacted through Carolyn Barrett, manager of Horizon Cottages (tel. 876/382-6384, info@barrettadventures.com).

Reliable Adventures Jamaica (tel. 876/955-8834, cell 876/421-7449, wolde99@yahoo.com, www.reliableadventuresjamaica.com) organizes community tours as well as birding, hiking and marine excursions with local fisherman led by Wolde Kristos.

Getting There and Around
Route taxis ply the coast all day long from Sav-la-Mar (US$1.50) and Black River (US$1.50) to Whitehouse. Karl (cell 876/368-0508) is a JUTA-licensed driver based in the area who offers tours and taxi service.

THE SOUTH COAST AND CENTRAL MOUNTAINS

The parishes of St. Elizabeth, Manchester, and Clarendon make up the southcentral part of the island, which is *the* place to get away from the tourist hubs and see some of Jamaica's farmland and less-frequented coastline. Locals in these parishes are less dependent on tourism and accordingly less pushy in soliciting business. While the region doesn't boast grandiose and glitzy resorts, the accommodations often make up for it in their rootsy charm and there are still plenty of comfortable lodging options, especially in Treasure Beach where villas and cottages range from rustic to unpretentious luxury. Languid fishing villages dot the St. Elizabeth coast, the most popular of which are found in Treasure Beach, and farther east in Alligator Pond, which straddles the St. Elizabeth–Manchester border. High above the plains, the cool air of Mandeville has been a draw in the heat of summer for centuries and is often referred to as the "retirement capital of Jamaica" for the number of repatriating Jamaicans who settle here. Over the past 50 years the bauxite industry has given Mandeville a strong economic base, while the 1970s saw the flight of many of the town's gentry during the Manley administration when socialist policies were feared. The old moneyed families in Mandeville were somewhat replaced by an influx of nouveau riche, some allegedly owing to drug money, who have arrived over the past few decades to fill uptown neighborhoods with concrete mansions.

PLANNING YOUR TIME

If your goal is to hit the main sights and take in a bit of the South Coast culture, a night

HIGHLIGHTS

◖ **Lower Black River Morass:** As one of Jamaica's largest wetlands, this mangrove and swamp is home to a variety of unique animals and plant life (page 269).

◖ **Pelican Bar:** Located on a sandbar about 1.5 kilometers offshore, this is the best place to spend an afternoon snorkeling and eating fresh fish (page 270).

◖ **Font Hill Beach Park and Wildlife Sanctuary:** An excellent beach park with a small coral-lined fine-sand beach and picnic facilities bordering miles of unspoiled coast (page 274).

◖ **Y.S. Falls:** The best-managed waterfall attraction in Jamaica offers swimming, tubing, and a heart-thumping zipline (page 275).

◖ **Bamboo Avenue:** A strip of road planted with giant bamboo groves shades jelly coconut and peanut vendors, making this a fantastic refreshment stop (page 276).

◖ **Appleton Estate:** Jamaica's most popular rum tour features the country's most important and timeless export at the distillery of its most recognized brand (page 278).

THE SOUTH COAST

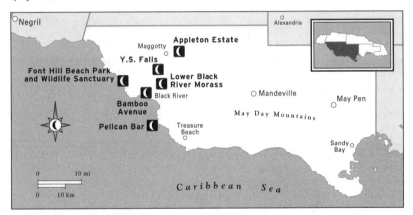

LOOK FOR ◖ TO FIND RECOMMENDED SIGHTS, ACTIVITIES, DINING, AND LODGING.

or two in Black River, a few days in Treasure Beach, and a night in Mandeville is probably sufficient. Treasure Beach is one of those places where a certain type of person falls into the groove immediately and finds it very difficult to leave. Others find that the area is too popularly off-the-beaten path and prefer seafront communities that are even more sedate, like Black River, a few kilometers away, or Belmont and Little Bay in Westmoreland. What is certain is that Treasure Beach has a unique feel with a land and people unto itself and the length of time visitors deem sufficient depends

on how easy they are entertained by the rough-edged natural beauty that gives the area its charm. The immediate surroundings of Treasure Beach lend themselves to long walks, hiking in the Santa Cruz Mountains, boat rides, and cautious swimming.

Most people visiting the South Coast choose Treasure Beach as a base, making easy day trips to surrounding attractions. This is probably the best option with the most variety of accommodations, a hipper-than-chic vibe, and several beaches and unique scenery to enjoy. Decent accommodation options are also available in

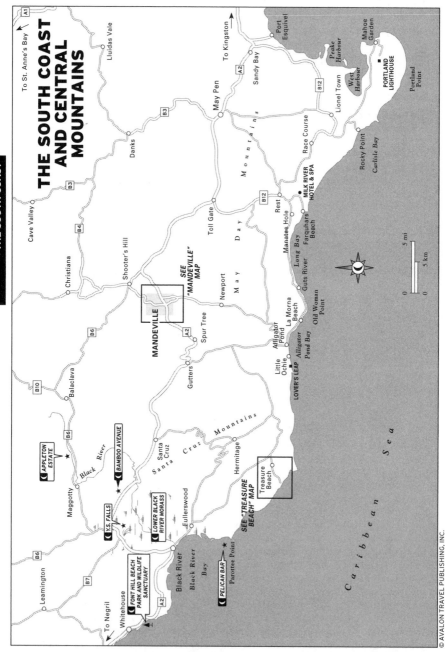

THE SOUTH COAST AND CENTRAL MOUNTAINS

To St. Anne's Bay

A1

To Kingston

Port Esquivel

Lluidas Vale

May Pen

A2

Sandy Bay

Peake Harbour

Mahoe Garden

B12

West Harbour

Lionel Town

PORTLAND LIGHTHOUSE

Portland Point

B3

Danks

Cave Valley

B3

M o u n t a i n s

Race Course

Rocky Point

Carlisle Bay

B4

Christiana

Shooter's Hill

Toll Gate

D a y

Rest

B12

MILK RIVER HOTEL & SPA

Manatee Hole

SEE "MANDEVILLE" MAP

Newport

M a y

Farquhars Beach

Long Bay

Guts River

MANDEVILLE

A2

Spur Tree

La Morna Beach

Old Woman Point

B6

Gutters

Alligator Pond

Alligator Pond Bay

B10

Balaclava

Little Ochie

LOVER'S LEAP

B6

Santa

M o u n t a i n s

APPLETON ESTATE

Black River

BAMBOO AVENUE

Cruz

Hermitage

Maggotty

Santa Cruz

Fullerswood

SEE "TREASURE BEACH" MAP

Treasure Beach

Y.S. FALLS

LOWER BLACK RIVER MORASS

C a r i b b e a n   S e a

Leamington

B6

Black River

Black River Bay

Parottee Point

B7

FONT HILL BEACH PARK AND WILDLIFE SANCTUARY

PELICAN BAR

Whitehouse

A2

To Negril

5 mi

5 km

0

0

Black River and at Font Hill farther west. Mandeville also has a smattering of decent hotels, and for those set on getting as much curative power as possible from the hot baths at Milk River, the hotel on-site has basic affordable rooms. Clarendon's capital, May Pen, also has a few decent hotels but there is little here that draws visitors.

Both Treasure Beach and Black River make convenient bases for exploring the interior with attractions like Accompong Town, Appleton Estate, and Y.S. Falls all within about an hour's drive.

DANGERS AND ANNOYANCES

Thankfully, Jamaica's South Coast is a welcome respite from the hustling that goes on in virtually every other area of the island that participates in the tourism industry. The most important dangers and annoyances in the region are accordingly more nature-oriented rather than human-related. Beaches along the South Coast are commonly deserted and swimming alone is therefore not the safest activity, especially in Treasure Beach, where every year the list of drowned fishermen seems to grow. The current and undertow in all the bays of Treasure Beach can be quite dangerous, and it's therefore safest to ask the locals about it before getting too comfortable in the water.

Also related to the sea, there are times when jackfish contains high levels of toxins. It is better to avoid this fish altogether to be safe. Lobster is widely available on the South Coast, and is the specialty at Little Ochie. Nevertheless, spiny lobster has a designated closed season (Apr.–June), which has been established to protect the species from over-harvesting. The ban on lobster fishing during this time should be acknowledged and supported first and foremost by visitors to discourage any potential breach of the seasonal ban by fishermen—who ultimately are more prone to responding to the market, rather than government regulations. It is illegal to land lobsters below 76.2 millimeters, the established minimum size for a mature female.

Black River to Parottee

An important economic center in years past, especially for the export of logwood and mahogany, Black River is today a quiet literal and littoral backwater parish capital, with the main tourist attraction being the river at the heart of town that serves as the entry point into the great morass. There are a few popular tourism attractions within a half-hour's drive and plenty of forlorn stretches of mediocre beach just east of town along the coast towards Parottee. A few minutes west, Font Hill offers horseback riding and great swimming on a beautiful small tract of sand surrounded by coral reef. A few interesting buildings around town are worth a look, most notably Invercauld Great House.

SIGHTS

Invercauld Great House and Hotel (66 High St., tel. 876/965-2750, invercauldgreat house@yahoo.com), with its Georgian architecture, is the most striking structure in Black River. The great house was built in 1894 by Patrick Leydon.

Luana Orchid Farm (across from Luana Sports Club, contact Dr. Bennett, cell 876/361-3252, admission US$5) offers formal tours by appointment only to check out the 150,000-odd local and foreign orchid plants at the 1.5-acre farm. Dr. Bennett has bred several new varieties himself. The farm is located on the northern outskirts of Black River.

◖ Lower Black River Morass

The Lower Black River Morass is one of Jamaica's largest wetlands, with 142 square kilometers of mangrove and swamp providing a rich habitat for a variety of animal and plant life. Turtles and crocodiles are still relatively abundant, while manatees, once relatively common around the mouth of the river, are gone today. It's the largest remaining undisturbed wetland in the English-speaking Caribbean at 7,285 hectares. The Black River Morass has 113 species of plants and 98 species of animals. The Anchovy Pear (*Grias cauliflora*) of the Brazil Nut family (*Lecythidaceae*) grows in the morass and sawgrass, or razor grass (*Cladium jamaicensis,*) first described by botanists in Jamaica and thus given the Latin name *jamaicensis,* covers about 60 percent of the wetlands area. Sable palm (*Sabal jamaicensis,*) or Thatch Palm, is another wetland plant abundant in the reserve that was also first described in Jamaica.

The crocodiles along the Black River are quite accustomed to being around people, to the point where many tourists think the ones sitting on the river's edge next to the restaurant are tame. While it's not recommended, some people swim in the same water as the crocs, who, according to one seasoned adventurer, are more afraid of us than we are of them. It's best to respect their space, however, and not give them the chance to prove they are anything but friendly.

The Black River and the Lower Black River Morass are best accessed by taking one of the river safari tours that start in the town of Black River, where three tours are offered from the river banks on pontoon boats.

Black River Safaris

Charles Swaby's **Black River Safari** (tel. 876/965-2513 or 876/965-2086, jcsafari@hotmail.com, www.jamaica-southcoast.com/blackriver, US$16.50 adult, US$8.25 children), run by parent company South Coast Safari, has a pontoon boat tour up the Black River for 75 minutes with a commentary by the captain. Tours run daily (9 A.M., 11 A.M., 12:30 P.M., 2 P.M., and 3:30 P.M.). Swaby started the tour in 1987. Lunch is served at the Bridge House Inn and at Riverside Dock.

Dr. Bennett, a local businessman, runs **St. Elizabeth Safari** (tel. 876/965-2374 or 876/965-2229, US$16/per person, US$8 children) on the opposite side of the river, operates a virtually identical 75-minute tour up the Black River. Both operations are located on the banks of the Black River.

Irie Safari (12 High St., tel. 876/965-2211, lintonirie@hotmail.com, 8:30 A.M.–5 P.M. Mon.–Sat., 9 A.M.–4 P.M. Sun.) offers a narrated tour on pontoon boats lasting 75 minutes (US$17 per person, minimum charge of US$40 per boat with two people). Proprietor Lloyd Linton is a wetland biologist who leads many of the tours himself. Irie is the smallest of the three tours, which can help avoid the long wait sometimes found at the competitors, which get more large groups. Irie Safari also offers sportfishing for tarpon and snook. The tour was established in 1993.

◖ Pelican Bar

One of the most unique attractions in all of Jamaica, Pelican Bar is a ramshackle structure less than 1.5 kilometers offshore on a sandbar off Parotee Point. Run by the charismatic Denever Forbes, known by everybody as Floyde (cell 876/354-4218), Pelican Bar serves drinks and cooks up excellent plates of fish (US$8.50) and lobster (US$13) accompanied by rice, bammy, or festival. The sandbar is an excellent spot to spend the day relaxing and snorkeling. The best way to reach the bar is by calling Daniel McLenon, known as Dee (cell 876/860-7277), who offers round-trip shuttle service in his fishing boat (US$8.50 per person) from Parotee. Dee leaves from near his yard past Basil's just after some houses with blue roofs. Turn right and park along a little lane that leads to the beach. Call Floyde before heading out to make sure he's around. Generally he keeps hours starting at 9 A.M. until the last customers are ready to leave in the evening. The bar is closed when bad weather requires. The only land tour operator servicing Pelican Bar on a regular basis is **Barrett Adventures** (contact Carolyn Barrett, cell 876/382-6384), which offers transport from MoBay or Negril and can also arrange snorkeling equipment.

ENTERTAINMENT AND EVENTS

The most popular annual event held in St. Elizabeth is **Rebel Salute** (Port Kaiser Sports Club, tel. 876/934-0827, tony_rebel@hot mail.com, www.tonyrebel.com), held in mid-January. It draws tens of thousands of reggae fans to an all-night stage show organized by Tony Rebel, and is intended to honor the more conscious artists of the genre. In recent years some spectators have been disappointed by an ever-growing crowd that has been deemed too disorderly for a roots reggae event.

Calabash Literary Festival (www.calabash festival.org) is a fun, free event held at Jake's Hotel in Treasure Beach (800-outpost, tel. 876/965-0635, jakes@cwjamaica.com, www .islandoutpost.com/jakes) that draws writers and attendees from across the Caribbean and African diasporas, as well as featuring some of Jamaica's own lyricists and authors.

Jake's Jamaican Off-Road Triathlon and Sunset Run (contact Jake's in Treasure Beach) is held every April, generally on the weekend before Easter.

BREDS (Kingfisher Plaza, Calabash Bay, contact Sean Chedda, assistant project manager, tel. 876/965-0748, info@breds.org, www.breds .org, 9 A.M.–5 P.M. Mon.–Fri., 9 A.M.–1 P.M. Sat.) is a community-based organization engaged in community betterment activities and staging events. The non-governmental organization is currently involved in bringing a couple benchmarking schemes to test for environmental integrity to keep the community green and sustainable and is also working to have life guards posted along the beaches. The group has already trained lifeguards who are posted at Frenchman's Beach, one of the area's most notorious, which has claimed the lives of many locals. There is no reef protection at Frenchman's Beach, and the currents tend to be very strong accordingly. Jason Henzell, of Jake's, is the BREDS chairman.

BREDS organizes **Jake's Annual Triathlon,** (last Sunday in April), which consists of a 500-meter swim, a 25-kilometer mountain bike ride, and a 7-kilometer run. The group also organizes

the **Hook 'n Line Canoe Tournament** held at the Calabash Bay Beach on Heroes weekend in October (second weekend of the month). The popular event starts on Saturday and goes into Sunday, when all the boats come in by noon to weigh in their catch. Whoever gets the largest fish (by weight) wins. Any kind of fish is fair game. Tourists participate by renting boats. The entry fee is kept low (around US$7 per boat) to ensure that the event remains decidedly local. The top prize ranges from an inflatable boat with an engine (2006) to other fishing-related equipment given in past years. Contact the BREDS office (tel. 876/965-0748).

Little Ochie Seafood Festival (tel. 876/961-4618, thelkar@cwjamaica.com), held in August, is a definite must and worth traveling from the other side of the island for the lobster, fish, oysters, and cultural activities that range from traditional dance to popular reggae acts.

ACCOMMODATIONS

The options for staying in Black River are not highly varied, with slightly better than basic rooms the order of the day. Most visitors come to town just for the day from either nearby Treasure Beach or Negril.

South Shore Guest House Bar & Restaurant (Crane Rd., tel. 876/965-2172) is wedged between the road and the beach with decent basic rooms facing the water (US$21 with fan, no hot water, no TV; US$28 with TV, fan, and hot water; US$46 for two double beds, hot water, TV and a/c). South Shore is owned by Rose Williams.

Bridge House Inn (14 Crane St., tel. 876/ 965-2361, US$21–26) has 13 basic rooms with either fan or air-conditioning. Private bathrooms have hot water. A restaurant on the property (8 A.M.–10 P.M. daily) serves chicken, beef, pork chop, curry goat, and fish (US$3.50–6).

Port of Call Hotel (136 Crane Rd., tel. 876/965-2360, US$31–36) has a variety of rooms, some with one double bed, others with one double and one single. All rooms have private bathroom with hot water and air-conditioning.

Waterloo Guest House (44 High St., tel. 876/965-2278, US$29–47) has basic rooms with ceiling fan, double beds or two single beds, and private bath; rooms with queen beds, TV, and air-conditioning; and rooms that have a small fridge and coffeemaker. The guesthouse has a popular restaurant and bar (7 A.M.–11 P.M. daily, US$2.50–7) serving chicken, pork, oxtail, fish, and fried rice. Keniesha is the sweet and helpful bartender.

Invercauld Great House and Hotel (66 High St., tel. 876/965-2750, invercauldgreat house@yahoo.com) offers rooms in both the historic great house, for those who wish to experience the antiquity firsthand in its old colonial charm, and nearby in straightforward, concrete-palace love nests across a little bridge facing well-kept gardens. All the modern rooms have air-conditioning, private bathrooms with hot water, TV, and balconies. Standards (US$59) have two single beds with standing shower, while executive suites have queen beds with walk-in closets and bathtubs (US$75). The junior suites (US$85) have a living room area with a sleeper sofa (max three persons) with a queen bed or three singles. A spacious deluxe room (US$97) has a king bed and large living room area. Food is served in the on-site restaurant (7 A.M.–10 A.M. for breakfast, 7 P.M.–10 P.M. for dinner) with local dishes like curry goat and fried chicken and more international cuisine like lasagna. There has been talk of owner Trevor Hamilton establishing a school behind the great house. Nickeisha Daley is the pleasant front desk manager.

Font Hill Villas Guest House (contact guest house manager, Kareem Reid, cell 876/462-9011) has comfortable and well-appointed rooms (US$50 for master with King Size, US$40 for the rest) which all have hot water, air-conditioning, and a kitchenette. Some have ceiling fans. This is a great place to get away from it all on the grounds of the expansive Font Hill Estate with great hiking and horseback riding and the Font Hill Beach Park minutes away.

Parottee Beach Resort (Crane Rd., tel. 876-383-3980) is a no-frills property toward the end of Parottee Point with four two-level buildings that have combinations of two rooms with two single beds or one king and two singles (US$95). One half of the duplex suites can also be rented alone (US$50).

Idlers Rest Beach Hotel (Crane Rd., tel. 876/965-9000) run by Diane Powell has spacious and well-decorated rooms with all the amenities (a/c, ceiling fans, cable TV, mosquito nets) along a pleasant and quiet beachfront stretch along the road to Parottee Point.

Ocean View Restaurant and Resort Cottages (74 Crane Rd., tel. 876/634-4602, U.S. tel. 404/402-3257, njgravity@yahoo.com) owned by Neville Jackson, has a restaurant serving fish tea, vegetable soup, steam/escoveitch/ brown stew/fried fish, shrimp, conch, lobster, chicken, curry goat and chow mien. Cottages are small and basic (US$50).

FOOD

Northside Jerk Centre (5 North St., tel. 876/965-9855, 8 A.M.–7 P.M. daily, US$2.50–5) aka Alvin's Fish & Jerk Pork Center, serves fried curry, stew, jerk chicken, stew jerk pork, curry goat, steam, brown stew and escoveitch fish.

Tasty Foods (2 Market St., tel. 876/634-4027, 8 A.M.–9 P.M. Mon.–Sat., US$2.50–7) serves ackee and saltfish, salt mackerel, chicken (stew, fried, baked, and curry), cabbage, calaloo, oxtail, slice brown stew fish, whole fish, garlic or curry shrimp, and fries. Eulalee Bennett, Dr. Bennett's (a local businessman) sister in law, runs the restaurant.

Riverside Dock (contact manager and executive chef Cathy Charlebois, tel. 876/965-9486; 9 A.M. till you say when, daily, US$3.50–21) is the most upscale restaurant in Black River. The restaurant specializes in seafood, salads, cheesecake, rum cake in the open-air restaurant along the river with view under the bridge out to sea. Riverside Dock reopened under new management March 2007, with a new calypso color scheme and Caribbean-international fusion menu with dishes like smoked salmon or marlin, or riverside salad with basil vinaigrette, quesadillas, tacos, lobster and filet mignon. Catering is also available anywhere on the island for events as large as 500 people.

Tern's Restaurant serves decent Jamaican dishes (US$2–4.50) right along the waterfront in the heart of town.

Bayside Restaurant and Pastry (19 North St., tel. 876/634-3663, 7 A.M.–9 P.M. daily, US$3.50) serves curry goat, stew pork, and fried chicken. Cakes are also served by the slice (US$1.25) or whole (from US$10). Dahlia is the helpful supervisor.

The Fish Pot Bistro and **Indies Irie Pizza** franchise (Riverside on the Black River, adjacent to Riverside Dock, tel. 876/965-2211 or contact Lloyd Linton, cell 876/472-4644; 9:30 A.M.–5 P.M. Mon.–Sat., US$6–15) predominantly serves fish: escoveitch, steamed, and brown stew—fried and cooked back down in a sauce accompanied by rice, festival, or bammy. It also has curried or garlic shrimp, as well as jerk chicken at times, and lobster in season. Pizza is also served at the same establishment (US$6–20). Toppings include pepperoni, ham, ground beef, and pineapple.

© OLIVER HILL

Cloggy's on the Beach is one of the best spots in the Black River area for seafood.

🄲 **Cloggy's on the Beach** (22 Crane Rd., tel. 876/634-2424, www.cloggys.com, US$3–11) is the quintessential beachfront bar and restaurant, serving a range of dishes from chicken to steamed fish, brown stew, or fried fish to lobster. This is a great place to kick back and unwind, though the beach is not the most beautiful or pristine for swimming.

Basil's Seafood Restaurant (cell 876/369-2565, 7 A.M.–midnight daily, US$6.50–13) in nearby Parottee has good seafood. The restaurant serves excellent fish, conch, and lobster. Basil Bennett is the congenial proprietor.

Pelican Bar is the most interesting restaurant around, but it requires a boat ride to reach. (See *Sights* for more information.)

Andrene's (1 Brigade St., tel. 876/634-0233, 8 A.M.–8 P.M. Mon.–Sat. US$3–15), operated by Andrene Quest, serves good Jamaican fare with a menu that includes curry goat, fried or baked chicken, stew pork, and cow foot, brown strew or steam fish, lobster and shrimp.

INFORMATION AND SERVICES

The **post office** (35 High St., tel. 876/634-3769) is open 8 A.M.–5 P.M. Mon.–Fri. **DHL** is at 17 High Street (tel. 876/965-2651, 9 A.M.–5 P.M. Mon.–Sat.).

The Internet Shop (13 North St., tel. 876/965-2534, 10 A.M.–6 P.M., US$2.25/hr) has DSL Internet access. **Surf D Net**(12 High St., tel. 876/634-4535, 9:30 A.M.–6 P.M. Mon.–Fri., 10 A.M.–6:30 P.M. Sat.) also offers Internet access. The **St. Elizabeth Parish Library** (64 High St., 8:45 A.M.–5:15 P.M. Mon.–Fri., 8:45 A.M.–3 P.M. Sat.) also offers Internet service (US$1.50/hr).

The Globe Store (17 High St., tel. 876/965-2161) sells souvenirs and computer parts.

Both **NCB** (13 High St., tel. 876/965-2207) and **ScotiaBank** (6 High St., tel. 876/965-2251) have branches with ATMs.

GETTING THERE AND AROUND

Black River is easily reached by route taxi from Sav-la-Mar in Westmoreland (US$3) or from

THE SOUTH COAST

THE SOUTH COAST

© OLIVER HILL

The escoveitch fish at Scott's Cove is a great reason to stop when passing through.

Santa Cruz in St. Elizabeth (US$2). If you're driving, there's a dodgy but interesting road along the coast to Treasure Beach that's much shorter and not too much more potholed than the long way around. To take the coastal route, head over the bridge east of Black River along Crane Road and turn off the main road toward the water after passing the communications tower east of Parottee. A left turn at a Y intersection leads along the coast to Treasure Beach.

WEST OF BLACK RIVER
Scott's Cove

One of the best road stops along the South Coast, Scott's Cove on the Westmoreland–St. Elizabeth border has several stands with friendly competition between vendors of fried escoveitch fish, conch soup, shrimp, and lobster. Check **Ras Collie-Bud** for an excellent cup of conch soup or **Carlene and her sister Marlene** for an excellent fried fish on the Westmoreland side of the cove. A beached boat wreck in the cove makes for interesting scenery to accompany the fresh seafood.

Font Hill Beach Park and Wildlife Sanctuary

Owned and operated by the Petroleum Corporation of Jamaica (PCJ), Font Hill has a beautiful little coral-lined sandy beach (contact park manager Conroy Graham, cell 876/405-8218, 9 A.M.–5 P.M., people can stay later, but no one admitted after 5 P.M. and lifeguards not on duty, US$3 adults, US$1.50 children) with picnic tables, grills, and bathroom facilities. The beach attracts a predominantly local crowd and is busy on weekends. Across the road, the Font Hill estate extends deep inland.

Outside the swimming area hundreds of hectares of protected coastline provide fantastic grounds for horseback riding, which is offered by a private concessionaire (876/396-4133, rides at 9 A.M. and 1 P.M., US$40 adults, US$30 children) near the guest cottages. Bird-watching and exploring the wildlife sanctuary is not officially offered by PCJ, but it may be possible to arrange access for these activities by contacting property manager Texbert (Tex) Gooden (cell 876/990-2930).

© OLIVER HILL

The coral-lined sand at Font Hill Beach Park is a favorite for locals in the area, who crowd in on weekends for picnics and swimming.

The nature reserve is not officially open to the public and the PCJ makes clear that those who enter do so at their own risk. Not long ago, a scientist member of a team, with years of observing the area's crocodiles under his belt, inadvertently stepped on one of the animals and received severe gashes in his leg. Crocodiles are not generally aggressive, but avoid stepping on them at all costs.

Newmarket

Straddling the Westmoreland–St. Elizabeth border and best accessed by turning inland along the road just east of Whitehouse just west of the South Sea Park subdivision, Newmarket has the best weekly market in the area, generally held on Mondays. When the incline levels out, turn right to reach Newmarket, passing the striking Carmel Moravian church sitting on a hill. It's well worth stopping to have a look around. The church is in a good state of repair with an impressive organ in its modest interior.

EAST OF BLACK RIVER

Middle Quarters is a favorite motorist stop where women line the road selling "pepper swimps" (shrimp) and Howie's roadside restaurant serves up typical Jamaican dishes out of huge pots to motorists. Michelle Williams' roadside shop is an excellent choice for fresh-out-the-pot swimps. Of course, Ms. Williams serves beer as well at her shop and has a good fruit and vegetable stand out front.

◖ Y.S. Falls

Y.S. Falls (www.ysfalls.com, ysfalls@cwjamaica .com, 9:30 A.M.–3:30 P.M. Tues.–Sun., US$13 adults, US$6.50 children 4–14 years) on the Y.S. Estate is by far the best conceived and organized waterfalls destination in Jamaica. It's been operated by Simon Browne since 1991. The Y.S. River changes with weather, crystal clear blue normally, and swelling after rain in the mountains to make the perfect venue for tubing (US$6). There is a bar and grill on the property, as well as gift shops with an excellent array of books, crafts, and Jamaica-inspired clothing. There is also a swimming pool just below the falls.

The latest development is the installation of a zipline over the falls (US$30 for first run, US$10 for each consecutive run), operated by the Chukka Caribbean Adventures crew.

It is a rush to say the least, and perhaps the most exhilarating of Chukka's three ziplines in Jamaica.

The origin of the name "Y.S." is somewhat disputed: one version is that it comes from the Gaelic word "wyess," meaning winding and twisting. The second version is that it comes from the last names of the two men who ran the estate in 1684, John Yates and Richard Scott, who branded the cattle and hogshead of sugar with "Y.S." The 3,238-hectare property was bought out of bankruptcy from the list of Encumbered Estates in London by Simon's great uncle, John Browne, in 1887 for 4000 pounds sterling—without Browne ever having seen the estate. Some of the land was sold, leaving 809 hectares today where champion thoroughbred racehorses are bred and Pedigree Red Poll cattle graze the Guango tree–lined fields. Sugarcane production was discontinued in the 1960s.

The Y.S. River originates in Cockpit Country and is fed by many springs on its course to where it meets the Black River. A spring on the estate is the original source of water for the town of Black River, 13 kilometers downstream.

Bamboo Avenue

One of the most beautiful four-kilometer stretches of road in Jamaica running from Middle Quarters to West Lacovia, Bamboo Avenue is also known as Holland Bamboo. The stretch is lined with Jamaica's largest bamboo species, the common bamboo (*Bambusa vulgaris*), brought from Haiti by the owners of the neighboring 1,780-hectare Holland sugar estate once belonging to John Gladstone (1764–1851). Gladstone went on to father 19th-century British prime minister William Gladstone. Bamboo Avenue provides shade for several jelly coconut and peanut vendors. On the eastern side of Bamboo Avenue is **Bamboo Ville,** a vibesy jerk center with big pots on open fires.

Southern Cockpit Country

The interior of St. James, St. Elizabeth, Manchester, and Clarendon parishes is rugged terrain, much of it forming part of Cockpit Country, which blankets pitted limestone hills full of caves and underground rivers. As the impassible interior descends to the sea, ridged hills taper down around lush valleys, which have proved some of the most fertile in Jamaica. The Y.S. and Appleton estates remain prized lands. The **Nassau Valley,** where Appleton Estate is located, is still heavily planted in sugarcane to feed the healthy rum business.

From Maggoty the main road (B6) heads east, skirting a large wetland area fed by the upper reaches of the Black River before rejoining the main south coast "highway" (A2) just east of Santa Cruz. From Balaclava, a turn to the north (B10) leads deep into the interior to Troy and then Warsop, passing by Ramgoat Cave before hitting Clarks Town, Trelawny. North of Clarks Town the road emerges on the

coast in Duncans. For extreme adventure-seekers, the **Troy Trail** is a challenging traverse of the most rugged part of Cockpit Country. The trail is best accessed with the help of a guide that can be set up through the **Jamaica Caves Organization** (info@jamaicancaves.org, www.jamaicancaves.org).

MAGGOTY

Apple Valley Park (contact Lucille Lee, cell 876/487-4521 or 876/963-950, or Andrea, cell 876/449-7718; www.applevaleypark.com, 10:30 A.M.–5 P.M. daily, reservations are imperative as the park is closed when none have been made) is one of those places where even locals aren't entirely sure whether it's open or not. Nonetheless paddle-boating around a manmade pond, swimming pools, a cold-water whirlpool tub, rope swing, and picnic area make it a potentially entertaining affair. The park offers a tractor tour and meals. The price of admission can include a jerk or fried chicken lunch, or visitors may bring their own food. Admission is US$8.50 adults, US$7 children under 12 with lunch included; US$5 adult, US$3.50 children under 12 for admission alone. Four cabins on the property (US$14) offer basic accommodation for up to three persons with private baths and cold water.

Apple Valley Guest House (contact Lucille Lee, cell 876/487-4521 or 876/963-9508), also run by Lucille Lee, has slightly less basic double-occupancy rooms (US$36) than those at the park, with hot water in private baths and air-conditioning or fans available by request.

ACCOMPONG

Home of the Leeward or Trelawny Maroons, Accompong (derived from Achumpun, or Acheumpun, from Twi language of Ghana) was named after a brother of the famous leader Cudjoe (Kojo) who signed a peace treaty with the British that granted his people autonomy from the crown on March 1, 1738. In exchange for their sovereignty, granted 100 years before emancipation, and free-

dom for the rest of the black population, the Maroons were called on repeatedly by the British to assist in the suppression of slave rebellions and to help capture runaways. Accompong falls within the borders of St. Elizabeth Parish, but it's really outside the confines of any parish as the land occupied by the Maroons predates the establishment of parishes by the British. Today Accompong is led by **Colonel Sydnie Peddie** (cell 876/464-0651) who was elected to his second five-year term in 2005. It's best to check in with the colonel so he can anticipate your arrival, as he'll help with the logistics and ensure fair treatment by representatives of the community.

The best time to visit is for the annual **Accompong Maroon Festival** (Jan. 5–6), when the village comes alive with traditional Maroon music and dance as well as stage shows more typical of the rest of Jamaica. During the rest of the year it's a great destination for getting some fresh air and spectacular views of a seldom-visited corner of St. Elizabeth. Guides from the community are available to take visitors to the cave (US$10/person) where the famous treaty

ACCOMPONG MAROONS

Jamaica's Maroons date back to the Spanish settlement of the island, when it came to be accepted that a fraction of the blacks brought from Africa as slaves would not succumb to live in perpetual subordination and would instead resist perpetually until granted their freedom. These so-called "runaway slaves" were termed "Cimarrones" by the Spaniards, a name later translated into English as Maroon. To name these warriors "runaway slaves" is to ignore the fact that not only did they flee the plantation, but they also beat into the most remote and mountainous regions of the island to claim land and hold it against assault. The Spaniards ultimately gave up in their attempt at putting down the Maroons, many of whom it is said descended from the warrior Ashanti people of West Africa. The British would also eventually sign a peace treaty in 1738, the legacy of which has left the Maroons with their sovereignty

to this day. The Maroon treaty was signed by Cudjoe (Kojo), whose repeated defeat of British forces led to granting the Maroons privilege to large swaths of Jamaica's highlands. Large Maroon settlements grew in Accompong, St. Elizabeth, as well as in Moore Town in the Rio Grande River Valley, and above Buff Bay in Charles Town, Portland, and in Scott's Hall, St. Mary. Today the Maroons are still a force to be courted by those representatives of government who have Maroon lands within their constituencies. While the communities themselves have been largely diluted since emancipation, the warrior spirit of the Maroons has permeated Jamaican society at large, influencing social movements like the Rastafarians, who draws on their experience as rebels against the status quo to present an alternate worldview based on principles that can be traced through the Maroon heritage to Africa.

was signed, as well to a few other important sites in the community like a burial ground and the church where English names were given to the Maroons after emancipation.

◖ APPLETON ESTATE

Appleton Estate (tel. 876/963-9215 or 876/963-9217, fax 876/963-9218, appleton@infochan.com, www.appletonrum.com, Tour hours: 9 A.M.–3:30 P.M. Mon.–Sat., US$15 admission includes a miniature bottle of rum) in Nassau Valley is one of the most popular tours in Jamaica and well worth a visit, both to sample the several grades of rum and to experience the most lush corner of St. Elizabeth with impressive topography. The distillery at Appleton Estate is run by Wray and Nephew, which makes Appleton's, Jamaica's most well-known rum. To get there, turn inland off the A2 towards Maggoty in West Lacovia after passing through Bamboo Avenue from the west or Lacovia from the east. Where the road splits keep right, following well-marked signs for Appleton Estate.

SANTA CRUZ

A bustling transportation hub more than a destination of any note, Santa Cruz can get congested during the day and if you're just passing through there is a very useful bypass around the town center that saves a lot of time. Arriving from the east, veer right off the main road at the Y where the road splits at the Total gas station before getting to town. Take the third left to rejoin the main at the stoplight on the western edge of town. Arriving from the west, follow the reverse route: a left at the first stoplight, and then a right until the road meets the main at the Total station on the eastern edge of town. The dusty bus terminal parking lot in the heart of Santa Cruz is a good place to catch a route taxi for Treasure Beach, Black River, or Mandeville.

Entertainment and Shopping

Toxic Night Club in Leddister's Plaza is the best spot in town to get your groove on at night should you be stranded in Santa Cruz.

Record Mart (right before Singer in Santa plaza, tel. 876/966-2564) sells both domestic and imports with plenty of reggae, R&B, and hip-hop.

Accommodations

Danbar Guesthouse (Trevmar Park, tel. 876/966-9382, US$38) has simple rooms with standing fan and hot water should you get stranded in Santa Cruz. Some guests are known to use the place on an hourly basis.

Chariots Hotel (Leeds, tel. 876/966-3860, US$37–74) has a pool, restaurant, and bar. Heading west, turn left at the stoplight onto Coke Drive, pass RBTT bank, then National Commercial Bank, four kilometers from Santa Cruz on the road to Malvern. It's the only hotel between Mandeville and Black River. The restaurant serves typical Jamaican dishes (US$4–8.50). All rooms have cable TV, air-conditioning, hot water, and floral print bed covers on either two double beds or one king. It's a decent, well-kept place.

Food

Miguel's Cafe (5 Jewel Close, tel. 876/966-4304, 8 am–9:30 P.M. Mon.–Sat., until 10 P.M. Fri. and Sat., US$2.50–3.75) in the heart of town just below KFC has fried chicken, baked chicken, curry goat, stewed peas, and pork chops.

Mother's (77 Main St., tel. 876/966-2857) is Jamaica's favorite local fast-food institution, serving vegetarian power patties as well as run-of-the-mill beef patties and other local dishes.

Hinds Restaurant & Bakery (Santa Cruz Plaza, tel. 876/966-2234, 7:30 A.M.–5 P.M. Mon.–Thurs., until 7 P.M. Fri. and Sat., US$3–5.50) has decent Jamaican dishes liked fried, stewed, and baked chicken, as well as oxtail, curry goat, stew pork, and escoveitch fish.

Services

G-Link World Internet Cafe is at Shop 21, Jakes Plaza (tel. 876/966-4497).

NCB (7 Coke Drive, tel. 876/966-2204) and **ScotiaBank** (77 Main St., tel. 876/966-2230) have small branches with ATMs. This is the closest place to get cash if you're staying in Treasure Beach.

Treasure Beach

Isolated from the rest of the island by the Santa Cruz mountains, which create the area's distinct coastal desert environment by capturing the westbound rainfall, Treasure Beach is a catch-all for a series of bays and fishing villages that extends from Fort Charles at the greater community's western edge, to Billy's Bay, Frenchman's Bay, and Great Bay on the eastern edge of the community. Treasure Beach prides itself on offering a different kind of tourism than that found in Jamaica's more built-up tourist centers. Local ownership of the guesthouses and restaurants is more the rule than the exception, and it's impossible not to interact with Jamaicans in a more substantial context than being served your cocktail.

The earth in St. Elizabeth is a deep red, and the people, thanks to a mix of Scottish and African blood, also have a reddish complexion often with striking blue or green eyes. These

Jamaicans are commonly referred to as "red" by the rest of the island's population with typical disregard for innuendos or connotations outsiders might deem as politically incorrect. In spite of St. Elizabeth receiving the least rainfall on the island, the parish is known as Jamaica's "breadbasket," not for any grain produced there per se, but mainly for vast quantities of vegetables it sends across the island.

Many of the bays have decent swimming areas, but it's best to inquire with locals about the safety of jumping in the water at any particular point until you get accustomed to the area. Remain vigilant of rip tides and strong currents generally.

History

The light complexion generally seen in Treasure Beach and St. Elizabeth is said to owe to Scots who had unsuccessfully settled in Darion Point,

THE SOUTH COAST

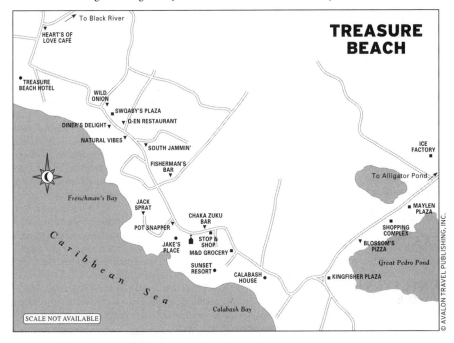

Panama, and were forced to flee. It is said that William III sent word that the Scots were not to come into any port, so they beached at Treasure Beach. Treasure Beach started to become an offbeat destination in the 1970s, and fortunately developed at a slow pace, giving the area a chance to develop an alternate approach that has been far more equitable for the community than other tourism developments around the island.

SIGHTS

As an off-the-beaten track destination, the main appeal of Treasure Beach is the community itself and the infectious sleepy pace that permeates the area. Despite their laid-back nature, residents of St. Elizabeth pride themselves on being some of the hardest working, from the fishermen who spend days out at sea to the farmers who take great care in mulching and watering their crops resisting the perpetual drought. Despite the lack of differentiable sights of interest along the Treasure Beach coast itself, there are several worthwhile excursions within an hour's drive, many of which are around Black River. East of Treasure Beach along the coast there are also a few notable attractions.

Lover's Leap (Southfield, tel. 876/965-6577, 9 A.M.–9 P.M. daily, closing later on Sun.) is a 480-meter drop to the sea less than 16 kilometers east of Treasure Beach along the coast. According to legend, a slave couple leapt to their deaths to avoid forced separation by their master, who was lusting after the girl. As the legend has it, an old woman who witnessed their leap said the moon caught them up in a golden net and they were last seen holding hands standing on the moon as it sank over the horizon. A lighthouse was built on the point in 1979, and can be seen from 35 kilometers out at sea. Peach is a very nice person who works at the restaurant and bar. Admission is US$3, or support the bar and restaurant in lieu of admission.

ENTERTAINMENT AND EVENTS

If you're looking for wild all-night parties, Treasure Beach is probably not the best desti-

nation. Romantic sunsets and quiet nights are more the norm than live music. Nonetheless, a few venues see regular activity on weekends. Most of these venues operate as restaurants as much as nightspots.

Treasure Beach comes alive for annual events like Calabash Literary Festival and the Hook 'n Line Fishing Tournament with bonfires on the beach and roots reggae pumping from sound systems well into the night. Rebel Salute, a massive reggae concert held annually in mid-February in nearby Port Kaiser, is another exception to the rule of calm and quiet nights along the South Coast.

Fisherman's Bar (cell 876/379-9780) is a club open nightly with dance hall and roots reggae booming. A pool table and domino area around back are popular with locals, while the restaurant around front serves typical Jamaican fare at reasonable prices. The venue occasionally hosts live music.

Wild Onion (contact business manager Lurline Rhodes, tel. 876/965-3619, 3 P.M.–2 A.M. Tues.–Sun., US$4–7) is a bar and restaurant serving Jamaican lunch and dinner items like rice and fish, curry goat, vegetable pasta, pork, and chicken. As a night spot Wild Onion contracts a selector on Friday, Saturday, and Sunday nights. In the high season the venue hosts live music once a month.

South Jammin' (contact owner/manager Christine Becks, cell 876/377-4825; open daily from 7 A.M. until the last person leaves, US$3–13), a centrally located restaurant, serves as a local hangout and nightspot with darts, billiards, and dominoes. Satellite TV and occasional live music are strong draws.

SHOPPING

Elizabeth Eyre Seltzer Designs (ees01@ earthlink.net, lizzie1@cwjamaica.com, www .eesdesigns.com) sells decidedly hip tie-dyes on fine cloth for funky women's outfits. Elizabeth also owns Calabash House.

Treasure Beach Women's Group makes handcrafted gift items while providing a forum for addressing issues affecting the community's matriarchs.

SPORTS AND RECREATION

People come to Treasure Beach to escape the busy tourist hubs of Ocho Rios, Negril, and Montego Bay. Swimming, fishing, long walks and yoga may be the most popular recreational activities.

Captain Dennis Adventure, run by Dennis Abrahams (cell 876/435-3779 or 876/965-3084, dennisabrahams@yahoo.com), offers excursions and fishing trips for US$120 to get to Black River Safari, Pelican Bar, (US$75 for two), or to a white-sand beach called Gallon Beach in Malcolm Bay just past Black River. Dennis also offers fishing (US$50/hr) and excursions to Little Ocho (US$120). Additional passengers can be added for an extra fee (US$45 per person).

Andy Nembhard (cell 876/438-1311, andytours@yahoo.com) leads hiking tours, rents Trek and Raleigh mountain bikes, and rents sea kayaks (US$60 for three), and does a hiking/biking tour (US$60/per person) to Great Bay or Fort Charles or to Lover's Leap.

Cindy Wimsatt (cell 876/889-3087) is a skilled massage therapist based in a neighboring parish who practices regularly in Treasure Beach upon request.

Beaches

Wherever you go in the water in Treasure Beach, it's best to have a companion and to inquire with locals to ensure it is safe. Treasure Beach maintains a growing list of locals who have fallen victim to the hungry sea, which can have strong currents and undertows. While Treasure Beach is not sought after specifically for the quality of its beaches (which aren't as suitable for Jamaica Tourist Board posters as those in other parts of the island), the beaches it has are picturesque in an entirely different way and romantic all the same.

Frenchman's Beach is a great beach for body surfing when the sea is a little rough. There is coral aplenty towards the edges of this beach even in shallow waters. The safest spot to swim is directly in front of Golden Sands Guest House.

Calabash Bay Beach is a fishermen's beach with a large, clear, sandy area good for swimming. The safest spot to swim is in front of Calabash House before you reach the boats. **Great Bay** also has a decent beach for a dip.

ACCOMMODATIONS

The popularity of Treasure Beach as an off-the-beaten track destination has led to a blossoming in the accommodation market, most of the guesthouses being remarkably affordable when compared with other tourist areas—with comfortable accommodations for two starting around US$30 per night. The only time of year it becomes hard to find a room is during Calabash Literary Festival, when those who haven't booked well in advance happily settle for whatever's available, even staying in Black River, Junction, or as far away as Mandeville if necessary. Rebecca Wiersma has over the past decade created a great online presence with her **Treasure Tours** website (tel. 876/965-0126, treasuretours@cwjamaica.com, www.treasurebeach.net), subscribed to by most of the accommodations in the area with prices and amenities listed. Unless otherwise noted, all the accommodations listed can be booked through Treasure Tours.

Rates in Treasure Beach are by and large far more reasonable than other tourist destinations on the island, even for the villas, where going in a small group or with a pair of couples makes them a bargain.

Under US$75

Ashanti Village (Frenchman's Bay area, contact Alieda Ebanks, cell 876/433-1593, cell 876/387-4887) is a great budget option with a one-bedroom (US$45) and a two-bedroom (US$65) sea-view cottage and four additional rooms (US$35) in the main house. The rooms come with a private bath, small fridge, fan, and electric kettles, with screens on the windows. The cottages have equipped kitchens, and verandas with a sea view. Meals are prepared by request. There is lots of garden space and play area great for kids. Ashanti is well situated in a very quiet location still within an easy stroll to most restaurants and bars and Frenchman's Beach.

Ital Rest (contact Frankie and Jean, tel.

876/863-3481; US$40/night, US$250/week) is about as roots as you can get. The property has limited electricity, supplied by solar panels to the smart wood cabins, nicely situated within an easy walk from several sandy coves. Mosquito nets are used in lieu of fans or air-conditioning, and a kitchen on the property is available for guest use while vegetarian food can also be prepared by request.

Nuestra Casa (Billy's Bay, tel. 876/965-0152, roger@billybay.com, www.billysbay.com, US$45/50 low/high) is a villa-style guesthouse run by Lillian Chamberlain and her son Roger that rents three rooms, two with a double bed, and a third with two twin beds. One room has a private bath, the other two sharing the bathroom. Amenities include ceiling and standing fans, and hot water. Dinner is prepared by request. Anika Elliott is the sweet housekeeper.

Lovers' Leap Guest House (Southfield, tel. 876/965-6004, US$36 upstairs, US$50 poolside) has decent, basic rooms with double beds and private bath, hot water, air-conditioning, and ceiling fans.

US$75-200

⟨ Villa Mutamba (tel. 876/920-8194, cell 876/868-4658, mutabarukax@hotmail.com, www.villamutamba.com, US$700/week) is a physical embodiment of the minimalist philosophy of dub poet Mutabaruka, who owns the property. African relics adorn the entrance after one of the longest staircases, dubbed the "stairway to heaven." Inside, simple and tasteful bamboo furnishings complement the funky master bathroom, which has a small window looking out to sea from the colorfully tiled tub.

⟨ Calabash House (Calabash Bay, tel. 876/965-0126, US$60/70 low/high per room or US$200/US$250 low/high for house) is a four-bedroom villa right on Calabash Bay, one of the best spots for swimming in Treasure Beach. Bedrooms have air-conditioning with hot water in the bathrooms. A housekeeper tidies up during the day while a cook can be arranged to prepare breakfast and dinner (additional US$25 daily for four persons). Two cute mini-cottages were recently added to the yard, where there's also a hammock for lazing the

Calabash House has a large villa as well as a few cute cottages on the waterfront.

days away and watching the fishermen bring in their catch. Owner Elizabeth Seltzer is an artist who brings a creative vibe to the house and its ambiance.

Sunset Resort Hotel (Calabash Bay, tel. 876/965-0143, srv@sunsetresort.com, www .sunsetresort.com, US$125 garden view, US$163 ocean view) basically defines "Butu," the Jamaican equivalent of kitsch, with its Jamaican nouveau-riche exaggerated decor. Floral bedcovers with matching lampshades seem to be transplanted straight from the home of a Kingston drug don. Nonetheless, it's hard to overlook the charm and care taken to make everything match so carefully, even if it is sorely lacking in taste.

Perhaps the best deal at Sunset Resort Hotel are the small villas adjacent to the main building, which rent for less (from US$97) and have more basic amenities—with appreciably less gaud strewn about.

Treasure Beach Hotel (Frenchman's Bay, tel. 876/965-0110, US$107/$119 low/high) is the closest thing you'll find to Sandals in Treasure Beach—with split-system air-conditioning in the tile-floor rooms, private balconies, and floral bedcovers matching the drapes. Rooms have either two singles or one king bed. This property sells itself on peace, quiet, and relaxation, as opposed to Sandals.

Over US$200

Jake's (tel. 876/965-0635 or 800-OUT-POST, jakes@cwjamaica.com, www.island outpost.com/jakes, US$113–385 low, US$136–468 high) has taken rustic chic to a new level, pouring on the kind of details sought out by those members of the jet set always on the prowl for the next in spot. To call Jake's rustic is to ignore the posh bedding and elaborate detailing reminiscent of an Arabian love lair. The honeymoon suites have outdoor showers and sunbathing decks on the roof. Jake's is the only Island Outpost property not run as an all-inclusive. The most unpretentiously hip accommodation at Jake's is the two-bedroom

THE SOUTH COAST

© OLIVER HILL

An old anchor salvaged from the sea decorates the waterfront at Jake's, the most decidedly upscale chic accommodation in Treasure Beach.

Jack Sprat (US$177/230 low/high), located right next to Frenchman's Beach with its iconic buttonwood tree adjacent to Jack Sprat Cafe.

The bold and classy architectural style at Jake's owes to the creativity of Sally Henzell, wife of the late Perry Henzell, who became Jamaica's biggest film icon after directing the cult classic *The Harder They Come* in the early '70s. Sally Henzell has an aesthetic that blends the old colonial charm found in the island's historic buildings with a windswept rustic edge one might associate more with the Maine coast of New England.

Sometimes described as "shabby shacks," the cottages at Jakes don't neglect the modern essentials, with hot water provided in all the rooms with solar energy. The Henzells bought the property in 1991 and opened and developed the rooms and cottages. Jake was a pet parrot of the Henzells, while Jake's is also a generic term used to call out to a white person.

Sparkling Waters (Billy Bay, tel. 876/927-8020, reservations@sparklingwaters villa.com, www.sparklingwatersvilla.com, US$250 for up to four) is an exquisitely decorated collection of three modern, two-bedroom duplex villas: Villa de la Sable, Villa de l'Ocean, and Villa du Soleil. The three villas share the grounds, which contain a pool, whirlpool tub, and a gorgeous private beach. The villas have comfortable and inviting bathrooms with hot water, satellite TV, stereos, and air-conditioning in the bedrooms. Spacious and comfortable living and dining rooms are found downstairs along with the kitchen. The bedrooms are on the second floor at the top of a spiral staircase.

Sun Splash Villa (contact Joyce Chang, tel. 802/484-5918, joyce.chang@valley.net; US$1,200/week for two persons, US$250 each additional) is a spacious three-bedroom, two-bath oceanfront villa with a pool and a staff of a cook and a gardener. An adjacent apartment can also be rented for larger parties.

Great Escape (Fort Charles Rd., tel. 574/707-0132 or 269/641-5451, greatescape@ jamaicavilla.com, www.jamaicavilla.com, from US$1,500/1,800 low/high) is a three-bedroom

house well-removed from the languid center of Treasure Beach, with queen beds in each room. A large pool overlooks the water with a clubhouse area. Great Escape is a good spot for families, with a small private beach and plenty of space to roam about.

FOOD

Thanks to Treasure Beach's popularity as Jamaica's number one off-the-beaten track destination, a wide variety of restaurants have popped up. They cater to both a local and tourist market, serving a mix of cautious international dishes and local favorites. Few of these restaurants have land lines, and addresses in Treasure Beach are somewhat relative.

Jack Sprat (adjacent to Jake's, tel. 876/965-3583, 10 A.M.–10 P.M.) is a favorite for fried fish, conch soup, pizza, and Devon House ice cream.

Hearts of Love Café serves fresh baked goods like pineapple upside-down cake, banana bread, baguettes, and chocolate cake, as well as breakfast items like calaloo, cheese omelets, and fresh juices.

Diner's Delight (across from Swaby's Plaza next to Golden Sands Resort, contact Andrea Wright, tel. 876/839-2586, 9 A.M.–10 P.M., US$3.50–13) serves typical Jamaica dishes including curried goat, peppered steak, brown stew chicken, shrimp, fish, and lobster at reasonable prices. Diner's Delight is a favorite among locals. Take-out is also available.

Natural Vibes (no phone) is a restaurant, bar, and souvenir shop in one serving local Jamaican dishes on an outdoor patio or for take-out. It's open for breakfast, lunch, and dinner.

The Gold Coast Restaurant (Kingfisher Plaza, cell 876/391-2458) serves Jamaican fare like fried chicken, curried goat, and steamed fish. It's open for lunch only.

South Jammin' (contact owner/manager Christine Becks, cell 876/377-4825; open daily from 7 A.M. until the last person leaves, US$3–13) serves breakfast, lunch, and dinner with a fixed menu and a large number of items that changes daily and is written on a blackboard out front.

Jerk is cooked on weekend, including chicken, pork, and fish.

Jake's Place (tel. 876/965-3000) is the restaurant at the hipper-than-hip accommodation, serving Jamaican and international cuisine for breakfast, lunch, and dinner daily.

Shantz Eating Place (towards Billy's Bay, no phone, open for lunch) serves quality, cheap eats with a rotating menu including items like fried chicken, pork, fish—plus curry goat on Saturdays—out of a little shacklike restaurant. The food is served for takeout in Styrofoam boxes.

⬤ Pot Snapper (cell 876/393-6377), a small restaurant located next to the entrance to Jack Sprat, prepares excellent fish, Jamaican dishes, and decent pizza at reasonable prices.

Sunset Resort (tel. 876/965-0143) serves Jamaican and American fare from steamed fish to pizza, with an all-you-can-eat buffet nights on Friday nights.

M&D Grocery (tel. 876/965-0070, 7 A.M.–8 P.M. daily) is a small grocery shop and bar good for basic supplies. Jerk chicken and pork as well as conch soup are prepared on Fridays and Saturdays.

Round the Clock Bar (contact owner Charmaine Moxam, cell 876/378-6690; open 24/7) is a small grocery shop and bar good for basic supplies and drinks located in Frenchman's Bay next to Jake's.

INFORMATION AND SERVICES

The Calabash Bay **post office** (five minutes east of Southern Supplies on foot, 10:30 A.M.–4:30 P.M. Mon–Fri, closed for lunch 1–2 P.M.) often lack stamps.

Kingfisher Plaza is a small shopping center and home to **The Bird's Nest Bar,** which has a billiards table, a grocery shop, and a supermarket.

Southern Supplies (eight minutes north of Kingfisher Plaza on foot, just before the ice factory) is the largest supermarket in Treasure Beach, selling among other essentials international phone cards, gift items, and music. The store also has an Internet café.

GETTING THERE AND AROUND

Treasure Beach is serviced by frequent route taxis from Santa Cruz, direct, and via Watchwell (US$2.50) and from Junction (US$1.50). If you're driving there are three routes to get there. From Black River there is a short, direct road along the coast that is a bit iffy in places, but still passable with a two-wheel-drive vehicle. Turn off the main towards the sea on a road just east of the communications tower east of Parottee. Driving from Mandeville take a left at the base of Spur Tree Hill and pass through Junction to reach Treasure Beach. From Santa Cruz, turn south towards the sea about 1.5 kilometers west of the stop light.

EAST OF TREASURE BEACH
Junction

A busy stopover point on the way over the Santa Cruz Mountains, Junction is the closest outpost of civilization to Treasure Beach with supermarkets and banks. The Junction Guest House offers basic accommodations, and several hole-in-the-wall restaurants serve Jamaican staples.

Junction Guest House (tel. 876/965-8668, US$25–100, simplepunkie@yahoo.com) has rooms ranging from basic with ceiling fan, private bath, TV, or carpeted with air-conditioning to the most luxurious, a suite with kitchen and verandah.

Supersad's Roti Restaurant (Pine Plaza, across from police station, tel. 876/965-8124, 8:30 A.M.–5 P.M. Mon.–Sat., US$3.50–11) serves dal pea roti and a variety of Jamaican dishes like curry goat, chicken, and beef. Conch, shrimp, and lobster dishes are also prepared.

The **Shopper's Fair** and **SuperPlus** are the best supermarkets in town for groceries.

Both **NCB** (tel. 876/965-8611) and **ScotiaBank** (tel. 876/965-8257, Shop #1, Tony Rowe Plaza) have branches with ATMs.

Alligator Pond

One of the busiest fishing villages on the South Coast, Alligator Pond has as its central attraction the Seafood Restaurant, Little Ochie, and the nearby Manatee Hole. **Sea Riv** (cell

876/539-3916) is the only place to stay in Alligator Pond with basic rooms (US$30) that have private baths, TV, and fans. D. Rochester is the owner.

To get to Alligator Pond, turn south at the bottom of Spur Tree Hill (a left coming from Mandeville, a right from Santa Cruz) and keep straight until reaching the coast.

⚔ Portview Restaurant and Bar at LaMorna Beach (contact owner/manager Philip Perkins, cell 876/852-7390, lamorna@ gmail.com, beach entry US$1.50) is on a gorgeous little beach seven kilometers east of Alligator Pond. There is one basic cottage on the property that can be rented (call Perkins for rates). The little beach is located in a cove that faces west along the coast to the lights in Alligator Pond and at the Port Kaiser aluminum terminal that glimmers as the sun sets. There are a few gazebos up a series of steps from the beach that make romantic hangouts.

Little Ochie

⚔ Little Ochie (tel. 876/965-4449, littleochie@ cwjamaica.com, www.littleochie.com, 9 A.M. until you say when, daily, US$7.50–14) is a seafood paradise, serving a wide range of dishes like jerk and garlic crab, fish, and lobster. Over 75 seafood recipes are utilized on a daily basis, with lobster cooked 15 different ways, the best of which could very well be the garlic lobster. Everald Christian, aka "Blacky" or Mr. Christian, is the founder who built the place in 1989 in a rustic style reminiscent of the good old days in Ocho Rios on the North Coast. At the inception of Jamaica's tourism economy, before it became dangerously over-developed, Ocho Rios (known locally as Ochie) had similar rustic thatch huts on the beach as the ones used today as the restaurant's boat-shaped dining areas. Little Ochie has since become wildly popular with uptown Jamaicans, who will drive from Kingston or MoBay just for the spectacular cuisine.

The first or second Sunday in July, Little Ochie hosts the annual Little Ochie Seafood Festival, which draws a good crowd for cultural shows and even more seafood than normal.

CANOE VALLEY WETLAND

Canoe Valley Protected Area (contact ranger Devon Douglas, tel. 876/441-6799) is a coastal wetlands area managed by Jamaica's National Environment and Planning Agency (NEPA) full of diverse plant and animal life. The manatees that live in semi-captivity along the river in the park are the highlight. **Row boat excursions** (US$10/person) to spot these manatees and snorkel in the surreal crystal blue waters are offered from the ranger station a few kilometers south of Milk River. The rangers at the station also offer hikes to remote Taino Caves (rates negotiable). Turtles and alligators also share the waters; swimmers are advised to keep their eyes peeled.

About five kilometers west, or about 16 kilometers east along the coast into Manchester from Alligator Pond, the **Guts River** creates a small pool as it emerges from the rocks with cool, crystal-clear waters said to have medicinal qualities. The deserted beach nearby is great for long strolls. Getting to Guts River requires chartering a taxi if you don't have your own vehicle, or hiring a boat from Treasure Beach if that's where you're based.

Mandeville

Manchester is Jamaica's sixth-largest parish, much of its land located at relatively high altitudes with three mountain ranges: the May Day Mountains, the Don Figuerero Mountains, and the Carpenters Mountains, where the highest peak in the parish stands at 844 meters. Any approach to Mandeville, the parish capital, entails steep climbs, which have fortunately been given some of Jamaica's best roads.

Manchester has been at the center of Jamaica's bauxite industry, led by Jamalco (Alcoa-Jamaican government joint venture), which has massive mines around Mandeville. It also has processing facilities across the border in Clarendon, as well as in St. Elizabeth, where Port Kaiser along the coast west of Little Ochie is an important export terminal.

The parish was named by the Duke of Manchester, who served as Governor General 1813–1821. Named after the Duke of Manchester's eldest son, William de Mandeville, the small city of Mandeville was at one time a British enclave where colonial government officials preferred to spend their summers in the high altitude's relatively cool climate.

The 1970s destroyed Mandeville as the gentry left when Manley came into power (they were scared off by his socialist lean). Bauxite has benefited the local economy and has created an income for skilled workers since the industry was established in the 1950s. The bauxite industry has trained and paid many Jamaicans while the lucky were educated at the Belair School, which remains one of Jamaica's best preparatory institutions.

SIGHTS

Mandeville's historic sights are concentrated around the town square, known as Cecil Charlton Park. These include the **Mandeville Courthouse,** which was built of limestone using slave labor and finished in 1820. The courthouse housed the town's first school on its ground floor. The **Mandeville Jail and Workhouse,** also among the first public buildings in town, is now in use as

the police station. Adjacent to the courthouse, the Mandeville Rectory is the oldest house of worship and the original Anglican rectory in Mandeville, having once also served as a tavern and guesthouse to the dismay of many parishioners.

Marshall's Pen

Marshall's Pen (contact owner Ann Sutton, tel. 876/904-5454, asutton@cwjamaica.com) has been a popular spot for serious birding for many years. Birders come especially to see the Jamaican owl, which can often be seen in its favorite easily accessible tree. Of Jamaica's 28 endemic birds, 23 have been spotted at Marshall's Pen, with a total of 110 species recorded on the property over the years.

At this point tourism is not the main business at Marshall's Pen. Only experienced birdwatchers should express interest in visiting.

Marshall's Pen was built in 1795 at the latest, the exact date being somewhat of a mystery. Originally the estate was about 809 hectares, whereas today is has dwindled to a still-respectable 121 hectares.

The origin of its name is a bit ambiguous, but it seems it does not refer to an identifiable previous owner. The present owner is Dr. Ann Sutton, widow of the late Robert Sutton, one of Jamaica's foremost ornithologists who created an audio catalogue of Jamaican bird songs that was released by Cornell University's ornithology department. Robert Sutton also co-authored *Birds of Jamaica,* the island's best bird guide. Dr. Ann Sutton is also an ornithologist, as well as being a conservationist and secretary of the Society for Conservation and Study of Caribbean Birds.

Marshall's Pen welcomes serious birders, who find warm hospitality and even accommodation sometimes. It is also possible to tour the great house and extensive gardens (US$10/person, minimum six persons) by appointment; visitors can find orchids, anthuriums, ferns, and other indigenous plant life. It's not a place to show up unannounced; call ahead to arrange a visit and for directions.

ENTERTAINMENT

Odeon Cineplex (Caledonia Rd., tel. 876/962-1354, movie times tel. 876/962-7646) is the local movie theatre and often the most entertaining venue in town for a night out.

Upper Level (Upper Level Plaza, Caledonia Rd.) is Mandeville's regular nightspot with pool tables.

The Ville Nightclub (22b Ward Ave., Steven Smith tel. 876/614-6135, cell 876/409-0734, 4:30 P.M.–midnight Mon.–Thurs., 6 P.M.–until

you say when Fri.–Sun.) is the newest nightspot in town, with pool table and a bar. On Fridays the bar hosts an after-work jam and karaoke. Saturdays are the ultimate party experience, while Sundays is oldies but goodies night with '70s and '80s music.

Kourtney's Jerk Krib (formerly Jerkey's, 10 A.M.–midnight Sun.–Thurs., 10 A.M.–4 A.M. Fri.–Sat.) is a dependable jerk center and bar located by the roundabout on the western end of town heading up towards Spur Tree Hill.

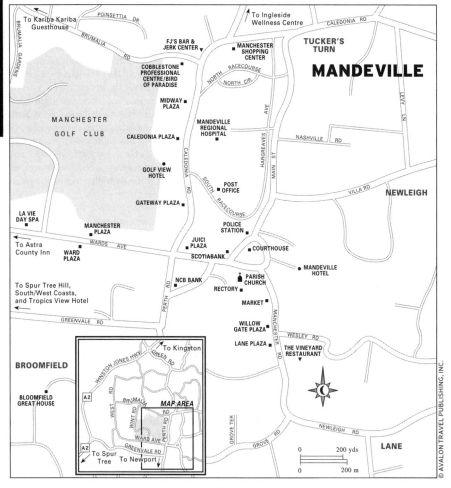

The bar holds occasional stage show performances and has a few billiards tables for the slower nights. Kourtney's has an Internet café out front with several terminals.

Shock Wave Sports Bar (Willow Gate Plaza, contact owner Mark Haughton, cell 876/866-6216, 10 A.M. till you say when, daily) is the most happening bar in town with a few billiard tables and dancehall blasting. The bar turns on the strobe lights as it heats up into the night.

SPORTS AND RECREATION

Manchester Club (Caledonia Rd., contact Janice Wright, tel. 876/962-2403) is the oldest golf course in the Western Hemisphere, going back 142 years. It remains the least expensive course in Jamaica (US$21.50 green fees, US$8.50 clubs, US$14 caddy per round), and perhaps in the hemisphere as well. The nine-hole course is well maintained, even if it is not the bright green of more popular courses on the island. For those staying in the area for a length of time, membership brings the fees down significantly.

Ingleside Wellness & Recreation Centre (Ingleside Dr., tel. 876/961-3632) has tennis courts, badminton, table tennis, weight lifting equipment, and a bar that no longer keeps regular hours. Day membership is available for use of the facilities. Call manager Janice Robinson for more details. Ingleside is the base for the Manchester Table Tennis Association.

La Vie Day Spa (28 Ward Ave., tel. 876/625-5766) opened in 2006 offering nail care (US$20 for mani/pedi), facials (US$21), waxing (US$7.50 for bikini), and massage (US$64 hot stones, US$21 for back). Carolyn Miller is the kind proprietor and Wendy, who does the manicures, is a sweetheart.

ACCOMMODATIONS
Under US$75

Crystal Palace Guest House & Restaurant (Spur Tree Hill, tel. 876/964-6766) is one of the most basic accommodations in the Mandeville area. Some guests are known to use the place for short-term visits. Overnight rates with fan run US$17, and overnight with fan and TV run US$28.

Castle View Guesthouse (87 Manchester Rd., tel. 876/961-3612,US$14–17) is a more centrally located dive guesthouse. Some rooms have TVs. It doesn't serve food but offers short-term rentals.

Kariba Kariba Guest House (tel. 876/962-8006, kariba@cwjamaica.com, US$45) was built about halfway in 1997 and has operated since '98 without any real appearance or sense of completion inside or out. Dobson the caretaker is friendly enough nonetheless, and the four rooms in operation have TV and ceiling fans and, while not immaculately maintained, are a decent value and come with breakfast. Baths are shared. Derrick O'Connor is the owner.

Golf View (7B Caledonia Rd., tel. 876/962-4471 or 876/962-4477, gviewrosi@cwjamaica.com, US$55) is a 62-room hotel near the center of town with basic rooms that have a ceiling fan, private bathrooms with hot water, as well as two-bedroom suites with air-conditioning (US$100).

Astra Country Inn (62 Ward Ave., tel. 876/962-7758, countrystyle@mail.infochan.com, www.countrystylecommunitytourism.com, US$47–56) is a decent inn that has clean rooms with cable, fans, private bathrooms with hot water, and either two double beds or one king. The amenities are on the same level as the Mandeville Hotel, which has the same owners.

US$75-200

Tropics View Hotel (Winston Jones Hwy., tel. 876/625-2452, tropicsview@cwjamaica.com, US$88–180) is the newest of Mandeville's hotels, with wireless Internet in the lobby. All rooms are in two-bedroom suites with a kitchen and two bathrooms. In the deluxe suites, one room has a king and the other a queen, whereas in the popular suites, there are queen beds in both rooms. There is a restaurant and bar on the property by the front gate.

Mandeville Hotel (4 Hotel St., tel. 876/962-2460, manhot@cwjamaica.com, mandeville hoteljamaica.com; rooms either have fan

(US$88) or a/c (US$94)) is the oldest hotel operating in Mandeville. It recently underwent a restoration that left it with nice parquet floors and soothing color schemes in many of the rooms, while it seems details in the bathrooms were overlooked. Clean sheets, ceiling fans, air-conditioning, a fridge, cable TV, and hot water round out this comfortable yet quite basic hotel in the heart of town. Bring your own soap and shampoo.

FOOD

Windies (Shop 1–2, James Plaza, tel. 876/ 962-9463, 8 A.M.–midnight Mon.–Sat., 8 A.M.– 10 P.M. Sun., US$3.50–6) serves ackee and saltfish, roti-wrap with boneless chicken, jerk chicken, curry chicken, curry goat, and festival.

Tweety's Fried Chicken (Perth Rd., tel. 876/962-3426) serves rotisserie chicken behind the Texaco station.

⦗ Bloomfield Great House (tel. 876/962-7130, bloomfield.g.h@cwjamaica.com, lunch and dinner Mon.–Sat.) is one of the most beautiful colonial-era houses in Mandeville. Bloomfield opened for business in 1997 following a two-year restoration by Aussie Ralph Pearce and his wife, Pamela Grant, whose father became the first Jamaican to own the property when he bought it in the 1960s. The panoramic view over Mandeville is spectacular, and food is excellent, albeit a bit pricey. A good bet is the local snapper, which is prepared in typical Jamaican fashion with onions, pepper, and okra. Bloomfield is a great spot for an evening cocktail and smoked marlin appetizer. There are tentative plans to build rooms off the back.

Mother's (28 Manchester Rd., tel. 876/625-8837, 7 A.M.–9:30 P.M. Mon.–Thurs., 7 A.M.– midnight Fri. and Sat., 7 A.M.–8 P.M. Sun.) is the favorite national fast-food restaurant serving patties and Jamaican staples.

Bamboo Garden Restaurant (35 Ward Ave., tel. 876/962-4515, noon–10 P.M. Mon.– Sat., 1–10 P.M. Sun., US$7–30) serves Chinese food that ranges from sweet and sour chicken to butterfly shrimp to lobster with butter and cola. The restaurant is located upstairs from Cash & Carry Supermarket.

International Chinese (117 Manchester Rd., opposite Guardsman, tel. 876/962-0527, noon–9 P.M. Mon.–Thurs., till 9:30 Fri. and Sat., noon–8 P.M. Sun., US$6–14) serves items like Cantonese-style lobster, cashew shrimp, and chicken with mushroom.

La Bella Italia (7B Caledonia Rd., tel. 876/962-8606, ferravale@yahoo.it, 10 A.M.– 7 P.M. Mon.–Sat.) makes the best ice cream and gelato in Jamaica, although Devon House fans would certainly beg to differ. The company was founded by Valerio Ferrari (cell 876/464-2832) and is based in Mandeville, where the small factory has a retail outlet (11 A.M.–9 P.M. Sat., noon–9 P.M. Sun. and holiday). Lee's, Megamart, and select Super-Plus and Shopper's Fare supermarkets carry the products in Kingston and around the island, while there are franchise outlets in Negril, Ocho Rios, and at Norman Manley Airport in Kingston. The company began operations in late 2002. The Otaheite Apple flavor is a favorite.

Merv's Restaurant and Coctail Lounge (4a Caledonia Rd., behind Juici Beef Plaza, tel. 876/961-0742, 8 A.M.–9 P.M. Mon.–Sat., until 6 P.M. Mon. and Wed., US$3–4) serves rotisseire chicken, cabbage, and stew/baked chicken. Merv's has a second branch at Midway Mall (tel. 876/961-6378, 8 A.M.–6 P.M. Mon.–Sat.).

Cake, Coffee and Ice Cream (59 Main St., 876/962-6636, 8 A.M.–10 P.M. daily) is the local Devon House franchise, owned and operated by Christopher Bird.

Early Bird (St. Elizabeth Bus Park, tel. 876/962-1046, 6 A.M. 7:30 P.M. Mon.–Sat., US$3) serves Jamaican dishes like chicken with rice and peas.

Cathay Chinese Restaurant (Brumalia Town Centre, across from Western Union, tel. 876/625-0850, 10:30 A.M.–9:30 P.M. Mon.– Sat., US$3) serves decent Chinese food with daily lunch specials like chicken lo mein and sweet and sour pork.

⦗ Bird of Paradise (1 Brumalia Rd., tel. 876/962-7251, 7 A.M.–10 P.M. Mon.–Sat., 10 A.M.–3:30 P.M. Sun. for brunch, 5–10 P.M.

Sun. for dinner, US$9–17) is an upscale restaurant with marble tables and a sleek bar serving a mix of vegetarian and meat dishes with appetizers like calamari al aioli, shrimp margarita, and spring rolls. Entrées range from snapper cutlet pan fried in caper butter to duckling breast. Bird of Paradise is located in Cobblestone Professional Centre, the first set of buildings on Brumalia Road on the left coming up from Caledonia Road.

Bennett's Restaurant (Elethe Mall, tel. 876/961-3464, 7:30 A.M.–8 P.M., US$2.50–4) serves typical Jamaican dishes with breakfast consisting of calaloo or ackee and saltfish, mackerel rundown, liver, baked beans and saltfish or stew chicken. Lunch and dinner items include baked, BBQ, or stir-fry chicken, stew pork, or peppered steak. It has delivery.

Foodz to Go (Shop 8, Elethe Mall, tel. 876/961-8646, 8 A.M.–8 P.M., US$3–5) has takeout and delivery service with dishes like curry, fried, or fricassee chicken, oxtail, brown stew fish, curry goat, stew peas. Breakfast is served in the mornings with stew chicken, ackee and saltfish, and mackerel rundown.

The Vineyard Restaurant & Bar (61 Manchester Rd., Perth Teacher's College, tel. 876/625-6113, noon–10:30 P.M. Mon.–Sat., 5–8 P.M. Sun., US$5.50–12) opened in 2003. It has Jamaican and international cuisine, with dishes including fish, chicken, ribs, and steak. On every last Friday of the month, a local band, Breeze, performs vintage reggae sprinkled with other musical genres (no cover).

Pat's Pizza & Restaurant (Lane Plaza, tel. 876/625-5171, 7 A.M.–11 P.M. Mon.–Sat., 3 –11 P.M. Sun.) serves pizza and a variety of other dishes like chicken and chips. Mr. Grant runs the place.

Sandra's Restaurant (Lane Plaza, tel. 876/625-4149, 7 A.M.–midnight daily) serves a changing menu of Jamaican dishes like fried chicken, curry goat, and stew pork (US$4–8).

Reidy's Restaurant (Lane Plaza, tel. 876/962-6533, 24 hours Mon.–Sat.,) serves stew chicken, brown stew fish and vegeta-ble, stew beef, cow head, chicken and fish (US$2–4).

FJ's Restaurant, Bar and Jerk Center (23 Caledonia Rd., tel. 876/961-4380, cell 876/360-2082, 10 A.M.–11 P.M. Mon.–Sat.) serves seafood and jerk dishes (US$2–11). Busta is the jerk chef.

Spur Tree Hill

The main road west from Mandeville (A2) rises over Spur Tree Hill, famous for being a dangerous stretch. From atop Spur Tree Hill, the views of Manchester's lowlands are spectacular, even if they are dominated by the scarred red earth of a bauxite facility. To the west the Santa Cruz Mountains can be seen tapering down to the sea.

Cool Shade Jerk Centre sits at the top of Spur Tree Hill and is run by Pauline, some kind of relation to Lloyd, who runs All Seasons.

Alex Curry Goat about 0.4 kilometers before All Seasons, is the oldest and best curry goat shop in town.

All Seasons Restaurant Bar and Jerk Centre (tel. 876/965-4030, 8 A.M.–11 P.M. daily) is considered by many to be the best jerk spot in Manchester, with other typical Jamaican dishes served as well. Perched on the steep slopes of Spur Tree Hill, All Seasons commands an impressive view of southern Manchester and St. Elizabeth down to where the sky meets the sea.

Hill View Jerk Centre is farther down Spur Tree Hill, but it still has a decent view. Hill View also serves jerk, while not as highly rated as its cousin farther up the hill.

Claudette's Top Class (Spur Tree Hill, tel. 876/964-6452) is a favorite local spot to get curry goat. The little sit-in restaurant is across the highway from Hood Daniel Well Company.

Gran's Seafood and Bar (tel. 876/603-4254, noon–midnight daily) is located in the Hopeton district between Kingsland and Hatfield going up Spur Tree Hill from Mandeville. Gran's is the best spot in town for seafood items like steamed, escoveitched, and fried fish, shrimp, and lobster (US$7–17).

INFORMATION AND SERVICES

The Real Thing Health Food (Shop 33, Mandeville Shopping Ctr., tel. 876/962-5664 or 876/625-7703, 9 A.M.–5 P.M. Mon.–Sat.) sells healthful groceries like rice cereal and some herbal soaps, shampoos and hair oils, teas, and nuts. Mr. and Mrs. Reid run the shop.

SuperPlus has four locations in Mandeville (17 Caledonia Rd., tel. 876/961-1624; 16 Manchester Rd., tel. 876/625-2310; 12 Ward Way, tel. 876/961-5702; 2 Park Crescent, tel. 876/625-0842).

Shoppers Fair supermarket is located at 5 Caledonia Rd (876/962-6217).

Finishing Touches (Shop 2, Midway Mall, tel. 876/961-3217) family grooming centre is a convenient place to stop for a haircut.

Express Laundromat is located at 30 Hargreaves Avenue (tel. 876/962-6701).

DHL is at Perth Road, Brumalia Town Mall (tel. 876/961-0744, 9 A.M.–5 P.M. Mon.–Fri.).

Medical

Hargreaves Memorial Hospital (Caledonia Ave., tel. 876/961-1589) is a private clinic with many of its staff also working at Mandeville regional.

Mandeville Regional Hospital (32 Hargreaves, tel. 876/962-2067) is the largest hospital for kilometers around with a good reputation.

Two pharmacies are available: **Villa Pharmacy** is at 29 Main Street (tel. 876/962-0892). **Gateway Medical Centre and Pharmacy** is located at 3A Caledonia Road (tel. 876/962-5292).

Vision Care Centre is at 2 Caledonia Road (tel. 876/961-6629).

Karene Blair (Suite 9, Cobblestone Professional Centre, 1 Brumalia Rd., tel. 876/961-4540) is a highly recommended dentist.

Money

Both **NCB** (9 Manchester Rd., tel. 876/962-2083; Mandeville Plaza, tel. 876/962-2618) and **ScotiaBank** (1A Caledonia Rd., tel. 876/962-2035) have branches with ATMs in Mandeville.

Internet

Manchester Parish Library (34 Hargreaves Ave., tel. 876/962-2972, manparlib@cwjamica.com, 9:30 A.M.–5:30 P.M. Mon.–Fri., until 4 P.M. Sat.) offers use of the Internet (US$1.50/hr).

Manchester Shopping Centre has an Internet café, along with a food court with a lot of hole-in-the-wall restaurants, and **Fontana Pharmacy** (tel. 876/962-3129).

GETTING THERE AND AROUND

Mandeville is served with regular buses from Kingston and May Pen and regular route taxis departing from the square for surrounding destinations including May Pen, Christiana, and Santa Cruz (US$2).

CHRISTIANA

A small community near the highest reaches of Manchester Parish, Christiana is a quiet town with one main drag and a single guest house. The most popular attraction in town is **Christiana Bottom,** a gorge located within walking distance from the center of the small village. **Gourie State Park** (contact Trevor Anderson for guiding services, tel. 876/964-5088, cell 876/771-4222, trevormanderson@hotmail.com, US$20 per person) is a recreational area on government land managed by Jamaica's Forestry Department, located between Christiana and Colleyville, about two miles past Christiana. Immediately after passing Bryce United Church, take the first left turn and then the first right until reaching the unmanned Forestry Department station and picnic area. **Gourie Cave,** the highlight of the park, is not actually inside the park but rather about a quarter mile down the hill to the left of the park entrance. By the cave entrance there's a picnic and camping area with a hut and tables and benches. There is one main trail through the park that leads to the community of Ticky Ticky, with excellent views along the way of the Santa Cruz Mountains, Spur Tree Hill, and the historic Bethany Moravian Church.

Gourie Cave was a hideout for runaway slaves. The cave follows the channels of an underground river about three- to four-feet deep, depending on how much rain has fallen. If you go north from the entrance and upstream against the current, you end up on the other side of Colleyville Mountain. A different route leads downstream along the underground river deep into the earth where there are several caverns along the way. If you're going to be exploring in the cave, you should monitor the weather and be aware of any fronts on the horizon. It's not wise to venture into the cave alone. Contact Trevor Anderson for his guide services.

In Christiana Bottom, there's a Blue Hole fed from underground streams with two waterfalls dumping into the pool. There's another waterfall at William Hole further downstream. To get to Christiana Bottom coming from Mandeville, turn right immediately after the NCB bank on Moravia Road, then take the first left around a blind corner, and then the first right, which leads to Christiana Bottom. Continue past the first left that leads to Tyme Town and park at the entrance to the second left, a wide path that leads down to the river. Ask for Mr. Jones for a guided tour (US$20) of Blue Hole and William Hole, and his farm where he grows ginger, yam, potato, pineapple, bananas, and sugarcane.

Accommodations

Villa Bella (tel. 876/964-2243, villabella@ cwjamaica.com, www.jamaica-southcoast .com/villabella) is billed as "Jamaica's original country inn." Located in a cool setting at 914 meters above sea level, you won't find a more comfortable temperate climate on the island. The hotel has a lot of old world charm in a gorgeous setting. The allure as an accommodation is somewhat shadowed by the tired state of its rooms. Owner Sherryl White-McDowell has initiated efforts to refurbish the property, which will be ongoing. The restaurant serves Jamaican dishes like ackee and salt fish, roast and jerk chicken, and steamed fish (US$6–12). A spa opened at the hotel in early 2007 offering services that include massage (US$50–90), body scrubs (US$55), facials (US$50), nails (US$5–30), and body wraps (US$55).

The **Pickapeppa Factory** (at base of Shooter's Hill beside Windalco plant; call in advance to arrange a visit, tel. 876/603-3441, fax 876/603-3440, pickapeppa@cwjamaica .com, www.pickapeppajamaica.com, US$3 adults, US$1.50 children) offers a half-hour educational tour (8:30 A.M.–3:30 P.M. Mon.–Thurs.) led by Diana Tomlinson or Noel Miller, which covers the company's founding in 1921 and the process involved in the manufacture of its world-famous sauces. The factory is closed for the first two weeks in August and between Christmas and New Year's, but at any other time of year a sampling of the Pickapeppa sauces is included in the tour. The sauces are made with all-natural ingredients and include cane vinegar, mango chutney, hot, spicy and gingery, mango sauces, and of course jerk seasoning. The only preservative agents used in Pickapeppa sauces are vinegar and pepper.

Scott's Pass (between Toll Gate and Porus) is the headquarters for the Nyabinghi house of Rastafari in Jamaica with the House of Elders based there. The land was bought by Bob Marley and given to the Binghi for that specific purpose. It has become one of Jamaica's most important Rastafarian communities where Nyabinghi drumming around Haile Selassie's July 23 birthday lasts for a week. The community members are for the most part welcoming of visitors, but you may get some evil eyes if you fail to recognize their customs for the Binghi celebrations: women must wear skirts or dresses (no pants) and cover their head, while men must uncover their head. To arrange a visit or learn about the birthday celebrations or other Nyabinghi events around the island contact the Rasta in Charge, Paul Reid, known as Iyatolah (cell 876/850-3469) or Charlena McKenzie, known as Daughter Dunan (cell 876/843-3227). Arts and crafts are sold throughout the year at Scott's Pass.

Other important Binghi's throughout the year include Ethiopian Christmas (January 7), one during Black History Month (a couple days sometime in February), commemoration of His Majesty's visit to Jamaica (April 21, 1966), All African Liberation Day (May 25), Marcus Garvey's birthday (three nights around

August 19), Ethiopian New Year's (3–7 days starting September 11) and Haile Selassie's coronoation (November 2).

To get to Scott's Pass take the first left heading west of the train line in Clarendon Park where the Juici Patties plant is located. Look out for a small bridge crossing the Milk River before reaching Porus.

Clarendon

The second most-populous parish, Clarendon is a major agricultural center with a lively market (Mon.–Sat.) by the square (or triangle) in May Pen. The parish, like all others in Jamaica was originally settled by the Tainos, who were later pushed out by the Spaniards who favored the area for cattle farming on their "hatos" or haciendas. Cotton and indigo became important crops during the early British period, before sugar took over later under British rule. The parish developed as British troops settled on land grants given to them as rewards for service by Charles II in the 17th century. Cudjoe, the Maroon leader, is said to have been the son of a slave on Sutton Plantation in Clarendon which was the sight of Jamaica's slave rebellion in 1690. Following emancipation, large numbers of Indian indentured laborers were brought in, forming the basis of a distinct cultural enclave that still exists today.

MAY PEN

Jamaica's second-largest inland town after Spanish Town, May Pen is strictly Jamaican—receiving few foreign visitors compared with other major population centers on the island.

May Pen is the parish capital with several heritage sites in its vicinity, including Halse Hall Great House, and the birthplace of acclaimed writer and poet Claude McKay, who went on to contribute to the Harlem Renaissance movement after moving to the United States. Unfortunately, Halse Hall is not open to the public.

May Pen was established on the banks of the Rio Minho and grew thanks to the river, which hampered travelers who took rest in the inns that were established on its banks. In the 1880s a railway station was built, further fueling the town's growth. Clarendon has a disproportionate population of East Indian descent, and is the location for **Hosay,** a traditional Indian festival that has been Jamaicanized (see sidebar).

The town gets its name from the Reverend William May, who owned the estate that predates the settlement. May served as rector in Kingston and his son went on to become custos of Clarendon and Vere. The second important annual event held in May Pen is the **Denbeigh Agricultural Show,** which is a fantastic display of the region's farming prowess.

Sights

Halse Hall Great House (contact Duane Malcolm manager, tel. 876/986-2215 or 876/986-2215, halsehallgreathouse@hotmail.com, http://halsehall.tripod.com) has been owned since 1969 by aluminum mining giant Alcoa. The property was named Hato de Buena Vista ("ranch with a nice view") by the Spaniards who laid the foundation on which the present structure stands. Major Thomas Halse arrived with the British forces in 1655 and was given the property as a land grant following the British takeover. The present structure was built by Halse in the fortified style of the time to defend against potential reprisals from the Spanish and their Maroon allies. A second story was added by his heirs in the 1740s. Perhaps the most distinguished owner of the property was Thomas Henry de la Beche, an English geologist who founded the geological survey of Great Britain Royal School of Mines and Mining Record Office and wrote *Remarks on the Geology of Jamaica.* Ownership passed from the hands of the family in the 1830s to settle debt. Halse Hall was not offering tours to the public at time of writing, being used only as a private residence for the likes of visiting aluminum execs.

Clarendon Park Garden (manager Alfred Gayle) is a well-maintained park right across

HOSAY

A traditional Shia Muslim festival that arrived with the indentured Indians brought to Jamaica in the years following emancipation, Hosay (oft-pronounced Hussay) used to be held in communities of significant East Indian populations across the island, including Kingston, Spanish Town, Sav-la-Mar, and Port Maria. Known as Moharram in other countries where the festival is observed, Hosay is today held only in Clarendon, with a procession from Lionel Town to the banks of the Rio Minho taking place every August.

Traditionally, Mahorram participants mourn the Prophet Mohammed's martyr grandsons Hosain and Hasan by whipping themselves and praying as they follow the Tazia or Tadjah, a giant bamboo and paper replica of the slain Hosain, with dancing and stick fighting until the figure is set on the river or sea to float away.

In the Caribbean, the festival has been creolized, starting with its name change, which derives from the chanting of Hosain during the festivities – interpreted as Hosay. The original dates of the festival were also changed from the first 10 days of the lunar cycle in January–February to August–September, when there was less work on the sugar estates and more time to allow for the personal pursuits of the workers. To a large extent the festival lost its religious connotations in Jamaica even while it was observed by non-Muslims in India as well. It has been suggested that the festival today represents an affirmation and remembrance of the struggle of the participants' ancestors as they left the lives they knew to come toil on the sugar estates. The festival is also observed in Suriname, Guyana, and Trinidad, also former sugar colonies where Indians were brought as cheap labor. Contact the **Museum of Ethnography** at the IOJ in Kingston for more information (tel. 876/922-0620, ioj.jam@mail.infochan .com, www.instituteofjamaica.org.jm).

the street from Alcojuice and next to the Juici Patties factory. This is a good place for a picnic and break from the road.

Practicalities

◖ Alcojuice Restaurant & Bar (Clarendon Park, tel. 876/987-1029, alcojuice@net comm-ja.com, 6:45 A.M.–8 P.M. daily, until 9 P.M. on weekends), managed by Madge Bowen (cell 876/876-6250), across from the Juici Patties factory has excellent juices and typical Jamaican dishes (US$2.50–6.50). Soups are also served (US$0.75–2.50).

Daily Delicious Restaurant & Sports Bar (28 Main St., next door to Island Grill, a Jamaican fast-food joint, tel. 876/986-9842, 8 A.M.–9:30 P.M. Mon.–Sat., weekends till 11 P.M., US$2.50–6) serves baked, stew, curry, and fried chicken; cow foot; cow head; oxtail; fish; pork; and curry goat.

Juici Patties (tel. 876/904-2618) has its factory and an adjacent outlet and drive-through in Clarendon Park.

Versalles Hotel (42 Longbridge Ave., tel. 876/986-2775) is reached by taking the second left from Mineral Lights Roundabouts. Suites with air-conditioning and hot water, cable TV, king or two double run US$56.

Bridge Palm Hotel (Toll Gate, tel. 876/987-1052, cell 876/819-4332, or U.S. tel. 905/963-3251, info@bridgepalm.com, US$50–64) has rooms with minifridge, air-conditioning, and ceiling fans. Some rooms have balconies and overlook the swimming pool.

NCB (876/986-2343) has a branch and ATM located at 41 Main Street, with a **ScotiaBank** (tel. 876/986-2212) branch at 36 Main Street.

Clarendon Parish Library (Main St., tel. 876/902-6294 claparlib@cwjamaica.com) offers DSL Internet access (US$1.50/hr).

SOUTH OF MAY PEN

The area south of May Pen is the prime agricultural land celebrated in the Denbeigh Agricultural Show each year. The area is dominated by cane production at the Moneymusk Sugar Estate. Few visitors to Jamaica make it to this remote side of Clarendon, and the few who do typically visit the somewhat rundown Milk River Baths. More interesting is the coastal region of Portland, where the Portland Lighthouse stands on the farthest point south on the island, which juts out into the sea. You will need to charter or rent a vehicle to properly explore this remote area.

Alley was the capital of the former parish of Vere, and remains the sugarcane-producing heartland of Clarendon. The area was once dominated by the Moneymusk Estate and is still largely covered in cane fields that feed the factory now located closer to **Lionel Town.**

Lionel Town is the largest and most bustling community in the region and the starting point during Hosay, which celebrates Jamaica's East Indian heritage with a procession all the way to May Pen.

Jackson Bay has some of Jamaica's deepest coastal caves, where legend has it the pirate Morgan stashed booty. The little-explored coastline around Jackson Bay is dotted with such caves while the beach is a popular spot with locals on weekends and holidays. A four-wheel-drive vehicle is very helpful for heavy exploring along this stretch of coast.

At **Salt River,** 10 minutes east of Lionel Town near the coast, there is a public mineral spring that is a favorite among locals. Dances are held on weekends for what they call **Early Sundays.** This is a far more popular bath spot than Milk River, although it's seldom visited by tourists. Unfortunately the lack of tourists also means upkeep is substandard, as the locals don't seem to mind the rubbish that litters the place. Nevertheless, it's a great spot to soak up the up the scene and eat some fried fish and festival. To get to Salt River, take the left turn before reaching Lionel Town heading south, or a left at the T junction after passing through Lionel Town. When the road splits in a Y about a kilometer from the junction, keep left, and then keep left at the following junction. Salt River will be on your right.

Sights

St. Peter's Church is one of the oldest churches in Jamaica. It was founded in 1671 as the parish church of the former parish of Vere. The present building was erected around 1715 on the foundation of the original. The church bell weighs a quarter ton and was commissioned by the same company that created Big Ben, London's most distinguishing landmark.

The original Moneymusk Sugar Estate windmill in nearby Amity Hall is an interesting octagonal brick structure that now houses a branch of the **parish library** (tel. 876/986-3128, 11 A.M.–5 P.M. Mon.–Fri.); Maxine Reid is the branch assistant. Internet service is offered (US$1.50/hr) on one terminal. The Moneymusk windmill was the only one in Jamaica to be constructed of brick, which begs the question of why the owners went through the trouble of importing such heavy materials from England when other estates were building the structures of locally quarried limestone.

Accommodations

Milk River Hotel and Spa (tel. 876/902-4657, milkriverhotel@yahoo.com) has three types of rooms. The first category has two twin beds and either shared bath (US$110), or private bath (US$117), both of which include breakfast, dinner, and bath access. The third room category has either a king or queen bed with private bath (US$137) and breakfast, dinner, and bath access. These can also be rented with just bath access included (US$48 shared bath, US$55 private bath, US$75 private bath and queen bed). One suite has a king and a twin bed (triple occupancy, US$112 room and bath alone, US$206 with bath, breakfast, and dinner). Most rooms have air-conditioning and TV. Rooms without air-conditioning have standing fans.

The **Milk River Baths** (7 A.M.–9 P.M. daily, US$4 per 15 minutes for adults, US$2 children 10 and under), located at the hotel, are spring fed with lukewarm water. A bath can be enjoyed whether or not you're staying at the hotel. For curative purposes, a minimum of three baths is recommended, but it is not advisable to stay in the water for longer than an hour because the water is highly radioactive, more so even than the springs at Vichy in France. To get to Milk River, turn south at the roundabout in Toll Gate before reaching Clarendon Park heading west from May Pen. Continue straight from Toll Gate without turning off until reaching the hotel on the right. Keep heading south in Rest, instead of turning east along the B12 toward Alligator Pond in St. Elizabeth.

Getting There and Around

Route taxis and buses serve May Pen from Kingston and Mandeville. May Pen is located at the western end of Highway 2000, one of Jamaica's best toll roads, making it a quick 45-minute drive from Kingston. From the taxi stand in the square in May Pen, route taxis for points south (like Milk River) leave sporadically once they fill up.

BACKGROUND

The Land

Jamaica enjoys a widely varied topography for its small size, ranging from tropical montane regions in the Blue and John Crow Mountains to temperate areas at the higher elevations of Manchester Parish, to lush tropical coastline along much of the coast to near-desert conditions south of the Santa Cruz Mountains in St. Elizabeth parish.

GEOGRAPHY

Jamaica is a relatively small island: 235 kilometers miles long and 93 kilometers miles at its widest point, covering an area of 10,992 square kilometers (slightly smaller than the state of Connecticut

in the United States). Distances in Jamaica can seem much greater than they really are thanks to mountainous terrain and poor roads.

CLIMATE

Jamaica has a tropical climate along the coast and lowlands, with average annual temperatures of 26–32°C. In the mountains, temperatures can drop down near freezing at night at the highest elevations. Jamaica has two loose rainy seasons: between May and June and then later, with heavier, more sustained rains and coinciding with hurricane season, from September to November.

Flora and Fauna

In terms of native biodiversity, Jamaica is surpassed in the Caribbean only by Cuba, a country many times its size. What's more, Jamaica has an extremely high rate of endemism, both in plant and animal life. Perhaps most noticeable are the endemic birds, some of the most striking of which are hard to miss. The national bird is the red-billed streamertail hummingbird (also called the doctor bird), which is ubiquitous across the island. Other endemic birds, like the Jamaican tody, are more rare—requiring excursions into remote areas to see.

FLORA

While agriculture has diminished in importance as bauxite and tourism have taken over as Jamaica's chief earners, the country still depends heavily on subsistence farming outside the largest cities and towns, where even still many houses have mango and ackee trees in the yard. Coffee remains an important export crop, the Blue Mountains fetching some of the highest (if not *the* highest) prices per pound in the world. In recent years, a growing number of entrepreneurs have begun developing cottage industries based on key agricultural crops. The market for Jamaica's niche products is strong both domestically and abroad. It helps that prices within the country are buoyed by heavy reliance on imported foodstuffs, which while posing a challenge for consumers, means producers can get a fair price for their goods even at home. Some of the most notable of these cottage industries based on natural products of Jamaica are Walkerswood, Starfish Oils, Pickapeppa, and Belcour Preserves. Look out for these in crafts shops and specialty supermarkets across the island. Many of these enterprises offer tours of their production facilities.

Jamaica's flora consists of a diverse mix of tropical and subtropical vegetation. Along the dry South Coast, the landscape resembles a

Ackee is the key ingredient in Jamaica's national dish, ackee and saltfish.

desert, while mangrove wetlands near Black River provide a sharp contrast within relatively close proximity. In the highlands of Manchester, temperate crops like potato, known as Irish, and carrots thrive.

Fruits and Plants

Ugli fruit is a hybrid between grapefruit *(Citrus paradisi)* and tangerine *(Citrus reticulata)* developed at Trout Hall, St. Catherine. It has a brainy-textured thick skin that is easily removed to reveal the juicy, orange-like inside. A few large citrus estates, most notably Good Hope in Trelawny, make this an important export.

Ackee *(Blighia sapida)* is a small-to-mid-size tree native to West Africa, its introduction to Jamaica having been recorded in 1778 when some plants were purchased from a slave ship captain. It is said to have been present earlier, however, owing to a slave who wouldn't relinquish his grasp of the fruit across the Middle Passage. Ackee is Jamaica's national fruit.

Anatto *(Bixa orellana)* is an important dye and food coloring, and was at one point an important Jamaican export, likely lending its name to Annotto Bay in St. Mary, which was a center of production and export.

Jimbalin is the Jamaican name for what is known as passion fruit in the United States. **Passion fruit** *(P. edulis flavicarpa)* has one of the world's most beautiful flowers and a delicious fruit not commonly seen fresh in northern countries.

Antidote cacoon *(Fevillea cordiflora)*, known as sabo, segra-seed and nhandiroba, is a perennial climbing vine whose fruit has been used for its medicinal and purgative qualities.

Agave *(Agave sabolifera)* is a succulent, its broad leaves edged with prickles, notable for its tremendous 5- to 10-meter flower shoot February–April. Bulbils fall from the shoots to develop into independent plants.

Arrowroot *(Maranta arundinacea)* was brought from South America by pre-Columbian populations and used medicinally. Later it was grown on plantations and used as a starch substitute and thickener.

Apple in Jamaica is a generic term that could refer to any number of fruits, starting with the delicious Otaheite apple. Other apples include star apple; custard apple (sweet sop, sour sop); mammee apple *(Mammea americana)*; crab apple, or coolie plum; rose apple *(Syzyguim jambos)*, used as a windbreak and for erosion control; golden apple *(Passiflora laurifolia)*; and velvet apple *(Diospyros discolor)*, aka the Philippine persimmon. The imported American or English apple, the common apple of the United States, has been slowly and unfortunately taking over from the more exotic varieties on fruit stands in recent years due to its exotic appeal.

Avocado *(Persea americana)* is known commonly in Jamaica as "pear." Avocado is a native of Mexico, from where it was taken by the Spaniards throughout the Americas and much of the world. The Spanish name, *aguacate,* is a substitute for the Aztec name, *ahucatl.* Avocados are in season in Jamaica from August to December with a few varieties ripening into February. Alligator, Simmonds, Lulu, Collinson, and Winslowson are some of the varieties grown on the island.

Banana *(Musa acuminata* x *balbisiana)* is the world's largest herb (non-woody plant), and became an important Jamaican export in the post-Emancipation period of 1876–1927. Jamaica was the world's foremost producer of the fruit during the period, with Gros Michel and later Cavendish varieties. The banana trade gave rise to Caribbean tourism when increasingly wealthy shippers began to offer passage on their empty boats returning to Jamaica from New England, where much of the produce was destined. In this way Portland, an important banana-growing region, became the Caribbean's first tourism destination with the Titchfield Hotel, built by a banana baron, exemplifying the relationship between the fruit and the economy that would come to replace it in importance. Several varieties of banana are still grown in Jamaica, including plantain, an important starch; boiled bananas are a necessary accompaniment in the typical Jamaican Sunday breakfast of ackee and saltfish, callaloo and dumpling.

Barringtonia *(Barrintonia asiatica)* is a large evergreen with its center of origin in Asia. Its large coconut-like fruit will float for up to two years and root on the shore where it lands. Known locally as the duppy coconut, the tree has been naturalized in Portland and 220-year-old trees grow at Bath Gardens in St. Thomas.

Wild basil *(Ocimum micranthum)* is a wild bush used in folk medicine and in cooking, popularly called barsley or baazli.

Bauhinia *(Bauhinia spp.)*, known locally as "poor man's orchid," Bauhinia is a favorite of the streamer-tail hummingbird, or doctor bird, which visits the orchid-like flowers. It grows as a shrub or mid-sized tree with pinkish flowers.

Madam Fate *(Hippobroma longiflora)* is a poisonous perennial herb with a five-petaled, star-shaped flower used in Obeah and folk medicine. Found along pastures or on riverbanks, it's commonly called star flower or horse poison.

Trees and Flowers

Kingston buttercup *(Tribulus cistoides)* is a low, spreading plant with bright yellow flowers. It's known commonly as "Kill Backra" because it was thought to have caused yellow fever, which killed many European settlers. It's also called "police macca" because of its thorns, and turkey blossom.

Blue mahoe *(Hibiscus elatus)* is a quality hardwood of the Malvaceae family. It grows native in the Blue Mountains and is the national tree.

Ironwood *(Lignum vitae)* is an extremely dense tropical hardwood that produces Jamaica's national flower.

Mahogany *(Swietenia mahagoni)* was and still is highly valued for its timber and has accordingly been unsustainably harvested since the Spanish colonial period, resulting in dwindling numbers today. Mahogany can still be seen growing, albeit sparsely, along the banks of the Black River, which was originally called the Mahogany River by the Spanish, or Rio Caobana.

© OLIVER HILL

Sorrel flowers are mixed with ginger and sugar to make a refreshing drink.

FAUNA
Mammals

The **coney** or Jamaican hutia *(Geocapromys brownii)* is Jamaica's only surviving indigenous land-dwelling mammal, the only other being bats. Conies are nocturnal and thus seldom seen. The animal is basically a large rodent with cousins inhabiting other Caribbean islands like Hispaniola. Its meat was prized by the Taino centuries ago, while it is still a delicacy for the mongoose today, which is blamed for pushing it towards extinction. Another threat is loss of habitat, owing to encroaching urbanization in its principal habitats in the Hellshire Hills and Worthy Park of St. Catherine. It is also found in the John Crow Mountains in Portland and St. Thomas.

Mongooses are today a common animal seen scurrying across the road. Widely regarded as pests, it is said that all mongooses in the Western Hemisphere are descendants of four males and five females introduced to Jamaica from India in 1872 to control the rat population on the sugar estate of one William Bancroft Espeut. They soon went on to outgrow their function, eventually being held responsible for killing off five endemic vertebrates, and bringing Jamaica's iguanas to the verge of extinction.

Bats

Jamaica has 23 species of bat, known locally as rat bats, bats being used for moths. Many species of the Bombacaceae family are bat-polinated, including the baobab, cottonwood, cannonball tree, and night cactus trees. Bats also go for other pulpy fruits like sweet sop, banana, naseberry, and mango. *Noctilio leporinus,* a fish-eating bat, can be seen swooping low over harbors and inlets at twilight.

Birds

Of the 280 species of birds that have been recorded in Jamaica, 30 species and 19 sub-species are endemic (found nowhere else). Of these 30, two are considered extinct. There are 116 species that use Jamaica as a breeding ground while around 80 species spend the northern

© OLIVER HILL

A male doctor bird perches for a meal of hibiscus nectar.

winter months on the island. The Jamaican tody, the ubiquitous "doctor bird," and the Jamaican mango hummingbird are especially colorful species to look out for.

Reptiles

Jamaica has 26 species of lizards, including the island's largest, the iguana, now protected in the Helshire Hills and in slow recovery after near extinction due to slaughter by farmers and mongooses. The Anolis genus includes seven of the most common species, often seen in hotel rooms and on verandas, their showy throat fan extending to attract females. The largest Anolis is the garmani, which prefers large trees to human dwellings. All Jamaica's lizards are harmless.

Six of Jamaica's seven snake species are endemic, and all of them are harmless. Mostly found in remote areas like Cockpit Country, snakes have fallen victim to the fear of country folk who generally kill them on sight, and to the introduced mongoose, famous for its ability to win a fight with the cobras of its native India.

The island's largest snake is the yellow snake, with yellow and black patterns across its back. The snake is a boa constrictor, known locally as nanka, which can grow up to 3.5 meters in length. The nanka is seldom seen, as it is only active at night when it emerges from hiding to feed on bats and rats. Other less impressive snakes include three species of grass snake of the *Arrhyton* genus and the two-headed or worm snake *(Typhlops jamaicensis)*, which burrows below ground with its tail end virtually indistinguishable from its head. The black snake is considered an extinct victim of the mongoose.

Crocodiles are Jamaica's biggest reptiles, and are often referred to on the island as alligators. The American crocodile *(Crocodylus acutus)* is found across the island in swampy mangrove areas like Font Hill Wildlife Sanctuary and the Lower Black River Morass. This is the same species of croc found in Florida and other coastal wetlands of the Caribbean. Crocodiles have a long tapering snout whereas alligators have a short, flat head.

SEALIFE
Marine Mammals
Jamaica has no large native mammals on land. The largest mammals are instead marine-based, namely dolphins and manatees, the latter being known locally as sea cows. Manatees are endangered and now protected under wildlife laws after having seen their population dwindle due to hunting.

Turtles
Of the six sea turtle species known worldwide, four were once common, and now less so, in Jamaican waters: the green turtle *(Chelonia midas)*, the hawksbill *(Eretmochelys imbricata)*, the leatherback *(Dermochelys coriacea)*, and the loggerhead *(Caretta caretta)*. Turtle meat formed an important part of the diet of the Tainos, and was later adopted as a delicacy by the colonial settlers. In keeping with Taino practice, they kept green turtles in large coastal pens known as turtle crawles to be killed and eaten at will.

Responsible Tourism

The most important thing to remember in any visit to a foreign country is that your dollar is your most substantive demonstration of support. Jamaica is an expensive place to live by any measure and foreign currency is the chief economic driver. The benefit, or lack thereof, that tourism brings to the island is dependent on where the incoming dollars end up. Though rock-bottom, all-inclusive packages are an easy way to control your vacation spending, it should be noted that the money that flows to these groups is not widely distributed and typically ends up lining the pockets of a few individuals. What's more, large resorts often pay their workers a pittance.

Jamaica has gone through several different eras of tourism development dating back to the booming banana trade in the late 1800s. Up until the 1960s Jamaica remained a niche destination for the early yacht set, which later became the jet set. In the late 1960s and early 1970s the hippie movement discovered Jamaica and large groups would tour around on motorbikes, reveling in the laid-back lifestyle and plentiful herb. Montego Bay was the upscale destination on the island, with Port Antonio the playground of movie stars and Negril a newly discovered fishing beach only just connected by road to the rest of Hanover Parish. In those days the numbers of visitors were low and, outside Montego Bay, the environmental impact of tourism was negligible. Then came the all-inclusive resorts, the largest of which, Sunset Jamaica Grande, had 750 rooms by 2006. Since 2006, several new hotels have been built along the North Coast with over 1,000 rooms. The water resources required by these facilities puts a huge strain on the environment, as does wastewater, which is often poorly or minimally treated before being dumped into the sea. The enormous demand for food at these establishments generally is insufficiently met by local producers. These hotels cite inconsistency in the local market as a factor in their heavy reliance on imported goods.

Perhaps the best way to make a positive impact with a visit to Jamaica is by promoting "community tourism" by staying in smaller, locally run establishments and eating at a variety of restaurants rather than heeding the fear tactics that keep so many tourists inside gated hotels. Treasure Beach in St. Elizabeth parish is a mecca for community tourism, where the few mid-size hotels are far outnumbered by boutique guesthouses and villas, many of which are locally owned.

ENVIRONMENTAL ISSUES

In the past 10 years the Jamaican government has opened the country to an incursion from multinational hotel groups that are some of the most blatant culprits of environmental destruction. Ever-larger all-inclusive resorts are covering what were a few years ago Jamaica's remaining untouched stretches of coastline. The absence of beaches has not inhibited developers from making their own, at incalculable environmental costs to the protective coral reefs and marine life they support along much of the coast. When scuba diving and snorkeling along Jamaica's reefs, make your impact minimal by not touching the coral.

Bauxite Mining

The bauxite industry is an important foreign exchange earner for Jamaica but the environmental costs are clear. The Ewarton Aluminum Plant in St. Ann is noticeable from its stench for kilometers around and from the heights of Mandeville several bauxite facilities scar the

ENDANGERED FISHERIES

The spiny lobster is one of Jamaica's most prized culinary delicacies, often prepared either grilled, with garlic sauce, or with a curry sauce. Lobsters fetch a high price, usually somewhere between US$10 and US$20 per pound at local grills and restaurants, and as high as US$40 per plate in many tourist establishments. The sustainability of lobster harvesting depends on allowing the creatures a safe period for reproduction, which has been acknowledged in Jamaica by the Fisheries Division in the Ministry of Agriculture and Land with a ban on harvesting between April 1 and June 30. It is crucial that visitors to the island respect this ban and in so doing support efforts to ensure that lobster populations are kept at a sustainable level so the delicacy can continue to be enjoyed in the future. Some establishments serve what is said to be frozen lobster during the closed season. Regardless, it's best to avoid ordering it during this period to be on the safe side and avoid adding incentive to any potential shortfall of integrity on the part of restaurateurs and anglers. The Fishing Industry Act of 1975 makes it illegal to catch lobster during closed season and also puts a general ban on landing undersized lobster (under 76.2 mm, or 3 inches) and those bearing eggs, throughout the year. As the Fisheries department has struggled in recent years under financial constraints, it's imperative to be supportive in the effort to curb illegal harvesting. Conch (Strombus gigas) is also protected from over-fishing and has a closed season from July 1 through October 31.

Jamaican waters are also becoming severely over harvested where finned fish are concerned. It's best to avoid buying fresh fish smaller than six inches unless it's a type of fish that doesn't grow to a larger size. The median size of the catch brought in from traditional line fishing and spear fishing in waters close to Jamaica's shores has decreased noticeably over the past decade. The situation becomes clear when snorkeling along Jamaica's coastal reefs as few large fish can be seen today, and snapper, once common, are increasingly scarce near to the shoreline.

landscape. Discovery Bay and Ocho Rios have important export terminals, as does Port Kaiser in St. Elizabeth with another bauxite port in Clarendon. Bauxite interests seeking to mine in Cockpit Country are being met with stiff resistance from local stakeholders including the Southern Trelawny Environmental Association and the Jamaica Caves Organization.

Litter

Environmental education in Jamaica is seriously lacking. Environmental awareness has only recently been directly linked to the island's tourist economy by some of the more responsible tourism groups. The difference in sanitation and upkeep between the leisure destinations frequented principally by Jamaicans rather than foreign tourists is marked. Choice spots like Salt River in Clarendon are littered with trash, while other popular local spots like Bluefields Beach Park in Westmoreland make greater efforts to clean up after their patrons. Regardless of how senseless it may seem to take a green stance when it comes to litter in the face of gross negligence on the part of Jamaicans themselves, it's important to be aware of the fact that Jamaicans watch visitors very carefully: Make a point of not trashing the country, even if you seem to be up against insurmountable odds.

Water Table Salination

Several coastal areas suffer salination of the water table when water is extracted more rapidly than it is replenished. While Jamaica is blessed with high rainfall in the east and abundant hydrology generally, there will likely be an increasing problem in drier northwest coast areas where new all-inclusive resorts are being built. Wherever you end up staying, the best way to lessen your impact on finite water resources is by not taking long showers and by heeding the calls made at many of the more responsible and proactive hotels to reuse towels during your stay rather than throwing them on the floor after a single use for housekeeping personnel to deal with.

Deforestation

Despite the known harm it causes and the ensuing potential for erosion, slash-and-burn agriculture remains the predominant means of smallholder cultivation in rural area. While significant portions of land have been designated as protected areas across Jamaica, pressure on the environment, especially around tourism boom towns like Ocho Rios, where little planning preceded the influx of workers from other parishes, is leaving the water supply under threat and causing erosion where forest lands on steep inclines are cut for ramshackle housing settlements.

History

EARLY INHABITANTS AND SPANISH DISCOVERY

Jamaica was first inhabited by the Tainos, sometimes referred to as Arawaks, who arrived from the northern coast of South America in dugout canoes around A.D. 900. The Tainos practiced subsistence agriculture to complement hunting, fishing, and foraging activities, forming mostly seaside settlements from where travel by dugout canoe remained an important mode of transport.

Upon his arrival on the island in 1494, the Italian explorer Christopher Columbus claimed the island on behalf of his financiers King Ferdinand and Queen Isabella of Spain—in spite of the presence of a large Taino population with whom the Europeans engaged in an easily-won battle. The exact point of his arrival is contested; it is likely the explorer landed in Rio Bueno, on the border of present-day St. Ann and Trelawny, where there is freshwater, rather than in Discovery Bay, which was named Puerto Seco, or Dry Harbour, by Columbus because it lacked freshwater—something historical observers say would have influenced where the ships came ashore.

The Taino paintings at Mountain River Cave have been recognized by the Jamaica National Heritage Trust as part of the island's Taino patrimony.

Jamaica was not deemed very important for Spain due to its relatively rugged terrain, and more importantly for the lack of gold that became the obsession for the Spanish crown as they focused their exploits on Mexico and Central and South America. Neighboring Hispaniola had more gold and was thus deemed more worthwhile, while Cuba, 145 kilometers to the north, was also of more import as it was easily settled with vast arable flat lands and a strategic position as the key to the Gulf of Mexico. While Cuba became increasingly important as a transshipment point for gold and other goods from the New World to Europe, Jamaica remained a backwater left largely under the control of Columbus' heirs. Within 50 years of "discovery," the indigenous Taino population, estimated at as much as one million inhabitants at time of contact, was virtually annihilated through forced labor and more importantly, European diseases to which the natives had no immunological resistance.

Four early Spanish settlements are known to have been established at Melilla, somewhere on the North Coast, at Oristan, near present-day Bluefields, Westmoreland, at Spanish Town, which grew into the principal city of Santiago de la Vega, and in Yallahs, near the border of St. Andrew and St. Thomas today. These settlements were mainly focused on cattle ranching, while horse breeding was also an important endeavor. Jamaica became a regular provisions stop for Spanish galleons heading to Colombia, among other important gold coasts. While a few inland routes were carved out of the tropical jungle, transportation around the island remained almost entirely sea-based with the long and navigable Martha Brae River also becoming an important route between the North and South Coasts. The lack of a centralized strategy for settlement and defense left Jamaica extremely vulnerable to attack from other early colonial powers, ultimately leading to an easy takeover by Britain's naval forces led by Cromwell. While it was the Spanish who first brought many of plants that would become key to the islands economy in following centuries including banana, sugar cane, and indigo, it was the

British who created an organized plantation system key to their effective exploitation and the lucrative trade with Europe.

THE ENGLISH TAKEOVER

In 1655 English naval forces, led by Oliver Cromwell, invaded Jamaica and easily captured Spanish Town, the colonial rival's capital. The Spanish colony had virtually no defense strategy in place, a fact known and exploited by Cromwell, who distributed vast tracts of land to his fellow officers as a reward for their service. These land grants would form the first plantation estates of the British Colony. The former Spanish rulers were loathe to abandon the island, waging guerilla warfare and reprisal attacks on the British with the help of loyal Maroons, led by Ysassi. The Spanish fled to the North Coast or left the island altogether for Hispaniola or Cuba.

Soon after Cromwell's forces seized Jamaica, the British began a policy of legitimizing the activity of pirates—in effect gaining their allegiance in exchange for allowing them to continue their raids on mostly Spanish ships as privateers instead of buccaneers. The alliance made Port Royal at the tip of the Palisadoes in Kingston harbor into a boomtown, fueled by bustling trade in slaves and rum in addition to commerce in luxury goods, some imported from England and beyond, others plundered from victim ships.

While the slave trade had been established on the island under Spanish rule, it wasn't until the British set up vast, well-organized sugarcane plantations that slave labor was imported en masse from Africa. Jamaica became the Caribbean's primary transshipment point for slaves to other parts of the New World, including the United States.

PLANTATION CULTURE AND THE SLAVE TRADE

As an incentive to see Jamaica reach its full potential as a plantation colony, the British offered land not only to those who had been involved in the successful takeover, but also to Britons from England and other British colonies, most notably Barbados. Vast estates covered thousands of acres, with many absentee landowners installing overseers to take care of business on the island while reaping the benefits from quiet England. The cultivation of sugar expanded during the 1700s to the point where Jamaica was the world's foremost producer and England's prized colony. But the economic boom was far from equitable, relying heavily on a slave trade set up first by the Portuguese and later by the Dutch and English along the Gold Coast of Ghana and Slave Coast of Nigeria. Slavery was not a new phenomenon in Africa, but with the arrival of European traders it was formalized and raids into the interior began to supplement the prisoners of war who were first exported as slaves. The slaves brought to Jamaica were a mix of different ethnicities, including Coromantee, Ibo, Mandingo, Yoruba, and Congo. Slaves of different ethnic backgrounds and tongues were intentionally put together to complicate any potential resistance.

Slaves were not only used in the fields on the plantations, but also as domestic workers, carpenters, masons, and coopers.

Government and Economy

The Jamaican central government is organized as a constitutional monarchy and member of the British Commonwealth with Queen Elizabeth II as its official head of state. On the island, the Queen is represented by the governor general, who is a signatory on all legislation passed by the bicameral Jamaican Parliament. The bicameral government is comprised of a Senate and a House of Representatives, known as the Upper and Lower Houses, respectively. Representatives are elected for five-year terms, one from each of the island's 60 constituencies. Of Jamaica's 50 senators, 21 are appointed by the governor general, 13 on the advice of the prime minister, and eight by the opposition leader. The cabinet consists of the prime minister and a minimum of 13 other ministers, including the minister of finance, who must also be an elected representative in the house, with not more than four cabinet ministers selected from the members of the senate.

Beyond the national government, Jamaica has been organized into parishes of ecclesiastical origin since the arrival of the British, who installed the Church of England as their watchdog and pacifier. The Church of England later became the Anglican Church, whose rectories are still some of the most impressive buildings in the more rural areas across the island. The 60 federal constituencies are subdivided into 275 electoral units, each of which has a parish councillor in the local government. The Corporate Area, as metropolitan Kingston is known, combines the parishes of Kingston and St. Andrew into one local government entity known as the Kingston and St. Andrew Corporation.

Local representation dates to 1662 when the Vestry system was installed to manage local affairs across the island. The Vestry was composed of clergy members and lay magistrates of each parish and was in effect indistinguishable from the Church of England insomuch as governance and policy were concerned as it operated almost exclusively for the benefit of the landed elite. The amalgamated ruling class of the planters, clergy, and magistrates became known as the plantocracy. After 200 years of the Vestry system, it was abandoned in favor of a system of Municipal and Road Boards following the Morant Bay Rebellion in 1866. During the period when Jamaica was ruled by the Vestry system, the number of parishes increased from seven at the outset to 22 by the time it was abandoned. In 1867, the number of parishes was reduced to the 14 recognized today. In 1886, a new representational system of local government was installed consisting of Parochial Boards, which merged the operations of the Municipal and Road Boards into one entity. A general decentralization occurred during the intermittent period before the Parochial Boards were established, leaving local governments in charge of public health, markets, fire services, and water supply. Following implementation of the Parochial Board system, the oversight of building regulations, public beaches, sanitation, slaughterhouses, and streetlights was also assigned to the local government bodies.

Jamaica's political system is notoriously bureaucratic and corrupt, with little to suggest this will ever change—regardless of which party comes to power. Many say this is a legacy of British rule, but the fact that money is the chief motivator behind decision-making at Gordon House is generally acknowledged, with favoritism a rampant and accepted part of the political operations.

POLITICAL PARTIES AND ELECTIONS

Jamaica's two political parties, the People's National Party (PNP) and the Jamaica Labour Party (JLP) were founded by cousins Norman Manley and Alexander Bustamante. Bustamante was a labor leader who came to some degree of wealth through his travels around Latin America before exploiting anti-colonial sentiment of the day to push for greater worker rights and ultimately Jamaican independence. The PNP has held on to power since the 1980s with JLP representatives taking every opportunity to voice their opposition to PNP policies.

Election time tends to be tense and tumultuous in Jamaica when memories of political violence in the 1970s become fresh again. Kingston's poor neighborhoods bear the brunt of the tension and are often barricaded during elections to prevent opposition loyalists from entering with their vehicles to stage drive-by shootings.

ECONOMY

Jamaica's economy is supported by agriculture, bauxite, tourism, and remittances (in order of increasing importance). The financial sector is closely tied to other English-speaking Caribbean countries with large banks and insurance companies. Jamaica has a serious balance of payments problem owing to high external debt dating back several decades. Austerity measures imposed by IMF restructuring packages during the political reign of Edward Seaga left little money for education and social programs, a situation which persists today. Universal education has been the most tragic victim, with the quality of schools deteriorating since British rule while fees have steadily increased. Failure to provide universal education is the most serious shortfall of both political parties and has directly impacted productivity. The flip side of the coin sees the country's best educated leaving for higher-paid jobs overseas.

Agriculture

Agriculture remains an important part of Jamaica's economy, if not in sheer numbers then for its role in providing sustenance. The cultivation of provision grounds established during slavery persists to some degree in rural areas, where most households grow some time of crop, even if it is limited to a few mango and ackee trees. Sugar production is still ongoing on a handful of large estates across the country, some of them private, others government-owned, but the end of preferential pricing for Jamaican sugar in England has affected the

crops viability just as it ruined the prospects for Jamaica's banana crop. Apart from sugar, important export crops include coffee, the Blue Mountain variety fetching some of the highest prices in the world, and citrus including oranges and ugli fruit.

Mining

Bauxite mining and processing in Jamaica is done through a joint venture between the government and Alcoa called Jamalco. Jamaica remains one of the most important bauxite sources in the world, ranked third in production of bauxite ore and fourth in alumina production. The bauxite industry accounts for 75 percent of the country's export earnings. Other less important mineral resources found in Jamaica include gypsum, limestone, marble, silica sand, clay peat, lignite, titanium, copper, lead, and zinc.

Tourism

Tourism remains the primary focus of economic growth, even if the emphasis has been misplaced on mega projects that employ large numbers at low wages and take profits offshore. There seems to be little interest in seeing tourism dollars more evenly distributed among the population at large with the government seemingly happy to collect its 16 percent general consumption tax for each guest that passes through the mass-market all-inclusive resorts. Despite the government's lack of effort to see tourism revenue more widely distributed, entrepreneurial Jamaicans see great benefits from tourism with a slew of niche attractions having been created and developed to serve this market.

Remittances

As a percentage of GDP contributed by remittances, Jamaica is ranked seventh in the world and second in the Caribbean after the Dominican Republic—with nearly US$2 billion entering the country in 2006. The "Jamaican Dream" pursued by many who are able consists in leaving the country to pursue a career abroad for however long it takes to make it and come back to flex pretty. Sometimes the required time lasts generations. Jamaica is heavily dependent on expatriates, the majority of whom live in Toronto, New York, Florida, and London.

DISTRIBUTION OF WEALTH

Some say there are two Jamaicas, comprised of the haves and the have nots. But in fact there are many more Jamaicas. You don't need a whole lot of money to have a high quality of life when the hot sun is shining; mangos, ackee and breadfruit are ripe on the trees; and the rivers are pleasantly cool for bathing. So in a sense how you live is based on how close you are to the natural resources that make this a tropical paradise.

But land isn't free, fruit goes out of season, and some days it rains. More importantly, there is a serious cash-flow problem in Jamaica, and as they say, what little there is goes like water. The reality is that many Jamaicans don't find the time, let alone the resources, to travel around and enjoy tourism centers in the focused and intensive way foreigners tend to on their two-week vacation. With nearly half of the island's population living in the Corporate Area and nearby Spanish Town, there gets to be competition for things that might otherwise be picked from the tree. But more overwhelming than the price of local produce from the market are imports, which basically covers everything else. With jobs hard to come by for under-qualified youth, and even for qualified youth, there is a desperate situation for many, especially as everyday prices for groceries and other basic goods keep rising. Add in the fact that it is not uncommon for a man to have several children from more than one woman, and the role of what's termed "social capital" becomes clear. If it weren't for the way Jamaicans help each other out—whether by raising children belonging to a niece or nephew, or employing a man around the house who really doesn't do much gardening but clearly has no better prospects—Jamaica would find itself in a far worse state. But it is this cycle of too many mouths to feed with too little to go around that maintains a steep class divide on the island. Education costs money, for school fees, books, and uniforms; and with competing interests vying for the limited resources in many cash-strapped homes, school can take the back seat. Without a proper education, the youth become stuck doing menial jobs or nothing at all, and to "breed one gyal" (a common albeit crass way to say "get a girl pregnant") may be the most rosy thing going for them.

People and Culture

Jamaica's national motto, "out of many one people," reflects the tolerance and appreciation for diversity promulgated from an institutional level. Meanwhile individuals and communities comprising Jamaica's myriad ethnic groups keep old prejudices and stereotypes very much alive, usually without the slightest hint of malice but still with names that are likely considered derogatory in other parts of the world. "Coolie" is the term generally used to refer to East Indians, or those of Indian descent, "Chiney" for those of East Asian descent, and "Syrian" for anyone of Middle Eastern descent. If you find yourself the victim of this kind of stereotyping, try not to be offended. Ethnic divisions and cultural prejudices in Jamaica are a result of a history steeped in confrontation and oppression. Rarely, if ever, do these prejudices lead to conflict or violence. While racism is still very much a baffling reality in a country with such an overwhelming black majority, Jamaica's African heritage is celebrated in popular music enjoyed across social and economic classes.

RACE AND CLASS

Race in Jamaican society is and has been of utmost importance in maintaining the strict class structure historically, while in contemporary society everything boils down to money.

Nonetheless, complexion and ethnic background still often form the basis of an individual's perception of self and place in society. While the island has an overwhelming black majority, other minority groups play an important, even dominant role in the local economy. Chinese and Indians who were brought to the island as indentured labor following the abolition of slavery became and remain prominent members of society as shopkeepers and traders, even in the smaller communities. Lebanese-Jamaicans have also played a significant role in business as well as in national politics. White Jamaicans still own some of the most beautiful and expansive estates. The British established the precedent of "complexionism" by putting lighter-skinned, or "brown," Jamaicans—often their own errant progeny—in managerial positions, a self-perpetuating phenomenon that continues today in the nepotism that pervades the political and economic elite. The Maroons, who initially put up fierce resistance to the British colonial government and forced a treaty giving them autonomy and freedom from slavery long before abolition, have been an important source of pride for Jamaicans, even while the issue of their collaboration with the British in suppressing slave rebellions remains somewhat of a cultural taboo.

RELIGION

Jamaica holds the Guinness record for most churches per capita. Virtually every religion and denomination on earth is represented on the island, with churches everywhere you turn. A common sight on weekends is large tents set up across the countryside for the open-air services preferred by the evangelical denominations. Only those churches that are unique to Jamaica or have played an important role in the country's history have been described, with listings in the destination chapters for those of historical or architectural significance.

Revival

Born as a distinctly Jamaican fusion between Christian and African beliefs during the Great Revival of 1860–1861, Revival today is composed of two different branches: Pukkumina (Pocomania or Poco) and Revival Zion, the former being further towards the African end of the merged spectrum, the latter incorporating more obviously Christian beliefs and practices. Revivalists wear colorful robes and turbans during energetic ceremonies during which trance-like states are reached with drumming singing and a wheeling dance that is said to induce possession by spirits. Revival has its roots in the Native Baptist and Myal movements that lie at the margins of Jamaica's more prominent Anglican and Baptist churches. Baptist churches were early venues for the emersion of what would become known as the Revival faith. Morant Bay rebellion leader Paul Bogle's church in Stony Gut was one such Native Baptist church where elements of African worship were incorporated into more typical Baptist practice. Today Revival is closely associated with the Pentecostal denomination and practitioners will generally attend one of the established churches in addition to observing Revival practices.

Core to Revival philosophy is the inseparability of the spirit and physical worlds. It is based on this belief that Revivalists can be possessed and influenced by ancestral spirits. Revivalists reinterpreted the Christian theme of the Father, the Son, and the Holy Spirit, placing emphasis on the latter, which manifests as the "Messenger" attending services and possessing believers.

Baptist Church

Significant in Jamaica for its role in fomenting abolitionist sentiment and fueling revolt, the Baptist church was first brought to the island by a freed American slave, Reverend George Liele, in 1738. Liele was baptized in Savannah, Georgia, before receiving a preacher's license and being ordained a minister. He brought his ministerial prowess to Jamaica, where he attracted large numbers of converts with his abolitionist sentiment that would prove indispensable in firstly attracting followers and ultimately in bringing about emancipation with the help of the British Baptist Mission, which arrived on the island in 1814. After emancipation the Baptist Church was instrumental in organizing the free villages that allowed the former slaves a new start after leaving the plantation and the church was also important in promoting education among the former slaves. Three of Jamaica's seven national heroes were Baptists, including rebellion leaders Sam Sharpe and Paul Bogle. Today Baptists remain one of Jamaica's strongest religious groups following their separation from the British Baptists in 1842.

Hinduism

Brought by indentured Indians, Hinduism is still practiced across the island but maintains an extremely low profile within tight-knit and economically stable Indian communities. There is a temple on Maxfield Avenue in Kingston that holds regular service on Sundays.

Judaism

The first Jews arrived in Jamaica early in the colonial period during the Spanish inquisition, when they were expelled by King Ferdinand and Queen Isabella and found refuge in Jamaica—in spite of not being officially allowed in the Spanish colonies. Many of these Jews outwardly converted to Catholicism while continuing to practice their own religion in secret. When the British arrived in 1655 to capture the island from the Spanish, they were aided by the Jews, who were subsequently free to practice their religion openly after the conquest. Sephardic Jews of Spanish, Portuguese, and North African descent were the first arrivals, followed in the 1770s by Ashkenazi who left Germany and Eastern Europe.

Ethiopian Orthodox Church

Brought to Jamaica in 1972, the Ethiopian Orthodox Church was the official state church of Ethiopia. Following Selassie's visit to the island in 1966, he instructed the establishment of a church in Kingston in an attempt to legitimize the Rastafarians with a bona fide institution. Many Rastafarians were drawn to the church, even while it does not recognize Selassie as a divine person beyond his own affiliation with the church and the divinity that would convey.

Obeah

Essentially the Jamaican version of Voodoo, Obeah plays an important role in Jamaica, evoking fear even among those who don't believe in it. The mysticism and use of natural concoctions that help bridge the physical and spiritual worlds has similar African roots as the Santeria or Voodoo found in neighboring Cuba and Haiti. While there are few who practice Obeah as priests or worshippers, it is a widespread phenomenon evidenced by markings and charms strewn about many Jamaican homes.

Rastafari

The name of Ethiopian Emperor Haile Selassie I prior to his coronation was Ras Tafari, Ras meaning Prince, and Tafari Makonnen his given name at birth. When Leonard Howell, a Jamaican follower of Marcus Garvey, saw Ras Tafari Makonnen crowned His Imperial Majesty Emperor Haile Selassie I on November 2, 1930, he viewed the coronation as the fulfillment of biblical prophecy, more so given the emperor's title, King of Kings, Lord of Lords, Conquering Lion of Tribe of Judah. The original prophecy that foretold of a black man rising in the East is attributed to black nationalist and Jamaican national hero Marcus Garvey, who had written a play performed in support of his movement in the United States where the now-famous line, "look to the East for the crowning of a black king" was supposedly gleaned from. It is interesting to note that Garvey never viewed Selassie as a god or claimed his coronation a fulfillment of prophecy at any point during his turbulent life, but this did not stop Leonard Howell from making the proclamation, which then fell upon eager ears among his own followers in rural Jamaica and sparked a global movement that continues to grow today.

Leonard Howell chose an opportune time to proclaim Selassie's divinity. Disillusionment by the masses of blacks descended from slaves was high in the 1920s and 1930s, fueling Jamaica's labor movement and the establishment of the two political parties. The Harlem Renaissance of the 1920s gave blacks in the United States a confidence that was exported to the Caribbean in the form of bold ideas that came to a people that never really forgot Africa. Thanks to the important role Jamaica's Maroons played in preserving African belief systems, and the persistence of Revivalist and Obeah religious practices even within the many Christian denominations that were established on the island, select segments of the Jamaican population were well primed for the proposition that the divine had manifested in an African king. Nevertheless, these select segments were predominantly poor blacks, essentially social outcasts seen as the "dreads of society." Dread locks, as the hairstyle became known to the chagrin of many adherents, who scorn the fear and criminality the term "dread" implies, predates the Rasta movement and was effectively a natural occurrence for those who neglected to use a comb. With the conversion to the Rastafarian philosophy among many up-and-coming reggae musicians during the 1960s and 1970s, the faith gained traction in Jamaica, and as the island's music became an increasingly important export, Rasta soon became almost synonymous with reggae and the philosophy spread around the world.

The Rastafarian movement can be traced directly to the recognition of the divinity of Selassie upon his coronation in 1930, but most Rastafarians assert their faith is far more ancient, going back at least to the Nazarenes mentioned in the Old Testament from whence they derive their aversion to razors and scissors, as well as to the eating of flesh. King Selassie has become the head of the movement by default as the most recent manifestation of divinity on earth, despite his own disagreement with being viewed as a God. But the line is traced straight back to the divine theocracy of the Old Testament, Selassie himself said to be the 225th descendant of King Solomon and the Queen of Sheba. Rastafarians essentially claim the Hebrew lineage as their own and have reinterpreted the Old Testament by identifying Africans as the Israelites of modern times, having

been enslaved just like the Jews in Babylon. In effect, Rastafarians espouse a natural lifestyle free of the contamination and corruption of modern society. Repatriation to Africa, whether spiritual or physical, forms a central theme.

Along the movement's course of development, charismatic leaders carved out the many "houses," or denominations, that can be found today across the island, including the Nyabinghi, Bobo Ashanti, and the Twelve Tribes of Israel.

The Nyabinghi evoke the warrior spirit of the African empress Iyabinghi; drum ceremonies that last for days around important dates are a central feature.

The Bobo Ashanti, or Bobo Shanti, is a group based at Bobo Hill in Nine Mile just east of Kingston along the coast. The Bobo live a ritualized lifestyle away from society putting emphasis on the teaching of Marcus Garvey and founder Prince Emmanuel. Themes of self-reliance and self-confidence are central to the Bobo philosophy. The group has gained as converts many contemporary dancehall reggae musicians including Sizzla and Capleton.

Perhaps the most international house of Rastafari is the Twelve Tribes of Israel founded by the late Vernon Carrington, known by his brethren as Brother Gad. Members of the Twelve Tribes are found across the world with the denomination having crossed social and economic barriers more than other houses perhaps due to its Christian lean. The Twelve Tribes of Israel embraces Christianity and views Haile Selassie I as representing the spirit of Christ.

Another important force within the Rastafarian movement has been that of Abuna, or Rasta priest, Ascento Fox, who has made strong inroads in society by establishing churches in Kingston, London, and New York. These churches are used as a base for maintaining a presence in the community and providing an alternative for convicts in the prison systems, where the group does a lot of work.

Rastafarians in Jamaica and "in foreign" (abroad) are viewed with a combination of respect and fear to this day. Many Rasta colloquialisms have become everyday parlance in Jamaican society as reggae music grew to a global force recognized and appreciated far beyond the Caribbean, with phrases like "one love," "blessed," and "irie" used commonly even by those who don't claim the faith as their own. Use of marijuana, or ganja, has been legitimized to some degree in society at large thanks to the important role it plays for Rastas as a sacrament, even while the ubiquitous herb remains officially prohibited.

LANGUAGE

In Jamaica, free speech is held as one of the foremost tenets of society. Nevertheless, using the wrong language in the wrong place can cause scorn, embarrassment, or even murder, and knowing how to speak under the given circumstances defines a Jamaican's identity and the reveals the layers of a highly classist society. Language use ranges from thick patois to the most eloquent of the Queen's English, and generally suggests to which tier of society the speaker belongs. Nevertheless, those raised in Jamaica to speak an impeccable form of English will often flip in mid-conversation to outwardly unintelligible patois. The rich flavor of Jamaica's language is the most apparent expression of feverous pride based on a 400-year struggle that spanned the country's anti-slavery, black power, and independence movements. The rise of the island as a cultural hotspot owes not disparagingly to the influence of Indians, Lebanese,

Syrians, Jews, and Chinese, and a remaining smattering of the old white plantocracy.

SEXUAL RELATIONSHIPS AND FAMILY LIFE

Uncommitted sexual relationships are commonplace in Jamaica, for both men and women, and particularly among those at the lower end of the economic spectrum. It takes little more than a visit to a nightclub to understand that women and men are quite comfortable flirting and flaunting their sexuality in a light-hearted game played out on a daily basis. The exchange of money is very common in relationships, where a man will often support, or "mind" his mistress by giving her money and buying her things. This regular occurrence offers no disincentive for a woman to keep a number of such suitors, just as it relieves the man of any need to keep the fact that he's married with kids a secret from his mistresses.

Prostitution, although it is illegal, is widespread in Jamaica and most conspicuous in tourist areas. In Negril especially, and to a lesser extent in Ocho Rios, prostitution is heavily solicited to tourists. It is quite common for Jamaican men and women to maintain a handful of steady relationships with repeat visitors who live abroad and support their romantic interest by sending regular money wires.

The Arts

MUSICAL HERITAGE

Music has been an integral element of Jamaican society for centuries—from use of song on the plantation to mitigate the torturous work, to funeral rituals that combine Christian and African elements in the traditional nine nights. Most of the instruments used in Jamaica have been borrowed or adapted from either European or African traditions, while some Taino influence surely occurred before their cultural annihilation.

Today music remains as important and central to Jamaican culture as ever. From the

beach resorts to the rural hills, sound systems blare out on weekends into the early dawn hours with a wide variety of genres appreciated on the airwaves.

Jonkunnu

Pronounced "John Canoe," Jonkunnu is a traditional music and skit-like dance performed primarily at Christmas, the Jonkunnu rhythm is played in 2/2 or 4/4 on the fife, a rattling drum with sticks, bass, and grater. Dancers wear costumes and masks representing characters like Pitchy Patchy, King, Queen, Horsehead, Cow-head, and Belly Woman that act out skits and dance.

The origin of Jonkunnu is revealed in the word's etymology: Jonkunnu is an adaptation of the Ghanaian words *dzon'ko* (sorcerer) *nu* (man), derived from secret societies found on the African mainland. Among the costumes found in Jonkunnu are pieced-together sacks similar to those seen in the Abakua, a secret society in neighboring Cuba that also uses dance and drumming.

In Jamaica, Jonkunnu became associated with Christmas time likely because it was the only real holiday for the slaves in the whole year, during which they would tour the plantation with their music, dance, and skits, typically with headgear consisting of ox horns. At the height of the British colonial period, plantation owners actively encouraged Jonkunnu and it took on European elements, including satire of the masters, and Morris dance jigs and polka steps. The importance of Jonkunnu declined as it was replaced by the emergence of "set girls" who would dance about to display of their beauty and sexual rivalry. Later following emancipation, non-conformist missionaries suppressed Jonkunnu and the mayor of Kingston banned the Jonkunnu parade in 1841, leading to riots. In the years leading up to Jamaican independence, as the country's cultural identity was being explored, Jonkunnu gained the support of the government, which still sponsors the folk form in annual carnival and Jamaica Cultural Development Commission events.

Kumina

The most distinctly African of Jamaica's musical forms, Kumina was brought to Jamaica after emancipation by indentured laborers from Congo and remains a strong tradition in Portland and St. Thomas. Kumina ceremonies are often held for wakes and burials, as well as for births and anniversaries and involve drumming and dancing.

Mento

Jamaica's original folk music, mento is a fusion of African and European musical elements played with a variety of instruments that as the genre developed were borrowed from plantation owners and fashioned by the slaves themselves. A variety of instruments have a place in mento, from stick and hand drums to stringed instruments, flutes, and brass. Mento was one of the most important foundations for reggae.

Reggae

Most people know Jamaica by its legendary son, Bob Marley. Marley brought international attention to the island, now popularly known as Jam Rock thanks to the Grammy-winning album of his youngest son Damian, or "Junior Gong." Yet apart from Marley, Jamaica's music has had limited impact beyond the country's expatriate communities in London, New York, and Miami. Only recently has dancehall reggae become mainstream internationally, thanks in part to crossover artist Sean Paul, who took hip-hop charts by storm with his 2003 hit, "Gimme the Light." The genre has its roots in the ska and rocksteady of the 1950s and 1960s, when radio brought American popular music to Jamaican shores and the country's creative musicians began to adapt American tunes to an indigenous swing.

After a decade of slackness in reggae during the late 1980s and early 1990s, several talented artists have managed to capitalize on a resurgence of conscious music by launching successful careers as "cultural" reggae artists in the one-drop sub-genre, sometimes using original musical tracks, sometimes singing on one of the more popular rhythms of the day. These include I-Wayne who came out with a huge hit critiquing the prostitution lifestyle with "Can't Satisfy Her" and the conscious tune, "Living in Love" on his 2005 breakout album *Lava Ground*. Richie Spice pays tribute to his ghetto roots with "Youth Dem Cold," an immensely popular hit. Chuck Fenda's "Gash Dem and Light Dem," released in 1995 and banned on the radio is still reverberating years later. Luciano, Capleton and Buju Banton top the pack of contemporary conscious reggae artists while roots artists like Jimmy Cliff, Toots and the Maytals, Burning

Spear, Israel Vibration, Third World, and Freddie McGregor continue to perform and churn out the occasional album. In 2006, Joseph Hill of the seminal reggae group Culture passed away while on tour in Germany, leaving the masses to mourn back home in Jamaica. Another artist of note is Tanya Stephens, whose eloquent lyrics are being appreciated around the globe following the success of her 2006 *Rebelution* release.

Dub, a form of remixed reggae that drops out much of the lyrics, was an offshoot of roots reggae pioneered by King Tubby and others, that led to the dub poetry genre whose best known artists include Mutabaruka and Linton Kwesi Johnson. The most accomplished new artist of the dub-poetry genre is DYCR, whose 2005 hit, "Chop Bush," won fans everywhere.

Dancehall

Clearly the most popular genre of music in Jamaica today, dancehall refers to the venue where it was born. Dancehall is a loose term, however, that has spilled out into the street, where the street dance is today the dancehall of yesteryear. Voicemail, Busy Signal, Movado, Vybz Kartel, Tony Matterhorn, Elephant Man, and Vegas have led the pack in popularity and influence in modern dancehall, while Beenie Man has well-established himself as the "King of Dancehall." Macka Diamond is a tremendously popular female artist whose raucous and raunchy lyrics have garnered fans, while her veteran counterpart Lady Saw maintains her top ranking as Jamaica's favorite female performer.

FINE ART

The Jamaican art world can be classified broadly into folk artists, schooled artists, and self-taught, or intuitive artists. Folk art has been around throughout Jamaica's history as far back as the Tainos, whose cave paintings can still be seen in a few locations on the island. European and African arrivals brought a new mix, with the planter class often commissioning works from visiting European portrait painters, while enslaved Africans carried on a wide range of traditions from their homeland, which included wood carving, fashioning musical instruments, and creating decorative masks and costumes for traditional celebrations like Jonkunnu. The annual Hosay celebrations, which date to the mid-1800s in Jamaica, as well as Maroon ceremonies, are considered living art. Folk art had a formative influence on Jamaica's intuitive artists.

The century after full emancipation in 1938 saw deep structural changes and growing pains for Jamaica, first as a colony struggling to maintain order and then more tumultuous years leading up to independence. Jamaican art as a concerted discipline arose in the late 1800s, and culminated with the establishment of formal training in 1940. In the early years, sculpture and painting reflected the mood of a country nursing fresh wounds of slavery, with progressive, renegade leaders and indigenous Revival and then Rastafari movements giving substance to the work of self-taught artists.

Edna Manley, wife of Jamaica's first prime minister, Norman Manley, is credited with formally establishing a homegrown Jamaican art scene. An accomplished artist herself, Edna Manley was born in England in 1900 to a Jamaican mother and English father and schooled at English art schools. On arrival in Jamaica, Manley was influenced by Jamaica's early intuitive sculptors like David Miller Sr. and David Miller Jr., Alvin Marriot, and Mallica Reynolds, a revival bishop better known as "Kapo." Edna Manley's 1935 sculpture *Negro Aroused* captured the mood of an era characterized by cultural nationalization where Afro-centric imagery and the establishment and tribulations of a black working class were often the focus. Manley began teaching formal classes in 1940 at the Junior Center of the Institute of Jamaica giving the structure necessary for the emergence of a slew of Jamaican painters including Albert Huie, David Pottinger, Ralph Campbell, and Henry Daley. Her school later developed into the Jamaica School of Art and Crafts, which was ultimately absorbed by Edna Manley College. Several other artists, who did not come out of Edna Manley's school, gained prominence in the early period, including Carl

Abrahams, Gloria Escofferey, and John Dunkley. Dunkley's works consistently use somber shades and clean lines with dark symbolism reflective of serious times, making them immediately recognizable.

Jamaican fine arts exploded in the fervent post-independence years along with the country's music industry, fueling the expansion of both the National Gallery as well as a slew of commercial galleries, many of which still exist in Kingston today. The post-independence period counts among its well-recognized artists Osmond Watson, Milton George, George Rodney, Alexander Cooper, and David Boxer. Black Nationalism and the exploration of a national identity remained important topics for artists like Omari Ra and Stanford Watson, while many other artists like the ubiquitous Ras Dizzy or Ken Abendana Spencer gained recognition during the period for the sheer abundance of their work, much of which celebrated Jamaica's rural landscape. In the late 1970s, the National Gallery launched an exhibition series called "The Intuitive Eye," which brought mainstream recognition to Jamaica's self-taught artists as key contributors to the development of Jamaican art. Some of the artists to gain exposure and wider recognition thanks to "The Intuitive Eye" series include William "Woody" Joseph, Gason Tabois, Sydney McLaren, Leonard Daley, John "Doc" Williamson, William Rhule, Errol McKenzie, and Allan "Zion" Johnson.

The Institute of Jamaica together with its various divisions continues to bring new exhibition space into use, notably opening a gallery in late 2006 on the top floor of the Natural History building where a very successful photo exhibit on the 1907 earthquake that ravaged Kingston was staged.

CRUCIAL REGGAE

The following selections are not intended as an exhaustive list of reggae releases, but are a few essentials for any reggae fan's collection and some of the author's favorites.

In the United States, the best source for reggae albums is Ernie B's, which has an excellent online catalogue of full albums and singles (www.ebreggae.com).

ROOTS

Abyssinians	*Satta Massagana*
Augustus Pablo	*King Tubbys Meets Rockers Uptown*
Black Uhuru	*Ironstorm*
Bunny Wailer	*Blackheart Man*
Burning Spear	*Marcus Garvey, Live in Paris*
Cocoa Tea	*One Cup*
The Congos	*Heart of the Congos*
Culture	*Two Sevens Clash*
Dennis Brown	*Revolution, Milk and Honey*
Desmond Decker	*Israelites*
Ernest Ranglin	*Below The Baseline*
Ethiopians	*All the Hits*
Freddie McGregor	*Bobby Babylon*
George Nooks	*Tribal War*
Gladiators	*Dreadlocks, the Time Is Now*
Gregory Isaacs	*Night Nurse*
Half Pint	*Half Pint*
I Jah Man	*Marcus Hero*
Israel Vibration	*Power of the Trinity*
Jimmy Cliff	*Wonderful World Beautiful People, Harder They Come* (various artists)
John Holt	*Stealin'/Ali Baba*

Cultural roots reggae icon Luciano performs at Portland Allfest at Somerset Falls in March 2007.

© OLIVER HILL

Junior Murvin	*Police and Thieves*
Ken Booth	*Everthing I Own,*
	Best of Ken Boothe
Lee Scratch Perry	*Roast Fish Collie Weed*
	& Corn Bread
Leroy Sibbles	*It's Not Over*
Max Romeo and	*War Ina Babylon*
the Upsetters	
Maxi Priest	*Best of Me*
Melodians	*Swing and Dine*
Morgan Heritage	*Family & Friends,*
	Protect Us Jah
Paragons	*Best of*
Peter Tosh	*Legalize It, Equal Rights*
Rita Marley	*Who Feels It Knows It*
Sugar Minott	*Inna Reggae Dancehall*
Third World	*96° in the Shade*
Tony Rebel	*If Jah*
Toots and	*Pressure Drop*
the Maytals	
Wailers	*Exodus, Burnin, Natty*
	Dread, Songs of Freedom

CONTEMPORARY ONE DROP

Anthony B	*Universal Struggle*
Bushman	*Higher Ground*
Capleton	*More Fire, Still Blazin*
Chuck Fenda	*The Living Flame*
Damian Marley	*Half Way Tree,*
	Welcome to Jamrock
Fanton Mojah	*Haile H.I.M.*
Garnett Silk	*Gold*
Gentleman	*Confidence, Intoxication*
Gyptian	*My Name is Gyptian*
I-Wayne	*Lava Ground*
Jah Cure	*Freedom Blues*
Jah Mason	*Wheat and Tear*
Junior Kelly	*Love So Nice, Tough Life*

Luciano	*Messenger*
Lutan Fyah	*Phantom War*
Perfect	*Bobbylon Bwoy*
Richie Spice	*In the Streets to Africa*
Sanchez	*One In A Million*
Sizzla	*Praise Ye Jah,*
	Da Real Thing
Tanya Stephens	*Gangsta Blues, Rebelution*
Turbulence	*Notorious*
VC	*By His Deeds* (single)
Warrior King	*Virtuous Woman*

EARLY DANCEHALL

Shabba Ranks	*As Raw as Ever*
Yellowman	*King Yellowman*

CONTEMPORARY DANCEHALL

Beenie Man	*From Kingston to King,*
	Undisputed
Bounty Killer	*Nah No Mercy:*
	The Warlord Scrolls
Busy Signal	*Step Out*
Lady G	*God Daughter*
Lady Saw	*Strip Tease*
Macka Diamond	*Money-O*
Mr. Vegas	*Heads High,*
	Hot Wuk (single)
Ms. Thing	*Miss Jamaica*
Red Rat	*Oh No It's Red Rat*
Sean Paul	*The Trinity*
Shaggy	*Mr. Lover Lover*
T.O.K.	*Unknown Language*
Tanto Metro	*Musically Inclined*
& Devonte	
Tony Matterhorn	*Dutty Whine* (single)
Voicemail	*Hey*
Vybez Kartel	*Up 2 Di Time*

ANNUAL EVENTS

revellers during the Bacchanal carnival festivities at Mas Camp in Kingston

JANUARY

Accompong Maroon Festival: (Jan. 5 and 6), Accompong, St. Elizabeth

Rebel Salute: (second Sat. in Jan.), Port Kaiser Sports Park, St. Elizabeth

Bacchanal J'ouvert: (launch second Fri. in Jan., each subsequent Fri. till Easter), Mas Camp, Kingston

FEBRUARY

Bob Marley's Birthday: (Feb. 6-12), Bob Marley Museum, Kingston and Nine Mile, St. Ann

Miss Jamaica Universe Competiton (first week in Feb.), Pulse Entertainment, Kingston

Fat Tire Festival: (Feb. 8-11), Ocho Rios, St. Ann

Fi Wi Sinting: (third Sun. in Feb.), Natures Way, Portland

Follow Di Arrow: (last Sat. in Feb.), James Bond Beach, Oracabessa, St. Mary

MARCH

Portland All Fest: (Sun. in mid-March), Somerset Falls, Hope Bay, Portland

Spring Orchid Show (last weekend in March), Assembly Hall, UWI Mona, Kingston

Bacchanal Beach J'ouvert: (March 22), James Bond Beach, Oracabessa, St. Mary

Bacchanal J'ouvert: (last Fri. of March), Mas Camp, Kingston

Bacchanal Road March: (last Sun. in March), Oxford Road, Kingston

APRIL

Luau (first Sat. in April), Reggae Beach, Tower Isle, St. Mary

J'ouvert: (first or second Sun. in April), Chukka Cove, St. Ann

Trelawny Yam Festival: (mid-April), Albert Town, Trelawny

Kite Festival: (Easter Monday), Seville Heritage Park, St Ann's Bay, St. Ann

Claremont Kite Festival: (Easter Saturday), Claremont, St. Ann

Jake's Annual Triathlon: (Second weekend in Apr.), Treasure Beach, St. Elizabeth

MAY

Belmont Crab Fest: (last Sunday in May), Belmont Marina, Belmont, Westmoreland

Take Me Away: (last Sunday in May), National Indoor Arena, Kingston

Calabash Literary Festival: (last weekend in May), Jake's, Treasure Beach, St. Elizabeth

Style Week: (last week in May), Kingston

JUNE
Caribbean Fashion Week: (second weekend in June), National Stadium, Kingston

Ocho Rios Jazz Festival: (second week in June), Ocho Rios, St. Ann

Epicurean Escape: (last weekend in June), Grand Lindo Negril, Westmoreland

JULY
International Reggae Day: (July 1), Kingston

Portland Jerk Festival: (first Sun. in July), Folly Oval, Port Antonio, Portland

Bling Dawg Summer Jam, Portland: (mid-July), Somerset Falls, Hope Bay, Portland

Reggae Sumfest: (third week in July), Montego Bay, St. James

Breadfruit Festival: Bath, St. Thomas

Emancipation Jubilee: (July 31), Seville Heritage Park, St Ann's Bay, St. Ann

Denbigh Agricultural Show: (third weekend in July), May Pen, Clarendon

Little Ochie Seafood Festival: (mid-July), Alligator Pond, St. Elizabeth

AUGUST
Emancipation Day: (Aug. 1), island-wide, festivities most pronounced in Negril and Kingston

Independence Day: (Aug. 6), island-wide, festivities most pronounced in Negril and Kingston

St. Mary Mi Come From: (first Sat. in Aug.), St. Mary

Bussu Festival: (second weekend in Aug.), Swift River, near Hope Bay, Portland

Cure Fest: (Aug. 24-26), Kingston and North Coast

Fully Loaded: (third week in Aug.), James Bond Beach, Oracabessa, St. Mary

Miss Jamaica World Competition: (third Sat. in Aug.), Kingston

Jamaica Cultural Development Competitions: (all month), Kingston

SEPTEMBER
Freshers Fete (second weekend in Sept.) UWI Mona, Kingston

OCTOBER
Best of Jamaica Heritage Festival: (first week in Oct.) Grand Lido Braco, Rio Bueno, Trelawny

Port Royal Seafood Festival: (second weekend in Oct.), Port Royal, St. Andrew

Old Harbour Fish & Bammy Festival: (second Sun. in Oct.), JPSCO Sports Club, Old Harbour, St. Catherine

World Championship of Dominoes: (third weekend in Oct.), Holiday Inn Sunspree, Rose Hall, Montego Bay

International Marlin Tournament: (third Saturday in Oct.), Port Antonio, Portland

NOVEMBER
Season of Dance: (all month), Movements Dance Company, Kingston

Kingston Restaurant Week: (mid-Nov.), Kingston

DECEMBER
Reggae Marathon: (first Sun. in Dec.), Negril, Westmoreland

East Fest: (Dec. 26), Goodyear Oval, Morant Bay, St. Thomas

Pepsi Teen Splash: (Dec. 26), James Bond Beach, Oracabessa, St. Mary

Sting: (Dec. 26), Jam World, Portmore, St. Catherine

ESSENTIALS

Getting There and Around

ARRIVING BY AIR

Regular airlines from the United States and Canada into Kingston's **Norman Manley International Airport** include Air Jamaica, Air Canada, American, Delta, Continental, and US Airways. Budget carrier Spirit flies once a day from major U.S. cities with all flights connecting through Fort Lauderdale, Florida.

Virgin Atlantic recently started direct service from London into Montego Bay with connections on Air Jamaica into Kingston.

Within the Caribbean, British West Indies Airways (BWIA) offers service to St. Kitts, Barbados, and St. Lucia while Cayman Airways and International AirLink also offer regional service. Copa is the best airline from Latin America, with service connecting through Panama City from most countries in Central and South America.

Sangster Airport in Montego Bay remains the most popular entry point for visitors to Jamaica. The arduous lines common in Kingston, where several flights land within a short time period, are thankfully absent.

Most accommodations can provide transportation from either airport, and the more remote accommodations often make an extra effort to help provide transportation to guests.

ARRANGING TRANSPORTATION

Public transportation is readily available and very affordable for those who are patient and adventurous. Buses run between major cities and towns, and route taxis run between even the smallest villages and their closest transport hubs. The inevitable drawbacks include blaring music, long waits, ripe body odor, and reckless drivers. Car rentals, JUTC charters, and internal flights are expensive, but well worth it under the right circumstances. Nothing compares with the freedom of a rental car, and for two or more people looking to explore the island, it can be affordable and indispensable. Many visitors are thrown off by the fact that traffic circulates on the left, and if that weren't confusing enough to pose a challenge, abundant, deep potholes leave little time to enjoy the scenery when also dodging the ubiquitous white route taxis careening around almost every corner.

Chartering a car is also very expensive; the standard rate of US$60 for the one-hour trip between Montego Bay and Negril is a good indication of typical charges island-wide. An excellent and affordable bus service, the Knutsford Express, runs twice daily between Kingston and Montego Bay (US$17 one-way booked a day in advance, or US$20 if booked the same day). Apart from the multiple internal flights that service the route for about three times the price (US$70), the bus service is the best option. Public buses and route taxis are the mass transport option used by most Jamaicans who don't have their own vehicle.

PUBLIC TRANSPORTATION

It can be challenging to get around Jamaica via public transportation and you will likely arrive at your destination a bit frazzled by the congested route taxis and buses, dangerously fast driving, and the inevitably loud R&B or dancehall blasting from the speakers. It's important to keep reminding yourself that this is all part of Jamaica's charm.

In and around Kingston, the public bus system is very functional—with bus stops along all the main roads and inexpensive fares based on the distance you travel along the route.

Route Taxis

Arriving with luggage or backpacks to hike up to the road and hail down a route taxi is perfectly feasible in Jamaica, even if it does make the locals laugh at you. Most taxis will want to give you a charter, however, when you are carrying luggage, and others won't stop. This makes getting a licensed taxi a good idea.

Route taxis are typically white Toyota Corolla station wagons with the origin and destination painted in small letters on the side by the front doors. These cars can be flagged down from the side of the road anywhere along their route and when not operating as route taxis will generally offer private charters at greatly inflated rates. Haggling is a must when chartering a car, while routes have fixed rates that are not typically inflated for tourists except in highly touristy areas like Negril or Ocho Rios.

Internal Flights

A few airlines operate internal flights around the island that are an affordable option between Kingston and Montego Bay if time is of concern (US$70 per person). Routes to smaller, less trafficked destinations are significantly higher priced, but for an extended stay with a small group, a charter from Negril to Port Antonio can make perfect sense.

RENTING A CAR

For those who can afford it and have the confidence and experience, a rental car is by far the best way to get around the island for several reasons, the most important being independence. However, rentals are expensive by international standards and you should expect to pay at least US$60 per day for a compact car, plus insurance and fuel. Options for different car rental agencies are included in the destination chapters.

Visas and Officialdom

As of January 2007, American citizens require a passport to reenter the United States after visiting Jamaica as part of a campaign to bolster security. Americans and EU citizens do not require a visa to enter Jamaica, and can stay for up to six months, although the actual length of stay stamped into your passport will be determined by the customs agent upon entry. For extensions, visit the immigration office in Half Way Tree (25 Constant Spring, 876/906-4402 or 876/906-1304).

EMBASSIES AND CONSULATES

Britain 28 Trafalgar Road, Kingston 10, tel. 876/510-0700, fax 876/511-0737, bhckingston@cwjamaica.com (general), consular.kingston@fco.gov.uk (consular), ukvisas.kingston@fco.gov.uk (visa)

Canada 3 West King's House Road, Kingston 10, tel. 876/926-1500 or 876/926-1507, fax 876/511-3491, kngtn@international.gc.ca

Cuba 9 Trafalgar Road, tel. 876/978-0931 or 876/978-0933, fax 876/978-5372, embacuba jam@cwjamaica.com

Dominican Republic 4 Hacienda Way, Norbrook, tel.: 876/931-0044, fax 876/925-1057, domeb@cwjamaica.com

European Union Delegation of the European Commission/European Union, 8 Oliver Road, P. O. Box 463, Kingston 8, tel. 876/924-6333 or 876/924-6337, fax 876/924-6339

France 13 Hillcrest Avenue, tel. 876/978-1297, 876/978-4881 or 876/978-4883, fax 876/927-4998 or 876/926-5570, french embassy@cwjamaica.com

Germany 10 Waterloo Road, Kingston 10, tel. 876/926-6728 or 876/926-5665, fax 876/929-8282, germanemb@cwjamaica.com

Mexico States, PCJ Building, 36 Trafalgar Road, tel. 876/926-6891 or 876/926-4242, fax 876/929-7995, embmexj@cwjamaica.com

Panama 1 St. Lucia Avenue, Spanish Court, Suite 26, tel. 876/968-2928, fax 876/960-1618, panaemba@cwjamaica.com

Spain 6th Floor Courtleigh Corporate Centre, 6–8 St. Lucia Avenue, tel. 876/929-5555, fax 876/929-8965, jamespa@cwjamaica.com, emb.kingston@mae.es

St. Kitts and Cedric Nevis 11A Opal Avenue, Golden Acres, P.O. Box 157, Kingston 7, tel. 876/944-3861, fax 876/945-0105, clr harper@yahoo.com

Trinidad and Tobago 60 Knutsford Boulevard, tel. 876/926-5730, 876/926-5739, or 876/968-0588, fax 876/926-5801, kgnhctt@cwjamaica.com

United States 142 Old Hope Road, tel. 876/702-6000, consularkingst@state.gov (visa/consular), opakgn@state.gov (general)

Venezuela PCJ Building, 36 Trafalgar Road, tel. 876/926-5510 or 876/926-5519, fax 876/926-7442

Accommodations

Jamaica offers a range of accommodation options to suit any budget and taste, from camping for US$10 per night, to hole-in-the-wall motels to luxurious villas that go for upwards of US$20,000 per week.

CAMPING

Camping has not been developed to its full potential by any means in Jamaica, perhaps because it is not considered a good way to make money in the tourism industry. Nevertheless, decent camping facilities can be found in the Blue Mountains, and in Portland and St. Mary parishes. It is unlikely you will be bothered for setting up a tent in any remote area of the island and the safety concerns that have likely been a factor in preventing camping from becoming more popular are more hype than well-founded warnings. Nonetheless, women traveling unaccompanied by men should stick to designated camping facilities at least until your comfort level in the specific region has been gauged. In touristy areas, camping will not be tolerated outside designated areas, and few designated areas exist.

GUESTHOUSES

Guesthouses vary in Jamaica from serious operations that register high occupancy levels throughout the year to more informal homestay arrangements like those available in the Winward Maroon stronghold of Moore Town. Guesthouses are defined by the on-site presence of the owners in either case, as opposed to hotels which typically have different ownership and management.

HOTELS

Hotels are for the most part locally owned in Jamaica with the exception of a few foreign-owned exceptions. Amenities range from shabby to world class at hotels across the island, with breakfast included at select accommodations. Many boutique hotels could be more accurately described as an assortment of cottages

or villas. In Negril and Treasure Beach certain properties have tailored their offerings to entice sophisticated travelers who swear by places like Tensing Pen, The Caves, and Jake's.

ALL-INCLUSIVE RESORTS

The all-inclusive phenomenon has, to the dismay of many, only accelerated in recent years with the arrival of several new chains including Excellence Resorts, Fiesta Group, Riu, and Principe. The well-established home-grown variety include Butch Stewart's Sandals and Beaches Resorts, Lee Issa's Couples Resorts, and his cousin John Issa's SuperClubs brands Hedonism, Grand Lido, and Starfish. All-inclusive resorts are a great way to cap your spending, even if they tend to be expensive, and if zoning out in a fantasyland with your partner is the goal, there's no better option. It's not a good way to see or get to know Jamaica, however, and you could just as well be on any other island with sun, sea, sand, and booze. While all-inclusive packages can be cut-rate and enticing, there are less expensive ways to see Jamaica without sacrificing first-world comforts. Nevertheless, there is an addictive allure to not worrying about where to eat and how much to tip the bartender. Couples stands out among the crowd as the most inviting all-inclusive chain for the discriminating vacationer, while SuperClubs has the most differentiated niches under its umbrella.

Differentiating Among the All-inclusive Resorts

Jamaica was a pioneer in the all-inclusive formula, which has since spread the world over. While it takes little planning to spend a week or two at an all-inclusive resort, there are certainly differences among the resorts that are reflected in the quality of service, food, and, of course, the cost. Many smaller accommodation options have started offering all-inclusive packages that make sense if you're not looking to explore the different food options in the area you're visiting, and most villas offer an all-inclusive option as well. At the right place, a package deal can certainly be worth it.

Many smaller all-inclusive accommodations include the Island Outpost properties, as well as some of the island's best cottages and villas. Where small properties offer an all-inclusive plan, it is indicated in the text under the accommodation listings in the chapter. All the all-inclusive resorts offer multiple pricing options within each location, which typically start at around US$150 per person per day and go up to US$400 per person for the high-end properties in the winter season.

COUPLES

Easily at the top of the all-inclusive options, Couples Resorts benefits from Lee Issa's hands-on approach and the exquisite taste of his wife Jane, who has been instrumental in ensuring tasteful decor and excellent food. Couples operates under the motto, "couples who play together stay together," and plenty of options are offered for "play," including nude beaches at the Sans Souci and Couples Ocho Rios properties. The other two properties, Couples Swept Away and Couples Negril, are within a few miles of each other, on Long Bay and Bloody Bay, respectively. Lee Issa is the son of Abe Issa, who pioneered Jamaica's tourism industry in the late 1940's and founded the first Couples Resort in 1978.

RIU

If the Spanish retained any bitterness about losing the island of Jamaica in the 17th century, perhaps it is in the 21st century when they will have their revenge, not on the British, but on the established all-inclusive resorts. The Spanish hotel group Riu aims to undercut across the island. Its owners entered the market by setting up hotels beside Sandals properties in Ocho Rios, and virtually taking over the whole of Bloody Bay in Negril. A fourth Riu Resort is being built in Montego Bay.

Riu offers some of the most competitive all-inclusive rates in Jamaica, attracting principally cost-minded American tourists. Unfortunately the quality of food at Riu Resorts leaves something to be desired in the "fine dining" à la carte restaurants, with long lines in the morning that make reservations mandatory. The American-style fare in the buffet dining areas is mediocre at best. On the other hand, rooms at Riu are well appointed and comfortable.

SUPERCLUBS

SuperClubs owner John Issa is a cousin of Lee Issa, the owner of Couples Resorts, and perhaps the more enterprising of the two when it comes to taking his hotels around the Caribbean Basin to Cuba, the Dominican Republic, Curaçao, and Brazil. SuperClubs is a much more diverse holding than Couples, with five different hotel names to uphold, and discernible differences in service and amenities at the different properties.

SuperClubs has targeted a variety of niche groups in shaping its appeal for each of its signature all-inclusive hotel chains: Breezes, Hedonism, Starfish, and the top-end, Grand Lido. Rooms on the beach in Ocho Rios is a SuperClubs foray into the European plan (a non-all-inclusive) market, and the Jamaica Pegasus in Kingston is also a SuperClubs holding owned in conjunction with the Jamaican government. In all the SuperClubs properties, there is a strong emphasis on activities, while there is no pressure to partake. From volleyball and trapeze contraptions on the beach to nude bathing at many of the properties, SuperClubs knows how to excite and entertain.

The Breezes properties in Jamaica, one in Montego Bay and the other on Runaway Bay, are open to everyone, from families to couples, to O. J. Simpson, who reportedly stayed in Runaway Bay on a recent trip to Jamaica. Breezes properties can be classified as mid-range in terms of amenities and quality of service, with good buffet-style food as well as better à la carte service for dinners served in the specialty restaurants. Liquor is mid-range, with no premium brands offered.

Starfish Trelawny is SuperClubs' answer to the ideal family vacation, with extra emphasis on engaging guests in activities like basketball, trapeze acrobatics, and water slides. Less attention is paid to quality and preparation of food at Starfish than at other SuperClubs properties, but it's still possible to eat a good dinner accompanied by wine and finished off with champagne. As a family-oriented property, the selection of alcohol is not as varied as at some of the other properties.

The **Hedonism** properties, Hedonism II in Negril and Hedonism III in Runaway Bay, need little explanation. Nevertheless, it's worth mentioning the abundance of nude beaches, mirrored ceilings, private whirlpool tubs, and notoriously naughty guests. Hedonism also engages special-interest groups like swingers (couples who exchange partners for a bit of a change), with theme weeks interspersed throughout the year. It's therefore best to be aware of the planned happenings when booking a stay, lest you should be expected to swap spouses with the next couple. Food at Hedo, as employees refer to the resort, is quite good, with the fluffy coconut bread a favorite.

Grand Lido operates two properties, Grand Lido Braco in Trelawny, and Grand Lido Negril, the SuperClubs flagship property. Grand Lido is quite deliberately a step up from the other SuperClubs properties, with large, luxurious suites, premium drinks, and special attention to the culinary arts. Braco sits on a large estate, which has stables where horseback riding tours are offered.

SUNSET RESORTS

Sunset Resorts has three properties: **Sunset Jamaica Grande** in Ocho Rios, **Sunset Beach** in Montego Bay, and best of all, **Sunset at the Palms,** a boutique property across Norman Manley Boulevard from Bloody Bay in Negril. Sunset Resorts make an attempt to appeal to everybody, with its motto, "always Jamaican, always for everyone," but the mass-market feel is palpable at the two larger properties. The rooms cover the basics nonetheless, and compared with other all-inclusive resorts the price point is attractive. The quality of food and booze is clearly not a priority at the larger

properties, while the service is consistently good throughout the chain. The Hendrickson family, which owns Sunset Resorts, also operates the Knutsford Court and the Courtleigh hotels in Kingston. In both Ocho Rios and Montego Bay, Sunset Resorts occupy choice beachfront real estate.

SANDALS AND BEACHES

Owned by Gordon "Butch" Stewart, the Sandals chain attracts couples, and the Beaches resorts cater to families. Newly built or refurbished properties like **Sandals Whitehouse** in Westmoreland, **Sandals Dunn's River Villagio** outside Ocho Rios, and **Sandals Royal Caribbean** in Montego Bay contrast with the more downscale properties in Negril and MoBay, **Sandals Negril, Sandals Montego Bay,** and **Sandals Inn.** The quality of each varies with the price point, some serving premium brand liquors and others offering a more basic package. Be sure to know what to expect as the baseline of quality varies greatly between locations.

Royal Caribbean is easily the best Sandals property, with a small private island just offshore and easy access to Montego Bay and its attractions. Meanwhile, Sandals Dunn's River Villagio has benefited greatly from recent renovations and is the most proximate Sandals property to Dunn's River Falls. Sandals Whitehouse is the newest property, but it is also the most remote and many guests find themselves too isolated for comfort when it comes to seeing Jamaica beyond the walled compound.

VILLAS

There is no better way to experience Jamaica than by staying in a staffed villa—and with proper planning and a small group, villas can be very affordable. Typically villas employees are long-term and become like family with each other and with guests. The warm interaction you can experience at many of these villas has no parallel and villas employ some of the best chefs on the island. Jamaica's best villas are concentrated around Montego Bay, Ocho Rios, and Port Antonio.

Food

Jamaican food is a reason in itself to visit the island. Home-cooked meals are generally the best so it's worth seeking out an invitation whenever possible. The traditional dishes were developed during the era of slavery and typically include a generous, even overwhelming, serving of starch, and at least a token of meat or seafood protein known historically as "the watchman." In recent years pan-Caribbean fusion has caught on as a new culinary trend, with creative dishes added to the traditional staple dishes.

Ackee is a central ingredient of the national dish, ackee and saltfish. The fruit contains dangerous levels of toxic amino acid hypoglycine until the fruit pods open naturally on the tree, or "dehisce," in horticultural terminology, at which point the yellow fleshy aril surrounding the glossy, black seed is safe to eat. Ackee has the consistency and color of scrambled eggs and is generally prepared with onion

© OLIVER HILL

steamed fish with okra, festival, and yam at Scotchie's

and rehydrated saltfish. Dried codfish was the original ingredient, which made an important dietary contribution during slavery when it was shipped from its abundant source off Cape Cod, Massachusetts. Today cod has become scarce and very expensive when available as a result of over-fishing and the fish is most often imported from Norway or replaced altogether with other saltfish substitutes.

Curry was brought to Jamaica by indentured Indians and quickly caught on as a popular flavoring for a variety of dishes, most commonly curry goat, but also including curry chicken, conch, shrimp, crab, and lobster. Curry rivals ganja as the most popular contribution from Indian to Jamaican culture.

Jerk is a seasoning that goes back as far as Jamaica's Tanios. The most common jerk dishes are chicken and pork, optimally barbecued using pimento wood which gives the meat a delicious smoky flavor complemented by the spicy seasoning that invariable contains hot scotch bonnet pepper.

Oxtail is a popularly dish that requires little explanation.

Mannish water is a popular broth with supposed aphrodisiac properties made of goat parts not suitable for other dishes (the head, testicles, legs) and cooked with green banana, spinners, and seasoned with pepper and sometimes rum.

Fish tea is similar to mannish water except it is made with boiled fish parts.

Starches are an inexpensive and important part of the Jamaican diet. The most commonly consumed starches include rice, yam, cassava, breadfruit, dumpling (fried or boiled balls of flour), boiled green banana, and fried plantain.

Bammy is derived from the Taino word *guyami,* which was a staple for the Tainos. Bammy is made from cassava, (known in many Spanish-speaking countries as *casabe*). In Jamaica, bammy is either steamed or fried and usually eaten as the starch accompaniment to fish.

Rice and peas is the most ubiquitous staple

served with any main dish. "Peas" in Jamaica is what the rest of the English-speaking world refers to as beans, and usually consist in either kidney beans sparsely distributed among the white rice, or gungo peas cooked with coconut milk and other seasoning.

Festival is another common starchy accompaniment to fish and jerk meals, consisting basically of fried dough shaped into a slender cylindrical sort of blob.

Dumpling is a round doughy mass that's either boiled or fried, generally to accompany breakfast. When boiled, there is little difference at the center from raw dough. **Spinners** are basically the same thing but rolled between the hands and boiled with conch or corn soup.

Saltfish was originally codfish that was shipped from New England in large quantities, with salt used as a preservative. It became a protein staple that helped sustain the slave trade. Despite the widespread use of refrigeration today, saltfish continues to be a sought-after item, even as the stocks of cod have been depleted of the Great Banks of Massachusetts and other salted fish has been substituted in its place.

Fresh seafood is readily available throughout Jamaica though fish, shrimp, and lobster are typically the most expensive items on any menu. Fish is generally either red snapper or parrot fish prepared steamed with okra, escoveitched, or fried. **Escoveitch** fish comes from the Spanish tradition of *escaveche* with vinegar used in the preparation. In Jamaica, scotch bonnet pepper and vinegar-infused onion is usually served with fried or escoveitch fish.

The most common Jamaican lobsters are actually marine crayfish belonging to the family Palinuridae *(Palinurus argus)*. Commonly known as the spiny lobster, two species are widely eaten, and, while noticeably different, are every bit as delicious as lobster caught in more northern waters.

Popular breakfast item include **hominy porridge** and **beef liver** in addition to ackee and saltfish typically eaten on Sundays.

Calaloo is a spinach-like green often served for breakfast steamed as a side dish either alone or sometimes mixed with saltfish.

Bulla is a heavy biscuit made with flour and molasses.

Easter bun is a tradition that has become popular enough to last throughout the year, so much so that by Easter there is little novelty left. Bun is typically eaten together with cheese.

Conduct and Customs

ETIQUETTE

Etiquette and manners are taken very seriously in Jamaica, although there's a lot of variation when it comes to individual concern over proper etiquette. Some people are so proper they might as well be the Queen, whereas others lack manners entirely. To a more exaggerated extent than many other places in the world where the same holds true, manners, etiquette, and speech in Jamaica are perceived as directly correlated to upbringing, socioeconomic class, and social status. Therefore it's important to be aware of the impression you make, especially with language. Cussing, for instance, is scorned by many educated Jamaicans, especially devout Christians. Meanwhile, as is the case everywhere, many people couldn't care less about the impression they make and speak quite freely and colorfully.

Photographing people in Jamaica can be touchy and should be done only after asking permission. That said, media professionals are highly respected and if you are walking with a camera, people will often ask you to take their picture regardless of whether they will ever see it. It makes a nice gesture to give people photos of themselves and is a great way to make friends. Photographing people without asking permission will often garner a request for monetary compensation. Asking permission often gets the same response. If the picture is worth it, placate your subject with whatever you think it's worth. Money is rarely turned down.

BEGGING

Begging in Jamaica is an everyday affair, from people voluntarily washing car windows at stoplights in Kingston and MoBay, to friends asking friends for money for this, that, or the other. It's important to balance altruism in providing whatever contribution you are able to offer based on your means with the practicality of perpetuating a dependence on others for monetary gifts. The truth of the matter is, underemployment is severely underreported in Jamaica and unfortunately poverty will not be eradicated anytime soon. Nevertheless, in tourist areas begging can be a nuisance, and it's best to discourage beggars by donating your money instead to a local organization or charity.

Tips for Travelers

OPPORTUNITIES FOR STUDY AND EMPLOYMENT

The University of the West Indies (UWI) has exchange programs with several regional institutions and alliances with US and UK-based universities.

INTERNATIONAL DEVELOPMENT AND VOLUNTEER OPPORTUNITIES

While work is often the last thing on people's minds on a trip to Jamaica, volunteering can be an immensely rewarding experience. It inevitably puts visitors in direct contact with real, working people as opposed to the forced smiles associated with the tourism industry. Several church groups offer volunteer opportunities, while there are also several secular options.

Jamaica Abode (28 Upper Waterloo, tel. 876/920-0509) is Jamaica's former Habitat for Humanity organization. It recently became independent from the international NGO but nonetheless continues to accept applicants for volunteer work across the island building accommodations for those in need.

The Peace Corps (www.peacecorps.gov) is quite active in Jamaica but generally requires an extensive application process, offering little or no opportunity for spontaneous or temporary volunteer work on the island. Nevertheless Americans looking to make a contribution to sensible development programs have found Jamaica a challenging and rewarding place to work.

The Blue Mountain Project (cell 876/474-6519 or U.S. tel. 260/571-0128, info@blue mountainproject.org, www.bluemountain project.org) actively supports volunteerism at a significant cost to participants (US$59/day) for short-term work, reduced to very reasonable for long-term work (US$19/day); accommodation and meals are provided. The U.S.-incorporated NGO carries out projects in the Blue Mountains to support basic community needs and sustainable development. Cash and donations in kind are also accepted by this group.

ACCESS FOR TRAVELERS WITH DISABILITIES

Travelers with disabilities should not be turned off by the lack of infrastructure on the island to accommodate special needs, but it is important to inquire exhaustively about facilities available. Most of the all-inclusive resorts have special facilities to accommodate wheelchairs and the like, but outside developed tourist areas, a visit will not be without its challenges.

TRAVELING WITH CHILDREN

Despite the stereotypes associated with Jamaica (leaving many who have never visited with the impression of a hedonistic partyland or a gun-slinging Wild West), the island is one of the most fascinating and engaging places for children. Beyond the obvious attraction of its beaches, Jamaica has a wealth of attractions that make learning fun, from jungle and mountain hikes teeming with wildlife, to farm tours that offer visitors a sampling of seasonal fruits. The activities available to engage children are endless. What makes the island an especially great destination for families is the love showered on children generally in Jamaica. Nannies are readily available virtually everywhere and can be easily arranged by inquiring at any accommodation, not just at those that tout it as a unique service.

WOMEN TRAVELERS

Jamaica is a raw and aggressive society, with little regard for political correctness and little awareness or respect for what is considered sexual harassment in the United States and Europe. Flirtation is literally a way of life, and women should not be alarmed if they find they are attracting an unusual degree of attention compared with what they are used to back home. On the street, catcalls are common, even when a woman is accompanied by her boyfriend or husband; in nightclubs women are the main attraction and dancing can be very sexual. Both on the street and in the club it's important to keep your wits about you and communicate interest or disinterest as clearly as possible. It is more the exception than the norm for men to persist after clearly communicating disinterest.

Jamaica depends overwhelmingly on the tourist dollar, and the authorities generally make an extra effort to ensure visitor safety. Nonetheless, if you are a woman traveling alone, it's best to exercise caution and avoid uncomfortable encounters. Suitors will inevitably offer any and every kind of enticing service: Accept only what you are 100 percent comfortable with and keep in mind that local men might make romantic advances because they're motivated by financial incentives.

GAY AND LESBIAN TRAVELERS

Jamaica is notoriously and outwardly anti-gay. Many Jamaicans will defend their anti-homosexual stance with religious or biological arguments, and many reggae artists use anti-gay lyrics as an easy sell, often instigating violence against gay men (whether metaphorically or literally, it's hard to tell the difference). Some of these artists—like Buju Banton, who had a hit titled "Boom Bye Bye" which suggested killing gay people—have toned down their rhetoric following tour cancellations abroad owing to their promulgated prejudice, while others, like Sizzla, continue unabated, indifferent to the potential for promoters abroad to affect their careers.

Though on the whole Jamaica is an extremely tolerant society, it is best for gay and lesbian travelers not to display their sexual preference publicly as a precautionary measure. Many all-inclusive resorts have in recent years altered their policies to welcome gay travelers, and still other high-end resorts have a noticeably gay lean.

Health and Safety

There are no special vaccinations required to enter Jamaica.

HEAT

Jamaica is a tropical country with temperatures rising well above 38°C in the middle of summer. Sensible precautions should be taken, especially for those not accustomed to being under such hot sun. A wide-brimmed hat is advisable for days at the beach, and a high-SPF sunblock essential. Being in the water exacerbates rather than mitigates the harmful rays—creating a risk for overexposure even while swimmers may be unaware until the evening when it becomes impossible to lay down on a burned back. While most hotels offer air conditioning, just as many have been constructed with cooling in mind to obviate the need for air-conditioning. Louvre windows with a fresh sea breeze or ceiling fan can be just as soothing as air-conditioning, while not putting such a strain on Jamaica's antiquated and inefficient electrical grid. In the summer months, air-conditioning is a well-appreciated luxury, especially for sleeping. If you are traveling between June and September, consider spending some time in the Blue Mountains, where there's a cool breeze year-round.

SEXUALLY TRANSMITTED DISEASES

Jamaican culture celebrates love, romance, and intimacy. While not everyone is promiscuous, keeping multiple sexual partners is common, and infidelity is generally treated as an inevitable reality by both men and women. The obvious danger in this attitude is reflected in a high incidence of STDs on the island, including underreported figures on AIDS/HIV infections. If you engage in sexual activity while in Jamaica, like anywhere else, condoms are indispensable and the best preventative measure you can take apart from abstinence.

CRIME

Unfortunately, criminal acts are a daily reality for a large number of Jamaicans, from the petty crimes committed by those who find themselves marginalized from the formal economy, to high-rolling politicians and drug dons who control the flow of capital, illegal substances, and arms on the island. In sharp contrast to other developing nations with high poverty rates, and perhaps contrary to what one might expect, random armed assault on individuals and muggings in Jamaica are quite rare. The crime that is most ingrained and more or less the order of the day is devious, petty thievery. Almost everybody who has stayed in Jamaica for any length of time has experienced the disappearance of personal effects, whether a wallet or a perfume or a cell phone, one of the most prized items. Stay vigilant and take every possible precaution and you will likely have no problem.

BRIBERY

Officially bribery is illegal, and people offering a bribe to an officer of the law can be arrested and tried in court. It's generally quite obvious when a police officer is seeking a pay-off. Phrases like, "do something for me nuh" or "gimme a lunch money" typically get the message across quite effectively. Do not try to bribe police when it is not solicited (or even when it is); there are officers of the law who will take offense and could even try to use this to add to the severity of the alleged offense.

There is a department, the **Office of Professional Responsibility** (OPR) within the Jamaican police force dedicated to routing out corruption. The office is based in Kingston (tel. 876/967-1909, 876/967-4347 or 876/924-9059) but has officers across the island. Be sure to take note of the badge number of the officer in question if you are planning to make a report.

DRUGS

Jamaica has a well-deserved reputation as a marijuana haven. Contrary to what many visitors believe, marijuana is classified by the Jamaican authorities as a drug and is illegal. Practically speaking, however, marijuana use is not criminalized and it's impossible to walk through Half Way Tree in Kingston or Sam Sharpe Square in MoBay without taking a whiff of ganja, as the herb is known locally. Nevertheless, if a police officer sees a tourist smoking, it often provides a good excuse for harassment and threats of imprisonment. These are generally not-so-subtle hints that a pay-off is in order. It's not generally a good policy to entertain bribes, but some tourists caught in this situation have found that US$20 can go a long way in preventing discomfort for all parties involved.

Beyond ganja, Jamaica has also gained a well-deserved reputation as a transshipment point for cocaine originating in Colombia. Crack addiction has been a problem in some coastal communities where cargo has inadvertently washed ashore. While marijuana use is tolerated on the island due to its widespread consumption and a Rastafarian culture that incorporates its use into religious and recreational practices as a sacrament, there is no good reason to use cocaine or any other hard drug in Jamaica, despite offers that will inevitably arise on a walk along Seven-Mile Beach in Negril.

Information and Services

MONEY

The best way to access funds in Jamaica is by using an ATM with your normal NYCE, Maestro, or Cirrus bankcard. "Express kidnappings" (where victims are taken to a cash machine to withdraw the maximum on their accounts) are not especially common in Jamaica, and the little effort involved in canceling a checking account card makes the ease of 24-hour access well worth the risk of getting it lost or stolen. Travelers checks are a good back-up option and can be cashed at most hotels for a small fee. Taking large amounts of cash to Jamaica is not advisable as it is likely to somehow disappear. ScotiaBank offers Jamaican or U.S. currency from many of its ATMs, although foreign bank fees can run as high as 6 percent of the amount withdrawn. U.S. dollars are accepted pretty much anywhere in Jamaica, though restaurants and other small businesses will generally not honor current exchange rates, usually taxing about J$5 per US$1. Currency trading houses, or cambios as they are often called, typically offer a few more Jamaican dollars for each U.S. dollar exchanged, which can make a significant difference when exchanging large amounts of cash.

ELECTRICITY

Jamaica operates on 110V, the same current as in the United States. Power outages are frequent in some areas, but for the most part seldom where resorts are based. Most tourism establishments have back-up generators.

COMMUNICATIONS AND MEDIA

Telephones

Fixed-line telephony in Jamaica was until recently a monopoly controlled by Cable & Wireless (C&W). As the Internet has become more widely available, voice over Internet protocol (VoIP) telephony has become increasingly important as a means of communicating with the outside world. Netstream Global began offering fixed-rate VoIP service, which compelled C&W to offer their own VoIP product; many households now enjoy this inexpensive way to keep in touch with family members in the United States, Canada, and the UK. Two new cellular providers, Megafone and MagicPhone, offer similar flat-rate calling abroad.

Cellular phones are more important than fixed lines in Jamaica due to the fact that C&W never installed lines in the more remote areas of the country before cellular obviated the need to. C&W was the first cellular provider but was soon overtaken in popularity by Digicel, which currently offers the best service island-wide in terms of reception. Both C&W and Digicel operate on GSM networks and cell prepaid SIM cards, as well as post-pay contractual service (which is more affordable in the long run, but few people use). A relatively new arrival on the scene is the third cellular carrier, MiPhone, which has established a spotty network with CDMA technology, focuses primarily on business customers who are courted by its strong data service, with coverage strongest in Kingston, Ocho Rios, and Montego Bay. The three cellular providers have roaming arrangements with select carriers in the United States, but the fees charged for roaming make buying a SIM card locally (US$5) the best option no matter your length of stay. Prepaid phone credit is sold in different increments starting at about US$1.50.

The cellular providers penalize their customers when calling outside their own network, and many Jamaicans will carry both C&W and Digicel phones to avoid out-of-network calling. Similarly, calling land lines from cell phones is more expensive, as is calling cell phones from land lines. In order to dial a cell phone from a fixed line you must dial 1 and then the number.

The 876 country code is never used for calls within the country, and calling land lines from cell phones does not require adding the 1 before the seven-digit number.

Radio

Kingston has some of the best radio stations anywhere, and it's not just reggae you'll find on the airwaves. Reggae in fact developed with the help of a strong tradition in radio, as young musicians were inspired by American music of the 1950s and 1960s, adapting the songs with a distinct Jamaican flavor. Radio stations of note include RJR, Power 106, Irie FM (which has been referred to as the daily soundtrack of the island), Fame FM, and Zip FM. Radio West broadcasts from Montego Bay, while KLAS FM is based in Mandeville and Irie FM in Ocho Rios. Radio Mona (93 FM) broadcasts from the communications department at the University of the West Indies, Mona. Hits 92 FM is a good station in Kingston for a wide range of contemporary music, from dancehall to hip-hop and R&B.

Radio broadcasting in Jamaica dates from World War II, when an American resident, John Grinan, gave his shortwave station to the government to comply with wartime regulations. From wartime programming of one hour weekly, the station quickly expanded to four hours daily including cultural programming. Radio would have a key impact on the development of Jamaican popular music in the 1940s and 1950s as the only means of dissemination for the new styles coming mainly out of the United States.

Television

Jamaica's main television stations are Television Jamaica (TVJ, www.televisionjamaica.com), formerly the Jamaica Broadcast Corporation (JBC); CVM (www.cvmtv.com); Reggae Entertainment Television (RETV); and Jamaica News Network (www.jnnntv.com). In 2006, TVJ acquired both JNN and RETV, consolidating its leadership in both news and entertainment programming on the island.

MAPS AND TOURIST INFORMATION

The map of Jamaica published by Shell (US$4.25) is the best and most easily accessible island-wide road map, with detailed inserts for major towns and cities. The city maps sold by the National Land Agency are less detailed and lack many of the road names included on the Shell map. The Land Agency does have good topographical maps on the other hand, which are sold for a hefty US$7 per sheet. Twenty sheets cover the whole island and the maps can be obtained on CD.

Handy tourism-oriented business brochures are available free of charge at the chamber of commerce offices in Ocho Rios, Montego Bay, and Negril.

WEIGHTS AND MEASURES

One of the most frustrating things in Jamaica is the lack of a consistent convention when it comes to measurements. On the road, where the majority of cars are imported from Japan and odometers read in kilometers, many of the signs are in miles while the newer ones are in kilometers. The mixed use of metrics in weights and measurements is also a problem complicating life in Jamaica, with chains used commonly when referring to distances, liters used at the gas pump, and pounds used for weight.

TIME

Jamaica operates on Eastern Standard Time (Greenwich Mean Time minus five or six hours), with no allowance made for daylight savings since the difference between day length in the winter and summer is nominal.

RESOURCES

Glossary

Jamaican patois is a creative and ever-evolving English dialect rooted in the mélange of African and European cultures that together comprise Jamaica's identity. Irish, English, and Scottish accents are clearly present, as is the influence of Spanish, with many words also of African origin. Patois carries a thick and warm twang that can be very difficult to understand for those unaccustomed to hearing it. After relaxing your ears for a few weeks however, Jamaican talk begins to make perfect sense.

Babylon used by Rastafarians to refer to any evil and oppressive system. Also used as a reference to the police.

bad man a thug or gangster

bad mind corrupt mentality; or a scheming person, as in, "dem bad mind, eeeh."

bakra a plantation overseer, often used to express resentment toward someone acting in an authoritarian manner.

baldhead a person with little or no hair on their head. Used in a derogatory sense by Rastafarians.

bangarang when hell breaks loose

bankra basket (of West African Twi origin)

bashment a party, celebration, any form of excitement

batty backside or derriere

batty man a gay man

beah only; derived from the word "pure," as in "a beah argument she a gimme."

biggup used as a showing of respect, a shout-out as in, "biggup to all mi fans."

blenda blender. A mixed-up situation rife with confusion.

blessed used as a greeting, as in "blessed love!"

blood used as a greeting between close friends considered like family, as in "whaapen blood?"

blouse and skirt an exclamation that usually sounds more like "blows and skirt!"

bly a chance or opportunity; to be let off the hook.

bomba claat an expletive; Sometimes used without the "claat" as a less vulgar exclamation.

boopsy a man or woman who takes their mate's things; a user (as in, "boops you out").

boots condom

brawta an extra something thrown into a deal when the haggling is done

bredda brother. Used in referring to a close friend, as in "yes mi bredda!"

bredren brethren, used when referring to a close friend, as in "mi bredren dem."

brownin a light-skinned black woman

buck up meet or run into someone

buddy male genitalia

bullet bullet! an exclamation; originated by dancehall musician Bounty Killer drawing on the popular obsession with guns; the predecessor to Bounty's musical rival Beenie Man's "Breed It, Breed It!"

bruk broken or broke, meaning not having any money

bruk out to let loose and be free

bulla a heavy biscuit made with flour and molasses

buss bust, as in a career break; to bust out and make it

bway a boy

catty a girl

cha a versatile exclamation that can indicate disgust or astonishment; also written as "cho"

chalice a water pipe used to smoke ganja

clash a battle; often used in the context of a sound clash where different sound systems or artists face off

chi chi an ant with a big behind that eats wood. Used commonly as a derogatory term for homosexual males, as in a "chi chi man."

collie marijuana

colon man a man who went off in the style of national hero Alexander Clarke, who came back from his sojourns through Latin America with a flashy style of dress, flashy gold watches, and a general cosmopolitan air.

copacetic cool, nice, criss

cotch to rest or lean up against; to brace something, as in the tire of a car to keep it from rolling. Also used to say where you stay or spend the night.

craven greedy

crawle pen, likely derived from the corral where animals were kept, such as a hog crawle or turtle crawle

criss nice (crisp)

dads used as a show of respect, as in "yes mi dads"

daughta daughter, a young lady

deh pon doing, as in "mi deh pon mi homework"; or in reference to a place, as in "mi deh pon di road."

dehso there, or over there

deejay a dancehall singer

dege-dege small

don from the Italian usage, a honcho or leader

downpress to suppress

dread a derogatory term used for someone who wears locks. Also used to describe hardship: "the time getting dread."

duppy a ghost

eeeeh an inflection used at the end of a phrase to denote a casual query of consensus, as in "she pretty, eeeeh... " ("She is pretty, isn't she?")

enz a hang-out spot, as in "mi deh pon di enz."

face to demonstrate interest, as in "di gyal deh a gimme beah face."

flex to profile or show off

forward come back, as in "mi soon forward."

front female genitalia

galiss a womanizer

ginnal a con artist or hustler, either male or female

give bun (burn) to cheat (on your spouse/ girlfriend)

grind pelvic gyrations central to popular dance

groundation a Nyabinghi session of drumming that can last for days; usually held around a significant date in the Rasta calendar, e.g., Selassie's birthday or Ethiopian Christmas.

gwaan go on, as in "wha gwaan?" ("What's happening?")

gweh go away, as in "gweh nuh, tek weh ya self!"

gyal girl, tends to be construed as somewhat derogatory

haffi have to, must

herb marijuana

higgler a trader in the market. Also referred to small-scale importers who bring goods to sell in Jamaica from Panama.

high-grade top-quality marijuana

hush an expression of sympathy

I and I the Rastafarian substitute for "me" referring to the individual's inseparability from the divine creator

idren used like "bredren"

irie to feel nice or high

Ital natural, derived from "vital"

jacket a child born outside an established relationship that is obviously from a different father

Jah Rastafarian term for the Almighty, derived from Jehovah in the Old Testament

John Crow turkey vulture, buzzard (Cathartes aura)

juk to cut, prick, or knock; a juking stick is used to knock ackee or mangoes off a tree.

junjo a type of mushroom once used as a meat substitute

leggo let go

likkle little, as in "a likkle more" for "see you later."

lime to hang out, also used as a noun for a laid-back gathering or party

macca thorn, as in "di macca juk mi." ("The thorn cut me")

mampi a heavy-set woman

massive the people, as in "the Kingston massive"

mawga meager, skinny, or thin

medi meditation, as in to "hold a medi"; to ponder or meditate on something

"Mi credit run out." what people will say when they place a phone call before hanging up so that the recipient will have to call back and pay for the call.

natty a person that wears locks in their hair

nuff enough

nyam to eat, as in "mi a nyam some food" ("I'm going to eat"). Also used in the context of getting what you need: "mi haffi go a wuk, cause me haffi nyam food." Nyam can be used in the context of to get something at any cost, sometimes neglecting the consequences.

obeah Jamaican sorcery or voodoo

par hang out with

payola bribe

pickney a child or children

pop-down shabby or disheveled, referring to a place or person

posse a group of friends; a crew that hangs out regularly.

pum pum female genitalia

raated an exclamation

ragamuffin a serious dude, used in referring to a true soldier, Rasta thug, or rude boy

ramp to hang out with or move with, as in "mi nah ramp wid dem people!"

ram-up packed with people

ras from Amharic, meaning "prince," as in Ras Tafari

rat-bat a bat; a bat usually refers to a moth.

rass a versitile expletive

reason to converse or hold a discussion; a reasoning

red used in reference to people of a ruddy complexion typical of the people in St. Elizabeth parish

respect a greeting or acknowledgment of appreciation

riddim rhythm

roots anything referring to something original. Roots reggae is the early form of the music considered the most traditional and authentic style.

roots tonic an herbal and root tonic consumed to uphold general health and stamina

rude boy a bad ass as popularized by the character of Jimmy Cliff in *The Harder They Come*

runnings the way things operate, as in "him don't understand di runnings roun' yahso."

selector a disc jockey

sell-off exclamation derived from sold out, as something in high demand. Used in the context of something that's immensely popular, as in "di dance sell-off!"

screw face an expression of bitterness

sensi, sensimilla marijuana, adapted from Spanish *sin semilla*, meaning without seeds

session party

set girls rival groups of female dancers who would sing and dance and compete in matching costumes against other such groups during the colonial period.

sistren a sister, the female version of "bredren" (brethren)

skank to dance

skettle a prostitute

skylark to laze away one's days rather than work or go to school.

slack loose, degrading, as in "pure slackness a gwaan."

soon come used to say, "I'll be there in a bit" or "I'll be back in a bit." This is a very loose phrase, however, and could mean in a few minutes, days, or years.

sound system often referred to as simply a "sound"

spliff, skliff a marijuana cigarette or joint

stageshow a musical concert typically featuring performances by many artists

stoosh snooty, uptown

swimp shrimp

tek to take

tekeisha a female name used in jest to refer to a girl who takes a man's money

uno you (plural), "one" in the third-person sense

vex upset, angry

whine wind; gyrating, sexually suggestive pelvic motion at the heart of the bumping and grinding seen in a typical club

wood male genitalia

wuk work, as in "wuk mi a wuk." Also used in a sexual sense, as in "you wuk mi out."

wukless worthless

yard home, as in "mi deh pon mi yard" ("I am at home"). Also used in referring to Jamaica.

Yahso here, as in "yahso mi deh" ("I am here")

"Yuzimiaseh." as in "you see what I'm saying."

Zion the holy land, as referred to by Rastafarians

Suggested Reading

HISTORY

Bryan, Patrick E. *Jamaica: The Aviation Story.* Arawak Publications, 2006. An interesting account of aviation and the role air travel has played in Jamaica's modern history.

Buckley, David. *The Right to be Proud—A Brief Guide to Jamaica Heritage Sites.* This book covers select sites from those listed by the Jamaica National Heritage trust. It is a good coffee-table book with interesting details.

Christie, Pauline. *Language in Jamaica.* Arawak Publications, 2003. An academic examination at the significance of language in Jamaica as it relates to history, class, and prejudice.

De Lisser, Herbert G. *White Witch of Rosehall.* Humanity Press, 1982. A fantastic account of Annie Palmer rooted in much historical truth. This is a great quick preparatory read for a visit to Rose Hall Great House near Montego Bay.

Emilie, Adams, L. *Understanding Jamaican Patois.* LMH Publishers, new ed., 1991. An introductory guide to Jamaican patois and phrases.

Goldman, Vivian. *The Book of Exodus: The Making and Meaning of Bob Marley and the Wailers' Album of the Century.* Three Rivers Press, 2006. An excellent account of the years surrounding Bob Marley's launch into international stardom with great anecdotes and lots of good context on the tumultuous 1970s.

Gottlieb, Karla. *The Mother of Us All: A History of Queen Nanny, Leader of the Windward Jamaican Maroons.* Africa World Press, 2000. The story of Nanny, Jamaica's most prominent Maroon leader and only national heroine.

Henzell, Perry. *Cane.* 10a Publications, 2003. A novel about a white slave from Barbados who becomes a member of the planter class and owner of the largest plantation in Jamaica. While the book is fiction, it accurately portrays class dynamics and gives an excellent sense of the brutal reality that characterized the colonial period.

Pariag, Florence. *East Indians in the Caribbean: An Illustrated History.* An illustrated look at the arrival of East Indians in the Caribbean basin—focused on Jamaica, Trinidad, and Guyana.

Price, Richard. *Maroon Societies: Rebel Slave Communities in the Americas.* The Johns Hopkins University Press, 3rd ed., 1996. An interesting look at the parallel development of Maroon societies in a number of Latin American countries.

Senior, Olive. *An Encyclopedia of Jamaican Heritage.* Twin Guinep Publishers, 2003. An A-to-Z of things, people, and places Jamaican and their historical relevance. An indispensable quick reference for scholars of Jamaica.

LITERATURE

Banks, Russell. *Rule of the Bone.* Minerva, new ed., 1996. An engaging novel that traces the growth of a somewhat troubled American youth who ends up in Jamaica.

Bennett, Louise. *Anancy and Miss Lou.* Sangster's Book Stores, Ltd., 1979. A must-have among Miss Lou's many printed works. The Anancy stories are folk tales rooted in Jamaica's African heritage. Miss Lou brings them to life in a book appreciated by children and adults alike.

Figueroa, John. *Caribbean Voices: An Anthology of West Indian Poetry: Dreams and Visions.* Evans Bros., 1966. This book is a good representative of Figueroa, one of the grandfathers of Jamaican literature.

Kennaway, Guy. *One People.* Canongate Books, new ed., 2001. A hilarious look at the idiosyncrasy of the Jamaican people.

McKay, Claude. *Selected Poems.* Dover Publications, 1999. Many of McKay's poems are written in colorful dialect ranging in theme from clever critiques on political and economic ills to love poetry.

McKenzie, Earl. *Boy Named Ossie: A Jamaican Childhood.* Heinemann, 1991. Earl McKenzie is one of Jamaica's most respected literary figures who grew up in the years leading up to independence.

Mutabaruka. *The First Poems / The Next Poems.* Paul Issa Publications, 2005. Mutabaruka's definitive collected printed works spanning many years of his career.

NATURE AND THE ENVIRONMENT

Fincham, Alan. *Jamaica Underground.* University Press of the West Indies, 1998. An essential guide to the sinkholes and caves of Cockpit Country. Diagram and plates of cave layouts complement anecdotal accounts and exploration logs.

Hodges, Margaret. *Guide to the Blue and John Crow Mountains.* Natural History Society of Jamaica. Ian Randle Publishers, second edition 2007. Edited by expert naturalist Margaret Hodges with chapters written by several members of Jamaica's Natural History Society, this book improves on the much-in-demand and out of print first edition, *Blue Mountain Guide* published in 1993. This is an essential guide for travelers looking to get intimately acquainted with Jamaica's most spectacular national park for which the Jamaica Conservation and Development Trust is seeking UNESCO endorsement. The book is divided into six regions making it especially practical for devising day-trip excursions.

Iremonger, Susan. *Guide to the Plants of the Blue Mountains of Jamaica.* University Press of the West Indies, 2002. A handy guide to the flora of the Blue Mountains.

BIRDING

Downer, Audrey and Robert Sutton. *Birds of Jamaica: A Photographic Field Guide.* Cambridge University Press, 1990. A good guide to Jamaica's birds.

Raffaele, Herbert, et al. *Birds of the West Indies.* Princeton University Press, 2003. This is the best bird guide for the Caribbean basin, with excellent plates.

FOOD

Burke, Virginia. *Eat Caribbean Cook Book.* Simon & Schuster, Ltd., export ed., 2005. Easily among the best Caribbean cookbooks on the market. Burke makes essential recipes easy to put together with widely available ingredients.

Quinn, Lucinda Scala. *Jamaican Cooking.* Wiley, rev ed.,2006. A selective cookbook with some excellent recipes for those seasoned in Jamaican cooking.

SPIRITUAL

Barrett, Leonard E. *The Rastafarians.* Beacon Press, 20th anniversary ed., 1997. A comprehensive study of the Rastafarian movement.

Bender, Wolfgang. *Rastafarian Art.* Ian Randle Publishers, 2004. Bender covers the contribution of Rastafarian philosophy to Jamaican contemporary art.

Bethel, Clement E. *Junkanoo.* Macmillan Caribbean, 1992. An in-depth look at Jonkunnu, a fascinating dance and music style closely associated with Jamaica's folk religions and performed for a few celebrations throughout the year, notably at Christmastime.

Chevannes, Barry. *Rastafari: Roots and Ideology.* University of West Indies Press, 1995. One of the best assessments in print of the Rastafarian movement, Chevannes is the top academic authority in Jamaica on the faith, having studied and lived amongst Rastas throughout his career.

Hausman, Gerald. *The Kebra Negast: The Lost Bible of Rastafarian Wisdom and Faith from Ethiopia and Jamaica.* St. Martin's Press, 1st ed., 1997. Considered the Rasta bible by many adherents, this is a must-have resource book for those with deep interest in the faith.

ESSENTIAL PERIODICALS

The Jamaican Magazine is an excellent periodical published by the University of Technology. Each edition highlights a different parish.

Jamaican Journal, Published by the Institute of Jamaica (IOJ), is a great, easy-to-read academic publication highlighting different aspects of Jamaican culture and heritage.

Internet Resources

TRAVEL INFORMATION

Jamaica Tourist Board
www.visitjamaica.com
This is the official website of the Jamaica Tourist Board. It is smartly designed and easy to navigate. Unfortunately many of the features were left undeveloped and for practical resources beyond the tourist board offices, the site falls short.

Funkingz
www.funkingz.com
A discount travel club served with a card for purchase that offers discounts at hundreds of participating establishments in Jamaica and a number of other select Caribbean destinations.

Negril.com
www.negril.com
One of the island's most active bulletin board–style sites with members both locally and abroad. Negril.com advertises for many tourism establishments in Negril with more and more coverage extending to other areas of Jamaica.

Insider's Jamaica
www.insidersjamaica.com
A well-designed site with some of the less commercial alternatives for accommodations and food listed and reviewed.

NEWSPAPERS

The Jamaica Gleaner
www.jamaica-gleaner.com
Jamaica's most widely circulated daily.

The Jamaica Observer
www.jamaicaobserver.com
The island's number two newspaper.

The Star
www.jamaica-star.com

Jamaica's entertainment daily is chock full of gossip and trash talk, making for good entertainment and little news.

FLIGHT INFORMATION

Norman Manley International Airport
www.manley-airport.com.jm

Norman Manley is the capital's international airport. The site has useful information, including airlines and flight schedules.

Sangster International Airport
www.mbjairport.com

Montego Bay's international airport receives the lion's share of the island's tourists. The airport's website provides complete travel information from arrivals and departures to local accommodations, shopping, and food options.

ECOTOURISM

The Jamaica Caves Organization (JCO)
www.jamaicancaves.org

The Jamaica Caves Organization is the most active scientific exploratory organization on the western side of the island, researching the caves and sinkholes of Cockpit Country on a continual basis. The JCO sells maps and offers guide services.

Jamaica Conservation and Development Trust (JCDT)
www.greenjamaica.org

The JCDT has charge of the Blue and John Crow Mountain National Park and is the go-to organization for matters related to hiking and staying at the park.

Southern Trelawny Environmental Agency (STEA)
www.stea.net

A regularly updated site dedicated to coverage of the activities of the STEA, which include the annual Yam Festival. The site also contains resources for exploring the Trelawny interior and contracting guide services.

Jamaica Scuba
www.jamaicascuba.com

A well-designed and useful site with some of the island's best dive sights highlighted. The site also provides an intro to Jamaica's marine life.

MUSIC AND ENTERTAINMENT

Irie FM
www.iriefm.net

Jamaica's most popular reggae station, Irie broadcasts on 107.5 and 107.9 FM as well as over the Internet.

What's On Jamaica
www.whatsonjamaica.com

A current-events website with island-wide listings.

Party Inc
www.partyinc.com

A site dedicated to Jamaican-style bashments around the globe, with listings and streaming mixes from top selectors.

Whata-Gwan
www.whata-gwan.com

A site dedicated to promoting the Jamaican parties in every part of the globe, but with a strong lean towards the Kingston and Miami areas.

Whaddat
www.whaddat.com

A decidedly Jamaica-focused party site covering events from "uptown to the garrison." The site is a good resource for staying abreast of the latest talk and cultural trends.

Muzik Media
www.muzikmedia.com

A New Jersey–based website that runs the top 10 music videos of the week as well as archiving contemporary classic videos.

Jammin Reggae Archives
www.niceup.com

A U.S.-based site with information on reggae artists and upcoming performances.

Bob Marley
www.bobmarley.com

The official Bob Marley family website with bios on individual family members, merchandise, and news. Most of the Marley progeny have their own sites as well.

Reggae Entertainment
www.reggaeentertainment.com

A site dedicated to the reggae industry with entertainment news and downloads.

Ernie B's
www.ebreggae.com

One of the best catalogs available for purchasing reggae on vinyl, both classics and new releases. Based in California.

ART AND CULTURE

Afflicted Yard
www.afflictedyard.com

A counterculture photography site that reflects the pulse of popular Jamaican culture with enticing visuals and selected writing.

Index

Acknowledgments

This book would not have been possible without the support of my parents, William Blaine Hill and Maria del Pilar Abaurrea, who kindled from day one my desire to see more, learn more, and travel the world. They taught me the virtue of understanding the way other people live beyond our borders, and the joy of indulging in new cultures, hearing fresh music, and tasting new foods. Most of all, my parents taught me to make every encounter a positive interaction. Of course my brother, Antonio, and sister, Paola, helped refine this doctrine and have also been supportive in my unorthodox ventures.

I am grateful to count many of the following people not merely as professional and respectable business associates, but also as friends in a common cause. These individuals greatly facilitated the logistics behind the fifth edition of *Moon Jamaica* and generously gave their time and assistance. Chief among those who deserve recognition are Daniel Barrett, who first introduced me to the runnings of his homeland; Mary Francis and Sheldon Davis, who have been real "fam" from the beginning; Gary Codner, who opened his home and helped with the links; Lance Watson, who is both *yahso* and *dehso* anytime you need him; Robin and Mike Lumsden, who shared their piece of paradise and vision; Carolyn Barrett, who knows where and how to enjoy Jamaica better than anyone; Rebecca Wiersma, my indispensable ally on the South Coast; Jason and Laura Henzell, who were always enthusiastic aides; Helmut and Charmaine Steiner, who made me feel like visiting royalty in Port Antonio; Yvonne Blakey, who has the best links in Portland; Mary Phillips, who wrote the book on how to entertain with class; Susan McManus, whose "God Bless!" at the end of our phone conversations always smoothed over the anguish I caused her; Andria Mitzakos and Darlene Salzer for perfectly coordinating my stays with their clients; Lee and Jane Issa, who bring the highest level of professionalism and taste to Jamaica's tourism industry; Robert Anderson, who is doing things right at Tiamo and showed me one of the area's best kept secrets; Lorna Robinson at the JTB; Donahue Jarrett for making me feel presidential at the Altamont; Angie Dickson, who has revitalized Green Castle Estate magnificently; and Blaise and Tammy Hart, some of the best people in the world; Charlotte and Cary Wallace, who embellished my time in Negril; Stephanie Chin, who knows how to project the family vibe from her perch over MoBay; Tony, whose Time N Place is a much needed bastion of another; and Michelle Rollins, whose vision and perseverance continue to transform Rose Hall.

For their assistance and generous hospitality, I would also like to extend my gratitude to Jenny Wood, Linda Smith, Clinese Prendergast, Charles Burberry, Cortina Byles, David Rosenstein, David Lowe, Frank Lawrence, Gaia, Jennifer Lyn, Jeremy Jones, John Issa, Sonia Gray-Clarke, Louis Grant, Michael Fox, Barry Chevannes, Wayne Modest, David Boxer, Bernard Jankee, Andrea Davis, Michael Gleason, Carol Reid, Jonathan and Paula Surtees, Klaus Peter, Michael Hoe-Knudsen, Michelle Hussey, Nancy Mclean, Nicole Henry, Peter Frazier, Richard Bourke, Rochelle Forbes, Burchell Henry, Sharon Powell, Sherryl White-McDowell, Sigi Fahmi, Ted Ruddock, Otis and Valerie Deans, Helga Stockart, and many more who have not been mentioned.

Lastly, but certainly not least, I need to acknowledge my employers, Avalon Travel Publishing and Mergermarket. My editor, Elizabeth McCue, and the entire team at Avalon were critical in putting the book together to the highest standards in a timely fashion. Mergermarket, and especially Charlie Welsh, was also instrumental in seeing the project to completion with his constant demand to "take the spliff out my mouth, come out from the Jacuzzi, and get back to work."

www.moon.com

For helpful advice on planning a trip, visit www.moon.com for the **TRAVEL PLANNER** and get access to useful travel strategies and valuable information about great places to visit. When you travel with Moon, expect an experience that is uncommon and truly unique.

MAP SYMBOLS

▦	Expressway	【	Highlight	✗,	Airfield	⚲	Golf Course
▬	Primary Road	○	City/Town	✈	Airport	🅿	Parking Area
▬	Secondary Road	◉	State Capital	▲	Mountain	⬟	Archaeological Site
▫▫▫	Unpaved Road	◉	National Capital	✛	Unique Natural Feature	⛪	Church
- - - -	Trail	★	Point of Interest			
··········	Ferry	•	Accommodation	🦢	Waterfall	⛽	Gas Station
—⊢—⊢—	Railroad	▼	Restaurant/Bar	▲	Park		Glacier
▰▰▰	Pedestrian Walkway	▪	Other Location	🆃	Trailhead		Mangrove
▮▮▮▮	Stairs	▲	Campground	�skiing	Skiing Area		Reef
							Swamp

CONVERSION TABLES

°C = (°F – 32) / 1.8
°F = (°C x 1.8) + 32
1 inch = 2.54 centimeters (cm)
1 foot = 0.304 meters (m)
1 yard = 0.914 meters
1 mile = 1.6093 kilometers (km)
1 km = 0.6214 miles
1 fathom = 1.8288 m
1 chain = 20.1168 m
1 furlong = 201.168 m
1 acre = 0.4047 hectares
1 sq km = 100 hectares
1 sq mile = 2.59 square km
1 ounce = 28.35 grams
1 pound = 0.4536 kilograms
1 short ton = 0.90718 metric ton
1 short ton = 2,000 pounds
1 long ton = 1.016 metric tons
1 long ton = 2,240 pounds
1 metric ton = 1,000 kilograms
1 quart = 0.94635 liters
1 US gallon = 3.7854 liters
1 Imperial gallon = 4.5459 liters
1 nautical mile = 1.852 km

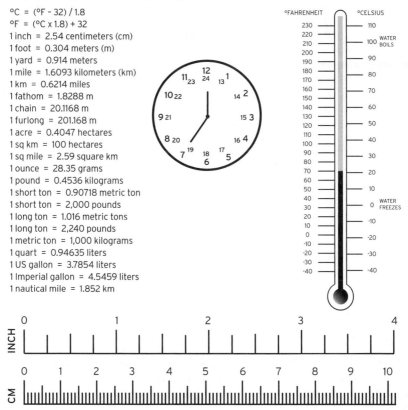

MOON JAMAICA

Avalon Travel Publishing
a member of the Perseus Books Group
1400 65th Street, Suite 250
Emeryville, CA 94608, USA
www.moon.com

Editor: Elizabeth McCue
Series Manager: Kathryn Ettinger
Copy Editor: Ellie Behrstock
Graphics Coordinator: Stefano Boni
Production Coordinator: Darren Alessi
Cover Designer: Stefano Boni
Map Editor: Albert Angulo
Cartographers: Chris Markiewicz, Kat Bennett
Cartography Director: Mike Morgenfeld
Indexer: Deana Shields

ISBN-10: 1-56691-569-4
ISBN-13: 978-1-56691-569-4
ISSN: 1088-0941

Printing History
1st Edition – 1991
5th Edition – November 2007
5 4 3 2 1

KEEPING CURRENT

If you have a favorite gem you'd like to see included in the next edition, or see anything
that needs updating, clarification, or correction, please drop us a line. Send your
comments via email to feedback@moon.com, or use the address above.